MEXICO

FODOR'S TRAVEL GUIDES

are compiled, researched, and edited by an international team of travel writers, field correspondents, and editors. The series, which now almost covers the globe, was founded by Eugene Fodor in 1936.

OFFICES

New York & London

Fodor's Mexico:

Fodor's Editor: Andrew E. Beresky
Area Editors: Jim Budd, John Busam, M. Susan Wagner
Editorial Contributors: Mary Joan Anderson, David Dodge, Margaret Medina, Kal Muller
Drawings: Edgar Blakeney
Maps: Marc Dinoir, Dyno Lowenstein

FODOR'S®

MEXICO 1987

FODOR'S TRAVEL GUIDES
New York & London

ISBN 0-679-01385-7
ISBN 0-340-40049-8 *Hodder & Stoughton, London*

The following Fodor's Guides are current; most are also available in a British edition published by Hodder & Stoughton.

Country and Area Guides

Australia, New Zealand & the South Pacific
Austria
Bahamas
Belgium & Luxembourg
Bermuda
Brazil
Canada
Canada's Maritime Provinces
Caribbean
Central America
Eastern Europe
Egypt
Europe
France
Germany
Great Britain
Greece
Holland
India, Nepal & Sri Lanka
Ireland
Israel
Italy
Japan
Jordan & the Holy Land
Kenya
Korea
Mexico
New Zealand
North Africa
People's Republic of China
Portugal
Province of Quebec
Scandinavia
Scotland
South America
South Pacific
Southeast Asia
Soviet Union
Spain
Sweden
Switzerland
Turkey
Yugoslavia

City Guides

Amsterdam
Beijing, Guangzhou, Shanghai
Boston
Chicago
Dallas & Fort Worth
Greater Miami & the Gold Coast
Hong Kong
Houston & Galveston
Lisbon
London
Los Angeles
Madrid
Mexico City & Acapulco
Munich
New Orleans
New York City
Paris
Philadelphia
Rome
San Diego
San Francisco
Singapore
Stockholm, Copenhagen, Oslo, Helsinki & Reykjavik
Sydney
Tokyo
Toronto
Vienna
Washington, D.C.

U.S.A. Guides

Alaska
Arizona
California
Cape Cod
Chesapeake
Colorado
Far West
Florida
Hawaii
I-95: Maine to Miami
New England
New Mexico
New York State
Pacific North Coast
South
Texas
U.S.A.
Virginia

Budget Travel

American Cities (30)
Britain
Canada
Caribbean
Europe
France
Germany
Hawaii
Italy
Japan
London
Mexico
Spain

Fun Guides

Acapulco
Bahamas
Las Vegas
London
Maui
Montreal
New Orleans
New York City
The Orlando Area
Paris
Puerto Rico
Rio
St. Martin/Sint Maarten
San Francisco
Waikiki

Special-Interest Guides

Selected Hotels of Europe
Ski Resorts of North America
Views to Dine by around the World

MANUFACTURED IN THE UNITED STATES OF AMERICA
10 9 8 7 6 5 4 3 2 1

CONTENTS

Editor's Foreword vii

FACTS AT YOUR FINGERTIPS

Physical Features, 1; Climate, 1; Population, 2; Language, 2; Major Cities and Resort Areas, 3; Where to Go, 4; Planning Your Trip, 6; Taking Money Abroad, 7; Insurance, 8; How to Get There, 9; Getting Around by Car, 11; Passports, 15; Travel Agents, 15; Tour Operators, 16; Tourist Information Services, 17; Meeting the Mexicans, 17; Tips for British Visitors, 17; When to Go, 18; Money, 18; What to Take, 18; What It Will Cost, 20; Seasonal Events, 21; Business Hours and Holiday Closings, 24; Traveling with Pets, 25; Hotels, 25; Dining Out, 26; Tipping, 26; Shopping, 27; Time Zones, 29; Electric Current, 29; Telephones, 30; Laundry and Dry Cleaning, 30; Senior Citizen/Student Travel, 30; Handicapped Travel, 31; Health, 32; Mail, 33; English Language Media, 33; Airport Departure Taxes, 33; Customs, 33

MEXICO

Mexico—The Land and Its People 37
An Insight into History, by Kal Muller 37
Insights into the Mexicans, by David Dodge 46
The Pre-Columbian Heritage: A Primer on Mexican Archaeology
by Kal Muller 56
Contemporary Arts of Mexico: Form Follows Revolution 71
Folklore: Blend of Several Cultures 83
Food and Drink: From Fiery to Subtle
by Margaret Medina 101
Bullfighting for Beginners: And Other Mexican Sports
by Mary Joan Anderson 108
Mexico City and Environs: The City That IS Mexico
by Jim Budd 120
Map of Mexico City 122–123
Map of Mexico City Metro System 125
The Heartland of Mexico: The Bajío and West Central
by Kal Muller 166
Guanajuato 168
León 173
San Miguel Allende 174
Querétaro 179
San Juan del Rio 183
Tequisquiapan 183
Morelia 185
Lake Pátzcuaro 189
Uruapan and Playa Azul 193

Guadalajara: Roses and Gentlemen Cowboys 200
Map of Guadalajara 202–203
The Lake Chapala Area 220
Aguascalientes 226
San Luis Potosí 230
Zacatecas 235
Acapulco: Playground Where Fun Reigns
by Susan Wagner 239
Map of Acapulco 241
Ixtapa/Zihuatanejo 263
Pacific Resorts: Puerto Vallarta, Manzanillo, Mazatlán, and More
by Kal Muller 272
Puerto Vallarta 273
Manzanillo 291
Mazatlán 306
Los Mochis and El Fuerte 317
The Famous San Blas and Tepic 320
Guaymas and Sonora 324
Baja California: A Peninsula of Paradoxes
by Jim Budd 334
Map of Tijuana 339
Map of Ensenada 343
Chihuahua and the Copper Canyon: Mexico's Wild North 371
Monterrey Area and the Gulf Coast to Veracruz Area
by Jim Budd 383
Map of Monterrey 386
The Indian South: Oaxaca and Chiapas: Resort Area in the Making
by Kal Muller 403
Yucatan and the Maya Country: Elegance Amongst the Ruins
by Jim Budd 432
Map of Isla Mujeres-Cancun-Cozumel-Tulum Area 434
Map of Cancun Hotel Zone 436
Map of Mérida 452
Useful Phrases and Vocabulary 493
Index 505
Map of Mexico 516–517
Map of Mexican States 518–519

Editor's Foreword

Magnificent Mexico! We *norteamericanos* should be forever grateful that we have on our continent a country so close to us yet so different from our own culture. We tend to take for granted the sheer volume, range, and quality of Mexico's attractions, both historical and modern.

Mexico's rich history encompasses three thousand years of continuous civilization, from the archaic cultures of the Olmec and Tlatilco Indians, dating from before 1000 B.C., to the pyramids, sacred temples, and giant urban communities of the Aztecs. These civilizations left behind a legacy of innumerable relics in some eleven thousand archaeological sites—treasures most of which await your viewing.

Unlike the rest of the continent, Mexico retains much of its Indian heritage. However, the country is also Latin American to the core, as proclaimed by every village church and the many *zocalas,* or village squares, so full of architectural gems. Modern Mexican history dates from the victorious wars of national liberation from Spain, which started in 1810 and ended in 1821. The country trembled for over a century from a succession of political eruptions, foreign interventions, and revolutionary convulsions, until a new nation and a new people emerged from the turmoil.

In the creative arts, Mexico's contributions have been stunning. Architects, painters, and musicians—such giants as Diego Rivera, Orozco, and Siqueiros—are contemporary heroes to their people. As regards the more popular forms of music and dance, the Mexicans are passionately devoted to fiestas, regional dancing, and all manner of festive activity.

That doesn't mean Mexico hasn't kept the pulse of the modern beat, as attested to by the lush hotels, sparkling beaches, and throbbing discos of Acapulco, booming Cancún, Puerto Vallarta, and other fun-filled vacation resorts.

Mexico can also boast of every variation of climate and terrain—from alpine to tropical, from mountains and plateaus to deserts to jungles. And in her cities as well as small villages, Mexico is a shopper's paradise. It remains a relatively inexpensive country for the American tourist.

In every travel guide, particularly one of this size and scope, errors are bound to creep in. Much change can and will occur even while we are on press, and also during the succeeding twelve months or so that this edition is on sale. We sincerely welcome letters from our readers on these changes or from those whose opinions differ from ours, and we are ready to revise our entries for next year's edition when the facts warrant it.

Please send your comments to the following addresses: In **North America,** Fodor's Travel Guides, 2 Park Ave., New York, NY 10016; in **Europe,** Fodor's Travel Guides, 9-10 Market Place, London, W1N 7AG, England.

FACTS AT YOUR FINGERTIPS

PHYSICAL FEATURES. Geographically, Mexico is a unique country encompassing towering mountain ranges, broad plateaus, and jungle lowlands. Mountains usually separate the important settlements, much to the despair of engineers and roadbuilders. Yet, this has helped the country maintain some of its rural charm.

Mexico's 8,300-mile boundary is contiguous to the United States on the north, the Gulf of Mexico and the Caribbean Sea on the east, Guatemala and Belize on the southeast, and the Pacific Ocean on the south and west. With its 759,000 square miles, this country is about one-quarter the size of the United States and ranks fourth in size among Western Hemisphere republics.

The central tableland of Mexico, the *altiplano,* is traversed by large mountain chains ranging in altitude from about 3,000 feet near the U.S. border to 8,000 and 9,000 feet around Mexico City. Thus Mexico has some of the highest inhabited areas in the world (second only to Tibet and the Andean countries).

The central area contains the highest peaks in the country and effectively divides the north from the south. Among the major peaks are Citlaltepetl or Orizaba, 18,851 feet, and Popocatépetl, 17,716 feet. They are exceeded in height in the Northern Hemisphere only by Mount Logan and Mount McKinley.

Other mountain ranges further divide the country. In the west, the Sierra Madre Occidental seals off both the peninsula of Baja California and the state of Sonora from the north central plains of Mexico. In the east, the Sierra Madre Oriental forms a forbidding barrier between the coastal plain of the Gulf of Mexico and the interior highlands.

A neo-volcanic axis of mountains cuts across Mexico from near Puerto Vallarta to a point just south of Veracruz. Several mountain ranges converge like crumpled paper in Oaxaca before falling off to the southeast at the narrow Isthmus of Tehuantepec. There the land mass reaches its narrowest point: 120 miles across, from the Gulf of Campeche in the Gulf of Mexico to the Laguna Superior, an inlet of the Pacific Ocean. Several projects to cut a canal through this neck of land failed before the Panama Canal was eventually built. To the southeast, the mountains start again in Chiapas to continue into Guatemala. The northern part of the Yucatán Peninsula is mostly flat limestone, broken only by the low Puuc hills. The Pacific coastal plain is crowded by the Sierra Madre Occidental; there is more space on the Gulf Coast. Tropical vegetation grows exuberantly in the southern latitudes.

Mexico contains few extensive rivers or lakes. The longest river is the Río Balsas, which rises in the state of Tlaxcala and flows into the Pacific Ocean but is navigable only for short distances. The country's largest lake is Lake Chapala near Guadalajara. Somewhat smaller, but noted for their beauty, are Lakes Pátzcuaro and Cuitzeo in Michoacán.

CLIMATE. Most people think of Mexico as being a hot, tropical area. Actually one-half of Mexico is north of the southernmost tip of the continental United States, and the country's temperature and rainfall depend more on variations in altitude than on latitudinal position.

The seacoast regions of Mexico as well as the lower altitudes of the interior are often very hot, except during the winter season. Temperatures range from 75° to 88° in winter to well over 100° in summer.

A more temperate area is found at altitudes from 4,000 to 6,000 feet, where the mean temperature ranges from 60° to 70°. The cool zone above 6,000 feet has a mean temperature of 58° to 60°.

In general, the high central plateau on which Mexico City, Guadalajara, and many of the country's colonial cities are located is springlike year-round—a bit cooler in the winter and a little warmer in the summer. The coastline is generally tropical in climate as you go south.

Rainfall ranges from a few drops a year in northern Sonora to an occasional annual precipitation of 16.4 feet in the Grijalva River Valley in the south. Throughout the country there is a rainy season from May to October. These rains are usually late afternoon or evening downpours, leaving the rest of the day for travel or sightseeing. It is during the rainy season that much of the countryside becomes a lush green, in marked contrast to the dry season's browns and yellows. From November to April, rains are rare. May is generally Mexico's hottest month.

POPULATION. Out of roughly twenty centuries of turmoil, invasion, occupation, and revolution, a new race of Mexicans has emerged. What is a Mexican? He is one of these species: Indian, *mestizo,* or *criollo.*

Before the Spaniards arrived in 1519 there were several million people (estimates range up to 20 million) in the area of present-day Mexico—all Indians. These various Indian nations produced some of the most brilliant civilizations in the world, along with the Incas by far the most advanced in the Western Hemisphere. Just stop to think that a true urban metropolis of 250,000 people—Teotihuacán—had already been *abandoned* in the seventh century by its inhabitants. When Cortés conquered the Aztecs in the sixteenth century, Tenochtitlán—a canal city of the magnitude of present-day Venice, with over 100,000 inhabitants—was completely destroyed and today's Mexico City founded on its site. All of this happened at a time when not a single city existed in the area that is now the United States.

No one knows exactly how many Indians there now are in Mexico. Their number is difficult to estimate, for lack of criteria. For census purposes, the government considers as Indian those who speak an Indian tongue among themselves. There are some 54 ethnic Indian groups, with a total of perhaps 4 to 5 million members.

The bulk of the nation consists of *mestizos,* a type which has existed for only four-and-a-half centuries. Most Mexicans you will meet are *mestizos,* the end product of the mixture of Indian and European stock, the latter largely of Spanish origin. A large proportion of *mestizos* remains Indian in outlook. Their cultural habits, tools, utensils, social organization, and, particularly, personal attitude are more Indian than European. *Machismo,* an exaggerated masculinity, is both an Indian and Spanish trait.

Immigrants, primarily from the U.S.A. and Europe, account for only about 3 percent of the population.

The total population (1985 estimate) is 78 million. Most of the population is concentrated in urban areas or in a few rich farming sections in northwest or central Mexico.

LANGUAGE. Spanish is the language of Mexico, though English is understood in tourist-oriented resorts and hotels. In some outlying areas, ancient Indian languages are still spoken.

Mexicans, unlike some other nationalities, are not scornful of visitors' mispronunciations and errors in grammar. Rather, they welcome even the most halting attempts to use their language. A few key words plus gestures can convey a world of meaning.

MAJOR CITIES AND RESORT AREAS. Mexico City's urban area of some 18 million people dwarfs all the country's other cities. Guadalajara is a distant second with 3.5 million, followed by industrial Monterrey in the northeast. Just as Mexico City concentrates population, industry, and government on a national scale, so do the state capitals at the regional level. Decentralization, long recognized as essential, is being spurred as a result of the 1985 earthquakes.

Most of the well-known resorts are on the Pacific Coast: Guaymas, Mazatlán, Puerto Vallarta, Manzanillo, Ixtapa/Zihuatanejo, and Acapulco. Farther south, Puerto Escondido is favored mainly by the young, as good accommodations are still scarce. There are no major resorts on the Gulf Coast, but on the eastern side of the Yucatán Peninsula the unmatched beaches of Cancún, backed by a string of luxury hotels, make for a winning combination. On the Baja California Peninsula, the luxurious hotels at the southern tip—Cabo San Lucas—are excellent, and Loreto, on the east coast of the peninsula, is a new resort that holds great promise.

THE MEXICAN STATES

State	*Abbreviation*	*Capital*
Aguascalientes	Ags.	Aguascalientes
Baja California	B.C.	Mexicali
Baja California Sur	B.C.S.	La Paz
Campeche	Camp.	Campeche
Chiapas	Chis.	T. Gutiérrez
Chihuahua	Chih.	Chihuahua
Coahuila	Coah.	Saltillo
Colima	Col.	Colima
Durango	Dgo.	Durango
Guanajuato		Guanajuato
Guerrero	Gro.	Chilpancingo (Ciudad Bravo)
Hidalgo	Hgo.	Pachuca
Jalisco	Jal.	Guadalajara
Mexico	Mex.	Toluca
Michoacán	Mich.	Morelia
Morelos	Mor.	Cuernavaca
Nayarit	Nay.	Tepic
Nuevo León	N.L.	Monterrey
Oaxaca	Oax.	Oaxaca
Puebla	Pue.	Puebla
Querétaro	Qro.	Querétaro
Quintana Roo	Q.R.	Chetumal
San Luis Potosí	S.L.P.	San Luis Potosí
Sinaloa	Sin.	Culiacán
Sonora	Son.	Hermosillo
Tabasco	Tab.	Villahermosa
Tamaulipas	Tamps.	Ciudad Victoria
Tlaxcala	Tlax.	Tlaxcala
Veracruz	Ver.	Jalapa
Yucatán	Yuc.	Mérida
Zacatecas	Zac.	Zacatecas
Federal District	D.F.	Mexico City

WHERE TO GO. Mexico offers a wide range of different types of vacations, from just lying on the beach sipping *cocolocos* to studying pre-Columbian ruins. And of course there's no reason not to combine several interests. As many first-time vacationers to Mexico find, there's a lot more to Mexico than is commonly known. Here are some broad categories of destinations to choose from, defined either geographically or by interest.

Mexico City area. This is the hub of the country's communications and transportation. Many flights arrive directly from the U.S. and connections are excellent to any destination within the country. Be forewarned: the two major problems in the city are smog and traffic. Using Mexico City as a base, many day trips can be taken to archaeological sites and to spectacular countryside featuring snowcapped volcanos. Some colonial cities can also be visited on a day trip—Cuernavaca to the south and Puebla to the east. Querétaro, three hours' drive or bus ride to the northwest, marks the beginning of a region known as El Bajío, a heartland dotted with many attractive colonial cities.

Seaside playgrounds. To many hardworking denizens of the cold northern latitudes, Mexico's beaches and sunshine are winter dreams. Most famous of all, Acapulco on the Pacific Coast is geared for large-scale tourism, with all the facilities and amenities found anywhere in the world. Prices cover a wide range of budgets, and many all-inclusive tours take the worry out of a vacation. Farther up the coast lies the new resort complex of Ixtapa, picked by computers and technocrats as the ideal spot. The nearby fishing village of Zihuatanejo has been spruced up and has sprouted plenty of lower-scale hotels, whereas Ixtapa boasts of top-of-the-line accommodations away from distracting hustle and bustle. Farther north, Manzanillo is a busy port and railhead, but just out of town, two bays separated by a peninsula have attracted hotels, mushrooming around the fabled Las Hadas complex. On to Puerto Vallarta, which has kept much of its original charm by requiring tourist developments to grow just to the north or south along the beaches. Just south is a spectacular stretch of coast which served as the set for filming *The Night of the Iguana.* Up the coast lies Mazatlán, a busy port and a semi-modern city. It has invested heavily in its coastal strip, which has blossomed into a major resort. Formerly only favored by knowledgeable deep-sea fishermen and awash with college students during school breaks, Mazatlán now caters to just about any budget. Finally, Guaymas, near the U.S. border, is favored by many Americans from the western states. Its condos and yacht marina have made San Carlos Bay almost an American enclave.

Aside from the major resorts, there are many smaller, usually less expensive ones dotting the Pacific Coast (described in detail in our "Pacific Resorts" chapter). On the eastern shores of Mexico, the Gulf Coast has no major resorts, but the Caribbean of eastern Yucatán boasts a true jewel of a beach at Cancún, backed by a long line of first-class hotels. Cozumel Island, best known for superb skin diving, doesn't have Cancún's fine beach, but the prices are lower and the atmosphere is more Mexican. A tour of the Yucatán's splendid Mayan ruins can easily be combined with a tan-and-relax vacation at Cancún or Cozumel.

Getaway resorts. Mexico has developed many seaside resorts aside from its world-famous ones. The quality of accommodations and cuisine varies greatly, as does cost and ease of access. Isla Mujeres, just off the northeastern tip of Yucatán, is an ideal place to relax and a convenient base for visiting bird sanctuaries and doing a bit of diving and Mayan sightseeing.

On the Pacific Coast of the state of Oaxaca, Puerto Escondido can be reached by air from Mexico City and Oaxaca City, or else by a long and rough, but cheap, bus ride. Surfing can be excellent there. The place is full of young people on tight budgets. Farther down the coast, Puerto Ángel is nestled in a cove, offering scant excitement but plenty of scenery and a quiet vacation in an unspoiled setting. Nearby, a huge new resort at Huatulco is in the planning stages; the first hotels are scheduled to open there possibly in 1987.

The Italy-length peninsula of Baja California was formerly the private preserve of four-wheel-drive-equipped adventurers and wealthy folks with private planes. No longer. Although well-off Californians and others still scoot down to the hotels' private strips at Cabo San Lucas, plenty of development and promotion have opened other areas on the southern edge of Baja. The town of La Paz, with its busy ferry harbor and airport, has many medium-priced hotels and shopping facilities, duty free. To the south of La Paz, San José del Cabo now offers an affordable alternative, although one a bit farther than Cabo San Lucas from the spectacular setting of huge stone arches in the ocean which marks the southern tip of Baja. Loreto, north of La Paz on the shore of the Sea of Cortés, is Mexico's latest resort area to receive all-out development and promotion, including direct flights from the U.S. and first-rate facilities in a tranquil setting.

Colonial cities. As opposed to the tourist-oriented resorts, the country's colonial cities represent much of the "real" Mexico. A bit of Spanish, although not essential, can come in handy in these cities, where the tidal wave of tourist hordes has not yet hit. However, all of the colonial cities have excellent hotels where English is spoken. There are also inexpensive accommodations available for tight budgets.

An hour east of Mexico City, Puebla is full of interesting colonial buildings, both civil and religious. There is plenty of shopping for crafts in town as well as for excellent woolen goods nearby. There are incredible Indian-colonial churches just out of town at San Francisco Acatepec and Tonantzintla. The biggest pyramid in Mexico is found at Cholula. Looking like a hill and covered with vegetation, it is tunneled through and topped by a church. The colonial town of Tlaxcala is also just a short distance away.

To the south of Mexico City is Cuernavaca of eternal spring. It was the favored winter resort of Aztec emperors. The conquistador Hernán Cortés built his fortress-palace here, now converted into an attractive museum. Today, many of the wealthier members of the Mexican power structure maintain vacation homes here, along with a colony of Americans, some retired. The silver city of Taxco, perched on a steep hillside, boasts the ornate baroque church of Santa Prisca, one of the finest in the country. Silver is still mined nearby, and excellent craftsmen fashion a plethora of utilitarian and decorative items from the precious metal. A sizeable group of Americans have made their homes here.

San Miguel de Allende is located in the heartland of Mexico, almost equidistant from Guadalajara and the capital. This is probably the best-known colonial city, due to its sizeable American community involved in the arts. English is widely spoken here. Without being spectacular, the little town is as charming as they come. South of San Miguel, Morelia, capital of the state of Michoacan, offers a well-preserved colonial downtown area dominated by a massive yet harmonious cathedral. Morelia is very close to Pátzcuaro, a miniature colonial gem complete with a bustling Tarascan Indian market. Guanajuato, one of the first silver towns, is also located in the heartland. With its underground roadways and steep, narrow streets, it is a stroller's paradise as well as being among the best-preserved colonial cities. Farther north, Zacatecas lies off most visitors' routes. This was the first Mexican city built on silver, producing tremendous quantities for the Spanish treasury with enough left over to build the most baroque of cathedrals. Another winding stroller's delight, Zacatecas provides a most unusual travel experience. Guadalajara, the road and air focus of northern central Mexico, combines the attractions of its colonial architecture, the paintings of Orozco, and rich cultural life with a whole gamut of accommodations and restaurants. The city provides a good starting point for visiting many of the colonial cities, as well as a launching pad for the half-hour flight to either of the Pacific resorts of Puerto Vallarta or Manzanillo.

Archaeological sites. Mexico's pre-Columbian civilizations represent one of mankind's most fascinating chapters—and one of the most mysterious. These civilizations developed and faded without leaving clearly written records. Much of what was written down was destroyed by the Spaniards. Much of the country's pre-Hispanic history has been pieced together by archaeologists. Visiting the ruins of many restored sites is a cultural and esthetic experience not to be missed. Mexico has literally hundreds of ancient sites, almost all of which are located in the center or the south.

Close to Mexico City, the ancient center Teotihuacan is one of the most important sites, as well as the easiest to visit. Two huge pyramids dominate the ancient complex which holds strong stone carvings and powerful paintings. Farther west is Tula, center of the Toltec empire. Tall stone figures perch on top of a pyramid with crude but interesting frieze-sculptures at the bottom. South of Mexico City is the Aztec military shrine of Malinalco, carved out of living rock. Farther in the same direction, between Cuernavaca and Taxco, are the hilltop ruins of Xochicalco, which could someday reveal interrelations between Mayans and central Mexican cultures. The city of Oaxaca is built at the foot of mountain whose top the Indians leveled for the spread of the sacred center Monte Albán, the most important and complex site in southern Mexico aside from the Yucatán Peninsula's numerous Mayan centers. Near Oaxaca, the ancient ritual complex of Mitla shows intricate stonework decorating the palaces.

Starting up the coast of Yucatán, the archaeological park of La Venta, on the outskirts of Villahermosa, holds the best carvings of the Olmecs. These include huge basalt heads as well as other monoliths by this "mother culture" of the Mexican civilizations. A couple of hours away, Palenque is surrounded by jungle. A Mayan site of exquisite beauty, Palenque's pyramid holds the elaborate tomb of a ruler. A four-story tower, built probably for astronomy, juts over a palace with the most delicate stucco figures. Some of the finest stone carvings also grace this site.

Mérida, in the northern Yucatán, is the closest city to the important classical Mayan site of Uxmal, a fantasy of elaborately decorated buildings and an unusual elliptical-base pyramid. Chichén Itzá, probably the most visited Mayan site, shows an overpowering Toltec influence in style and design, quite different from other sites in the region and more closely akin to Tula. A well-restored pyramid holds a tomb at this extensive site full of carved warriors, jaguars, and eagles. The country's largest sacred ball court is here, along with a huge natural well—used for sacrifices—with the water some 75 feet below ground level.

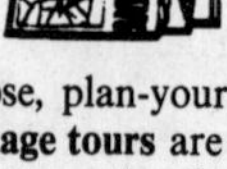

PLANNING YOUR TRIP. Package tour or independent travel. Time, convenience, cost, and the type of travel that most interests you are the factors to consider when it comes to choosing an all-inclusive, fully escorted tour; a loose, plan-your-own-itinerary package tour; or totally independent travel. **Package tours** are the easiest to arrange and probably the most economical and efficient mode of travel for first-time visitors to Mexico, especially since most tourists want to divide their time between lying in the sun and visiting ruins and other sites. The operator will arrange for all plane, rail, motorcoach, and other transportation, transfers wherever needed, tour guides, and generally commodious accommodations. Flight-plus-lodging with many such tours often works out to be less expensive than the flight alone as a regular economy fare. Thus, even if you prefer accommodations at someplace other than that offered by the tour operator (who usually has a selection of hotels to choose from according to the price-plan selected), and even if you have no intention of participating in any group sightseeing or other package activities, it may still be in your best interests to buy the entire package.

Among the general items to check when considering any package are these:

1) Does the price quoted cover air as well as land arrangements? If airfare is not included, does the tour operator have a special rate available?

2) How many meals are included?

3) How tied to the tour are you? If it is a motorcoach tour, for example, must you stay with the tour city-by-city or can you leave and rejoin it at will?

4) Does the rate for an automobile included in the package carry an additional per-mile fee or is mileage unlimited? Is the car in the base rate exactly what you need? Air conditioning may or may not be necessary for you, but there is a substantial difference in charges for standard and automatic shifts. Driving a standard can save a great deal of money.

5) What is the tour operator's responsibility for getting you home on time (within reason, considering weather delays, etc.)?

In other words, read the fine print **very carefully.**

Traveling independently allows for greater freedom than tour travel, but it is almost always more expensive for comparable accommodations and services. However, you will almost always get better value for your money (that does not necessarily mean it will be cheaper) when dining on your own, assuming you are not limiting your visit to a single resort hotel. Tour operators have arrangements with particular establishments that can handle busloads of tourists at a time; in order to serve them simultaneously and at a reduced rate, there will usually be a fixed menu offered or a limited selection from the full menu. The food in such places also tends to play on stereotypes; both your options and the quality of the food you get are likely to be better if you go it on your own.

If you have not tied yourself to a tour and do require en-route assistance in finding accommodations within your budget, go directly to the information kiosk at a rail, ship, or air terminal in the place where you wish to stay. The people manning these kiosks are among the most helpful and reliable sources of information concerning available rooms.

In booking a package tour it is best to go through a travel agent; indeed, except for the likes of *American Express, Cook,* and the airlines, most packagers do not handle their own reservations.

$P£

TAKING MONEY ABROAD. Traveler's checks are still the standard and best way to safeguard your travel funds; and you will usually get a better exchange rate for them than for cash. In the U.S., many of the larger banks issue their own traveler's checks, which are just about as universally recognized as those of *American Express* and other top firms. In most instances there is a 1 percent charge for the checks; there is no fee for Barclays checks. Some banks also issue them free if you are a regular customer. The best-known British checks are those of *Cook* and *Barclays, Lloyds, Midland,* and *National Westminster* banks. It is also a good idea to have some local currency upon arrival. Some American banks will provide this service; alternatively, contact *Deak-Pererra,*

630 5th Ave., New York, NY 10036 (212–757–0100; call for additional branches). Major credit cards are accepted in Mexico in most large hotels, restaurants, and shops.

INSURANCE. The different varieties of travel insurance cover everything from health and accident costs to lost baggage to trip cancellation. Sometimes they can all be obtained with one blanket policy; sometimes they overlap with existing coverage you might have for health or home; and sometimes it is best to buy policies tailored to very specific needs. Insurance is available from numerous sources, and many travelers unwittingly end up with redundant coverage. Before purchasing separate travel insurance of any kind, be sure to check your regular policies carefully.

It is best to take care of your insurance needs before embarking on your trip. You'll pay more for less coverage—and have less chance to read the fine print—if you wait until the last minute and make your purchase from, say, an airport vending machine or insurance-company counter. If you have a regular insurance agent, he or she is the person to consult first.

Flight insurance, which is often included in the price of the ticket when the fare is paid via *American Express, Visa,* or certain other major credit cards, is also often included in package policies. Such policies, which provide accident coverage as well, are available from most tour operators and insurance companies. While it is a good idea to have health and accident insurance when traveling, be careful not to spend money to duplicate coverage you may already have. Then again, be careful not to neglect some eventuality which could end up costing a small fortune.

For example, basic *Blue Cross–Blue Shield* policies do cover health costs incurred while traveling. They will not, however, cover the cost of emergency transportation, which can often add up to several thousand dollars. Emergency transportation *is* covered, in part at least, by many major-medical policies, such as those underwritten by *Prudential, Metropolitan,* and *New York Life.* Again, we can't urge you too strongly to be sure you are getting the coverage you need and to check any policy carefully before buying. Another important example: Most insurance issued specifically for travel does not cover preexisting health conditions, such as a heart condition.

Several organizations offer coverage designed to supplement existing health insurance and help defray costs not covered by many standard policies, such as emergency transportation. Some of the more prominent are these:

NEAR (Nationwide Emergency Ambulance Return), 1900 N. McArthur Blvd., Suite 210, Oklahoma City, OK 73127 (800–654–6700). Rates range from $70 a person for 1–8 days, to $360 for a year.

Carefree Travel Insurance, c/o ARM Coverage, Inc., 9 E. 37th St., New York, NY 10016 (212–683–2622), offers medical evacuation arranged through Europe Assistance of Paris. Carefree's coverage is available from many travel agents.

International SOS Assistance, Inc., Box 11568, Philadelphia, PA 19116 (800–523–8930), has fees from $15 a person for 7 days to $195 for a year.

IAMAT (International Association for Medical Assistance to Travelers), 736 Center St., Lewiston, NY 14092 (716–754–4883) in the U.S.; or 188 Nicklin Road, Guelph, Ontario N1H 7L5 (519–836–0102) in Canada.

Another frequent inconvenience to travelers is loss of baggage. It is possible—though often it is a complicated affair—to insure your luggage against loss through theft or negligence. Insurance companies are reluctant to sell such coverage alone, however, since it is often a losing proposition for them. Instead, it is most often included as part of a package that would also cover accidents or health. Remuneration is often determined by weight, regardless of the value of the specific contents of the luggage. Insurance companies usually require documentation; should you lose your luggage or some other personal possession, be sure to report it to the local police immediately. Without documentation of such a report, your insurance company might be very stingy. Also, before buying baggage insurance, check your homeowners policy. Some such policies offer "off-premises theft" coverage, including loss of luggage while traveling.

The last major area of traveler's insurance is trip cancellation coverage. This is especially important to travelers on APEX or charter flights. Should you get sick abroad, or for some other reason be unable to continue your trip, you may be stuck having to buy a new one-way fare home, plus pay for space on the charter you're not using. You can guard against this with trip cancellation insurance, usually available from travel agents. Most of these policies will also cover last-minute cancellations.

HOW TO GET THERE. By Air: Air fares are in a constant state of flux, and our best advice is to have your reservations made by a travel agent. Agents are familiar with the latest changes in fare structures—ever more confusing despite "deregulation" among U.S. carriers, who now allegedly base prices on distance traveled—as well as with the rules governing various discount plans. Among those rules are: booking (usually) 21–30 days in advance, minimum stay requirements, maximum stay allowances, a payment in advance (sometimes) for land arrangements. Lowest prices overall will, of course, be during the off-season.

Generally, on regularly scheduled flights, you have the option, in descending order of cost, of First Class, Club or Business Class, or APEX. APEX is by far the most used and the most useful of these categories. Some charter service is still available; again, an agent will be able to recommend which ones are reliable. Sometimes it is also worth investigating package tours for flights even if you do not wish to use a tour's other services (hotels, meals, etc.). Because a packager can block-book seats, the price of a flight-plus-lodging package can actually be less than the cost of air fare that is booked separately.

If you have the flexibility, you can sometimes benefit from last-minute sales which tour operators have in order to fill a plane or bus. A number of brokers specializing in such discount sales have also sprung up. All charge an annual membership fee, usually about $35–$45. Among these are *Stand-Buys Ltd.,* Box 2088, Southfield, MI 48037 (800–621–5839); *Moments Notice,* 40 E. 49th St., New York, NY 10017 (212–486–0503); *Discount Travel Intl.,* 114 Forrest Ave., Narbeth, PA 19072 (800–458–5200); and *Worldwide Discount Travel Club,* 1674 Meridian Ave., Miami Beach, FL 33139 (305–895–2082). Sometimes tour and charter-flight operators themselves advertise in Sunday travel supplements, as well. Do try to find out whether the tour operator is reputable, and, specifically, whether you are tied to a precise round trip or whether you will have to wait until the operator has a spare seat in order to return.

Airlines specifically serving Mexico from major U.S. cities include:

Aeromexico, 8390 NW 53rd St., Miami, FL 33166 (305–592–1300), flies from Miami, New York, Houston, Tucson and Los Angeles. *Mexicana,* 9841 Airport Blvd., Los Angeles, CA 90045 (800–421–2214), flies from Los Angeles, San Francisco, Seattle, Denver, San Antonio, Dallas, and Miami. *Pan Am,* Pan Am Building, New York, NY 10017 (212–687–2600), flies in from Miami and Houston. *Continental,* 2929 Allen Pkwy., Houston, TX 77210, flies in from Houston. *Western,* 6060 Avion Dr., Los Angeles, CA 90009 (213–636–2345), flies in from Los Angeles and Phoenix. *United,* P.O. Box 66100, Chicago, IL 60666 (312–569–3000), flies from Chicago to Cancun and Cozumel.

From Canada: *Aeromexico* operates a weekly flight from Toronto to Mexico City and Acapulco. *Japan Airlines* has three weekly flights from Vancouver.

Typical excursion fares to Mexico City: from New York, $380; Chicago, $319; Dallas, $277; Denver, $449; Philadelphia, $339; Houston, $190; Los Angeles, $359; Miami, $225; San Francisco, $419; Seattle, $469. Lower promotional fares often are available.

From Britain: *Air France,* 158 New Bond St., London W1 (tel. 01–499–9511), flies to Mexico City via Paris and New York, and can arrange onward flights within Mexico.

Iberia, 169 Regent St., London W1 (tel. 01–437–5622), flies to Mexico City three to four times a week from Madrid. They have two flights daily from London to Madrid.

K.L.M., Time and Life Building, New Bond Street, London W1 (tel. 01–568–9144), flies to Mexico City most days of the week, via Amsterdam, and will arrange onward internal flights if requested.

Typical fares as of mid-1985:

London to Mexico City, £1,000 Economy year-round, no restrictions; £576 PEX/Budget low season, restrictions on length of stay, etc.; £633 PEX/Budget high season, restrictions on length of stay.

By Sea: Many cruises include Mexico as part of their itinerary. Most originate from across the Gulf of Mexico, usually at Miami, stopping in Key West, Cancún, and Cozumel. Others sail from Los Angeles along the Acapulco coastline. Still others include both coastlines, passing through the Panama Canal.

Empress Travel's cruise packages to Cancún, Acapulco, Mexico City, and Puerto Vallarta feature choice of hotel and round trip via Aeromexico from New York. Cruises leave from either San Francisco or Tampa. Trips are eight days and priced at $491–$1,305.

Fantasy Cruises offers a five-night cruise aboard the SS *Galileo,* starting in Miami and visiting Key West, Playa del Carmen, and Cozumel before returning to Miami. $169 to $795 per person, double occupancy depending on accommodations and season.

Cruise operators you may wish to contact (though bookings are generally handled through a travel agent) include *Carnival Cruise Line,* 800–327–9051; *Eastern Cruise Line,* 305–374–1611; *Holland American Lines,* 800–426–0327; *Norwegian Caribbean Lines,* 800–317–9020; *Princess Cruises,* 213–553–1770; *Royal Caribbean Cruise Line,* 305–379–2601; *Royal Viking Line,* 800–422–8000; *Sitmar Cruises,* 800–421–0880; and *Sundance Cruises,* 800–222–5505.

For details on the possibility of freighter travel to or from Mexico, consult either of the following specialists: *Air Marine Travel Service,* 501 Madison Ave., New York, NY 10022, publisher of the *Trip Log Quick Reference Freighter Guide;* or *Pearl's Freighter Tips,* 175 Great Neck Rd., Great Neck, NY 11021.

By Bus or Rail: Strictly for the adventurous or budget conscious, bus or rail travel into Mexico involves a transfer at one of the Texas border cities such as El Paso or Laredo or one of the bigger southern Texas cities such as San Antonio. A number of small private bus lines leave from these cities, as do the larger *Greyhound* and *Continental Trailways* lines. As for rail lines, the Mexican pullman *Aztec Eagle* leaves Nuevo Laredo, across from Texas' Laredo, once daily for Mexico City. *Amtrak's* train from Chicago requires an overnight stay in Laredo. For rail connections to the *National Railways of Mexico,* U.S. passenger representatives are located at 1100 17th St. NW, Suite 907, Washington, DC

20036 (202-347-4518/19); and 1500 Broadway, New York, NY 10036 (212-382-2262).

GETTING AROUND BY CAR. With unleaded (Pemex *Extra*) fuel often unavailable, the number of Americans driving into Mexico is declining. The government has been promising to remedy this situation, but checking with an auto club first is a good idea. Beyond that, it should be kept in mind that Mexico is part of the Third World, where Indiana Jones may be at home behind the wheel but where you might feel uneasy. Also, Mexican insurance (U.S. policies are no good in Mexico) can run $150 a month, and even regular gas is expensive. Then, too, spare parts often are hard to find. Except for quick trips to destinations near the border, it usually is better to fly down and then rent a car.

There are several major highways into Mexico from the American border. From California, at Tijuana, a good highway (#1) runs over 1,000 miles down the length of Baja California, with ferries to the mainland at Santa Rosalía, La Paz, and Los Cabos. From Arizona, at Nogales, Highway 15 follows the Gulf of California coast on the mainland for 750 miles to Mazatlán on the Pacific, then turns gradually inland to Guadalajara. From Texas, starting in El Paso, Highway 45 runs between Mexico's two great northern mountain ranges, the Sierra Madre Occidental and Sierra Madre Oriental. This road leads to the cities of Chihuahua, Torreón, Durango, and Zacatecas on the central highland, 750 miles from the Texas border. In northeastern Mexico, two main highways head south, one (#57) from Piedras Negras to Saltillo and the other, the Pan-American Highway (#85), from Laredo to Monterrey. From Saltillo, you can head to either Durango, Zacatecas, or San Luis Potosí (just about at the geographical center of the country). From Monterrey, the Pan-American Highway drops south through Ciudad Victoria and Mante down to Pachuca and then Mexico City. At Mante, Highway 80 branches off toward Tampico and the Gulf Coast. Note that the Sierra Madre Occidental's ruggedness prevents any highway from crossing it north of the spectacular Durango–Mazatlán road (#40). The farther south you get, the more east–west links exist, tying together the major north–south arteries.

Practical tips to drivers. There are two absolutely essential things to remember about driving in Mexico. First and foremost is to carry Mexican auto insurance, which can be purchased in the States from *Sanborn's,* 2011 South Tenth, McAllen, TX 78502 (512-682-3401). If you injure anyone in an accident, you could well be jailed—whether it was your fault or not—unless you have insurance. This is part of the country's *Code Napoléon:* guilty until proven innocent.

The second item is that if you enter Mexico with a car, you must leave with it. The fact that you drove in with a car is stamped on your tourist card, which you must give to immigration authorities at departure. If an emergency arises and you must fly home, there are complicated procedures to face with customs. The reason is that cars are much cheaper in the U.S., and you are not allowed to sell your vehicle in Mexico. The authorities at the airport assume that, unless you have a customs release, you have sold your car for a hefty profit. Explaining that your beloved mother-in-law is in the hospital or that your business is about to collapse cuts no ice. If such a situation should arise, contact the customs officials at the airport to see if you may leave your car in their special parking lot.

Mileage and speed limits are given in kilometers; 100 kph and 80 kph (62 and 50 miles, respectively) are the most common maximum speeds. A few of the newer toll roads allow 110 kph (approx. 68.4 mph). Cities and towns may have posted speed limits of 40 kph (25 miles), sometimes even 30 kph (18 miles), and it's best to observe them. To convert kilometers to miles, multiply by .62, or get a rough idea by remembering that 100 kilometers is about 60 miles.

The one-way street is widely used in most communities through which you may drive. Your guide is an arrow posted on the sides of corner buildings, its point indicating the direction of traffic flow. A two-pointed arrow means two-way traffic. The arrow may have the words *tránsito* or *circulación* printed on it.

In town a sign with a large *E* inside a circle stands for *estacionamiento,* or parking. Much more frequently seen is the same sign with a strong bar diagonally through the *E* and maybe the word *NO* underneath—no parking!

When you approach a narrow bridge *(puente angosto)* at the same time another car approaches the opposite end, the first one to flick his lights has the right of way.

Don't drive at night unless absolutely necessary, and even then only on the superhighways. The hazards are too many—you can't see perambulating animals soon enough; large rocks may have been left on the pavement by some motorist who had car trouble and braced his wheels with them, and then unthinkingly drove off without removing them; a pedestrian or cyclist appears around a sudden curve; new rock slides occur in mountain areas during the rainy season; potholes abound—the list is a long one and the risk not worth the little mileage gained.

During the day be alert to cattle crossings. Free-grazing animals may decide to amble across the highway just as you approach. Domestic animals frequently graze along the shoulders and the sight or sound of an approaching car could cause one or more to bolt—not always away from the pavement. Advises a Mexican, "An older animal is wise to the dangers of the highway and will seldom move fast, but watch for the young ones, like calves. They're nervous and easily frightened into bolting."

There are several toll roads in Mexico, covering mostly the last stretches of major highways leading to the capital. Some of these roads are two-lane affairs but most are four-lane with a divider strip. These highways have non-toll roads running roughly parallel. The toll roads have signs that say *cuota* and give the destination (usually *Mexico,* meaning Mexico City and perhaps an intermediary city) while the parallel routes have signs saying *libre* (free) with the destination. These two signs, with arrows pointing in different directions, are usually posted before the road splits. Remember that because of the mountainous nature of central and southern Mexico and the many trucks on the highways, driving times are longer than for comparable distances in the U.S. There are also toll bridges in various parts of the country.

When you buy insurance, you will probably receive a folder showing Mexican road signs. The essential markers are obvious even if your Spanish is nonexistent. *No* means no, and arrows show what's forbidden. Take a good look at the sign diagrams and keep them handy until you have them memorized. Here are a few words on the road signs that you should know: *alto*—stop; *no rebase*—do not pass; *ceda el paso*—yield right of way; *conserva su derecha*—keep to the right; *curva peligrosa*—dangerous curve; *derrumbes*—landslide zone; *despacio* (sometimes also *disminuye su velocidad*)—slow down; *tramo en reparacion*—road work ahead; *puente angosto*—narrow bridge; *no hay paso*—road closed; *desviacion*—detour.

Topes, meaning bumps, are indicated by a sign showing a series of bumps. As many highways—sometimes even major ones—cut through towns and villages, these bumps are the only way to slow down the speeding traffic to protect life and livestock. At times the bumps are so worn down that you don't even have to slow down, but elsewhere you have to come to an almost complete halt to make it over without damage to your vehicle, especially if it is low slung. Best to slow down when approaching any village—at times the bumps are there but the signs are not.

If an oncoming vehicle flicks its lights at you during daytime, it could mean trouble ahead. Best to slow down for a while and see what's around the curves, so that you won't run into a landslide, a stalled truck, or an accident.

As you climb into the highlands of central Mexico, your car might not feel quite right due to the altitude. This could be a result of the lower octane gasoline or your carburetor's needing adjustment.

Road maps are handy for those travelling by car or on foot in Mexico. A large selection of the most up-to-date maps are available from Bradt Enterprises, 95 Harvey St., Cambridge, MA 02140.

Aid to Motorists: The "Green Angels." The Mexican Tourism Secretariat operates a fleet of more than 227 special pickup trucks on all the nation's major highways to render assistance to motorists. Known officially as the *Radio Patrol Tourist Assistance Service,* one and all, familiarly and with affection, call them the *Green Angels.* The bilingual drivers are equipped to offer mechanical first aid to your car, medical first aid to you, communication through a two-way radio-telephone network, basic supplies of all types, towing if needed, adjustment and changing of tires, tourist information, and protection. The trucks are white with two shades of green and have a flashing red light atop the cab. The doors carry printed identification in English and Spanish.

How to hail one in case of need? Pull off the road as far as possible and lift the hood of your car. If on an isolated section of highway, then hail the first passing car in either direction and ask the driver to notify the patrol of your trouble. Bus drivers and drivers of heavy trucks will also be helpful in this respect.

The patrol's services are rendered free of charge; tips, however, are appreciated. Any spare parts, fuel, or lubricants they supply to get your car back on the road are provided at cost.

The Green Angels patrol fixed sections of highway, passing a given spot several times a day. The service is provided from 8 A.M. to around 8 P.M. every day on major highways. But remember, this is Mexico, not Switzerland. Most likely, a Green Angel will come along if you have mechanical problems, but you can't always count on it.

Insurance. Remember that your foreign car insurance coverage is not good in Mexico. Purchase enough Mexican automobile insurance at the border to cover your estimated trip. It's sold by the day, and if your trip is shorter than your original estimate, a prorated refund for the unused time will be issued to you upon application after you exit the country. *Dan Sanborn's Insurance* and *Seguros Atlantico* (Allstate reps) have offices in most border cities. Also, you might try *Instant Mexico Auto Insurance,* San Ysidro and Chula Vista, CA, and Nogales, AZ. All three are experienced, reliable.

Always lock your car securely in Mexico when no one's in it. *Never* leave valuable items in the body of the car; either lock them in the truck compartment or carry them into your hotel or motel with you at night.

At a service station. Pemex, the government oil company, franchises all the gas stations in Mexico. They are not plentiful and they do not accept credit cards or dollars.

Fuel prices are the same at all stations and are about the same as in the U.S. Regular gas is sold from blue pumps, unleaded *Extra* (when available) from silver pumps. The metric system is used; 3.7 liters equals a gallon.

Oil: Pemex's Faja de Oro (black and gold can), *Esso, Shell, Quaker State,* and *Mobiloil* are best grades of motor oil. Pemex products usually cost less. Mexican-made tires are of good quality but more expensive than in the U.S. and Canada.

Restrooms tend to be filthy, although promises are made that cleaner facilities and unleaded fuel will become available along major highways. If you must ask for the key to a locked restroom, for women it's "*la llave para damas, por favor*" (lah yah-vay pah-rah dam-mahs, pohr fah-vohr); for men, "*caballeros*" (cah-bah-YEHR-ohs).

Tell the attendant "*Lleno, por favor*" (YAH-noh)—that is, "Fill'er up." Point out the pump you want. Most cars do well on the *Nova* (blue pump), but if yours is a late U.S. model you'll need the *Extra* (nonleaded, in silver pump). Check to be sure the pump gauge is turned back to zero before the attendant starts pumping your gas; as soon as the tank is filled write down the amount of pesos shown as due. In a busy station—and most highway stations are—a second attendant may turn the gauge back to zero to service another car and your amount due may be forgotten (or escalated). Write it down to be on the safe side.

Attendants don't jump to clean your windshield the moment you pull in. As a general rule you must ask to have this done. Also, you may have to ask for under-the-hood inspection and checking of tire pressure. A tip of 50 or 100 pesos for these extra services is customary and expected. The gas stations do not have mechanics.

Automobile repair. You may have heard tales about how Mexican mechanics put motors back together with bobby pins and glue. True, the mechanics are resourceful and capable, as evidenced by the large numbers of vintage automobiles still daily plying the streets. Finding U.S.-made spare parts can be a major problem—so is trying to locate an English-speaking mechanic. We suggest that you ask for help at your hotel if you need mechanical work done on your car.

Parking. In cities, finding space on the street is often difficult. Worse, illegally parked cars are likely to be towed away. We suggest parking in pay lots, usually called *estacionamiento* (parking).

Those missing license plates. Mexican police have always employed a most effective means for punishing those who park their automobiles in forbidden areas—they remove one license plate. Redeeming it requires a trip to the local *tránsito* headquarters and the payment of a fine. In Mexico City, the officers are now supposed to write out a ticket, placing it under the wiper, but leaving the plates intact. They *do* write the ticket in most instances, but they still remove a plate, too.

Witnessing an accident. When you see an accident or an injured person, don't stop to help. Instead, notify the first policeman you see or, if on the highway the first Green Angel Tourism Secretariat truck or highway patrol car. Not helping personally is against one's instincts and training, but it can get you seriously involved, even thrown in jail. You can be accused of *mal medicina,* for instance, if you move an injured person. He, or the police, can later charge you made things worse for him, or, in the extreme, if he dies you could be accused of causing it. Far better to locate the nearest official and *then* offer your help.

Police. The color and cut of police uniforms vary throughout the Mexican Republic. Mexico City traffic and civil police all wear blue uniforms—with the addition of white gloves for dress occasions. Other special police units in the capital: park police (including young women), navy blue and grey; parking police, khaki; bank and other guards, navy blue. The city fathers have striven to assign bilingual officers along downtown Juárez Avenue, Reforma Boulevard, and the Pink Zone, the better to offer directions and any other assistance to tourists.

Some Mexican cities have added specially trained young women to their police ranks. They direct traffic and offer bilingual assistance.

Fly and drive. Not much vacation time? Fly to any major Mexican city and rent an automobile to get around in. Your travel agent can make advance reservations, and your car will be waiting for you at the airport of arrival. If you require automatic transmission, say so. It is not standard in Mexico.

Another suggestion: Make the fullest use of your available time and see more of the countryside by alternating flying and driving to various key cities, always making advance reservations to avoid possible delay. The larger auto rental firms in Mexico publish folders in English outlining such suggested Fly-Drive Tours.

Volkswagen, Nissan, and Renault produce most of the cars sold in Mexico (their prices are lower), but Chevrolet, Ford, Chrysler, and Jeep vehicles also are manufactured in the country.

Car rental, however, is not cheap. Even subcompacts run $50 per day once insurance and taxes are included. Shopping around can pay off; large discounts are available during slow periods. Check to see if mileage is free or extra; unless you are planning a long trip, usually it costs less to pay by the mile (actually, by the kilometer, since Mexico is metric).

Requirements: over 24 years of age, valid driver's license, passport or tourist card, and a major credit card.

The central reservations numbers in Mexico City for major companies are given below. Most of the auto rental firms have service stands at the international airport, as well as several outlets in the capital and in major cities throughout the republic.

Avis, tel: 578–1044; *Budget,* tel: 566–6800; *Hertz,* tel: 566–0099; *National Car Rental,* tel: 533–0375; *Romano Rent-a-Car,* tel: 250–0055 and 545–5722; *Quick Rent-a-Car,* tel: 533–4908 and 533–5335.

PASSPORTS. Passports are not formally required for entry into Mexico by U.S. citizens, though some form of identification is. Also suitable is a birth certificate or voter registration card, plus tourist card. The latter can be obtained from a travel agent or an airline agent at the airport or from local Mexican consulates.

Canadian citizens need only their provincial birth certificate and tourist card. Again, the latter is available from travel agents and airlines.

British subjects need a valid passport and a Mexican tourist card. Passport may be secured from the Passport Office, London, from passport offices in Glasgow, Liverpool, Newport, and Peterborough, or from any British consulate abroad. It is valid for ten years. Mexican tourist card may be secured from the Mexican Embassy, 8 Halkin St., London S.W.1, or the Tourist Office, 7 Cork St., London W.1; or, if already abroad, from any Mexican embassy and national airlines. Students wishing to study in Mexico and business travelers must inquire at the consulate for additional requirements. Passport or other proof of citizenship must be presented to reenter Great Britain. No limit on amount of money carried out of the country for pleasure travel.

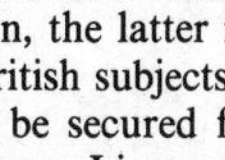

TRAVEL AGENTS. The critical issues in choosing a travel agent are how knowledgeable that person is about travel and how reliable his or her bookings are, regardless of whether you are looking for a package tour or planning to go it independently. The cost will be substantially the same whether you go to a major tour operator such as *Maupintour, American Express, Thos.*

Cook & Son, or *Olson's* or to the small agency around the corner. Most commissions are paid by airlines, hotels, and tour operators. In Europe there may be a small general service charge or fee-per-reservation; in the U.S. only out-of-the-ordinary telephone or telex charges are ever paid by the client.

The importance of a travel agent is not merely for making reservations, however. A good travel agent booking a flight for you will know what general discounts are in effect based on how long your stay will be, how far in advance you are able to make your reservations, whether you are making a simple round trip or adding extra stops, and other factors. He or she will also likely be able to suggest suitable accommodations or packages that offer the kind of services you want.

In the case of package tours, you want to be sure that the tour operator can deliver the package being offered. Here again, a travel agent can be helpful. Certainly the organizations named above have established their reputations based on reliability—the inevitable occasional foul-up notwithstanding.

Not all U.S. travel agents are licensed, as the laws vary from state to state, but membership in the American Society of Travel Agents (ASTA) is a safeguard. Similarly, U.K. agents belong to the Association of British Travel Agents (ABTA). Members prominently display ASTA or ABTA shields.

TOUR OPERATORS. In addition to airlines, cruise lines, and hotel chains, a number of tour operators—known in the trade as "wholesalers"—offer a variety of package programs to numerous Mexican destinations. In most cases these call for independent travel, although groups are handled as well. A typical package includes air transportation, airport transfers, hotels, and sightseeing. Tour operators generally market their packages only through retail travel agents, but since not all retailers handle all tour operators, you might wish to contact the various organizations to learn what they have available.

American Express, 822 Lexington Ave., New York, NY 10021; 800–241–1700.

American Leisure, 9800 Centre Parkway, Houston, TX 77036; 800–231–5804.

Asti Tours, 21 East 40th St., New York, NY 10016; 800–223–7728.

Betanzos OK Tours, 323 Geary St., San Francisco, CA 94930; 415–421–0955.

Cartan Travel, One Crossroad of Commerce, Rolling Meadows, IL 60008; 800–323–7888.

Club Universe, 1671 Wilshire Blvd., Los Angeles, CA 90017; 800–252–0862.

Compass Tours, 330 Seventh Ave., New York, NY 10001; 212–714–0200.

First Family of Travel, 3530 Forest Lane, Dallas, TX 75234; 800–527–6366.

Firstours, 1341 W. Mockingbird Lane, Dallas, TX 75247; 800–423–3118.

Four Winds Travel, 175 Fifth Ave., New York, NY 10010; 212–777–0260.

Friendly Holidays, 118–21 Queens Blvd., Forest Hills, NY, 11375; 800–221–9748.

Garza Tours, 14103 Riverside Dr., Sherman Oaks, CA 91423; 800–423–3178.

GoGo Travel, 432 Park Ave. South, New York, NY 10016; 212–683–7744.

Intersol, 3303 Harbor Blvd., Costa Mesa, CA 92626; 800–421–5365.

Mexican Representatives Inc., 3355 West Alabama, Houston, TX 77098; 800–231–6333.

Mexico Travel Advisors, 1717 N. Highland Ave., Los Angeles, CA 90028; 800–421–4037.

Thompson Vacations, 401 N. Michigan Ave., Chicago, IL 60611; 800–621–6400.

Tour Express, 5472 Leetsdale Dr., Denver, CO 80222; 800–525–1948.

Packages may include a single city or beach resort, or a combination of both (three nights in Guadalajara and three more in Manzanillo) as well as a variety of coach tours (Mexico City-Taxco-Acapulco; the Colonial Highlands; or the archaeological sites on the Yucatan Peninsula). There are rail packages that take in the Copper Canyon in northern Mexico, and fishing packages for sportsmen who want to hook a marlin off Mazatlán or Baja California. And there are special interest tours for photographers, bird watchers, bullfight aficionados, and others.

TOURIST INFORMATION SERVICES. The *Mexican Government Tourist Office* at 405 Park Ave., New York, NY 10022 (212–755–7212), and its branches, can provide only scanty, noncommercial data. Travel agencies and airlines serving the country do far better when it comes to answering questions.

Mexico City. The *Federal District Tourism Board* has counters at the International and domestic arrivals area at the airport and in the Pink Zone at Londres and Amberes (525–9380). The *Secretariat of Tourism,* Avenida Masaryk 172, Polanco (250–0123), has information on the rest of the country. Most localities in Mexico have their own tourist offices; some are better than others.

MEETING THE MEXICANS. The best way to get the feel of a country is to spend some time with its native inhabitants, learning their ways and native customs. In Mexico, for example, formality and tradition are very important. Yet Mexicans are easygoing and relaxed, and the notion of things moving rather slowly down there is not a stereotype.

Some organizations in Mexico City that can help you get to know your hosts: *Mexican-North American Cultural Institute,* Hamburgo 115, tel. 511–4720; *Anglo-Mexican Cultural Institute,* Antonio Caso 127, tel. 566–4500; *University Club,* Reforma 150, tel. 566–2266. Arrange for a guest card through your hotel.

TIPS FOR BRITISH VISITORS. National Tourist Office. 7 Cork St., London W1 (tel. 01–734–1058/9). **Insurance.** We heartily recommend that you insure yourself to cover health and motoring mishaps, with *Europ Assistance,* 252 High St., Croydon CR0 1NF (tel. 01–680–1234). When you need help, there is a 24-hour, seven days a week (all holidays included) telephone service staffed by multilingual personnel.

Money Matters. It is best to provide yourself with U.S. traveler's checks or dollar bills, as they are much easier to change than European currencies.

Electricity. Usually 110 volts. You should take along an adaptor, as razor and hair-dryer sockets are usually of the American style, taking flat-pronged plugs.

Tour Operators. *Bales Tours,* Bales House, Barrington Rd., Dorking, Surrey RH4 (tel. 0306–885–991) offers a 15-day escorted tour which concentrates on archaeological sites in Central Mexico and the jungles of the Yucatan. Cost £1,146 including some meals.

Kuoni Travel, 33 Maddox St., London W1 (tel. 01–499–8636) has a "Mexican Panorama" tour to Mexico City, Merida, Oaxaca, and Acapulco; 12 nights from £1,120. They also offer 10 nights in Acapulco, with a stop-over in Mexico City on the way, starting at £867.

Sovereign Holidays (British Airways), reservations and inquiries tel. 01–897–4545, arrange a Mexican Riviera Cruise, beginning in San Francisco 17 days later. Cost including return flight from London, from £1,796.

Speedbird Holidays, 152 King St., London W6 (tel. 01–741–8041) offer seven nights in Mexico City, from £575; seven nights in Acapulco, from £648; 14 nights visiting both places, from £748; or a 14-night tour "Down Mexico Way" staying in Mexico City, Taxco and Acapulco, with sightseeing tours and a driver/guide, from £810.

Swan Hellenic, Canberra House, 47 Middlesex St., London E1 (tel. 01–247–0401) offers an 18-day tour looking at the art treasures of Mexico, accompanied by a tour manager and a guest lecturer. £1,827.

WHEN TO GO. The peak tourist season is from mid-December through April. Rates at beach resorts usually drop between May 1 and December 15. Spring and fall are pleasant and generally uncrowded. Summer is when Mexicans themselves travel, schools being on holiday at that time of year. The rainy season runs from June into October, although rain seldom falls for more than two or three hours a day.

MONEY. The Mexican peso floats, and its relationship to the dollar and other currencies changes from day to day. Inflation has been running at an annual rate of about 80% in recent years. All this can be confusing. Hotel rates are not changed from day to day, but other prices, including those appearing in restaurant menus, frequently are. The good news is that while the purchasing power of the peso constantly is slipping, that of the dollar tends to grow.

Dollars and traveler's checks may be exchanged for pesos at banks, exchange houses *(casas de cambio),* or at most hotels. Hotels give the poorest rate. Funds should be carried in traveler's checks and exchanged sparingly, since converting pesos back into dollars is difficult.

Most major U.S. credit cards are accepted in popular resorts and the bigger cities—in the better hotels and restaurants—but as policies change, it is advisable to check before planning a credit card splurge. In smaller towns and rural areas, forget about using credit cards unless at a foreign tourist-oriented hotel or restaurant.

Traveler's checks are widely accepted. Banks usually provide the best rate of exchange, but you might lose time if things are busy. Most airports have money exchanges at the same rate as banks. You can usually get more pesos for your dollars at Mexican airports or banks than at U.S. airports, which often charge a 1% commission.

We advise that you change your traveler's checks gradually, as you need them, throughout your vacation. This will protect you in case of theft and you will receive a bit more for your dollars the longer you wait, due to the gradual slide (devaluation). Although it is not advisable to keep large amounts of cash on you, private money exchangers in resorts or the big cities can give you 10 to 20 pesos more to the dollar (cash only) than the banks.

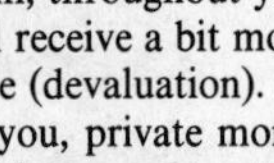

WHAT TO TAKE. Every guidebook ever published has set forth the same advice to anyone contemplating a foreign trip: *travel light!* And every tourist always takes too much anyway.

If traveling by air to Mexico, or to Central and South America, you are limited to 2 bags not to exceed 132 lbs. Of course, if you are driving your own automobile or taking a ship cruise, you have greater flexibility. Yet it is never wise to burden yourself with more than you, one person, can comfortably carry.

For air travel two average-size suitcases, or one spacious suitcase and one fold-over garment bag, should be sufficient and should come within the allowable weight limits. The suitcases should preferably be of the flexible, lightweight types especially manufactured for air travel.

When coming to Mexico by plane, we recommend your two suitcases be packed very lightly, enabling you later on to put the bulk of your clothing into one and your purchases into the other. (Carry-on cases or bags are presumably limited to a size that will fit under your seat, and some carriers are strict about enforcing this.) If driving, it's not a bad idea to bring one entirely empty suitcase or other sturdy container for the same purpose—to hold all your purchases.

What to bring to wear depends on personal choice and your vacation destination or destinations. Going to Puerto Vallarta and Acapulco? Or Zihuatanejo? Mazatlán? Cozumel? All are beach resorts calling for swim suits and lightweight sport clothes. And not too many of those, either, because all these places sell wonderful, high-style resort clothing, and you are not going to be able to resist buying some. Prices range from reasonable to outrageous. So, shop well before buying.

Other than that: a pair of comfortable sandals (or for women, two or three pairs), tennis shoes, a sweater, light raincoat and hat, and folding umbrella during the summer months (the rain comes, sometimes in buckets, and then quickly passes) will do nicely. Acapulco and Puerto Vallarta are casual to the extreme—anything goes in the line of dress, and the wilder the better. The other resort cities are slightly more conservative, but for cocktails and evenings out dress is always on the elegant-casual side—like pantsuits or caftans for women.

Mexico City is, and has always been, both dressy and conservative-minded. Here women will need a small supply of street dresses—all those marvelous new fabrics that are drip-dry, wrinkleproof, and so on—plus one lightweight wool suit, a sweater or two, at least two simple cocktail dresses or dressy pantsuits. In the winter, an all-weather coat and perhaps something to protect the head (Mexican rebozos do beautifully here!). Always, at least one pair of dress shoes, one or two pairs of comfortable, well-broken-in walking shoes; other shoes as desired, or as packing space allows.

Until recently women were warned of Mexico City's extreme conservatism—no wearing of shorts, slacks, nothing way-out in the way of personal street wear. This is no longer entirely true. Mexican women have adopted pantsuits for day and evening wear with great enthusiasm, hence their visiting counterparts should be allowed the same latitude. Keep current styles in mind when preparing to come to Mexico's capital. The city has become very fashion conscious in recent years.

Strangely, the familiar warning against either men or women wearing ordinary walking shorts on Mexico City streets is still valid. Nor do you wear such items in the provincial towns. Save street and sport shorts for the resort cities alone. Mexican city women in pantsuits, however, by traveling through the countrysides on weekends and vacations, have done a good job of inuring the conservative natives to the sight of "a woman in men's pants!"

Normally, formal wear will not be needed, unless you may be invited to a dressy diplomatic affair. Long cotton dresses are popular all around the country for evenings in a home or out on the town. A light wrap, if not too bulky, may come in handy for chilly evenings. But why not save precious packing space and buy a pretty Mexican *rebozo* (shawl) after arrival.

Men will need one dark suit, with appropriate accessories, for dress. Otherwise, a plentiful supply of slacks, one or two sport jackets, sport shirts, one or two long-sleeved, drip-dry shirts, a sweater or two, and at least one pair of sandals, tennis shoes, or comfortable walking shoes. During the winter, a light topcoat. During the summer: a raincoat or light all-weather coat that can serve in rain, as well as some type of cap. One or two ties—some city restaurants will not admit a man without jacket and tie. Men will want to buy at least one *Guayabera* shirt while in Mexico. Called the most practical men's shirt ever invented, it is worn outside the trousers.

Except for visiting country Indians who always wear them, neither men nor women wear hats in Mexico City as a general rule. It is no longer a requirement for women to cover their heads when entering a church or cathedral, but many still feel more at ease with a handkerchief or light scarf over their hair.

Both men and women: A pair of tennis shoes or other sturdy, rubber-soled footgear is a necessity if you plan to go pyramid climbing, or if a visit to the cobblestone-streeted cities of Guanajuato, San Miguel Allende, or Taxco is included in your itinerary. The centuries-old pyramid steps and cobblestones are well worn and slippery under leather soles.

If you're driving about the country in your own car, dress for comfort, by all means, but remember: no shorts outside of the resort cities.

Precaution for automobile travel: If you are getting around via car with a guide-driver, one of the first things he will tell you is not to leave any of your possessions in sight in the body of the car when you are not occupying it. This means, when sightseeing or shopping during the day, lock everything in the car trunk.

The warning is even more important when you are driving your own automobile, that is, one with foreign license plates. Discourage thievery by taking anything expensive—camera, tape recorder, radio, and the like—into your motel or hotel room at night. Keep your luggage locked when you are out of your room. Try not to park your car overnight on the street—most motels and hotels have garages or parking lots with night guards—and always lock your car unless you need to leave your key with the parking attendant. These simple precautions have become a modern necessity almost anywhere in the world, and Mexico is no exception.

Other helpful items to bring: Your camera, of course. No country is more photogenic than Mexico. Each person is allowed to bring in one regular and one movie camera, with 12 rolls of film for each, and it's a good idea to bring the limit because you might not find your favorite make of film. Your citizens band radio is now allowed free entry. A small flashlight will prove its value many times over—the electric power about the country sometimes goes on and off like a yo-yo.

Bring at least one can of spray insect repellant with you. Mosquitoes are plentiful in many areas, and so are the *jejenes,* a tiny, nearly invisible, pesky native insect that bites like fury. The red welts and itching last for days. The *jejene* favors the warm archaeological zones, grassy areas and the seashore.

Also, among smaller items: a tweezers, small scissors, a roll of cellophane or magic transparent tape, a few rubber bands, a notebook or two and ballpoint pens, and a sewing kit that includes a few spare buttons. A plentiful supply of paper tissues or a roll of toilet tissue, a bar of soap in a small plastic container, and maybe a small quantity of paper towels. As in so many parts of the world, public restrooms in Mexico often lack these items. A small-size plastic bottle or other container of your favorite powdered detergent—avoid liquids if possible. Cream or powder perfumes and colognes are preferable to the liquid; if you do bring the liquid variety, be sure to seal the top with cellophane.

WHAT IT WILL COST. Cost for a typical day for two in a top resort such as Acapulco, Cancun, Cabo San Lucas, or Puerto Vallarta:

Double room at a top hotel, with taxes	$125
Meals for two with moderate drinking	105
Drinks and show at a nightclub	55
Cocktails	15
Tips	20
	$320

This is the big splurge. You can easily cut costs in half by staying in a less expensive hotel, and eating at a less expensive restaurant. In major cities such as Guadalajara, Monterrey, and Mexico City, you can easily lop off 30% from the above prices. In other important cities, figure 35–40% less, while in the rest of the country, you will not need to spend even half of the costs quoted above. It is perfectly feasible to travel around Mexico for $40 to $100 per day (excluding car rental) without any belt tightening. The main items in your budget will be hotels and restaurants, covered below. In general, the more Spanish you speak, the cheaper it will be to travel, especially if you are willing to risk eating Mexican cuisine and going without confirmed reservations.

SEASONAL EVENTS. Mexico's provincial heart beats for fiesta time, and the Spaniards' centuries-long efforts to eradicate the "pagan" and instill their own version of culture served only to bring about a haphazard, but happy, amalgamation of the traditional and the enforced. The Mexicans adopted those forms they liked, combining them with those they already knew, and rejecting the others. Mexico's fiestas, then, are uniquely Mexican, a blend of religious mysticism, gaiety, pageantry, fantasy, and history. And if the Mexican could have his way, he'd schedule a fiesta every other day of the year!

Fiesta time in a village or town invariably centers around the church and the main plaza, or *zocalo,* both always gaily decorated, with elaborately costumed folk dances and constant fireworks displays the main bill of fare.

The following calendar gives but a selection of the types of fiestas to be found about the country.

January 1—Mitla, state of Oaxaca, celebration by Zapotec Indians with all-night fires. In the city of Oaxaca itself, New Year's Trade Fair, with serenades in Hidalgo Park, many games, fireworks, and other events.

January 6—Three Kings Day (Santos Reyes), observed all over Mexico. This is the traditional date when Mexican children set out their shoes, expecting them to be filled with gifts.

January 17—San Antonio Abad and Blessing of the Animals. All over Mexico not only household pets, but cows, pigs, and chickens, all flower- and ribbon-bedecked, are carried or led to the churches for priestly blessing.

January 18—Santa Prisca, in Taxco, state of Guerrero; fiesta of the silver town's patroness.

January 20—San Sebastián (St. Sebastian)—in Chiapa de Corzo, state of Chiapas, and in cities of León and Guanajuato, state of Guanajuato, a fair and folk dances. In Tehuantepec from 18th on: dances of the Isthmus and processions by women. Chiapa de Corzo's fiesta lasts through the 23rd.

February-March (variable dates)—Carnival (Carnaval) in Mazatlán, state of Sinaloa; Veracruz, state of Veracruz; Huejotzingo, state of Puebla; Mérida, Yucatán, and Tepoztlán, state of Morelos. Lasts 7 days, merrymaking includes lavish masquerade dances, battles of flowers, election of queen and parades of floats.

February 2—Dia de la Candelaria, dances, parades, bullfights all over Mexico.

This Festival ("Candelaria" means Candlemas) is particularly colorful in Tlacotalpan, Veracruz. Fair and Exposition, public dancing featuring "La Bamba," horse races, water-sports competition on the Papaloapan River, and the Pamplona-like "running of the bulls" (turned loose in the streets to help spectators hone their bullfighting skills).

February 19—Cuautla, Morelos, celebrates the breaking of Spanish siege of city during the War of Independence in early 1800's. All-out fiesta.

March-April (variable date)—Holy Week, widely observed with special passion play presentations all over Mexico, especially in Taxco, state of Guerrero (all week); in Ixtapalapa, near Mexico City, on Good Friday, in Pátzcuaro, Michoacán, and at El Cubilete near Guanajuato city.

March-April—during Easter Week annual handicraft and native costume exhibition and competition in Uruapan, Michoacán.

March 10–21—Irapuato, Guanajuato (on toll Highways 57-D and 45-D from Mexico City), Mexico's strawberry capital, holds its annual Strawberry Fair and Agricultural, Livestock, Industrial and Handicrafts Exposition.

March 21—Guelatao, Oaxaca—Commemorates birth of Benito Juarez with popular fair, fireworks, other events.

April 1–7—San Cristóbal de Las Casas, Chiapas—Celebrates founding of city with participation of natives in colorful regional costumes.

April 15-May 5—Aguascalientes—"Feria de San Marcos" (Fair of St. Mark) actually falls on April 25, but fete is one of most important in Mexico, celebrated accordingly. Features native "Matachines" dances, "mariachis," bullfights, etc.

April 15–17—Fortin de las Flores, Veracruz, offers a Flower Fair, popular festival in town renowned for its gardenia-filled swimming pools.

April 23–30—Villahermosa, Tabasco—Annual Agricultural, Livestock, Industrial, Trade and Cultural Fair with horse races, bullfights, and even regattas on scenic Las Ilusiones lake.

April 28—Chumayel, Yucatán—Festival of the Holy Christ, usually lasting through first days of May; all the usual festivities plus the typical Yucatecan dances called "Jaranas." Biggest plus, though, is that one of the very few extant *Chilam Balaam* chronicles—Books of the Mayan Soothsayers—was discovered here.

May 3—La Santa Cruz (The Holy Cross)—Fair and folk dances in Milpa Alta, of the Federal District, and in Valle de Bravo, state of Mexico.

May 3–4—Felipe Carrillo Puerto, Quintana Roo—Religious festival with Mayan dances, cockfights, etc. in town once better known as Chan Santa Cruz, stronghold of insurrectionist Mayans until well into 20th Century.

May 15—All over Mexico: San Isidro Day, dances, livestock decorated with flowers.

May 10–20—Etchojoa, Sonora—Religious festival of the Holy Ghost, featuring "The Deer" and "La Pascola" dances, popular fair.

May 20–28—Tecoh, Yucatan—Festival of the Hammocks, with Fair, regional dances, other events.

May 31—Tehuantepec, Oaxaca—Beginning month-long fete with dances, processions and Grand Fair featuring regional arts and crafts. High spots of celebration are June 21, 24 and 29. On Highway 190.

May-June (variable date)—Corpus Christi Day. In Mexico City children, including babes in arms, are dressed in native costumes and taken to the cathedral on the *zocalo* for blessing. Afterward they'll pose for anyone in and about the *zocalo*—it's a field day for the photographer, amateur and professional. In Papantla, Veracruz, all-day presentation of Dance of the Flying Birdmen, a pre-Hispanic ritual to the sun.

June 1—Navy Day, celebrated in all of the more important ports in the country.

June 4–13—Cardenas, Tabasco—Fete honors St. Anthony of Padua with large fair. 30 miles from Villahermosa.

June 24—Dia de San Juan (St. John the Baptist)—anywhere in Mexico you might get doused with a bucket of water. In some towns important formal celebrations begin earlier and/or last beyond this date. Examples: Guanajuato, June 15–24; Navojoa, Sonora, June 23–24; Tehuantepec, Oax., June 23–27.

July 7–15—Comitan, Chiapas—Festival of St. Fermín, also known as Festival of Lights because of the offerings of beautifully-fashioned candles deposited in and around the church. Scenic Montebello Lagoons nearby.

July 15–31—Cd. del Carmen, Campeche—Traditional July festival in honor of Our Lady of Carmen (also celebrated in Mexico City and many other parts of the country). A really swinging fiesta featuring fireworks, games, bullfights, aquatic contests, even an important fishing tournament.

July 22—Uruapan, Michoacán—Fete honors St. Mary Magdalen with regional dances, colorful procession. Lovely National Park on city's outskirts plus unique Tzaráracua Falls. On Highway 37 from Carapan, Mich.

July 28—Tlalpan, Federal District—Traditional Fair dates back to colonial days held in main square. Southern outskirts of Mexico City.

July 31—Chetumal, Quintana Roo—Festival of St. Ignatius, though festivities actually begin week earlier on July 25. Reached from Merida or via Highway 186 from Villahermosa, Tabasco.

August 1–15—Aguascalientes, Ags.—Regional Grape Fair, varied festivities.

August 8—Paracho, Mich.—Traditional Festival in town noted for quality of its handmade musical stringed instruments. A flower-bedecked steer is sacrificed, cooked with special ingredients to prepare a ceremonial food called "Shuripo" in accordance with pre-conquest pagan custom. Reached via Highway 15 to Carapan, thence #37 to Paracho.

August 12–19—Villa Escalante, Mich. (better known as "Santa Clara del Cobre"), famed for its beautiful handmade copper articles, annual Copper Fair with exhibitions, dances, parades, many other special events. From Mexico City, Highway 15 to Morelia, then #120.

August 14–29—Córdoba, Ver.—Celebrates signing of Córdoba Treaties which recognized Mexican Independence in 1821. Sports events, bullfights, music, etc. On toll Highway 150-D.

August 15—Assumption Day—observed in Huamantla, state of Tlaxcala; Cholula, state of Puebla, and in Milpa Alta, Federal District.

August 15–16—Huamantla, Tlaxcala—Annual fair with exhibits of regional handicrafts, wool-woven products, features beautiful carpets made of flowers and sawdust "paving" the streets. On Highway 136.

August 21—Dances all day at Cuauhtémoc Circle on Reforma Blvd., Mexico City—also on Aug. 13.

August 23—San Bartolo Naucalpan, State of Mexico—(An industrial suburb of Mexico City on NW outskirts), another traditional fete with all the trimmings.

August 25—San Luis Potosí—Festival honors St. Louis with regional dances of "Matachines" and "Malinches," serenades, etc. Highway 57.

August 27–31—Zacatecas, Zac.—Traditional Festival of "La Morisma" with re-enactment of battles between Moors and Christians.

August 28—Puebla—Festival of St. Augustine, dazzling fireworks, city decorated with colorful paper hangings, seasonal fruits and nuts abundant.

September 6–9—Cholula, Pue.—Festival of Our Lady of the Remedies featuring native dances in the atrium of that church, sitting atop largest pyramid in the world. Highway 190, 9 miles this side of Puebla.

September 7–8—Nativity of the Virgin Mary in Tepoztlán, state of Morelos.

September 14–30—Campeche, Camp. dedicates fete to the Christ of San Roman with raffles, serenades, regional musical comedies. Highway 180.

September 16—Independence Day—starts the night before when all over Mexico public officials give the "grito," Father Hidalgo's original cry for independence.

September 29—San Miguel (St. Michael)—in San Miguel de Allende, state of Guanajuato, and in every other town or village with Miguel in its name, bullfights, fireworks, folk dances and concerts on the Saturday following.

September (last Sunday)—Fiesta of Atlixcáyotl in Atlixco, Puebla, with exhibitions of traditional regional dances. Very colorful. From Mexico City, #150/150D to Puebla, marked turnoff to Atlixco.

October—Guadalajara, Jalisco—Month-long festival of cultural events, music, dance, fair in Parque Agua Azul, opera, theater.

October 1–8—San Francisco (St. Francis), a coffee growers' fair featuring folk dances in Cuetzalán, state of Puebla.

October 12—Columbus Day (Día de la Raza). Festivals in Guadalajara, state of Jalisco, and religious celebration in nearby Zapopan.

October 22—Apatzingán, Mich.—Fete commemorates date of Mexico's first constitution, written here. State Fair. Reached via Uruapan going south on Highway 37.

November 1–2—All Souls' Day and Day of the Dead—in Mixquic, Federal District; the island of Janitzio, state of Michoacán, and in much of provincial Mexico, candlelit all-night vigils at cemeteries, graves decorated with offerings of food and flowers for the departed.

November 15—Halacho, Yucatán—Festival in honor of St. Santiago with bullfights, dances, other diversions. On Highway 180 near Mérida.

November 20—Anniversary of the Mexican Revolution.

November (last week, or early December)—Silver fair in Taxco, Guerrero.

December—In Acapulco during the first two weeks of the month, the *Nao de China* (China Ship) recalls when ships came in from the Orient during colonial times.

December 8—Nuestra Señora de la Salud (Our Lady of Health), in Pátzcuaro, state of Michoacán, festival in honor of the town's patroness, featuring folk dances, an arts and crafts fair, much more.

December 12—Día de Guadalupe (Day of Our Lady of Guadalupe), Mexico's patroness saint, observed all over the country, but especially at the shrine in Mexico City with processions, native folk dances, etc.

December 16–25—Christmas season, widely observed all over the country with *posada* processions leading to Christmas parties, nativity plays, fireworks. Mexico City is decorated throughout like a brilliant Christmas tree.

December 18—Nuestra Señora de la Soledad (Our Lady of Solitude), in Oaxaca, state of Oaxaca, festival and folk dances in honor of the city's patroness. Celebrations start as early as November 25.

BUSINESS HOURS AND HOLIDAY CLOSINGS. Banks are open from 9 A.M. to 1:30 P.M. Monday through Friday. In some larger cities, a few banks open their offices Saturday mornings. Stores are generally open from 9 or 10 A.M. to 7 or 8 P.M. In many areas, businesses close for the lunch hour, from 2 to 4 P.M.

National Holidays. (All government offices, banks, and most private offices are closed).

January 1—New Year's Day (Año Nuevo).

February 5—Constitution Day, observing the framing of the Constitutions of 1857 and 1917.
March 21—Birthday of Benito Juárez, known as the "Abraham Lincoln of Mexico."
May 1—Labor Day—parades.
May 5—Anniversary of the Battle of Puebla in 1862, when the Mexicans defeated the French Army.
September 16—Independence Day—starts the night before when all over Mexico public officials give the "grito," Father Hidalgo's original cry for independence.
October 12—Columbus Day (Día de la Raza).
November 20—Anniversary of the Mexican Revolution.
December 25—Christmas Day.

The following additional dates are not official national holidays but are so widely observed that businesses may be closed on some of them:

Holy Week (prior to Easter) sees commercial activity slow down on Monday and come to a full halt on Thursday; resorts are crowded.
May 10—Mother's Day, always observed on the same date and featuring special celebrations all over the country.
June 29—Day of St. Peter and St. Paul.
July 16—Day of the Virgen del Carmen.
July 25—St. James.
August 13—Fall of Tenochtitlán (Aztec capital which became Mexico City).
August 15—Day of the Virgen de la Asuncion.
August 25—Day of San Luis (St. Louis).
September 1—President's annual report to the nation; banks and government offices close.
November 22—St. Cecilia's Day.
Christmas Week (following Christmas)—Most business and government offices close until January 2.

TRAVELING WITH PETS. Not recommended. If you choose to travel with a pet, you must have a statement of good health from a licensed veterinarian that is certified by a Mexican consul.

HOTELS. Hotels and other accommodations in this guide are divided into categories, arranged primarily by price. These categories are *Gran Turismo,* or *Super Deluxe,* where the visitor can expect all amenities in a special, luxurious atmosphere, particularly in the larger cities and posh resort areas; *Deluxe; Expensive; Moderate;* and *Inexpensive.* Although the names of the various hotel categories are standard throughout this book, the prices under each category may vary from zone to zone. This variation is meant to reflect local price standards, and takes into account the fact that a moderate price in a large urban area might be considered quite expensive in a rural region. In every case, however, the dollar ranges for each category are clearly stated before each listing of establishments. Costs are given for a double room and exclude tips and other extras.

Note: Hotel rates are set and approved by the *Government Tourist Secretariat;* no hotel can raise its prices without official permission. However, due to inflation, hotel rates are raised frequently to meet increased costs. Current approved rates are posted in each hotel room.

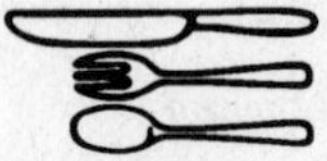

DINING OUT. The cost of dining out can vary a great deal in Mexico but it never comes close to top New York prices. Most resort areas and larger cities are filled with restaurants that serve a type of food called "international," which, if not very exciting, at least has the redeeming feature of familiarity. The same restaurants will also have a selection of Mexican dishes, toned down for the tourist trade. Just to make certain, you could say *sin picante* (no hot stuff) when ordering. If you try a non-tourist restaurant (no English menus) you can generally tell if it's a good place by seeing how crowded with locals it is. Many of these places feature a set menu lunch (with some choices) called *comida corrida* from about 1 to 4 P.M.—quite filling and inexpensive. Remember the general rule that if a place looks clean, you probably won't have tummy problems, but you can never be 100% certain, even in a hotel restaurant. Stick to bottled beverages to be on the safe side. And forget about a good French wine with your meal; it's not available except at a few top restaurants, where it costs much more than in the U.S. You could try Mexican wine (Okay, without being anything special—the whites are generally better than the reds), Chilean (more expensive but not outrageously so) or Spanish (often quite passable). Or stick to the excellent Mexican beers.

Mexicans have their big meal in the afternoon, sitting down to a leisurely feed around 2:30 or 3. At night, few self-respecting restaurants really get going before 7:30. Many of the dining places will have live music during the busy hours. Mariachis are favored, but in most parts of the south there are marimba bands and quiet singing or instrumentals.

In the *Practical Information* sections of the various chapters, we list the restaurants, along with the basic price of a meal that includes an entree, main course and dessert *without* drinks, or tip; the 15% federal sales tax is included in the price, but many restaurants list it separately so that figuring the tip is easier. As elsewhere, seafood tends to be more expensive, especially large shrimp or lobster. Resort areas and the bigger cities often have quite passable restaurants, including Italian, inexpensive Chinese, Japanese (good but expensive), and Argentine (where you can get a good-sized hunk of meat).

Credit cards are in wide use in the better restaurants. Ask if yours is accepted when you make a reservation. Most places that accept the Mexican *Bancomer* credit card will also accept *Visa; Carnet* in Mexico corresponds to *Mastercard* and *Banamex* to *Mastercharge.*

TIPPING. In Mexico you will be on safe ground to use the same percentages you would back home. Remember that in this country service charges are seldom added to hotel, restaurant, or bar bills. It is, therefore, up to you to remember the waiters, bellboys, maids, bartenders, porters, and any others rendering personal service.

The following is a suggested guide for individuals:

Waiters—15% of restaurant or bar bill.

Bellboys—100 pesos per bag or other item.

Porters—Same as above.

Hotel maids—100 pesos per day.

Taxis—a tip is not expected, although many passengers give the driver the small change left over from the fare.

Ushers at major shows or sporting events—50 pesos.

Parking policemen and car-watchers 20 to 30 pesos, and usually same per hour (important to remember when visiting museums and the like).

Shoeshine boys—their fee, not a tip, is 100 pesos in Mexico City.

Tourist guides—for meeting service for 1 or 2 persons at airport or railroad station, $1 U.S. per person. For ½-day tour (3 to 4 hrs.), $2 U.S. per person; full day, $4. per person. Use your own judgment for longer trips (a week or two, for instance); much will depend on your guide's service and general excellence. A fair tip for a 6-day tour would be $20–$24 U.S. per person.

Bus groups, in addition to tipping their guide, usually make up a small pool for the driver. Not essential, but always much appreciated.

Additional tipping hints: Always try to carry with you a bunch of 5-, 10- and 20-peso coins. Don't tip less than 5 pesos. Don't overtip.

SHOPPING. The sentence has been repeated so often it's become a cliché, but it's absolutely true, nonetheless: Mexico is a shopper's paradise. It's the land where the beautiful or unusual item lovingly created and decorated by hand is still considered king—where new materials, paints, and finishes are, often reluctantly, adopted only where they enhance the final effect of traditional, time-honored designs. It's the land, too, of the small, family-run handicraft workshop where quality, not quantity, remains the watchword.

It's also inhabited, unfortunately, by the entrepreneur who turns out cheap, shoddy merchandise masquerading as "native handicraft" to satisfy the souvenir hunter looking for a bargain. The shopper needs a discerning eye to sort out the chaff, selecting only those pieces worth buying and carrying home to treasure. (As an example, when buying copper elsewhere than in Santa Clara del Cobre, examine it carefully to be sure it's not just sprayed iron, which would be heavier than the real thing.)

Bargaining? Of course. It's a game of fluctuating values that can be played to the hilt with roadside vendors and in the native markets. Some items sold by Indians at street-side in places like Oaxaca and Chiapas are so low in price that it's a shame to even try bargaining—they are so poor and, in comparison, you are so rich. Along beach areas, it's just the opposite—they overcharge. Try offering half of the asking price and come up very slowly. Unless you just must have the item, never pay more than 70% of the asking price. Show interest but not too much. Walking away will almost always result in your last offer being accepted. Shops have fixed prices but it can't hurt to ask for a discount; you can often get 10% off at all but the most exclusive shops. For U.S. Customs purposes, Mexico is classified as a "developing" country. This means that many of its local products may enter the U.S. entirely free of Customs duties, that they do not count on your $300 exemption. Since the list of products is long, and is reviewed every year, you should write to: Department of the Treasury, U.S. Customs Service, Washington, D.C. 20229, for the latest edition of the brochure, *GSP & the Traveler.*

Driving down through Mexico, one finds woolen serapes, rugs, in Saltillo. Certain villages in this state weave rebozos only of silk (a rebozo is the Mexican version of the stole), some of them reputedly of such fine thread they can be slipped through a woman's finger ring.

Semiprecious stones—delicately purple amethysts, opals in a range of colors —are found in the Querétaro region. You will be approached here by ambulatory vendors who bring handkerchief-wrapped stones out of their pockets, but confine your purchases to reputable stores in town to be sure of the quality.

The expanses of the country to the east and west of Querétaro are craft wonderlands. Off to the east is Mexico's Mezquital region, land of the Otomi and Huastecan Indians, who create a wide assortment of hand-embroidered and handpainted items ranging from woodenware to pillows, bedspreads and sash-belts—and who gather, bottle, and sell wild honey.

To the west lie some of the richest handicraft-producing states of the entire country: Michoacán, Jalisco, and Guanajuato, with Aguascalientes, a bit north of these, noted for fine embroidery. Many villages throughout these states make variations of one item, according to a plan originally devised by an enlightened Spanish bishop who wanted the townspeople to become fine artisans by specializing.

Thus, one finds highly decorated, durable lacquerware in Uruapan, Pátzcuaro, Olinalá, and Quiroga; pottery in many villages, each producing its unique type; copperware in Santa Clara del Cobre (near Pátzcuaro); guitars in Paracho; handmade blouses and exquisite embroideries in Morelia, Pátzcuaro, Erongarícuaro, and Guadalajara (as well as Aguascalientes, mentioned above). Hand-woven textiles of unusual design are found throughout these states, as are woolen and silk rebozos, woolen serapes, ponchos, and rugs.

Jocotopec, on Lake Chapala in Jalisco state, is famous for fine white wool serapes, most of them woven in traditional designs, but some with a surprisingly modern feel. Uruapan, noted for its lacquerware, is also becoming known as the home of the weaving studio of the Ilsleys, an American couple who work with native artists and follow traditional techniques to produce unusual textiles.

Pátzcuaro, lying in the heart of the Tarascan Indian country, is a most versatile craft center, producing pottery, lacquerware, wood carvings, serapes, rebozos, baskets, jewelry, copperware, and henequen (sisal) rugs in lovely designs and all sizes. Guanajuato offers its own type of pottery, some jewelry, baskets and fiber purses.

Fine quality ceramic ware is found in Guadalajara's neighboring towns of Tlaquepaque and Tonalá, as well as colonial-style furniture, hand-tooled leather work, and stylish fashions for women based on native designs. Guadalajara's artisan suburb of Tlaquepague has hand-blown glass factories (so does Mexico City).

Guadalajara and its border village of Zapopan, lying near the almost inaccessible Huichol Indian country, are the best sources for authentic Huichol craft—the cross-shaped "God's Eyes" and striking yarn paintings of wool in brilliant colors, the woven sash-belts and small, over-the-shoulder purses (both worn by the Indian men, not the women).

Coming farther south, Valle de Bravo, in the state of Mexico, makes a different type of pottery, sold only through its native market. Toluca, also in the state of Mexico and one of the highest cities in the country (8,710 feet), offers at its Friday market a bewildering array of handloomed cloth, serapes, baskets of all shapes and sizes, jewelry of bone, fiber rugs and mats, and reed furniture, among many others.

Nearby Metepec is noted for its "trees-of-life" and other ceramic figures, as well as cooking pottery of all types. Puebla produces fine ceramic ware in shades of blue, yellow, and white and is famous for its Talavera tiles.

Taxco produces fine silver jewelry and table items, as well as "wedded metal" ware (silver and brass) in a variety of styles—traditional or modern Mexican, Danish modern, some even Oriental in feel. Don't buy cheap silver—yes, it's available. Good silver is not pliable in the fingers, and the products of all reputable factories (many of them small home affairs) bear the stamp of a spread eagle—the hallmark of Mexican sterling. Taxco also produces a line of fine ceramics.

A wide variety of good silver is also available in Guadalajara, Guanajuato, San Miguel de Allende, and Mexico City. Authentic handicrafts from every corner of the country can, in fact, be found in the capital, for about the same price.

Cuernavaca and Acapulco shops feature smart resort wear for men and women—tailored pants, pantsuits, simple dresses—both short and long—with stunning embroidery, lacy beach coats and sun hats, and the popular *chaleco* jacket—a cotton, pleated-front, long-sleeved sport shirt (girls use them for beach jackets).

The entire state of Oaxaca abounds in native crafts. Oaxacan pottery is black, slightly green-glazed, and of excellent quality. Its serapes are of soft, beautifully designed and woven wool. Its jewelry is like no other—gold filigree pieces modeled after the ancient treasures found in Monte Albán tombs, and dangly gold-coin earrings and necklaces, highly favored by Oaxacan women. Leathercraft, rebozos, wood carvings, baskets, daggers, and knives with intricately designed handles, and hand-woven textiles are plentiful. Native dresses are favorite carry-home items for women visitors—the state has more than 100 distinct and different regional female costumes.

Neighboring Chiapas, perhaps the least known and least developed of all Mexican states, produces exquisite and sturdy cross-stitch work and embroideries. Mérida has basketware of all sizes, shapes, and colors, and is the home of the handsome Guayabera shirt (straight bottom, worn outside trousers). This is also the place to buy fine hammocks and Panama-type hats.

Like the fiesta calendar, this is only a sampling of what's available throughout Mexico. Shopping through native markets and city stores alike is such fun one needs either an extra-roomy car trunk or a few of the strong, dyed-fiber carryall bags readily available everywhere—each one a souvenir in itself.

TIME ZONES. Mexico stays on standard time all year. Most of the country is on central time; there are two other time zones, as follows:

Pacific standard—Northern Baja California (Tijuana, Mexicali, Ensenada and San Felipe).

Mountain standard—Baja California south of the 28th parallel; west coast of mainland south to, but not including, Puerto Vallarta.

If you are vacationing in Mexico during daylight savings summer months in the United States and wish to make a phone call to the Eastern U.S., remember that their clocks are 2 hours ahead from the bulk of Mexico, 3 hours ahead if you're in Baja, and 4 from Tijuana or Mexicali.

ELECTRIC CURRENT. All Mexico is on 60-cycle, 120 voltage current. This means that your small electric appliances (shaver, hair dryer, electric hair-rollers, etc.) will operate as well and as safely anywhere in Mexico as they do at home. Plugs are the same as in the U.S. but you might want to take an extension cord, as outlets are not always conveniently located.

In any event, we advise that both men and women carry with them a hand razor for emergency use when the electric power goes off—which happens frequently in every corner of Mexico. Nobody understands exactly why, but that's the reason every hotel and motel room is equipped with a candle. Just in case you wondered! Power failures are most frequent during the violent downpours of the rainy season—and this happens in all parts of Mexico.

TELEPHONES. The country's telephone system works most of the time, but as there are too few lines, you might have to wait a bit to get through during peak business hours in Mexico City. Before making a long-distance call from your hotel, it might be a good idea to find out how much the surcharges run. It is often cheaper to make your international call from a long-distance concessionary, called *caseta de larga distancia.* The problem is that they are sometimes hard to find and it's unlikely that much English will be spoken. In smaller towns, these casetas could be in a corner of a bustling store, where it is not easy to hear over the usual bustle.

To call Mexico from the U.S., dial 01152 and the local area code; within Mexico dial 91 and the local area code. To call the U.S. from Mexico, dial 95 and the area code, or dial 09 for an English-speaking international operator who will assist you (collect calls, as they are not subject to hefty Mexican taxes, are less expensive than calling direct, but the caller is subject to a service charge if the call is not accepted or the person called cannot be reached). Domestic long-distance operators in Mexico (who rarely speak English) may be reached by dialing 02.

The government owns and runs the telephone system with no competition. Long-distance calls abroad cost much more than domestic calls—about twice. Collect calls are usually accepted only to the U.S., Britain and a few European countries. Within Mexico, long-distance calls are more reasonable, but still expensive by U.S. standards. In a person-to-person call (national or international), you will be charged the equivalent of a one-minute station call, even if the party you asked for is not there. This is to prevent cheating by the use of some previously agreed-upon code.

Local calls from a coin booth are a ridiculously cheap one peso, which works out to something like five calls for a penny.

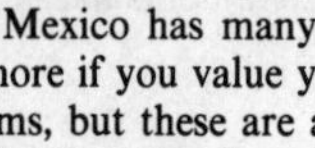

LAUNDRY AND DRY CLEANING. Service here can range from good to impossible. Best to send items out through your hotel, or ask at the front desk which place they recommend.

Self-service laundromats have mushroomed recently in the larger cities, but all still have at least one attendant to assist you. For a small service charge you can leave your dirty laundry at the laundromat and pick it up several hours later—the attendant will handle it for you. Prices are reasonable.

Mexico has many hole-in-the-wall dry-cleaning establishments it's best to ignore if you value your clothing. At the same time, there are many excellent firms, but these are all located in the larger cities. Try to avoid having items either laundered or dry-cleaned in the smaller towns.

SENIOR CITIZEN/STUDENT TRAVEL. Senior citizens should always have an identification card with them, even though resort areas do not generally offer any special discounts. All student travelers should obtain an *International Student Identity Card,* which is in most instances needed to get student discounts, youth rail passes, and Intra-European student charter flights. Apply to *Council On International Educational Exchange,* 205 East 42 St., New York, NY 10017, 212–661–1414, or 312 Sutter St., San Francisco, CA 94108, 415–421–3472. Canadian students should apply to the *Association of Student Councils,* 44 St. George St., Toronto, Ontario M5S QE4, 416–979–2604.

The following organizations can also be helpful in finding student flights, educational opportunities, and other information. Most deal with international student travel generally, but materials offered by those listed do cover Mexico.

Council on International Educational Exchange (CIEE), 205 East 42 St., New York, NY 10017, 212–661–1414; and 312 Sutter St., San Francisco, CA 94108, 415–421–3472, provides information on summer study, work/travel programs, and travel services for college and high school students, and a free charter flights guide booklet. Their *Whole World Handbook* ($6.95 plus $1 postage) is the best listing of both work and study possibilities.

Institute of International Education, 809 United Nations Plaza, New York, NY 10017, 212–883–8200 is primarily concerned with study opportunities and administers scholarships and fellowships for international study and training. The New York office has a counseling service and library; satellite offices are located in Chicago, Denver, Houston, San Francisco, and Washington. *Vacation Study Abroad* is an annually revised guide to over 900 courses offered by both foreign and American colleges and universities. *U.S. College-Sponsored Programs Abroad* gives details on foreign study programs run by American schools, for academic credit. These publications are $9.95 each, including first-class postage and handling.

Arista Student Travel Assoc., Inc., 1 Rockefeller Plaza, New York, NY 10020, 212–541–9190, is a specialist in the field of youth travel, offering student and young adult tours.

Your World Travel Services, Inc., 2050 West Good Hope Road, Milwaukee, WI 53209–2889, 414–351–6363, has an eight-day tour to Mexico for students.

Specific information and rail and other discounts are listed in the appropriate sections.

In Canada: *AOSC (Association of Student Councils),* 44 St. George St., Toronto, Ontario M5S 2E4, 416–979–2604 is a nonprofit student service cooperative owned and operated by over 50 college and university student unions. Its travel bureau provides transportation tours and work camps worldwide.

HANDICAPPED TRAVEL. *Access to the World: A Travel Guide for the Handicapped,* by Louise Weiss, is an outstanding book that covers all aspects of travel for anyone with health or medical problems; it features extensive listings and suggestions on everything from availability of special diets to wheelchair accessibility. Order from Facts on File, 460 Park Ave. South, New York, NY 10003 ($14.95).

Tours specially designed for the handicapped generally parallel those of the nonhandicapped traveler, but at a more leisurely pace. For a complete list of tour operators who arrange such travel, write to the *Society for the Advancement of Travel for the Handicapped,* 26 Court St., Brooklyn, NY 11242. Another excellent source of information is *Rehabilitation International U.S.A.,* 1123 Broadway, New York, NY 10010, which publishes the "International Directory of Access Guides." *Moss Rehabilitation Hospital,* 12th St. and Tabor Rd., Philadelphia, PA 19141, answers inquiries regarding specific cities and countries and provides toll-free telephone numbers for airlines that have special lines for the hearing impaired. They also have listings of selected tour operators.

International Air Transport Association (IATA) publishes a free pamphlet entitled "Incapacitated Passengers' Air Travel Guide" that explains the various arrangements to be made and how to make them. Write IATA, 2000 Teel Street, Montreal, Quebec H3A 2R4.

HEALTH. Most travelers to Mexico are eventually hit with a diarrheal intestinal ailment known facetiously as Montezuma's Revenge or the Aztec Two-Step. Tolerate it as best you can, for it generally lasts no more than three days. If it is going to hit, it will usually come early in your trip. Most victims suffer only a few watery stools for a day or two. Others may have nausea and abdominal pain, while a few develop a fever. The best anti-diarrheal agent seems to be paregoric, which generally dulls or even eliminates the abdominal cramps. Most doctors advise taking one and one-half tablespoons followed by a teaspoonful after each bowel movement until the diarrhea ceases. This usually will not take more than four or five hours. If this is your own personal remedy, bring it with you; it requires a doctor's prescription in Mexico. Some doctors recommend Kaomycin, a liquid, 1 tbsp. to be taken every 4 hours. This contains neomycin (antibiotic) and kaopectate. It can be bought without prescription at Mexican *farmacias* (drug stores). Another favorite remedy is Lomotil, available in Mexico without prescription.

A recent panel at the National Institutes of Health recommended against the use of antibiotic drugs (such as enterovioform, available without prescription in Mexico) as a means of **preventing** travelers' diarrhea. The two major antimicrobial agents tested as preventatives—doxycycline and trimethoprim, taken alone or with sulfamethoxazole—were cited by the panel as useful and effective. Pepto-Bismol and two antimotility drugs, diphenoxylate (Lomotil) and loperamide (Imodium) were suggested for mild cases. If you come down with it anyway, rest as much as possible, since traveling and strain makes the bug last longer. Drink lots of tea (without milk) or, in severe cases, a salt-sugar mixture added to water to rehydrate yourself.

Health and Medical Supplies

1. Carry with you on your trip a small supply of whatever medical products you customarily use at home—aspirin, throat lozenges, vitamins, and such. The same brands may not be available in Mexico.

2. If some of the above are on prescription, be sure to have the prescription with you and handy to show at the border on your return trip to the U.S., or the American customs agents may seize your pills or powders.

3. Tetanus and typhoid shots are not required, but, if they make you feel safer, have them administered well before your departure from home. Also gamma globulin to prevent hepatitis (maybe) if you plan on going to out-of-the-way places.

4. If you wear prescription glasses, prescription sunglasses, or contact lenses, be sure to carry one extra pair of each with you, as well as a copy of your eye prescription.

5. If you have a serious medical problem of any kind (like diabetes or epilepsy), wear a neck or wrist tag to this effect—a *MedicAlert* tag is good.

6. Be sure to carry with you an identification card showing whom to notify in case of serious illness or death, your Social Security number, and identification card for any insurance, especially medical. It's also a good idea to note your blood type on the ID card, especially if yours is a rare type.

7. Many English-speaking doctors, dentists and other specialists live in Mexico. U. S. Embassy in Mexico City has a list of approved physicians. Call 553–3333 day or night. Same at the British Embassy, 511–4880. The U.S. consulate in Guadalajara also has a similar list. In other cities your hotel may be able to help.

Mosquito and other nuisance bites can be prevented by liberal applications of insect repellent. If you get bitten, an antihistamine cream can reduce swelling and itching. Rubbing wet soap on a bite and letting it dry is also good first-aid for itching. There have been recent cases of malaria on the southern Pacific coast and in a few other areas, so ask your doctor about prophylactic quinine tablets. In Mexico, you can purchase malaria-preventive Aralen without a prescription. These tablets should be taken regularly, according to instructions, before entering a malarial region.

MAIL. Usually letters and postcards reach their destinations within a week, or sometimes two weeks. Postage rates go up periodically with no advance warning (compensating for inflation). Hotel news stands usually have stamps for sale, but charge more than face value. Post office hours are from 8 A.M. to 6 P.M.

ENGLISH LANGUAGE MEDIA. *The News,* published in Mexico City, is a good general newspaper distributed in larger cities and resorts. Local English newspapers will be covered in the various chapters. There's an occasional undubbed English-language film on TV but just about everything else on TV or at movie houses is in Spanish. Mexico City has an English-language FM radio station, affiliated with CBS. Many first class and luxury hotels pick up U.S. television programs beamed by satellite.

AIRPORT DEPARTURE TAXES. Known as the Airport Use Fee, this is U.S. $10 or the equivalent in pesos on the day of departure. The fee for domestic departures is included in the ticket price.

Most flights open for check-in two hours before departure time. It is suggested that you arrive early, as reserved seats are given on a first-come, first-served basis. Many internal flights have open seating and Mexican politeness does not extend to queues. During holidays, airports are madhouses and waiting lists are long. On crowded flights, even confirmed reservations can be cancelled if you don't show up at least 30 min. before departure. Not quite as punctual as their U.S. or European counterparts, Mexican flights usually do leave on time. Don't plan on tight connections, because your checked luggage might not accompany you. On domestic flights there is a penalty of up to 50% of the value of the ticket charged to no-shows. When you are booked on a flight, it pays not to miss it.

CUSTOMS. U.S. residents may bring in $400 worth of foreign merchandise as gifts or for personal use without having to pay duty, provided they have been out of the country more than 48 hours and provided they have not claimed a similar exemption within the previous 30 days. Every member of a family is entitled to the same exemption, regardless of age, and the exemptions can be pooled. For the next $1,000 worth of goods a flat 10% rate is assessed.

Included in the $400 allowance for travelers over the age of 21 are one liter of alcohol, 100 non-Cuban cigars and 200 cigarettes. Only one bottle of perfume trademarked in the U.S. may be brought in. However, there is no duty on antiques or art over 100 years old. You may not bring home meats, fruits, plants, soil or other agricultural products.

Gifts valued at under $50 may be mailed to friends or relatives at home, but not more than one per day of receipt to any one addressee. These gifts must not include perfumes costing more than $5, tobacco or liquor.

Canada. In addition to personal effects, and over and above the regular exemption of $150 per year, the following may be brought into Canada duty-free: a maximum of 50 cigars, 200 cigarettes, 2 pounds of tobacco and 40 ounces of liquor, provided these are declared in writing to customs on arrival. Canadian customs regulations are strictly enforced; you are advised to check what your allowances are and to make sure you have kept receipts for whatever you may have brought abroad. Small gifts can be mailed and should be marked "unsolicited gift, value under $25 in Canadian funds." (You should also include the nature of the gift.) For other details ask for the Canada Customs brochure "I Declare."

British residents. Returning from Mexico (or any other non-E.E.C. country), you may import duty free: 200 cigarettes or 100 cigarillos or 50 cigars or 250 grammes of tobacco (*Note* if you live outside Europe, these allowances are doubled); plus one liter of alcoholic drinks over 22% vol. (38.8% proof) or two liters of alcoholic drinks not over 22% vol. or fortified or sparkling wine; plus two liters of still table wine; plus 50 grammes of perfume; plus nine fluid ounces of toilet water; plus other goods to the value of £28.

In addition, no animals or pets of any kind may be brought into the U.K. The penalties for doing so are severe and are strictly enforced; there are *no* exceptions. Similarly, fresh meats, plants and vegetables, controlled drugs and firearms and ammunition may not be brought into the U.K. There are no restrictions on the import or export of British and foreign currencies.

MEXICO

MEXICO—THE LAND AND ITS PEOPLE

An Insight into History

by
KAL MULLER

A native of Hungary, Kal Muller became a resident of Mexico in 1973, after visiting some eighty countries. He has two books to his credit (with two more in the works) and many magazine articles, including some in the National Geographic. *A photographer as well as travel writer and researcher, Kal has accompanied three peyote pilgrimages with Mexico's Huichol Indians. He lives in Guadalajara with his Mexican wife and their two children.*

A French historian once defined the concept of country by calling it an aggregate formed, above all, by shared suffering. If that is the case, Mexico has had more than its ration of traumas to forge the nation.

Before the arrival of the Spaniards, there were several brilliant and complex Indian cultures in this country. All were authoritarian and, with the possible exception of the early Aztecs, there was no trace of democracy—Greek, British, or American style. Conformity was the norm, not individuality. Technological advances were not sought. These factors were to plague the nation later on. On the positive side, there was a tradition of mutual help and strong bonding within the extended family and community. Sadly, some of this has been lost in contemporary Mexico, except in Indian groups who hold to their traditions.

Another critical problem has been a lack of initiative, on both the individual and the community level. Mexicans became used to a strong central government throughout their history, with a leader controlling the purse strings and telling people what to do. There is a definite line of absolute authority from the Aztec emperors through the Spanish viceroys to the contemporary presidents. The worst mess the country was ever in—at least since the Spanish conquest—came during the three decades after independence when a strong central authority was lacking: There was endless internal fighting and Mexico lost half of her territory to a self-justifying American concept called manifest destiny.

The Conquest

Shortly before the arrival of Hernán Cortés, the Aztec empire was in full expansion, artistically, architecturally, and militarily. There had been, to be sure, some reversals. The Tarascans of Michoacán had twice stopped the Aztec war machine in its tracks. The Zapotecs and Mixtecs, reluctant tribute payers, had withstood an Aztec siege at Tehuantepec. Close to home base, the Tlaxcalans had never been conquered. But by and large, no group was strong enough outside its home territory to challenge Aztec domination of the region. Many communities were paying onerous tribute to the Aztec capital of Tenochtitlán.

The Conquest of Mexico by Cortés is an epic saga in the history of military conquests. Burning his ships and venturing into unknown territory, at first with only four hundred men and a few horses, Cortés combined tough fighting with diplomacy to exploit the weaknesses of the Aztecs. The Spaniards' weapons were superior, as were their military tactics. The Aztec emperor Montezuma II believed that Cortés was a god returning to claim his kingdom. All of this makes a fascinating story. The Spanish view of the conquest was best rendered by the common foot soldier Bernal Díaz del Castillo in his *Conquest of New Spain.* The Aztec perspective is found in *The Broken Spears* by Miguel Leon Portilla.

The conquest left an important psychological legacy called *malinchismo* which bedevils Mexico to this day. The term refers to La Malinche—also known as Doña Marina—Cortés's native mistress-interpreter-advisor. Her paramount importance in the Spanish victory is undeniable. She is hated as a traitor to her race, and her name has become associated with the trait of rejecting one's cultural and material heritage, finding anything foreign better than the Mexican. (This trait, sad to say, may be partially justified in view of the shoddy manufactured goods often produced in Mexico today.)

After the fall of Tenochtitlán, the conquistadores embarked on the exploration and conquest of the rest of New Spain. There was tough fighting in Yucatán, which was not subjugated for three decades, but by and large the small Spanish forces swept away opposition after a few sharp battles. Then, when the Spanish Crown decided that the conquistadores were getting too big for their britches, power was concentrated in the hands of viceroys, who proceeded to rule Mexico for three centuries in the name of the Crown, administering it as private royal property.

Mexico as a Colony

The disciplined and well-organized Indians of central Mexico accepted their new white lords and exchanged a sort of folk Catholicism for their old religions. The Indians and their lands were divided up among Spaniards favored by the Crown or its representatives. In return for labor and tribute from the Indians, the Spaniards were supposed to protect their charges and instruct them in the Catholic faith. There were, however, shocking abuses, which continued in spite of the good intentions of the Crown, whose directives for better treatment of the Indians were often ignored. The worst scourge for the natives was a succession of epidemics of European origin—smallpox, typhus, cholera—which wiped out from 50 to 90 percent of the Indians, according to various accounts. (Excellent descriptions of the colonial land-grabbing patterns are found in Leslie Byrd Simpson's *The Encomienda in New Spain* and François Chevalier's *Land and Society in Colonial Mexico.*)

The only recourse that the Indians had against the power structure was through the missionaries, who often were able to mitigate some of the worst abuses. Several of the early priests and friars also took a genuine interest in the traditional cultures. A great amount of knowledge comes from their writings, especially Father Bernardino Sahagun's monumental work, written in conjunction with surviving Aztec elders, *General History of the Things of New Spain.* Despite this interest, the priests also burned all the Indian writings they could find, considering them the work of the devil. No one was more zealous in this pyromania than Diego de Landa, bishop of Yucatán, who, however, wrote enough about the Mayas to help later scholars unravel the mysteries of this very special group.

Three missionary orders split up Mexico among themselves, with the Dominicans pushing into the south, the Franciscans taking the center, and the Jesuits moving north. (This was not a rigid division, but today you can see the different architectural styles of these three orders in the respective regions.) It is undeniable that the Catholic church played a leading role in the assimilation of the Indians into the Spanish framework and culture, although many Indian groups have maintained to this day elements of their traditional culture or synthesized outside influences with their own values. (The role of the Catholic church in colonial Mexico is best described by Robert Ricard in his *Spiritual Conquest of Mexico.*)

If the Indians of central Mexico accepted Spanish domination, the "wild" tribes of the northern part of the territory were less easily subjugated. They had no central authority which could be crushed with one military blow. However, once the silver mines of Guanajuato, Zacatecas, Santa Barbara, and other places were discovered, the bonanza made the push to the north inevitable. Slowly the Indians were more or less subdued through force, diplomacy, and religion, but occasional bloody rebellions occurred. Parts of Chihuahua had their "Indian problems" through much of the nineteenth century.

During the three centuries of colonial rule, the Spanish Crown exploited Mexico, taking out huge amounts of silver, which financed often fruitless European adventures such as the disastrous Armada attack on England which was so decisively defeated. The river of silver pouring in prevented Spain from developing a manufacturing infrastructure similar to that of northern Europe, as it was easier simply to purchase needed items. Mexican silver was also the main trade item for the Manila Galleon, which brought Asia's riches to Mexico and Spain. But the working of the mines exacted a terrible toll in the lives of the Indians, who were forced to work in atrocious conditions.

During colonial times initiative was often stifled by the necessity of waiting for approval of projects from Spain. Nepotism and favoritism bred a stifling bureaucracy. In desperate attempts to raise more and more funds from Mexico, the Spanish Crown sold important government positions in which the officeholder was free to enrich himself as much as circumstances permitted. One needed then as now to grease palms to get things done or circumvent laws and regulations. With a few notable exceptions, officials were seldom chosen on the basis of ability. Much of the above is still true in contemporary Mexico.

Social problems and frustrations finally ended the colonial period. While the Indians were mostly docile and obedient, other segments of Mexican society resented the domination of the *gachupines,* Spaniards born in the Iberian peninsula who by law received all the best positions in Mexico. *Criollos,* pure-blooded Spaniards born in Mexico, were denied the opportunity to advance to the most prestigous posts. *Mestizos,* mixed-bloods, were much lower on the totem pole, followed by the pure-blooded Indians and the blacks, who had been imported to work in the mines.

Independence and Pandora's Box

Although the War of Independence was started in 1810 by the radical priest Father Miguel Hidalgo, after some initial victories at Guanajuato and Guadalajara his rabble was soon defeated by royalist forces. Small-scale guerrilla warfare continued, but, ironically enough, independence from Spain would finally be achieved by the most conservative elements of Mexican society. Under the impulse of new ideas from France, the Spanish *cortes,* or parliament, wrote a new, liberal constitution. Then Napoléon imposed his drunkard of a brother, Joseph, on the Spanish throne. Mexican conservatives reacted by supporting their own rebellion, into which guerrilla forces were assimilated. A Mexican emperor was installed. That did not last long, however. Mexico embarked on several decades of turmoil, the worst in the country's history.

From 1821, when independence was at last achieved, until 1855, when the liberals took over the country, Mexico had atrocious growing pains. The conservatives advocated a strong central government, allied themselves with the Catholic church, and aimed to keep class privileges. The liberals were anticlerical and took as models both the U.S. and France. The battles, mini-revolutions, and coups of the period are too numerous to even list. Only one name stands out, that of the perpetual dictator Antonio López de Santa Anna, who loved power, whose convictions changed with circumstances, and who appeared and reappeared in the presidential seat like a jack-in-the-box.

Mexico's most traumatic experience was the loss of half of her territory in the period 1835–1853. Problems started when Mexico forbade slavery in Texas, which then belonged to her. Santa Ana led the troops at the Alamo and San Jacinto, meeting defeat at the latter. Texas declared independence, and in 1845 became part of the U.S. In 1846 began the War of Intervention, more familiarly known in the U.S. as the Mexican War. In 1848 Mexico surrendered, and ceded to the U.S. her northwest territories: present-day California, Arizona, New Mexico, Nevada, Utah, and Colorado. Baja California just missed being grabbed by Big Brother.

If Texans remember the Alamo, the Mexicans remember Chapultepec Castle. In the final stages of fighting between the U.S. forces under General Winfield Scott and the Mexicans, the military school cadets fought to the last boy. Sixteen-year-old Juan Escutia grabbed the flag and leaped to his death from the highest rampart rather than face the disgrace of capture.

In spite of having lost the war, Santa Ana managed to become president again. But finally even he made one mistake too many. In order to support himself in the luxurious style he loved, he sold a chunk of his country—the southernmost part of Arizona—to the U.S., which transaction is known up north as the Gadsden Purchase. After this, Santa Ana could no longer be tolerated by his countrymen. The liberals under Benito Juárez took the reins of power.

Juárez as President

Juárez was a pure-blooded Zapotec Indian from Oaxaca. He is often considered the Abraham Lincoln of Mexico for having held his country together at a time of crisis. Juárez was a liberal who made his convictions into law. He attacked the special privileges of the Catholic church, and offered enormous tracts of church land for sale. This plan backfired, however: The church retaliated by excommunicating the buyers of its property. This meant that the peasants for whom the land was meant were afraid to go through with the purchases, while unscrupulous speculators grabbed enormous properties. Juárez also made the mistake of insisting on private property for the Indians instead of the traditional communal lands. As a result, more tracts were bought by the speculators. The conservatives fought back against Juárez; the bitter War of Reform lasted from 1858 to 1861. The liberals won but the treasury was exhausted. Foreign debts went unpaid.

Britain, France, and Spain then mounted a joint military expedition to collect their due. Britain and Spain soon pulled out of the venture, but Napoléon III of France persisted. Meanwhile, the Mexican conservatives convinced the nobleman Maximilian of Austria to become emperor of Mexico. Supported by Napoléon III and imposed by the force of French arms, Maximilian turned out to be a closet liberal in resplendent conservative clothes. To the dismay of the conservatives, the emperor restricted working hours and child labor, forbade corporal punishment of criminals, and—horrors—not only restored communal property to the Indians but went after abusive hacienda owners. Maximilian, who loved Mexico, never understood that he was unacceptable to the liberals just because he was an imposed foreigner. He thought he was really wanted by the Mexican people.

Juárez had holed up in northern Chihuahua, in what is now Ciudad Juárez. Soon, the conservatives were giving none but the most tepid of support to the emperor. The U.S., having finished its civil war, now had the power once more to enforce the Monroe Doctrine. Napoléon III judged it prudent to withdraw French forces from Mexico. Juárez came back at the head of the liberals and in 1867 had poor Maximilian executed. He was president until his death in 1872. But the liberal comeback was not to last much longer.

Dictator from Oaxaca

Porfirio Díaz, a *mestizo* general from Oaxaca, became president in 1877. He dominated Mexican politics for the next thirty-four years, most of it from the presidential chair. He took the country in an iron grip and tolerated no opposition. Lots of strict administration and no politics were the order of the day. Political liberty would be granted when Díaz judged that it would be compatible with the progress of the nation—a typically empty dictatorial statement. Any challenge to Díaz's authority was quickly crushed, as decisively as were the bandits (who had become a plague). The Catholic church was given back some of its lands and privileges.

As the internal situation stabilized, foreign investments poured in, thanks to generous concessions to foreigners for mining, banking, oil drilling, and, above all, railroad building. Manufacturing increased by leaps and bounds. Díaz, fully aware of the United States's power and domineering tendencies, tried to balance American investments with those of Britain and France. He is credited with a still often-used saying which conveys his country's plight: "Poor Mexico. So far from God and so close to the United States."

Most of the productive land became concentrated in the hands of a few thousand *latifundistas,* owners of huge tracts. Emphasis was on cash crops such as coffee, tobacco, sugar, and hennequin. A group of advisors, called *científicos* or scientists, applied rational ideas in order to turn Mexico into a modern nation. It all sounded wonderful, on paper anyway. Mexican newspapers were allowed only to praise the regime. The American newspaper baron, William Randolph Hearst, acquired a 2.5-million-acre spread in Chihuahua for a song—or rather for eulogies of Díaz in his newspapers.

Very few leaders paid attention to the conditions of the working stiffs. The peon on the hacienda, the miner, the factory worker were given starvation wages and no voice whatsoever in politics. It was the worst of repressive regimes. Strikes were handled by the army, with bullets the most persuasive of arguments. The inhuman working conditions were described in horrible detail by the American writer John Kenneth Turner in his *Barbarous Mexico.*

Eventually Don Porfirio made a fatal mistake. He said in an interview with an American newspaper that Mexico was ready for a real election. A wealthy landowner from the state of Coahuila, Francisco Madero, took up the challenge. When Madero began to campaign, Díaz finally realized that his long regime was not very popular. He had Madero arrested, but it was too late. Armed revolt broke out.

Revolution

The Mexican Revolution, which lasted from 1911 to 1920, was a complex and bloody affair. While Pancho Villa and Emiliano Zapata are known to everyone, several other figures loomed large in the struggle, men who were more important in the long run than either of these popular folk heroes.

It is not easy to keep track of the winners. Mexico was not blessed or cursed in this conflict with a single revolutionary leader. So who won in the end? Madero was elected president in 1911, and Díaz took a ship to France to live in exile. Madero, vacillating and afraid to make a clean sweep of Díaz's supporters, was murdered in 1913 by the reactionary general Victorian Huerta, who received the backing of the U.S. ambassador. (This episode of U.S. meddling on the conservative side still does not sit well with Mexicans.) Huerta assumed the presidency. The governor of Coahuila, Venustiano Carranza, put himself at the head of the opposition. His right-hand man was General Alvaro Obregón, and his unruly and reluctant allies were Villa and Zapata. General Huerta represented the conservative status quo, while his enemies advocated land reform and were anticlerical. High-minded President Woodrow Wilson went about helping the rebels, but in the worst way possible: He sent U.S. troops to occupy Veracruz to cut off Huerta's supplies. Carranza joined Huerta in denouncing the intervention. The U.S. troops left Veracruz and the Mexicans went at each other again. After some tough fighting, the good guys won—that is, the revolutionaries Carranza, Obregón, Villa, and Zapata.

Now the plot thickens. The good guys started to fight among themselves: Carranza and Obregón versus Villa and Zapata. Villa was defeated by Obregón; Zapata was treacherously murdered. Carranza proceeded to father the 1917 constitution, but failed to move quickly on the paramount problem of land reform. He then picked his successor, wishing to remain the power behind the presidential throne. In the elections, Obregón opposed Carranza's puppet. When it looked as though Obregón would win, Carranza had him arrested. Obregón escaped and gathered his forces together. Carranza tried to escape by train but was caught and shot. End of revolution.

President Obregón set the pattern for much of postrevolutionary Mexico. He had the support of the peasants and workers, but he also realized that his country needed foreign capital as well as native businessmen. So he compromised, as do most politicians under difficult circumstances. Obregón carried out land reform in some areas but not very much in his native north (except as regards the Yaqui Indians, who had been part of his loyal troops). He also encouraged foreign mining and oil companies, in violation of the constitution, which clearly states that the subsoil belongs to the nation. Obregón renegotiated the foreign debt, making peace with the bankers. He was thus able to secure the arms necessary to put down a couple of nasty little rebellions led by cashiered military leaders. Politicians began an association with businessmen which lasts to this day—with resulting corruption which also lasts. Labor unions were given some rights, but under government supervision.

The toughest problem was the Catholic Church. Its power had to be broken. In 1923 the Vatican's nuncio was expelled, as were all foreign-born priests. Convents and Catholic schools were closed. Church properties were confiscated. (See Graham Greene's *The Power and the Glory.*) The Catholic hierarchy reacted by closing the churches and encouraging a rebellion. Obregón's successor, Plutarco Elías Calles, tried to crush the rebels and met with mixed success. After his presidential term was up in 1928, Calles remained the paramount political power in the country—until Lázaro Cárdenas became president in 1934.

According to many liberal historians, Cárdenas was the best president that Mexico ever had. He carried out large-scale land reform and brought some order to the corrupt labor unions. With the backing of the constitution and the Supreme Court, he nationalized the oil industry. Diplomatic relations were broken off with Britain, whose nationals owned the lion's share of the oil wells. For once, America was not the villain. After a quiet request for compensation, President Franklin Roosevelt kept to his "Good Neighbor" policy. This bore fruit when Mexico cooperated with the U.S. during World War II.

The legacy of the Revolution is definitely positive, although many basic problems remain. It is undeniable that the lot of the common man has improved tremendously since the days of Porfirio Díaz. A majority of peasants work their own land, most children go to school, and much of the population has access to medical services. Mexico has one of the largest middle classes of any developing country.

Contemporary Mexico

Agriculture and land reform are still major headaches. Whether to emphasize land distribution or efficient production—that is the question. As part of the agricultural reform laws, haciendas were broken up and land redistributed—not with titles to individuals but to associations of *campesinos* called *ejidos.* This land can be passed from father to son but cannot be sold, nor can it be used as collateral for a loan. A special rural bank was created for farm loans, but bureaucracy, inefficiency, and lack of funds have often prevented loans to the *ejida-*

tarios from coming through on time. There are still tracts of land that are illegally large, belonging to men who have managed to keep what they had before the Revolution or acquire large spreads afterwards. (These men are sometimes politicians or their relatives.) In the northwest, especially the state of Sinaloa, modern, efficient, export-oriented farming is carried out on irrigated land. Should these large-scale operations be broken up into small, inefficient units? The owners of these large farms are theoretically small landowners, who, by means legal and illegal, have managed to control areas large enough to make modern agricultural techniques worthwhile. They have done this sometimes by renting lands belonging to *ejidos,* a practice which goes against the law. No one denies the efficiency of these spreads. Nor does financing these operations present problems. (For a thorough description of this issue and much more, see Lamartine Yates's *Mexico's Agricultural Dilemma.*)

Another continuing problem is the high birthrate, which produces a larger work force than the economy can absorb. Many Mexicans seek work in the U.S., an arrangement which is convenient for both countries. It eases the unemployment problem in Mexico and provides hard workers for the U.S. But, more important for both countries, employment in the U.S. serves as a safety valve—a large, poor group of unemployed workers in Mexico could easily fall under the spell of left-wing ideologies, perhaps starting a Central American type of rebellion. If Cuba, Nicaragua, and El Salvador are getting uncomfortably close to home base for us gringos, it should be remembered that Mexico shares a fifteen-hundred-mile border with the U.S. It is in the long-term interest of Americans to allow the immigration of "wetbacks" as well as to have the U.S. market open to Mexican agricultural products, steel, and other items; all of this contributes to the stability of our neighbor. If occasionally Mexico comes out with some uncomfortably left-wing rhetoric, one must consider how much power socialists and communists have within the country: practically none, for now.

A humorous Mexican publication once asked the rhetorical question: Who won the revolution? The answer, after many blind alleys, was the PRI, the Partido Revolucionario Institucionalisado, the official government party. So far, the PRI has never lost an important election for the presidency or the governorships. By means fair or foul, it always comes out the winner. The candidates campaign as if their lives depend on it, but the outcome is a foregone conclusion. The process of selecting the PRI's candidates goes on out of sight, sheltered from public scrutiny, let alone participation. The candidate is unveiled at the appropriate moment and that's it. It is generally known that the president chooses his successor, but he must not pick a man unacceptable to leaders of the *campesinos* and unions. Although he wields almost absolute power for his one legal term of six years, when the president steps down from office he must fade from sight.

As long as there are no major economic crises, most Mexicans accept the PRI, just like death and taxes, as something not very pleasant but inevitable. When the oil boom was in full swing, the government had lots of money to spread around, some of which trickled quite far down the socioeconomic ladder. International bankers were falling all over themselves to lend money to Mexico, and the government was only too happy to oblige. Then the debt crisis hit. Prices and demand for petroleum, Mexico's chief export, plummeted.

Mexico now has the dubious distinction of having the second-highest foreign debt in the world. (Brazil's is first.) The International Monetary Fund has imposed some drastic belt-tightening measures. Most citizens have had to accept a lower standard of living. Opposition political parties have begun to make waves.

The left recently won municipal elections in the important town of Juchitán in the state of Oaxaca, but the PRI forced its officials out of city hall. The right won elections in the state capitals of Chihuahua, Guanajuato, San Luis Potosí, and Hermosillo, and these new mayors and city councils *were* allowed to function, albeit with problems from the governors, always loyal to the central government. The PRI has realized that it can no longer present just any candidate and be assured of an automatic victory. Better-qualified men have been selected by the PRI for various government posts. It remains to be seen if the electoral process is to be fair and honest. The current moral-renovation campaign is making little headway against the entrenched system of corruption, but some fairly big fish from the last administration have been indicted and even jailed, often on charges of becoming rich for "inexplicable reasons."

The future of Mexico depends on its internal reforms as well as the help and tolerance of the U.S. Efficiency within the country is desperately needed, and some very tough economic and political problems must be resolved. Exports to the U.S., acceptable foreign loan terms, and no outside interference in internal affairs are essential keys to the continued stability of Mexico.

Insights into the Mexicans

by
DAVID DODGE

Mexicans are a brand-new race, historically speaking. Their paternal ancestors were the conquistadores; their maternal ancestors were the descendants of Indians native to this part of the world for several thousand years: Aztecs, Mayans, Tlaxcalans, others. As their name implies, the conquistadores were inclined to grab what they wanted without regard to prior property rights or the wishes of the grabbee, and their sons in some cases grew up with the same affection for their fathers as their mothers had—namely, none at all. They invented a name for the conquerors of Nueva España, as Mexico was called in colonial days. The name was *gachupín,* derived from an Aztec word meaning "man who wears shoes with spines sticking out of them" (since the Aztecs had never seen spurs, or horses, until the Spaniards brought both to the New World, and had no word in their language for either). The war cry, "*Muerte a los gachupines!*"—"Death to the *gachupines!*"—later regularly rallied their descendants during Mexico's bloody struggles to throw off the Spanish yoke.

Los gachupines, at times, looked down upon their mixed-blood offspring as worthless cattle, and bragged of their own simon-pure Castilian blood, even though it wasn't any purer or was even more mixed than any other national blood-strain in Europe. The constant humiliations of this superior-inferior relationship, the institution of peonage fastened on the country by *gachupín* landholders, other repeated reminders to the Mexican that in his own land he was second low man on the totem pole—a degree above an Indian slave—crushed any pride of race he might have felt at an early date in his history.

He, too, when he was able to fight his way out from under the burdens of poverty, illiteracy, and savage exploitation by his aristocratic betters, bragged of the pure *castellano* blood of his forebears, explaining away the Indian darkness of his skin as the effect of tropic sun—as indeed it had been in his ancestors. He couldn't claim to be *gachupín,* because *gachupines* were by definition born in Spain. He became *criollo,* Creole, a man of "pure" Spanish blood born in Nueva España, and in his own turn was able to look down on the other, lowly *mestizos,* or mixed-bloods, and the Indians—to both of whom he was kin.

All this has changed. Caste levels still survive in Mexico, and *gachupinismo* lingers on in a modified form that expresses itself in pride—sometimes exaggerated pride—of name, family, heritage. Everybody has this in him, to some extent. It's reasonable and normal. But the values in which today's Mexican takes pride are Mexican values, no longer transplants from Spain, and his roots are firm in his native soil. He is a man in his own right on his own native land.

Ask him about his *puro castellano* blood and he's as liable as not to ask you about your *puro* English or French or German or Italian or Chinese or Negro or Irish or Greek or Portuguese blood—you name it. Traces of these have crept into his own veins over the generations, too. The admixture, with all its components, is *puro mexicano,* as "pure" as ours or any other in the Americas. The exception to this "pure mix" is the population of several million Indians living in the southern and southeastern parts of the Mexican republic. Here the woods are thick and a nimble-footed Indian maiden four-and-a-half centuries ago could successfully hide out from her would-be *conquistador.* But these indigenes do not think of themselves as *mexicanos* in the national sense. They call themselves Chamula, Zoque, Huave, Totonac, Huasteca. They speak their own language, sometimes to the exclusion of Spanish, mind their own business, breed true, and don't cotton much to strangers.

You will also hear in Mexico natives deny, or seem to deny, the fact of their nativity. This takes a special understanding, in view of their pride in themselves and their country. When asked if he is a Mexican, a man from Veracruz may well reply, "No, I am *jarocho,*" and, if you fail to understand the colloquialism, go on to explain that he is *veracruzano.* Similarly, a man from Guadalajara might describe himself as a *tapatío,* or perhaps as *jalicense* (from the state of Jalisco). A man from Jalapa would call himself *jalapeño,* a woman *jalapeña,* and so on. The residents of that unmanageable urban mess, Mexico City, are called *chilangos.* These distinctions show pride in one's *patria chica* or small country.

The Mexican Way

The typical Mexican, *al contrario,* takes to strangers quite readily, in his own way. His friendship isn't as quick to flower or as intimate as with us in the U.S., where a casual curbstone introduction may lead within minutes to a suggestion by Joe to Al (they're on first-name terms from the very beginning) that Al come home with Joe for cocktails and a home-cooked dinner (preceded, not unnaturally, by hard private words to Joe from Mrs. Joe, who has to do the home cooking and was kind of hoping to be taken out for a feed that evening). Mexicans do not entertain in this informal fashion or readily take strangers into their homes. It is possible to know a Mexican closely and well over such a long period that you have come to *tutear* each other—that refers to the use of "thou" verb-forms between close friends, family members, and lovers—drink with him, dine with him, and habitually play golf with him, yet never meet his wife or darken the door of his house.

Invitations to home-cooked meals are just not part of the Mexican way of doing business. Outside his home and away from his home life, which are private things not to be shared, he can be as staunch a friend and as good a companion as you will find anywhere; by and large gracious, courteous, generous, and proud to welcome you as a guest of his homeland even if his home is not readily open to you.

Exceptions there are, sure. Plenty of them, in Mexico as elsewhere. The exceptions run in both directions. You may be taken into a Mexican home during your first few days in the country, which is so much to the good for you. Or you may instead simply be taken, which is so much to the bad. Every land, including our own, has its quota of sharpshooters on the lookout for pigeons. Mexico differs from other tourist areas in this respect only in that it is better than most. The average Mexican's attitude toward his fellowman, whether of domestic or foreign parentage, is basically an honest one, in large part because he is a simple person and it is simpler to be honest than to be a crook. The small dishonesties he may stoop to now and then are most often in the class of petty pilferage or its equivalent, and often stem from hunger. He is usually struggling too hard to bring home the daily bread for a large family to have time for thoughts of grand schemes to con suckers with pie in the sky.

Friendships aren't as quick to form as in the U.S., but all *mexicanos —jarochos, tapatíos, jalapeños,* and *chilangos* alike—make good friends when you get to know them.

Possibly one of the most widely held misconceptions of the Mexican character is the stereotype of the lazy peon asleep in the sun, his sombrero tipped forward over his eyes, a bookend figure propping up the side of his ramshackle hut. Nothing could be further from the mark. The average Mexican working stiff, be he factory hand or farmhand, grinds away like merry hell from dawn to dark. He must, to survive. His wage scale is not generous by our standards. He and his wife and kids can get by if the old man applies his *nariz* steadily to the *amolad-*

era, and that's about it; getting by. Luxuries call for an extra effort, sometimes on the part of the wife and kids as well as the old man. As a people Mexicans are among the hardest and most indefatigable toilers you can find anywhere.

Siesta Time

It is true that the institution of the siesta, that enjoyable break for a short nap after the big midday meal, still survives here. You can easily get into the habit yourself after you have been in Mexico awhile, since most business offices, government offices, and commercial establishments shut their doors for a couple of hours at 1 or 2 P.M. But in my town, a representative small community, the wake-up whistle and the church bells for early morning mass sound off together at 5:30, winter and summer, and most workdays in towns and cities end at 7 or 8 P.M., not 5. Farmers and other outdoor laborers, since they can only work while there is light to see by, generally forgo the siesta and put their time in from sunup to sundown. The bookend-peon figure could hardly account for the fact that the annual rate of growth for Mexico's gross national product was—up to the 1982 economic crisis—one of the highest in the world. That takes sweat, in a country with more manpower than investment capital and not as much arable land as it could use to feed itself.

Only in Mexico—and you had best get into the habit of hearing "Mexico City" when somebody says "Mexico" down here, because when we mean *la república* we most often say *la república*—has the institution of the siesta virtually vanished. The reason for this is probably that Mexico has become too busy, too noisy. The city is growing too fast. There's too much hurtling traffic for daytime restfulness. But the siesta break, the two-hour vacation knocked out of the middle of the day originally for the big midday meal followed by a snooze, survives. Mexico by and large shuts up shop around 1 or 2 P.M. to go home for *la comida* even when it doesn't sleep it off afterwards. This does not mean you will be unable to find a clerk to wait on you in a department store in the early afternoon or that hotel switchboard operators will be any less—or more—alert to answer your call during the same hours. It does mean that business and professional appointments and such are best made before 1 P.M. or else late in the day. The later in the morning or afternoon, the better. Mexican government officials, business executives, professional men, and such, unlike their proletarian *paisanos* of the factories and fields, rarely show up on the job before 10 or 11 A.M., nor do they hurry back to it in the afternoon simply because the door to the office has been opened for business by an underling.

In addition to the still-surviving siesta break, originally a device to postpone work from the heat of the tropic midday to the cool of the evening—a kind of twilight saving time, you might call it—there is also the matter of Mexico's *mañana* to adapt to. *Mañana-ismo* is everything you may have heard about it and then some.

Mexicans are normally so concerned with making you feel loved and cared for that they will tell you what they think you want to hear, regardless of the facts. It isn't deceptiveness, simply good manners. A Mexican will *always* stop to give you polite directions if you ask for them, even when he doesn't know which way is *arriba.* For him to say he doesn't know would be churlish. Far better to point you in the wrong direction and receive and acknowledge your thanks with the courtesy of the gentleman he truly is.

The same goes for plumbers, carpenters, electricians, housebuilders, and the man who repairs leaks in the roof. You want him to come to work *mañana* at 8 A.M.? *"Sí, señor, sin falta, con todo gusto, mañana por la mañana a las ocho."* He means it too, bless him. The trouble is, *mañana* doesn't have the same meaning for him as it does for you. In your mind it means the day after today—right?—the next solar cycle. In his vocabulary it means anything at all later than tonight: tomorrow, the day after, next week, next year, any old time—whenever he gets around to it. He's right and you're wrong, of course. It's his country and his word. Until you get used to it, it can drive you mad. Afterwards—but that's *mañana,* friend, and *mañana* can never be rigidly defined, or confined.

Similarly with business appointments, promises, many oral contracts, and all conventional expressions like "My house is yours." Commitments like these are courtesies, no more. We make the same kind of gesture when we say, "How do you do?" or "Pleased to meet you." Most often we don't give a damn how you're doing and would be bored silly if you took the time to tell us.

The Mexican Male

To begin to know the Mexican male, you have to know first the meaning and usage of *macho,* a word you will hear often. Basically it means nothing more than virile, sexually competent, potent—as a bull or ram or boar is potent. A man who has fathered kids is *macho.* But another man who has no kids may be fully as *macho* as the paterfamilias, because there is much more to the concept of *machismo* than mere reproductive capacity. *Macho* connotes—in addition to virility—all of the virtues of manhood: gutsiness, self-reliance, the ability to take care of oneself against opposition, pride of person, a touch of swagger to point up the image. You can see *machismo* in action at any hour of the day on the Paseo de la Reforma in Mexico City, when two cabdrivers start jockeying for position against each other in a stream of hurtling traffic. Nothing material is to be gained by the contest, and some danger exists in it—enough to whiten the hair of *gringo* passengers riding in the taxis. But *machismo* compels each driver to out-risk the other guy, at whatever peril to himself, his hack, his passengers, or innocent by-hurtlers, and the winner's day is made by his triumph even if it costs him a crumpled fender or two.

Machismo evidences itself in other, less physical ways. It is *macho* for a Mexican whom you have invited to lunch to try to pick up the check, even though it may be beyond his means. In our hometowns this could lead to a friendly argument ending with a division of the check down the middle and both parties content. Not in Mexico. You either pick up the tab or he does, and if he does he has demonstrated his *machismo.* The demonstration is not a conscious one, simply a reflection of the Mexican male's compulsion to prove himself. You don't have to know the reasons for it. They are too complex to go into here. Just remember that the trait is a dominant one in the character of the Mexican—masculine gender—and you will begin to understand what makes him tick.

Religion

It was easy for the Franciscan friars to convert the Indians of central Mexico, who were used to taking orders and were further fascinated by the Catholic ritual: the gold of the altars, the chants, the smell of incense, and the tolling of bells.

When the Mexicans got their own "Dark Virgin" in the person of Our Lady of Guadalupe in 1531, the new religion became an integral part of the country. In their fight for independence, the revolutionaries were urged on to victory under the banner of the Virgin of Guadalupe.

Nowadays among the poorer Mexicans, whereas the males turn to alcohol for release, their wives turn to religion. Mexico is almost solidly Roman Catholic in its faith, for all that the country has had no official state religion for over a hundred years. Benito Juárez, a contemporary of Abraham Lincoln and like Lincoln a man of humble origins and great ideals who became president of his country, dedicated himself early in life to the destruction of what he referred to as "the doleful power of the privileged classes." One of the most privileged of all in his day was the clergy. The church and its hierarchy owned enormous properties, in all a considerable portion of the entire Mexican republic, and exercised a great secular power in the making and unmaking of governments. Juárez led the fight to break their power, nationalize their holdings, institute a civil marriage ceremony to replace the established religious ceremony, and bring about other clerical reforms.

He succeeded, at some cost to the land, the republic, and himself. Since his time Mexico's people have been free in religion in theory and as solidly Catholic as before in practice. To the Mexican male, his religion is largely a formality. He is born in the church, christened in it, married in it—the civil marriage is obligatory, a supplementary religious one optional but common—and buried by it. Otherwise he tips his hat respectfully as he passes a church door but does not often enter it. To his woman the church is clubhouse, social center, spiritual refuge, and solace of her sorrows when they are too much for her to bear alone and her man cannot help her. Juárez would have no objection to the choice made by either, as long as the choice remains free. That freedom is what he was striving to give his people when he expropriated the church's privileges.

What Is a Gringo?

This is as good a place as any to discuss the meaning and use of that word *gringo.* It carries a misconception to many American minds. In its own way *American* reflects the same kind of misconception, as we normally use it to denote a citizen of the United States of America as distinguished, let's say, from a citizen of the United States of Mexico. All natives of the Americas, from Tierra del Fuego to Ellesmere Island, are Americans, properly speaking. Mexicans, furthermore, are North Americans like us, since they live on the North American continent together with us and the Canadians. Likewise they are themselves *estadounidenses*—"United-Statesers"—as we are. It's hard to come up with a strictly accurate English word to distinguish ourselves from our neighbors north and south. The *mexicano* frequently reserves *norteamericano* to describe us and Canadians collectively, as *mexicano* describes him.

An easier word for us from north of the Rio Grande—which, incidentally, is the Rio Bravo on Mexican maps—is *gringo,* very gradually coming into common usage after years of border-town, back-alley existence as a hard word, an ugly word, and a challenge. Older Mexicans still won't use it where *gringo* ears might hear and resent it. The former connotation is still in their minds; native courtesy prevents them from risking possible offense. Among younger *mexicanos* as well as many *gringos* who live here it is increasingly used as commonly and inoffensively as a New York cabdriver's "Mac" to address a fare whose name he doesn't know. *Señor* is more polite, more respectful, and more to be expected of cabdrivers and their ilk here, since Mexican class levels still survive to an extent unknown to New York cabdrivers and *their* ilk. But within your own social stratum *gringo*—*gringa* in the feminine—is as friendly and harmless as "pal," "doc," or "chum," and although your Mexican maid may not herself choose to use it within your hearing any more than she would use "pal," "doc," or "chum," if she tells you that you had visitors while you were out of the house and you say, "*Gringos?*" she knows exactly what you are asking her. If you hear the word used of or to yourself, don't misinterpret it, as some *gringos* are prone to do because of its former connotation and usage. Somebody may be asking you to have a friendly drink with him.

The word, incidentally, is old, legitimate, and honorable, deriving from Spanish *griego,* meaning Greek. It has nothing to do with "Green Grow the Rushes, Oh," or any of the other various American folk-etymologies attributed to it.

As the social and economic status of the middle-class *mexicano* and that of the average *norteamericano* become more nearly equal, there is a growing respect for the American in Mexico. No "Gringo—go home!" here of late.

As a matter of fact, the average Mexican is now beginning to commiserate with the American and his increasingly desperate social situation encompassing racism, poverty, drugs, war, pollution, and youth rebellion.

Learn the Language

Mexico richly rewards those of its visitors and guests who take the trouble to learn something of its language as well as its customs and conventions. This is not to say that you have to be fluent in Spanish, or even that a smattering of it is necessary to get by—if getting by is enough to satisfy you. In my own village I have *gringo* friends who have lived here for years and still don't know how to say "waiter" in the native speech of the man who brings them food in a restaurant. My friends are decent people, kindly people, who love Mexico and its people and treat their Mexican house servants with consideration and generosity. (Although to hear the lady of the house try to explain a complicated recipe to her cook without knowing even the word for mixing bowl, much less the names of the ingredients that are to go into it, is like watching somebody else get his teeth yanked in a dentist's chair: It hurts you even if he is numb to what is going on in his mouth.) But my friends' attitude is that waiters and cooks should acquire a working knowledge of *their* language if waiters and cooks want to receive good *gringo* tips and salaries, and they do have an argument on their side.

So it is with many other *gringos,* visitors here, who patronize almost exclusively those hotels, restaurants, bars, nightclubs, resorts, and other establishments where they will regularly be able to speak and hear their own familiar language. They often consume familiar food and drink in these places, too, and pay far too familiar high prices for everything they get. But they certainly aren't experiencing much of Mexico and its people. The best way you can begin to know and appreciate Mexicans is to reach them through some means of reciprocal communication. Most of them, off the established tourist beat, are not going to be able to read you loud and clear or even tune you in when you talk English at them.

These truths should be self-evident, although they don't seem to be to a lot of people who find themselves confined to the treadmill of the established tourist track by their inability to break through the language barrier that hems them in. Even a little Spanish provides the key to let you out of that treadmill. It is one of the simplest of languages to learn because of the rigidity of its rules for pronunciation and accent. It can also save you a comfortable bundle of scratch by giving you the tool with which to shop around and bargain, and scratch often seems to be a matter of some interest to some people.

I note that I have misused a word, *Spanish. Mexican* should be substituted for *Spanish* in reference to this language. Mexican-Spanish is not Spanish-Spanish, although they are related in the same way that American-English is related to English-English. Vocabulary is different, usage is different, some pronunciation is different. The Spanish *ceceo,* the lisp given to *z* and soft *c,* is never used habitually by any native of Latin America. Both soft *c* and *z* are invariably pronounced like *s* in Mexico, as any half-decent phrase book will inform you.

Mexican Law and You

Some small knowledge of basic Mexican law would be another useful bit of lore for a *gringo* to have with him when he visits the country, although few of us take the trouble to acquire this unless and until we are forced to do so by circumstances—i.e., the hard way. Guests of the Mexican house are sometimes shocked, bewildered, and dismayed to find themselves guests of the Mexican *policía* as well without quite realizing how and why it happened to them. Neither Mexico's legal precedents nor its statutes are founded on the Bill of Rights or the principles for which our forefathers fought, bled, and died to bring forth on this continent a new nation, as the Mexicans fought, bled, and died to bring forth *their* new nation on the same continent not many years later.

Their system, inherited from Spain during the colonial days, is based on the *Code Napoléon,* which says in effect that you are guilty of everything possible until proved innocent, instead of the other way around. There is no trial by jury as we know it, and there are other very fundamental differences. Since jurisprudence is a field in which I am highly qualified to have no worthwhile opinion, I will offer no personal views as to the merits of one system compared to the other. But as a present resident of Mexico and former resident of my own country, as well as of several other countries which embrace the principles of the *Code Napoléon* rather than our own (as more do than not), I have never observed or suffered any more or less injustice under one system than the other. They're just different. Sometimes you are better off under one system than the other, but not consistently.

Possibly the most important thing to bear in mind about Mexican law—above all if you drive an automobile (other than a rented car, which is taken care of by someone else)—is that third-party liability insurance, although in no way compulsory anywhere in Mexico, can save you unhappy hours in some less-than-sumptuous village sneezer with the local *juez* taking his time to sort out responsibility for an accident, as he must. Many Mexicans, perhaps a majority of Mexican drivers, carry no such insurance, relying instead on fleetness of foot to carry them from the immediate scene of a smackup before the law arrives. This is not recommended for *gringos,* for whom going on the dodge in a country to which they are conspicuously not native is more difficult. You can scream for help from your own embassy in Mexico City, and, if you are a U.S. national, any of eleven consulates located here and there around the countryside. (Canadians have only their embassy, so far.)

If, in spite of precautions, care, and the best of intentions you do nevertheless manage to become involved with the law in Mexico, you have an open sesame available to you which in most cases is as good as a bail bond to spring you out of your difficulties; and in other cases it is even better because it costs you absolutely nothing. The magic word, then, is "tourist."

This is another usage which in some ears and some countries has taken on unhappy overtones. It connotes rube and rubberneck, if nothing worse. Most people dislike thinking of themselves as tourists. To be a tourist even in our own country, certainly in the minds of many of us, is to be something of an easy mark and a joke.

This is in no way true of Mexico. *Turista* is a respectable and well-meant word in this country. (It is also used commonly to describe the mild passing ailment referred to less commonly as Montezuma's Revenge, but that's another subject.) One sound reason for this is the fact that *turismo* is Mexico's greatest single source of dollar income, a sum that now approaches two-and-a-half billion dollars annually and increases from year to year.

On top of this amount there is a further bonus of four to five billion dollars' worth of peso income generated in Mexico each year by the creation of new jobs, new business, new plants, new developments to meet the demands of the burgeoning *turista* market. Mexico calls tourists collectively, with respect and gratitude, *La industria sin chimeneas* or The Industry Without Chimneys, and when a Mexican asks if you are a *turista* he is asking you, in effect, to identify yourself as an honored and welcome visitor of his country.

Mexico, above all, is a land to tour, literally. It contains such an infinite variety of attractions that it is inexhaustible within a lifetime. It is a country with something in it for everybody, from the turned-on swinger to the turned-off sourpuss; a land of promise and reward for the young, the middle-aged, and the old; for the sportsman and the scholar; the swinger and the sightseer; the painter, the writer, and the sculptor; the archaeologist; the camera bug; the egghead and the meatball; the traveler with money and the traveler with none. If we from the north are *La industria sin chimeneas,* then surely Mexico is for us *El país sin límites:* The Land Without Limits.

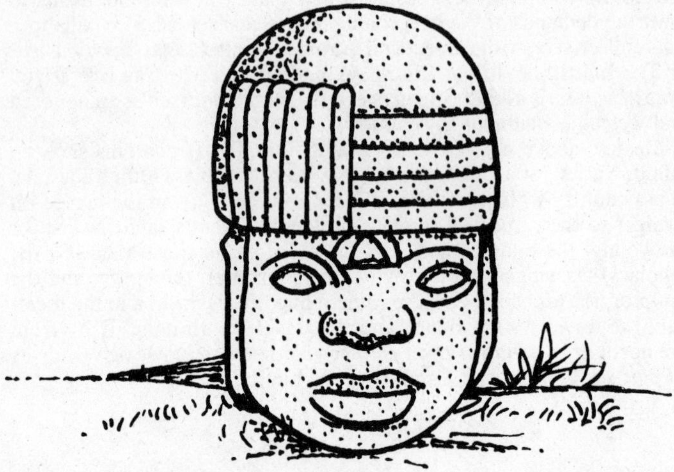

THE PRE-COLUMBIAN HERITAGE

A Primer on Mexican Archaeology

by
KAL MULLER

The ancient art of Mexico can be disconcerting if not downright monstrous—or it can be exquisite. Architecture is overwhelming in scale—just massive in some places, refined and harmonious elsewhere. For the western mind, pre-Columbian Mexico is arguably the most difficult culture to appreciate. Yet any effort toward understanding is rewarded by an expanding of one's aesthetic horizons.

Primitive man trekked overland into the Americas from Siberia, following big game across what is now the Bering Strait. Starting in Alaska perhaps 30,000 years ago, mankind pushed into the New World, reaching southern Chile around 7000 B.C.

Drastic changes in climate began with the end of the last glaciation, around 9000 B.C. The Indians in Mexico were forced to change their lifestyle from that of big game hunters when the warmer, dryer climate wiped out the ecology of their prey. They had to make do with smaller game, and edible fruit, seeds, and roots became an important part of their diet. Some 8,000 years ago, gathering of these foods began to lead to the domestication of plants.

These adaptations are pretty much the history of mankind everywhere. But then Mexico's pre-history becomes special, as does that of a few other areas in the world unusually well-blessed by nature. Much of central and southern Mexico is a mosaic of climates and ecologies favoring a diversity of plant and animal life. Of the roughly 50 families of land mammals in the New World, 35 are found in Mexico. A small area in the southern highlands has more kinds of corn and a greater number of bird species than the entire U.S. This kind of diversity, much greater than to the north or south, led the Indians to several inviting valleys. The environment was favorable to a semisedentary existence.

Plant domestication, the essential condition of civilization, began around 6000 B.C., but some four millenia passed before full-fledged agriculturists appeared. Pumpkins and beans were the first plants cultivated, followed by corn, the Indians' staff of life, and chile to make food interesting. Along the way, the Indians stumbled upon such revolutionary technologies as pottery-making and the weaving of cotton.

At a time over 3,000 years ago, parts of Mexico were ready for what we loosely call civilization. There was some excess agricultural production, which allowed a number of individuals to follow pursuits not strictly necessary for physical survival—religion and government. There had been attempts to manipulate deified forces of nature, shamanism and the most basic rules of society, but these efforts were at the most rudimentary of levels.

Olmecs' Origin a Mystery

Around 1500 B.C. we come across the first and greatest of mysteries in ancient Mexico: Where did the Olmecs originate? The Olmecs began the most ancient of the advanced cultures of Mexico, but so far the experts cannot trace the major transition of their evolution. Although Olmec-type artifacts from a formative period have been found in many areas of central and southern Mexico, there is an unexplained quantum jump in their achievements around 1100 B.C., when they began to build religious centers on the Gulf Coast, in what is now southern Veracruz and Tabasco. They seem to have burst on the scene with a full-fledged civilization.

Many outstanding features of the Olmecs are as disconcerting as the enigma of their origins. Their megalithic sculptures include heads with negroid as well as Mongolian features, up to 10 feet high and weighing 20 tons. These and other megasculptures, some over 25 tons, were transported, probably by rafts, over 60 miles. At the site of La Venta, the best known Olmec ceremonial center, a circular pyramid reached toward the gods. With a base of over 500 feet in diameter and a height of 100 feet, its man-made volume equals some 100,000 cubic yards. At La Venta, there were also offerings of great underground floor mosaics representing jaguar faces and covered with layers of different-colored clays.

The Olmecs' intellectual achievements were just as advanced as their architectural prowess. Hieroglyphic writing appeared in an incipient form, time was calculated, and astronomy developed to direct the agricultural calendar as well as to orient religious structures. These amazing feats were, until recently, attributed to the later Mayas, who actually only perfected this cultural heritage.

The jaguar seems to have held the predominant position in the Olmec religion. The sculptures show a jaguar fixation with many examples of a "haunting mixture of human and feline characteristics in varying degrees," according to one expert. The representation of a jaguar copulating with a human may give us a clue as to the mythical origins of the Olmecs and explain why there are so many representations of man becoming a jaguar—or the jaguar becoming a man.

The complex of La Venta was to become the prototype for later ceremonial centers in many parts of Mexico. The building began at the Olmec site around 1100 B.C., reached its climax some three centuries later and was ritually demolished without explanation about 400 B.C.

For all the unknown aspects of the Olmec culture, it would be a mistake to opt for facile and unsubstantiated solutions—that the origins are to be sought in Atlantis, China, or extraterrestrial contacts. Archaeologists are patiently unraveling the thread of continuity and answers are slowly emerging. Progress is hampered by grave-robbers who find a ready market in Europe and the U.S. Important pieces emerge on the art market with no knowledge as to their provenance, then disappear into private collections.

The archaeological park of La Venta, on the outskirts of Villahermosa, is the best place to admire a variety of massive Olmec sculptures. The pieces were transferred there from the original site of La Venta, which was difficult to reach. Petroleum had also been found at the original location. The outdoor museum of La Venta boasts, among other marvels, a large mosaic made of serpentine stones representing a jaguar face, an altar depicting a sitting priest holding an infant with both humans in the open mouth of a jaguar, a tomb of large basalt slabs, and one of the massive heads. The museums of Villahermosa and Mexico City hold most of the best smaller pieces.

Monte Alban

The civilization that was centered in Monte Alban, Oaxaca, gives the Olmecs a run for their money in the race for the intellectual honors of pre-Columbian Mexico. Monte Alban's precise relation with the Olmecs has not been established, but some degree of influence was certainly present. For all we know, Monte Alban could have been one of several sites from which the Olmec culture finally coalesced.

The principal buildings of Monte Alban top a hill which rises 1,200 feet to dominate the fertile valley of Oaxaca. It was an important ceremonial center for hundreds of years for the surrounding urban area and today it remains as one of the prime drawing cards for visitors interested in Mexico's Indian past.

Archaeologists have divided the site's history into five periods. Monte Alban I developed from an unimpressive local culture around

800 B.C. There must have been some form of association with the Olmecs on the Gulf coast. Some experts think that Monte Alban was the originator of America's first calendar and writing system as well as where the deities were first individualized, gods who under different names and representations were to rule Mexico until the advent of the Spaniards. At the moment, there are no known antecedents to the writing system of Monte Alban, where a complex set of religious constructions began around 600 B.C. The *danzantes* are the most spectacular remains of this period: low relief sculptures on hard stone, depicting human figures in contorted positions.

Around 300 B.C., a different group of Indians, perhaps from Guatemala or the Highlands of Chiapas, took over the site to begin Monte Alban II. A building boom was set off, leveling most of the hilltop. The Great Plaza was built and plastered while the off-axis astronomical observatory was erected. A superb jade mask mosaic of a bat god dates from this period.

The Zapotecs began their domination of Monte Alban shortly after the birth of Christ. This period lasted close to a millenium. The greater part of the sacred complex as we see it today was raised during this period, Monte Alban III. The main phase of the construction, from 200 to 600 A.D., resulted in a huge patio surrounded by buildings. Gods proliferated and ornate baroque pottery was fashioned in their likenesses.

The first part of this period was characterized by strong links with the great city of Teotihuancan to the north. The urban area around Monte Alban reached over 40 square kilometers. Then a decline set in about 1000 A.D. The ceremonial sections of Monte Alban were abandoned and the Zapotecs retreated into a relative cultural isolation. The next period, Monte Alban IV, is known only for its tombs within the complex.

The demise of the Zapotecs as a vigorous civilization was perhaps due in part to the southward expansion of tough warriors from the north. But we must not think of this as an Attila-the-Hun campaign, sweeping all cultures from its swift, bloody path. It was rather a set of gradual pressures by groups of tough nomads shifting south out of unproductive northern Mexico and into the settled agricultural areas of the central plateau.

Whatever the causes, the Mixtec Indians, who had been living in the area of present-day Puebla and northern Oaxaca, shifted south. Although there were some battles, the Mixtecs did not conquer the Zapotecs, but settled into the Valley of Oaxaca without displacing the bulk of its occupants.

Rich Archaeological Find

The Mixtecs did not build grand monuments. They concentrated their talents on the perfection of the finish, lavishing attention on small, fine objects of gold, silver, rock crystal, jade, amber, and obsidian. With one possible exception, the Mixtecs had no rulers that led the tribe. Small, independent units were the norm.

Monte Alban, in its fifth and last period, was used only as a cemetery for Mixtec nobles. One of their tombs, justly called the richest Mexican archaeological scoop ever, yielded a wealth of art: 121 gold objects, practically the only silver pieces on record, intricately carved jaguar bones, ear ornaments of obsidian less than a millimeter thick, an exquisite cup of rock crystal, a jade-mosaic covered skull, and the list of marvels goes on. Here's how the discovery was described:

"A stone slab from the vaulted ceiling was removed. The beam of a flashlight revealed glittering objects in the darkness of the chamber, a first glance at the treasure that was to make history as the richest archaeological find in the New World: a fabulous cache of splendid gold jewelry, a mask of solid gold, strings of pearls as big as pigeon's eggs, carved jades, mosaics of turquoise, ornaments of rock crystal and alabaster . . . . over 30 narrow strips of jaguar bone, exquisitely carved with mythological scenes and calendrical signs and inlaid with minute pieces of turquoise."

Nine skeletons—eight men and a woman—shared the tomb. The most important of these was a hunchback with a syphilitic brain tumor.

The discovery of the fabulous hoard made news in the world press of 1932 and the treasure traveled to Mexico City under military guard, then to the U.S. for exhibition at the 1936 World's Fair. The riches raised an ownership controversy between the federal government and the state of Oaxaca, ending in a surprising local victory. This enabled the state to proudly display the contents of the tomb at the Regianal Museum, now housed in the former convent of Santo Domingo.

Pyramids of Teotihuacan

Teotihuacan is the most visited pre-Columbian site in Mexico. This is partially due to its closeness to Mexico City and certainly because the most monumental set of structures built by Indians are found here. Teotihuacan was the most important culture in central Mexico with an influence that continued after its demise. Over seven centuries later, Montezuma and his priests worshipped here. The original name has been lost; Teotihuacan is in the language of the Aztecs, meaning "the place where men become gods." The two major pyramids, the Sun and the Moon, were also Aztec designations as it was believed that these sacred heavenly bodies were born here, the reincarnation of two gods who had the courage to throw themselves into a fire.

The Pyramid of the Sun dominates the area. Its base, almost square with 225 meters on each side, is just about equal to the Pyramid of Cheops. The resemblance stops there. The Mexican pyramid's height of 70 meters, half that of Cheops, gives it a much bulkier appearance than its Egyptian counterpart. Also, the Pyramid of the Sun is truncated—the flat top supported a temple that disappeared a long time ago.

The wide "Street of the Dead," the main axis of Teotihuancan, is a series of joined plazas and has nothing to do with death. This axis begins with the "Citadel," so named by the Spaniards for no good reason as it had no military function. It is a huge, built-up square, some 1,200 feet on each side, surrounded by four platforms crowned with small pyramids. From here, the Street of the Dead runs past several platforms and unimposing structures, past the Pyramid of the Sun to end at the bottom of the Pyramid of the Moon. This pyramid is much smaller but since it is built on higher ground, the tops are just about even. Most of what has been excavated and restored lies on either side of the central axis. But it has been estimated that the excavations represent only 5% of the Teotihuacan urban area.

The Pyramid of Quetzalcoatl, located in the southeast corner of the Citadel, is adorned with the most impressive stone sculptures of Teotihuacan. A series of carvings thrust out of the inclined slope. These alternatively represent the rain god Tlaloc and Quetzalcoatl, perhaps symbolizing earthly waters. This facade has no Mexican competition in power and composition. At the other end of the Street of the Dead, a complex of "palaces"—perhaps priests' living quarters—are graced with low-relief sculptures on columns and surprisingly expressive and artistic red-based paintings.

The architecture of Teotihuacan is much more grandiose when compared with that of the Mayas, who are renowned for their exuberant, baroque buildings. At Teotihuacan, the ceremonial structures are built on earth and stone fill, covered with a sloping base called talud and topped by a vertical plane named tablero. All outer surfaces were covered by multicolored lime plaster, requiring huge quantities of quicklime.

The sculptures of Teotihuacan, powerful as they may be, do not even approach the quality of Olmec megaliths or the refined carvings of the Mayas. It was in the art of painting that Teotihuacan was unrivaled in Mexico. Murals were found not only on the walls of temples and palaces but also on the dwellings of the common people. Although no artist discovered perspective, outstanding are the use of flowing lines and themes from nature such as geographical features, vegetation, and animals. Most visitors see only the frieze in the Temple of the Jaguars, near the Pyramid of the Moon. Two remarkable series of murals are found to the west of the main ceremonial center of Teotihuacan—Tetitla and Atetelco. You have to insist that the guide lead you there. The most famous of paintings is located in an edifice called Tepantitla, just behind the Pyramid of the Sun. The mural has been named Tlalocan, the Aztec name for the paradise of Tlaloc, the Rain God, logically paramount in a dry, agriculture-based economy. This heavenly spot, Tlalocan, was reserved for Tlaloc's elected—those who died by drowning, epilepsy, or venereal disease. The element of water pervades the scene where Tlaloc rules over humans who are enjoying the god's favor. They bathe, chase butterflies, pick flowers, go fishing, or dance. Only a part of the original mural has been preserved. An excellent copy of the original was painted at the National Museum in Mexico City.

A Real City Emerges

Teotihuacan began around 600 B.C. and lasted four centuries as a large village. The obsidian industry, a mainstay of the economy, began during this period. The next 200 years, up to the birth of Christ, saw the birth of a true city whose population reached 50,000. The ceremonial center was laid out with a north-south orientation of the Street of the Dead, perhaps to face the setting Pleiades. The two great pyramids were built in continuous construction, not superimposed on earlier structures, which was the usual technique elsewhere in Mexico. In the next period, to 350 A.D., the city grew into a metropolis with an urban area bigger than contemporary Imperial Rome. Thin Orange pottery, a particular kind of high quality vessel, was manufactured as an essential trade item, the Temple of Quetzalcoatl was erected, and the great plaza completed. The dates of 350 to 650 A.D. mark the greatest power and glory of Teotihuacan, whose population reached 200,000. The best murals were painted during this period. The last century, one of decline, ended with furious wrecking and burning, perhaps under the orders of the city's elite, perhaps by outsiders.

At its height, Teotihuacan was densely populated and spread over more than eight square miles. Only a small portion of the urban spread, the main ceremonial center, has been cleared and restored. Enough digging around has revealed that most of the inhabitants lived in apartment compounds, grouped by profession (such as potters or obsidian workers) or by ethnic origins.

Unlike Monte Alban, whose influence never went much beyond regional boundaries, Teotihuacan's culture spread far and wide. Kaminaljuyu, now partially covered by a suburb of Guatemala City, is almost a replica of Teotihuacan circa 400 A.D. Both the Gulf Coast and the Pacific show too many influences to have come from trade alone. Of course, commerce must have been an important factor in spreading the ideas and styles of Teotihuacan. Thin Orange has been found in innumerable places far from its home base, and obsidian implements from Teotihuacan followed the same routes. In return, the tropical lowlands furnished plumes (especially those of the quetzal bird), jaguar skins, jade, and shells, all luxuries required for religious purposes. Cacao for chocolate was also a major import.

It is still uncertain if Teotihuacan can be considered a true empire but at the very least it must have exerted a degree of control over strategic points. The priest, who developed astronomy and the cult of Quetzalcoatl, undoubtedly played a leading role both at home and far afield. During the final century before the definitive collapse, military orders began their importance and the religion started to require human sacrifices. New tribes with different values pushed their way into central Mexico, ending the glory of Teotihuacan's civilization.

Toltec Influence

The Toltec culture, centered at Tula (about two hours' drive northwest of Mexico City), followed Teotihuacan as the major power in central Mexico. The Toltec influence was of relatively short duration, from the mid-10th to the mid-12th centuries. The history of Tula is complicated by later conflicting texts, where myths and facts are inextricably bound. For the Aztecs, who adopted the Toltecs as their ancestors to gain legitimacy, a place called Tollan was the source of all the beauty and positive elements of their culture. Tula has been identified as Tollan, but in reality was far less rosy than the Aztecs' idealized picture.

A city whose maximum population never surpassed 60,000, Tula had the natural advantage of a nearby river with fertile banks insuring a reliable food supply. Tulan values centered around warfare, as shown in art—warriors, skullracks, sacrificial stones, jaguars, and eagles devouring human hearts.

The Central Plaza of Tula is dominated by the pyramid and temple of Quetzalcoatl. Huge stone warrior figures graze ahead without expression from the top of the pyramid, formerly supports of a temple roof. Behind the pyramid, a long wall's repeating frieze shows skeletons being swallowed by snakes. All is grim, executed with poor, almost shoddy, workmanship.

It was at Tula that the cult of Quetzalcoatl became dominant. The deity was the patron of a warrior society, only vaguely resembling the whitewashed version given to the Spanish friars by the Aztecs, who had to impress their new rulers with at least one benevolent god who did not require human sacrifices. The numerous attributes of Quetzalcoatl are further complicated by human ruler-priests who took the deity's name and whose actions and fate often blended with the god's.

The inhabitants of Tula were probably made up of two distinct ethnic groups—settled former nomads from the north and a relatively advanced group of Nonoalcas from what is now Tabasco state. It is possible that these two groups never fused, different outlooks giving rise to rivalry which might well have led to Tula's downfall.

Whatever the reasons for Tula's demise, early in the city's history a link was established with the sacred site of far-off Chichen Itza in the Yucatan peninsula. Similarities between the two sites are many. But the Mayan workmanship at Chichen is far superior to Tula's, giving speculation that the Toltec ideals of militarism and human sacrifice might have developed in the Yucatan before art forms were transferred back to home base. Or it could be that Mayan artisans were just more skillful than their Toltec counterparts and at Chichen they merely perfected an already-established style.

After the fall of Tula, no major culture dominated the central plateau of Mexico until the advent of the Aztecs, some two centuries later. Influences from both Teotihuacan and Tula are evident in El Tajin, a tropical site in northern Veracruz. The extensive ceremonial center is dominated by an unusual pyramid with 365 niches.

Xochicalco, a ceremonial center near present-day Taxco, was at the crossroads of many major cultural currents. Ideas, gods, styles, and trends converged here—Teotihuacan, Monte Alban, Maya, Toltec all contributed or took something from this hilltop center. The most imposing remain is a long, low relief frieze going around a small pyramid. Suspiciously Mayan looking dignitaries sit cross-legged between the coils of a serpent. Elsewhere, gods from Teotihuacan do not seem to mind mingling with upstart deities from a more recent tradition.

Mayan Ruins Prompt Studies

No culture has excited as much romantic imagination, or inspired the loads of hard work, as much as the Mayas. Starting in the early 19th century, a stream of adventurers—some with crackpot theories, others with surprisingly accurate insights—studied the Mayan ruins. They were drawn by the intricate buildings and the fact that by the time the Spaniards arrived in the New World, the high culture of the Mayas had disintegrated back into subsistence farming and quarreling fiefdoms.

John Lloyd Stephens was the foremost popularizer of the Mayas. Accompanied by the artist Frederick Catherwood, he traveled to Mayaland and published a superbly illustrated two-volume best-seller in the mid-19th century. A series of expeditions led by competent and enthusiastic archaeologists was sponsored by American institutions such as Harvard's Peabody Museum, the Carnegie Institute, Tulane, National Geographic, the Smithsonian, and the University of Pennsylvania. No other Indian culture has received this much high-powered attention.

Although the Aztecs' buildings were leveled by the Spaniards, Aztec civilization was still accurately chronicled, beginning just after its demise at the zenith of its culture. The Mayas' case was just the reverse. Their constructions were left alone, already overgrown by jungle in areas of scant economic potential. But accurate early historians of the Mayas were lacking. Only one stands out—Bishop Landa, who also burned just about all existing ancient Mayan codices, their illustrated books. Only three have survived his rage at the heathen religion. Landa's writings, which lay gathering dust in Spain for over three centuries, gave the only accurate basis for scientific work necessary to understand the ancient Mayas and their accomplishments.

The Mayas lived, and continue their existence, in three diametrically opposed ecological zones—the dry savannah of the Yucatan, the tropical lowlands of the Gulf of Mexico, the Caribbean, and highlands of Chiapas and Guatemala. Although lifestyles responded to environment and there never existed a ruler who controlled all the Mayas, the culture shows a remarkable set of similarities over an extensive area.

The passage of time was the great theme of the Mayas. Time was conceived as an endless cyclical procession of gods who were also numbers. As many as five different gods of conflicting attributes battled in a particular day's arena to determine the world's fate. The calendar, which was probably adopted from the Olmecs', first developed to regulate the agricultural cycle before acquiring the complexities that only specialized priests could understand. From a mythological past, a date corresponding to our August 10, 3114 B.C., was picked as the beginning, just like the birth of Christ in our culture. From then on, history moved in repeating katuns or 260-year cycles. Taking this and many other factors into account, the priests directed the timing for all kinds of activity—inaugurations, rituals, hunting, planting, warfare. Dates, names, and activities were recorded with hieroglyphs with some phonetic elements and not yet thoroughly understood.

The accumulated knowledge of generations of priest-astronomers, the basis of intricate time divisions, is truly amazing. The precise length of the solar year was found to be exactly 365.2420 days. Our instruments record it at 365.2422 days. The lunar cycle was set at 29.5209 days and the movements of Venus were analyzed with similar accuracy.

The Mayas excelled in many practical endeavors but, with the possible exception of agriculture, they failed in practical technologies along with their Mexican cousins. Except for jewelry and a limited number of the crudest copper tools, metallurgy was never developed in the New World. Nor was wheeled transport invented due to the terrain and the lack of draught animals. No early genius hit upon a truly phonetic writing system, making for endless speculation about pre-Columbian man in Mexico. That the Mayas and other Mexican cultures could have developed without the essential technologies of the Old World only reinforces our admiration of mankind's genius.

Palenque, Uxmal, and Chichen Itza are the most fascinating and popular of the Mayan ceremonial sites. These restored complexes are the highlights of any visit to the Yucatan area for archaeology buffs or travelers with the slightest interest in the cultures of Mexico.

Palenque—Artistic Achievement

Palenque is characterized by a well-thought-out concept and attention to delicate detail. According to many experts, it is the highest architectural-artistic achievement of the pre-Columbian world. Palenque, which means "palisade" in Spanish, spreads in a tropical rain forest on a ledge in the foothills of Chiapas state's mountainous side. The original name of the complex of buildings has been long forgotten but it is known that the site flourished during the 7th and 8th centuries of our era.

The Pyramid of the Inscriptions and the Palace physically dominate the site. The pyramid had been drawn, explored, and even lived in by amateurs and archaeologists when the keen eye of Alberto Ruz Lhullier noticed something unusual in 1952. One of the rock slabs forming the floor of a temple set on the roof of the pyramid had a double row of holes plugged with stone stoppers. Carefully lifting the heavy slab, he found a rubble-filled passageway leading downwards. After four seasons of careful clearing, Ruz and his team had their patience rewarded. They found an antechamber with the skeletons of several young men and beyond it a richly painted royal burial chamber. The team saw a large sarcophagus covered by a huge, beautifully carved five-ton lid. The cover was carefully raised to reveal a skeleton with a jade mosaic mask. It was later determined that this was the man who ruled Palenque from sixth or seventh century A.D.

The adjacent "Palace" is a complex of buildings and courtyards dominated by a unique four-story tower, probably used for astronomical observations. Stucco decorations on the various buildings show this specialty at its pinnacle. The extract of a bark was added to the wet plaster in order to retard drying so that intricate details could be worked at leisure. The figures were first modeled in the nude, then layers of clothing added one at a time. Parts of the palace are also decorated with stone sculptures, including precise, artistic glyphs, some yet to be deciphered.

Aside from the pyramid and the palace, there are many other religious buildings, only some of which have been restored. The most interesting of these is the Temple of the Sun with a large stone carving of the sun represented as the jaguar god. Also the Temple of the

Foliated Cross with its fine sculpture of a ceiba shown as a life-giving world-tree.

While Palenque has an over-abundance of rainfall, a lack of water is the main problem in much of northern Yucatan. The land is flat, made up of porous limestone which quickly absorbs any rain. There is only a thin layer of soil. At times the ground collapses, revealing large natural wells called cenotes. It is obvious that whoever dominated these cenotes held sway over the population of the surrounding countryside.

Chichen Itza

The sacred cenote of Chichen Itza is one of the largest of these natural wells and it is the *raison d'être* of the ceremonial center which grew around it. The precious fluid, lying some 75 feet below ground level, provided a permanent, unfailing supply of drinking water. For centuries it was the prime destination of religious pilgrimages. Whenever the gods failed to provide rain, victims were sacrificed and thrown into the cenote along with precious offerings. Children of both sexes were the most frequent victims, not the beautiful virgins of fertile imaginations. The exploration and dredging of the cenote was first carried out under the direction of Edward Thompson who for many years was the American consul of the Yucatan. Late in the 19th century, Thompson bought the whole sacred site of Chichen Itza, lock, stock, pyramid, and cenote. Many precious offerings were lifted from the cenote, including carved jades and gold figurines. Thompson illegally shipped his hoard to the Peabody Museum in diplomatic pouches, creating a legal storm which abated somewhat when part of the loot was returned to Mexico. A more through, and legal, exploration of the cenote took place under the sponsorship of the National Geographic Society during the early 1960s.

Chichen Itza was already an established religious center when around 980 A.D. the Toltecs of central Mexico invaded northern Yucatan, supported by the Itza, a Mayan group. The Toltecs were led by a ruler-priest named Quetzalcoatl, in honor of the god he served. At this time, Chichen Itza, along with the leading Maya city-states, were no longer basking in splendor as they had during the Classic period which had lasted roughly from 300 to 900 A.D. No definitive answers have yet been given as to why the Mayan culture went into a decline. Be that as it may, the scattered population succumbed to the invaders' better discipline, organization, and superior weapons.

The Toltecs and their Itza allies made their capital at Chichen Itza. It is probable that the Toltecs introduced their architectural style as well as the cult of Quetzalcoatl, the Feathered Serpent, whose name was rendered as Kukulcan in the Mayan language. Some scholars think that perhaps it was Chichen Itza which influenced the architecture and art of Tula rather than the other way around. The restored ceremonial site is spectacular on a grand, muscular scale. The only pre-Toltec building of any importance is the "Caracol" (Snail), an astronomical observatory, so named for its spiral staircase. Chichen is replete with Toltec-style buildings, decorated with the invaders' signatures: warriors, eagles, plumed serpents, skulls.

The pyramid which dominates Chichen Itza is a huge pre-Columbian calendar. The 91 steps of each of the four sides, plus the top platform, add up to the 365 days of the solar year. The 52 panels on the sides represent the Indians' sacred 52-year "century" cycle. And the 18 sections of terraces correspond to the 18-month religious year. On the spring and fall equinoxes (March 21 and September 21), the shadows from the terraces form an undulating snake body which ends at the giant snake heads at the base of the ballustrade. Within the body of the pyramid, there is an earlier pyramid with a room holding a red jaguar throne with jade discs for the feline's spots.

Next to the pyramid, the complex of the Temple of the Warriors covers five acres. It is a large-scale replica of (or model for) the one built in Tula, the Toltec capital. Hundreds of plumed warrior-columns used to hold up a roof. On top of the stairway, between two massive stone snakes, reclines the most photographed man in the Americas. This stone figure, called chac-mool (thus baptized by a 19th-century Frenchman from the Mayan words for "claw" and "red") was used for receiving the hearts of sacrificed victims.

The sacred ball court, the largest ever found, has low relief sculptures showing the fate of the losers—decapitation. The religious "game" was played with a rubber ball which could only be stuck with the forearms, knees, and hips. The object was to propel the ball through a stone ring some 20 feet up on the side wall. The ball court has incredible acoustics.

Ruins at Uxmal

If Chichen Itza is replete with Toltec motifs, the ruins at Uxmal represent classical Puuc-style Mayan architecture and decorations par excellence. Uxmal is unsurpassed for intricate but harmonious stonework combined with simple architectural lines which set off details in lavish variety. The word "uxmal" means "thrice built" in Mayan but archaeologists have found five different periods of construction here. The problem at Uxmal—and perhaps the main reason for its periodic abandonment—was lack of water. There are no cenotes and rainwater had to be stored in lime coated reservoirs and lidded cisterns.

The Pyramid of the Magician, with an unusual elliptical base, dominates both the site and the surrounding flat countryside. It faces the setting sun at the summer stolstice. Legend says that the pyramid was built overnight by a dwarf with some magic helping to speed up the construction. Actually, there are five superimposed layers within the pyramid, corresponding to the site's five periods of activity. A climb to the top may be tiring but well worth the effort for the panoramic view and to orientate yourself for your subsequent wanderings among the ruins. Warning: the sides are very steep and not built for modest skirt-wearing women. Here, as at other sites, slacks are recommended for all women.

The Palace of the Governor displays what is often called the most beautiful Mayan facade, with over 20,000 carved and fitted stones in a geometric frieze 320 feet long. The late Mayan expert Sylvanus Morley called this palace "the most magnificent, the most spectacular single building in all pre-Columbian America."

The Nunnery Quadrangle, so named for its cell-like chambers in four long buildings surrounding a courtyard, almost matches the Palace of the Governor. The nunnery's facades explode in detailed, high-relief decorations. The lattice-panneled friezes represent Chacs (rain gods), typical humble Mayan huts which have not changed to this day, large nude male figures and undulating double-headed serpents. Other musts at Uxmal include the House of the Turtles and the House of the Doves, named for their motifs.

It was after visiting Uxmal that Stephens became fully convinced—as are all serious students of the Maya—of the indigenous nature of the architecture and the culture. He wrote: "They are different from the works of other known people, of a new order, entirely and absolutely . . . . without models or masters, having a distinct, separate, independent existence; they were constructed by the races who occupied the country at the time of the invasion by the Spaniards."

Unlike that of the Mayas, there never was any doubt that the Aztec culture was influenced by any but Mexican currents. Stephens' accurate appraisal was unfortunately disregarded by following travelers, some of whom ascribed the Mayas' achievements to lost Israeli tribes, Atlantis, and recently to extraterrestial beings. These wild theories never began in central Mexico, thanks to the collaboration of some Aztec elders who survived the conquest and historian-friars. The knowledge of the last indigenous Mexican culture is quite complete.

The Aztec Migration

According to their mythologies, the Aztecs issued from the Seven Caves and started their migration from a place called Aztlan, whence their name. Somewhere in their history, the tribe adopted the name Mexica (May-she-ka) whose etymology is still open to dispute but whose mispronounced Spanish form became the country's name.

Carrying their god Huitzilopochtli, the Aztecs wandered for many generations, stopping at times to grow crops, then urged on by the priests who interpreted the deity's wishes. The migrations finally led them to the Valley of Mexico, probably in the late 12th century. The civilized settlers in the area, heirs to the Toltec culture, did not welcome the new group of semi-barbarians. The Aztecs had to settle in the least desirable places along the shores of what was then several interconnected lakes. After some warfare and shifting around, the permanent spot to build their city was pointed out by a long awaited sign, an eagle perched on a cactus while devouring a serpent. Later, this sign was adopted as the symbol of the Mexican nation. The year for settling down was 1345 although tradition has it in 1325.

During the next 83 years, the Aztecs paid tribute and built up their city to become a lakeside power. The nobles took wives from nearby cities, from lineages which claimed descent from the Toltecs who were considered the source of legitimacy as well as learning and art. The Aztecs built up a system of *chinampas,* highly fertile plots of raised land filled with rich soil from the lake bottom. Mistakenly called "floating" gardens, the chinampas are still in use at Xochimilco, now a southern suburb of Mexico City.

The next major turning point in Aztec history occurred in 1428 when the Aztecs and a coalition of lakeside city-states defeated the Tepanecs of Azapotzalco, the paramount power of the region. From then on, the Aztecs in a Triple Alliance with Texcoco and Tlacopan, set out on a path of conquest which, in less than 100 years, resulted in an empire encompassing most of central Mexico and reaching down the Pacific coast to Guatemala. The Aztec war machine was not always successful: the Tarascans of Michoacan twice defeated the onslaught and the city-state of Tlaxcala resisted all attacks. Tlaxcala, as the principal ally of the Spaniards, was to become one of the most important factors in the ultimate defeat of the Aztecs.

Warfare, the main purpose of the Aztec state, had a philosophical justification. The Aztecs believed that they were the Chosen People of the Sun and that this celestial body needed human sacrifices in order to make its daily way across the sky and through the dangerous underworld each night. In order to ensure a sufficient supply of potential sacrificial victims close to home, the Aztecs initiated "Wars of Flowers" with nearby city-states where the capture of victims was paramount, not conquest. During the wars of conquest, the main purpose was to defeat far-flung enemies to force them to pay regular tribute such as cotton cloth, foodstuffs, gold, and precious feathers. Of course, captives were also brought back for sacrifices but the defeated towns were usually left alone as long as they regularly delivered the heavy tribute.

As the Aztec empire grew, their social organization evolved to give increasing power to the nobles and especially to the emperor who was elected by a select portion of the nobility. The majority of the inhabitants were commoners belonging to 20 clans, each with its own ward in the city. These commoners could greatly improve their lot and status by capturing victims for sacrifices during the incessant wars. Children of both nobles and commoners attended compulsory schools. Bondsmen or serfs tilled the nobles' lands while a small group of slaves were treated well and could not be inherited. The *pochteca* were a small but important group of long distance traders who doubled as spies in nations prior to a prospective Aztec take-over.

Cortés Crushes an Empire

When Cortés and his small band of conquistadores first saw the Aztec capital of Tenochtitlan, the city was in full bloom, a jewel sitting lightly on the lake. Great causeways joined the city to shore and aqueducts brought drinking water. A ten-mile long dike set off Tenochtitlan to prevent flooding and to hold back the brackish part of the lake from the fresh water around the city. The market of Tlatelolco, full of daily and luxury products, was greater than any the Spaniards had seen in Europe. The sacred precinct, surrounded by a Snake Wall, was dominated by two imposing pyramids, one dedicated to Huitzilopochtli, the other to Taloc, the Rain God. This holy area was completed 32 years earlier and dedicated, according to one source, with the sacrifice of 80,400 victims. (The still incredible figure of 20,000 is more likely.) Even the gold-hungry conquistadores, anxious to impose their religion, were amazed by the grandeur of the Aztec capital. The city's population was between 200,000 and 300,000, including the adjoining market town of Tlatelolco.

The reasons for the Spanish defeat of the Aztecs should be sought in the fields of psychology and politics as well as the military. The Aztec emperor Motecuhzoma (the English Montezuma is a corruption of the Spanish Moctezuma, itself a mispronunciation) was a deeply religious man who was swayed by a series of ill omens and thought that Cortés might be the god Quezalcoatl, returning to claim his empire. Only the most vacillating of oppositions was directed by the Aztec emperor while Cortés knew what he wanted and shrewdly exploited changing situations. Cortés allied himself with the tribute-oppressed Totonacs on the coast, then the Aztec-hating Tlaxcalans of the highlands as well as other groups. The Spanish fighting men, skillfully using superior weapons and tactics, were far superior to the Aztec warriors. In the final siege of Tenochtitlan, a 2½-month bloody battle, the Spaniards could count on thousands of well armed Indian allies, a small fleet of brigantines which isolated the city from supplies, and the just-introduced smallpox which killed more defenders than the weapons did.

Shortly after the Spanish victory, what was left of the city was razed to make room for the conquerors' new town. Or so it was thought until 1978 when workers digging next to the cathedral to lay electrical lines struck archaeological pay dirt. Extensive excavations in this downtown area revealed that the Templo Mayor, the sacred precinct, was centered here. The excavated ruins are not very impressive but one major sculpture was discovered—a huge eight-ton andesite disc representing Coyolxauqui, sister of Huitzilopochtili. The piece was left in situ while the many offerings were moved the Anthropological Museum. The site is worth a look but it is at the museum where, through scale models, you can have an idea of the sacred precinct and the great market, the lost splendors of Tenochtitlan. Aztec sculptures at the same museum graphically display power and grandeur as well as sensitivity, giving us a better idea of the genius of the nation. Malinalco, about an hour's drive from Mexico City, is the best, and about the only, surviving example of Aztec architecture. The highlight here is the small temple of the Eagle and Jaguar Knights, carved out of solid rock. A very special atmosphere permeates the place, most propitious for reflection on the achievements and grandeur of the vanished cultures of Mexico.

CONTEMPORARY ARTS OF MEXICO

Form Follows Revolution

The Spanish conquistadores and colonists did a good job of wiping out the pre-Columbian art forms. These men were not keen on strange art. They melted down exquisite gold objects, broke up sacred sculptures, burned the codices and shrugged their shoulders at the intricate featherwork. Throughout colonial times and in the 19th century, talent in Mexico was chaneled to European styles with very little originality.

Modern Mexican art was born of the revolution that overthrew the Diaz dictatorship in 1910. Mural painting with heavy political overtones was revived between 1920 and 1925, principally by the Big Three, neither generals nor politicians but painters, José Clemente Orozco, Diego Rivera, and David Alfaro Siqueiros. During the past two decades it has been fashionable to decry the work of this famed trio, but perhaps the school they led could free contemporary artists from their involvement with an undistinguished international style. Their art sprang from a deep need during times that bred a heroic generation of painters who were uplifted by the force of the movement they expressed. Mexican muralism has been a unique contribution to art of the 20th century. Perhaps no other school of painting based largely upon a political esthetic has ever, anywhere, achieved such success or exercised such influence.

If it is true that easel painting has been a weak echo of murals and graphics, and that modern abstract expressionism has hardly affected Mexican painting—with the notable exceptions of Rufino Tamayo and Carlos Merida—it is also beyond doubt that engravers and lithographers were powerful influences during and after the revolution.

José Guadalupe Posada worked for a conservative publishing house but was an illustrator of various periodicals opposed to the Diaz regime. In the 1890s he had an open shop in the city where both Orozco and Rivera, boys on their way to or from school, watched him working on metal plates. Posada produced skeleton pictures, cut in wood or type metal. The technique had been used by Santiago Hernandez, but Posada applied it to every kind of social and political problem, anticipating the caricaturists of the revolution and founding a school that still endures.

Such was the Workshop of Popular Graphic Arts, formed during the administration of President Lazaro Cardenas. The League of Revolutionary Artists and Writers (Leopoldo Mendez, Pablo O'Higgins, Alfredo Zalce, Antonio Tujol, Angel Bracho, Siqueiros, Orozco, and Tamayo were among its members) also brought Luis Arenal, Ignacio Aguirre, Raul Anguiano, Jesus Escobedo, and Everardo Ramirez into the Workshop, where techniques derived from Posada were utilized to illustrate political events throughout the world.

Engraving much less political in content also is encouraged by the Salon of Mexican Plastic Arts that, since its founding by the National Institute of Fine Arts in 1953, has staged more than 20 individual exhibitions each year, and Annual Salons of painting, engraving, and sculpture. Its membership numbers about 140.

Rivera

Diego Rivera, born in Guanajuato, showed such a talent for drawing that he entered the San Carlos Academy at the age of 10. Eleven years later he traveled in Europe and stayed in Paris until 1921, painting under the influence of Cézanne, the Cubists, Renoir, and others, but notably engaging, in 1919, in discussion with Siqueiros of plans for transforming art in Mexico into a popular, national movement. On his return home at the invitation of the Ministry of Education, he painted a sentimental-philosophical mural *The Creation* in the Preparatory School. Immediately afterward, he began the extensive murals in the two three-story patios of the Ministry—a task that occupied five years—and the murals that still attract visitors to an agricultural school at Chapingo, near the capital. He entered the field of social-minded art in one step, painting his people and portraying their hopes, their needs, in large simple forms and areas of bold color.

He tempered the content of his work to adverse political winds that were blowing, but on his return from a visit to Moscow in 1927, his work demonstrated more concern with political message than with esthetic quality and seemed to regard the Mexican Revolution as part of a world revolution. Although the U.S.A. was the subject of criticism or outright attack in the Ministry of Education murals, Rivera accepted a commission from U.S. Ambassador Dwight Morrow and painted, on the walls of an open balcony corridor of the Palace of Cortés in Cuernavaca, a long series of incidents from the history of Mexico, the enslavement of the Indian, and the uprising of Zapata, a hero of the state of Morelos.

Decoration of the Council Room of the Ministry of Health in Mexico City, in 1929–30, satisfied neither artist nor public, but the vast murals in the National Palace, begun in 1929, instantly retrieved and enhanced Rivera's international reputation. Basically, they relate the history of Mexico from pre-Columbian times to the revolution, but as post-revolutionary figures began to appear in uncomplimentary poses, the artist perhaps thought it politic to accept invitations to visit the U.S.A. His one-man show in San Francisco, California, in 1930; the staircase mural in the San Francisco Stock Exchange; a mural at the California School of Fine Arts; a fresco in a private home, the completion of four panels that he would carry to the Museum of Modern Art in New York, made 1931 a year of social and, to a lesser degree, artistic success. Rivera glorified industry in a mural in the courtyard of the Detroit Institute of Arts before engaging in battle with the owners of Rockefeller Center. His mural there was destroyed when Orozco was completing one at Dartmouth College, but he was to reconstruct it later in the Palace of Fine Arts in Mexico City and to paint 21 fresco panels at the New Workers School before leaving New York to complete the National Palace murals.

Orozco

Orozco, imbued with deep sympathy for the poor and oppressed, lived through months of fighting during the revolution and evolved his own characteristic expressionist form of protest.

Born in Ciudad Guzmán (formerly Zapotlán el Grande), he died in Mexico City in 1949. As a child, he met the famous José Guadalupe Posada whose engravings led to his interest in painting. But Orozco studied agriculture for three years before setting down to study his life's calling at the San Carlos Academy. In 1914 he joined the team of illustrators in "La Vanguardia," published by General Carranza's army in Orizaba.

"La Vanguardia" was founded by another artist from Jalisco, Gerardo Murillo, who is better known by his adopted name of Dr. Atl (atl means water in náhuatl, spoken by the Aztecs and other groups). Dr. Atl's fame rests on his many paintings of volcanos and for starting a new genre: landscapes from airplanes.

Under Dr. Atl's influence, Orozco got into trouble over the politics and anticlericalism evident in his art. He prudently left for the U.S.

After returning to Mexico, in the early 1920s he covered with paintings the inner walls of the great patio of the ex-Jesuit College of San Ildefonso, now the National Preparatory School (open free of charge to visitors on school days). Dozens of masterpieces unfold on the ground level as well as on the first and second floors. His themes are not meant to please conservatives, with Justice portrayed as a drunken female figure and God flanked by extravagantly dressed bourgeois, later defaced by religious zealots.

Orozco traveled to the U.S. on several occasions. In 1930, he painted at the New School for Social Research an explicit mural portraying the global social situation and the revolutionary movement in, particularly, Russia, Mexico, and India. Earlier in that year he had completed "Prometheus" at Pomona College, and in 1932 he began the murals that at Dartmouth College offer a history of America as a blend of aboriginal and European elements and, in juxtaposition, the accomplishments of the pre-colonial peoples and of the white man.

Siqueiros

During the period 1934–40, the relative positions of Mexico's leading painters changed. Orozco emerged as the outstanding muralist, Tamayo became recognized as an easel painter, and Siqueiros, caught up as always in a multitude of activities, dominated the politically oriented artists.

The highly individualistic Siqueiros, born in Chihuahua in 1896, was involved in a student strike in Mexico City in 1911. In the same year, at the age of 15, encouraged by Dr. Atl, he joined the Constitutionalist army and quickly became a lieutenant. A captain in 1919, he was sent to Europe, officially as military attaché of his embassy in Paris, but in fact to develop his demonstrated talent as a painter. He became a friend of Rivera, issued from Barcelona in 1921 a Manifesto to the Artists of America and, back home in 1922, helped to found the Syndicate of Technical Workers, Painters, and Sculptors.

From late in 1922 until mid-1924, Siqueiros painted his staircase murals in the patio of the Preparatory School. Then, as ever since, he treated the mural as an integral part of the building, insisting that the mural should be the painting of architectural space and not of flat walls in two dimensions. But art was to be almost abandoned for six hectic years during which Siqueiros organized unions of miners, led a delegation of Mexican miners to an international congress in Moscow and another to Uruguay, on which trip he was expelled from Argentina. May Day 1930 marked the beginning of one year's imprisonment in Mexico City and a further year under police surveillance in Taxco. The artist produced there a series of woodcuts and easel paintings on proletarian themes. Politics, controversy as to the place of painting within the class struggle, the introduction of pyroxilin paints in murals in California and Argentina, the formation of the Experimental Workshop in New York, all restricted his artistic production to a series of canvases—a self-portrait, *Birth of Fascism, Stop the War, Frightened Child, Negro Woman,* among them—before he departed for Spain where he became a colonel in the Republican forces. Back in Mexico in 1939 he was again, but briefly, imprisoned. Yet he was painting as well, for a show at the Pierre Matisse Gallery in New York and a mural called *The Trial of Fascism* in the building of the Electrical Workers Union, done in pyrixilin and achieving in it his first complete synthesis of modern techniques and political ideas.

Guadalajara Murals

While Siqueiros was so busy, Rivera completed one mural in the Palace of Fine Arts and one, *Sunday in the Park,* in the Del Prado Hotel, and peacefully sat at his easel, painting portraits, imaginative landscapes, and a variety of other canvases, all of meticulous workmanship.

Orozco was just beginning a series of stupendous murals. In 1934, he pictured the violence of the conflict between modern man and the chaotic, mechanized world, and successfully incorporated into this work, in the Palace of Fine Arts, symbols of class war, of the oppression of the poor by the rich. During 1936–39, he painted the dome and end wall of the auditorium of the University of Guadalajara. His stairwell at the Palacio (Government Palace) features an enormous Father Hidalgo brandishing a torch, seemingly coming out of the wall with a sad but resolute expression. The inner walls and dome of the ex-orphanage Cabañas (now the Centro Cultural Cabañas) boasts what many critics consider Orozco's best murals. The central cupola features "man in flames," consumed by his burning drive for self-realization.

While painting another mural in the Gabino Ortiz Library in Jiquilpan, birthplace of President Lazaro Cardenas, Orozco began *Dive Bomber,* a portable mural that he completed in the Museum of Modern Art, New York: a vivid reflection of the condition of mankind at the time of its painting, mid-1940.

Orozco began early in 1941 to decorate four large areas in the entrance hall of the Supreme Court and in the following year the vault and walls of the choir of the former church of the ancient Hospital de Jesus. The latter work was unfinished when the artist faced a wall 95 feet high and 72 feet wide in the open-air auditorium of the National School for Teachers. This mural, *National Allegory,* comprises large geometric forms. Stone and metal were used, and ethyl silicate as paint.

Toward the end of 1948, Orozco started to decorate the concert hall of the newly built National Conservatory of Music, only to be called to Guadalajara, where his last completed work was accomplished on the dome of the Chamber of Deputies. He left unfinished his decoration of the Alemán housing development in Mexico City, but he produced, in the extraordinarily fruitful last nine years of his life, numerous distinguished easel paintings.

More Rivera

Rivera as a muralist revived in 1943, when he painted two walls in the Institute of Cardiology and one in a popular nightclub. Then he returned to the National Palace, to work on a series of impressive panels in an upper corridor leading from the head of the staircase he had so brilliantly adorned in 1935. *The Nightmare of War and the Dream of Peace,* 50 square meters in area, was finished in 1952, and during that year and the following one Rivera was commissioned to decorate a large wall space at the University City, another at the Social

Security Hospital Number One, and a mosaic mural on the exterior of the Insurgentes Theater.

Siqueiros in Action

The far-ranging Siqueiros went to Chile in 1941, where he worked for a whole year on a set of murals in the city of Chillán—250 square meters of decoration of the Escuela Mexicana. His friend and associate Xavier Guerrero painted smaller murals in the same school. Traveling by way of Peru, Ecuador, Colombia, and Panama, Siqueiros executed one fixed mural and two transportable ones, in Cuba. Back in Mexico, he produced *Cuauhtemoc Against the Myth,* a 75-meter square mural done on a concave surface joined to a plane surface and part of a ceiling. Murals were planned and sketched for a Mexico City hotel and the state capitol of Chihuahua, but were not realized. Portraits, landscapes, and compositions fairly tumbled from his easel, characterized by the sculptured form he had achieved with synthetic paints.

The New Democracy joined the Rivera and Orozco murals in the Fine Arts Theater in 1945. During 1946 and 1947, Siqueiros completed some 70 easel pictures; in 1951, two panels on the general theme of *Cuauhtemoc Reborn;* in 1952, one of his most active years as an artist, one mural in a new building of the National Polytechnical Institute and another at the Social Security Hospital Number One. Half a dozen other projects were begun that year at the National University. In 1953, a mural depicting the excommunication and execution of Hidalgo, Father of Independence, was finished for the University of Morelia, and shortly thereafter Siqueiros rushed off to Poland, to do "the world's largest mural" in a sports stadium—a work now far surpassed in size, in Mexico City, by the same artist, who asserts that mural painting has reached a new stage through modern rather than traditional architecture, dynamic rather than static surfaces, and exposure to the public view rather than confinement to interior walls. These three principles dramatically apply to the monumental work Siqueiros has achieved in the Siqueiros Polyforum (the name of the mural-structure was chosen by the former owner of a tall hotel which has risen on the site but whose interior never seems to get completed—except for a revolving restaurant on top): the theme, humanity's struggle through the ages; the size, overwhelming.

The Current Scene

Although the work of the Big Three has overshadowed that of other Mexican artists, it accounts for only a part of the whole. Juan O'Gorman planned and built the library of the National University, and designed and constructed the mosaics that cover the four sides of the ten-story tower of closed stacks and extend over 4450 square yards. The violence of anti-clerical and anti-Fascist statements contained in frescos he painted in the Mexico City airport led to the destruction of the work. He collaborated with Julio Castellanos on a mural in the Gabriela Mistral school; achieved an elaborate mural in the Gertrudis Bocanegra Library at Pátzcuaro, with José Chavez Morado did the mosaics that adorn the exterior of the Ministry of Communications; and in recent years has added two murals, historical in character, to the nation's notable collection at Chapultepec Castle. He was commissioned in 1971 to paint more murals in the castle.

Alfredo Zalce's murals adorn a secondary school in the capital and the Museum of Morelia. Rina Lazo, Arturo Garcia Bustos, Diego Rosales, and Marco Antonio Borregui have followed the Rivera approach. Siqueiros, impossible to follow, much less to imitate, has influenced Federico Silva and Francisco Pego. Armando Lopez Carmona, Ramon Sanchez Garcia, and Guillermo Monroy are of the Orozco tradition.

Jorge Gonzalez Camarena's career as a muralist illustrated a new trend, a demand for artistic decoration of banks, offices, hotels, a brewery, although he also has painted in churches and museums, and in the lobby of the Institute of Social Security.

José Chavez Morado, a notable easel painter and muralist, has tried, individually and under government aegis, to integrate painting, sculpture, and architecture.

Modern Mexico City fairly teems with art galleries. The fact that the capital has no museum comparable to the Metropolitan, the Louvre, or the National Gallery perhaps serves to illustrate the magnitude and the influence of the murals in the history of painting in Mexico.

LITERATURE

Literature, as represented by the codices—the painted books—of Mesoamerica, was rudely obliterated from the history of human thought and expression.

The life of even the smallest township was recorded on paper made from the inner bark of various trees or on deer or jaguar skin parchment. Very many codices were destroyed when the conquering Spaniards set towns on fire. Their systematic destruction began with the arrival of missionaries and officers of the Inquisition.

Each codex was a long, single sheet, folded between decorated wooden ends. Principal religious documents presumably were inscribed and kept by priests, but from surviving codices, most of which are in Europe, it can be assumed that few events or human experiences went unrecorded.

The Dresden and other codices pictorially or in hieroglyphics depict and describe plants, animals, songs, rites, customs, historical events, laws, regional trade, tax returns, topographical notes from which maps could be compiled, the findings of astronomers and astrologers and their relation to agriculture, myth, dance, births, and deaths. Most of Mesoamerica's recorded knowledge and belief lay between those carved and painted wooden covers.

The Maya, however, compiled the Popol Vuh—the *Book of the Counsel*—in the Quiché language using Latin characters, about 1554, and their *Books of Chilam Balam,* concerned with religion, medicine, astrology, and history, also were composed after the conquest.

First Press

The first printing press to be operated in the Americas meanwhile had reached Mexico, sent to the capital by Juan Cromberger from Seville in 1536.

Sixteenth-century literature for obvious reasons recorded exploration, discoveries, and conquest; poetry was epic or lyric. Missionaries, observing the inclination of the native peoples toward performance and dance during religious ritual, tried to convert this pageantry and spectacle into an appropriate channel for propagating Christian doctrine, particularly at such ceremonial centers as Tlaxcala, Cholula, and Teotihuacán.

Colonial Latin America's foremost poet, Sister Juana Ines de la Cruz, born in 1651 on a ranch at Nepantla near the capital, was learned also in philosophy, theology, the humanities, and music.

La Gaceta de Mexico, the country's first formal newspaper, began publication in 1784.

The novel was a late starter. A decree issued in 1531 prohibited the sending of novels to New Spain, and the first were not written until the beginning of the 19th century, as the movement toward independence from Spain gathered momentum. Literature then became political. In the course of 1820, some 500 pamphlets discussing freedom of thought, social ills, and the constitutional regime were published. The first profoundly Mexican novel, *El Periquillo Sarniento* (published in English under the title *The Itching Parrot*) was written in 1816 by José Joaquin Fernandez de Lizardi, founder of an influential newspaper *El Pensador Mexicano (The Mexican Thinker).*

French romanticism was discernible in invariably sentimental novels and short stories by 1830, and a decade later the same school, but now Spanish, was expressed by such writers as Espronceda and Garcia Gutierrez.

Political Involvement

From the middle of the 19th century until the collapse of the Diaz dictatorship in 1910, a period during which Mexico endured the Reform War, French occupation, and domestic oppression that led to the revolution, intellectuals were searching for expression of nationhood but paying much more attention to politics than to literature.

The complete poems of Salvador Diaz Miron, composed between 1876 and 1928, were published as late as 1941. The poet Ramon Lopez Velarde was to die in his prime, in 1921. Prose, but principally poetry, comprised the seven volumes of the work of Luis G. Urbina. Armando Nervo, an outstanding poet and essayist, was published in Madrid between 1920 and 1928 by Alfonso Reyes—in 29 volumes.

Dramas, novels, and an autobiography were written by Federico Gamboa, whose *Santa,* a novel with a sentimental approach to the life of a prostitute, first published in Barcelona in 1902, since has gone into innumerable editions in many languages and has been staged and screened.

In the years immediately preceding and following the outbreak of revolution in 1910, intellectuals who were to become famous in Latin America and elsewhere but then were deeply involved in politics included the writers Jose Vasconcelos, Alfonso Reyes, Antonio Caso, and Pedro Henriquez Ureña; the poets Luis Urbina and Gonzalez Martinez, and the novelist and essayist Carlos Gonzalez Peña, author of a superior history of Mexican literature that was published in 1928. Federico Gamboa, Marcelino Davalos, and José Joaquin Gamboa were the best-known dramatists of those turbulent times. More poets emerged, Carlos Pellicer, Ortiz de Montellano, Gonzalez Rojo, Jose Gorostiza, and Jaime Torres Bodet founding a Forum in 1919 and Salvador Novo and Xavier Villaurrutia another, in 1927.

Contemporary Voices

The magazine *Taller (Workshop),* founded in the late 30s by Rafael Solana, became the voice of contemporary poets Octavio Paz and Efrain Huerta. Between 1940 and 1942, another magazine, *Tierra Nueva,* brought together the philosopher Leopoldo Zea, Jose Luis Martinez, a literary critic, and the poet Ali Chumacero.

In the aftermath of the revolution, realism found its principal expression in the novel. Mariano Azuela's *Los de Abajo (The Underdogs)* was instantly translated into English and French, as were Martín Luis Guzmán's *Eagle and Serpent* and *Shadow of the Caudillo.*

Carlos Fuentes is the best known of Mexico's contemporary novelists. Two of his major novels, *The Death of Artemio Cruz* and *Where the Air Is Clear* have been widely translated. They make excellent reading as well as providing an insight into the upper—and often seamier—side of Mexican society and politics. Whereas Fuentes sets his novels in the nation's capital, two regionalist novelists, Augustín Yáñez and Juan Rulfo, develop their work in the state of Jalisco. Yáñez, who was governor of his native state and Mexico's Secretary of Education, wrote of the impoverished, proud northern part of his state in *The Lean Lands* and *The Edge of the Storm.* Both are powerful novels with a gripping atmosphere. Juan Rulfo, a strange character, wrote only a volume of short stories, *The Burning Plain,* and a novelette, *Pedro Páramo.* You can read these two works in a couple of hours but a strange feeling will haunt you for a long time. Never again will you fall for the misconception of Mexico-is-machismo or Mexico-is-a-sleeping-peon. If you like your psychology straight but not clinical, Ocavio Paz's *Labyrinth of Solitude* is an absolute must to understand Mexico and the meaning of such abused terms as machismo and malinchismo. The well-known Nobelist, Gabriel Garcia Marquez, is an adopted son of Mexico, having spent a decade in this country.

A surprising number of well-known British and American authors have written about Mexico or set their plots in this country. The list, which has surprises for all but a few professors, includes Sherwood Anderson, Saul Bellow, Ray Bradbury, William Burroughs, Hart Crane, Jon Dos Passos, Lawrence Ferlinghetti, Allen Ginsberg, Graham Greene, H. Rider Haggard, Aldous Huxley, Jack Kerouac, D.H. Lawrence, Oscar Lewis, Jack London, Malcolm Lowry, Norman Mail-er, Anais Nin, Katherine Porter, John Reed, John Steinbeck, B. Traven, and Tennessee Williams. The work of these authors is well described by Drewey Gunn in *American and British Writers in Mexico, 1556–1973.*

Upon reading the literary works, one is surprised how few foreign writers understood Mexico—language barrier, social isolation, and a lack of time all contributing. That is not to say that the production is worthless, but it is often the writer's talent, not knowledge of the country, which makes the material worthwhile. Of course, there are some exceptions. Oscar Lewis has accurately chronicled Mexico's "culture of poverty" in the capital, to the surprise—and sometimes anger—of some local, out-of-touch intellectuals. The mysterious B. Traven, best known for his *Treasure of the Sierra Madre* (the least "Mexican" of his novels), has remarkably captured the southern part of the country—especially the feelings of the Indians—in novels such as *The Bridge in the Jungle, The General from the Jungle* and *Rebellion of the Hanged.*

MUSIC

The peoples of Mesoamerica learned and perpetuated their history by singing it. Until the practice was prohibited by the Spaniards, they sang of the history of the tribes, of earthquake, famine, and plague, of comets, deities, the hunt, of love, afterlife, and ancient tradition.

Spanish chroniclers not only omitted to write down a single melody, they also failed to translate a single song—because, as Sahagun put it: "these songs are full of things of the devil." In the same spirit, the conquistadores forbade community dancing, for which the participants wore special dress.

Whistles, flutes, percussion instruments, drums, giant conch shells, rattles, trumpets, and notched deer bones were the instruments of music, and the earliest, made of bone or of baked clay, date from about 1500 B.C. Ceremony was always accompanied by music, and parties could not begin until the arrival of the drummers. The *teponaztli,* a large, round drum, was played for dancing. The *huehuetl,* a drum up to four feet in height and played vertically, was made from a hollowed log over which membrane was stretched and frequently was elaborately carved or painted in bright colors. War drums came in many sizes.

Whistles of bamboo, clay, bone, or wood were carved in representation of gods, dogs, monkeys, birds. The *ayotl,* a percussion instrument made from turtle shell, was common throughout the area in the classic period, and on the eastern coast drums were made from the same type of shell, carved, painted, and occasionally decorated with gold. Rattles were most often made from gourds, painted and decorated. The Spaniards could not be blamed for disdaining the only five tones known to the Aztecs. But elsewhere, flutes with double or triple mouthpieces and sounding up to 16 tones were played.

Outstanding Composers

Elements of pre-Columbian music have been introduced by several of the Mexican composers who have achieved international reputations.

Rodolfo Halffter, a native Spaniard who became a Mexican citizen, and Carlos Chavez, who composed his first symphony in 1918 at the tender age of 19, were two outstanding Mexican musical leaders of the first half of this century. Younger musicians influenced by them who became prominent in their own right include Daniel Alaya, Blas Galindo, Luis Sandi, and José Pablo Moncaya, who composed "Huapango."

Silvestre Revueltas, a child prodigy in his native Durango, studied in Chicago and Spain, then returned to Mexico to write symphonic poems and other compositions with very Mexican themes such as the cries of the street merchants, the problems of the poor, and Pancho Villa.

Mexico's Most Popular Music

Surprisingly good Indian bands are found in the states of Oaxaca and Michoacán, livening many a fiesta until the musicians can no longer resist the numerous invitations to imbibe with their fellow villagers.

The "musica ranchera" was more typical of the north and center of Mexico but now has invaded all corners of the country, thanks to the radio. The closest American equivalent is the country and western music. The rancheras sing of unrequited love and machismo. Among the popular songs, known to most Mexicans, there's one about a man whose word is the law and another one telling of a macho who murdered his wife's lover and faces death with no qualms as in the afterlife he will seek out his victim to murder him again.

Although modern music is in plentiful supply in Mexico, to the delight of the younger generation, the music longest, and most fondly, remembered by foreign visitors is that of the mariachis. Reputedly born in the state of Jalisco, but now spread well over all the republic, mariachi music has become popularly known as the "tipico" music of Mexico.

And popular it is! No home party, wedding, public fiesta or special occasion is complete without its mariachi troubadors. The musical groups, each numbering anywhere from three to more than a dozen musicians, cut dashing, romantic figures in their huge sombreros, tight dark suits well adorned with silver, frilly shirts, and cowboy boots. To the visitor they are truly Mexico's "gay *caballeros.*"

Trumpets, guitars and violins predominate among the instruments played. Most groups can deliver vocally and instrumentally, about 100 standard pieces, largely of a sentimental, sadly romantic vein. In Mexico City the mariachis gather each evening in Garibaldi Square, playing for their own enjoyment and that of the passersby while waiting to be hired for other locations. Other major cities, especially Guadalajara, have their own Garibaldi Squares.

About ten years ago the capital's mayor fell into disfavor with the populace when he outlawed night serenading claiming it was a public nuisance. His successor wisely canceled the ordinance, stating, "Serenading is a part of our Mexican tradition. Let it continue!" It has. A suitor hires mariachis to serenade his love of the moment, a husband thus remembers his wife's or daughter's saint's day.

Most popular serenading hours are between 2 A.M. and 4 A.M. No foreign visitor who has been wakened by the haunting, romantic strains flowing through the night air will ever forget the unique experience.

FOLKLORE

Blend of Several Cultures

Since Cortés first marveled at the craftsmen and cuisine of Tenochtitlán, its fabled marketplace, and the dancers and musicians of Montezuma's court, travelers have found Mexico's folklore a source of fascination. Today, four-and-a-half centuries after the Spanish Conquest, many of the ancient folkways still endure, sometimes as remote from the mainstream of contemporary life as they were from sixteenth-century Europe.

Indian tribes in the high sierra worship their ancient deities of sun and rain, wind and fire. Villagers a few miles from the capital affectionately call Our Lady of Guadalupe, Tonantzin, after the Aztec mother-goddess. Pregnant women all over Mexico carry something made of iron under their belts to ward off the ill effects of an eclipse of the moon on their unborn children.

In the cities too, folkways still persist. Middle-class housewives in high-rise apartments try out folk remedies suggested by their servants. In village huts and city restaurants, Mexicans of every class dine on *tortillas,* piquant *chile* sauces, black beans, hot chocolate, *tamales*—all of it pre-Columbian fare. On a garden wall in a Mexico City residential street, stalks of maize grow in the niche normally reserved for a statue of the household patron saint.

European customs never supplanted the vigorous native folkways. The indigenous peoples, steeped in their culture, chose what suited them from the strange new ways of the conquerors, but kept what they needed from the old. They accepted Christianity because it proved as useful to them as their own religion had been; but even Mexican Catholicism—like handicrafts and music—is a unique blend of two cultures.

Because so many aspects of Mexican folklore—fiesta, music and dance, even textile design—are tied to religious beliefs, the key to understanding the folk consciousness lies in the native religion and the alloy it formed with Catholicism.

For the ancient Aztecs, the universe was a hostile place. A man's fate was determined by heavenly signs on the day he was born. The gods, who represented the natural elements, had to be placated if man was to survive. The sun itself, so taught the priests, would cease to shine if not appeased with an abundant diet of human hearts.

Both Aztecs and Mayas had developed a complicated mythology with a vast pantheon of deities, a high ranking priestly class, and an extensive calendar of holy days. Each of the 18 months of the Aztec solar calendar had its specific rites, all of which were vitally important, for they assured the coming of rain, the orderly procession of the seasons, the very light of day itself. In short, the activities of men and gods were intimately related. Without sun and rain, man would perish; without ritual, life on earth would end. Man's life was one long process of propitiation: his holidays, his music, even the patterns he wove into his clothing were amulets against an unhappy fate.

Christianity ended this strict interdependence of god and man: human sacrifice was stopped, and the sun kept shining. But much of the native religion remained. For one thing, there were many similarities between Christianity and the Mexican forms of worship. The cross was already a potent symbol when the Spaniards came. Baptism with water was practiced in ancient Mexico, and so was confession, fasting, incense burning, and the chastity of priests.

Catholic saints took over the functions of the Aztec gods, but the saints were treated as idols, and in many ways they still are. A village that is suffering from a drought may hold a special fiesta in honor of its patron saint, complete with a mass for rain, fireworks, and a religious procession.

Many of the more isolated indigenous groups, in spite of being nominal converts to Christianity, still prefer to honor the gods in the old way. Chinantecos and Cuicatecos of the State of Oaxaca offer *tamales* and the sugarcane liquor, *aguardiente,* to the earth to insure good crops. The Mixes of the same state sacrifice birds and sprinkle the fields with their blood before sowing the seeds. The Huichol Indians sacrifice an ox or, better yet, a deer as part of their rain ceremonies.

Most Indian groups made Christianity a part of their own ancient beliefs. The Yaquis of the northwest, who were not converted until the 18th century, believe that Christ was a Yaqui who came to save them from the flood, give them their lands, find their eight villages and establish their religious and civil authorities. The Tzotzils, a Mayan group living in the Chiapas highlands, believe that the sun was cold before the birth of Christ. They blend the Christian story with the legend of their supreme god, Chultotic, the sun, who was born of his virgin mother, Chulmetic, the moon.

No matter how Christianity is translated, the role of the Virgin and the saints is always the same: they are champions of the people, benevolent beings who intercede for the faithful in Heaven. They are held in abiding affection, and the annual fiesta honoring a town's patron is the climax of the holiday calendar. In many Indian villages, the saints are more important than the Holy Trinity.

Fiestas and Ferias

Mexicans have always had a fondness for celebration. In pre-Hispanic times, the calendar brimmed with holidays, each with its processions, singing and dancing. Probably no country has invented as many occasions for celebrating as modern Mexico. Religious festivals, patriotic holidays, special dates honoring the mailman, the traffic cop, the newsboy—each is an opportunity for parties, days off, long weekends, and that peculiarly Mexican event, the fiesta.

A fiesta's mainspring is often religious, but this does not mean that devotion is the order of the day. Mingling fairground with spectacle, commerce with prayer, a fiesta is a chance to sell a few baskets, share a meal with friends or imbibe *pulque,* buy the children pink skeins of spun sugar, and pay one's respects to the patron saint.

Mexico celebrates more fiestas than any other Latin American country, and there is almost always one going on somewhere, any day of the year.

If you are planning a visit to a popular fiesta or *feria,* or an outing during Carnival, or Holy Week, it is well to have hotel reservations. If not, be ready to accept a farmer's invitation to stay at his family's one-room cottage, or share the mayor's splendid village house. Mexicans can be wonderfully hospitable, especially in the provinces, and the very poor are often the kindest and most generous of all.

The task of organizing a town patron's annual fiesta falls to village religious brotherhoods called *mayordomías,* organizations that date back to the early colonial period. Membership in these groups is considered a great honor, for preparing a fiesta is an absorbing part of community life, an activity that involves the collaboration of all. *Mayordomía* members often dip heavily into their own modest savings for fireworks, new clothes for the saint's image, and floral decorations for the church entrance.

A fiesta usually lasts one or two days, but if the saint is especially important, festivities may go on for a week or more, and include many other activities, such as bullfights, cockfights, art shows, and commercial and agricultural exhibits. These lengthy fiestas are called *ferias,* or fairs. No matter how small the village, at fiesta time there will be a marketplace, a carousel and other rides for the children, a *castillo* (tower) of fireworks, and usually regional dancing in front of the church.

Nationally, the most important of the annual fiestas is the one that honors Mexico's patroness, Our Lady of Guadalupe. It is celebrated everywhere, but the most important ceremony is held at the Basilica of Guadalupe on the northern edge of Mexico City, on December 12, the anniversary of one of the days Juan Diego saw the Virgin. According to the legend, the Virgin's miraculous appearances occurred in the very place where the pagan temple of Tonantzin had been destroyed on the orders of Mexico's first bishop. Like Tonantzin, Guadalupe was a virgin. One was the mother of Aztec gods, the other, the mother of Christ. Guadalupe had come to look after her people in place of the fallen mother-goddess.

Guadalupe's day is a national holiday, and the festival draws thousands of the faithful to her shrine. They begin arriving the evening before, many crawling on their knees up the long avenue that leads to the Basilica. Some have come walking all the way from their villages.

In spite of the religious nature of the day, and the depressing sight of the pilgrims struggling with bleeding knees up to the shrine, a carnival atmosphere prevails around the church. Fruit vendors peddle tangerines and sugar cane from blankets spread on the pavement. Because it is close to Christmas, the crisp cookies called Buñuelos are frying in cauldrons set up along the sidewalks, ready to be served with a sweet brown sugar sauce. Children, dressed in miniature native costumes, get photographed in Santa's sleigh—an import from the north. A block away, the lights of a ferris wheel spin through the dark, while in the church atrium, dancers from many regions prepare their homage to the Virgin. Splendidly costumed Concheros form circles for their dance, which will last most of the night and all the next day.

Many of the pilgrims camp out on the concrete or stone spaces around the Basilica. The next day they attend mass, watch the dancers again, socialize, eat and drink. If they must thank the Virgin for a favor granted, they may leave a small *milagro* near the altar. (These miniature silver figures come in the form of eyes, hearts, legs—anything that might have been healed through a saint's intercession.) At nightfall, they head for home, while vendors still offer their last few oranges, and one or two exhausted penitents continue their lonely acts of faith.

Christmas Season

Soon after Guadalupe Day comes the Christmas season, a miscellany of customs transplanted from Spain, left over from the colonial period, and imported from the United States. There was apparently no winter solstice festival before the conquest (there being no real winter season), and Mexicans still do not seem sure how they want to celebrate Christmas. Children write to Santa Claus and the Three Kings, and get toys on Christmas Day and Epiphany, as well. A crèche, or *nacimiento,* is set up under the Christmas tree. And the *posada,* in big cities anyway, has largely turned into a cocktail party.

The *posada* dates from colonial times, when missionaries sought to dramatize the Christmas story for their new converts. The nine days of *posadas* (inns), beginning December 16, represent the wanderings of Mary and Joseph and their search for lodgings. The traditional *posada* begins with a procession. Half the guests, carrying lighted candles and a tray bearing the images of the Holy Family, march around outside of the house, finally arriving at the door, where they sing the first stanza of the *posada* litany, begging for a place to stay. From behind the closed door, the other guests refuse. The dialogue goes on for several stanzas, until the group outside reveals its identity, and the door is opened.

The sacred portion of the evening now over, a party begins, with the breaking of those goody-filled, decorated jugs called *piñatas,* the drinking of a hot, fruit-laden and rum-laced punch, and the eating of a traditional Christmas salad and other holiday fare. (In Mexico City, the Villa Jones International Cultural Center usually gives at least one *posada* for its members and interested visitors. Check *The News* for dates.)

Humorous Death View

Many have puzzled over the Mexican's humorous, ironic, unconstrained view of death, and nowhere is this more evident than on the Day of the Dead, a combined observance of pre-conquest ceremonies, All Saints' Day, and All Souls' Day. Weeks before, bakeries have painted their windows with comic scenes of skeleton families enjoying "*Exquisito Pan de Muerto*"—delicious bread of the dead. This morsel is a round, somewhat dry coffee cake, decorated with small mounds of dough and sprinkled with sugar. Candy shops display piles of white sugar skulls, benignly decorated in pink and blue icing. Flower stalls overflow with *flores de muerto,* bright yellow marigolds, for traditional graveside offerings.

On October 31, villagers hurry back to their native towns to await the "*muertitos chicos,*" the souls of dead children. A toy, cakes, hot chocolate, and honey are left out to sweeten their visit to earth.

The return of the adult souls is anticipated the following night, and for them a marvelous repast is prepared. Among the traditional dishes are bread, *pulque,* and some kind of fowl prepared in *mole,* a piquant sauce of chocolate and chili. The food is placed on a specially decorated table often featuring a photo of the deceased, along with flowers and other offerings.

Often an all-night, candle-lit vigil is kept in the town cemetery, each family gathering on the graves of its departed to accompany the souls on their annual sojourn. Drinking for the health of the dead keeps everyone warm throughout the night.

One of the most traditional Day of the Dead observances is held in Janitzio, an island fishing village on Lake Pátzcuaro, Michoacán. A spirited duck hunt on the lake the day before provides fowl for the souls' banquet; housewives spend all day scrubbing their floors and their children, and preparing the *ofrendas,* and tourists pour in to inspect this most curious of festivals. For Janitzio, reservations are essential, either in Pátzcuaro or Morelia. There is a similar spectacle in Mixquic, near Mexico City.

In July, the City of Oaxaca holds a festival which is part Catholic feast day, part pre-Hispanic rite, and part modern civic celebration. This is *La Guelaguetza.* The word *guelaguetza* was originally applied to mutual help within a community whereby families cooperated in tasks such as harvests or festive preparations for a wedding or a funeral. The ancient homage to Centeotl, the god of maize, was recast as the fiesta of Our Lady of Mount Carmel, *La Virgen del Carmen,* which begins on July 16. The anniversary of the death of President Juárez (an Indian from Oaxaca) has also gotten mixed up in this act. More recently, a conscientious state governor, interested in preserving indigenous custom, established a statewide competition of regional songs and dances. *La Guelaguetza* amounts to a gathering of tribes from all areas of the state, dressed in their finest fiesta garb, and the effect is spectacular.

From this very abridged look at Mexico's fiesta calendar, it should be obvious that almost anything can be a fiesta; the wild indulgence in toys on Christmas and Three Kings' Day, the solemn pilgrimages to the shrines of the many Virgins and miracle saints, the formally organized dance festivals like the Guelaguetza and the celebration of St. Michael's Day in San Miguel de Atlixco, Puebla.

In a latitude where seasons slide imperceptibly into each other, there are only holidays to mark the progress of the year. In January, the feast day of St. Anthony the Abbott calls forth kittens in new gingham dresses and polka-dot painted pigs for a blessing from the animals' own patron. February brings Lent, but it is close to planting time and there are seeds to be blessed on Candlemas Day, as well as the many fiestas in honor of *La Virgen de la Candelaria.*

Carnival is celebrated almost everywhere in some way, from the hopping of Chinelo dancers in the dusty village of Tepotzlán, Morelos, to the parades and costume balls of Mérida, Mazatlán and Veracruz. Holy Week, a vacation period for most of the nation, is the time for solemn passion plays like the one in Mexico City's Ixtapalapa district, and the processions of black-hooded *penitentes* in Taxco.

April brings the ten-day Feria of San Marcos in Aguascalientes; May, the masons' rooftop revelry on Holy Cross Day; June the feast of San Juan (and the rain god Chac) in San Juan Chamula, Chiapas. Santiago is honored in July, and in August, the people of Huamantla, Tlaxcala, spend two weeks making fabulous carpets of flowers and colored sawdust to honor the Feast of the Assumption.

September 14 belongs to *charros,* October 4 to San Francisco, November 20 to the Mexican revolution; and so the year winds on, an endless circle of holidays, religious, national, occupational.

Folk Music and Dance

Whatever occasions them, one thing most fiestas have in common is music. In fact, Mexicans seem to need a musical accompaniment to almost everything they do. A bus driver races to a sultry tropical tune on his portable radio, while a wandering guitarist mounts the bus and serenades the passengers. A decrepit street singer in rags and a frayed *charro* hat, peddles a song in the public market. A marimba group sets up its instruments on a shady residential street, plays one hopeful song, and then waits to see if the neighbors are pleased enough to ask for more.

Mexicans have had music in their blood since remote antiquity. Pre-Columbian legend had it that music was divine in origin, a gift from the god-king Quetzalcoatl. Never performed for art's sake alone, music and dance were always a part of religious rite, and this is still true among the most conservative indigenous groups. Their ritual chants, accompanied by instruments which in many cases have not changed in centuries, suggest the vanished melodies of pre-conquest days.

Sounds of ancient instruments are all that remain of pre-Hispanic music: the windy tones of the *chirimía,* the trumpeting notes of the conch shell, the sonorous drumming of the *huehuetl.* But these and hundreds of other wind and percussion instruments reflect the astounding ingenuity of pre-conquest musicians and their considerable knowledge of musical theory.

The Spaniards brought new musical forms and a variety of stringed instruments to an already fertile musical tradition. Strings spread quickly to every corner of Mexico, and are found everywhere, from the rustic violins of the Huichols to the gourd mandolins of the Lacandons.

During the colonial period, troupes of Spanish musicians and dancers toured Mexico, entertaining the colonists with the popular music of the day. The *romances, malagueñas,* and *fandangos* of Old Spain took root, and through the years an entirely new kind of music came into being.

As with cookery and handicrafts, each region has its own musical specialties, but five areas stand out for the richness and variety of their folk repertoires. These are the state of Jalisco; *tierra caliente,* the hot country, near the coast of the state of Michoacán; the state of Guerrero; the coastal region of the state of Veracruz, called *La Jarocha;* and La Huasteca, in the northeast, an area which includes parts of the states of Veracruz, Hidalgo, San Luis Potosí, Tamaulipas, Querétaro, and Puebla. Each of these regions has its *sones,* tunes, which accompany lyrics, or *coplas,* and often a dance as well—usually a rhythmic *zapateado.* Instrumentation, rhythm, musical themes, and execution of the dance vary according to the region.

Son jalisciense, native to the state of Jalisco, is widely known outside Mexico for its association with the mariachi groups, with their silver-studded *charro* costumes and blaring trumpets. The trumpets are actually a fairly recent addition to the instrumentation, which also includes violins, *guitarra de golpe,* the small four-stringed *vihuela,* and the *gui-*

tarrón, a four-stringed bass guitar. The word mariachi, from the French *mariage,* refers to the original vocation of the group, which was the provision of music for weddings and balls. Mariachi bands are still favored by young men for serenading their girl friends, and regularly awaken whole neighborhoods with midnight trumpets under the beloved's window.

Forerunner of the *son jalisciense* and similar to it in rhythm, instrumentation, and musical themes, is the *son* of *tierra caliente,* Michoacán. The two areas are contiguous and probably made up a single cultural region centuries ago. The distinctive feature of many of these *sones* is a large, rustic harp, whose resonance box is used as a drum, giving a strong rhythmic accompaniment to the melodic lines of the violins, *vihuela,* and *guitarra de golpe.*

Son guerrerense, unique among the *sones* for its inclusion of a drum along with the strings, is the product of a variety of different influences, including, according to legend, the songs of a group of Chilean sailors shipwrecked off the Guerrero coast. The tunes they left behind are variations of the *son,* traditionally called *chilenas.* The *gusto,* another variant, is typical of the coastal region where, at fiesta time, dancers stamp out their rhythms on a raised platform called an *artesa.*

The *son jarocho,* from the Veracruz coast, is one of the richest, most varied, and best known of all types of Mexican folk music. Its origin is Spanish, and the mixture of African blood among the people of the region shows up in its rhythmic complexity.

Lyricists of the *son jarocho* have always favored improvisation and new stanzas are continually being invented to fit traditional songs. Many of the *sones* deal with love, and the dance they accompany is a tableau of courtship. Others are comic tales of birds and animals, like *El Pajaro Carpintero* or *La Iguana,* told in something very close to a nonsense verse.

Son huasteco and the regional dance called *huapango,* have their roots in the fandango of Spain. Vivid rhythms of violin, *jarana,* and the eight-stringed *huapanguera* accompany a vivid, complicated *zapateado* danced on a raised wooden platform that enhances the din of pounding feet.

National rather than regional, the *corrido,* a narrative ballad related to the Spanish romance, is traditional throughout most of Mexico. In the days before mass communications, *corrido* singers provided a kind of musical newscast, spreading the word of current events from village to village. The words of the *corridos* were printed up on broadsides, which the singer would sell to his audience for a few centavos each.

The *corrido* came into its own as a form during the Mexican revolution, when things were happening fast, and every new exploit of Pancho Villa served as the theme for a ballad. Any good story was *corrido* material: from a catastrophic train wreck *(El Descarrilamiento de Tematle)* to the tale of an incestuous father *(Delgadina).* The *corrido* is still a vital form, especially in small villages. During the clashes between the students and the Mexican government in the fall of 1968, someone wrote a *corrido* sympathetic to the student cause—*Mexico 68*—which is still sung and played in student circles.

The Ballet Folklorico has made world famous two haunting melodies from the Isthmus of Tehuantepec: *La Zandunga* and *La Llorona.* Among the loveliest of Mexican folk songs, they are also the best known representatives of the music of southern Mexico, homeland of the marimba and its slow, gracious dance rhythms.

Although the marimba was believed to have been African in origin, recent evidence seems to indicate that it was known in pre-Hispanic times. Marimba music is native to the Isthmus of Tehuantepec, the states of Tabasco, Chiapas, and Yucatán, and Quintana Roo. Three or four musicians divide the keyboard; one plays the melody, one the harmony, and the other two elaborate counterpoint motifs and vibrato effects. Each village has one or two marimba groups, and takes great pride in their virtuosity.

Besides the regional *sones,* the *corrido,* and the marimba composition, there are other minor types of folk song, like the Tarascan *pirecuas,* the satiric *valona* of Michoacán's *Tierra Caliente,* and the *tambora* played by the brass bands of the northern states. No matter what the region, even the smallest village usually has its own little band of unlettered but often very talented musicians, and to them Mexico owes the variety and vitality of its folk music.

The Festive Dances

Legions of dancers, their costumes defiant splashes of color against the buff tones of the village church, whirl without tiring for the pleasure of the Virgin. The coquette, on the other hand, tosses her head, lifting frilled petticoats to display the flashing steps of a *jarabe.* These two very different types of dances reflect the disparity of cultural influences that infuse Mexican folk dance.

A number of the dances derive more or less directly from European forms, like the *jarabes* of Jalisco and Michoacán, the *jarana Yucateca,* and the *polca norteña,* Mexico's version of the polka, which is traditional in the northern border states. Most of these symbolize courtship, and are danced by couples. Parties and weddings are the occasions for such dances, the sole purpose of which is pleasure.

Closer to ritual than to amusement are the regional indigenous dances that flood the villages with color at fiesta time. The execution of these dances is taken as seriously as any other aspect of religious observance. In many areas, young men form special associations dedicated to the performance of one or another dance, take certain oaths of ethical conduct, bring their new costumes to be blessed at church, and vow to perform the dance for a certain number of years.

The custom of dancing in the church atrium dates from colonial times, when early missionaries encouraged the Indians to continue their ancient songs and dances—but to dedicate them to God and the saints. The Church attracted more converts, and dancing for the saints' pleasure has been an important part of fiestas ever since.

Most spectacular of all Mexico's dances, *El Volador,* the "flying pole dance" of Papantla, has been performed by agile young men since pre-Hispanic times. Part dance, part acrobatics, *El Volador* is thought to suggest pre-conquest sun worship. The towering pole is the sun; the four dancers, swooping downward in ever-widening circles, make 13 revolutions to reach the ground, where they land lightly on their feet. (Four times 13 is 52, the number of years in the Aztec century.) The best place to see the dance is in Papantla itself during the Corpus Christi Day festival in late May or early June or on St. Francis' day, October 4, in Quetzalan, Puebla.

Two splendidly and similarly costumed dances are *Los Guaguas* of Papantla and *Los Quetzales* of Puebla, Hidalgo, and the Totonac area of Veracruz. The costumes of both feature a conical hat topped by a circular headdress more than a yard in diameter, made of strips of colored paper woven on a reed frame trimmed with feathers. Because of the unwieldy headdress, steps are necessarily slow and simple. The dancers are accompanied by the music of a reed flute and a small drum. *Los Guaguas,* like *El Volador,* involves a kind of stunt that may once have had religious meaning. At the end of the performance, four dancers mount a large revolving cross and turn on it, wheel fashion. In pre-conquest days, both the cross and the number four had represented the gods of the four cardinal directions.

The Yaqui Indians of Mexico's northwest, now mostly settled down to village life, recall their days as warriors and hunters in *El Venado,* the deer dance. Conceived as an homage to the deer—a sacred animal in Yaqui lore—the dance also dramatizes the struggle of good and evil. The leading dancer wears a headdress fashioned out of a deer's antlers, and leggings of dried cocoons filled with pebbles that rattle as he moves, imitating to perfection the grace of the animal.

One of the largest organizations of dancers in Mexico is the Los Concheros group of Mexico City and the central states, with several thousand members, a strict hierarchy, and rigidly enforced membership rules. Los Concheros takes its name from the *concha,* one of the group's musical instruments, a kind of mandolin made from an armadillo shell. The costumes, consisting of a velvet tunic, cloak, and feathered headdress, are meant to be replicas of the Aztec nobleman's costume, and are quite spectacular.

Several of Mexico's regional dances grew out of attempts by the early missionaries to convert the Indians to Christianity or to introduce them to Spanish history. One of these, variations of which are performed in several different areas, is *Moros y Cristianos,* the Dance of the Moors and Christians, a dramatization of the Spanish struggle to drive the Moors out of Spain. According to legend, the battle was won through the intervention of St. James and the heroic Santiago is always represented in the dance. In the dance of *Los Santigueros,* traditional in the Puebla highlands, he fends off the "Moors," a large wooden horse fitted around his waist.

Los Diablitos, a dance native to the eastern part of the state of Guerrero, grew out of dramatic charades akin to the medieval miracle plays, showing the repudiation of the devil and the seven deadly sins. Eventually, the dance came to include 16 participants, each representing another aspect of sin. One, dressed as Death, wears a black suit painted with a white skeleton. The dancers accompany themselves on a curious percussion instrument, a wooden box that in Colonial times represented the sin of avarice.

One of the most amusing of the regional dances is *Los Viejitos* (The Little Old Men) of the State of Michoacán. It can be seen in the Tarascan villages around Lake Patzcuaro at religious festivals. The dancers wear pink masks of wood or clay, with straggly hair and beards of sisal fiber. They carry canes, and begin the dance by hobbling along, imitating a rheumatic, limping gait. The pretense of age soon disappears as they begin to do the most complicated steps with great agility and vigor.

Folk Costume

Thirty years ago or so, Mexico had a national folk costume: *charro* outfits for the men, and *china poblana* dress for the women, both of them popular party outfits among young people. The *charro,* or horseman's suit, with its fitted jacket and trousers of fine suede or deerskin, accented with rows of silver buttons; its frilled shirt and wide-brimmed felt hat richly embroidered in gold and silver, was originally the gala dress of wealthy ranchers. Even today, a *charro* suit is acceptable formal wear, but is not often seen outside the *charro* organizations. The adoption of the *charro* suit as the official uniform for mariachi bands probably accounts for its decline in popularity.

China poblana dress, consisting of a red and green sequin-embroidered skirt worn over many petticoats, a white blouse and a *rebozo* worn crossed in the front, is said originally to have been the costume of Puebla servant girls (then called *chinas*). It is rarely seen today, except at costume balls. Modern Mexico no longer has a national costume, but the extraordinary variety of native Indian dress more than makes up for the lack of one.

One of the greatest pleasures in store for the traveler who ventures outside of Mexico's large urban centers is the sight of Indian women wearing costumes whose origins go back to antiquity. Even city-bound visitors can tour indigenous Mexico via the National Anthropology Museum's ethnographic section, an excellent introduction to the magnificence of Mexican Indian costume.

The ancient Mexicans were great weavers and one of Montezuma's first gifts to Cortés was several bales of "white cloth made of cotton and feathers—a marvelous sight," as Bernal Díaz describes it in *The Conquest of New Spain.*

Indian women today, especially those who live in the more isolated sections of Mexico, still conserve pre-Hispanic traditions in textile design and manufacture. Spinning and weaving techniques have changed little since ancient times, and one can still see country women spinning cotton thread or *henequen* fiber on a hand spindle, consisting of a shaft and a disk that serves as a flywheel. Women kneel patiently at the backyard waist loom, or *otate,* as they have done for hundreds of years, weaving lengths of cloth for family use. On this most primitive device, consisting of two sticks with the lengthwise warp threads stretched between, the indigenous artisan can create the most extraordinary textiles, often with handspun thread and homemade dyes.

Unfortunately, commercial chemical dyes are replacing the natural dyes extracted from plants and minerals, as well as insects, which

Mexico once produced in such profusion. Collectors must go far afield for cloth dyed with famed red *cochineal* or the even rarer purple *caracól.*

Especially rich and traditional garments are conserved in Oaxaca and Chiapas, but even in Indian communities on the fringes of Mexico City, the women still preserve certain elements of folk dress. The masculine costume has been increasingly modernized over the centuries. Shirts and trousers replaced the native loincloth; the warm wool *serape* took the place of cotton cloaks and animal skin coverings; and the Spanish straw *sombrero* was universally adopted. (Hats did exist in pre-Columbian times, probably more as ceremonial headgear than as a simple head covering, and suggestions of this remain in the fancifully decorated hats of the Huichols and Tzotzils.)

Many Indian men, no matter from what region, wear white loose *manta* (homespun) shirts and trousers, accented by a woven sash around the waist and usually some kind of embroidered design at the neckline or shirtfront. Heavy wool *serapes* with geometric designs in earth colors, keep the wearer warm and rainproof. Men of the Gulf Coast, from Veracruz to Yucatán, keep cool in loose fitting shirts, with many pockets and tiny pleats, called *guayaberas.*

The costume of the Tarahumara men of the north, while not particularly distinguished in any other way, is interesting for its resemblance to pre-Hispanic costume. They do wear shirts, but often go without trousers, using a loincloth with a hip-cloth tied over it. The hip-cloth, which is in effect a bandana tied around the waist, may be tied into a bag or used as a head covering.

Among the Tzotzil tribes of the Chiapas highlands, the men's costumes have preserved much of the ancient finery. They wear an incredibly wide, knee-length garment gathered into a kind of pantaloon, a fine *manta* shirt with embroidery at the collar and cuffs, a bright woven sash, and a palm hat with many colored ribbons flying from the crown.

Mexico's Dandies

The Huichols consider that a fine embroidery on their clothing symbolizes sacred motifs—although in some communities the embroidery has degenerated to copying designs from magazines. Huichol men are Mexico's dandies: they love to dress well, for ceremonial occasions and they keep their women busy embroidering trousers and shirts and weaving belts and bags. This is the one group where the masculine costume surpasses the feminine in brilliance.

Huichol men wear natural white cotton trousers and shirts with bands of red and black cross-stitch embroidery. The designs are traditional geometric forms and figures of birds and animals. Wide, colorful woven sashes circle their waists, as well as small embroidered bags decorated with woolen tassels. Larger bags, also richly embroidered or woven of wool, hang from their shoulders. Their wide-brimmed straw hats are trimmed with crosses and borders of felt and tassels of wool. Ceremonial hats are also adorned with turkey feathers for those who have made a pilgrimage to gather the hallucinogenic peyote. Most of the elements in the costume are thought to have some kind of magical significance: they act as amulets or ways of pleasing the gods.

Like the Hindu woman with her sari, the Mexican Indian woman evolved a costume that would serve her well through childhood, as a bride, during pregnancy, and into old age with very little variation in mode. Her clothing reflects inherent good taste in color and style, and she wears her clothes with pride. Within any given region it is usually possible to distinguish a woman's native village by the small variations in her costume.

The typical feminine costume consists of a *huipil* or *quechquemetl,* a wrapped skirt, a waistband, headdress and some kind of jewelry. Occasionally you see an Indian woman wearing sandals, but in general they preserve their ancient tradition of going barefoot.

The *huipil,* a rectangular dress with openings for the head and arms, is generally used throughout southern Mexico, from Oaxaca down to the Guatemalan border. It may be of wool or cotton, long or short, narrow or full. It may be woven in several colors, simply or heavily embroidered, made of a single length of cloth or of several sewn together with ribbons or decorative strips. It may be worn open at the sides, as it is in Chiapas, but is usually sewn closed.

The *quechquemetl* (from the Nahuatl word *quechtli,* neck, and *quemetl,* that which covers) is a triangular garment which covers the upper part of the body and was used in pre-Hispanic Mexico where modesty required it, blouses being unknown. It is usually made of two rectangular pieces of cloth, the short side of each piece sewn to the long side of the other, with an opening formed for the neck. Sometimes the points fall in front, sometimes at the sides, depending on the region. Generally speaking, the *quechquemetl* is worn (now over a blouse) throughout northern and central Mexico.

A headdress may be as simple as a napkin folded into a pad for carrying loads on the head (in the southern states) or just some satin ribbons braided into the hair and wound about the crown of the head. They can also be very elaborate. In parts of Oaxaca, the women wear great piled and twisted skeins of black yarn, which gives them a decidedly Japanese air. When the Tehuanas, women of the Isthmus of Tehuantepec, get dressed for a fiesta, they put on magnificent lace headgear that looks like a white hooded cape, which covers their shoulders and frames their faces in a burst of tiny lace pleats.

Most Indian women love jewelry, and when they can afford it and custom sanctions it, they wear a great deal. In Oaxaca, strings of colored glass beads are worn in masses; or necklaces of coral and silver with pendant triple crosses, or coin necklaces.

European additions to the Indian woman's wardrobe are the blouse, the pleated skirt, and possibly the *rebozo,* or stole, which may have had its pre-Hispanic counterpart. The *rebozo* is commonly thought to have come into use through the need to keep the head covered in church. It is now an essential part of the feminine costume. The sight of a baby (or any bundle for that matter) bobbing along in a *rebozo* slung from a woman's shoulders is a familiar one almost anywhere. The *rebozo* doubles as baby carrier, hat and coat, and blanket.

Regional interpretations of these basic garments make for an endless parade of distinctive costumes. Seri and Tarahumara women of Mexico's north, with their brightly colored blouses and long, full skirts, look like 19th-century pioneer women of the American West. In the cool pine forests of Michoacán, Tarascan women dress conservatively in a square necked white blouse with colored embroidery on the sleeves and around the neckline, a heavy black wool skirt held in place by a bright sash, and a black wool *rebozo* with narrow blue and white stripes.

The Totonacs of the Gulf Coast have been wealthy vanilla growers since the mid-19th century, and can afford to dress their women well. Their clothes are of fine, white imported cotton cloth. For fiesta wear, they use organdy and tulle, and a splendid diaphanous *quechquemetl* embroidered in white. In the hot Mayan lands of the Yucatan peninsula, the women dress in white *huipils* delicately embroidered with flowers around the square-cut neckline.

In Oaxaca, the variety of costumes is startling. Women of the Amusgo area are noted for their ankle-length, natural white *huipils,* brocaded in wide horizontal bands with certain traditional patterns, especially a stylized, eight-petalled flower. Some Mixtec women in the southwestern part of the state go bare breasted, wearing only a long skirt striped in dark blues and reds and wrapped sarong-fashion. Chinanteca weavers make some of the most colorful costumes in Mexico—*huipils* woven in many-hued alternating stripes and geometric patterns—and then paint parts of the finished goods with a deep purple dye.

Women of Yalalag, a small Zapotec village near Oaxaca City, wear a striking white *huipil* embroidered down the front with floral designs in brightly colored silk and accented at the throat with heavy silk tassels. The imposing Tehuanas dress in dark velvet—purple, blue, or red—embroidered with large, splashy flowers said to have been copied from imported shawls. At fiesta time they exchange their everyday skirts for ones embroidered to match the velvet *huipil* and hemmed with a deep lace ruffle.

All these garments, with their rich color, fine weaving, and painstaking embroidery, are among the most remarkable of Mexico's folk arts.

The Popular Arts

Mexican artisans are heirs to a tradition that goes back to Quetzalcoatl, the legendary source of knowledge in the crafts and sciences. The ancient Mexicans were fine gold and silversmiths, skilled cutters of precious stones, excellent potters, fashioners of feather mosaics, weavers and dyers of cloth, makers of musical instruments. They created works of art with the most primitive tools.

The Spaniards put the Indian's skill to work while expanding his techniques and introducing new materials and new handicrafts: woolen cloth, wrought iron, wheel-thrown pottery, textiles woven on the semiautomatic European loom. This meeting of two craft traditions resulted in an almost inexhaustible variety of arts and crafts. And the creative process is still going on.

In spite of an expanding industrial culture, Mexico's contemporary craftsmen continue to turn out hundreds of delightful handmade items —and invent new ones—often using implements and techniques that were perfected hundreds of years ago. Handicrafts are usually a family enterprise, and even the youngest children are given small workshop tasks. Often the economy of an entire village depends on the production of one or another handicraft. A craft village—like Santa Clara del Cobre (Saint Claire of the Copper)—may even be named for its particular specialty.

For the large majority of Mexicans, earthenware casseroles and handwoven *serapes* are not "folk arts" at all. They are just useful, everyday objects essential for keeping house and keeping warm. The enormous vitality of handicrafts in Mexico today is explained in part by the fact that hundreds of thousands of Mexican families furnish their homes and their wardrobes with objects they or the neighbors make by hand.

In one case, craft products being sold for decorative purposes are actually copies of sacred objects usually jazzed up to attract buyers. These are the "ofrendas" of the Huichol Indians—votive offerings in the form of colorful yarn "paintings" of birds and animals, beaded gourd bowls, and the diamond-shaped "god eyes" made of colored wool.

In spite of the artisan's importance to village economy and the fact that exportation of Mexican handicrafts has become a profitable enterprise, the average craftsman remains a poor man all his life. He generally asks a very modest price for his creations, and rarely recognizes the worth of his own time. He is happy to make a small profit on his materials.

The native craftsman uses whatever materials his native soil provides —and uses them to the full. The Otomis of the arid Mezquital region, whose bare desert lands nourish almost nothing but the spiky *maguey* cactus, have found ways to extract from this plant almost everything they need: building materials, rope, sleeping mats, rough thread for bags and cloth, and of course *pulque.* Ingenuity is the artisan's watchword. He is highly individualistic; he never makes two objects exactly alike and if he tires of a particular design, he may well stop making it altogether.

A thorough study of Mexican folk art has never been attempted, but it would entail a lifetime's work and go on for volumes, and necessitate an extensive tour of every part of the country.

There is sculptured tinwork from San Miguel de Allende: lanterns, frames for mirrors, and candelabra. Something new from Mexico City tin craftsmen are large, decorative soldiers—blowing trumpets, waving flags, riding horseback.

Encrusted lacquerware comes from Olinalá, Guerrero and Uruapan, Michoacán; copper from Santa Clara del Cobre, Michoacán; guitars and wooden masks from Michoacán's Tarascan region; elaborate bamboo birdcages from Oaxaca, blown glass from Guadalajara's suburb of Tlaquepaque.

There is furniture: Jalisco's pigskin-covered barrel-shaped chairs made of crossed rustic wooden slats; the ivory-white wooden pieces carved in Michoacán; the hardwood and palm furniture from the Toluca area.

There are toys: straw carousels, miniature copper saucepans, clay animals that whistle, fanciful piñatas.

Candy can be so attractive that it deserves its place on the list: bite-size doves made of marzipan, heavily sugared fruits, wheel-shaped concoctions of pink sugar and pumpkin seeds.

Pottery, Textiles and Straw

Mexico can be one huge, scintillating bazaar for those who are tempted into collecting folk crafts. But of all the myriad products of the native artisans, three stand out: pottery, textiles, and straw goods.

Pottery—for cooking, table use, and decoration—is a crowded field in Mexico. Inexpensive earthen casseroles, mugs, and dishes can be found in profusion in any public market. This is everyday pottery—from huge vats the size of dishtubs down to doll-sized tea sets, gaily flowered piggy banks, plain terra cotta flower pots.

Good glazed dinnerware is made in three main centers: Tonalá and its neighbor village, Tlaquepaque (both near Guadalajara), Puebla, and Querétaro. Glazing was a technique introduced by the Spaniards, along with molds and the potter's wheel, and the production of such ware is usually a highly commercial enterprise. The designs vary greatly, but they are distinctly Spanish colonial in feeling.

Tonalá and Tlaquepaque potters produce an excellent ware of a distinctive gray-beige color, painted with charming, curlicued brown and blue birds. In addition to dinnerware, they produce a variety of vases, decorative bowls, and lamp bases.

From Puebla come the *talavera* dinnerware and tiles. The dishes are usually a creamy white, decorated in blue, yellow, orange, or green. The Querétaro product is a similar shade of white, but more heavily decorated in combinations of blue, brown, green, and yellow.

Dishes that are less durable but no less charming are made in the villages around Lake Pátzcuaro. Tzintzuntzan potters make coffee-brown and cream-colored plates, pitchers, cups and bowls decorated with naively outlined birds, fish, and animals. From Santa Fe comes an attractive green-glazed brown ware decorated with silhouettes of birds and fish. These rustic dishes reflect the Indian's link to nature and his special sense of humor, a quality that makes them as valuable in their own way as the more sophisticated work of city potters.

Decorative ceramics abound in Mexico, and the most colorful come from Metepec, near Toluca in the State of Mexico. The women and children of the potters' families transform the staid terra cotta into glistening marvels of shocking pink, gold, green, and blue. There are humorous bulls and horses, crèche figures, grinning suns with bushy eyebrows, skeleton orchestras for the Day of the Dead. The Metepec craftsmen's masterpieces are the towering "trees of life"—literally ceramic trees containing in their branches the story of Adam and Eve's fall from Paradise. The wily serpent with his apple, the birds and flowers of Eden, the crestfallen Adam and Eve and the cherubim with flaming swords bring the Biblical tale to life in blazing colors.

In Oaxaca, the "black pottery" town of San Bartolo Coyotepec is rapidly becoming world famous for its smooth, hand-polished, smoky black ceramics. Guitar-playing mermaids, angels that are also candlesticks, and humorous animal figures are frequent subjects.

Textiles were so prized by the ancient Aztecs that they exacted bales of cloth and finished garments as tribute from their subject provinces. Among Montezuma's gifts to Cortés were "thirty loads of beautiful cotton cloth of various patterns." Mexico's hand-loomed fabrics are still nice things to take home from a trip. To start with there are the magnificent regional costumes: *huipils* from Oaxaca, *rebozos* from Tenancingo. There are the fine embroidery and drawn work from Aguascalientes and the colorful, informal cottons of Toluca, Oaxaca, and Patzcuaro.

There are *serapes:* the distinctive ones from the Mixe region of Oaxaca, woven in slender stripes of beige and natural white; the creamy white ones from Teotitlán de Valle, Oaxaca, with a gray deer or stylized rosette in the center; the footprint-splashed ones from San Miguel Chiconcuac near Texcoco.

The making of straw goods is Mexico's third major craft occupation. Wherever there are reeds, *maguey* or *henequen* fiber, or any suitable grasses, these are transformed into rugs, mats, baskets for every use, furniture, suitcases and shopping bags, purses and toys. Straw weaving is very often a part-time job. It can be done on the back of a market-bound burro, and an Indian may measure the distance between two towns in terms of the number of hats he can weave enroute.

Every market has straw goods, but Toluca's Friday *tianguis,* one of the largest and most varied Indian markets in Mexico, overflows with baskets, hats, and mats from the many straw weaving towns in the region. Superior in quality and design are the baskets made of built-up coils with in-woven brightly colored geometric patterns.

Fine palm hats are woven on the coast of Veracruz; from the hot springs resort of Tequisquiapan come good wicker baskets, charming cradles and bassinets. Ingenious Tarascan craftsmen use reeds from Lake Pátzcuaro to fashion humorous toys: musicians, birds and animals, merry-go-rounds, and doll houses complete with reed furniture.

No one paid much attention to Mexican crafts until after the revolution more or less ended in 1919. In 1921, President Alvaro Obregón opened the first-ever crafts exhibition, giving unexpected recognition to native artisans. The great trinity of muralists—Orozco, Rivera, Siqueiros—all praised the talent and workmanship of their humble countrymen. With that kind of backing, middle-class Mexicans started to buy crafts for decoration. American visitors followed suit.

Of course, the most fun is to purchase the craft items in the villages where they are produced. But if time, language barrier, and other inhibitions prevent this, there are many government and private stores where you can make your selection in a sanitized atmosphere.

The village artisan, with his easygoing manner and boundless creativity, is a part of what pessimists think is a vanishing Mexico. The exotic panorama of Mexican folklore is bound to disappear, they say, as roads and schools introduce modern ways into remote villages and the country moves toward a fully industrialized society.

Will gorgeous native costumes disappear as the latest city fashions become available to all? Will folk remedies be forgotten? Will the artisan gear his workshop to mass production?

The answers lie in old musicians who sing the traditional *sones* and young men who compose new ones; in the old potter who on his deathbed is said to have ordered the breaking of his molds, and the young one who goes to the city for a course in glazing methods. Folklore is never static. It is traditional, yet capable of change; as dynamic—and as enduring—as the folk themselves.

FOOD AND DRINK

From Fiery to Subtle

by
MARGARET MEDINA

Margaret Medina lived in Mexico for 16 years. An Iowa State University graduate, and food consultant to several major U.S. corporations, she is a former art critic and for several years wrote all foods material in the Mexican edition of Reader's Digest.

Mexican cuisine is one of the world's most exciting kinds of cookery. It is also one of the most difficult to eat, not just because of its unique blend of fire, fat and fancy, but also because—unless you happen to be a Mexican, living in Mexico and part of a Mexican family with a vast and ancient cooking tradition—it is exceedingly difficult to find. Even in Mexico City, with its eight million inhabitants and two or three thousand restaurants, really superb Mexican cooking is the exception rather than the rule. In provincial cities and towns, where almost everybody goes home for dinner at midday and restaurants exist for tourists and the homeless few, food tends to be simply something to eat and not something that makes you (the superb Mexican accolade) "lick your fingers." Outside of the country, so-called Mexican cooking—the tacos and chili con carne and hot tamales of the American Southwest or an occasional big city restaurant—bear somewhat the same uncomfortable resemblance to real Mexican cooking that a howling monkey bears to man.

This is not because the United States, a country with a growing gourmet focus and a genuine interest in things foreign and exotic, would not relish fine Mexican cooking, but simply because the cuisine depends not only on unique techniques but also on unique ingredients, most of which grow only in Mexico and have never been successfully exported.

The basic technique is grinding, done traditionally on a stone grinding slab called a *metate* or in a stone grinding bowl called a *molcajete.* To a great extent, mechanical mills have replaced the *metate:* shortly after dawn, almost anywhere in the country, you can see lines of women and children carrying buckets of soaked corn ready to be ground into dough. To nearly as great an extent, the electric blender has replaced the *molcajete:* all the intricate sauces of fresh or dried chilis ground with herbs, spices, nuts, vegetables, fruits and sometimes chocolate, can be whirred together in a few moments with this appliance that is more popular in Mexico than in any other country in the world—and with good reason. Thanks to it, and to the neighborhood mill for grinding *masa,* Mexican women have at last gotten off their knees after thousands of years during which the most time-consuming activity of every day was the grinding of food. If you are served somewhat paperlike tortillas, it could be that the cob was ground with the corn to make the *masa*—an unfortunate way to economize.

What gets ground, however, has changed not a bit: corn is still the base and backbone of the Mexican diet. Almost all corn cookery starts by soaking the dried kernels in lime water to soften them, after which they are ground into a dough called masa. Some varieties of corn are simply soaked, peeled and boiled to make a number of different hominy soups all called *pozole.* Masa is the dough from which tortillas are patted or pressed and then baked on a clay or metal griddle, but *masa* can also be diluted with water and boiled to make a thickened beverage called *atole,* or it can be beaten with lard and leavening to make the fluffy dough for tamales (steam cooked with goodies inside), or it can be flavored or enriched with other ingredients and used to make a host of different snacks.

The second most important food in the Mexican diet is chili, which adds vitamins to the diet and flavor to bland tortillas. At least 80 different commonly-eaten chilies run the gamut from pea-sized to pear-sized, and come fresh in shades of green, yellow, orange and red, or dried in tones of red, brown and black. In flavor, chilies vary enormously: they can blister not only your tongue but any part of your lips they touch in passing, or they can be fresh and mild, warm and aromatic, sweet and spicy or smoky and rich. Be careful of the chili habañero, especially popular in the Yucatan.

Nearly as important are tomatoes: Mexico has the reddest, roundest, ripest tomatoes in the world, and exports them in large quantities, but it also has a tiny green wild tomato that grows inside a papery husk like a Japanese lantern, of which it exports very few, and those only in cans.

Other foods which were gifts from Mexico to the Old World include avocados, chocolate, peanuts, squash, beans, vanilla, turkey and many tropical fruits, all of which have enormous importance in Mexican cookery, as do numerous herbs, vegetables and fruits which still grow only in this country.

In return for what Mexico contributed to world cookery, this country's cuisine has absorbed foods and influences from many lands. Such Spanish imports as onion, garlic, sugar, beef, pork, chicken and cheese have become wholly identified with Mexican cooking, and later invaders added further riches not the least of which is bread. The crisp-crusted French roll, as delicious in Mexico as in its native land, is nearly as popular as the tortilla, and so are the endless number of sweet rolls. Here Mexican artistry has worked the same extraordinary variations on bread that Mexican artisans worked on imported Spanish architectural forms. The Germans contributed a deft touch to sausage-making and honey production, but their greatest contribution is a liquid asset: Mexico's beer, from such light ale-types as Bohemia, Superior, Yucatan's Carta Clara or XXX Clara ("Tres Equis Clara") to heady dark bock-types such as XX ("Dos Equis") and Nochebuena, is rightly world-famous. Italy's pasta has become a daily staple in most Mexican homes. And American hamburgers, hotcakes, pies and doughnuts are still making inroads.

Real Mexican Cooking Rare

It is strange but true that you can find almost any of these imported cuisines in Mexico City, and even Guadalajara and Monterrey and other big cities, more easily than you can find really well-prepared Mexican cooking. Traditional Mexican foods are laborious and time-consuming to make, but that isn't the real reason why restaurants feature "international" cooking. After decades of dealing with flocks of tourists, Mexican restaurant and hotel owners have come to the conclusion that most people want to eat what they're used to eating. If a lavish *mole,* lovingly blended and slowly simmered, is going to produce shrieks of dismay, it's better to offer roast beef and be done with it.

A few Mexican specialties have proved to be popular with almost all tourists, so many good restaurants do feature *carne asada,* which is a thin strip of beef fillet quickly broiled and served with fried beans, sauteed strips of hot green pepper, the rich avocado sauce called *guacamole,* and perhaps other garnishes such as an enchilada or two.

Or you can find *tacos de pollo,* which will surprise you if you are used to California "tacos," and will delight you whether or not you've ever heard the word before. Usually, such tacos are tortillas rolled into tubes around a filling of shredded chicken, fried until crisp, and served with guacamole, a spoonful of heavy sour cream, fried beans, and assorted garnishes such as radishes and onions.

In reality, this is only one special version of the taco, for in Mexico, anything rolled up in a tortilla is a taco, and the tacos sold from street stands (rarely to be recommended to any traveler) are neither fried nor garnished. The Hotel Camino Real in Mexico City offers appetizer-sized tacos with assorted fillings, a fine snack to go with drinks before dinner. But two restaurants in the capital make a real specialty of Mexican food at its best, beautifully served in a charming environment. One is the Fonda El Refugio, at Liverpool 166; the other is the Restaurant Jardín del Angel, at Florencia 32. Both are in the Pink Zone and easy to get to from any hotel. Less elegant, less costly and also delightful is the Círculo del Sureste, at Lucerna 12, which serves better Yucatecan food than you're likely to find in Yucatán. And, for men only, a fine place to taste Mexican *antojitos* or snacks at their best is in men's bars, such as El León de Oro at Martí 101, which still features a continuous and abundant free lunch to keep you drinking.

But anyone who really wants to get acquainted with Mexican cooking will venture out into the provinces to discover the astonishing variations which can be played on a basic theme of corn, chili, tomatoes and beans. In this country, the traveling gourmet moves with a caution composed of equal parts of temptation, frustration and dread. Like many other countries, Mexico is full of stories about famous regional specialties, which turn out to be either impossible to find or else perfectly findable, but also tough, leathery, greasy, caustic, cathartic or at the least, perturbing. This perfectly normal picture of average highway cookery in many parts of the world is further complicated by that standard piece of tourist equipment in Mexico, fear of bugs.

Surely nothing in the world smells more enticing than a griddle full of *sopes,* which are little rimmed dishes of corn dough, fried and filled with beans and cheese and chile, and covered with shredded lettuce and fried spicy sausage and more cheese and chili. Fit that, if you can, into the cautious recommendation that you should eat "only cooked vegetables, fruits that can be peeled, no pork, no cheese and no chili" in Mexico.

Because so many tourists travel with this excessive caution, few hotels and tourist-oriented restaurants in the provinces offer much in the way of their region's special dishes. Restaurants catering to the local inhabitants usually do serve the regional specialties, and these are often found at their best in or around the town marketplace. If you are practical, realistic, self-disciplined and have eliminated both the gambler and the reckless hedonist in yourself, you will be able to walk through the marketplace filled with soft-boiled eggs and hard-boiled righteousness. If you are wholly mindless, you will succumb to the first seven tantalizing offerings placed in your path and immediately thereafter to at least five of the interesting variations on the normal functioning of the gastrointestinal system that abound in this land.

There are, on the other hand, hundreds of thousands of foreigners who have traveled through Mexico with open eyes, a lively curiosity and a real desire to taste and know a kind of cookery which has been called one of the ancient world's three original cuisines and the contemporary world's least known, with no misadventures whatsoever.

The rules for this kind of adventure are simple, composed mostly of moderation, respect and good judgment. Avoid any place which is not absolutely clean. When in doubt about the drinking water, choose bottled beverages and drink them without ice, or select something which has been boiled: coffee, tea, and any of the leaf—or flower—teas which might be offered to you. *Café con leche* made with freshly boiled milk is safe, almost always perfectly delicious, and a comforting way to end a long day's journey. Experiment with tropical juices made fresh to your order at many attractive small fruit stands, but avoid absolutely the large jugs of prepared drinks you'll see in many places. In good city restaurants that use purified water and ice, be sure to try these delicious drinks of tamarind, jamaica flower, or lemonade speckled with tiny seeds called *chía.* But don't risk them on the street.

Avoid, and with conviction, foods known to have considerable risk. Unrefrigerated dairy products including fresh cheese, can cause too much trouble to be worth playing about with, and so can lettuce (except in top-quality restaurants), unrefrigerated protein foods, or uncovered or unwrapped foods sold in the open, except for things prepared right before your eyes.

But don't be startled by unusual wrapping. Steaming tamales wrapped in corn husks are just as protected as anything covered with cellophane, and so are the little bundles of *barbacoa* (mutton wrapped in the parchment-like lining of maguey leaves) you may find in the State of Mexico and other parts of the high central plateau. As your travels take you into other regions of the Republic, you might, with a judicious blend of zest and caution, pursue some of these famed specialties:

In the North

Mexican restaurants in the U.S. seem to be operated almost entirely by former inhabitants of the Mexican states of Sonora and Chihuahua, so at least some of the food you will find in these areas may be familiar to you. Tamales tend to be fat and fully-stuffed, tacos look like turnovers, enchiladas are mostly red and filled with fine Cheddar-type Chihuahua cheese and raw onion. Tortillas are frequently made from wheat flour, and *burritos* are made from these tortillas, wrapped around a filling of scrambled egg with beef jerky. Nice things are done with beans in this part of the country—they may have cheese stirred into them, or tomatoes and onions or *chorizo.* Chihuahua fattens fine beef, makes great cheese and grows beautiful apples. Sonora is a clean and beautiful state where good cooks prosper: try *chili con queso,* one of the world's noble soups.

As you move toward the Gulf of Mexico, these same dishes continue to be popular—jerky (called *machacado*), wheat tortillas and red chili sauces. Coahuila is a grape state, which means wine, and is also noted for its pecan candies, rolls of caramel fudge covered with pecan halves, cones of panocha studded with nuts, pralines. Broiled young kid, kid simmered in a sinister-sounding but delicious blood sauce, and broiled ribs of beef are specialties of *Nuevo León,* which also grows Mexico's sweetest oranges. Tamaulipas, on the Gulf, adds the fine freshness of seafood and tropical fruits to the hotly sauced foods of the arid North. Most of the entire Northern desert country has some favorite way of serving tripe in a thick soup. Names vary: you may run into *birria, menudo* or *café de hueso.* These dishes are hearty and delicious. San

Luis Potosí makes one of the best of them, and even better *quesadillas,* which are turnovers made of stuffed corn dough. But this state's real fame comes from its cactus fruit, which is made into a fermented drink, into flat little cakes called *queso de tuna,* and into a lovely sticky preserve called *melcocha.*

Central and Coastal Mexico

Some states are best known for what they produce, such as Sinaloa and Nayarit, with their long Pacific coastline, fine shellfish, and many varieties of bananas. Mazatlán's seafood is superb, particularly the giant oysters that are at once tender and almost crisp, opened before your eyes in restaurants right on the beach.

The regions of greatest cooking fame in Mexico are Guadalajara and Puebla, with traditions that are heavily Colonial and as loaded with history as with ingredients. Puebla is the home of Mexico's national dish, mole, with its 20 or 30 different spices, nuts, chilies, fruits and so forth. It also makes some strange and intriguing wild fruit liqueurs and a whole host of exciting things to eat, including *chalupas* and *sopes,* all laced with carefully blended sauces that carry a heady dash of cloves and cinnamon in a rich chile base. In Guadalajara, you should try Jalisco's *pozole,* which is a good antidote to Jalisco's tequila.

Veracruz does wonderful things with seafood—fish, shellfish and turtle, cooked in tomato sauces laced with sherry, almonds, raisins and capers. Even better are the freshly boiled shrimp, as pink as a baby's thumbnail, sold from baskets in the central plaza. At Boca del Río near Veracruz you can try all the abundance of Gulf seafood.

Across the country on the Pacific coast, Acapulco involves itself in "international" cooking and tends to be disappointing when it comes to fish, with the exception of *ceviche,* an entirely marvelous sort of eat-it-anytime made of raw fish "cooked" by marinating it in lime juice, and seasoned with a symphony of oil, orégano, onion, chile and tomato, plus olives, maybe, and avocado, almost always.

One fresh-water fish in Mexico is exceptional, and has brought gourmets from many parts of the world to sample it: this is the white fish of Lakes Pátzcuaro and Chapala. The raw fish is scaleless and nearly translucent; the cooked fish is unbelievably delicate in texture and flavor.

Move from Pátzcuaro to nearby Morelia and you're in the heart of candy land. Regional sweet specialties vary from old-fashioned chocolate ground on stone and seasoned with cinnamon or almonds to blocks and sheets of fruit pastes made from guavas, apples, strawberries or quinces, to sticky, creamy or chewy candies made of caramelized milk and sugar flavored with wine. Not too far away is Celaya, famed for its thick caramel sold in little boxes as well as in jugs and jars, but named for the boxes: *cajeta.* And a step further on is Irapuato, which exports tons of frozen strawberries but keeps a few for its local specialty, crystallized strawberries.

Southeast Mexico

Oaxaca, Chiapas and Yucatán are jungle country, and the cooking is different and delicious. Tamales are no longer rolled in corn leaves: you'll find square, flat little puddings wrapped in banana leaves, tasting marvelously of artichoke. Oaxaca's *mole* is black, milder than Puebla's, and at its best in the public market. Chiapas has mountains above its jungles and thus such high-country specialties as ham and a unique cheese the shape of a cannonball, good plain, and even better stuffed with a spicy meat filling. Yucatecan cooking is wholly unique, fragrant rather than hot, seasoned with *achiote* and the juice of sour Seville oranges mixed with garlic and black pepper. Look, especially, for *cochinita pibil,* which is suckling pig rubbed with these seasonings and slowly baked in a banana leaf wrapping.

You may be offered venison in Yucatán, Quintana Roo or Campeche, and you will almost surely be offered baby shark, called *cazón.* Never pass up an opportunity to try Moro crab in this area: it is unbelievably sweet and succulent.

Or you can avoid all these strange new foods and travel through Mexico subsisting happily on steak, eggs, fine bread and soups so universally excellent that you will rediscover the reason for eating soup, just as you can stay in the capital city and feast on Swiss fondues, French duck à l'orange, Italian osso bucco, German bratwurst, or American tunafish sandwiches. What you miss will be the unique flavor of a country with a cuisine truly its own, that mellows by a marriage of continents a taste as wild and raw as dripping jungles, parched deserts, and ancient pyramids against the sun.

BULLFIGHTING FOR BEGINNERS

And Other Mexican Sports

by
MARY JOAN ANDERSON

Mary Joan Anderson, a specialist on Mexican bullfighting, is a former sports editor on the Mexico City daily News *staff.*

(The bullfight can arouse other kinds of passion than that described in the following article, which was written from the Mexican point of view. Many persons, particularly in North America and England, abhor bullfighting as a cruel and unfair practice in which, they feel, the animal is made to suffer unnecessarily. While the editors understand those who criticize bullfighting, it is nonetheless an integral part of the Mexican scene. They feel, therefore, they should report on it.)

Anglo-Saxons, on their first introduction to bullfighting, customarily voice an objection to it that indicates their lack of understanding of its basic nature. They consider that it is unfair. It is a contest between a man and a bull, in which the bull always dies. There is something wrong, they feel, in a sport in which the identity of the winner is fixed in advance.

So there would be, if bullfighting were a sport. Bullfighting is a spectacle. In a sense it is a play with a plot. The plot calls for the bull to die. To object to that is as pointless as to object that the plot of *Julius Caesar* calls for Caesar to die. In another sense, it is a ballet. One of its essential features is the performance of stylized traditional movements, and a by-product of their accurate performance is grace. In still another sense, it is an exhibition of physical dexterity, with the risk of injury or death accepted as the penalty for clumsiness, like the art of a trapeze performer. But in its essence, it is a demonstration of the mastery of a human being over two living organisms—over the bull, for the point of the torero's art is to maneuver a thousand pounds of recalcitrant, combative armed muscle according to his will, and over himself, for perhaps the basic meaning of the bullfight is that it is an ordeal of the quality most prized by Mexicans, courage. The bullfighter must master his own fear before he can master the bull.

The brave man is not the one who does not feel fear; he is the man who feels fear and still faces the danger that frightens him. Bullfighters are invariably afraid when they enter the ring. Make no mistake about that. They are afraid, and they are right to be afraid. They know that their chance of dying in the ring is 1 in 10. They know that their chance of being crippled is about 1 in 4. They know, usually, what the horn ripping through the flesh feels like; no bullfighters finish their careers completely unscathed.

The bull may die in the ring. He can avoid that fate by demonstrating either extraordinary cowardice or courage. If the bull refuses to fight, he is exchanged for a substitute animal and butchered in the corrals. In the latter case, the outstanding bull receives the *indulto,* or indulgence, and is spared for breeding purposes. Thus bullfighting bears some resemblance to a sport. But you will understand it better if you cease to regard it as such and look upon it instead as a spectacle—a magnificent spectacle and the most elemental one that still exists in this humanitarian era of regard for human life, since it is the only one in which death can be, on occasion, not an interruption to the spectacle, not an accident incidental to the spectacle, but an element of the spectacle.

The Plot

Bullfighting is highly ritualized. All its details have been developed over a long period into a pattern that now never varies, each one ticketed with its own label in the extensive vocabulary of bullfighting. To begin with, the bullfight is not a fight—it is a *corrida,* a "running" of the bulls. It is divided, like a play, into three acts, the *tercios*—the act of the picadors, the act of the banderillas, and the act of death. There is also a prelude, the parade across the ring, in which all the participants in the coming spectacle take part, even the men who will drag the dead bulls out of the arena.

The act of the picadors has three scenes: the *doblando,* the first luring of the bull with the capes; the matador's first playing of the bull; the arrival of the mounted picadors to challenge the bull with their lances; and the *quites,* which is the work of the matadors in luring the bull away from the picador after the former has reacted in natural fashion to the bite of the lance. The fine points of these maneuvers will be explained below.

The act of the banderillas also has three scenes, in the sense that three pairs of gaily decorated darts are thrust into the bull's shoulders, but each of these scenes is basically the same when performed as usual by the matador's assistants, the banderilleros.

The act of death, the *faena,* has two scenes: first, the playing of the bull with the small red flannel *muleta,* which replaces the billowing capes at this stage of the fight, and the killing with the sword, "the moment of truth."

All of this you will see in every bullfight, good, bad, or indifferent. How is a novice to know whether the manner in which it is performed is skillful or inept?

You may be surprised, at your first bullfight, to hear the crowd roar its approval for a maneuver that, to you, looks no different from those that preceded it, and were allowed to pass in silence. You may be baffled when seat cushions start flying into the ring, hurled by an angry crowd whose method of showing its ire is to attempt to strike the matador. The details that arouse the admiration or the contempt of the crowd (and the crowd, at a Mexican bullfight, provides a spectacle second only to what is going on in the ring) cannot be expected to be obvious to a newcomer. You will undoubtedly know whether the performance you are watching is, in general, skillful or clumsy, for deft movements are graceful and awkward ones are not, and it takes no expert to appreciate the difference between the single clean sword thrust that sends the bull down as though he had been struck by lightning and the blundering butchery marked by thrust after thrust, with the sword spinning into the air as it strikes the shoulder blade of the bull instead of piercing through the opening that leads to the heart. But in order to know why a performance is good or bad, you will need some coaching in what to look for.

What to Look For

The three elements by which the critics judge bullfights (and the bullfight critic, in Mexico, is a powerful individual, whose verdicts can make or break a matador's career) are *parar, mandar,* and *templar. Parar* is style, and consists in standing straight, firmly planted, unyielding, bringing the bull past in his thundering rush with a gracefulness that gives no ground. *Mandar* is mastery of the bull, controlling his every move and spinning him about like a puppet. *Templar* is timing, and the acme of skill in this respect is to perform the maneuvers of the fight in slow, rhythmic motion. The more slowly the bull is moving as he passes the matador, the longer the time of dangerous propinquity lasts, and the more opportunity is granted to the animal to change tactics and go for the man instead of the lure.

Watch the matador's feet. He should not move them as the bull thunders past. If he really has control of the animal, he will make it avoid him; he will not have to move to avoid it. Watch how closely he works to the bull. Distance is relative to the class of pass a matador is giving; also the style and armory of the bull is considered. In general, however, his mastery of the beast must be more exact if he lets the horns graze his chest than if he pulls it by several feet away. Closeness can be faked. If the torero holds his arms with the cape far out from his body, if he leans well forward so that, without moving his feet, he can still bring the upper part of his body back when the bull reaches him, then he is not performing with the same bravery as if he were standing ramrod-straight and maneuvering the bull without budging.

The question of when and to what degree danger truly exists is a complex one. It begins with proximity to a fighting bull and increases according to the amount of awareness and attention he directs toward whatever he considers the enemy. People have been killed simply standing in the outer ring by a bull that has leapt over the barrier. However, fantastic stunts can be pulled off in the center of the ring, as long as the bull is not actually involved, with little risk. The basic classic lances and passes involve considerable danger, kept in check by the matador's dominance of the animal.

Spectacular actions are almost always reserved as adornments, performed once complete control over the bull has been achieved, for success is based upon the assumption that the bull will charge perfectly straight without halting or hooking. The elements of these passes are reduced mobility on the part of the bullfighter, as in kneeling passes; loss of sight of the bull at a critical moment, as in back passes or when a matador will deliberately gaze away into the stands as the beast passes; and sudden movement of the target, as in change passes in which the bull, charging toward one side of the torero, is drawn across his body to pass on the other side. Only the most confident or daring matador will perform a pass that contains more than one of these elements, though such passes do exist.

Psychology of the Bull

On the other hand, standing with one's back against the fence, which looks dangerous, often isn't. It depends on the bull. Most bulls have no desire to bang their heads against a hard wooden wall. It is often more dangerous to be close to the fence, to allow the bull to pass between it and the bullfighter; bulls have a tendency to swerve outward from the fence. If you notice that the bull returns habitually to a certain spot in the arena after various charges, it is more dangerous to fight him in that part of the ring than elsewhere; he has instinctively elected it as his home ground, and is on the defensive there. When he is returning to his base, he is intent upon getting back "home." He is paying no attention to the obstacles along the edge of the path he is following. Bullfighters know that and sometimes take advantage of the bull's rush past to draw applause from spectators who haven't grasped the situation.

Paradoxically, the bull who looks most dangerous to you is the one who looks least dangerous to the torero—the one who comes charging into the ring full of fight and makes a vicious dash for the first moving object he sees. The bull that is confidently out to kill is the type of bull the torero can handle. He has a quixotically one-track mind, and like that tragic knight, is predictable. You can tell what he will do. Therefore you can control him. Bullfighters like a fighting animal, one that is going to charge hard and straight. It is the inferior animal that makes the torero "sweat the big drops." Due to the shortage of fighting stock, however, it is more probable that the majority of bulls entering the ring today will have some defect—physical, such as weakness or poor vision; or hereditary, that would affect bravery, alertness, or mobility. If sufficiently pronounced, any of these characteristics can eliminate possibilities of an artistic performance. But the responsible and accomplished matador can still give a lucid technical demonstration of much merit; for indeed, he is handling a much more dangerous sort of bull here.

You now know some of the things to look for. In order not to miss them, you should know when to be alert.

When the bull first charges into the arena, one of the bullfighters will wave his cape at him and very probably, at the bull's rush, will dart behind one of the bulwarks that guard the openings into the corridor behind the barrier. Don't mark him down as a coward for that. It is all part of the ritual. The bull is not yet actually being played. He is being studied. Perhaps the first cape will be waved by the man closest to him, to find out if his near vision is good. Then a man on the other side of the ring will try, testing his vision at a distance. The matador is watching how he charges, and whether he has a tendency to hook to the left or right. Upon his correct interpretation of the bull's reaction to these preliminary flaggings will depend his success in the rest of the fight.

After these opening maneuvers, the matador usually comes out to demonstrate his skill with the cape. This is your first real chance to witness the art of the bullfighter. If, in reading bullfight stories, you have come across the term *veronica,* and wondered what it meant, it is probably what you are watching now. The veronica is the purest and most basic of the various lances performed with the cape, and it is almost always the one with which the matador begins. The torero holds the cape before him, more or less gathered into folds, his profile toward the bull, and as the animal charges, he spreads the cloth before the animal's snout, swings it by his body, and the bull follows it past. Ordinarily, as the bewildered bull turns, he swings him by again, then perhaps a third, fourth, or fifth time, each time a little closer as he becomes acquainted with the animal's reactions, and acquires *mandar,* and perhaps finishes by gathering the cape in against his body in a half veronica as the bull passes. This usually stops the bull short, and the matador can turn his back disdainfully on the horns and walk away, a display of mastery over the bull that always brings a roar of "*Olé!*"

The Picador

With the end of this scene, the picadors, the mounted bullfighters with lances, appear. The object of this part of the fight is to test and tire the animal's ferocity. Until that tremendous hump of flesh on the top of the bull's neck, the tossing muscle, has been tired, so that the bull will drop his head, he cannot be killed with the sword. The way to the animal's heart is opened only when the front feet are together and the head is down.

Astride mattressed nags, the picadors challenge the bull, then drive the small, sharp metal point of their lances into the tossing muscle as he charges. The junior picador delivers the first punishment, then the animal is led to the older, more experienced man, who normally "stops" him; but if more lancing is required, the bull is returned to the first horseman. The bull breeder beams with pride if the representative of his ranch has had the strength and bravery to literally push the picadors around, even overthrow horse and rider. The matador is also pleased, for in so doing, the bull has spent about a third of his force.

The picador, though it is part of his job, isn't happy about the spill. When his horse is tossed, he goes down, sometimes beneath his mount. The picador, unlike the horse, has no mattress. He does have a heavy piece of armor on the leg that is going to be on the side from which the bull will charge. This, in addition to the rest of his costume, weighs as much as 77 pounds, and he can't easily get up unaided. He depends on his colleagues to draw the bull away.

Forty-odd years ago, of course, the picador was even more vulnerable, because his horse had no protection at all against the bull. Everything depended on the picador's skill at holding off the bull with his lance. So many horses were gored, however, that the *peto* or mattress was prescribed. This last grew longer and longer until finally it began to scrape the ground. Picadors grew careless and sometimes jabbed away at a bull until he was half-dead from lance wounds alone. The regulations later cut down the size of the *peto,* thus making the horse somewhat vulnerable and restoring greater skill to the picador's task. Presently, the *peto* weighs a maximum of 95 pounds, as taurine laws have grown lax. Horses are still injured internally, though, and even occasionally gored, and the next phase of this debate remains to be seen. But back to our bullfight.

Watch closely now, for here it is probable that you will have an opportunity to see some dexterous capework. The scene of the *quites*—drawing the bull away from the picadors—is principally the performing matador's show, though he may allow his alternates to enter into a competition with him here. The usual bullfight program calls for the killing of six bulls by three matadors. Although each matador has two bulls definitely assigned to him for the kill, if one bull has a good style, at least one of the other matadors will request permission to take a *quite.* Should a duel of artistry develop, you may see exeptional brilliance displayed at this time.

Now you are likely to see some of the most elegant lances (passes with the cape), though the chances are that at your first fight they will all look much alike. Although there are many lovely *quites,* the two most commonly used today are the *chicuelina* (the modern version) and the *gaonera,* named for their respective inventors, Manual Jiménez "Chicuelo" and Rodolfo Gaona. In the *chicuelina,* the matador gathers in the cloth just as the bull is passing, turning against the animal's charge, wrapping it around his body. The *gaonera* technically works like a veronica, but the cape is held behind the torero's back and offered from one side. These *quites* are usually done in groups. They may begin with a showy swinging of the cape into the desired position, and always end with a *remate*—a lance that will cut off the bull's return charge. The flowing *revolera* is highly favored for this purpose. It is executed by rapidly swinging the cape around the matador's waist in first one hand, then the other, so that it stands up like the skirt of a pirouetting dancer. You would be indeed fortunate to see other more complicated, artistic, or perilous *quites.* But most matadors prefer economy in this scene today to save themselves and the bull for the more serious business of the last act.

The planting of the banderillas—the pairs of decorated, barbed sticks that are thrust into the bull's shoulders—comes next. Ordinarily the responsibility of the banderilleros, it is one of the least dangerous parts of the fight. Watch closely, however, if you see the matador himself preparing to perform this maneuver. That means he is particularly expert with the darts, and you may see anything from blatant showmanship to breathtaking artistry.

The Climax

The last stage of the fight is the *faena*—the final playing of the bull leading up to the kill. This is when the matador, at least if he feels he has a good bull, a responsive animal, bold and aggressive, will put on his best show. First, the matador, hat in one hand, sword and *muleta* in the other, will ask formal permission of the plaza authority to kill the bull. Next comes the dedication—to a friend, a celebrity, or the entire plaza, holding his hat aloft and turning slowly around to salute the whole audience. No matter to whom the torero dedicates the death of the bull, the recipient is expected to respond in some way. The bullfighter's hat, the *montera,* is constructed with a special little pocket in the lining where a 50-dollar bill fits nicely. On the other hand, if a lovely lady catches the *montera,* there is considerable neck-craning to see who she is. Finally, if the matador toasts the bull to the crowd, he must be prepared to give an outstanding performance, for the public will pay him with cushions (rotten fruit and broken bottles in the provinces) if he fails to fulfill his promise adequately.

This is the most serious part of the fight. For the large cape the *muleta* is now substituted, a small piece of red cloth doubled over a stick that offers a much less conspicuous target for the bull's attention than the magenta lure. It is now that the matador's skill will be exerted to its utmost and now that you will want to follow most closely his every movement until at last the great black hulk of the bull goes crashing down onto the sand.

You may think that the quality of the bullfighting has suddenly decreased at the beginning of the *faena,* for the opening passes may be more harsh than graceful. That is because their object is to attain complete mastery over the bull. He is being fixed in the smaller lure, and this is done with technical "punishment" passes rather than by grace. Once the bull has been shown again who is master, however, you may see some of the most daring and elegant passes of the whole *corrida.* Passes in which the matador stands erect holding the *muleta* with both hands, as though flagging the animal by, are called "statues" —*estatuarios.* These, and the more common variety of high passes, serve a dual purpose. While artistic, they also tire the bull's neck muscles, causing him to follow the lure even more smoothly.

Now you will see the *faena*'s counterpart of the opening act's veronica, the most basic passes of this part of the fight. The *derechazo* consists in presenting the *muleta,* held out in the right hand and extended by the sword, and swinging it before the bull's muzzle as he charges. This is more dangerous when done on the left side, and called *un natural*—a natural pass—for it is done with the cloth in its natural position, unaided by the sword. In constructing a *faena,* the matador tries to link these classic passes into series, ended traditionally with the chest pass. It is at this stage that you may see the adornment passes—the *manolitina,* for one, or the *molinete,* which is the *faena*'s answer to the *chicuelina.* More impressive are passes done from the knees and change passes such as the *arrucina* and *chicharrina,* which are done behind the body. These two last passes are rarely used now that their inventors are respectively deceased and retired, and very few other toreros care to take the excessive risks they involve. Also fairly risky and presently popular is the *pendulo,* in which the *muleta* is swung from a front side position to the matador's back. It is occasionally used to initiate the *faena* of an accomplished matador with great success. The bull charges from a long distance and therefore the shifting of the lure has less effect on him. This, and other spectacular passes, are open invitations for gorings when attempted by inexperienced boys, however, and it is a sad state of affairs that they are most popular with the young toreros, eager to make an impression on the public.

At the end of this demonstration, the time comes for the kill. First, it is necessary to square *(cuadrar)* the bull, that is, to maneuver him into a head-on position with the two front feet together. If the matador has handled the bull properly during the entire fight, this is a simple matter, employing some of the same technical passes with which he began the *faena* to double the bull.

The Kill

The kill is called "the moment of truth" because there is absolutely no way of cheating here and getting away with it unnoted. An unscrupulous matador may have played to the gallery all afternoon, but when he takes the blade in hand, he exposes himself to something worse than the fury of the crowd—the waiting horns of a bull that has not been dominated. Assuming that the bull has been properly fought and lined up, the matador profiles, aiming down the curved-tipped steel, and drives it in over the horns with his right hand, while his left, with the *muleta,* sweeps under the bull's eyes and pulls his head down. It is a moment as dangerous for the man as for the bull; if the swing of the *muleta* fails to hold that head down, instead of sword into bull it can be horn into man. But if the matador has made no mistakes, the bull crumples to the ground after a few moments' courageous last stand.

Just as there are various approaches in placing banderillas, there are several styles of killing, but the method described above *(volapie)* is the most practical and frequently used. A special sword with a crossbar about four inches from the point is used by the matador to dispatch the dying bull if the regular sword thrust has not taken immediate effect. A final *coup de grâce* is given by the matador's dagger-man. The matador has had twelve minutes in which to prepare the bull for the kill, from the beginning of his *faena.* If the animal is not dead in the allotted time, a bugle sounds from the judge's box as a warning—an *aviso.* In another five minutes a second *aviso* sounds, and if the matador has not been able to kill his bull after another three minutes the third and final *aviso* sounds, and the bull is led out of the arena alive and slaughtered in the corrals. The matador is in total disgrace.

In an expert kill, the matador profiles several feet away from the bull and enters with moderate speed, passing his stomach inches over the horns, to leave a full sword thrust passing through the bull's shoulder blades to sever the artery to the heart. This is a prompt kill, but the bull falls even more rapidly when the lung is penetrated, which is usually the case.

What the judge of the fight thinks of the bullfighter's performance will be indicated now. In plazas outside of the capital, his judgment is often influenced by the reaction of the crowd. If the matador did well, he is awarded an ear; exceptionally well, both ears; and for a really superlative performance, the ears and tail. This is ordinarily as far as recognition goes, but there have been historic occasions on which hooves have been given. This award system evolved from the disused symbolic custom of rewarding a matador's expert performance with the gift of the dead animal as additional payment. The lifeless bull may be dragged around the ring and cheered in tribute to his courage. This in no way reflects upon the performance of the matador—indeed, quite the contrary.

A Few Odd Items of Information

When you buy a ticket for a bullfight, you will be asked if you prefer *sol* or *sombra*—the sunny side of the ring or the shady side. The sunny side is cheaper traditionally, a Spanish custom with less significance in Mexico, where the sun is not as unbearable. The main advantage of a shady-side seat here is in the closer proximity to the matadors' base of action. The more aristocratic fans choose this location, while the colorful crowd prefers the sunny side. Ringside seats are *barreras.* A sign over the box office reading "*agotado*" means that the seats are sold out. However, much to the chagrin of the management, that is rarely the case. Even so, should this occur, it does not mean you cannot get in, only that you can't get your ticket at the box office, but will have to deal with ticket speculators.

If you want to go to the bullring in any Mexican city, ask for the Plaza de Toros. The fence around the arena is the *barrera,* the corridor behind it, before the seats begin, the *callejon,* the shields that guard the openings in the *barrera* are the *burladeros.* A bullfighter is a *torero* (never, except in *Carmen,* a toreador) and only the star, who kills the bull, is a *matador.* The matador's attendant group, which works together as a unit, is the *cuadrilla. Novilladas* are fights with young bulls—*novillos*—and aspirant matadors—*novilleros.*

Summer is the little season. Appearing in the plazas will be novices, albeit the most experienced novices in the country. They will be boys, perhaps still in their teens, who have been fighting bulls for perhaps two or three years. To them, a chance to appear in Mexico City is the opportunity of a lifetime. What they lack in artistry they will make up in bravery.

The best of the novices eventually become full-fledged matadors (the word means "killer"). As matadors, they appear in Mexico City only during the big season in the winter. During the summer many of them do their bloody work in Spain.

You will want to identify the matadors at the beginning, to follow the fight. They will be the men walking in front of the opening procession into the arena, just behind the mounted bailiff. The matador with most seniority will be on the right, and will kill the first and fourth bulls, the junior in the center, who will kill the third and sixth bulls. The matadors are also listed in this order of seniority on the programs.

The formal bullfight season in Mexico City runs from the end of November through April. The capital is naturally the place where the most famous fighters are to be seen most often, and the best fights are staged here for the holiday season. Artistically, the second most important place and time is Guadalajara during the season that runs concurrent to Mexico City's. Border fights in Tijuana and Juárez, from May through October, often present attractive programs, though geared to the tourism that supports them.

Aficionados will argue the relative merits of Spanish versus Mexican bulls. About the only point of agreement is that the bulls of Spain might be slightly bigger but not enough to make a real difference. Spanish bullfighters do well in Mexico and vice versa. The fighting spirit and courage of the bulls have caused as many post-mortems as the World Series or the Super Bowl.

It is well known that bullfighting in Mexico arrived with the conquistadores. The first *corrida* was held in 1526 to celebrate Cortés' return from Honduras. Throughout colonial times, bullfights were an integral element of civil and religious celebrations. But Anglo-Saxon sensibilities are not the only ones opposed to bullfighting—some Mexicans don't like it either. President Juárez prohibited bullfighting but dictator Díaz lifted the ban for political and personal reasons. Carranza forbade the *corrida,* but then he was assassinated (not by an afficionado).

The first of the larger-than-life *toreros* was the superstar Bernardo Gaviño. On his way to Chihuahua for a bullfight in the 19th century, he and his party were ambushed by the Comanches. The fighting lasted all day, with only Gaviño and two other survivors out of a party of 64. Yet a couple of days afterwards, Gaviño gave such a rousing performance that at least one priest died of a heart attack from the excitement. Gaviño kept at the bulls until he was 75 years old when he was gored for the umpteenth time and died from the infection. Rodolfo Goana was perhaps the greatest of the Mexican bullfighters. His perfect technique of planting the *bandilleras* is still remembered in Pamplona, Spain as well as Mexico.

OTHER MEXICAN SPORTS

Jai Alai

In the small towns of Mexico, you may come upon an open court with a couple of walls, smooth and not too high. If it happened to be Sunday, you would catch on right away. It is a special Mexican handball court, and the friends and neighbors participating are following an age-old custom of Mexican men.

Sometimes called fronton, pelota vasca, or even Basque ball, the game they are playing is best known as jai alai. It is fast and fascinating. You can play singles or doubles. In metropolitan areas the game has become more sophisticated. It is played by professionals in a block-long 3-walled court with all the modern conveniences, including the bookies who call and take bets with astonishing rapidity.

Instead of bare hands, the professionals use a spoon-shaped wicker basket called a cesta. The ball, which travels like a bullet, is about the size of a golf ball. It is trapped in a sliding catch in the cesta and then shot out at dazzling speed.

To watch the professionals, take a knowledgeable friend along to Mexico City's Fronton Mexico near the Revolution Monument (Plaza de la Republica and Ramos Arizpe Street) any Tuesday, Wednesday, Thursday, Saturday, or Sunday about 7:30 P.M. Get an inexpensive ticket at the *entrada general* window, walk through the lobby, pick up a beer at the bar and go upstairs. This upper area is the one corresponding to your ticket; below, the price is double and not really worth it unless you want to do some betting.

If you want to watch the fair sex play this fast game, go to the Fronton Metropolitano at Bahia de Todos los Santos 190 in Mexico City. The star performance begins about 4 P.M., and three others, as a rule doubles, follow in quick succession. Admission prices are inexpensive and betting is heavy.

Soccer

Fans may jam the bullrings at times, but the biggest consistent spectator sport in Mexico is *futbol*—English-style football, called soccer in the United States. The new Azteca Stadium in Mexico City has room for 100,000 fans and is in itself a showpiece worth seeing.

Mexican teams, organized into leagues, are good, and topnotch European and South American teams often participate in international tournaments. Games are played during the fall and summer on Sunday afternoon and Thursday evening. The Azteca Stadium is easily accessible on Calzada Tlalpan, just about straight south from the Zocalo. The 1986 World Cup will be held in Mexico with matches in the capital and some of the bigger cities.

Typically Mexican

Other sports that are Mexican favorites are the *charreada* or *jaripeo,* a rodeo featuring gentlemen riders in a small town or a large one. They usually go with fiestas. Or, you can see a fancy one at the Rancho del Charro most Sundays in Mexico City. Here Charro riders put on quite a show, not the least part of which is the horses they ride and the gold- and silver-studded clothes they wear. In Guadalajara, *charreadas* are held on Sundays, starting around 11 A.M. at the Lienzo Charro, next to the Agua Azul Park. The best charreadas are held during the city's October Festival.

While it is illegal in the United States, Canada, and many other countries, *cockfighting* is a popular Mexican sport. A cockfight takes place in an enclosed pit, usually outdoors. Spectators place bets on their favorite gamecocks. At the start of the fight, handlers hold their birds and allow them to peck at each other just out of range. When the birds become angry, they are released and allowed to fight.

The best place to see cockfighting is at Guadalajara in the Nueve Palenque Tapatío, at Revolucion 2120, just outside of town on the way to Tlaquepaque. The Palenque has a restaurant and mariachi music and plenty of color with grizzled ranchers and dashing cowboy types in the audience. Fights are every night at 8:30 with cabaret-type entertainment of Friday and Saturday.

MEXICO CITY AND ENVIRONS

The City That IS Mexico

by
JIM BUDD

Jim Budd, Mexico City bureau chief for Murdoch Magazines (Travel Weekly, Meetings & Conventions, *and* Incentive World), *has lived in the Mexican capital since 1958. A former editor of the* Mexico City News *and the Spanish-language business magazine* Expansión, *he has concentrated on travel writing for the past fifteen years.*

Founded by the Aztecs in 1325, Mexico City is the oldest capital in the New World. Of late is also has become the center of the largest metropolitan area on earth. According to some estimates as many as 18 million people live crowded into the Valley of Mexico at a breathtaking altitude of more than 7,000 feet.

To the people of the country, Mexico City is Mexico. That is what they call it, simply "México." The rest of the nation is "La Republica," The Republic.

Yet, technically speaking, Mexico City does not exist. It is the Federal District or *Distrito Federal,* governed directly by the President of the Republic through a mayor he appoints. Next door, to add to the confusion, is the State of Mexico with all its many suburbs.

To the south lies Cuernavaca, that "sunny spot for shady people" which at 5,000 feet is a tropical weekend haven for the capital's wealthy. Beyond is Taxco, a silvermining town of cobbled lanes and whitewashed houses roofed with tile. Taxco is picturebook Mexico. East is Puebla, regal and Iberian. North are the Pyramids at San Juan de Teotihuacan. North, too, are the ruins at Tula, fabled capital of the Toltecs.

Most of what is now Mexico has been ruled from the central valleys for time immemorial.

Teotihuacan was a contemporary of Imperial Rome, but an even grander city. Too big and too grand perhaps. Some 1,500 years ago it was the heart of an empire that extended nearly from Texas to Guatemala. No one can really say what led to its fall.

Best guess is that Teotihuacan was overrun by barbaric hordes from the north. These may have been the Toltecs, warriors who forged a great empire of their own a millenium ago. The Toltecs, too, are a vanished people. Many migrated to Yucatan where they conquered the Maya city states only to be absorbed by the people they had vanquished. Once again, it appears, barbaric hordes from the north drove them out.

The Aztecs, who called themselves Mexicas and claimed to have come from a place called Aztlán, were part of this horde. Miserable nomads who settled on what was then an island in a lake, the Aztecs arrived in the 14th century and within a hundred years or so had defeated their neighbors and established a realm that spanned the continent.

It was to overthrow the Aztec regime that thousands of Indians allied themselves in 1520 with Hernan Cortés and his little band of adventurers. On the rubble on Montezuma's halls arose a new Mexico City, capital of New Spain, famed as the city of palaces and in the 1700s the grandest metropolis in the New World.

Three centuries of foreign rule came to an end with the uprisings in 1810. What had been New Spain became a free nation, taking the name of its Aztec-founded capital city. Yet independence brought with it decades of turmoil. A brief attempt to place the government in the hands of a European prince failed and cost Austria's Maximilian his life. Thirty years of dictatorship followed, ending with the Revolution of 1910 that ousted Porfirio Díaz. Modern Mexico was born in that revolution.

Mexico City today is a capsule of eons of history. Glorified is the ancient past, magnificent murals lauding the achievements of long ago, statues of Aztec rulers standing on the boulevards. Nor is Spain forgotten. The downtown area, formally decreed the Historic Center, is one great outdoor museum of palaces and churches from the Iberian era.

But most of all Mexico City is modern. A vibrant capital that rarely slumbers, it is a metropolis of fine shops, wonderful restaurants, magnificent museums and tree-shaded avenues. One of the most exciting metropolises in the world, it is a promise of an afternoon at the races,

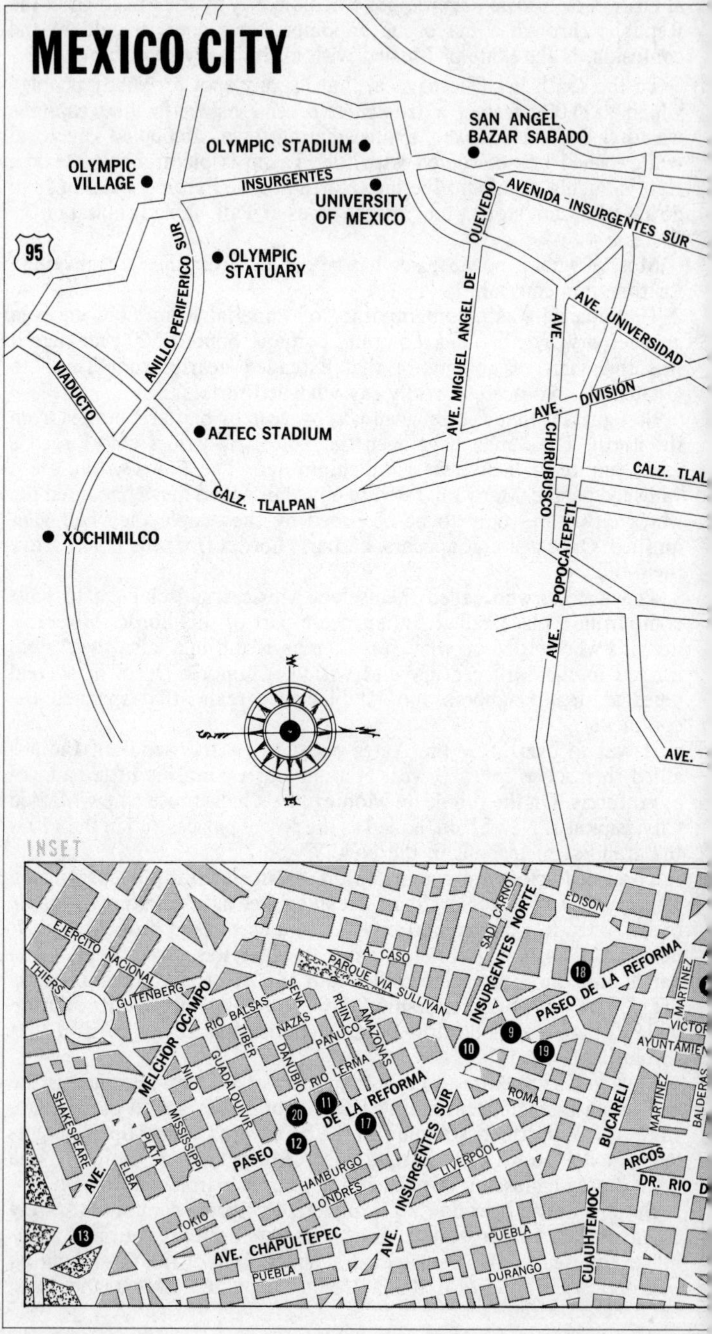
MEXICO CITY
SAN ANGEL
BAZAR SABADO
OLYMPIC STADIUM
OLYMPIC
VILLAGE
INSURGENTES
UNIVERSITY
OF MEXICO
AVENIDA INSURGENTES SUR
QUEVEDO
95
ANILLO PERIFERICO SUR
OLYMPIC
STATUARY
AVE. MIGUEL ANGEL DE
AVE. UNIVERSIDAD
AVE.
VIADUCTO
AVE. DIVISION
AZTEC STADIUM
CHURUBUSCO
CALZ. TLAL
CALZ. TLALPAN
XOCHIMILCO
POPOCATEPETL
AVE.
AVE.
INSET
EJERCITO NACIONAL
THIERS
GUTENBERG
MELCHOR OCAMPO
RIO BALSAS
SENA
A. CASO
PARQUE VIA SULLIVAN
SADI CARNOT
INSURGENTES NORTE
EDISON
18
PASEO DE LA REFORMA
MARTINEZ
VICTOR
AYUNTAMIEN
TIBER
NAZAS
RHIN
PANUCO
AMAZONAS
10
9
19
NILO
GUADALQUIVIR
DANUBIO
RIO LERMA
DE LA REFORMA
ROMA
BUCARELI
MARTINEZ
BALDERAS
SHAKESPEARE
MISSISSIPPI
20
11
17
12
INSURGENTES SUR
PLATA
PASEO
AVE.
ELBA
HAMBURGO
LIVERPOOL
ARCOS
DR. RIO D
LONDRES
CUAUHTEMOC
13
TOKIO
AVE. CHAPULTEPEC
AVE.
PUEBLA
PUEBLA
DURANGO

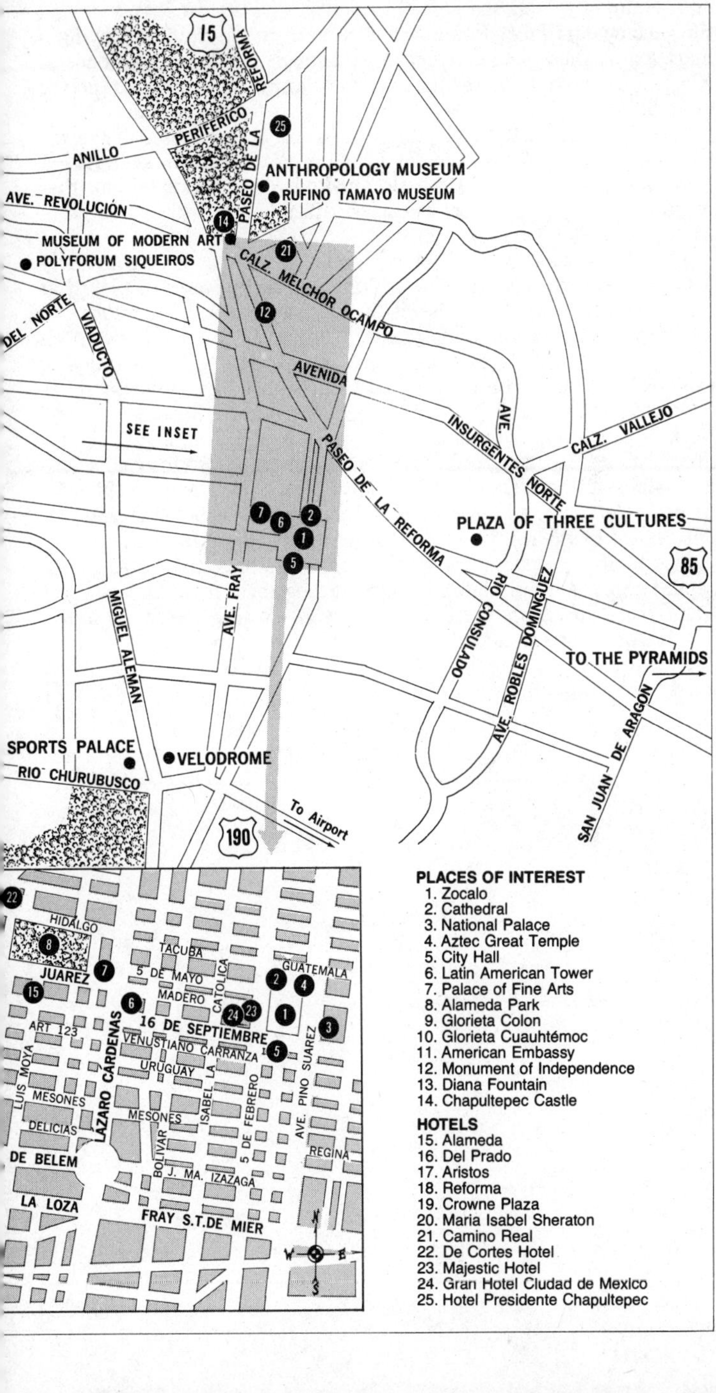

PLACES OF INTEREST
1. Zocalo
2. Cathedral
3. National Palace
4. Aztec Great Temple
5. City Hall
6. Latin American Tower
7. Palace of Fine Arts
8. Alameda Park
9. Glorieta Colon
10. Glorieta Cuauhtémoc
11. American Embassy
12. Monument of Independence
13. Diana Fountain
14. Chapultepec Castle

HOTELS

15. Alameda
16. Del Prado
17. Aristos
18. Reforma
19. Crowne Plaza
20. Maria Isabel Sheraton
21. Camino Real
22. De Cortes Hotel
23. Majestic Hotel
24. Gran Hotel Ciudad de Mexico
25. Hotel Presidente Chapultepec

an evening at the jai alai games, a night at the discos. It is watching the spectacular Ballet Folklorico at nine in the morning, enjoying a mariachi serenade while being poled through the floating gardens at Xochimilco, and then thrilling to the daring of a matador at the bullfights.

Shopping often is the high point of a vacation; it always is in Mexico City, where one can start the day haggling at a native market and end it negotiating a discount at an elegant Pink Zone boutique. Not that haggling or negotiating are necessary; these days any price quoted in Mexico City is a bargain.

The art is breathtaking. The vivid colors of the murals at University City are never to be forgotten. Striking are the canvases displayed at outdoor exhibits on Saturdays and Sundays, as well as those at the posh galleries on Reforma and Juarez.

Then, for a change of pace, there are the day trips that may be extended to overnight excursions to Taxco, Puebla, or the many other nearby points. Especially nice are brief holidays at the hacienda resorts. Back in the days before agrarian reform, haciendas were vast plantations, estates the size of dukedoms, where owners lived in regal splendor. Many of those stately homes have been converted into splendid hotels in the country, complete with tennis courts, bridle trails, and golf links, most of them little more than an hour's drive from the city.

Eventually, of course, the bright lights lure back the restless. The capital really is a destination in itself. Smog there is, to be sure, and traffic jams. Residents grumble about overcrowding and much more, but visitors scarcely notice. They are too busy having a good time. Ancient and grand, modern and dynamic, Mexico City is one of the most fascinating cities on earth.

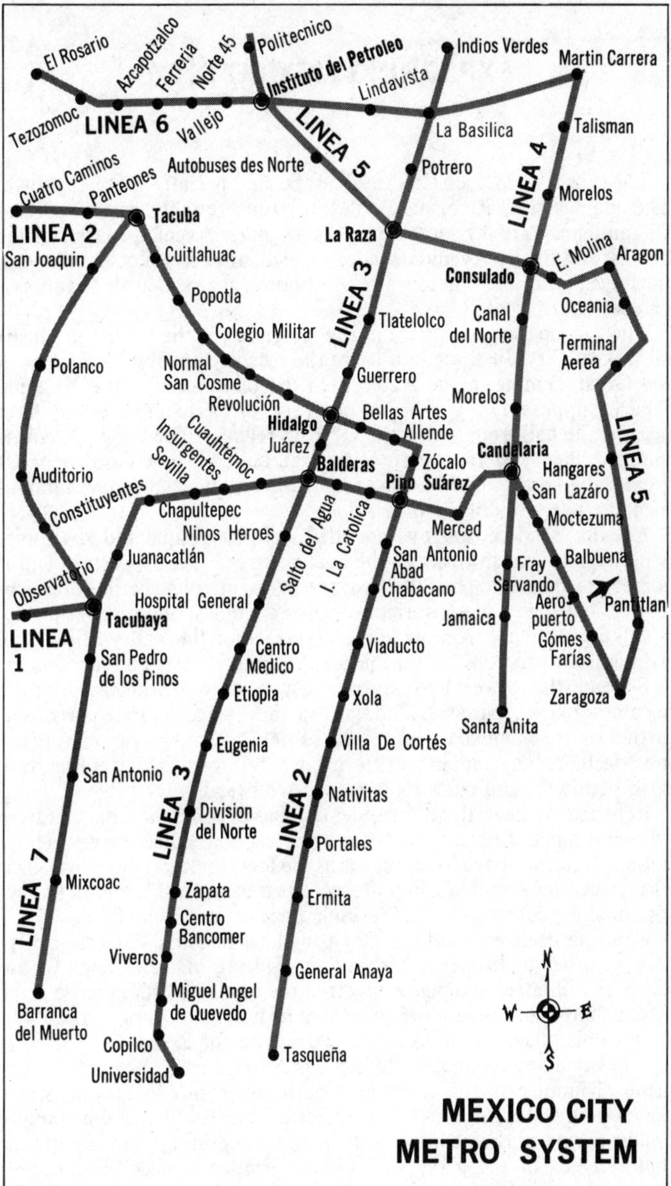

MEXICO CITY METRO SYSTEM

EXPLORING MEXICO CITY

Large as it is, Mexico City need not be an especially confusing town. The main street, Reforma Boulevard, runs roughly eastward from Chapultepec Park for some 30 blocks, becomes Avenida Juarez for ten blocks, and finally Avenida Madero which, after five blocks spills into the huge plaza called the Zocalo. Most hotels are located along this axis or near it.

The Zocalo, largest square in the Americas, is the traditional heart of Mexico City. Just north of it are the recently uncovered remains of the Great Temple of the Aztecs. On the plaza itself is the National Palace; supposedly it was begun on orders of Hernan Cortés and later became the hall from which the viceroys reigned. Towering above it is the magnificent Metropolitan Cathedral, built to show God's glory is greater than man's. For blocks around all is colonial splendor, a monument to 300 years of Spanish rule.

Avenida Madero, narrow, crowded, yet picturesque and charming, is perhaps the most lovely of the ancient streets. At its western end it comes crashing into the 20th century at the big blue Latin American Tower. The tower, at 44 stories no longer the tallest building in the city, is still a good place from which to get a feel for the Valley of Mexico. Admission to the observation floors on the top costs about a dollar.

Beyond the tower and across busy Lazaro Cardenas, Madero becomes Juarez. Notable landmark is the Palace of Fine Arts, and farther on the Alameda Park. Some 25 or 30 years ago Juarez was the most fashionable shopping street in town, but over the years the more posh boutiques and cafes have moved westward.

Reforma Boulevard, once residential, has become the smart address for today's better shops, restaurants, hotels, and office towers. Those not on Reforma strive to be near it in the few blocks bounded by Niza, Florencia, and Avenida Chapultepec, the trendy neighborhood known for some obscure reason as the Pink Zone or the *Zona Rosa.*

Reforma itself was laid out along the lines of Paris' Champs d'Élysées by order of Emperor Maximilian. During his brief reign in the 1860s the ill-fated Austrian converted the castle in Chapultepec Park into his imperial residence. From there he was wont to ride grandly in state to his offices in the National Palace on the Zocalo.

Midway along its length, Reforma is intersected by Avenida Insurgentes. Running roughly north and south, Insurgentes is the only street that actually bisects the city. To the north is the Basilica of Guadalupe, holiest shrine in the country. Beyond are the grand pyramids and all that remains of the great vanished civilization called Teotihuacan. Insurgentes Sur (*sur* meaning south) becomes the capital's restaurant row. It leads to San Angel, a charmingly colonial residential area. The bull ring is out this way, as is University City. Those who continue onward eventually will reach Cuernavaca and Taxco.

EXPLORING THE ENVIRONS OF MEXICO CITY

The Cuernavaca–Taxco route long has been a favorite with those venturing outside Mexico City.

Less than 50 miles from Mexico City, Cuernavaca, legend has it, has been a resort since Aztec times. Lower in altitude, at 5,000 feet, it is tropical without being oppressively hot. The locals claim Cuernavaca has the best climate in the world. Cortes built himself a palace there and conquerors of all sorts have been following his example ever since. Tycoons weekend in Cuernavaca, princes holiday there, and Americans have made it a retirement community. Tourists delight in sampling its many pleasant inns and restaurants.

Taxco, about a 90-minute drive farther on, is more the postcard Mexico one hopes to find south of the border. Cuernavaca at first glance is an ugly place; it hides its beauty behind walls. Taxco, on the other hand, is a winner from the moment it is first glimpsed, all red-tiled and whitewashed, clinging to the hills. Silver is what brings people to Taxco. The ore has been mined there since colonial times, but it was only half a century ago that New Orleans' Bill Spratling brought his jewelry-making techniques to the village. Scores of little silver shops remain as a monument to Spratling's having lived and taught there.

Two roads lead north out of Mexico City, one being the old Pan American Highway (Route 85) and the other the Queretaro Turnpike (Highway 57). A nice circle trip is heading up 85 and turning off to see the Pyramids at Teotihuacan along the way and possibly overnighting there. Then a night can be spent in Pachuca, a pretty little mining town not many travelers take the time to see. Nice up this way is San Miguel Regla, a resort in the mountains. From Pachuca a back road cuts over to Tula where the ruins of the ancient capital of the Toltecs are to be seen. Tula is just off the turnpike that heads back toward Mexico City.

East, about 80 miles away, is Puebla. While it can easily enough be visited in a day, spending a couple of nights is not a bad idea. There is much to see, from the splendid baroque churches that are in themselves works of art to the huge, still-buried pyramid at Cholula and lions and tigers roaming free at Africam, a zoo that is not a zoo. Beyond Puebla is Tehuacan, the spa town from which most of Mexico's bottled water comes and where some still seek cures.

PRACTICAL INFORMATION FOR MEXICO CITY AND ENVIRONS

HOW TO GET THERE. All roads, railways and air routes (well, nearly all) within Mexico lead to Mexico City. Most international visitors these days arrive by plane; few U.S. gateway cities are even as much as five hours flying time from the capital. By road from the closest U.S. border points the trip takes a day and a half (20 hours driving time or more). Trains are even slower.

By Air. From the U.S. *Aeromexico* flies into Mexico City from Houston, Los Angeles, Miami, New York, and Tucson while *Mexicana* flies from Chicago, Dallas/Fort Worth, Denver, Los Angeles, Miami, Philadelphia, San Antonio, San Francisco, San Juan, and Seattle. U.S. carriers serving Mexico City include *American Airlines, Continental, Pan American* and *Western.* From the rest of the world flying into Mexico City are *Air France, Air Panama, Aeroflot, Aerolineas Argentinas, Aeronica, Aeroperu, Avianca, Aviateca, Iberia, Japan Air Lines, KLM, Lacsa, Lufthansa, Taca, Tan,* and *Viasa.*

From Canada the only service is a once-a-week flight operated by *Aeromexico* via Acapulco.

Promotional fares in an almost endless variety frequently are available. Tour packages usually include substantial air fare discounts. Often considerable savings may be made by flying from border points within Mexico. Airline tour packages purchased within Mexico also can be quite attractive. Bear in mind, however, that no-shows lose 50% of the ticket price in penalties on Mexican domestic flights.

By Bus. Travel by bus in Mexico is quite cheap; however, you get what you pay for and little more. Even for those fluent in Spanish it can be confusing, and the garbled platform announcements are made only in Spanish. Passengers desiring to stop over en route should buy a ticket only to the city where they wish to stop and on arrival reserve a seat aboard the bus they wish to depart on; this costs no more. The good side of bus travel, aside from saving money, is the opportunity to see and get the feel of the country.

From **Matamoros** (across from Brownsville) the trip to Mexico City takes about 14 hours; from **Laredo** 15 hours; from **Ciudad Juarez** (El Paso) 24 hours; from **Nogales** 40 hours; from **Tijuana** 44 hours. Buses depart these border cities every hour on the hour from 6 A.M. until 10 P.M.

By Train. Slower and cheaper (sleeping births are extra) are the railroads which are operated by the government as a social service. Again you get what you pay for. Bring food and be prepared to tip the conductor to help you find the space you have booked. From **Laredo** the trip takes 24 hours; from **Juarez** 36 hours; from **Nogales** and **Mexicali** allow two days. Trains often arrive many hours behind schedule.

By Car. Driving time from the border is about the same as it is for the buses, which really roll along. Highways are fair to good, although in most cases only two lanes. Distances between towns are considerable. It is wise to top off the tank at every opportunity. It also is wise to drive only during daylight hours when the roads are patrolled by the *Green Angels,* who are out to watch for motorists in distress (cattle, among other things, make nighttime driving dangerous). Buy Mexican insurance at the border; uninsured drivers involved in accidents can wind up in jail. While speed limits usually do not exist, pretend they do and hold the line at 55; you won't regret it. Directional signs at times are lacking; when in doubt, ask. A questioning "MeHEEco?" (as everyone calls Mexico City) should bring either a nod or a finger pointing in another direction. No matter where on the border you are coming from you almost certainly will arrive via Queretaro on Highway 57. This is an expressway that passes through miles of suburbs. Turn off at the *Reforma Centro* ("centro" means downtown) exit and you will be headed for the heart of the city.

EMERGENCY TELEPHONE NUMBERS. The area code for Mexico City is 5; for Cuernavaca 731; for Pachuca 771; for Puebla 22; for Taxco 732 and for Tehuacan 238. Within Mexico dial 91 for access to long distance lines. To call Mexico from abroad first dial 01132.

Only local calls can be dialed directly from hotels. International calls should be made collect whenever possible in order to avoid exhorbitant Mexican taxes and hefty hotel service charges.

Calls from public telephones cost only a peso, an exceptional bargain. From public phones long distance calls must be made collect. Dial 09 to reach an international operator (they speak English as well as Spanish) and 02 for domestic calls (operators speak only Spanish). Directory assistance is 04; only Spanish is spoken.

The Federal District (Mexico City) Tourism Office hotline, *Protectur,* is 516–0490; it exists to help tourists with any kind of problem. Emergencies are best handled through hotels; people on the staff know both the ropes and the language. *Locatel,* 658–1111, is the general emergency number in Mexico City, but its operators speak only Spanish. When there is nowhere else to turn, dial 09, international long distance; these operators do speak English and should be able to summon help.

The *American-British Cowdray Hospital,* also known as the *ABC* and the *Hospital Inglés,* has English-speaking personnel on its staff and can handle any emergency medical situation for a price. Telephone 277–5000. The *Mexican Red Cross,* 557–5758, has its own hospital and ambulance fleet; there are no charges for it services but personnel seldom speak English. The *American Benevolent Society,* 514–5465, tries to help visitors in financial difficulties.

Embassy consular sections will respond in cases of death or tangles with the law. The *U.S. Embassy* phone is 211–0042, the Canadian 533–0610, the British 514–3886.

HOTELS. Within the national capital every possible type of hotel may be found; in the nearby cities the selection is somewhat more limited. Roadside motels are almost unknown. In this area there are no seasonal fluctuations in prices.

Mexico City

While Mexico City is big and spread out, most hotels are within walking distance of Reforma Boulevard (some, of course, are right on it) or of Avenidas Juarez and Madero, which are extensions of Reforma. Reforma-Juarez-Madero leads from Chapultepec Park to the Zocalo, the historic heart of the capital. The Zocalo is about three miles from the park. The Zona Rosa or Pink Zone is a trendy neighborhood on the south side of Reforma noted for its cafes, night spots, and boutiques.

Hotels classified as *Super Deluxe* at press time were authorized to charge up to $85 for a double room; *Deluxe,* $65; *First Class,* $35; *Moderate,* $20, and *Inexpensive,* $12.

Super Deluxe

Camino Real. Mariano Escobedo 700; 545–6960. An elegant prestige address near Reforma and the park. 700 rooms in a low rise spread out over 7½ acres. Four pools, tennis club, U.S. television, ten bars and restaurants including *Fouquet's de Paris.*

Maria Isabel Sheraton. Reforma 325; 211–0001. Next to the U.S. Embassy and across from the Pink Zone. With 850 rooms, this is Mexico City's largest hotel and a favorite convention venue. Rooftop pool, health club, U.S. television, seven bars and restaurants.

Deluxe

Airport Holiday Inn. Boulevard Aeropuerto; 762–4088. At the moment the city's only airport hotel; 324 rooms, two restaurants, piano bar, and a delightful pool. Quite pleasant.

Airport Fiesta Americana. Boulevard Aeropuerto; 762–0199. New, with 270 large rooms, coffee shop, and excellent restaurant, plus entertainment evenings.

Alameda. Juarez 50; 518–0620. The first Westin hotel in Mexico; 345 rooms, imaginative restaurants and plenty of evening entertainment in the bars and discos. The midtown location is close to the Palace of Fine Arts.

Aristos. Reforma 276; 211–0112. A Pink Zone favorite with 276 rooms, good restaurants, night club and disco. The location is ideal.

Century. Liverpool at Amberes; 584–7111; in the Pink Zone. New, small, with 142 rooms, luxurious bathrooms, small balconies, pool, sauna, restaurants, and night clubs.

Crowne Plaza Holiday Inn. Reforma 80; 566–7777. This is the renamed **Fiesta Palace,** much renovated but under the same management. Several bars and restaurants with some of the best nighttime entertainment in the city.

Galeria Plaza. Corner of Hamburgo and Varsovia; 211–0014. A 360-room Westin hotel in the Pink Zone. Exceptionally well run. Pool, two restaurants, piano bar, and disco.

Krystal. Liverpool 155; 211–0092. An attractive Pink Zone hotel with 355 rooms, in-house movies, pool, two restaurants, bars, and a nightclub.

Marco Polo. Amberes 27; 511–1839. Small and elegant, with a hot plate, wet bar, and U.S. television in all the attractively furnished rooms.

El Presidente Chapultepec. Campos Eliseos 218; 250–7700. 777-room high-rise on the edge of the park, near Reforma and the Anthropology Museum. U.S. television. Half a dozen bars and restaurants including *Maxim's,* a disco and jazz bar.

El Presidente Internacional. Circuito Interior and Marina Nacional; 254–4400. One of Mexico City's newest hotels, a 400-room establishment built with traveling executives in mind. A bit out of the way for tourists. Pool and health club; next to big shopping mall.

First Class

Calinda Geneve. Londres 130; 211–0071. Pink Zone location. A 378-room Quality Inn originally opened in 1912 and recently refurbished. Excellent restaurant, pleasant garden bar and entertainment in the evenings.

Corinto. Vallarta 24; 566–6555. A small hotel just a block from Reforma with 155 rooms, restaurant and bar. Discounts are available for extended stays.

Emporio. Reforma 124; 566–7766. The location is good, the modernistic space age decor unusual. Most clients are Mexicans from the provinces. Coffee shop.

Plaza. Insurgentes Centro 149; 546–4540. An older establishment, with curious architecture, trying to make a comeback.

Plaza Florencia. Florencia 61; 533–6540. The 130 rooms are quite luxurious and the Pink Zone location convenient. Restaurant and bar with plenty more close by.

Reforma. Reforma and Paris; 546–9680. Once the smartest address in the city, now past its prime but reeking of nostalgic charm. Good location and old-fashioned service. Coffee shop, restaurant and show bar.

Royal. Amberes 78; 525–4850. Modern and attractive, with a nice restaurant, all in the heart of the Pink Zone.

Ritz. Madero 30; 518–1340. All 158 rooms are somewhat shabby and the financial district location is not the best, but the food is good and the bar fascinating.

Romano Diana. Mississippi and Lerma; 211–0109. A block from Reforma, this is a modern tourist hotel with a restaurant and bar where there is nightly entertainment.

Moderate

Del Angel. Lerma 154; 533–1032. "The poor man's **Maria Isabel,"** with 100 rooms, is just across from one of the capital's posher hostelries. Reforma and the Pink Zone are a block away. Coffee shop, pool.

Brasilia. Avenida Cien Metros No. 4823; 587–8577. Close to the big Northern Bus Terminal; new, with 130 rooms.

Bristol. Plaza Nacaxa 17; 533–6060. Modern and pleasant, with 150 rooms, three or four blocks from Reforma and the Pink Zone. Coffee shop and cocktail lounge.

Cortes. Hidalgo 85; 585–0322; on Alemeda Park a block from Juarez. Built in the 18th century, and with just 28 rooms, this is the smallest and oldest hotel in the city. Rooms face out on a colonial patio. Restaurant, bar.

Diplomatico. Insurgentes Sur 1105; 563–6066. A bit off by itself, but handy to the bullring and some of Mexico City's best restaurants.

El Ejecutivo. Viena 8; 566–6422. The 190 rooms are furnished with business travelers in mind. Near Reforma and the Pink Zone. Restaurant, bar, and pool.

Gran Hotel de la Ciudad de México. Calle 16 de Septiembre 82; 510–4040. Interesting, a former department store; the *belle époque* lobby is a showplace, the restaurant and bar quite good, but the rooms are shabby.

Guardiola. Madero 5; 521–8580. Old, but the 85 rooms have been refurbished. Interesting location across from the Palace of Fine Arts and next door to the Latin American Tower.

Majestic. Madero 73; 521–8600. On the Zocalo, rather dreary at night, but in the heart of things during the day. The 80 rooms are well worn, but the rooftop dining is most pleasant.

Maria Cristina. Lerma 31; 546–9880. A charming old-fashioned Mexican inn with 110 rooms a block from Reforma, two from the Pink Zone. Garden restaurant, piano bar.

Prim. Versailles 46; 592–1609. Modern and attractive, with 160 rooms, nightly entertainment; close to Reforma and the Pink Zone.

Vasco de Quiroga. Londres 15; 546–2614. A 50-room gem in a residential neighborhood near Reforma and the Pink Zone. Good bar and restaurant.

Inexpensive

Edison. Edison 106; 566–0933. A 45-room hotel fairly near Reforma and a favorite with visitors planning long stays.

Fleming. Revillagigedo 35; 510–4530. A block from Juarez with 75 rooms and a restaurant. Modern with an inviting lobby and a fair restaurant.

Isabel. Isabel la Catolica 63; 518–1213. Downtown, near the Zocalo, with 74 rooms and old-fashioned Mexican surroundings.

Maria Angelos. Lerma 11; 545–6705. A favorite with repeat visitors not necessarily on a budget. The 20 rooms are shabby but homey atmosphere makes up for a lot. Dining room. A block from Reforma.

Monte Carlo. Uruguay 69; 585–1222. The glamourous name is misleading, but this downtown 59-room inn attracts many tourists on a budget.

Panuco. Ayuntamento 148; 585–1355. Near both Reforma and Juarez, unimpressive for outside but pleasant and cheap within.

Polanco. Edgar Allan Poe No. 8; 520–2085. Out of the way and rather Bohemian in a posh residential neighborhood.

Regente. Paris 9; 566–8933. Near Reforma, with 133 rooms, bar and restaurant. A favorite with budget tourists.

Del Valle. Independencia 35; 585–2399. A 50-room hotel a block from Juarez with a dining room and budget restaurants nearby. (Closed for minor repairs).

Suites

For the price of a first-class room these establishments provide sleeping quarters, living room, kitchenette, and maid service. They are ideal for families and guests planning a long stay.

Amberes. Amberes 64; 518–3306. Small, with 28 units in the heart of the Pink Zone.

Junior Executive. Rhin 54; 566–3000. A block from Reforma, two from the Pink Zone, with 24 attractive kitchenette suites.

Mi Casa. General Prim 106; 566–6711. Close to Reforma, with 27 newly furnished units.

Orleans. Hamburgo 67; 533–6880. In the Pink Zone and handy to everything. The 41 units are attractively furnished.

Palacio Real. Napoles 62; 533–0535. With 30 units in the Pink Zone; restaurant and a rooftop piano bar.

Del Parque. Dakota 155; 536–1450. One of the few nice places to stay in the fashionable southern part of the city.

San Marcos. Rio Po 125; 533–6772. Near Reforma and the Pink Zone with 26 units (four to a floor), balconies, and marble baths.

Silver Suites. Sullivan 163; 566–7522. American owned with a bar and pleasant restaurant. Location, five blocks from Reforma is slightly inconvenient.

Motels

Most motels around Mexico City cater to romantics. Visitors who arrive by car usually prefer to park their vehicles and get around by taxi rather than wrestle with Mexico City traffic. The following are quite respectable, and prices are moderate.

Dawn. Highway 57 north of the city; 373–2155. Much like the Maria Barbara with restaurant, bar, and pool.

Maria Barbara. Highway 57 just north of the city; 397–4544. Pleasant rooms, restaurant, bar, and pool. Handy when arriving tired and late.

Parque Villa. Gomez Pedraza 68; 217–4637. In a residential neighborhood near Chapultepec Park. Garden setting and a most pleasant restaurant.

Cuernavaca

A favorite weekend retreat from Mexico City, Cuernavaca is some 2,000 feet lower in altitude, hence quite tropical. At first glance it is not especially attractive, but behind the walls the homes and hotels are beautiful. A double room in a *Deluxe* resort will run up to $45 per night; *First Class,* $30; *Moderate,* $15; and *Inexpensive,* $10.

Deluxe

Hacienda Cocoyoc. Yautepec (20 miles east of Cuernavaca); 12–2000. A 16th-century hacienda with 260 rooms (some with private pools) spread out over 70 acres. Facilities include nine holes of golf, riding horses, tennis, swimming, a disco, and a nightclub. Big with convention groups.

Hacienda Vista Hermosa. San José Vista Hermosa (about 15 miles south of town); 12–0300. Another 16th-century hacienda that is now a resort. Tennis, squash, and a large pool. Tour buses stop here for lunch and on weekends many people stop in just for the day.

Casino de la Selva. Avenida Gobernadores; 12–4700. In town, big and brassy with 228 rooms; cinema on the premises as well as a bowling alley plus riding horses, swimming pools, restaurants, and a night club.

First Class

Las Mañanitas. Ricardo Linares 107; 12–4646. Better known for its magnificent garden restaurant, this establishment has 28 large and delightful rooms plus a big pool for guests only. Near downtown. No credit cards.

Las Quintas. Avenida Las Quintas 107; 12–8800. 45 units set around lovely gardens. Two pools, bar, and an excellent restaurant. A few minutes from downtown.

Jacarandas. Cuauhtemoc 805; 15–7777. The 90 terraced rooms look out over beautiful gardens and an inviting pool. Tennis, squash, and evening entertainment.

Posada de Xochiquetzal. Leyva 300; 12–0220. A 14-room inn built around a lovely garden and pool. The food is outstanding. Piano bar.

Racquet Club. Francisco Villa 100; 12–2180. Nine tennis courts and 32 marvelous rooms all in a club-like setting on what was once a sumptuous retreat built for Nobel Prize winners.

Hacienda de Cortes. Plaza Kennedy 70, Atlacomulco (five miles south of town); 15–9944. Lovely, small, with 20 units on the grounds of what supposedly was Hernan Cortes' hideaway. Pool, tennis, and golf nearby.

Moderate

Las Espadas. Rio Papaloapan at Rio Panuco; 15–3049. A garden resort, with a Jacuzzi, pool, and U.S. television. Nice restaurant.

Villa del Conquistador. Calzada Conquistador 134; 3–1055. Bungalows and cabañas set around a pool in a huge garden. Tennis, squash; restaurant and piano bar.

El Mirador. Francisco Villa; 15–1900. Cuernavaca's newest; large, with 100 rooms. Tennis, pool, restaurant.

Ancira Holiday. Paseo de Conquistador; 13–1010. A small 27-room inn with a panoramic view, heated pool, restaurant, and bar.

Inexpensive

Palacio. Calle Morrow 204; 12–0553. A downtown hotel with 16 rooms, restaurant and garden.

Papagayo. Motolinia 13; near downtown; 12–4694. Big with 90 rooms, a large pool plus restaurant and bar. Crowded with day-trippers on weekends.

OK Inn. Emiliano Zapata 825; 13–1270. A 46-room motel, some units with kitchenettes. Pool, restaurant. Tennis nearby.

Taxco

Perhaps 90 minutes south of Cuernavaca, Taxco can be either an overnight stop or an entire vacation. The choice of hotels is wide. The larger resorts are a bit out of town, while the smaller inns cling to narrow cobbled streets in town. The one *Deluxe* resort charges $40 for a double room; the *First Class* places cost $30; *Moderate,* $20; *Inexpensive,* $14.

Deluxe

Montetaxco. Lomas de Taxco; 2–1300. Quite splendid with 160 large rooms, in-house movies, and a magnificent view. Nine holes of golf, tennis, riding horses. Mexican and international cuisine. Nightly entertainment.

First Class

De la Borda. Cerro del Pedregal 21. Long a Taxco landmark, its 150 rooms looking out from a hillside over the town. Pool, nice restaurant, and entertainment nightly. Gets many bus tours en route to Acapulco.

Rancho Taxco Victoria. Carlos J. Nibbi 14; 2–0063. Under the same management as De la Borda but in town with 100 rooms. Classically Mexican with a lovely view. Two pools, restaurant, and bar.

Hacienda del Solar. Highway 95 south of town; 2–0323. Intimate, with 17 well-furnished rooms, tennis, riding horses, and pool. Outstanding restaurant with music in the evenings.

Posada de la Misión. Cerro de la Misión 32; 2–0063. Close to town with 90 rooms laid out like a Mexican village. Pool and tennis; disco. The murals in the dining room are masterworks by Juan O'Gorman.

Moderate

Los Arcos. Juan Ruis de Alarcon 12; 2–1836. An in-town inn with 30 rooms, heated pool, restaurant, and entertainment evenings in the piano bar.

Loma Linda. Avenida Kennedy 52; 2–0206. A motel on the highway just below town with 90 units, pool, restaurant, and bar. Well-run but rather ordinary.

Inexpensive

Los Castillo. Juan Ruiz de Alarcon 3; 2–1396. The 15 rooms in this in-town inn are worth more than they cost. Small but delightful with bar and restaurant.

Sancta Prisca. Cena Obscuras 1; 2–0080. Also worth more than is charged, with 40 spacious rooms, colonial decor. The patio garden is lovely. Restaurant and bar.

Melendez. Cuauhtemoc 3; 2–0006. Just of the Zocalo, a 40-room commercial hotel, but quite nice and close to everything.

Pachuca

An easy day trip from Mexico City, Pachuca does not attract many overnight tourists. On the road there and beyond, however, are some interesting places to stop and pleasant places to stay.

Villa Arqueologica. San Juan de Teotihuacan (en route from Mexico City to Pachuca); 511–1284. The famed Pyramids of Teotihuacan can be seen in a few hours, but stopping over is rewarding. Managed by Club Med, this hotel has 40 rooms, pool, tennis, and continental dining. About $35.

San Miguel Regla. Huasca (ten miles beyond Pachuca); 0–0053. A lovely 18th-century hacienda in the pine forests, now a 53-room resort with pool, riding horses, tennis, and putting green. Somewhat lonely except on weekends. About $40 with meals.

Emily. Plaza Independencia; 2–6617. A good downtown Pachuca hotel within walking distance of about all there is to see and a bargain at $15 per night.

Puebla

Although it is only a two-hour drive from Mexico City, Puebla is worth a one- or two-night stay. There is much to see and do and a good selection of hotels. A double in a *First Class* establishment will cost $35; *Moderate,* $20; *Inexpensive,* $10.

First Class

Mision. Cinco Poniente 2514; 48–9600. The city's newest with 225 rooms, U.S. television, pool, three bars, restaurant, and evening entertainment.

Meson del Angel. Hermanos Serdan 807; 48–2100. A resort on the edge of the city with 190 rooms, tennis, bowling, restaurant, and bar. Entertainment evenings.

Villa Arqueologica. Dos Poniente 601, Cholula (about five miles from downtown Puebla); 47–1508. Adjacent to the Toltec ruins, run by Club Med with 40 rooms, pool, tennis, and an excellent dining room.

Moderate

Lastra. Calzada de los Fuertes 2633; 35–9755. Small, with 55 rooms on the edge of town, roof garden, pool, and good food.

Gilfer. Dos Oriente 11; 40–6611. A modern 90-room hotel downtown. Quite nice and close to everything. Restaurant, bar, and nightclub.

Palacio San Leonardo. Dos Oriente 211; 48–0555. Colonial in atmosphere with modern appointments. Rooftop pool, restaurant, and bar.

Posada San Pedro. Dos Oriente 202; 46–5077. Another charming downtown hotel with 80 rooms, restaurant, bar, and pool.

Royalty. Portal Hidalgo 8; 42–4740. With 46 rooms, many overlooking the Zocalo. Sidewalk cafe, restaurant, and bar.

Inexpensive

Cabrera. Diez Oriente6; 41–8625. Not very impressive from the outside, but the 60 rooms are clean and comfortable. Lobby and coffee shop are one flight up.

Palacio de Puebla. Dos Oriente 13; 41–2430. Close to the center of town. Adequate, but no restaurant.

Virrey de Mendoza. Tres Poniente 912; 42–3903. Cozy and friendly with just 18 rooms. No restaurant.

Agua Azul. Prolongación Once Súr and Calzada Mayorazgo; 43–1288. A working class resort with garden and pool. Crowded weekends but not bad the rest of the time.

Tehuacan

Mexico's most famous spa town is rather ghostly now. People do not take the waters as they once did. Still, Tehuacan has a special rundown charm. Rates are about the same as for hotels in Puebla.

First Class

Spa Peñafiel. Carretera Puebla; 2–0190. A rambling old resort that someone should turn into a movie set. Ample grounds, pool, tennis, bowling. Restaurant and bar.

Hotel México. Reforma and Independencia; 2–0019. A nice old place reminiscent of the German *bads.* The 50 rooms are well kept up and the dining room is good.

Inexpensive

Posada Tehuacan. Reforma Norte 211; 2–0491. A small, pleasant inn with home-style cooking, clean and comfortable rooms.

SPECIAL EVENTS. January 17. Blessing of the animals *(Feast of St. Anthony)* with pets and working beasts decked out in their finery. Ceremonies at the Metropolitan Cathedral on the Zocalo and at other churches.

Mid-January. *Santa Prisca Fiesta* in Taxco honoring the town's patroness. Three days of outdoor dances by the Zocalo, fireworks, and general merrymaking.

February. *Pre-Lenten Carnaval* celebrated in a semipagan fashion at Teploztlán, roughly midway between Mexico City and Cuernavaca. Also, on a smaller scale in some Mexico City neighborhoods.

Easter Week. The *Passion of Christ* is reenacted in Ixtapalapa, a neighborhood in eastern Mexico City, beginning with the Last Supper on Thursday evening and going through a mock crucifixion on Friday. In Taxco the commemoration is even more impressive. Hooded penitents, black gowned and bare to the waist, flagellate themselves in an eerie candlelit procession through town.

May 1. *Labor Day.* Parade up Madero, Juarez and Reforma.

May 3. *Feast of the Holy Cross,* celebrated by construction workers as their day. Building sites are decorated with crosses and there is much exploding of fireworks.

May 5. In Puebla the *Battle of Puebla* is reënacted. It was in 1862 that Mexican forces successfully defended the city against the invading French. The month-long state fair gets started on this day.

July. On the weekend nearest the Fourth the American community marks U.S. independence with a fiesta of its own including a parade, patriotic speeches, carnival rides, food stalls and all the rest. At the American School.

Mid-August. Ten-day fiesta marking the Assumption, at Huamantla, Tlaxcala (between Mexico City and Puebla). Floral carpets made from petals and sawdust make this one of Mexico's most colorful fiestas. Also bullfights, charro rodeos, street dancing and fireworks.

August 13. *The Defense of Tlatelolco,* where the Aztecs fought their final battle, is marked by Indian dancing at the Plaza of the Three Cultures.

August 21. Tribute is paid to Cuauhtemoc, last of the Aztec rulers, at his statue on the intersection of Reforma and Insurgentes. Speeches and Indian dancing.

September 15. *Independence Eve* in Mexico City is another New Year's Eve, celebrations getting started at 11 P.M. when at the National Palace on the Zocalo the president rings the Liberty Bell, waves the flag and reënacts the original Cry of Liberty. Restaurants and night clubs stage grand and expensive celebrations.

September 16. *Independence Day.* Parade up Madero, Juarez, Reforma.

November 2. *Day of the Dead (All Souls' Day),* marked by the sale of special bread and candies. Candlelight vigil at the suburban Mixquic graveyard includes huge figures of skeletons.

November 20. *Revolution Day,* a national holiday, is marked by a spectacular parade of performing athletes down Madero, Juarez, and Reforma.

Last week in November. *Silver Fair* in Taxco with outdoor shows, dances, a beauty contest and, naturally, prizes to the Silver City's best silversmiths.

December 12. *Virgin of Guadalupe Day* brings pilgrims from throughout the country to the basilica to honor the Patroness of Mexico. Ceremonies start around midnight; crowds are huge.

December 16. The first *posada* and beginning of a Christmas season that lasts through Jan. 6, *Twelfth Night.* Yule lights go on and parties blast into full swing. *Posada* means inn and refers to the nightly search for shelter by Joseph and Mary; the search is reënacted at parties in many Mexico City hotels.

HOW TO GET AROUND. Huge as it is, Mexico City is not difficult to negotiate. Much of what people want to see is within walking distance of the hotels, and when feet get weary taxis are cheap. For sightseeing, organized tours are the best bet. Visitors staying awhile will want to master the subway (Metro) and a couple of bus lines.

From the Airport. Taxis are available at both the domestic and international arrivals areas. These cabs charge about $5 to most hotels, much less than the gypsy cab touts try to steer tourists to. Rental car agencies have booths at both arrivals areas; however, unless you are heading out of town or know Mexico City very well, renting a car is not recommended.

Porters are available in the customs hall and just outside is a bank that will exchange dollars for pesos at the most favorable rate (better still, arrive with a couple of thousand pesos in notes and coins). The Mexico City tourist office and the Hotel Association both have stands in the arrivals area and will provide information and help the reservationless find a room.

By Taxi. Cabs come in many colors and sizes in Mexico City; the color and size will give you an idea of the fare. Large, unmarked cars with hooded meters are found outside the major hotels. These usually are driven by licensed English –speaking guides and may charge a minimum of $5 for a fairly short trip.

Red and white taxis operate out of stands, take radio calls and when picking up passengers on the street are authorized to charge a premium. Yellow and white cabs, often VW bugs with one front seat removed, cruise the streets looking for business. Meters no longer are readjusted to keep up with inflation; instead, new tariffs are pasted to a window advising if the meter says $2.50 the fare will be $500 (pesos). Often, however, passengers are told the meter is broken. Cabbies will quote fares in advance, which is fine if you speak Spanish. Yet, even if you are overcharged, the trip will cost less (or should) than a cab ride back home. Tips are not expected.

By Subway. By the time you read this, a ride on the Metro may cost more than a peso, but no doubt it still will be the least expensive subway in the world. It is worth seeing, too, but avoid the rush hour. Between 10 A.M. and 4 P.M. the crowds are not too bad, but pickpockets are always a worry. Nice are the brightly–lit marble and onyx stations, good signing and the sleek French–designed trains that run on rubber tires. The Metro runs from 6 A.M. until midnight.

The various lines are indicated by color. Most used by tourists is the red line, Line 1, linking Reforma (Chaputepec station), the Pink Zone (Insurgentes station) and the Zocalo (Pino Suarez station).

By Bus. At this writing bus fares are three pesos and all the pickpockets not on the subway seem to be on the buses. In Mexican Spanish the word for bus and truck is the same: *camion.* In fact there is little difference between them.

The only bus route of interest to most people runs along Reforma, Juarez and Madero from Chapultepec Park to the Zocalo. Stops are clearly indicated by attractive shelters and queues of waiting passengers. A bus also may be taken out Insurgentes Sur to San Angel and University City or out Insurgentes Norte to the Guadalupe Basilica. One can get anywhere in the city by bus; call 525–9380 for route directions. Trolley buses and trolley cars are found only in outlying areas.

Intercity bus tickets may be purchased at the Mexicorama office in the Plaza del Angel arcade which may be entered either from Londres or Hamburgo between Florencia and Amberes; 533–0298. Personnel speak English.

Buses depart from four outlying terminals: North, Avenida Cien Metros 4907; South, Tazqueña 1320; East, Zaragoza 200 and West, Rio Tacubaya and Sur 122. Subways run to all these terminals but passengers are not allowed to carry luggage on subways.

By Peseros. Painted green, these are cabs and vans operating on a fixed route, charging a flat rate (a peso once upon a time, hence the name) and cramming in as many passengers as they can hold. *Peseros* run along Reforma from Chapultepec Park to the Zocalo as well as along Insurgentes. There are many other routes as well, each with its own fare.

By Car. Millions of people drive around Mexico City every day and survive, but for out-of-towners the experience can be traumatic. Streets are confusing, traffic nightmarish and parking places almost nonexistent. Police tow trucks constantly are hauling away illegally parked vehicles; finding them takes fluency in Spanish plus many hours of hunting (call 658–1111 for clues on where to start looking). Visitors can hire a chauffeur for their cars for about $25 per day by calling *Drive Power* at 524–8512; many hotels also can arrange for drivers.

An automobile is the most comfortable way to reach such nearby communities as Cuernavaca, Taxco, Pachuca, Puebla and Tehuacan.

TOURIST INFORMATION SERVICES. The Mexico City (Federal District) Tourist Office maintains information booths at both the international and domestic arrivals areas at the airport as well as on highways leading into the city. In town information is available in the lobby of the building at Amberes and Londres, in the Pink Zone. By telephone information is available from 8 A.M. to 8 P.M. by calling 525–9380.

The **Mexico City Chamber of Commerce,** Reforma 42 (phone 592–2677) publishes a variety of material distributed free to visitors. Open 10 A.M. to 2 P.M. and 4 to 6 P.M. weekdays.

In **Cuernavaca** the state tourist office is at the Borda Garden, Morelos 205; phone 2–1815. Open 10 A.M. to 2 P.M. daily except Sunday.

The **Taxco** tourist office is on Avenida Kennedy (the main highway) by the town's one big service station; phone 2–0979. Open 10 A.M. to 2 P.M., 4 to 7 P.M. weekdays.

In **Puebla** the tourist office is located at Reforma and Calle Siete Norte, phone 46–0928. Open 10 A.M. to 2 P.M. and 4 to 7 P.M.

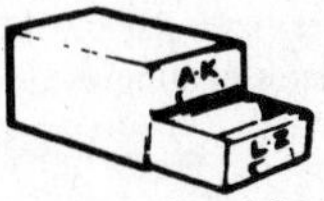

USEFUL ADDRESSES. *U.S. Embassy,* Reforma 305; 211–0042. Open 8:30 A.M. to 5:30 P.M. weekdays; closed for American and Mexican holidays. *Canadian Embassy,* Schiller 529; 254–3288. Open 9 A.M. to 5 P.M. weekdays; closed for Mexican and Canadian holidays. *British Embassy,* Lerma 71; 511–4880. Open 9:30 A.M. to 1 P.M. and 3:30 to 6 P.M.

The main Post Office is on the corner of Lazaro Cardenas and Tacuba; mail marked 'general delivery' *(lista de correos)*) may be picked up here. Near most hotels is the post office on the corner of Varsovia and Londres in the Pink Zone.

The *American British Cowdray Hospital* is at Observatorio and Sur 136; 515 8359.

Aeromexico has a ticket office at Reforma 64 and at Estocolmo 4 just off Reforma in the Pink Zone; 553–1577. *Mexicana* at Reforma and Amberes in the Pink Zone; 585–8933. *American* at Reforma 300; 566–2500. *Continental* at Reforma 325; 511–4988. *Eastern* at Reforma 30; 546–0722. *Pan American* at Reforma 35; 546 5715. *Western* at Reforma 243; 533–2000.

ENGLISH LANGUAGE MEDIA. *The News,* an excellent daily published in Mexico City, provides a good rundown on what is happening in Mexico and the rest of the world. It is available at hotel newsstands as well as at stands on the street in tourist areas.

Sanborns, which has three branches along Reforma and more elsewhere, is a good place to pick up U.S. newspapers and magazines as well as paperback books. The **American Book Store** at Madero 44, has even more.

U.S. network television is received by cable in Mexico City and many deluxe hotels offer this service. An increasing number of hotels have installed parabolic antennas which provide U.S. films, round-the-clock news and more. Radio VIP, which is FM, is Mexico's English-language station. It broadcasts CBS news on the hour. The station is the first on the left of the dial.

TOURS. There are more than three dozen tour operators in Mexico City running sightseeing excursions within the capital and its surrounding areas. They can arrange for trips anywhere else in the country as well. The better hotels all have travel desks that can set up tours. There also is *American Express* at Hamburgo 75; 533–0380; *Mexicorama,* Londres 161 (in the Del Angel arcade), 525–2346; *Mexico Travel Advisors (MTA),* Genova 30, 525–7520; *Linea Gris,* Londres 166, 533–1540, and *Turismo Del Paseo,* Reforma 185; 535–4408. Most tours are similar as are prices. Rates quoted here are per person in a bus; automobiles also are available at about $10 more per person.

City sightseeing. Includes the Zocalo, National Palace, Metropolitan Cathedral and Chapultepec Park; four hours, $10.

Pyramids. Takes in the Basilica of Guadalupe as well as a look at the major ruins at Teotihuacan; four hours, $12.

Pyramids plus Light and Sound. Similar to the above with the light and sound show added. Available only Oct. 15 through May 31; six hours, $14.

Ballet Folklorico, University City and Xochimilco. Available Sundays only, takes in a morning performance of the folkloric dances at the Palace of Fine Arts, goes on for a boat ride along the canals of Xochimilco's floating gardens, and continues to the modernistic campus of the National University; seven hours, $22.

Bullfights. Sundays only. Transportation to the bullring and back with a guide to explain the finer points of the spectacle. Four hours, $12. (Can also be combined with the Ballet Folklorico-Xochimilco tour.)

Night life. The best of these includes transfers by private car rather than bus, dinner at an elegant restaurant (frequently Del Lago), a drink and show at the Plaza Santa Cecelia where mariachis play, and a nightcap at Gitanerias, which features the best flamenco dancers in Mexico. Five hours, $50.

Cuernavaca and Taxco. Long considered the classic route with sightseeing in Cuernavaca and shopping in Taxco. Lunch is included. Twelve hours, $25. (Overnight stay in Taxco can be arranged for the price of a hotel room.)

Puebla and Cholula. Sightseeing in Puebla takes in the Cathedral and the Secret Convent; Cholula, a Toltec religious center, is the site of the world's largest pyramid (by volume, not by height). Lunch is included. Twelve hours, $25. (Overnight stays can also be arranged.)

Toluca Market. Fridays only, this trip is to one of the largest and most colorful Indian markets in the Mexico City area. Toluca is capital of the neighboring State of Mexico. The tour includes a stop at the Desert of the Lions, an attractive national park. $16.

PARKS AND GARDENS. Chapultepec, spread out over 40 square miles on the western edge of the capital, is the world's largest metropolitan park. It also is the oldest park in the Americas, having been set aside as a reserve for Aztec nobility in 1435; they gave the place its name, which means Grasshopper Hill. Chapultepec has eight museums, three lakes, a zoo, and an amusement park. Also there are two good restaurants, several snack stands, theaters, the National Auditorium, and Los Pinos, official residence of the President of the Republic. Open until dark, Chapultepec always delights, but takes on a special festive air on weekends when scores of thousands of families come out to enjoy it.

Alameda, which means poplar grove (an *alamo* is a poplar tree), stretching from the Palace of Fine Arts over a four–block area along one side of Avenida Juarez, dates back to the 17th century. It was laid out by order of the viceroy, Luis de Velasco. The western corner is where heretics were put to death during the Inquisition. In the late 19th century the Alameda was where fashionable folk would stroll on a Sunday to see and be seen. The Diego Rivera mural in the lobby of the Hotel del Prado satirizes the custom. Today the crowds are more bourgeoise, but the park remains every bit as lovely.

Xochimilco, the floating gardens, is part of the standard Sunday tour. Actually the gardens can be enjoyed any day. Visitors pile into gondolas and are poled along through the canals while boats bearing tacos and mariachi bands come by to sell their wares. It may sound too touristy, but foreigners always are vastly outnumbered by locals enjoying a day off. The gardens, by the way, no longer float. In Aztec times, when Mexico City was surrounded by a lake, rafts covered with soil were anchored out this way; flowers and vegetables were grown on the rafts. Today the rafts have disappeared but the vegetables and flowers are still grown in abundance out this way.

Desierto de los Leones translates into to Desert of the Lions which it is not. Rather, this cool pine forest was once owned by a family named Leon (Lion) who, since they never settled there, left the area deserted. Friday tours to the Toluca market often include a stop here to visit the remains of a Carmelite monestary built in the early 1600s. The park, less than ten miles from downtown, is a lovely place for a picnic.

Reino Aventura, on the southern edge of the city, is a theme park. The 100-acre spread encompasses six "villages": Mexican, French, Swiss, Polynesian, American, and Children's World. Admission fee ($3 at press time) includes most of the rides. There are also shows including performances by trained dolphins. And, of course, there a number of places to eat. The park is open 10 A.M. to 6 P.M. except Monday.

Cuernavaca

Borda Garden, by the Cathedral, was laid out along classic French lines by José de la Borda, a foremost 18th-century silver barron. In the 1860s, legend has it, the Emperor Maximilian would rendezvous in the shade of its great trees with a local girl who has gone down in history as La India Bonita. These days the garden is but a ghostly reminder of past glories.

Jardin Juarez or Juarez Garden, with its trees and benches, is an extension of Cuernavaca's main plaza. There are band concerts here Sunday nights.

Chapultepec, a smaller version of the Mexico City park, is more tropical and quite lovely, a favorite spot for family outings.

ZOOS. Chapultepec. Spread out over 60 acres, the park zoo is home for some 2,600 animals representing nearly 300 species. Most famous is the panda family; the two offspring are the only pandas known to have been born outside China. Another inhabitant is one of the first chimpanzees to return from outer space. The grounds include a children's area with a baby elephant, lion cubs, a llama, a donkey, turtle, and more. Youngsters can play with the animals, ride ponies, climb tree houses, and in general have a fine time. Smallers zoos are located in Pedregal and San Juan Aragon, outlying neighborhoods few tourists are likely to visit. The three Mexico City zoos are open from 8 A.M. until 6 P.M.; admission is free.

Puebla

Africam. Located some miles from town, but zebra-striped minibuses depart for Africam every 30 minutes. They arrive at 275 acres spread on the shores of

Lake Valsequillo where 2,000 animals, some 500 species, roam free. Those driving in their own cars are urged to keep their windows rolled up. The few fences, which are scarcely noticible, prevent the lions and tigers from gobbling up the giraffes, zebras, and antelopes. Mornings and afternoons, the elephants put on a show. The park is open daily from 10 A.M. to 5 P.M.; admission at press time was $2.50 plus $1 more for those taking the minibus tour.

PARTICIPANT SPORTS. Golf. The five 18-hole courses around Mexico City are private but the better hotels can arrange guest privileges except on weekends. *Cuernavaca* has three 18-hole golf clubs open to the public on weekdays and the nearby *Hotel Hacienda Cocoyoc* has its own nine-hole course. Taxco's *Hotel Montetaxco* has a rather spectacular nine-hole course on a mountaintop.

Tennis. All the golf spots have tennis courts as well. Best bet, of course, is for players to stay at a hotel that has its own courts (see *Accommodations*). Or they can play at *Club Reyes,* just three blocks from Chapultepec Park, 7 A.M. to 9 P.M. (phone 277–2690 for reservations). In Cuernavaca the *Hacienda Temixco* has public tennis courts.

Swimming. Again, the best bet is to check into a hotel with a pool; all the golf spots also have swimming pools. In Cuernavaca the *Hacienda Temixco* and *Hacienda Real del Puente* both have several pools as well as restaurants and bars open to the public (neither is a hotel). In Puebla the *Spa Agua Azul* has a public pool.

Jogging. *Chapultepec Park* in Mexico City is crowded with runners early in the morning and *Alameda Park* gets its share as well (athletes should take into consideration the capital's 7,200-foot altitude). In Cuernavaca joggers will feel most at home at the *Racquet Club, Casino de la Selva* or *Hacienda Cocoyoc.* Puebla's Zocalo is another good place to run as is the *Hacienda San Miguel Regla* near Pachuca.

Cyclists and Rowers can ply their sport in *Chapultepec Park* where both bikes and boats may be rented.

Horseback riding is featured at several resort hotels outside Mexico City (see *Accommodations*). There are horses for rent at the Desert of the Lions National Park.

Mountain climbing expeditions up the Popocatépetl volcano with guides can be arranged through tour operators. The season is November through May and only experienced climbers need apply.

SPECTATOR SPORTS. Charreadas or *charro* rodeos are a Mexican original, true exhibitions of riding and roping skill. *Charros* are Mexican cowboys, although these days many are amateurs, wealthy executives and professional people who can afford the sport. *Charro* associations usually hold competitions on Sunday mornings to see who can most rapidly rope a calf or bring down a steer by its tale. Venues vary from week to week. Admission usually is free. Going with a guide is recommended in order to understand what is happening. One can, of course, go unaccompanied. Rodeos usually are held at the *Rancho del Charro,* Constituyentes 500 on the western edge of Chapultepec Park, or at the *Lienzo del Charro* in Pedregal in the southern part of town. Have your hotel call 277–8706 for time and information. There are also *charreadas* in Puebla.

Bullfights take place almost every Sunday at 4:30 P.M. in Mexico City's Plaza México. Easiest way to go is with a tour group so as not to worry about transportation or finding your seat in the world's largest bullring. Individuals may buy tickets (for as much as $10 for seats on the shady side) from hotel travel desks, or at the ring itself on the day of the event. The bullring is just off Insurgentes Sur about two miles south of Reforma and reached easily by bus or taxi.

Jai Alai is played every evening except Monday and Friday at the *Fronton México* on the Plaza de la Revolución just north of Reforma. The first game usually starts at 7 P.M. This is a Basque variety of handball with wicker basket-gloves enabling the ball to be hurled at tremendous speed. Betting on the outcome is as fast and furious as the game itself. Admission is about $1 and program notes explain, in English, what is going on.

Horse racing takes place at the *Hipodromo de las Americas* starting at 3:30 P.M. on Tuesday, Thursday and Friday, 2:30 on weekends. The admission price is minimal and you can place a bet for less than a dollar (or much more, if you wish). Extra nice is having lunch at the *Derby Club* (phone 557–4700 for reservations) while watching the races. Open throughout the year (except Christmas and Easter weeks), the track is a few miles north of Reforma, about a fifteen minute taxi ride from most hotels (buses run back to town).

Soccer is Mexico's most popular sport, some people claiming it was invented here in prehispanic times, transported to Europe and then brought back. Throughout most of the year games are played on Thursday evenings and Sunday noon at huge, 100,000-seat *Aztec Stadium* on the southern edge of the city, the *Olympic Stadium* in University City, or at the *Sports City Stadium* near the bullring.

Baseball is played almost every night and Sunday afternoon from April through August by the Tigers or Red Devils, the capital's two teams in the AAA Mexican League. A number of Americans on their way up, or on their way down, are to be found in the lineups. The games are at the *Social Security Park* on Avenida Cuauhtemoc, about a 15-minute taxi ride from Reforma.

Boxing and Wrestling matches are held Saturday evenings in one of two or three arenas around town. Although Mexico is the cradle of many champions, attending the matches is not recommended. The crowds are not very refined; often more punches are thrown in the stands than in the ring.

HISTORIC SITES. Great Temple of the Aztecs, by the Zocalo, was discovered in 1978 and fully excavated four years later. Actually this is the base of twin temples to the gods of war and rain. Both structures were reduced to rubble during the Spanish siege in 1521. Cortes ordered an Iberian-style city built over the site. During their digging, archaeologists found countless sculptures and artifacts, many of which are to be seen here. Open from 10 A.M. to 1 P.M. except Mondays. Brochures explaining the site in detail are on sale, but it is more rewarding to go with a guide; there are no guides at the temple itself.

National Palace, on the Zocalo, is almost next door to the Great Temple. Originally it was constructed on Cortes' orders using Aztec rubble, and since rebuilt and modified considerably, the third story having been added in the early 1900s. This was the official residence of the Spanish viceroys and now houses the offices of the President of the Republic and the Finance Ministry. The murals over the principal stairway are by Diego Rivera. The bell above the central balcony is the one rung in Dolores, Guanajuato, by Father Miguel Hidalgo in 1810 when he launched the War on Independence. Open daily from 8 A.M. until 6 P.M.

Metropolitan Cathedral, on the Zocalo, was begun in 1573 and completed two centuries later. This is the largest church in Mexico. Within are 16 chapels and 21 altars, not to mention a crypt containing 3,000 tombs. It is best to come with a guide who can point out the subtleties in the baroque and *churrigueresque* decor. Open daily until 8 P.M.

National Pawn Shop on the Zocalo is the headquarters of a federal institution with many branches. This 18th-century palace was turned into a pawnshop by the Count of Regla as a bank for the poor. It continues to serve as just that and within many pawned items are for sale. Closed on weekends.

Historic Center of the City. Much of the area around the Zocalo has been restored to its colonial splendor. In many ways it is a vast outdoor museum of the viceregal era when Mexico City was known as the City of Palaces. Public buildings, churches, and aristocratic mansions have been refurbished. The entire area covers more than 600 blocks.

Legislative Palace, about ten blocks east of the Zocalo at Corregodora and Morazan, is the equivalent of the capitol in Washington, D.C. Dedicated in 1981, it is state of the art in the lawmaking industry, a marvel of electronic gagetry and a monument to the days when Mexico was flush with oil riches. Closed weekends.

Hospital de Jesus, about three blocks south of the Zocalo at Pino Suarez and El Salvador, was the first hospital in Mexico. Buried within its chapel, almost unnoticed, lie the remains of Hernan Cortes.

Iturbide Palace, Madero between Boliva and Gante, west of the Zocalo, is a 17th-century residence that served as the imperial mansion of the first ruler of independent Mexico, Augustin de Iturbide, who styled himself Emperor Augustin I and ended up, like the next emperor, before a firing squad. Today the palace is a bank.

House of Tiles at Madero and Lazaro Cardenas on the western edge of the old city, is the most lavish of the 18th-century palaces. This was the metropolitan seat of the counts of Orizaba; today it houses the original Sanborns, a chain of upscale American-style drug stores. The restaurant in the now-roofed patio retains much of the mansion's original grandeur.

Monument of the Revolution. Beyond the House of Tiles, Madero becomes Avenida Juarez, which runs west 15 blocks to this 200 foot high monolithic domed monument. Originally this was to have been the Capitol or Legislative Palace. Construction was begun in 1910 by Porfirio Diaz to mark the centennial of Mexican Independence; Diaz had ruled Mexico for some 30 years. It was in 1910 that the Diaz regime was toppled and construction on the project stopped. In the end what was to have been testimonial to a dictatorship ended up as a memorial to its downfall.

Chapultepec Castle is another monument to fallen dreams. It was begun in 1785, designed to be a viceregal retreat, but never completed. By 1810 Mexico had declared its independence and in the years the followed the castle became the National Military Academy. In 1847 it was one of the last Mexican strongholds during the American invasion; a monument to the defenders, the Boy Heros, stands below the castle. Maximilian, during his brief reign, made the castle his imperial palace. Later it served as the home of several presidents, many of whom came to a sorry end. In 1940 Los Pinos was built nearby as the official residence of the nation's chief executives and all have fared better. The castle is open daily except Tuesday 9 A.M. to 5 P.M. There is a small entrance fee.

Plaza of the Three Cultures, Lazaro Cardenas and Flores Magón near Reforma Norte. This is in Tlatelolco where the Aztecs fought their final battle against the Spanish. Here are to be seen the ruins of an Aztec ceremonial center and, towering above it the fortress-like 16th-century Church of Santiago. Soaring over both is the gleaming white headquarters of the Mexican Foreign Ministry. Thus three cultures—pre-Hispanic, colonial, and contemporary—are represented at the plaza.

Basilica of Guadalupe. Calzada Misterios near Insurgentes Norte toward the northern edge of the city. This is the holiest shrine in Mexico. Here in Aztec times stood the Temple of Tonantzin, mother of the gods. Shortly after the conquest, in 1531, the Virgin Mary is said to have appeared before a recently converted Indian, one Juan Diego, requesting that a chapel be built on the site. To convice the skeptical bishop, the Virgin instructed Juan Diego to pluck some roses from the site and bring them to the cleric. The Indian did so, carrying the flowers in his tunic; when he opened the garment he and the bishop discovered a portrait of Mary painted on the cloth. That miraculous tunic, framed in gold, hangs over the white marble altar in the new basilica, dedicated in 1976. The new ultramodern basilica is an architectural marvel, although not everybody likes it. The old basilica, built in the 18th century, had been damaged in several earthquakes and was considered structurally unsafe. The old basilica replaced the original chapel built at the Virgin's request.

Teotihuacan

About 30 miles north of Mexico City, Teotihuacan, famed for its pyramids, was, some 1,500 years ago, perhaps the largest city on earth and capital of an empire that extended from the Texas border to Guatemala. It was a remarkably well planned metropolis extending over eight square miles. Sometime in the 8th century it was abandoned, probably following either an invasion or internal rebellion. The Aztecs believed it had been built as the gathering place of the gods. The site is open daily from 9 A.M. until 5 P.M. There is a small admission fee. English-speaking guides are available.

Pyramid of the Sun, nearly 2,000 years old, is the grandest and one of the most ancient structures at the site. It is 210 feet high and has been considerably reconstructed. The pyramid stands over a cave which, archaeologists theorize, the Tetotihuacanos believed to have been the center of the universe.

Pyramid of the Moon. Dominating a plaza surrounded by what are taken to have been shrines, this is a somewhat newer and more sophisticated structure. Pyramids in Mexico were built as a base for temples and apparently elaborate ceremonies were carried out on the steps leading to the temples. The Moon Pyramid has not been as completely restored as its neighbor.

The Avenue of the Dead, leading south from the Pyramid of the Moon, is misnamed. What once were taken to be tombs lining the street later turned out to be temples and priestly homes. This was the main boulevard and probably the marketplace for a city of 200,000. The avenue leads to a complex of shrines known as the *Citadel* and on to the *Temple of Quetzacoatl* (the Plummed Serpent God).

Acolman, on the road to Teotihuacan, is one of the monasteries built in Mexico. Dating from the early 16th century, it was built by the Augustinians and rather resembles a medieval castle. What makes it quite special is the fact that in the mid-1700s the monastery was flooded, half-buried in mud and abandoned. Since restored, it is something of a fossil depicting exactly the artful surroundings enjoyed by the brothers some 200 years ago. Acolman is open from 10 A.M. to 6 P.M. except on Friday; there is a small entrance fee.

Pachuca

Casa de Caja, downtown, was built in 1670 to hold "the king's fifth," the 20% of all silver mined that was paid into the Royal Treasury. So productive were the mines of the region that the Counts of Regla sent great amounts of silver to Rome to help pay for the construction of the Vatican.

Casa Colorado, downtown, is the Red House that was built in the late 1600s as the seat of the Counts of Regla.

Tula

Although it is in Hidalgo State, of which Pachca is capital, Tula is most easily reached by Highway 57 which runs north from Mexico City to Queretaro. Here are to be found the ruins of what was the capital of the Toltec Empire. The once grand city was sacked and destroyed by raiding barbarian hordes in the 13th century and the site virtually unknown until archaeologists discovered it in 1938. Reconstructed since then is the Pyramid of Quetzacoatl topped with several 15-foot-high columns carved as warriors; these figures are some of the best known pre-Hispanic sculptures. The site attracts few visitors and has a feeling of eerie desolation. Open 8 A.M. until 6 P.M.; there is a small admission fee.

Cuernavaca

Palace of Cortes, on the Zocalo, is the city's most famous landmark. Construction of the building began in 1530 and while it no doubt has been modified over the centuries, the palace looks as old as it is. Once the seat of the Morelos state legislature, it now contains a museum. Especially worth seeing are the Diego Riviera murals within, commissioned by Dwight Morrow when he was U.S. Ambassador to Mexico. Open 10:30 A.M. to 6 P.M. daily except Sunday. Small admission charge.

Cathedral, Hidalgo and Morelos, was begun in 1525 and completed a quarter of a century later. The bell towers were built much later. Unlike most Mexican churches, the Cuernavaca Cathedral is almost starkly barren within. Once lavish, the building was frequently sacked during the rebellions and civil wars of the 19th century. Today the decor is stark and handsomely modern. One wall displays recently discovered murals depicting the martyrdom of 25 missionaries who sailed to Japan from what was then New Spain in the 16th century.

Teopanzolco Pyramid, at the end of Calle Rio Balsas near the railway station. An Aztec structure, this was a smaller version of the *Great Temple* in Mexico City. The remains of two shrines are to be seen at the top, one honoring the god of war, the other the god of rain. Open from 9 A.M. to 6 P.M. except Thursdays; small admission fee.

Xochicalo Ruins, about 30 miles southeast of the city, are fascinating, handsomely restored, and, for some reason, little visited. A city of perhaps 20,000, Xochicalco was inhabited from 200 B.C. to 1000 A.D. and may well have been the only center of civilization following the demise of Teotihuacan and the rise of the Toltec Empire and Tula. Baffling to archaeologists are the indications of a strong Maya influence so far from Yucatan and Central America. The site is open daily from 9 A.M. to 6 P.M.; small admission fee.

Taxco

Santa Prisca Church, on the Zocalo. A baroque classic, Santa Prisca was built at the behest of José de la Borda, a European adventurer who struck it rich in Taxco when he stumbled on a large vein of silver. In ordering the construction of the church he declared grandly, "God gives to Borda; Borda gives to God." Within are two of the finest paintings executed by Miguel Cabrera, one of the best Mexican artists of the colonial area.

Casa Figueroa, Guadalupe 2, is a colonial structure originally known as the House of Tears; a local official had it built using forced labor. It was restored to its former grandeur by an artist named Figueroa as a gallery to display his paintings. Open 10 A.M. to 1 P.M. and 3 to 7 P.M.; admission charge.

Casa Humboldt, Alarcon near Pineda, takes its name from the German traveler Alexander von Humboldt who sojourned there briefly in 1803. Moorish in design, this was once an inn used by those struggling between Acapulco and Mexico City. Today it contains a government run crafts shop. Open daily except Sunday during business hours.

Puebla

Cathedral. The most imposing structure in the city, the Cathedral, on the Zocalo, was completed in 1650 after 75 years of work. There are 14 chapels within. The high altar in onyx, marble, and gold, is the work of Manuel Tolsa, a master colonial architect.

Rosary Chapel, Church of Santo Domingo, Cinco de Mayo and Cuatro Poniente. Dazzling and splendid, a masterpiece in carved wood, gold leaf, marble and tile, the chapel was dedicated to the Virgin of the Rosary in 1690. Other religious art in Mexico pales in comparison.

Loreto and Guadalupe Forts, Avenida Ocho Norte on the outskirts of town, mark the spot where in 1862 Gen. Ignacio Zaragoza defeated a French expeditionary force. This was the only major victory ever won by Mexicans over a foreign army and the anniversary, May 5th *(Cinco de Mayo)* is still celebrated as a holiday.

Cholula Pyramid in Cholula, about five miles west of Puebla, is by sheer volume the largest pyramid in the world. Covering 45 acres, it resembles a grassy hill topped by a church. The Spaniards attempted to destroy this pagan structure, leaving only what they believed was earthen fill in its place. Actually a smaller pyramid—one still larger than the *Pyramid of the Moon* at Teotihuacan—lay buried within. In pre-Hispanic times new pyramids frequently were built over older ones. Visitors now can go through tunnels to the interior. Cholula was a great holy city in Aztec times. The Spaniards set about destroying its temples and replacing them with churches, giving rise to the story that the little town has a church for every day of the year. Actually, there are only 46 and most are in a sad state of disrepair. Near the pyramid itself is the *Patio of the Altars* with the remains of some fascinating paintings, including one picturing a drunken orgy that took place back in the second or third century. Open 10 A.M. to 5 P.M.; small admission charge.

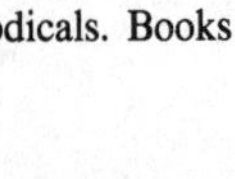

LIBRARIES. *The Benjamin Franklin Library* at Londres 16 (tel. 591–0244), near the Pink Zone and Reforma, is the closest thing in Mexico City to an American public library. Open Mondays through Fridays 10 A.M. to 6 P.M., it has an excellent reference section and a wide selection of current periodicals. Books are loaned only to residents. *The Anglo-Mexican Cultural*

Institute, Antonio Caso 127 (tel. 566–6739), a few blocks north of Reforma, is similar but with a British orientation. The *American Chamber of Commerce,* Lucerna 78 (tel. 566–0866)), a block south of Reforma, has a small library of publications of interest to business people. Open weekdays 9 A.M. to 1 P.M. and 3 to 5 P.M. *The National Library of Anthropology and History* at Reforma and Gandhi in Chapultepec Park (tel. 288–0700), usually has an exhibit relating to the country's past. Open weekdays 9 A.M. to 6 P.M. *The National Archives* at Eduardo Molina and Albañiles (tel. 789–5915) near the Zocalo is interesting both for its exhibits and the fact that it is housed in what was Mexico City's most notorious prison. Open weekdays 10 A.M. to 6 P.M.

Puebla's Palafox Library on Cinco Oriente behind the Cathedral, is a shrine for bibliophiles. Within are some 50,000 volumes dating from the colonial period as well as globes and maps from that era. The library is in a 17th-century palace and is open 9 A.M. to 3 P.M. weekdays and 10 A.M. to 1 P.M. weekends.

MUSEUMS. A visitor could go to one of Mexico City's museums every day for a month and not see all of them. The selection is enormous and there are more in the cities and towns surrounding the capital. In almost all cases admission charges, where they exist, are less than a dollar. Labels and explanations are, of course, in Spanish.

National Museum of Anthropology and History, on Reforma in Chapultepec Park, is perhaps the most outstanding institution of its kind in the world. Within is the Aztec Calendar Stone, unofficial symbol of the country, giant Olmec sculptured heads carved nearly 3,000 years ago in the steamy jungles of Veracruz' Gulf Coast, a replica of the painted temples of Bonampak (the original, in much worse condition, is in the wilds of Chiapas), along with treasures rescued from the Well of Sacrifice in Chichen Itza, Yucatan. The second floor contains ethnological displays depicting life as it is lived today in Mexico's more primitive villages. Multilingual guides are available. Open 10 A.M. to 7 P.M. except Mondays; entrance fee.

National Museum of History in Chapultepec Castle traces Mexico's past from the time of the conquest through the 1910 Revolution. Bringing the past to life are murals by José Climente Orozco, David Alfaro Siquieros, Juan O'Gorman and others. Especially interesting are the imperial apartments occupied by Maximilian and Carlota during their brief reign. The museum is open daily from 9 A.M. to 5 P.M.; entrance fee. Guides are available.

Gallery of Mexican History, near the Castle, contains a series of three-dimensional scenes out of the past including Father Hidalgo giving his Cry of Liberty and various battles. It is designed for school children, but worth a visit as it puts the country's history in focus. Admission is free.

Museum of Modern Art, on Reforma in the park, has a permanent exhibit of post-independence artists as well as temporary exhibits by both Mexican and foreign contemporaries. Entrance fee.

Rufino Tamayo Museum, Reforma and Gandhi in the park, is the newest in Mexico City. Built around a collection of works by Tamayo (considered the dean of Mexican modernists) and a permanent exhibition of 300 paintings from around the world, the institution usually also puts on the most exciting art shows in the capital. Open daily except Mondays 10 A.M. to 6 P.M.; entrance fee.

Museum of Fine Arts, Palace of Fine Arts by Alameda Park, Juarez and Lazaro Cardenas. The exhibition includes Diego Rivera's second version of his Rockefeller Center mural. The original was smashed because it contained a portrait of Lenin; in this one Rivera added Marx and Trotsky as well, along with an unflattering representation of old John D. There are usually some interesting temporary exhibits here as well. Open daily except Monday, 10:30 A.M. to 4:30 P.M.

National Art Museum, Tacuba 8, near Lazaro Cardenas and the Fine Arts Museum. Opened in 1983 in an elegant 19th-century ministry, this museum concentrates on works by Mexican artists from prehispanic times to the present. Previous visitors to the capital will recognize the equestrian piece outside as *El Caballito,* the Little Horse that stood for decades at the intersection of Juarez and Reforma. The horse carries Charles IV of Spain, but Mexicans studiously ignore His Majesty; indeed a plaque on the base explains the sculpture is shown not out of any love of royalty but because it is a work of art. A work of art it is, too, 30 tons of bronze that has been acclaimed as one of the finest equestrian works ever produced. It was sculpted by Manuel Tolsa in 1802. Open daily except Monday 10 A.M. to 6 P.M.; entrance fee.

Mexico City Museum, Pino Suarez at El Salvador (south of the Zocalo). Once the seat of the Counts of Santiago de Calimaya, this aristocratic mansion dates back to 1528, the walls built of rubble from Aztec palaces. It was considerably restored in the late 18th century. The exhibits within trace the history of Mexico City from pre-Hispanic times to the present. Open daily except Mondays 9 A.M. to 6 P.M. Free.

National Museum of Folk Art, Juarez 44, is one place where many of the exhibits are for sale. Shown are the best works by artisans from all over the country. Blown glass, copperware, pottery, and weavings are among the items fabricated the old-fashioned way that are on display. Open daily from 10 A.M. to 6 P.M. Free.

Polyforum, Insurgentes Sur and Filadelfia, stands by the towering, long unfinished Hotel de México. The area is surrounded by a violent, huge three-dimensional mural, "The March of Humanity," that was the final work by David Alfaro Siquieros. Within, there is an art gallery, theater, and dance hall as well as a display of fine handicrafts which may be purchased. Open daily 10 A.M. to 9 P.M. Free.

Carmelite Convent, Avenida Revolución in San Angel is a 17th-century nunnery with a notable collection of religious art from that era. Convents were numerous in colonial Mexico, serving as repositories for young ladies of breeding who could not come up with enough of a dowry to land a husband. Necrophiles will enjoy the crypt where the mummified remains of several priests and nuns are on display (the mummification was accidental and discovered only when tombs were opened during a construction project). Open daily except Mondays 10 A.M. to 5 P.M.; admission fee.

Museum of Intervention, Xicoténcatl and Viente de Agosto in Coyocan. Something of a Mexican original, this institution, housed in a former monastery, displays weapons, flags and other implements of war left behind by the various foreign armies that have invaded Mexico. The site is where the Battle of Churubusco was fought during the Mexican–American War in 1847. Open 9 A.M. to 9 P.M. daily; entrance fee.

Mexico City Wax Museum, Londres 6, near the Pink Zone. Many famous figures in Mexican and world history are brought nearly to life here. There are a few Hollywood types as well, along with a chamber of horrors. The museum is housed in a 19th-century Gothic mansion Charles Addams might have designed. Open daily 10 A.M. to 7 P.M. Entrance fee.

Cuernavaca

Cuauhnahuac Museum, Cortes Palace on the Zocalo. The building itself and its Rivera murals (see *Historical Sites*) are more interesting than the actual contents of the museum. The exhibits, which go from prehispanic times through the Revolution, seem to have been gathered from attics and cellars. Cuauhnahuac is the original Aztec name of Cuernavaca; Cuernavaca (which means 'cow horn') is the Spanish version of the word. Open weekdays 11 A.M. to 6 P.M., weekends 11:30 A.M. to 7 P.M.; small entrance fee.

Museum of Herbal and Traditional Medicine, Matamoros 200. Herbal medicine has been used in Mexico since prehispanic times and still is preferred by many country people. Herbalists are found selling their wares at most Mexican markets. The museum exhibits some 60 medicinal plants and explains their properties in a scientific manner. The house where it is located is fascinating, too. It was built in 1865, supposedly on orders of the Emperor Maximilian who installed here his mistress, the Cuernavaca native known to history as La India Bonita. The museum is open daily from 10 A.M. to 6 P.M. Free.

Taxco

Sprating Museum, behind the Santa Prisca Church and one block from the Zocalo. William Spratling arrived in Taxco from New Orleans, settled down there to become the town's first silversmith. He gave birth to what is now the community's leading industry. Much of his life was spent collecting prehispanic artifacts and these are displayed in the museum, as are models of colonial mines and how they were worked. Open daily 10 A.M. to 5 P.M.; small entrance fee.

Puebla

Secret Convent, Avenida Diezyocho Poniente 203, is a museum depicting either devotion or fanaticism, depending how you and your guide see things. The Reform Laws of 1857 outlawed convents and monasteries. In pious Puebla many of the religious went underground until, during a fresh wave of persecution, three secret convents were discovered in Puebla alone (the government today is more tolerant of these institutions). The Santa Monica Convent has been opened as a museum. The entrance originally was hidden behind a cabinet and the sisters attended mass while hiding behind grillwork in the wall. On view are the cells in which they lived and the basement crypts in which many were buried. Open daily 10 A.M. to 4 P.M.; Saturdays 10 A.M. to 2 P.M. Small admission fee. English-speaking guides on the premises.

Santa Rosa Convent, Tres Norte and Catorce Poniente. Said to be where *móle poblano* was invented, this is a shrine to Mexican cuisine. The convent itself no longer is a religious institution, but the kitchen has been preserved. The tiles, clay pots and stone stoves should fascinate gastrophiles. *Molé,* a spicy sauce with a chocolate base, is Mexico's national dish. The convent is open daily from 10 A.M. to 5 P.M. and there is a shop next door. Free.

Alfeñique, Cuatro Oriente and Seis Norte. This is the state museum, but its interest lies primarily in the architecture of the building; *Alfeñique* translates roughly as "gingerbread," for as one observer had it, the structure seemed more the creation of a baker than an architect. The upper floors are maintained as they were when this was the home of local grandees. Open daily except Mondays 10 A.M. to 5 P.M.; small admission charge.

Bello Museum, Tres Poniente and Tres Sur. A motley collection of wonderful colonial paintings, tile artesanry (a Puebla specialty), colonial furniture plus iron locks and iron keys. Open daily 11 A.M. to 5 P.M. Free.

Pachuca

National Photographic Archives, Former Monastery of San Francisco, Calle Convento. The finest collection of photographic Mexicaniana is to be found here in the care of the National Institute of Anthropology and History. Pachuca was selected because its cool climate will not contribute to the deterioration of the photos. The old monastery itself is interesting. Built in the 1600s, two centuries later it was seized by the military and converted into a stable, then a slaughterhouse, and finally a prison. Open weekdays 10 A.M. to 2 P.M. Free.

Tepotzotlan

Museum of the Viceregal Era, lies about 35 miles north of Mexico City just off Highway 57. A Jesuit church and monastery really comprise a small village founded around 1600. The former church is a masterwork in elaborate *churrigueresque.* The finest works of art done in the colonial period were created for the church and many of these treasures are to be seen at Tepotzotlan. Open daily except Mondays 11 A.M. to 6 P.M.; small admission charge.

ART GALLERIES. The streets of Mexico City's Pink Zone are almost lined with galleries where works of art are for sale. *Estela Shapirio* at Varsovia 23; *Galeria Circulo,* Hamburgo 112; *Solaris,* Estrasburgo 19; *Tere Haas,* Genova 2; *Pecanis,* Hamburgo 103 and *Galeria de Arte* Mexicano, Milan 18, are among the most outstanding establishments. Also quite good are the art galleries in the hotels *Maria Isabel-Sheraton, Camino Real* and *El Presidente Chapultepec.* On Sunday at midday the *Art Garden* in Sullivan Park just north of Reforma displays work by budding hopefuls.

Cuernavaca's art shops are all one might expect at a weekend retreat for the wealthy. Best are *Galeria Akari* at Jardines de Tlaltenango 49, and *Van Gelder's* at Galeana 102. In Taxco there is a gallery run by the Fine Arts Institute on the premises of the *Montetaxco Hotel.* Puebla has its *Barrio de Artistas* or Artists' Quarter with outdoor exhibitions around the corner of Cuatro Oriente and Ocho Norte.

STAGE. English-language theater understandably is limited in a Spanish-speaking country. An amateur group, *Theater Workshop,* puts on half a dozen programs throughout the year and they are quite good. Performances are weekends only at the Vasco de Quiroga Hotel, Londres 15 (tel. 546–2514).

Vaudeville is alive and thriving in Mexico City and language is not much of a barrier to enjoying it. The *Teatro Blanquita* at Lazaro Cardenas 16 (tel. 510–0751), a block or so east of Juarez, puts on two shows a day at 7 and 10 P.M. Mondays through Saturday with an extra 4 P.M. show on Sundays. Best seats in the house cost less than $5.

Visitors with a grasp of Spanish will find a wide choice of theatrical entertainment available, including translations of recent Broadway hits. Prices are quite low. Mexico City has no theater district as such; many of the best playhouses are a 15- to 30-minute taxi ride from most hotels.

Among Mexico City's top theaters are the *San Rafael* at Viginia Fabregas 40 (tel. 592–2954); *Manolo Fabregas* at Serapio Rendon 15 (tel. 556–1644); *Insurgentes,* at Insurgentes Sur 1537 (tel. 524–7871); *Julio Prieto,* Nicolas San

Juan at Xola (tel. 543–3478); *Polyforum Siquieros,* Insurgentes Sur at Filadelfia (tel. 536–4521) and *Hidalgo,* Avenida Hidalgo 23 (tel. 512–0810).

MUSIC. The Palace of Fine Arts with its main auditorium and its Manuel Ponce concert hall is the center of classical musical activity in Mexico City. The Palace is at Juarez and Lazaro Cardenas (tel. 512–3333). Here the National Opera's seasons run from January through March and August through October. The *National Symphony Orchestra* has a spring and autumn season at the Palace.

The *Mexico City Philharmonic* presents several concerts throughout the year at the Ollin Yoliztli concert hall, Periferico Sur 1541 (tel. 573–3366). The *State of Mexico Symphony* gives performances at Nezahualcoyotl Hall in University City. Seasons vary from year to year.

The **Teatro de la Ciudad** at Donceles 36 (tel. 510–2197) downtown is the venue for a number of musical programs, both classical and popular, throughout the year.

The **Sala Chopin** at Alvaro Obregon (tel. 556–7411) presents a number of free musical entertainments evenings throughout the week.

Sundays at 1 P.M. there generally is a free concert at Chapultepec Castle.

In addition, on any given evening there are likely to be several musical events taking place in the city, and on Sundays there are several free presentations around town.

DANCE. The *Ballet Folklorico* performs at 9:30 A.M. and 9 P.M. on Sundays and at 6 and 9 P.M. on Wednesdays at the Palace of Fine Arts. The ballet, which has toured the world, is a stylized presentation of Mexican regional folkdances and is one of the most spectacular shows to be seen in Mexico. Hotels and travel agencies can arrange tickets.

The *National Dance Theater,* part of the National Auditorium complex in Chapultepec Park, and the Dance Center, Campos Eliseos 480 (tel. 520–2271) frequently put on dance programs. Other performances are listed in *The News.*

SHOPPING. One comes to Mexico City to see the sights, but one can very easily end up seeing mostly stores. Temptations are found at every turn, especially in the capital. The best the country has to offer is to be found here at ragged markets and glittering malls, in swank boutiques and peddled on the streets. There are more than a few tips to remember, however. The first is that "let the buyer beware" is the prevailing philosophy; selling plate and claiming it is sterling is considered shrewd business. Only the largest, most reputable establishments stand behind their products. Then, too, anything imported is likely to carry a staggeringly high price tag; duties in Mexico are hefty. Hotel shops as a rule charge more than their neighbors; they have to if they are to pay the rent. Tour guides almost always get a commission on anything their clients buy, hence they steer their people to whoever pays them the most. The Pink Zone is where most of the shops appealing to tourists are located, with many more along the Reforma-Juarez-Madero route running down to the Zocalo. The streets around the Zocalo downtown are a maze of little shops many visitors delight in discovering. San Angel, in the southern part of the city, is a colonial neighborhood with quite a sprinkling of elegant shops and boutiques. Polanco, just north of Chapultepec Park, is Mexico City's Upper East Side (northwest side in this case), address of many of the finest department stores and

Mexican National Tourist Council

Architectural wonders can be found in Mexico's gleaming towers, rotundas, and plaza fountains.

Mexican National Tourist Council

From a dazzling La Paz sunset to a hotel's flower-decked swimming pool, Mexican sights are always awe-inspiring.

Mexican National Tourist Council

Guanajuato is the most Iberian city in North America, as these scenes attest.

Mexican National Tourist Council

Mexican National Tourist Council

Among the attractions in the capital's National Museum of Anthropology is this forked-tongued diety.

specialty shops. In the capital stores are open from 10 A.M. to 6 P.M. weekdays and until 8 P.M. on Saturdays. In the surrounding cities most shops close for lunch from 2 to 4 (sometimes from 1 to 5) and stay open later in the evening. Bargaining is an accepted practice almost everywhere but in department stores and supermarkets. Those who do not want to be blatant about it can ask what discount is available if they pay in cash or what exchange rate will be given for their dollars. In the markets haggling is expected, sellers often quoting twice the price they expect to get.

Handicrafts

Londres Market, Londres near Florencia, in the Pink Zone, is a typical neighborhood public market with one big difference. Many of the stalls sell a wide selection of crafts ranging from serapes and ponchos to baskets and pottery.

Centro Artesanal, San Juan Market, Ayuntamiento at Miranda, downtown. San Juan is a major wholesale produce market, its *Centro Artesanal* being a distribution center for baskets, leather goods, woolens, *piñatas* and the like. One can buy here retail as well, although the prices, even after dickering, are not especially low.

Ciudadela Market, Balderas at Plaza Ciudadela, about five blocks west of Juarez, specializes in handicrafts ranging from pottery and copperware to guitars. Prices are attractive as it is not too well known.

Fonart, Juarez 89. Other stores at Juarez 70 and Juarez 92 and Londres 136 in the Pink Zone. Run by the government agency charged with fomenting handicrafts, this chain of shops offers quality products at fixed prices.

Sanborns, Madero 4. Other stores at Reforma and Lafragua, by the Maria Isabel Sheraton and on Reforma across from the Chapultepec cinema, to mention but a few. The shop on Madero is the original, in the famed House of Tiles, and has a large, attractively priced selection of handicrafts.

Buenavista, Aldama at Degollado (take a taxi), is a virtual handicrafts warehouse, with a huge selection at wholesale prices. Open Sundays until 3.

Bazar Sabado, Plaza San Jacinto 11, San Angel, is open Saturdays only and worth staying over to visit. Only the highest calibre artisans are permitted to rent stalls here and almost everything imaginable in the line of crafts is available.

Casart, Juarez 18, is run by an agency in the neighboring State of Mexico and features crafts from that state including heavy woolen sweaters and rugs knotted (not woven) in the Oriental manner.

Janus, Niza 20 in the Pink Zone, specializes in hand-loomed and hand-embroidered textiles along with paintings and sculptures.

Muller's, Londres at Florencia, Pink Zone. Onyx in all its glory is found here, from bookends and chessboards to tabletops. The store will handle shipping.

Silver and Jewelry

Los Castillo, Amberes 41 in the Pink Zone and Palmas 50, San Angel. Taxco silver at its best, much of it forged with copper and gold. An excellent place to buy special gifts.

Joyas de Plata, Copenhague 31, Pink Zone, also Taxco silver of exceptional style. Here the emphasis is on jewelry, fine stones set in silver. Many of the designs are inspired by pre-Hispanic art.

Paul Flato, Amberes 21, Pink Zone, features fine golden jewelry designed by the owner. Fancy stuff at fancy prices.

Tane, Amberes 70, Pink Zone. Jewelry and flatware in silver by a Taxco firm that now has shops in Houston and Palm Beach.

Mexican Opal Company, Hamburgo 203, is run by Japanese, who are very big on opals. Set and unset stones are available as well as a selection of jewelry in silver and gold.

Kimberly, Niza and Hamburgo, Pink Zone, is one of Mexico City's oldest and most respected jewelry shops.

Clothing

Girasol, Genova 39, Pink Zone, specializes in originally designed resortwear fashioned from hand-embroidered and hand-loomed cloth.

Aca Joe, Amberes 9, Pink Zone, began in Acapulco and now is everywhere. Sports clothes here are unisex, very mod and lots of fun.

Ruben Torres, Amberes 9, Pink Zone, has more sportswear from jerseys and jump suits to T shirts and shorts, all nicely designed and well made.

Ralph Lauren, Amberes 21, in the Pink Zone, is the home of Polo sports wear made in Mexico under license at Mexican prices.

Paris Londres, Horacio 250, Polanco, bills itself as the Grand Boutique and is really a department store of fine feminine fashions.

Palacio de Hierro, Durango 230 (south of the Pink Zone) is the capital's most elegant department store. It specializes in labels signed by internationally known designers at Mexican prices.

Piña Colada, Leibnitz 11, across from the Hotel Camino Real, specializes in originally designed sports clothes for the family.

Leather

Aries, Florencia 14, Pink Zone, and Palmas 50, San Angel. An excellent assortment of shoes, bags, billfolds, belts, skirts jackets, and suits, all attractively fashioned. Many gift items as well. Prices are high.

Gucci, Hamburgo 136, Pink Zone. The name is a rip-off but the quality is excellent. Shoes, boots, luggage, and other attractive items made to demanding standards.

Ginatai, located at Niza 46 and at Londres 91, both in Pink Zone, specializes in boots and features custom made leather garments for both men and women as well as accessories

Castalia, Insurgentes Sur 318 (south of the Pink Zone) is a good place to find brief cases and hand bags at moderate prices.

Antil, Florencia 22, has a nice selection of leather clothing and accessories.

Or, Londres 157, in the Pink Zone, features suede and leather items for men and women.

Furnishings and Antiques

Lagunilla Market, Ecuador between Allende and Chile downtown, on Sundays is one vast garage sale. Not all the used tables and chairs are so old to be valuable, but many are.

Arte y Fauna, Copenhague 30, Pink Zone, is the local zoo housing fantastic animal sculptures by Sergio Bustamante. Worth a visit if only just to look.

La Granja, Bolivar 16, downtown, is Mexico's largest antique shop. To buy well one needs a discriminating eye and bargaining skills.

El Pabellon, Amberes 52, Pink Zone, is a small store filled with unusual furnishings and bric-a-brac.

Colonialart, Estocolmo 37, Pink Zone, is virtually a museum of antique furnishings and works of art. No bargains here.

Tamacani, Amberes 38, Pink Zone, is big with wall hangings and upholstry textiles. The looming is done by hand.

Artesanos de México, Amberes 61, Pink Zone, is a good place to buy traditional Mexican colonial furniture which can be made to order. They also have items in wrought iron and will arrange to ship.

Cuernavaca

The main shopping street is Avenida Guerrero, which runs off the main plaza. Along this avenue are to be found **Martha Bazar** with a nice selection of women's wear; **Artesanias Mexicanas** and **La China Poblana,** specializing in handicrafts, and **Casa Beltran,** a good place to shop for leather. Guerrero leads into the Cuernavaca market, one of the largest in Mexico. **Tianguis,** by the plaza, is a good place to find textiles and lacquered objects. **Ceramica Santa Maria** on Avenida Zapata, has several attractive lines of dishes and dinnerware. Modernistic religious art, some of it silver on wood and made by **Emaus,** is on sale at the Cuernavaca Cathedral. Best bargains in gifts are to be found at **Harry's Boutique** in the state penitentiary.

Taxco

This town of silversmiths is in reality a community of shopkeepers. Most are clustered around the Zocalo or the streets running into it, although a few good places are on Avenida Kennedy, which is what the main highway is called as it passes through town. **Los Castillo** and **Antonio Pineda** generally are recognized as having the best silver shops. **Emma** is quite good but not so expensive. All are around the Zocalo. **La Mina,** on Avenida Kennedy by the gas station, is a silver shop in an old silver mine and is fascinating. The **Spratling Workshop** south of town continues to turn out Spratling silver using the master's designs and molds. Handicrafts of all kinds are found at the **Casa Humboldt** by the plaza. Sunday is market day right on the plaza and this is a good time to hunt for huarache sandals, baskets of all kinds, leather goods, pottery, and wood carvings.

Puebla

Tile and other ceramics are Puebla's most famous products. The white and blue dinnerware used in good Mexican restaurants likely came from Puebla, as did the tile covering the domes of so many churches around the country. **La Purisma,** Cuatro Poniente 723; **Uriarte,** Cuatro Poniente 900, and **La Trinidad,** Viente Poniente 305, all are tile and ceramic factories that will arrange for shipping. **Talavera de Puebla,** in the centrally located Parian Market, is another good place to shop for tile. Onyx is another Puebla specialty and is sold is many shops. **El Parian** on the corner of Cuatro Oriente and Seis Norte is a good place to find low priced bowls, ashtrays and chess sets made of onyx. **Creart,** at Calle 16 de Septiembre 506, features an excellent assortment of handicrafts. Antiques also are plentiful in ancient Puebla. **Los Sapos** on Siete Oriente 401, and **Bazar del Sapo** on Plaza de los Sapos (a *sapo* is a toad) between Cinco Oriente and Siete Oriente, are good places to begin a treasure hunt.

RESTAURANTS. As befits the world's biggest metropolis, Mexico City offers a wide selection of restaurants, many of them outstanding. Hours are a bit later than in Anglo-Saxon lands and even in fast food joints service is never rushed. One can settle in for luncheon at a fine restaurant at 1 P.M. although it will be rather lonely until 2 and not crowded until 3. Stop in for dinner at 7 and some of the luncheon crowd may well be lingering over brandy (almost nowhere is the check presented until it is asked for). The fashionable hour for dinner is 9. There are American-style coffee shops (**Denny's, Vips, Toks** and others) all over the city and many of these never close. The Pink Zone has the greatest collection of restaurants. Insurgentes Sur, however, qualifies as Mexico City's restaurant row. San Angel in the southern part of the city, is noted for some outstanding places to eat as is Polanco, the fashionable neighborhood just north of Chapultepec Park. Reservations are a good idea in *Deluxe* and *Expensive* establishments. Jackets are required in these places and ties appreciated. Expect to pay $25 for a meal in a *Deluxe* restaurant, $20 in an *Expensive* place, $15 in a *Moderate* restaurant, and $10 or less in an *Inexpensive* cafe. Some of the capital's finest restaurants are open for breakfast and this offers a good way to try them while on a budget. Visa (V) and MasterCard (MC) are almost universally accepted, followed by American Express (AE), and Diners Club (D).

Mexican

Mexican food is much more than tacos and tortas, just as American food is more than hamburgers and hot dogs. Nor is Mexican food always hot and spicy. The country that gave the world vanilla, chocolate, turkey, tomato, and avocado has an extensive cuisine that will delight the most demanding gourmet.

Deluxe

San Angel Inn, Palmas 50, San Angel; 548–6746. Gracious living from the past is found at this restored mansion, a Mexico City landmark. The menu lists many international dishes, but the specialties include tortilla soup and pampano baked in maguey leaves. Open daily. V, MC, AE, D.

Hacienda de los Morales, Vasquez de Mella 525, Polanco; 540–3225. The manor house of a 17th-century hacienda, this is one of the capital's most elegant dining spots. International as well as Mexican dishes are served. Closed Sundays. V, MC, AE, D.

Expensive

Hacienda de Tlalpan, Calzada de Tlalpan 4619 on the southern edge of the city; 573–9959. A wonderful place for a garden lunch or a romantic dinner (violins at night). International as well as Mexican fare. Open daily. V, MC, AE.

La Cava, Insurgentes Sur 2465, San Angel; 548–8276. An attractive, elegant establishment featuring such dishes as stuffed chiles and roast duck in wine sauce. Very fashionable. Open daily. V, MC, AE, D.

Nicolasa, Insurgentes Sur 1874; 524–1624. Mexican creole cooking served in an elegant 19th-century townhouse. The kitchen is highly regarded. Open daily for luncheon and dinner, for breakfast and luncheon on Sundays. V, MC, AE, D.

Fonda del Refugio, Liverpool 166, Pink Zone; 528–5823. Modest in appearance, gourmets regard this spot as a shrine to Mexican cooking. Closed Sundays. V, MC, AE, D.

Moderate

Meson de Caballo Bayo, Conscripto 360, near the racetrack; 589–3000. A huge ranch-style Mexican restaurant right out of the movies with strolling trios and mariachi bands. Lunches here have a way of going on until midnight. Open daily. V, MC, AE.

Fonda del Recuerdo, Bahia Las Palmas 39, north of Polanco; 545–1652. A large Veracruz-style seafood house where there always is a party going on. The musicians, too, are from Veracruz. Open daily. V, MC, AE, D.

Las Mercedes, Darwin 113 (near the Camino Real); 525–2099. Classic Mexican cuisine prepared to please gourmets.

Inexpensive

Beatriz, Varsovia 24, Pink Zone; 511–6054. Plain and simple, but with a reputation for serving the best tacos and tortas in town. A favorite with executives grabbing a quick snack. Open daily.

Cafe Tacuba, Tacuba 28, downtown; 518–4950. Open for breakfast, this is a marvelous spot to start the day or to drop in later for coffee and sweet rolls. Nice, too, for a light supper of hot chocolate and tamales. Open daily.

Las Casuelas, Colombia 69, downtown; 522–0689. Very Mexican, featuring all kinds of stews (which can be peppery) this is a good place for lunch when strolling through the old part of town. Open daily.

Circulo Sureste, Lucerna 12, a few blocks from Juarez and Reforma; 525–2704. Unimpressive, but regarded as the capital's best Yucatan-style restaurant. Open daily.

Spanish

There is surprisingly little similarity between the rather heavy cuisine of Spain and Mexico's lighter, more seasoned dishes. Mexicans, however, have a great fondness for Spanish food.

Deluxe

El Parador de José Luis, Niza 17, Pink Zone; 533–1840. The best and usually crowded with executives at lunch time, but quiet and romantic for dinner. Nice is ordering while enjoying a glass of sherry and a bit of Spanish torta in the bar. Closed Sundays. V, MC, AE, D.

Expensive

Meson del Cid, Humboldt 61, a few steps off Juarez; 512–7629. The decor is right out of Iberria and the medieval dinners Saturday evenings spectacular. Roast baby pig is a specialty. Closed Sundays. V, MC, AE, D.

Prendes, Calle 16 de Septiembre 10, downtown; 585–4199. A big barn of a place, Prendes has been packing in the crowds for nearly a century. Leon Trotsky had his last supper here. Hectic for lunch, relaxed for dinner. Open daily. V, MC, AE, D.

Moderate

Lincoln Grill, Revillagigedo 24, a few blocks from Juarez; 510–1468. The name comes from the old Lincoln Hotel, but the restaurant is authentically Spanish. An old standby, it shows its years, but the food is excellent. Breakfast served. Open daily. V, MC, AE, D.

Meson del Perro Andaluz, Copenhague 26, Pink Zone; 533–5306. A sidewalk cafe on a pedestrian mall, this *meson* attracts customers more for its setting than its food. *Moderate.* V, MC, AE, D.

Hosteria del Rey, Copenhague 2, Pink Zone; 514–6715. Also a sidewalk cafe but with an attractive interior designed along the lines of a 16th-century Spanish inn. Excellent kitchen. Open daily. V, MC, AE.

Tasca Española, Londres 101, Pink Zone; 511–3303. A Madrid tavern in Mexico with music and flamenco dancing Friday nights (when reservations are suggested). Open daily; lunch only on Sundays. *Moderate.* V, MC, AE, D.

Meson del Castellano, Bolivar 51, downtown; 510–8821. A good place to order *caldo gallego* and *fabada* in an authentic Spanish setting. Open daily. V, MC, D, CB.

El Vasco, Diezyseis de Septiembre 51, downtown; 513–0938. One flight up and a favorite with Basques who crowd in for lunch. Open daily. V, MC.

Argentine

South American steak houses are favorites throughout Mexico. Baby beef and churrasco is grilled right at the table.

Expensive

Rincón Gaucho, Copilco 3, just off Insurgentes Sur in the San Angel area; 548–3065. Run by an Argentine movie star who hit the big time in Mexico. Evening entertainment. Open daily. V, MC, AE, D.

Corrientes 3–4–8, Miguel Angel de Quevedo 401, toward San Angel; tel 554–8703. A good place for a late lunch or dinner with shows from 3 to 5 P.M. and midnight until 3 A.M. Big on atmosphere. Entertainment afternoons and evenings. Closed Sundays. V, MC, AE, D.

Moderate

El Fogón, Leibnitz at Darwin, Polanco area; 511–0814. Charming, with terrace dining a lunchtime, romantic indoor nooks evenings. Open daily. V, MC, AE.

La Mansion, Insurgentes Sur 778; 520–0202. Mexico City's original Argentine steak house remains a favorite. Indoor and outdoor dining. Open daily. MC, AE, D.

La Troje, Insurgentes Sur 1217; 598–4739. Argentine fare served country style. Piano music in the evenings. Open daily. V, MC, AE, D.

British

The hearty fare and clubby ambience of Great Britain's drinking and dining establishments are much prized and much imitated in Mexico City.

Deluxe

Sir Winston Churchill, Avila Camacho 67 (Periferico), Polanco; 520–0065. A rare Tudor mansion, wainscoted and regal within. Roast beef and meat pies are better than in the Old Country. Closed Sundays. V, MC, AE, D.

Expensive

Piccadilly Pub, Copenhague 23, Pink Zone; 514–1515. Both a sidewalk cafe and indoor restaurant, a big of England as it should be. Lager is served by the yard. Closed Sundays. V, MC, AE, D.

Sir Mark, Ameyalco 10, just off Insurgentes Sur; 687–1373. Descended from a restaurant founded by Sir Mark Hylesford, this is a British-run establishment, Victorian and elegant in decor. The lamb is excellent. Closed Sundays. V, MC, AE, D.

Calesa de Londres, Londres 102; Pink Zone; 533–6625. Classic, in a turn-of-the-century town house, with an English bar and English chops and roasts. Open daily. V, MC, AE, D.

Lancers, Insurgentes Sur 2018; 548–8736. Scots rather than English is this attractive establishment (the best British beef is from Scotland). Open daily. V, MC, AE, D.

Cochera del Bentley, Insurgentes Sur 1650; 534–8474. Open for breakfast, when it is especially nice. Organ music evening. Open daily. V, MC, AE.

King's Pub, Arquimedes 31, Polanco; 254–2655. An American-style English pub run by a former Mexican ad man. Most convivial. Piano music in the evening. Mexican buffet Sundays. Open daily. V, MC, AE, D.

French

Deluxe

Fouquet's, Hotel Camino Real, Mariano Escobedo 700, Polanco area; 545–6960. The only branch of the famed Parisienne restaurant, and in many ways the best restaurant in Mexico City. Romantic dance music at night. Closed Sundays. V, MC, AE, D.

Maxim's, Hotel El Presidente Chapultepec, Campos Eliseos 218, Polanco; 254–0033. A licensed replica of the Paris original with an outstanding menu to match the decor. Closed Sundays. V, MC, AE, D.

Del Lago, Chapultepec Park; 515–9585. Considered by many the most beautiful restaurant in the capital. Excellent kitchen. Quiet dance music in the evening. Closed Sundays. V, MC, AE, D.

Expensive

Rivoli, Hamburgo 123, Pink Zone; 525–6862. Established in 1953 by Dario Borzani and now managed by his son, the Rivoli is a gourmet landmark. Closed Sundays. V, MC, AE, D.

Ambassadeurs, Reforma 12; 566–9400. A gathering place for the elite of Mexico City for more than 40 years. These days it is a favorite of newspaper executives. Open daily (evenings only on weekends). V, MC, AE, D.

Champs Elysees, Reforma and Amberes, Pink Zone; 514–0450. Where real men eat quiche. Extremely fashionable and usually crowded (less so at night). Closed weekends. V, MC, AE, D.

Passy, Amberes 10, Pink Zone; 511–0257. Another fashionable meeting place, the main dining room overlooking an enclosed terrace. More relaxed at night. Closed Sundays. V, MC, D.

Villa Lorraine, Insurgentes Sur 1759; 524–5949. The elegant former home of the Papal Nuncio, noted for its desserts. Open for breakfast daily. V, MC, AE.

Moderate

Estoril, Genova 75, Pink Zone; 511–3421. The management is French, the ambience exclusive and sophisticated. Crowded at lunch. Closed Sundays. V, MC, AE, D.

Toulouse-Lautrec, Genova 74 (arcade), Pink Zone; 533–4786. An informal bistro with an especially appealing bar. Relaxed, pleasant service. Open daily. V, MC, AE, D, CB.

La Casserole, Insurgentes Sur 1880; 524–7190. Provencal country dining. A good place for snails. Open daily; lunch only on Sundays. V, MC, AE, D.

Italian

Expensive

La Pergola, Genova and Londres, Pink Zone; 511–3049. Nicely appointed, a favorite for business lunches. Romantic at night. Closed Sundays. V, MC, AE, D.

La Scala, Periferico Sur and Insurgentes Sur on the southern edge of the city; 573–6974. A show place with live music for dancing in the evenings. Closed Sundays. V, MC, AE, D.

Mediterráneo, Palmas 210, Polanco area; 520–8244. Dishes from many Mediterranean countries are served here, but Italian cuisine is the specialty. Nice for breakfast. Open daily. V, MC, AE, D.

Moderate

La Gondola, Genova 21, Pink Zone; 511–6908. One of Mexico City's first Italian restaurants. Attractive decor and excellent pasta. Closed Sundays. V, MC, AE, D.

Alfredo, Genova 74 (arcade), Pink Zone; 511–3864. Alfredo Conti, a Sicilian, is the owner and chief cook and host. His place is very popular. Open daily. V, MC, AE, D.

Cardini, Insurgentes Sur 523; 564–5446. Founded in 1952 by Gaudencio Cardini, who claimed to have created the Caesar Salad; still a popular hideaway. Open daily. V, MC, AE, D.

European

Deluxe

Mazurka, Nueva York 150 near Insurgentes Sur; 523–8811. One of the finest Polish restaurants anywhere and worth a special trip. A chamber music quartet plays at night. Open daily. V, MC, AE, D.

Expensive

Paprika, Chipancingo 16, near Insurgentes Sur; 574–2856. The capital's only Hungarian restaurant, and a good one. Closed Sundays. V, MC, AE, D.

Piccolo Suizo, Mariano Escobedo 539, Polanco area; 531–1298. Swiss owned, featuring a number of international dishes; boullabaisse on Fridays. Open daily (lunch only on Sundays). V, MC, AE.

Bellinghausen, Londres 96, Pink Zone; 511–1096. A big, masculine German restaurant with a beer garden in back. Jammed at lunch. Open daily. V, MC, AE.

Moderate

Chalet Suizo, Niza 37, Pink Zone; 511–7529. The specialty at this long-time favorite is cheese fondue. Open daily. V, MC, AE, D.

Sep's, Insurgentes and Paris, a few blocks north of Reforma; 511–0012. Alsatian cooking, beginning with rich pates and sauerkraut, is featured. Open daily. V, MC, AE, D.

Konditori, Genova 61, Pink Zone; 511–1589. Indoor-outdoor snacking at a Danish-style cafe. Good breakfasts and light lunches. Open daily. V, MC.

American

Deluxe

Delmonico's, Londres 87; Pink Zone. A show place established by Nick Noyes in 1954. Roast beef, excellent steaks and seafood. Wonderful breakfasts. Open daily. V, MC, AE, D.

Villa Reforma, Reforma 2210, west of the park; 596–0123. In an elegant residential neighborhood. Attractive glass covered terrace. Sumptuous breakfasts. Open daily. V, MC, AE, D.

Les Moustaches, Rio Sena 88, near Reforma and Pink Zone; 533–3390. New Orleans creole cuisine in a lovely but snobbish setting. Closed Sundays. V, MC, AE, D.

Expensive

Carlos Anderson's, Reforma at Oxford; 511–5187. Flagship of the country's best and largest restaurant organization. Zany, friendly, but with good food. Open daily. V, MC, AE, D.

Moderate

Shirley's, Londres 102, Pink Zone; 584–7111. Hamburgers, french fries, malts, and banana splits for the homesick. Open daily.

Oriental

Deluxe

Mauna Loa, San Jeronimo 240 in the south of the city; 548–6884. A Polynesian delight with Cantonese and Mandarin dishes. Hula dancers entertain at night. Open daily. V, MC, AE, D.

Suntory, Torres Adalide 14, just off Insurgentes Sur; 536–7754. One of the seven Suntory restaurants in the world, serving traditional Japanese dishes with flair and elegance. Closed Sundays. V, MC, AE, D.

Moderate

Luau, Niza 38, Pink Zone; 533–6058. A longtime favorite with lovers of Cantonese food. Open daily. V, MC, AE.

Mikado, Reforma at Guadalquivir, an authentic Japanese cafe just a block or so from the Japanese Embassy. Closed Sundays. V, MC.

Inexpensive

Yi-Yen, Hamburgo 140, Pink Zone; 528–6966. A pleasant, unassuming Cantonese restaurant. Closed Sundays. V, MC.

CUERNAVACA

Deluxe

Las Mañanitas, Ricardo Linares 107; 12–4646. A splendid garden is the setting for one of the country's top restaurants. The international menu includes Mexican specialties. Open daily.

Expensive

Chateau Rene, Atzingo 11; 13–1201. Country dining in the European manner. One of the best. Open daily. V, MC.

Sumiya, in Juitepec; 15–3055. The Japanese palace built for Barbara Hutton is a magnificent place to see. The food is international, with a few Oriental items on the menu. Open daily. MC, V, AE, D.

Moderate

Harry's Grill, Gutenberg 3; 12–7679. A happy-go-lucky Carlos Anderson place on the main plaza. Closed Mondays. V, MC, AE, D.

La India Bonita, Morrow 6; 12–1266. Modest, but easily the best place in town for Mexican food.

Xochiquetzal, Leiva 200; 12–0220. A 16th-century hacienda, now an American-owned inn specializing in Mexican dishes. Open daily. V, MC, AE.

TAXCO

Expensive

Ventana de Taxco, Highway 95 south of town; 2–1300. Spectacular view (the name means "Window on Taxco") and fine North Italy cuisine. Open daily. V, MC, AE, D.

Moderate

Señor Costilla, Plaza Borda; 2–3215. Ribs, chops and Mexican specialties in one of Anderson's zany places. Open daily. V, MC, AE, D, CB.

Arnoldo, Plaza de los Gallos; 2–1272. Good, hearty fare in handy spot. Open daily, breakfast through dinner. V, MC, AE.

Celito Lindo, Plaza Borda; 2–0603. A charming little place with Mexican and international dishes. Open for breakfast.

Inexpensive

Los Balcones, Plazuela San Juan; 2–0680. Plain and simple, but a favorite with Americans living in Taxco. Open daily.

PUEBLA

Moderate

Max Internacional, Juarez 2915; 48–9503. One of Puebla's more attractive restaurants featuring international cuisine. Closed Mondays. V, MC.

Charlie's China Poblana, Juarez 1918; 46–3184. The best of Anderson's several establishments in Puebla. Closed Mondays. V, MC, AE, D.

D'Armandos, Juarez 2105; 41–8161. An attractive continental cafe serving local specialties as well. Open daily. V, MC, AE, D.

Fonda Santa Clara, Tres Poniente 307; 42–2659. Top spot for molé poblano and other regional dishes. Open daily. MC, AE, D.

NIGHTLIFE. The emphasis is on night when it comes to nightlife in Mexico City. People meet for cocktails at 7 or 8 P.M., take in a dinner and show at 10 or 11 P.M., stop in for a bit of disco dancing at midnight and then find a spot for a nightcap at 3 A.M. The easy way to do this is on a night club tour (such tours sound unsophisticated, but they take in the best places and there is never any hassle over reservations or getting a good table, nor any worry about how much to tip). Those who want to go out on their own should have no trouble getting around; waiters will arrange for taxis to be summoned. The big hotels offer the best selection when it comes to night life; they are where most of the locals head. Outside the hotels the Pink Zone, Reforma-Juarez and Insurgentes Sur have the greatest concentration of night spots. Liquor, it should be remembered, packs a heavy wallop at the capital's 7,000 foot altitude but drunkeness is considered bad form. Imported booze is staggeringly expensive. Mexico City is probably safer after dark than most other towns, but muggings are not unknown. Going out bejeweled or flashing a wad is asking for trouble. Unescorted women no longer are considered shocking, but they may be subjected to attentions they do not want.

Bars with Entertainment

Lobby Bar, Hotel Maria Isabel-Sheraton, Reforma 325. Open from noon to midnight with mariachis playing from 7 to 10 P.M. Something of a refined singles scene.

Lobby Bar, Hotel El Presidente Chapultepec, Campos Eliseos 218, Polanco. Various musical groups perform throughout the day from 1 until 11 P.M. Quite crowded early in the evening.

Lobby Bar, Hotel Camino Real, Mariano Escobedo 700, Polanco area. Open noon to 10 P.M., with piano music early in the evening. Meeting place for the capital's elite.

Ritz Bar, Hotel Ritz, Madero 30, open noon until 10 P.M. with piano entertainment evenings except weekends. A favorite with bankers and politicians.

Karisma, Campos Eliseos 219, Polanco. A cozy place where couples meet after a hard day at the office. The music is romantic.

Show Lounges

The entertainment is the draw at these spots, most of which are pleasant either before or after dinner.

Caballo Negro, Crowne Plaza, Reforma 80; 566–7777. Continuous entertainment until 1 A.M. Closed Sundays. Cover charge $2.

77, Londres 77; 518–3539. A Pink Zone dive where the entertainment is sexy.

La Peña de Gabriel del Rio, Balderas 33, just off Juarez; 510–0032. Bohemian and intellectual, everything from tangos to poets reciting. From 8 P.M. until midnight except Mondays. No cover, no minimum.

La Dilligencia, Hotel Alameda, Juarez 50; 518–0620. Mariachis and other Mexican musicians from 7 P.M. until 2 A.M.; full show at 10:30 P.M. Closed Sundays. Cover $2.50. (Closed temporarily).

JB, corner of Londres and Niza, Pink Zone, 211–0112. Beer is served by the yard and the music is rock or jazz.

Guernica, Hotel Krystal, Liverpool and Amberes, Pink Zone; 211–0092. Imaginative and fashionable. Cover $2. Open 7 P.M. to 1 A.M. except Sundays.

Parjaro Loco, Hamburgo 188, Pink Zone; 511–9770. Part of *El Señorial,* a complex of night spots, this one a favorite of well-heeled youth. Cover $3.50. Open 7 P.M. to 3 A.M. except Sundays.

Feeling, Hotel Century, Liverpool 152, Pink Zone; 584–7111. A lively penthouse hotspot open from 8 P.M. until 2 A.M. except Sundays. No cover, no minimum. (Closed temporarily).

Gatsby's, Hotel El Presidente Chapultepec, Campos Eliseos 218. Polanco; 250–7700. The city's best jazz bar swings from 7 P.M. until 3 A.M. except Sundays. Cover $4.

Dinner and Show

La Veranda, Hotel Maria Isabel Sheraton, Reforma 325; 211–0001. A top supper club, often with international performers, plus a dance floor. Shows at 10 P.M. and midnight except Sundays. Cover varies.

Regine, Hotel Century, Londres at Amberes; 584–7111. Strolling violins, elegant surroundings, a rooftop view, and passable food.

Casablanca, Florencia 36, Pink Zone; 525–2020. Part of the Marrakesh night spot complex. Dinner and dancing with a big, splashy show at midnight. Closed Sundays. Minimum $25.

Salon Luz, Leibnitz 14, Polanco area; 545–2562. Andrik, a Dutch crooner, is the fixture here. Good Teutonic food. Shows twice a night except Sundays. Minimum $15.

Stelaris, Hotel Crowne Plaza, Reforma 80; 566–7777. Top names usually perform at midnight except Sundays. Good food and music for dancing. Minimum $25.

Plaza Santa Cecilia, Callejon de la Amargura 30, near Juarez; 526–2455. Typically Mexican and a standard stop on night life tours. Close to Plaza

Garibaldi where mariachi bands congregate, the show here is all regional dances and folklore. Open until 3 A.M. except Sundays. Cover $3.

Verona, Copenhague 20, Pink Zone; 525–4110. If you can't find your waiter, he may be up front singing a Verdi number. Dinner show at 11 P.M.

Maquiavelo, Hotel Krystal, Pink Zone; 211–0092. Mexican headliners perform at 11 P.M. and 1 A.M. nightly except Sundays. Cover varies according to the show.

Carrousel, Niaza and Hamburgo, Pink Zone; 528–8764. The entertainment starts early, keeps going, with music for dancing.

Discos

La Boule Blanche, Insurgentes Sur 1333. Open from 9 P.M. until 3 A.M. except Sundays and the place to try breakdancing. Tries to be the most exclusive disco in town with a $15 cover.

Valentino's, Florencia 36; Pink Zone; 525–2020. Part of the Marrakesh complex. The emphasis here is on romantic music and touch dancing. Open 9 P.M. until 4 A.M. except Sundays. Cover $5.

Cero Cero, Hotel Camino Real, Mariano Escobedo 700, Polanco area; 545–6560. Live music as well as records. Bright lights and loud sounds. Open nightly 9 P.M. to 4 A.M. Cover $4.

News, San Jerónimo 252, in San Angel; 548–1636. Way out on the southern edge of the city but also very *in.* Nice after dinner at the *Mauna Loa* next door.

Gay Disco, Hamburgo 41, Pink Zone area. The name says it all. Open Sundays. No cover.

Disco Club, El Presidente Chapultepec, Campos Eliseos 218, Polanco; 250–7700. Recently renovated with a new sound system. Very popular. Open 9 P.M. to 3 A.M. except Mondays. Cover $5.

Le Chic, Hotel Galeria Plaza, Hamburgo at Varsovia, Pink Zone; 211–0014. Small, elegant, with stuffed chairs and modern sounds that deafen only the dancers. Open 9 P.M. to 3 A.M. except Sundays. Cover $5.

Late Night

Gitanerias, Oaxaca 15, just south of the Pink Zone; 511–1762. Flamenco dancing that does not get started until after midnight, goes on until nearly 4 A.M. Closed Sundays. Cover $2.50.

Afro Tramonto, Insurgentes and Sullivan (north side of Reforma); 546–8807. Rather wicked but not too rowdy. Appeals to gentlemen alone, but escorted ladies are welcome. Open from 10 P.M. to 4 A.M. except Sundays. Cover $2.

Guadalajara de Noche, Plaza Garibaldi (east of Juarez); 526–5521. A mariachi hangout that is the traditional last stop after an evening's revels. Open nightly until 4 A.M.

Cuernavaca

Action after dark in Cuernavaca is pretty much limited to discos which are usually open only over the weekends. Among the best are **Barba Azul** at Prado 10 (tel. 12–3255) which opens at 10 P.M. with a $2 cover; **Kaova,** Leyva 5 (tel. 14–3547), open at 9 P.M. but admitting couples only at $2 per person, and **Maximiliano's,** Juan Ruiz de Alarcon 7 (tel. 4–3547) with a $3 cover. The **Hotel Casino de la Selva** has a nightclub as does the **Hacienda de Cocoyoc,** but the latter is 30 minutes out of town.

Taxco

Best place to spend an evening is at **El Jumil,** the disco club up at the Hotel Monte Taxco. Frequently on weekends there is live entertainment at the club, for which a cover is charged. **The Hotel de la Borda** sometimes has nighttime entertainment. In town the top discos are **La Lechuza** on the plaza (tel. 2–2565), and **Bugambillas** at Juan Ruiz de Alarcon 7 (tel. 2–1836).

Puebla

There is frequently evening entertainment at the hotels **Misión** and **Meson del Angel. Flamingos,** at Teziutlan Norte 1 (tel. 48–0399) features shows at dinner on Friday and Saturday evenings. Discos include **D'Artagnan** at Juarez 2923 (tel. 48–6306), **Porthos** on the Cholula Road (tel. 48–9455) and **Midae** in Cholula (tel. 47–0638).

THE HEARTLAND OF MEXICO

The Bajio and West Central

by
KAL MULLER

This chunk of territory, centered on the Bajío region, contains the greatest concentration of the most varied attractions in the country with the possible exception of the capital and its vicinity. Yet none of Mexico's greatest drawing cards is found here: no beaches nor spectacular ruins. So we are reluctant to recommend this area for first-time visitors with limited time available. It is rather for the travel cogniscenti, for those who want to get a feel for the essence of Mexico.

There are two "musts" here: the colonial mining town of Guanajuato and idyllic lake-side Pátzcuaro with its colorful Tarascan Indians. Other important cities, all filled with colonial architecture, include San Miguel Allende with its foreign art colony and neo-Gothic church, the historic city of Querétaro, and Morelia, the capital of Michoacán state which produces the nation's finest crafts. There are vistas here as spectacular as any in the country (except for Chihuahua), including the Paricutín, a new if no longer threatening volcano. The far northeastern part of Michoacán is the winter home of millions of monarch butterflies, fluttering south every year from Canada and northern U.S.

The geography of the heartland shows marked contrasts. Whereas the Bajío—Mexico's breadbasket—lies flat, irrigated and fertile, the surrounding area is mountainous. The range to the north holds some of the world's richest silver deposits while the south is bound by a neo-volcanic arc which cuts across the whole country. Elevations are high, 6,500 feet on the average. The lowest city is Uruapan at 5,500 feet, while nearby Pátzcuaro perches at 7,250 feet. These altitudes, combined with the southern latitude, make for a pleasant, bracing climate. Winter nights are sometimes cold in Pátzcuaro, but bearable. Summer days are seldom hot, refreshed by almost predictable late afternoon showers which turn the dry, brown countryside to a lush shade of green.

Steeped in History

While the heartland represents but a small part of Mexico's huge geography, much of the country's history was written here. After the conquest of the Aztec capital, the Tarascan country of Michoacán was among the first to be taken. Gold-seeking soldiers preceded a gentle, visionary bishop. The wealth of the silver mines from Zacatecas and Gunajuato determined the main thrust of the Spanish expansion to the west, then toward the north of Mexico.

The plot leading to independence was hatched in Querétaro, led by Father Hidalgo from the town of Dolores (now called Dolores Hidalgo). The rebels scored their first major military victory by capturing wealthy Guanajuato. After the defeats and executions of the first leaders, the torch of independence was carried on by Morelos who could well claim a position equal to Hidalgo's as the Father of Mexico. Later, the years of French occupation were ended by the Mexican victory at Querétaro and the execution of Emperor Maximilian on the nearby Cerro de las Campanas (Hill of the Churchbells). And the ultimate fate of the Mexican Revolution was sealed by Pancho Villa's defeat at Celaya by Alvaro Obregon.

This region is relatively close to both Mexico City and Guadalajara. Highway 90 between these cities serves as the main axis of the Bajío as well as the road with the heaviest traffic. Querétaro lies but three hours' drive away. From Guadalajara, either Morelia or Guanajuato can be reached in some five hours. Within the heartland, all points of interest are close by.

The towns of León and Morelia have the only major airports in this area. There are daily flights to León from Mexico City, Acapulco, Ixtapa/Zihuatanejo, Mazatlán, and Tijuana while Morelia is connected daily with Mexico City and Acapulco with more flights planned to the north of the country.

The road network here is quite good and improving steadily. The ideal way to travel is by car but for budget-minded travelers, bus connections to all major points are frequent and inexpensive. Daily passenger trains connect Mexico City with Querétaro and Guadalajara, but its night schedule is not opportune for this area. A more convenient nightly train leaves Mexico City at 6 P.M., arriving at Morelia at 9 A.M.

It goes on to Pátzcuaro, Uruapan, and Apatzingan. Beds are available on this train but there are no dining facilities.

A wide range of hotels caters to all pocketbooks, from plush, renovated colonial mansions to pleasantly clean and most reasonably priced establishments. Although not famous for its gourmet cuisine, a good selection of international dishes as well as underrated but excellent Mexican cooking are available in all major cities.

Although in the process of being discovered by international tourism, the heartland of Mexico still holds to the traditional value of courtesy and does not exploit the trusting traveler as in the better known resorts. The states are receptive to visitors and a call to the local tourism offices will produce helpful, up-to-date information.

The shopping highlight is Michoacán which produces a plethora of excellent items, including copperware, ceramics, laquered objects, furniture, and musical instruments. Gem hounds will find opals and other semi-precious stones in and around Querétaro. Bargains in antiques could reward a search in Guanajuato while artsy-craftsy shops abound in San Miguel Allende, some with well-made and useful items as well as decorative junk.

EXPLORING THE HEARTLAND

GUANAJUATO

Guanajuato (pop. 100,000) is the most famous of Mexico's silver-mining cities, holding a wealth of colonial architecture as well as a fascinating jumble of winding streets, narrow alleys, plazas, and tunnels. The city is tucked into the sierras at 6,700 feet, just off the northeast end of a fertile plain called the Bajío. Due to a lack of flat space close by, the nearest airport is in León, 35 miles to the west. The only convenient way to reach this state capital is by bus or private car.

Guanajuato is a city planner's nightmare and a walker's delight. Most of the attractions are within easy strolling distance of each other, with alluring glances up narrow alleys lined with pastel-walled houses often sprouting potted flowers—color combinations which only Mexicans can get away with.

The city provides surprises underground as well. After the last of the disastrous floods in 1905, the river which cuts deep through the city was diverted and a roadway now twists in the old riverbed. Running under most of the town, the curving tunnels alternate with open stretches along basements. You see massive walls everywhere with cantilevered porches high above. There is an occasional exit, but if you are driving, just keep going. When you emerge, follow the one-way signs back to the downtown area.

To mitigate some of inevitable confusion in this crazy quilt patchwork of a city, keep in mind that the axis of the valley is north-south. The downtown area starts at the Jardín de la Union, runs within a few blocks east of Juárez Avenue to end for sightseeing purposes at the Hidalgo market and the Alhondiga. You will probably still get lost but that's part of the fun and by ambling a bit more or asking a usually friendly native, you will be set aright.

The tiny, tree-filled Jardín de la Union—one of Guanajuato's 15 plazas—has to make do as a sort of central square which focuses most Mexican towns. There are a couple of hotels facing the Jardín, an outdoor restaurant and two highlights. The San Diego Church (1633) shows the typically sculptured baroque facade in its Mexican churriguresque phase. The carved wooden doors are usually open but don't bother to go inside unless it's to cool off. It's all exterior show with nothing worthwhile inside. The church's incongruous neighbor, the Teatro Juárez, displays a muse-crowned 19th-century French style with a super-plush interior. By some miracle, the theater fits the setting.

A block south of the Jardín, the Basilica of Our Lady of Guanajuato sits at an odd angle in front of the Plaza de la Paz. The church's massive bulk and improbable strong yellow color combine to make it one of the city's three landmarks. (The other two are the university and the Alhondiga.) A 16th-century Spanish statue of the Virgin dominates the altar. According to one version, this was a gift to Guanajuato from King Phillip II of Spain, in grateful thanks for his royal fifth of the town's silver which financed his (ruinous) European meddling. Another version describes the statue as a gift from a lucky miner. Appropriately, this Virgin stands on a base of locally mined silver, as does the town of which she is the patron saint.

The university literally looms over town, huge and unavoidable, up a side street from the basilica. Built under Jesuit orders during the first part of the 18th century, its enormous crenelated white walls stand out like a sore thumb. That the Jesuits usually had better taste is proved right next door in their Church of the Compania de Jesus, impressive both inside and out.

It was perhaps the esthetic horror of the university's architecture which set the famous painter Diego Rivera out of town and on his way to a gargantuan way of life to fulfill sensual desires while covering acres of walls with didactic murals, one of which cries out that "God does not exist." Rivera was born next to the university, on Calle Positos. The house is now a museum showing some of his early paintings and sketches, proving his talent before his Marxism and consciousness-raising tendencies came to dominate style and content. Rivera moved to Mexico City when he was six years old and Guanajuato's conservative Catholic society ignores its most famous native son.

First Rebel Victory Site

The Alhondiga (granary) is as massively impressive as they come. It was built as a government grain storage facility during the 18th century to insure the supply in times of famine. The Alhondiga was the site of a most heroic deed in the War of Independence. When Father Hidalgo's rabble army of a 20,000 swooped down on defenseless Guanajuato, the Spanish soldiers and royalists barricaded themselves inside the Alhondiga. When you look at the building, it will be obvious how a few riflemen were able to hold off the horde which was armed only with spears and pitchforks. Then a tough young miner named Pipila grabbed a slab of stone for a shield and rushed the door of the Alhondiga, setting it on fire before dying in a hail of bullets. The rebels flooded inside, giving the independence forces their first major military victory. Later, when Hidalgo and three of the main leaders had been captured and executed, their heads were hung for several years on each of the upper corners of the building.

Today, the Alhondiga houses the state museum. The lower floor displays a permanent craft exhibit, temporary shows of photos, paintings, and other art along with a shrine with an eternal flame to the four independence leaders whose heads on grisly exhibit reminded the folks not to mess with authority. The upper floor, reached by a massive stairwell with an awful mural painting, houses a wide-ranging collection of pre-Columbian ceramics and a well displayed set of memorabilia from Guanajuato's history. The spacious, arch-lined inner courtyard contrasts pleasantly with the building's stark exterior.

The Mercado Hidalgo, a central market, spreads its orderly bustle under the equivalent of a turn-of-the-century French or Victorian railroad station. The cavernous iron edifice brightens with fresh fruit and vegetables on the ground floor where a plethora of every day utilitarian items also vie for the housewives' attention. A wide upper balcony gives an expansive overview of the lower level, along with inexpensive craft items whose price will depend on your ability to bargain.

Hardy walkers can climb from the Jardín de la Union to the Pípila monument, straight up in back of the San Diego Church. It's not as tough as it looks as the path zigs and zags to provide a gentle slope, but it still takes time. The Pípila monument is as monumentally pretentious as they come but the view of Guanajuato is stunning and good for photography at any time of day.

If you have a car (or join a local tour in a minibus), take the Carratera Panoramica whose best starting point is at the northern outskirts of town, off the Irapuato road. This scenic route snakes in a roughly oval form around Guanajuato. The cobblestone road starts by climbing to the Pípila, then becomes paved. A few miles farther, it drops down to a dam, the Presa de la Olla, and its two lakes, favored by local weekenders. The Panoramica then rises around the southern end of town, leading to mining areas. You first go through some of the ruins of the Las Ranas mine, still being partially worked. One can look down its endless main shaft by peering over a low stone wall. Farther on, this route joins the highway to Dolores Hidalgo with its half-dozen hotels just at the edge of town. By continuing uphill a couple of miles, you reach the La Valenciana Church and mine.

Valenciana Silver Mine

The first count of Valenciana bought his title of nobility from the King of Spain in the 18th century. He also tried to buy his way into God's favor by building a magnificent church, super-ornate churriguresque, graced with golden retablos in the interior and with plenty of also golden fancy doodads. A half mile down a dirt road, and you're at the mine which, according to one account, produced a fifth of all the world's silver for over 200 years.

Silver, Guanajuato's raison d'être, was first discovered in mid-16th century, supposedly by mule drivers who built a fire and saw almost pure ore run in rivulets from the heat. A bonanza followed with dozens of mines in operation during colonial times. These mines were shut down several times during the wars of the 19th century and the Revolution of 1910.

The Valenciana mine is now worked by a cooperative. You can stroll around the ruined former buildings and peek down into the abyss of the octagonal main shaft, dropping down a straight—shudder!—1,700-plus feet. The lowest 80 feet or so are filled with water while the horizontal working shafts branch out just above this water line.

After driving back to town, you can see what has given Guanajuato a ghoulish fame: the mummies in the municipal cemetery. Located at the top of a hill in the northern end of town and at the end of the Calzada del Panteon, you know that it's there when you see the dozens of souvenir shops catering to busloads of morbid tourists. It seems that an unusual dryness of the air plus the composition of the soil mummifies bodies in some parts of the cemetery. After several decades of decent burial, when it's time to make room for new corpses, the old ones are dug up and a committee decides if they are gruesome enough for public display. Leathery skin and hideous expressions stare at you from behind the safety of glass panels (whose safety?). If that's not creepy enough, read Ray Bradbury's short story, *The Next In Line.* The cemetery is open from 9 A.M. to 6 P.M. every day except Monday.

The cultural life of Guanjuato, usually as somnolent as most small provincial capitals, explodes once a year during the Cervantes Festival. A small square called the Plaza de San Roque had acquired fame over the years as the stage for *entremeses Cervantinos,* short farces by the most famous of Spanish writers. A few years ago, official support expanded these light plays into a full-bloom international festival with world-renowned actors, musicians, and dance groups which have included the Bolshoi Ballet. Numerous events are staged in various parts of town from late October to mid-November. A warning: tickets to the top billed events as well as hotel rooms are at a premium during these three weeks, so reserve at least a month ahead if you are planning to attend.

From a practical point of view, you might want to take a guided tour of Guanajuato. Some of the better hotels either have English-speaking guides on a permanent basis or can call one quickly. A cheaper alternative would be to contact a travel agency called *Turisticos Collectivos.* They have a booth at Juarez Ave. and 5 de Mayo as well as in the first-class waiting room at the bus station. (tel. 24735) They take small groups in VW vans on various tours which include the city, its environs, and longer trips within the state. The State Tourism Office (maps, general information) is also on Ave. Juárez and 5 de Mayo, and they are open every day from 9 A.M. to 7:30 P.M.

PRACTICAL INFORMATION FOR GUANAJUATO

Since few people in Guanjuato have a good command of English, for any emergencies we recommend that you contact the manager of your hotel or the tourism office.

HOTELS. Throughout the state of Guanajuato hotels classified as *Deluxe* at press time were authorized to charge, on the average, $48 for a double room; *First Class,* $29; *Expensive,* $19; *Moderate,* $13; and *Inexpensive,* $8. Due to inflation, however, hotel rates are raised frequently to meet increased costs.

First Class

Parador San Javier, highway to Dolores Hidalgo km. 1, tel. 20626; the lower part of the hotel with its garden, pool, reception area, and superb dining room are in the town's best colonial setting; a five-story tower hold 117 units of varying sizes; two discos; Galeria and Sanchos; restaurant with its special filet cuts; licensed guides available; their own bullring where you can try out your skills on a minibull.

Castillo Santa Cecilia, highway to Dolores Hidalgo km. 1, tel. 20485; a solid kitch castle built on top of an old mining hacienda; 87 rooms; the Comedor Real restaurant; La Cava bar, restaurant and nightclub, pleasant outdoor terrace overlooking pool; sauna; licensed guides.

Paseo de la Presa, on the Carretera Panoramica, just over one km. past the statue of Pípila, tel. 23761; a Best Western affiliate; 60 rooms with a panoramic view but not over the most attractive part of town; one lit tennis court, split-level restaurant, bar, parking, pool, nightclub.

Real de Minas, on the main highway into town from Silao and Irapuato, tel. 21460; a new 183-unit highrise with a good pool; bar with plenty of locals, restaurant, travel agency, parking, shops, convention facilities, tennis court, night club.

El Presidente, just off the main highway to town from Irapuato, about 1.5 miles before the city, tel. 23980; tastefully renovated hacienda now with 139 rooms in colonial style; one tennis court and a small pool; conference rooms, good restaurant, bar, crafts shop.

Expensive

El Carruaje, highway to Dolores Hidalgo km. 1, tel. 22140; neo-colonial with 50 rooms; pool, bar, restaurant, parking.

Motel Guanajuato, highway to Dolores Hidalgo km. 2.5, tel. 20689; 50 units with interesting domes and other attractive architectural features; good view over town, pool, meeting rooms, steam bath, restaurant, cafeteria;

Valenciana, highway to Dolores Hidalgo km. 2.5, tel. 20799; perched by the side of the steep road with 51 rooms, pool, good restaurant.

Villa de la Plata, highway to Dolores Hidalgo km. 3, tel. 21173; with 47 units, restaurant, cafeteria, pool, parking.

Hostería del Fraile, Sopeña 3, tel. 21179; central location with 37 rooms, restaurant, bar.

El Conde, Rangel de Alba #1, tel. 21465; downtown in front of the Alhondiga with 58 rooms, restaurant, bar.

Posada Santa Fe, Jardín de la Union 12, tel. 20284; excellent location with 48 rooms of varying quality; indoor/outdoor restaurant, cafeteria, bar, conventions room, parking.

San Diego, Jardín de la Union #1, tel. 21300; a former convent with 55 rooms, great rooftop terrace, restaurant, friendly cocktail lounge made to look like a Spanish wine cellar.

El Insurgente, Ave. Juárez 224, tel. 23192; on a noisy passage but good location with 82 rooms, two restaurants, closed-circuit TV, parking.

Hacienda de Cobos, Juárez 153, tel. 20350; tastefully remodeled hacienda from the 18th century with 43 rooms, restaurant, cafeteria, bar, parking, authorized guides.

Embajadoras, Parque Embajadoras, tel. 20081; quiet 27 units located a short distance from the downtown area; restaurant/bar, gardens, parking.

Moderate

Posada San Francisco, Av. Juárez and Gavira, next to the central market; somewhat noisy with 20 rooms; tel. 22084.

Mineral de Rayas, Calle Alhondiga #7, tel. 20543; fair location with 82 rooms near the bus station.

RESTAURANTS. The best restaurants are concentrated in the more expensive hotels where there is a wide variety of Mexican and international dishes. These hotels are located just a bit out of town, on the highway to Dolores Hidalgo: *Motel Guanajuato* (excellent view and cuisine); *Carruajes; Parador San Javier* (superb decor); *Motel Valenciana* (good view) and *El Castillo de Santa Cecilia.* In town, the Jardín de la Union faces the *Valdes* (Mexican, inexpensive) and the *Posada Santa Fe* (outdoors as well as inside facilities). On the Plaza de la Paz, *La Tasca de los Santos* (set menu, inexpensive). Argentine style: *Los Gauchos* (towards the suburb of Marfil) and *La Pampa,* on the way up to the **Pípila** monument. Past the Pípila, the *Hotel Paseo de la Presa* (split level dining room, Mexican and international).

EXPLORING THE VICINITY OF GUANAJUATO

Many trips can be taken from Guanajuato, either short jaunts or to reach another destination. From the city you can see a huge Christ figure on a mountain in the distance. It is a short drive from town to this hilltop, El Cubilets, said to be the geographical center of Mexico. On a clear day, there is a stupendous view from here over the country's breadbasket and largest valley, El Bajío.

LEÓN

The city of León is close by. It is the state's most populous urban area, with a population of over a million. The town is also the hub of the heartland's most important center for agriculture, cattle raising, industry, and commerce with the busiest airport between Mexico City and Guadalajara. León is famous to all Mexicans as their shoemaking capital and if you know about footwear, excellent purchases are available at a fraction of stateside prices. The colonial cathedral is nothing unusual by Mexican standards but you might want to peek inside to look at the woodcarvings of the priests' choir. The Panteon Taurino (Calzada de los Heroes 408) is a must for anyone with the slightest interest in bullfighting. This restaurant and bar is made up like a bullring, full of decorations from the fiesta brava.

PRACTICAL INFORMATION FOR LEÓN

HOTELS. For price category descriptions, see *Practical Information for Guanajuato.* **Real de Minas,** Blvd. Lopez Mateos Oriente, in front of the fairgrounds, tel. 43677. One of the Real de Minas chain, 150 units with both A/C and heating, bar, restaurant, pool, weekend disco, parking tennis, beauty shop, sauna, miniature golf, travel agency, nightclub, ladies' bar, convention facilities, shops, squash. *First Class.*

Motel La Estancia, Blvd. Lopez Mateos Oriente, tel. 63939. With 78 units, pool, restaurant/bar, gardens. *First Class.*

Condesa, Portal Bravo 14 on the main plaza, tel. 31120; large, marble lobby, bar, restaurant, parking.

Balneario Comanjilla, about 16 miles towards Silao at km. 387 on the Pan-American Highway. A spa hotel with thermal waters in the rooms, gardens, bar, restaurant, pools, horseback riding, golf. *First Class.*

León, Madero 113, tel. 41050; a traditional downtown favorite with 110 units A/C, restaurant, bar, parking, convention facilities. *Expensive.*

RESTAURANTS. **Los Venados,** L. Mateos 511, Mexican style; **Cafe León,** Colon 105 (on the pedestrian walkway), Mexican cuisine; **Panteon Taurino** (see text), meats, Mexican dishes; two Argentine style restaurants, owned by retired players from the local pro team: **El Rincon Gaucho** on the road towards Silao, and **La Parilla Gaucha,** Calzada de los Heroes 302.

Excursion Eastward

From Guanajuato, there are two logical roads to continue our exploration of the heartland. A good highway leads south to Morelia, about 100 miles away, then it's but a hop to Pátzcuaro, one of the two highlights in this region. If you take this alternative, you will pass Irapuato (many roadside strawberry stands), Salamanca (huge Pemex refinery; truly outstanding convent of San Augustin) and Yuriria (excellent 16th-century church, especially the facade) before cutting across Lake Cuitzeo, just north of Morelia.

Highway 110 heads in the opposite direction from Guanajuato, towards Dolores Hidalgo and San Miguel Allende. There is also a much faster road to San Miguel Allende which heads almost straight east from Guanajuato. If you have a bit of time to spare, we recommend Highway 110 which leaves Guanajuato, climbs to the La Valencia church and mine, then continues climbing with spectacular overviews of the valley and city far below. The road cuts through mountain woodlands before dropping down to the town of Dolores Hidalgo. There is a bypass around the urban area. The town is worth a stop only for history buffs. It was from the parish church that Father Hidalgo made his proclamation of independence, called the Grito (Cry) of Dolores. A museum houses independence memorabilia. From Dolores Hidalgo, it's an easy one hour drive to the plaza of San Miguel Allende.

SAN MIGUEL ALLENDE

San Miguel Allende holds a greater concentration of artistically active Americans than any other Mexican City. The Lake Chapala area has more gringos, Taxco fewer, while Mexico City is the headquarters of most norteamericanos who have to work for a living. In San Miguel you will find some serious writers and artists but most just dabble in the arts, supported by social security, retirement benefits, scholarships, or parents. While the esthetic quality of the artistic production might be spotty, life in San Miguel can be very pleasant indeed, especially for those on dollar incomes.

The town, with a population of about 25,000, is neither so big that you need a car nor too small to support cultural events for its artsy population. The 6134-foot elevation makes for a cool, pleasant climate. Restaurants and stores cater to the 3–4,000 foreign residents, often speaking English and providing the required necessities for non-Mexican tastes. We found one of the best English-language bookstores outside of Mexico City (it's on the main plaza). Townspeople have become used to strangers, happy with the added possibilities of income. Craft shops dot the streets around the plaza.

There are several colonial churches, nothing outstanding but worth a visit for those with time to spare. A scaled-down, neo-Gothic late 19th-century church dominates the town, worthy of either a laugh or admiration. All of this is pleasant and interesting but certainly not all that unusual. Traveling cognoscenti rightly prefer nearby Guanajuato and Pátzcuaro. Other towns have have history, better churches. So why is San Miguel Allende chosen by so many Americans?

It all started in the late 1930s when Stirling Dickinson and prominent locals founded an art school. It attracted a growing number of foreigners to what had been a village remote enough that a visitor from Mexico City would have been a rarity. With the end of World War II, the G. I. Bill swelled enrollment to the point that Enrique Fernández Martínez, a former governor of the state, turned over what had once been the 18th-century palace of the Counts of Canal to be the campus of what became the Instituto Allende. The school was incorporated as a part of the state-run University of Guanajuato and has prospered for many years. It also offers summer art classes. You can also register for a week or a month. Spanish is taught on several levels, along with several arts and crafts courses which can earn credits tranferrable to American or Canadian institutions.

Jewel of the Bajío

San Miguel has been transformed into the jewel of the Bajío, a town so delightful the federal government has declared it a national monument. Few state capitals boast the cultural sophistication of this mountain backwater. It has, for example, one of the very few lending libraries to be found anywhere in the Mexican Republic. The Ignacio Ramírez Cultural Center is tied in with the National Institute of Fine Arts, largely because the people in the town support it. This is a center of craftsmen who gathered in San Miguel because the foreigners were there to learn from them and then teach to them. Also called the El Nigromante, the cultural center is located in the colonial cloisters which were part of the contiguous Concepcionistas Church. The center boasts of several murals by Siquieros.

The Academia Hispano-Americana is the most serious of the town's schools. It emphasizes the teaching of Spanish as well as Mexican literature, history, and folklore. Students are encouraged to live in the homes of local families in order to improve their language skills.

San Miguel is like no other place in Mexico. Small, quaint, and picturesque, it is casually sophisticated, highly intellectual in a relaxed way all its own. This is Carmel South or where Cape Cod spends the winter. This is a melting pot of young people on their way up and old people who have quit the ratrace. Added to these are the Mexicans who somehow have adapted very nicely to all these human imports from the north.

Outsiders first made their way to the town a scant 20 years after the fall of the Aztec Empire. It was in 1540 that one Fray Juan de San Miguel showed up and established a parish. He named it after his own patron saint and, as the years passed, the community came to be known as San Miguel el Grande, the biggest of many towns named San Miguel scattered around Mexico.

The town became the marketplace for haciendas that were established in the area. The haciendas were vast fiefdoms, plantations measured in square miles, not acres, on which a thousand or more families lived as virtual serfs. As a result of the Mexican Revolution, almost all of these great estates have been divided up among the people who work them. The great manor houses today are mostly nothing more than ruined shells, although many have been restored as private homes or even hotels.

Mingling with the rich landowners of the 18th century were the wealthy miners from Guanajuato. Best-known of these were the Counts of Canal. The House of the Counts of Canal is one of San Miguel's most imposing buildings.

Historic plaques and markers can be found on buildings and fountains everywhere. For instance, the house at the corner of Hernández Macías and Pila Seca streets has an ornate green cross that marks it as the one-time headquarters of the dreaded Spanish Inquisition. The house directly across the street was the Inquisition jail.

Today, once again, San Miguel is a town of lovely homes. In the tradition of Spain, the houses are least imposing from the street, for, following what was originally a Moorish custom, Mexico lives behind walls. One of the delights of a visit to San Miguel is the chance to join in house and garden tours run each Sunday to raise funds for the public library. These tours start at 11:30 A.M. from the public library and cost $6.00.

The most famous house in town is the birthplace of the community's other namesake, Ignacio Allende. It's located on one corner of the main plaza. Allende, a captain in the Spanish colonial army, was as much a leader in Mexico's early struggle for independence as was Father Hidalgo. A member of the "literary society" which met in Querétaro, he provided the military leadership in the first triumphant battles. Later battles did not go as well. Allende, along with Hidalgo, was captured and shot.

Most famous landmark in San Miguel de Allende is the parish church, known simply as La Parroquia. It is quite new as Mexican churches go. Although the foundations were laid in the 17th century, the present façade was begun only in 1880. The builder, Ceferino Gutiérrez, was an uneducated mason who is said to have been inspired by picture postcards of European Gothic cathedrals. He sketched his designs in the sand with a stick and the church was built. There is nothing quite like it anywhere in the world.

Basically, the main activity in San Miguel is simply to wander the little streets, shop, relax at one of the many delightful hotels, and enjoy life.

Fray Juan taught the Indians handicrafts shortly after he established San Miguel. The town has been a citadel for artisans ever since. The simplest work involves straw, with weavers turning out a wide variety of items ranging from place mats to floor coverings. Toys and birdcages are other items made out of straw. *Artes de México,* Calzada Aurora 49, and *Casa Dolores,* Mesones 48, are good spots to stop for products from straw weavers.

Noted for Tinsmiths

Where Taxco is famed for its silver, San Miguel is noted for its tinsmiths. During the colonial era, Indians were prohibited from working in precious metals. Hence they turned to tin, producing tableware, picture and mirror frames, and a variety of other items. These people today pursue their ancient trade. They also do excellent work in wrought iron produced at crude backyard forges. Work is now also being done in a wide variety of other metals, including copper and brass as well as silver and gold. *Llamas Brothers,* Zacateros 11, and *Cerroblanco,* Correo 9, are good places to look for tinware; *Artes de Tequis,* on the plaza, has some most attractive work done in wire (yes, wire); *Casa Beckman,* Macías 105, and *David Salazar,* Canal 22, are two of the best places to look for jewelry and work done in silver. There are also charming brass items at *Casa Cohen* on Calle Reloj and at *Herco,* Canal 34. For all kinds of metalwork (and shipping the bigger pieces back home), try *Antonio Llamas* on Zacateros 26A.

There is a story that the serape was invented in San Miguel—no other place has claimed credit for this garment. Whether or not the story is true, the fact remains San Miguel has long been noted for its weaving and embroidery. The arrival of arty residents from abroad has spurred this industry. Today, a wide variety of textiles can be found in San Miguel, ranging from the traditional to variations on the original theme. *Garcia Zavala,* San Francisco 13; *Anguiano,* Canal 28, *Tequis* and *Casa Isa* on the plaza offer a wide selection of textiles, embroidery, and needlework. For a wide selection of wool blankets, rugs and sweaters, *Laura* at Zacateros 41.

Finally, San Miguel is justifiably noted for the output of its artists. There are five galleries in the town, surely the heaviest concentration of art shops anywhere in the country. The *Galeria San Miguel* on the plaza, *Galeria Princesa* at San Francisco 5, and *Galeria Xanadu* at Jesus 7 are the best spots. Take a look at the two government-run galleries—the *Bellas Artes* and the one at the Instituto Allende. There is a great deal of variation in the quality of the work. *Los Leones,* on Canal St., has batiks as well as other paintings.

Stop in at the new Studio 88 "Cadena del Destino," Hernández Macías 88, for stained and blown glass, both crafted by artists on the premises while you watch. For milady who yearns for a hand-embroidered Mexican dress of good quality, it's *Casa Canal* at Canal 3 (designs by Josefa). *Casa Maxwell,* across the street at Canal 14, has Mexican designs for men and women and handicrafts from all Mexico.

Something new in the area is water sports. The Ignacio Allende Dam has been built just five miles south of town, flooding over what was Fray

Juan's original settlement. The lake, formed by the Laja River, is something of a marvel, for San Miguel, while not in a desert, was not part of any fertile rain forest, either. Now motor boats whiz water-skiers around the lake during the summer months.

Overlooking the dam is the 9-hole *Club de Golf Malanquin* with a heated pool, steam baths, tennis courts, dining room and bar, and children's playground. Greens fees on daily, weekly, and longer basis. Location is km. 5 of the Celaya Highway.

PRACTICAL INFORMATION FOR SAN MIGUEL ALLENDE

Hotels

First Class

Posada La Ermita, Pedro Vargas 64 (on the highway to Querétaro), tel. 20777; with 25 tasteful bungalows, pool, restaurant, bar, gardens.

Hacienda Taboada, km. 7 on the Dolores Hidalgo Highway, tel. 21798; with 60 units on beautifully landscaped grounds; bar, restaurant, pools with thermal mineral waters, horseback riding. MAP rates; no pets.

Posada La Aldea, Calle Ancha de San Antonio, tel. 21022; good location, with 66 rooms, restaurant, bar.

Mision de los Angeles, km. 2 on highway to Celaya, tel. 21026; a bit out of town with 65 units, restaurant, bar with live music, large pool, gardens, golf.

Expensive

Aristos/Parador San Miguel, Calle Ancha de San Antonio, in front of the Instituto Allende, tel. 20149; a relaxing place to stay amid trees and gardens; pool, tennis courts, large restaurant; bungalows with kitchens may be rented by the month.

Rancho El Atascadero, Prolongacion Santo Domingo, on a hill overlooking the town, tel. 20206; with 51 units and several bungalows, bar and excellent restaurant, heated pool, spacious grounds.

Villas El Molino, on the highway to Querétaro just east of town, tel. 21818; with 60 units, restaurant, bar, pool in the center of a pleasant patio garden.

Posada San Francisco, on the main plaza, tel. 20072; with 40 rooms and 4 suites, charmingly colonial, fireplaces in some rooms, restaurant, bar; best location for strolling but noisy on weekends.

Villa Jacaranda, Aldama 53, tel. 21015; small place with 4 rooms and 5 suites, near the main square but quiet; excellent dining room.

Casa Sierra Nevada, Hospicio 35, tel. 20415; with 20 units in three former haciendas, total elegance; exceptional dining room, ties required; well-maintained gardens. Excellent management and service; no credit cards.

Mansion del Bosque, Aldama 65 on Juarez Park, tel. 20277; with 24 rooms in a small inn; good dining; MAP.

Hacienda de las Flores, Hospicio 16, tel. 21808; with 10 suites and 23 rooms; top quality small inn with a gourmet restaurant; privacy, heated pool; childen welcome but no credit cards.

Motel La Siesta, km. 1 on highway to Celaya, tel. 20207; with 28 comfortable rooms, each with fireplace, space for trailers and campers, pool, tennis, other recreational facilities; continental breakfast provided for guests.

Posada Las Monjas, Canal 37 just past the overhead bridge, tel. 20171; clean, 63 room colonial castle, lots of interior parking; large dining room.

Posada La Aldea, Calle Ancha de San Antonio, across from the Instituto Allende, tel. 21022; white motel village with ample parking, 66 rooms heated in winter, all with tubs restaurant, bar, lounge, pool.

Moderate

Meson de San Antonio, Mesones 80, tel. 20580; one block from the plaza with 16 pleasant rooms, small, attractive dining room.

Posada Carmina, Cuna de Allende 4, tel. 20458; with 10 rooms in a former historic mansion with a lovely patio and restaurant near the main plaza.

Vista Hermosa, Cuna de Allende 11, near the main plaza, tel. 20437; with 19 rooms in a converted home; affilitated with the Hacienda Taboada; guests are entitled to use its facilities; restaurant/bar.

Quinta Loreto, Callejon de Loreto 13, tel. 20042; with 30 rooms in a friendly place with gardens and trees; restaurant, unheated pool, games room; low monthly rates for students.

RESTAURANTS. El Patio, Calle Correo 10, just off the plaza, good for a snack or a meal anytime; bar with occasional entertainment; an old, comfortable favorite.

Chez Max, Zacateros 21, tel. 20728; specialties; seafood, international, Italian; indoors and outside in their patio; open 1 to 11 P.M. except on Mondays.

Sierra Nevada, Hospicio 35 just in back of the main church, tel. 20415; snails à la provençale and international dishes; excellent in every respect; ties recommended and reservations essential.

La Princesa, Recreo 5, tel. 21403; romantic atmosphere, excellent food, piano bar, dancing; open noon to 11 P.M.

Hacienda de las Flores, Hospicio 16, tel. 21408; a dining experience in intimate, traditional setting with outstanding view of city.

Señor Plato, Jesus 7, tel. 20626; specialties: bone marrow to suck on, international; fine decor, expensive by local standards; closed Mondays.

La Casona, Canal 21, tel. 21062; international, on the expensive side.

La Cartuja, Hernandez Macias 107, tel. 22057; especially for Spanish dishes.

Meson de Bugambilias, Hidalgo 42, just off the main square, tel. 20127; good piano bar with plenty of space in two rooms; international dishes; closed Wednesdays.

QUERÉTARO

The most historic city in Mexico is Querétaro (pop. 370,000). This is not to say it is a town of museums and placemarkers, either, for Querétaro seems to be unchanged from the days when it was making history.

This is the aristocrat of Bajío cities. Too often it has been passed over in favor of its more publicized neighbors, Guanajuato and San Miguel, a pair of towns that seem to live on tourism. Querétaro is an industrial center (with the industry carefully kept on the outskirts) whose charm seems a well-kept secret.

Querétaro owes much of its charm to two 18th-century residents, Eduardo Tresguerras, an architect, and the Marqués de la Villa del Valle del Aguila, his patron. With the Marqués paying the bill, Tresguerras designed and built the magnificent aqueduct, its 74 towering arches carrying water, ending in the lovely Neptune Fountain. He also added to the San Francisco Church, originally built in 1545. The Church of Santa Rosa is entirely his work.

Churches are the most remarkable landmarks, but the splendid mansions and handsome plazas blend in setting the tone for this noble city. One of the loveliest of these honors Querétaro's greatest hero, a woman often referred to simply as La Corregidora. She was Josefa Ortiz, wife of the Corregidor (mayor-magistrate) in 1810. It was she who, in effect, launched Mexico's war for independence.

Those were adventurous days. The creoles—Spaniards born in Mexico—had long been restless, living, as they were, like second-class citizens. With turmoil in Europe and the very legality of the viceregal government in question, they met and talked and planned and plotted about declaring independence.

In Querétaro the plotters often met at the home of Doña Josefa. They were discussing, the lady would explain to her husband, literary matters. The Corregidor was pleased that his wife had a "salon" to keep her interested, but he managed to keep himself busy with anything else when the guests arrived. The students of literature were a motley lot. They included a young officer from San Miguel, one Ignacio Allende. And from the town of Dolores came a parish priest, Father Miguel Hidalgo.

War for Independence Begun

Then came the day when the plotting was discovered. Loyalist troops were being readied to round up the rebels. The Corregidor locked his wife in a room at the municipal palace. Somehow, Doña Josefa managed to whisper a warning through a keyhole to a fellow conspirator. A messenger galloped off to San Miguel and then Dolores to warn the others. The time had come to stop talking and start fighting. In the wee hours of September 16, Father Hidalgo tolled the bell of his church, summoning his parishioners, calling on them to rise up and fight for freedom. The war for independence had begun.

It was to Querétaro that ill-fated, Austrian-born Emperor Maximilian fled with the remnants of his government in 1867, hoping to maintain the empire, although Napoleon had withdrawn all French troops from Mexico in March of that year. Betrayed by General López on the night of May 14, 1867, he was court-martialed and executed June 19, the final act in a long tragedy.

Maximilian, archduke and admiral, brother of Austria's Franz Josef, died a well-intentioned pawn of scheming men. He accepted the throne of Mexico (in fact, a nonexistent chair) from men who would make him a puppet. Mexican reactionaries, enemies of the liberal President Benito Juárez, joined with France's Louis Napoleon to turn this country into a glorified colony of Paris. Although crowned an emperor, Maximilian was to have been little more than a viceroy.

To the Austrian's credit, he would not play the game. He came to Mexico to rule and began, much to the horror of his Mexican supporters, by asking Juárez to join him. Juárez refused, and the Emperor, with the help of French troops, came close to driving him from the country.

His time ran out. In the United States, the Civil War came to an end. Washington demanded a halt to the French intervention, and Louis Napoleon, aware Maximilian would take no orders from Paris, acceded. Juárez moved in with all Mexico behind him. The Imperial Government fled to Querétaro and there the Emperor surrendered.

His place of execution is enshrined by a small chapel built on the spot by the Austrian government. It stands near the summit of the Hill of Bells. Towering over it nearby is a monolithic monument to the man who defeated him, the Indian shepherd who became a president, Benito Juárez.

Juárez was followed into office by Porfirio Díaz, who remained there, a dictator, for 34 years. He was ousted by the Mexican Revolution which began in 1910. Seven years later the men who made this revolution chose Querétaro as the place to meet and write a new constitution. This document remains the fundamental law of the land even now.

PRACTICAL INFORMATION FOR QUERÉTARO

WHAT TO SEE. The Regional Museum, downtown on Juárez Street, is definitely worth a visit. It is housed in the 16th-century former monastery of San Francisco, a huge edifice with two stories of arcades around an inner patio with a majestic stairwell. There are many colonial and European paintings along with historical memorabilia, all well displayed. An ornate table with caryatid legs held up the signatures which ended the Mexican War, giving the U.S. its huge chunk of territory west of the Mississippi. An upstairs hall holds several huge, finely carved pieces of colonial furniture. (Open Tuesday through Saturday from 10 A.M. to 2:30 P.M. and 4 to 6 P.M.; Sunday, 10 A.M. to 4 P.M.)

The Palacio Federal has taken over a former Augustinian monastery. Bureaucrats now pass the time here, amidst harmomous columns and arches, no more concerned with austerity than the monks who preceded them. It is reported that the gargoyles grimacing from the walls are not really leering at the secretaries but praying the Hail Mary in sign language.

As there is plenty of mining in the hills around town several stores specialize in setting semiprecious stones, especially opals. Aside from the usual rings, bracelets and necklaces, there are well crafted jewelry boxes and other objets d'art. Try Lapidaria Queretaro on the corner of Pasteur and 15 de Mayo.

The State Tourism Office is located in a side room of City Hall at Pasteur Sur #6. They have good maps of the city and lots of literature, all in Spanish however. Check here for any special events, especially for local bullfights, famous throughout Mexico. Open weekdays from 9 A.M. to 3 P.M. and 5 to 9 P.M.; Saturdays from 10 A.M. to 4 P.M. (tel. 43078, or 29100 ext. 268, or 22802).

HOTELS. For price category descriptions, see *Practical Information for Guanajuato.*

Deluxe

Holiday Inn, on Hwy. 57, Ave. Constituyentes Sur, tel. 60202. 172 handsome rooms, restaurant, cafeteria, lobby bar, pool, disco, convention salon, tennis courts. A welcome addition to this city's facilities.

Jurica Hacienda, north of town, off Hwy. 57, at km. 9, tel. 21081, with 186 units; a historic jewel established in 1551. Set in 25 acres of beautifully landscaped grounds and gardens, it offers swimming pool and sunning, golf, tennis, squash, badminton, horseback riding, and even donkey polo. Evening bar entertainment and disco dancing. Convention meeting facilities for up to 1,500. A delightful, self-contained inland resort offering the atmosphere and graciousness of the past complemented by all modern comforts. Now managed by Camino Real (Westin) Hotels.

Meson de Santa Rosa, Pasteur Sur 17, Plaza de Armas, tel. 20415; total elegance, excellent formal dining, European service in majestic traditional setting.

First Class

Real De Minas, adjacent to the bullring just off Hwy. 57, Ave. Constituyentes 124, tel. 60444; with 227 units a handsome facility, restaurant, lobby bar, pool, tennis courts, game salon, plenty of parking, pretty gardens.

Mirabel, new 171-room hotel, in town at Constituyentes 2 Oriente. Good reports on restaurant; small convention salon, heating, FM, TV, parking.

Expensive

Azteca, a 45-room (and 1-suite) clean and pretty motel on Hwy. 57, km. 15 at north edge of town. Gardens, swimming pool, tennis court, restaurant, bar, handicrafts store, gas station. Accommodations for campers and trailers.

Moderate

Gran, Ave. Madero 6 on the plaza downtown, is a clean inexpensive home away from home for traveling salesmen and the occasional tourist who wants to get off the tourist circuit. One disadvantage: it tends to be chilly; restaurant/bar.

San Francisco and **Corregidora** hotels, along the main street, are also clean and comfortable.

RESTAURANTS. Josecho, next to the bullring, tel. 60201; frequented by well-to-do locals; seafood and international cuisine; bullfight crowd when there are corridas; open 8 A.M.–11 P.M.

La Cabaña del Tio Tom, Zaragoza Poniente 132, tel. 62311; so named because it is located in a wooden cabin-like building with rural American decorations; speciality: American cuts of meat.

La Fontana, in the Hotel Jurica, tel. 21081; excellent but expensive international cuisine in tasteful colonial decor.

La Costa Cantabrica at Colon 16, tel. 29771; specializes in seafood; family atmosphere, popular prices.

El Museo, Prolongacion Corregidora Sur 25, for Querétano's elite, excellent international food, service but expensive; disco here on weekends.

Fonda del Refugio, on Corregidora, is tucked away in a nook of the city that reminds one of the Left Bank in Paris. A fine place to linger over pozole or quesadillas; live music Fridays and Saturdays, 9 P.M.--2 A.M.

NIGHTLIFE. Discos: **L'Opera,** Circuito Jardin Sur #1, Colonia Alamos, tel. 43832 (off the highway to San Luis Potosi); **Zero's** at the Holiday Inn, Constituyentes sur #13, tel. 41202; **Emiliano's,** Ave. Tecnologico Sur 140 tel. 41041. Nightclub: **La Cava,** Corregidora Sur #27, tel. 41888.

CAR RENTAL. National, Ave. 13 de Septiembre #34, Colonia Las Campanas, tel. 24768 and 20734; **Budget,** Ave. Constituyentes #46, on the corner of Ocampo, tel. 21570; **Autorent,** Ave. Tecnologico Norte, tel. 62152.

SAN JUAN DEL RIO

Two hours north of Mexico City, the Bajío begins. While the turnpike avoids the town, the easy-going traveler can well afford to swing off the highway for a while. This is a neighborhood in which a day or two can be spent enjoyably and calmly.

Ancient buildings cluster about tree-shaded plazas, old men lounge on benches, and the women amble slowly on their shopping rounds. Down side streets are several balnearios, spa hotels for taking the thermal waters. The pace of life is relaxed, tranquil.

In pre-turnpike days, when all north-south traffic funneled through the town, it was one great handicraft market, with emphasis on basketry. Baskets of all sizes and types are still on display at stands along the brick-mosaic sidewalks, tempting the strolling shopper, but prices are up.

San Juan is the hub of a prosperous agricultural area. Several local wineries produce vinos of consistently good quality. Local cheeses are excellent. Nearby opal mines have made San Juan a town of stonecutters, who've branched out to include other semiprecious gems—amethyst, topaz, turquoise, ruby. Two stone shops, La Lapidaria Guerrero on the main street and La Guadalupana (16 September #5) have good selections.

TEQUISQUIAPAN

Twelve miles east of San Juan, away from the turnpike, lies Tequisquiapan, a delightful spa village too few foreign travelers have discovered. A charming town of cobbled streets winding among one-story adobe houses, Tequisquiapan is a village of hotels. The lure here is the radioactive water, of volcanic origin, said to ease the pain of arthritis, cure insomnia, improve digestion, and ease gout.

Medical men have some doubt about the curing powers of the local water, but there is general agreement that a stay in this restful community will improve the health of most harried city dwellers. The climate is ideal: warm in the day, cool at night; seldom does a day pass without sunshine.

About all there is to do is relax by one of the many pools, amble the tree-shaded streets, or perhaps mount one of the many tame horses for a quiet ride along the river bank. The restless can arrange to go fishing in the waters of a nearby dam, or hunt small game.

For day-trippers, activities can pretty much be limited to taking the waters and dining. If you are around in mid-August, check out the town's wine-and-cheese festival.

PRACTICAL INFORMATION FOR TEQUISQUIAPAN AND SAN JUAN DEL RIO

HOTELS. For descriptions of price categories, see *Practical Information for Guanajuato.*

Tequisquiapan

Las Cavas, on Calzada de Media Luna, is a lovely new addition, in colonial décor throughout. Has 88 unusually large rooms (including 2 suites), all A/C, a restaurant-bar, a pool, disco, and its own wine cellar. Also a small convention salon. EP Mon.-Thurs., full AP on weekends. *First Class.*

Maridelfi, on the plaza; Moctezuma 4, with 34 rooms, large, clean, comfortable and grounds are ample. 3 swimming pools, restaurant, parking. *Expensive.*

La Calesa, on the plaza, Juarez 10, tel. 30279; old section very Spanish, 20 modern rooms; pool, flowered patio, restaurant, inside parking. *First Class.*

Rio, Niños Heroes 33, tel. 30047; with 30 rooms, thermal pools and a lovely garden. Family-style dining room with checkered tablecloths. *Expensive.*

Relox, Morelos 8, tel. 30066; oldest and most comfortable, favorite with those who go to take the waters, the 108-room Relox has 3 big pools and 17 "supertubs" for those who seek a cure in private. *Expensive.*

Posada Del Virrey, G. Prieto #9 norte, tel. 20239; with 11 clean, plain rooms, pool, inside parking. *Expensive.*

Poza Real, M. Mateos ½ block from plaza; tel. 30454; 10 clean, attractive rooms, each with kitchenette, some with thermal Roman tub. Inside parking. *Moderate.*

San Juan Del Rio

La Estancia de San Juan (formerly **Exelaris La Mansion**), km. 172 of Hwy. 57 from Mexico City to Queretaro, tel. 20120. 110-room resort in 16th-century hacienda. A favorite for weekending residents of Mexico City. Amenities include 6 clay tennis courts, putting green, restaurants, bars, live entertainment, stables, pool, boutiques. *Deluxe.*

Hotel La Mansion Galindo (formerly **Exelaris Hacienda Mansion Galindo**), km. 172 of Hwy. 57 from Mexico City to Queretaro, 3 miles south via Hwy. 120 in village Galindo, tel. 20050. A reconstructed historic hacienda that is now a complete country resort on a fresh-water lake. 166 quality rooms, 3 restaurants, 3 bars, near-Olympic-size swimming pool, 6 clay tennis courts, putting green, horseback riding. Its fully equipped convention wing can handle groups from 10 to 800. Priceless 16th-century antiques adorn the majestic halls. Absolute elegance. *Deluxe.*

El Retiro, north of San Juan at km. 195, has 24 delightful bungalows set amid ample gardens. The pool is heated. Restaurant and cocktail lounge. *First Class.*

Restaurants

Tequisquiapan

Restaurant of **La Calesa Hotel,** dining inside or in charming outodor patio; inside parking; closed Monday. **El Cid,** close to plaza on M. Mateos. **Maridelfi Hotel Restaurant,** on the plaza, is a favorite.

San Juan Del Río

Centro Vasco, on the plaza; Italian, Spanish, Mexican dishes. Cheerful. Quality at medium price.

Madeus, Juarez 26, popular restaurant and disco.

Los Corseles, Av. Juarez Oriente 28, international and Mexican goodies.

Fonda del Camino, on the highway north of town at km. 195 is a delightful Mexican-style roadhouse of which there are far too few. Try the grilled cheese sprinkled with Spanish sausage for an appetizer.

MORELIA

Morelia (pop. 400,000) is the capital of Michoacán, a state where a long time could be spent before the attractions are exhausted. Michoacán, although medium-size by Mexican standards, is still larger than 60 nations, including Belgium, Holland, Lebanon, or Switzerland. Most of the state's spots are concentrated in the north-center, around Morelia and Lake Pátzcuaro. There is also an incredible coastal drive along the Pacific. (See chapter on Coastal Resorts.)

Transportation between Mexico City and Morelia has improved considerably. There are now daily flights and a new highway cuts down on driving time. It's a bit under four hours by road, going through Toluca, Atlacomulco, and Maravatio, a distance of just over 300 km. Although it is only a few kilometers farther to Guadalajara—through Zamora and La Barca—this adds up to an extra hour, due to traffic and road conditions. To the north, Guanajuato is some 160 km. and almost three hours away while the Pacific Coast lies 240 km. and 5½ hours to the south. Buses are frequent to all these points but will take somewhat longer, depending on the number of intermediate stops. Morelia can be reached by an overnight train from Mexico City, a train which then continues to Pátzcuaro and Uruapan. It has dormitory cars but no dining facilities. Don't trust the schedule—if you are in a hurry, take the bus.

We suggest passing a day or two in Morelia then using Pátzcuaro as a base for exploring during your remaining time. There are many nearby points of interest. While Morelia is a medium-sized city with some life after dark, Pátzcuaro is much smaller with practically no night action.

Morelia was founded in 1541 and originally known as Valladolid.

Set at a bracing altitude of 6,235 feet, Morelia is the state capital of Michoacán and one of Mexico's most gracious cities. Well planned and laid out, Morelia is not a difficult city to explore. The majority of its attractions are within a 6-block radius of the cathedral, one of the most impressive in Mexico.

Knowing travelers long ago discovered Morelia. While novice voyagers often pass it by, a select few have settled down here in retirement while others make a yearly pilgrimage for an extended stay at one of the two lovely if misnamed motels atop a hill overlooking the city. Accommodations in Morelia are excellent.

The city takes its present name from José Maria Morelos, its most illustrous son. Morelos was a muleskinner-turned-priest who seized the banner of independence when Hidalgo fell and gave the country's freedom-fighters a philosophy as well as a cause. His thinking has deeply influenced Mexican politics even to this day. In a manner of speaking, Morelos played much the same role in Mexico as Thomas Jefferson did in the United States.

Valladolid was founded by Antonio de Mendoza, first viceroy of New Spain. At the time, Michoacán had only recently come under outside domination. Previously, it had been the kingdom of the Tarascans, a people who, while more primitive than their neighbors, successfully resisted Aztec domination.

Here, once again, a priest had a powerful impact. He was Vasco de Quiroga, first bishop of Michoacán. He came, saw what had been conquered, and set about restoring the economy. Before Don Vasco's arrival the Tarascans had been brutally oppressed by Nuño de Guzmán, cruelest and greediest of the conquistadores. The Tarascans were a simple folk—farmers, fishermen, and artisans. Don Vasco set out to learn from them and teach them. He quickly established the College of San Nicolas, surely the oldest state university in the Americas. In the villages he promoted handicrafts so that even today Michoacán ranks as a leading area of folk art in Mexico.

Earthenware pottery comes in a wide variety in Michoacán. Complete sets of dishes in a multitude of colors are available. From ancient times, the Tarascans have done marvelous work with vegetable dyes. Along with pottery, they turn out lacquerware prized around the world. The best of this is done on carved plates, trays, and boxes, the colors carefully set in and then glazed over. This, in turn, led to wood carving in general, ranging from handsome candlesticks to room dividers and screens as well as an assortment of furniture. Don Vasco taught the woodworkers the art of making guitars and violins so that today the finest instruments in the country come from a little town called Paracho in Michoacán.

The Sights

The cathedral is the most imposing building in town. Exceedingly handsome, it sets the regal tone for the rest of the city. A marvelous example of tender loving care, the cathedral was started in 1640 but not completed until 1744. Exclusively Plateresque in design, it is constructed of pinkish-brown trachyte with brown and gold predominating on the inside. Combining majesty and delicacy, the towers are an esthetic triumph—massively based but pleasingly graceful at the same time. Though the interior was redecorated in 1899, it remained in tasteful harmony with the building's original design. Make sure to look up at the 4,600-pipe organ, one of the finest in the world. An international organ festival takes place here every May. In front of the Cathedral, you can't miss the Palacio de Gobierno (Government Palace). This handsome structure dates back to 1770, when it was built as a Tridentine Seminary. Go inside to take a peek at the patio and the murals by the local artist Alfredo Zalce.

There are many who travel to Morelia simply to visit the Church of the Child of Health which contains an image said to have healing powers. The church was built especially to contain this image. Originally the image is said to have belonged to a poor woman who was unable to keep it in clothing. The image apparently grew. Word of this miracle got out and visitors showed up. In some cases, the ailing reported they were cured and the healing powers were generally accepted. The hierarchy was skeptical, but eventually permitted the church to be built.

There are two houses in downtown Morelia associated with the liberator Morelos, one in which he was born and the other which he bought after he gained fame.

The patriot first saw the light of day in the entranceway of a house near San Agustín Church. This building is on the corner of Corregidora and García Obeso streets, a block south of the cathedral. Later, when he achieved prominence, Morelos bought a house on what is today the corner of Morelos Sur and Aldama. This residence is now a museum containing a number of Morelos's effects, manuscripts, a camp bed used by his colleague Allende and even the blindfold he wore when he was executed.

Occupying the block west of the cathedral is the Plaza de Martíres, Morelia's zócalo. Beautifully tended and shaded by tall trees, the plaza features popular band concerts on Sundays and holidays.

Catercorner from the plaza's southwestern end is the Michoacán Museum, formerly an 18th-century palace. The ground floor contains an art gallery plus archeological exhibits from Michoacán and other parts of the country. On the second floor you'll find a wide variety of colonial objects, among them furniture, weapons, and religious paintings. A balcony on the same floor contains a mural depicting the Four Horsemen of the Apocalypse. The museum is flanked by two blocks containing government buildings—the Municipal Palace on the west and the Palace of Justice to the east. The Palace of Justice dates from the late 17th century with a recent stairwell mural by Augustin Cardenas. The Municipal Palace was built in the 18th century. Slavery in Mexico was officially abolished in this edifice by Father Hidalgo in 1810.

On the block northwest of the plaza is the Universidad de San Nicolás. It is superseded in age only by Mexico City's College of Santa Cruz Tlateloco, founded in 1537. The original site of San Nicolás was Pátzcuaro, where the college was inaugurated by Bishop Vasco de Quiroga in 1540. Forty years later it was moved to Morelia. Two of San Nicolás's alumni went on to make a lasting mark in Mexican history. One was Morelos himself and the other his old philosophy teacher, Father Hidalgo. The renovation of the inner patio, with its interesting collection of frescoes, was scheduled for completion in 1985.

The monumental Palacio Clavijero is next to San Nicolas. Built by the Jesuits in the 17th century, it is the most majestic in a city where there's plenty of colonial competition. Its huge arcaded inner courtyard is a must to see. Government offices now fill the edifice. The state tourism office is located on the east side. The portals on the outer west side are filled with regional candies and crafts.

The Church of Santa Rosa was part of the city's first convent, founded in 1590. The church itself has interesting sculptures on its exterior and a rich, baroque interior. The rest of the convent is now a conservatory of music and the home of the famed Morelia Children's Choir. This choir has sung in Rome and Carnegie Hall, and visitors are welcome to attend their rehearsals at Las Rosas. From the northwest corner of the main plaza you reach Las Rosas by going 2 blocks north of Guillermo Prieto. The choir often performs on national and religious holidays. For more information, check at the state tourism office or call 21469.

Two blocks east of Santa Rosa, turn left on Juarez. The Museo de Arte Colonial is down a half a block on Juárez. The paintings and Christ figures are displayed in several well-lit rooms.

Another must is the Casa de la Cultura, located 3 blocks north of the cathedral. Once a Carmelite convent, it has 3 cupolas reminiscent of 17th- and 18th-century architecture. Before restoration, the building suffered a period of neglect, serving alternately as a bus station, blacksmith shop, and junk yard. Today, this cultural center holds temporary art and graphic shows, dance classes, literature workshops, plays, musical performances and the state's best pre-Columbian art and artifact collection.

You will find one of the best crafts emporiums—if not the best—of all of Mexico just three blocks west of the cathedral. It is housed in the ex-convent of San Francisco, next to a church on Humboldt Street. The Casa de las Artesanias faces a large plaza where crafts are also sold. On the Casa's ground floor, the best handmade items from all the state are sold at fixed prices: copperware, ceramics in all forms and shapes, lackerware, embroidered clothing, and lots more. Upstairs, the various villages specializing in a particular craft. There is also a small museum and sets of plastic hands showing how the various items are made. The Casa de las Artesanias is worth a visit even if you are not in the mood for purchases. You get a quick idea of the range of items available as well as prices. With time, luck, and perseverence, you could find the same crafts elsewhere and—if you know how to bargain—obtain them cheaper than here. But don't count on it.

Not least among Morelia's attractions is a dazzling planetarium, completed in 1970 and located on Calzada Ventura Puente. Close to the planetarium are three newer attractions—the Teatro Morelos, a convention center, and an orchidareum with over 3,000 varieties. All were completed in 1980. The planetarium is open from 6–8 P.M. and has shows at noon and 6:30 P.M. on Friday, Saturday, and Sunday.

Morelia is proud of its several parks. To the east, Bosques Cuauhtémoc (Cuahtemoc Woods) is found next to the 250-arch colonial aqueduct which used to be the city's main source of drinking water.

The Spaniards traditionally followed the Roman example of building aqueducts in places they colonized. This one, on the eastern outskirts of the city, is one mile long and dates back to 1785. A massively imposing structure, it contains arches up to 30 feet in height.

The Bosque Cuauhtémoc is Morelia's largest park, a favored location for Sunday family outings. Band concerts take place here on Sunday. A museum of contemporary art is located next to the park.

Heading south from downtown, the Parque Juárez is parallel to the Calzada Juárez. Sunday concerts here also and a small but excellent zoo. Continuing south from the park, you can keep going to Pátzcuaro or ride up to Santa Maria, a suburb on a hillside where some delightful little resort hotels are located where one would be hardpressed to go and spend merely one night. The hotels downtown are better for those who need be on their way quickly and want no temptations to delay their travels. Santa María filters the water that comes from the Morelia reservoir.

The Casa de las Artesanias at Plaza Valladolid, has a wide display of handicrafts from all over the state. Government-run, this is a combined museum and store, a highly recommended stop for shoppers. *Senal,* in the suburb of Santa Maria, has taken advantage of the local talents to turn out wonderful modern furniture in handsome leather combined with exotic hardwoods. Another good bet is the gift shop at Villa Montaña.

If you have a sweet tooth you'll be right at home in Morelia. This city is the candy capital of Mexico, with what the English call "tuck shops" scattered all over town. So strong is the sweet-eating tradition here that the city harbors a *Mercado de Dulcería* (sweets market). This installation is located on Gomez Farías, 2 blocks west and a half block north of the plaza.

The Vicinity of Morelia

Most people head to Pátzcuaro from Morelia, about an hour away. A trip in the opposite direction holds many attractions for those with a day or two to spare. Highway 15, formerly the main road to Mexico City, heads east as a continuation of Avenida Acueducto It soon starts climbing among pine forests. The spectacular lookout point of Mil Cumbres (Thousand Peaks) is some 75 km. from Morelia. Morning fog often shrouds the panoramic view but usually by 11 A.M. the sun has managed to clear things up.

Another 55 km. on Highway 15, you will see a sign to San José Purua, one of Mexico's best known spas. In the 4½-mile downhill roller coaster ride between the highway and San Jose Perua you will lose 2,132 feet in altitude. (Make sure that your brakes are in good condition.) This drop represents a difference between arid highlands and a region sometimes bursting with flowers and tropical vegetation.

San José Purua is a spa center with a town almost incidentally tacked on. At one time the village was so tiny that its inhabitants were outnumbered by guests coming to enjoy the spa's fine climate and healing waters. Though this is no longer the case, you still at times get the impression that you're witnessing a situation where the thermal tail wags the municipal dog.

Back to Highway 15, you head for Zitacuaro. It it's between early November and late March, you could take in one of nature's marvels: millions of monarch butterflies spending the winter here after flying down 3,500 miles from Canada and the northern U.S. The most accessible of the sanctuaries is north of the main road. About ten miles before Zitacuaro, take the side road towards San Felipe and Angangueo. When you reach the village of Ocampo, ask for directions to the "mariposas" (butterflies)—it will be about 45 minutes on a dirt road from there. Once you return to Highway 15, it will lead you to Toluca and Mexico City—or back to Morelia.

LAKE PÁTZCUARO

Searchers for the primitive life will find paradise in Pátzcuaro. A handsome town not far from Morelia, it somehow defies Morelia, for

Morelia may be the official capital of Michoacán, but Pátzcuaro, its spiritual capital, is clearly where the heart of the Tarascan people lies.

A town, a lake, a way of life is Pátzcuaro. It lies little more than an hour away from Morelia by bus or car; somewhat more by train, but the train can be great fun.

The highway from Morelia leads west to Quiroga, which is something like San Juan del Rio, a bus stop of a town, its streets lined with curio shops. Though such roadside communities inevitably market schlock, there are good buys here in leather and handicrafts.

Turn south at Quiroga and it's about 5 miles to Tzintzuntzan (Place of the Hummingbirds). This was the capital of the ancient Tarascan kingdom. Attractions here are a 16th-century Franciscan monastery and the pyramids of the Las Yacatas archeological site. Tzintzuntzan is also a shopper's paradise, with most outlets concentrated near the town's borders. Driving through Tzintzuntzan we encountered 10 outlets at the northern end of town and 11 to the south.

There are two ways of getting to Pátzcuaro from Morelia. One is a direct road for about 35 miles over the mountains. The other, covering a total 36¼ miles, runs approximately 21 miles from Morelia to Quiroga and approximately 17 miles from Quiroga to Pátzcuaro.

As for Pátzcuaro itself, it begs for an artist to put it on canvas. Other places in Mexico are easily photographed, but Pátzcuaro cries for more. There is a mood to the place that defies film, for Pátzcuaro is not so much a place as a state of mind. For all the cobbled streets and tiled roofs of almost Oriental shape, there is something of the Highlands here, the fisherfolk being poor yet proud.

This is where you'll see the famed butterfly fishermen ply the waters, their nets like the wings of insects as they dip on first one side of a canoe and then the other. Nowadays, these nets are seldom used for work but remain as a tourist attraction.

Pátzcuaro (pop. 58,000) figures in Mexican colonial history by having its fate linked with both the most sadistic and the most enlightened figure of that era.

The former was one of Cortés's lieutenants, infamous Nuño de Guzmán. Guzmán, the Himmler of his day, committed hideous atrocities on the local Tarascan population in his attempt to conquer Western Mexico. He was eventually arrested by the Spanish authorities, and in 1537 the humane prelate, Vasco de Quiroga, was appointed Bishop of Michoacán. In an effort to undo the havoc wreaked by Guzmán, Quiroga created a number of model villages in the area and promoted development of commerce among the Indians to make them self-supporting. He died in 1565 and his remains were consecrated in the Basilica of La Virgen de la Salud, a church that he founded. Today a statue of Don Vasco dominates Pátzcuaro's main plaza.

Exploring the Town

The town is surprisingly big, or, at least, spread out. The center is compact enough, but the best hotel is quite far out while the lake itself is nowhere near being within walking distance.

The plaza is as good a place as any to begin our orientation tour of the town. Facing the plaza to the west is a small tourist office located in the Town Hall (Palacio Municipal). Another tourism office is in the Casa de los Once Patios.

The basilica can be found by walking a block east from the northeast end of the plaza and then 2 blocks north. As you face in that direction, the basilica is on your right. Overlooking the main altar is a statue of the Virgin made of cornstalk paste and liquid obtained from orchids. This unorthodox mixture was popular among Indians in making religious statues. The Tarascans were used to carrying representations of their gods to battle. Stone statues would have created logistical problems, hence the lightweight cornstalk-cum-orchid mixture. The Spanish friars adapted the material and workmanship to the making of Catholic ikons.

On your way to the basilica is the ancient site of San Nicolás College set up by Vasco de Quiroga. Today the building houses Pátzcuaro's tasteful Museum of Popular Arts. Here you'll find collections of ceramics, masks, lacquerware, and handicrafts so famous that some have been exhibited in New York. Nearby is the House of the Eleven Patios, once a convent. Today there are many shops selling the area's crafts and a few artisans make their wares on the premises. A state tourism office is located upstairs in one of the second floors of this amorphous building which has spread itself haphazardly.

A block north of the main plaza is another square, the attractive Plaza de Gertrudis Bocanegra. Facing San Agustín from the north is the public library. This building, named for independence heroine Gertrudis Bocanegra, contains a famous fresco by Juan O'Gorman depicting the history of the area. (O'Gorman also designed the mosaic library at the National University in Mexico City.) Gertrudis was shot in 1814 for refusing to divulge information concerning revolutionary activity to the Spaniards.

Rounding out the list of in-town attractions is the ceramics market, containing mainly pottery. This facility is located on the east side of San Francisco Church. To get there you go a block north from the northwestern end of the main square and a block west. Only on Friday.

From the center of town a cobbled road leads up a hill to a delightful picnic spot known as El Estribo which means the (saddle's) pommel in Spanish. From here the town can be seen nestling below, and beyond is the lake itself with its five islands. In the placid waters fishermen in crude canoes fish mainly with nets set overnight and gathered up at dawn. The small whitefish they catch are a delicacy prized all over Mexico.

Dominating the lake is the island of Janitzio, a volcanic elevation jutting up through the waters and crowned with a rather ugly monolith representing José Maria Morelos of independence fame. Despite its unprepossessing appearance, this figure is bigger than the Statue of Liberty. A trip to the island is virtually a must, a pilgrimage all Pátzcuaro visitors are expected to make. Though boats provide year-round service to this island town, the best time to go is the night of November 1st, preceding what is known in Mexico as the Day of the Dead. In a fantastic ceremony that might seem ghoulish by our standards, villagers troop out to the graveyard at midnight with lighted candles and baskets of food for their deceased relatives.

The dead return to their village on this one day of the year. Here, they are received with their favorite food which often includes wild duck. These ducks are still occasionally hunted in the ancient way: with a spear propelled by a spear thrower, similar to the technique used by Australian aborigines.

If you decide to visit Janítzio on the day—and night—of the dead, bear in mind that there may well be more tourists than natives and it can get mighty chilly at night. Also, there might be a long wait to catch a boat back to Pátzcuaro, It might be a better idea to visit the graveyard of some other lakeside community. Today, Janitzio is something of a touristy Indian village, its one cobbled street a stairway to the summit lined with junky shops, rudimentary beer gardens, and soft-drink stands. But "civilization" has yet to triumph. The government-built laundry stands empty while the hausfraus of the island huddle on the shore washing shirts in the waters of the lake. It's a short but breathtaking climb to the top of the island, due to the altitude. The blocklike statue of Morelos dominates the scene. The interior is covered with murals but they are worth only the most cursory of glances.

Later, scarf down some whitefish while you enjoy the view from a small restaurant overlooking the lake from the top of the island. Ask to take a look at the fish before it's cooked. The fresh catch from the lake is far better than the frozen variety "imported" from Lake Chapala and passed off as local. The whitefish from Pátzcuaro have a greenish form inside the top of their transparent heads. It is said that this form represents the Virgin who imparts an unmatchable flavor. (Most restaurants on the island, near the mainland wharf and in town also serve the renowned whitefish.)

There are three smaller islands in the lake that can also be visited—Yunuén, Jarácuaro, and La Pacanda. Jarácuaro, connected to the mainland by a causeway, is a major producer of the Mexican sombrero.

Into this idyllic lake setting the United Nations has moved. Just outside of Pátzcuaro, UNESCO and the Mexican government operates the Regional Center for Fundamental Education for Latin America, known usually by its Spanish acronymn, Crefal. The place is an experimental center in community-development projects, started long before the Peace Corps or the Alliance for Progress, and likely to remain for a long time after. The idea is to try out new theories that can be applied in the rest of Latin America, rather than attempt to ram untried schemes down unwilling communal throats.

Students from the Crefal center have gone all over the hemisphere, aiding communities from Guatemala to Uruguay. In this respect, Pátzcuaro has made notable contributions to better living.

Pátzcuaro does provide an ideal setting. The people in the area are poor more by tradition than necessity. The Tarascans live on the bit of corn they can grow and the fish they can net because this is what their people have always done. Convincing them to change their ways is not easy and not always wise. An attempt to get people to whitewash their adobe houses, for example, boomeranged as the whitewash peeled off, giving the painted homes a far more seedy appearance than their neighbors. On the other hand, the establishment of a cooperative henhouse was highly successful, bringing scores of marginal families into the money economy.

Although all sorts of things are available in Pátzcuaro, pottery is the specialty. Vasco de Quiroga, when he went to Michoacán, decided each town should have its specialty. The villages around the lake were put to work making dishes and plates.

While potters in other parts of the country tend to concentrate on vases and bowls and ashtrays, those around Pátzcuaro produce table settings. They use a wide variety of clay to turn out handsome dishes in dark green or burnished red, carefully decorating each piece by hand. Sadly, all this is remarkably fragile stuff that can be easily chipped or shattered.

With a decent vehicle, you can now drive all around Lake Pátzcuaro. The dirt road running along the western side of the lake is passable, especially during the dry season and by going slowly over the rough spots. The adobe villages are all Tarascan and the Indian language is widely used although almost everyone speaks Spanish. All day, but especially in the late afternoon, you will have stunning views of the lake.

Nearby Pátzcuaro is Santa Clara del Cobre, a town famed for its copperware. This is another monument to Vasco de Quiroga, who wanted native workers to produce goods in the great tradition of the Romans. Products range from exceptionally striking handcrafted jewelry to pitchers and candlesticks made on primitive hand-operated forges. The "factories" are in homes. Again, the articles in Santa Clara are the very best. There is a tendency in other parts of the country to spray ironware with copper paint and let the buyer beware. But not in Santa Clara. To honor a local revolutionary hero, the Mexican Government has tried to change the town's name to Villa Escalante. A compromise was finally reached in which the municipality became Villa Escalante while the town remained Santa Clara del Cobre.

URUAPAN AND PLAYA AZUL

Through the pine woods from the Black Forest setting of Pátzcuaro, Uruapan (pop. 180,000) is in the subtropics less than 40 miles away on a good road. At 5,300 feet, Uruapan enjoys a milder climate than 7,200-foot Pátzcuaro. The name derives from the Tarascan word *urupan* ("where the flowers bloom") and the name is apt. The gentler climate may well account for the fact that Urapan has a much larger population than Pátzcuaro.

The Paricutín volcano, Mexico's newest, was born in in 1943 near Uruapan. The lava flow and ashes which attended its birth wiped out the village of San Juan Parangaricutiro. Literally growing up in a cornfield, the mountain rose 2,000 feet high, for nine years spewed fire and brimstone, then suddenly calmed down to fumerole-only activity, but not before it sent 4,000 people fleeing their homes forever. It is possible to drive out this way to catch a glimpse of hell frozen over. The dirt road ends 4 miles from the volcano itself, but one can hire a guide and horses to go right up to the place and view all that remains of the village—a church spire sticking up above the cold lava. Since volcanic ash is a great natural fertilizer, it's a sobering thought that much of the area's natural beauty and incredible fertility was caused by a destructive act of nature.

Uruapan's center is marked by three differently named plazas which are really just one large open space. The western plaza is the Jardín de Martíres, in honor of military heroes. Stage center is the Plaza Principal, and east the Plaza Fray San Miguel. The latter is named after Juan de San Miguel, the Franciscan friar who founded the city.

Facing the plaza area is La Huatapera, formerly a chapel and hospital but now a local crafts museum. This facility is sponsored by La Huatapera, the Museum of Folk Arts, and contains some of the region's most skillful Tarascan workmanship. La Huatapera is next to the 17th century San Francisco Church, in one corner of the plaza area.

Uruapan is famed for its lacquerware. Trays, boxes, little chests, and wooden plates are produced here in a manner similar to work done in the Orient. It is a complicated process involving the use of sage oil and boiled plant lice, with designed actually carved into the wood, the colors set into the niches and finally the lacquer applied. The process is long and tedious, involving much careful work and long hours of rubbing. In recent years there has been a tendency to skip all this bother and simply use a bit of paint following the traditional designs. But in Uruapan, the old ways are still followed. However, tradition is beginning to give way in the face of economic necessity as few buyers are willing to pay for all the labor required in the rubbing process.

The city's northern outskirts are bracketed by Eduardo Ruíz National Park. Reflecting the wild fertility of the region, the park abounds in streams, springs, and proliferating vegetation. It is the source of the Cupatitzio River ("the river that sings") described by many old Mexican hands as the most beautiful in the world. Six miles downriver are the 90-foot Tzaráracua Falls, amid a verdant location enormously popular with picknickers.

About 30 minutes by auto from Uruapan is the spectacular waterfall at Tzaráracua. The waterfall bursts through holes and crevices in the face of a sheer rock cliff about 150 feet above the lower river bed, the roar of the cascading water is nigh deafening, and a lovely rainbow hangs perpetually over it all. It's very much off the beaten path. There's a good entry road, concrete steps lead down to the falls, and horses are available for those who don't care to walk. A bridge has now been constructed across the bottom of the falls itself. Sadly, this natural beauty spot is marred by literally mountains of modern man's trash. There seems to be no one to clean it up.

Thirty kilometers due north of Urapan is Paracho, a town of violin makers and the home of the finest Mexican guitars. Sixty percent of the country's guitars are manufactured here. The instruments are compared favorably with the best produced in Spain, and it is to this little Michoacán community that the finest musicians in Mexico make pilgrimages when they go to shop. In the approximately 18 miles between Uruapan and Paracho you encounter a complete climatic change. Paracho, at an altitude of 7,150 feet, is almost 2,000 feet higher than subtropical Uruapan. Lacking a lake to regulate temperature, Paracho is even colder than Pátzcuaro.

At the nearby village of Angahuán one can rent gentle mountain ponies and ride to the buried village of San Juan Parangaricutiro just below the volcano. Even the most timid visitors who may never have straddled a horse can feel at ease riding these "ponies for people who can't ride." Local Tarascan Indian boys lead the mounts. A word to the wise: try to obtain a good saddle or you might have problems sitting in the next few days.

Northwest of Uruapan, in the direction of Zamora, lies the Sierra de Patamban and the village of the same name. According to *House and Garden* magazine, it is here that the world's finest pottery is produced. But Patamban is not easy to reach. The nearest town in or near a main highway is Tagancícuaro, about 10 miles southeast of Zamora and just off Route 15.

On the way to Patamban, you will pass the village of Ocumicho, famed for their clay figures of devils in hilarious representations, such as on a motorcycle or enjoying a banquet with lady campanions.

Uruapan is also the avocado capital of the world. It is undoubtedly this fact that prompted local financing for improvement of the airport. There are now four weekly departures to Mexico City, connecting with flights to Acapulco, Ixtapa/Zihuatanejo, Merida and Monterrey.

From Uruapan, you can hurry to Guadalajara through Zamora and La Barca. Or, for something entirely different, head south to the Pacific through Neuva Italia. It's about 150 miles to the sea but it will take about five hours' driving. Lots of curves and dropping down as you leave Uruapan and again before you reach the ocean.

The southeast coast of Michoacán is in full economic bloom thanks to a huge new steel mill and port complex at the town of Lazaro Cardenas. The Infiernillo (Little Hell) dam provides the hydroelectric energy and nearby mines have tremendous reserves of iron ore. Only coal is missing. (It's brought down by railroad from Coahuila.) The main problem is too much steel on the world markets.

A few miles west of the steel town, Playa Azul is an inexpensive black-beach resort where hotels are adequate but swimming difficult due to heavy surf and undertow. In 1983 the coastal highway linking Playa Azul with the state of Colima was completed. The only hotel along the way is at Caleta de Campos, a delightful bay and fishing village. Many hotels and much development are in the planning stages. The completely paved road hugs the coast, sometimes at sea level, sometimes up on the sides of mountains whose slopes plunge directly into the Pacific. Spectacular views.

PRACTICAL INFORMATION FOR MORELIA, PÁTZCUARO, AND URUAPAN

HOTELS. As in the state of Guanajuato, hotels throughout Michoacàn classified as *Deluxe* at press time were authorized to charge up to $46 per room; *First Class,* $29; *Expensive,* $19; *Moderate,* $12; and *Inexpensive,* $9.

Morelia

Calinda Morelia Quality Inn, Ave. de las Camelias, tel. 41427; luxury hotel with 126 rooms, restaurant, bar, pool, remote control color TV in all units. *Deluxe.*

Villa Capri, Madero Pte. 2069 on exit road to Guadalajara, tel. 27293; excellent Boccaccio restaurant, bar, parking. *First Class.*

Virrey de Mendoza, Portal de Matamoros 16, tel. 20633; attractive colonial hotel downtown, facing the main square, with 52 rooms, bar, restaurant. *First Class.*

Villa del Sol, Tecnológico 1811, tel. 24034; with 80 units, bar, restaurant, pool, tennis courts. *First Class.*

Alameda, Madero Poniente and Guillermo Prieto, tel. 22023; with 75 units, bar, restaurant, coffee shop, nightclub; a friendly, commercial hotel. *First Class.*

Catedral, Zaragoza 37, next to the zocalo, tel. 30783; with 44 units, modern baths; glass-roofed atrium, excellent restaurant, bar. *First Class.*

De la Soledad, Zaragoza 90 and Ocampo, tel. 21888; the most authentically Mexican place to stay, with 65 rooms, all the modernity combined in an 18th-century building; restaurant, bar, central heating. *First Class.*

Real Victoria, Guadalupe Victoria 245, tel. 32511; bar, restaurant, pool. *First Class.*

Villa Montaña, Calle Galeana, 2 miles south of Hwy. 15, tel. 40231; with 60 units overlooking city, most with fireplaces; popular with the elderly; hotel discourages children under 10. Good restaurant, pool, gift shop. American Plan during high season. *First Class.*

Presidente, Aquiles Serdan 647, tel. 22626; a 90-room hotel with restaurant, bar, extensive convention facilities. *Expensive.*

Posada Vista Bella, Colonia Vista Bella, next to the Villa Montaña; with 57 rooms, all with shower or bath and most with fireplaces; parking, restaurant, bar, pool. *Expensive.*

Meson Tarasco, km. 7 on highway to Guadalajara, tel. 27624; with 24 units, restaurant, bar, pool, rooms with fireplace. *Expensive.*

Casino, Portal Hidalgo 229, tel. 31003; on the main square with 50 clean rooms, large restaurant and bar. *Expensive.*

Concordia, Gomez Farias 328, tel. 23052; very close to the bus station, relatively modern and spacious; not too noisy for its location. *Moderate.*

Plaza, Gomez Farias 278, tel. 23095, with 33 clean rooms, next to the bus station, restaurant. *Moderate.*

Pàtzcuaro

Don Vasco, Ave. Lazaro Cardenas 450, tel. 20227; a combination of hotel and motel located on the road between the town and the lake, charmingly colonial, an especially pleasant place to stay. Along with 102 comfortably furnished rooms, it has a swimming pool, tennis courts, and bowling lanes. Twice a week exhibitions of folkloric dances are given and on two other nights English-language films are shown (otherwise, there isn't much to do in Pátzcuaro after dark). CP, MAP, AP. *First Class.*

Las Redes, Ave. Americas 6, tel. 21275. *First Class.*

Hosteria San Felipe, Lázaro Cárdenas 321, tel. 21298; on the main road entering town, with 12 rooms, bar, restaurant, parking. *Expensive.*

Meson del Gallo, Dr. Jose María Coss, tel. 21474; downtown with 25 rooms and 5 suites; makes up in quality for what it lacks in size; restaurant, cafeteria, bar, pool. *Expensive.*

Meson del Cortijo, Prolongacion Alvaro Obregon, tel. 21295; with 14 rooms on the outskirts of town; bar, restaurant, cafeteria, parking. *Expensive.*

Posada de San Rafael, Portal Aldama 18, tel. 20770; with 104 units on the main square; a copy of a colonial inn; dining room with beer only; friendly staff but slow service in the restaurant. *Expensive.*

Posada de la Basilica, Arciga 6, tel. 21108; facing the square of the basilica, with 11 rooms of which 7 have fireplaces; excellent restaurant, garage. *Expensive.*

Los Escudos, Portal Hidalgo 73, tel. 20138; on the main square with 30 rooms with fireplace in an engagingly colonial building with an excellent, inexpensive restaurant. *Expensive.*

Mansion San Manuel, Portal Aldama 12, tel. 21313; on the main square with 42 rooms, restaurant, bar, parking. *Expensive.*

Mansion Iturbide, Portal Morelos 59, tel. 20368; simple and colonial on the main plaza with 12 rooms and a popular restaurant. *Expensive.*

Gran Hotel, Portal Regules 6, tel. 20443; with 26 rooms on the busy market plaza named for the independence heroine Gertrudis Bocanegra; restaurant with inexpensive set menu. *Moderate.*

Valmen, Lloreda 34, tel. 21161; with 17 fairly modern rooms; quaint colonial motif, ideal for those on a budget. *Inexpensive.*

Uruapan

Mansion de Cupatitzio, Apartado Postal 63, tel. 32070; located in a nearby national park, with 56 rooms, bar, restaurant, pool, artisan shop. *First Class.*

Tarasco, Independencia 2, tel. 21680; newest midtown hotel with 52 units, bar, pool, restaurant, parking. *First Class.*

Victoria, Cupatitzio 11, tel. 36611; large 5-story modern hotel near the main plaza with good view of city and surroundings from rooftop terrace; bar, restaurant. *Expensive.*

Regis, Portal Carillo on the main square, tel. 35844; with 32 units, restaurant, bar. *Expensive.*

Nuevo Alameda, 5 de Febrero 15, tel. 34100; with 46 units and cafeteria; top choice. *Expensive.*

Concordia, Portal Carillo 8, tel. 30400; with 71 rooms, bar, restaurant. *Expensive.*

Hernandez, Portal Matamoros 19, tel. 21600; with 50 units, bar, restaurant. *Expensive.*

Paraiso Uruapan, at km. 2 on the Pátzcuaro Highway; a Best Western with 64 units, restaurant, heated pool, gardens, playground. *Expensive.*

Plaza Uruapan, centrally located on Ocampo, tel. 30333; with 124 units and 9 suites, 2 restaurants, bar. *Expensive.*

Pie de la Sierra, 2 km. north of town on Highway 37 towards Zamora; 38 ample rooms, heated pool, restaurant, plenty of grounds, parking. *Expensive.*

Villa de Flores, Carranza 15, tel. 21650; with 29 rooms; restaurant excels in regional cuisine. *Moderate.*

Restaurants

Morelia

Good centrally located restaurants are **Monterrey, Los Canarios, Pollocoa, La Huacana and Los Comenzales, La Cabaña,** and **Grill de Enrique,** plus leading hotel restaurants. Farther out are **Los Adobes, La Llave, Jimmy's Cafeteria, Fish del Mar, Master Chef, Pollo, Queso y Vino, Las Morelianas, El Zaguán** (seafood), **Sanborn, Casa Blanca, Casa Paya** (Spanish), **Bar-Grill Frol's,** and **Solar de Villagran.** We found the best combination of atmosphere and international dishes at **La Cabaña de Vic,** Ave. Carmelinas 1535 (tel. 40979) and **El Solar de Villagran,** Rincon de las Comadres 7 (tel. 45647). For the best local dishes, try **La Huacana,** Garcia Obeso 15, (tel. 25312).

Pátzcuaro

Hostería San Felipe, between the Don Vasco and the town, might be the best restaurant in Michoacán. A typical Mexican inn, it boasts excellent cuisine in pleasant surroundings. The Tarascan soup, a specialty of the house, should win some kind of prize. **El Tarasco,** reflects the charm of the area, with décor that is very Tarascan. Also recommended are **Misión del Arriero, El Cortijo, La Carreta, Fonda del Sol, Del Monje, Gallo, Manjares de Caltzontzín,** and dining rooms at the Gran Hotel, San Carlos, Posada de la Basilica, and Mansión Iturbe. Also **Zirahuen** on Uruapan Hwy. **Los Escudos,** Portal Hidalgo 73 (tel. 20138) for inexpensive, excellent local dishes. **El Patio,** on Plaza Vasco de Quiroga 19 (tel. 20884) for inexpensive regional cooking and dinner music. If you are down by the lakeside and have a few minutes to kill while waiting for a boat to Janitzio, there are many stands just outside the wharf area serving whitefish. Nearby, with the same speciality, try **Los Redes,** Ave. las Americas 6, tel. 21275, and **El Gordo,** Ave. las Americas 2, tel. 20501.

Uruapan

Downtown: **El Emperador** (meats) at Plaza Uruapan (tel. 30333), and **Las Ventas** at the Tarasco Hotel, (tel. 21680); also **Las Palmas** (inexpensive, Mexican) and **Restauran Vegetariano** (lots of choice, delicious, clean, and very cheap). Farther out: **La Ronda, Jardín Steak House** (tel. 33241), **Manjares de Caltzontzín** (tel. 33178) and **La Cueva de Victor.**

Museums

Morelia

Casa de Morelos, Morelos Sur and Aldama. Former home of patriot José María Morelos. A tasteful example of colonial architecture, it contains a number of the liberator's personal effects. Open weekdays from 9 A.M.–1 P.M. and 4–6 P.M.

Museo Michoacano (State Museum), on Allende near southwest corner of main plaza; housed in an 18th-century palace, full of historical odds and ends and 19th-century paintings by locals. Only for history buffs except for the architecture. Open as above.

Casa de la Cultura, Ave. Morelos Norte and Ave. del Trabajo, with the best collection of pre-Columbian artifacts from the state, Taracscan and earlier, well displayed.

Museo de Arte Contemporaneo, Ave. de los Arcos near the Bosque Cuahtemoc, with permanent and temporary exhibits of mostly local painters.

Museo de Arte Colonial, on Juárez and Santiago Tapia; a small, well lit display of colonial paintings and religious objects, especially Christ figures.

Pátzcuaro

Museo de Artes Populares, on Lerin and Alcantarillas, near the Basilica; housed in the former Colegio de San Nicolas, a museum of fine crafts from the lake region.

Uruapan

Museo Huatapera, next to the Immaculate Conception Church on the main square, with several large rooms filled with the region's craft, mainly ceramics and lacquerware.

FIESTAS. The state of Michoacán is probably the most fiesta-filled in the nation. Check at the tourism offices and at your hotels to see if any will be held along your route. We list only a selection of the most important ones. **Morelia.** First two weeks of May, the state's biggest fair with many events all over town; Sept. 30, Morelos' birthday, celebrated with a long, colorful, float-filled parade, dancing, gigantic fireworks.

Pátzcuaro. Market days Sunday, Tuesday, Thursday, and Friday. Late December, parade of canoes with butterfly nets, folk dances. Villages near Pátzcuaro: Santa Clara del Cobre, annual copper fair August 12–19 with exhibitions, parades, dances. Janitzio, on the island with the Morelos statue in the lake, fantastic candlelight ceremony in the cemetery on November 2, the Day of the Dead, but remember the cold and innumerable tourists; the same ritual also takes place in all the lakeside villages.

Uruapan. Market day is Sunday. Palm Sunday to Easter, handicrafts fair, native costume exhibition, band music, folk dancing. July 22, festival of St. Mary Magdalene, parade with decorated ox-pulled floats, a queen and her court, clown dressed as vegetables, dance of the ancients (inside a barrio church), and many other folk dances.

ARCHAEOLOGICAL ZONES. Ihuatzio, on the eastern shore of Lake Pátzcuaro, off the highway to Quiroga; follow the dirt road to the village of Ihuatzio and beyond until you see the sign to the archaeological zone—a bit of a rocky climb, then about 1 km further; three small truncated Tarascan pyramids with a good view from the tops to the Morelos statue on Janitzio island.

Tzintzuntzan, on the main road between Pátzcuaro and Quiroga, just off Lake Pátzcuaro; a series of rounded pyramids on a huge base, good view of the lake. The Tarascans used to keep eternal fires going on top of these pyramids called yacatas: the pyres were to appease their Sun God, Curicaueri, the "great burner," so that the deity would keep the volcanos quiet.

Tingambato, a Tarascan ceremonial complex with a small pyramid, ballcourt, and two plazas, all set among fruit trees in a lovely site; located halfway between Pátzcuaro and Uruapan; take the main cobble-stoned street through the village of Tingambato and keep going until you see the sign pointing to your right; follow the dirt road to the car parking area, then it's another 50 yards walk in a path among trees.

USEFUL ADDRESSES. State Tourism Offices. Morelia: Palacio Clavijero, Nigromante 79, tel. 32654. Pátzcuaro: Casa de los Once Patios, tel. 21214, and on the main square, in the Palacio Municipal, tel. 21888. Uruapan: 5 de febrero 17, tel. 20633.

Airlines. *Aeromexico.* Morelia: Guillermo Prieto and Madero Poniente (in the Hotel Alameda), tel. 36533. Uruapan: Hotel Plaza Uruapan, tel. 21578, and Ocampo 64, tel. 31080.

Bus Service. Morelia: Main terminal at Eduardo Ruiz and Gomez Farias, tel. 22664. Pátzcuaro: Tres Estrellas de Oro and Flecha Amarilla, both at Ahumada 63, tel. 21460 and 20960 respectively; *Autobuses de Occidente,* Lloreda and Titere 1A, tel. 20052. Uruapan: at the edge of town, on the highway to Pátzcuaro and Morelia.

Car Rental. Morelia. *Quick* (Morelia Rent), Ave. Madero Poniente 1818A, tel. 31551; *Auto Renta Chevrolet,* Ave. Madero Poniente 1540, tel. 21431. Uruapan. *Budget,* tel. 25907.

GUADALAJARA

Roses and Gentlemen Cowboys

Guadalajara: the Pearl of the West, the City of Roses, the land of the mariachis, ideal climate, lovely señoritas, the *charro,* the gentleman cowboy (*fuerte, feo, y formal:* strong, ugly, and formal). Some 25,000 Americans have chosen the Guadalajara area as their home after looking things over pretty carefully. And in spite of all that, it's still a liveable city. Not too many pimples accompany the growing pains. Almost year-round temperatures in the 70s and 80s, thanks to the southern latitude combined with a 1,500-meter elevation (5,000 feet). Many parts of the city abound with trees, flowers, and fountains. The industrial zone has been carefully located away from the city, downwind. Much needed roads and bypasses have been completed and downtown renovated. No one has ever thought of the city as "*el monstro*"—the monster—an epithet reserved for that ungovernable morass called Mexico City.

Of course, it's impossible to have a three-million-plus city with a growing indistrual sector and not run into some problems. Rush-hour traffic can be sometimes frustrating and occasionally smog drifts over parts of the city. But these are minor irritants when compared to the awful quality of life in the nation's capital. The real price that Guadalajara pays for its beauty is provincialism. Yes, Placido Domingo did come to sing here. This city boasts two major universities and several smaller ones, superb cultural programs created and presented by the Instituto Cabanas, and nine matches of the 1986 World Soccer Cup. Yet, Guadalajara loses its best and brightest to Mexico City, which may be a monster but it's a dynamic one.

Guadalajara was founded in 1541 as an outpost of Spanish expansion in an area of scant Indian population. It was no bonanza town. For a short while it exercised control over the river of silver pouring out of Zacatecas but soon that wealth went directly to Mexico City and on to Spain. Guadalajara grew slowly over the centuries as a commercial center for its farming and ranching hinterland, and industry was slow in rearing its ugly head. Few movers and shakers lasted long here. Conservatism is still dominant.

EXPLORING GUADALAJARA

As a visitor, your prime interest will be the downtown section which concentrates most of the attractions within walking distance. The suburb of Tlaquepaque is a must, even for the most inveterate non-shoppers. Another suburb, Zapopan, holds the tiny Virgin of Zapopan of miraculous fame, housed in a colonial basilica. Just out of town, the Barance de los Oblatos offers grandiose scenery. A bit farther afield, you have a town called Tequila and Lake Chapala, the country's largest.

The heart of the city, an excellent example of Spanish colonial planning, is dominated by the cathedral which is surrounded by four plazas. The Plaza de los Laureles (Laurels) lies just in front of the cathedral. Continuing clockwise, we find the Rotunda de los Hombres Ilustres (Jalisco's famous native sons), the Plaza de los Tres Poderes (the Three Powers; formerly called Liberación) and the Plaza de Armas, the usual main town square.

The cathedral was begun in 1568 and inaugurated in 1618 without being architecturally completed. The huge building's style is as eclectic as they come: a bewildering combination of Gothic, Byzantine, Tuscan, Corinthian, Doric, and Baroque, reflecting changes in fashion as the cathedral took its final shape over the centuries. If the exterior leaves something to be desired in the way of harmony, the interior is well integrated, huge and splendid. Take a look at the fine retablos, especially the painting by the famous Spanish artist Murillo, the "Assumption of the Virgin," over the door of the sacristy.

The Plaza de Armas is graced by an excellent kiosk or sort of bandstand-pavillion hosting late Sunday afternoon concerts. The kiosk is pure 19th-century French with pillars disguised as luscious, unclad maidens. The 18th-century Palacio de Gobierno faces this square. The policemen guarding the entrance will let you by to see, just to the right, the stairwell painting of Father Hidalgo by the most celebrated son of Guadalajara, the painter José Clemente Orozco. Thanks to his use of space, you are encompassed by the powerful, torch-wielding Hidalgo who is surrounded by figures portraying the artist's views of the atrocity of war and the stupidity of right and left wing ideologies.

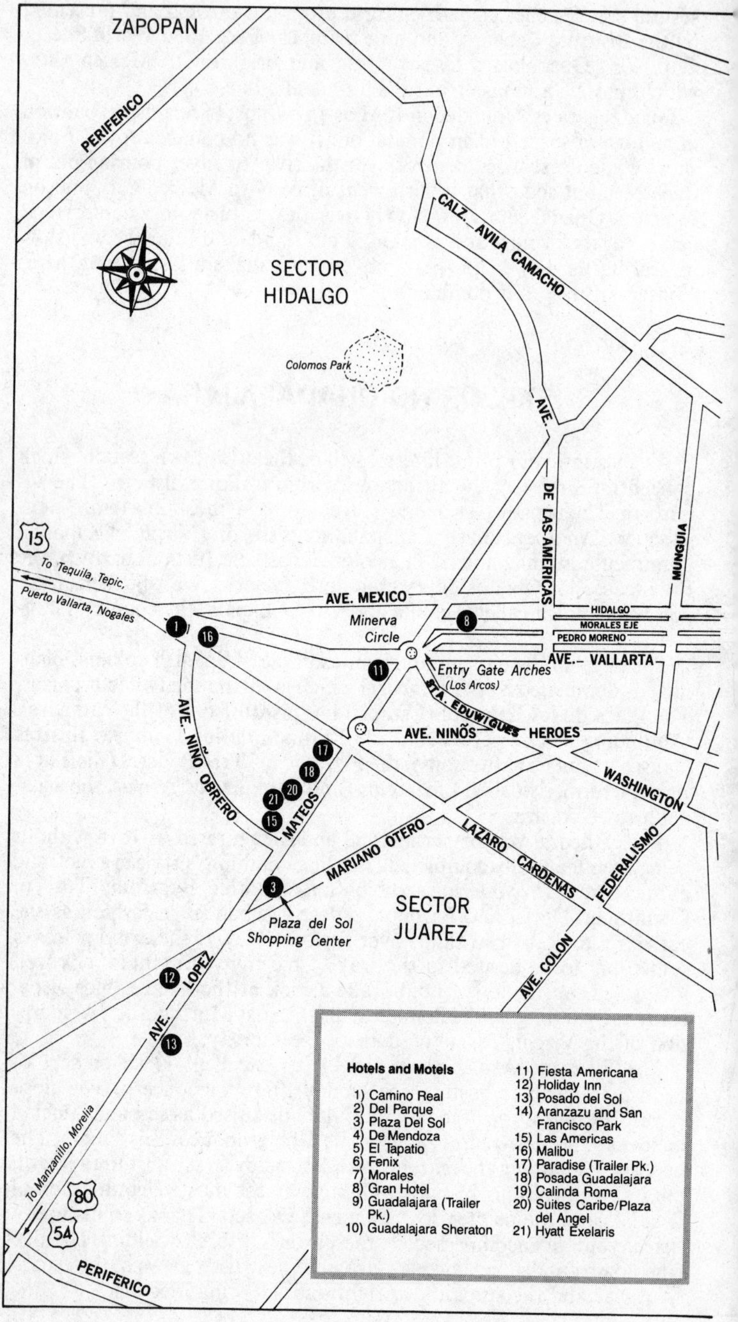
ZAPOPAN
PERIFERICO
SECTOR HIDALGO
CALZ. AVILA CAMACHO
Colomos Park
AVE. DE LAS AMERICAS
MUNGUIA
15
To Tequila, Tepic, Puerto Vallarta, Nogales
AVE. MEXICO
HIDALGO
MORALES EJE
PEDRO MORENO
Minerva Circle
AVE. VALLARTA
Entry Gate Arches (Los Arcos)
STA. EDUWIGUES
AVE. NIÑOS HEROES
AVE. NIÑO OBRERO
MATEOS
WASHINGTON
MARIANO OTERO
LAZARO CARDENAS
FEDERALISMO
Plaza del Sol Shopping Center
SECTOR JUAREZ
AVE. LOPEZ
AVE. COLON
To Manzanillo, Morelia
80
54
PERIFERICO
Hotels and Motels
1) Camino Real
2) Del Parque
3) Plaza Del Sol
4) De Mendoza
5) El Tapatio
6) Fenix
7) Morales
8) Gran Hotel
9) Guadalajara (Trailer Pk.)
10) Guadalajara Sheraton
11) Fiesta Americana
12) Holiday Inn
13) Posado del Sol
14) Aranzazu and San Francisco Park
15) Las Americas
16) Malibu
17) Paradise (Trailer Pk.)
18) Posada Guadalajara
19) Calinda Roma
20) Suites Caribe/Plaza del Angel
21) Hyatt Exelaris

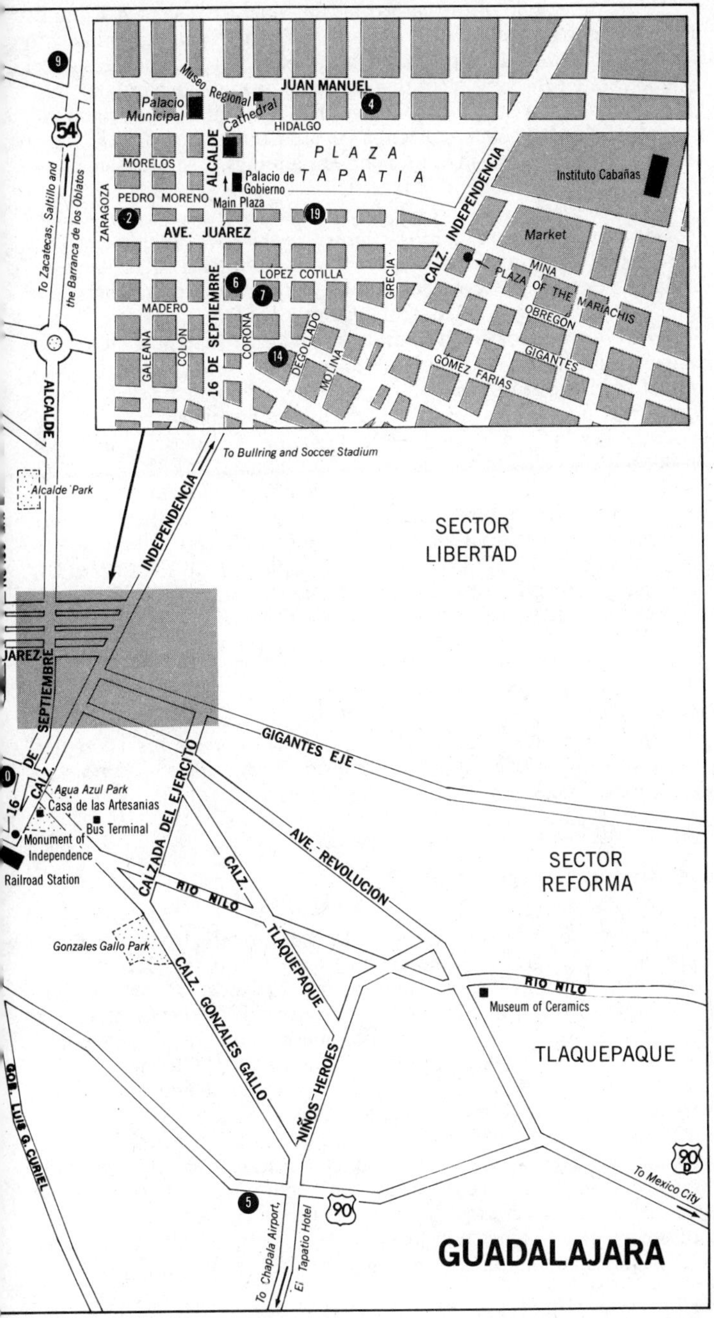

JUAN MANUEL
Museo Regional
Palacio Municipal
Cathedral
HIDALGO
PLAZA TAPATIA
ALCALDE
MORELOS
Palacio de Gobierno
Main Plaza
PEDRO MORENO
ZARAGOZA
AVE. JUÁREZ
CALZ. INDEPENDENCIA
Instituto Cabañas
Market
MINA
PLAZA OF THE MARIACHIS
LOPEZ COTILLA
GRECIA
16 DE SEPTIEMBRE
MADERO
GALEANA
COLON
CORONA
DEGOLLADO
MOLINA
OBREGON
GIGANTES
GOMEZ FARIAS
To Zacatecas, Saltillo and the Barranca de los Oblatos
54
ALCALDE
To Bullring and Soccer Stadium
INDEPENDENCIA
Alcalde Park
SECTOR LIBERTAD
JAREZ
16 DE SEPTIEMBRE
GIGANTES EJE
CALZ.
Agua Azul Park
Casa de las Artesanias
Bus Terminal
Monument of Independence
Railroad Station
CALZADA DEL EJERCITO
AVE. REVOLUCION
SECTOR REFORMA
RIO NILO
CALZ. TLAQUEPAQUE
Gonzales Gallo Park
CALZ. GONZALES GALLO
Museum of Ceramics
TLAQUEPAQUE
NIÑOS HEROES
GOB. LUIS G. CURIEL
To Mexico City
90
To Chapala Airport, El Tapatio Hotel
GUADALAJARA

On the other side of the cathedral, the quiet, tree-shaded Rotunda de los Hombres Ilustres features statues of people you are unlikely to know. The Museo Regional, sometimes referred to as the Museo del Estado (State Museum) faces this square. The massive baroque building dates from the early 18th century. The exhibition halls around the courtyard display a fine collection of pre-Columbian ceramics from western Mexico, Spanish, and colonial paintings, historical memorabilia, and some ethnographic material.

The large Plaza de los Tres Poderes in back of the cathedral reaches the Degollado Theater, a 19th-century neoclassic, complete with a muse-fulled frieze above the two columns. Modeled on Milan's La Scala, the interior reeks of gilded doors, doodads and chandeliers. The ceiling is covered by a well executed painting of Dante's Divine Comedy. The Unitersity of Guadalajara's folk ballet troupe puts on a lively show in this theater every Sunday morning. Stuck on the exterior back wall of the Degollado, there's a large fountain with a long metal sculpture depicting the conquest of Jalisco by the Spaniards.

At the head of the Plaza Tapatía (feminine of Tapatío, a nickname of varying etymologies for the natives of Guadalajara), this large, 10-block area holds shops, stores, the state tourism office, fountains, and sculptures. There is plenty of parking space underneath. The plaza stretches above the busy Calzada Independencia to end at the Instituto Cultural Cabañas. Built originally as an orphanage at the turn of the 19th century, its prime claim to fame is the former chapel whose inner walls are covered with Orozco's paintings. The walls' tableaux, painted in somber colors, depict the Spanish conquest with its power and despotism. Most impressive is the "Man of Fire" on the central dome where colors and perspective show what artistic power can achieve. Many of Orozco's smaller works are displayed in an adjoining gallery. Countless patios surround the chapel, all part of the cultural complex which presents a varied program of music, theater, films, lectures, and exhibitions. Check at the entrance to see what's on during your stay.

Market on a Grand Scale

The Mercado Libertad can be reached directly from the Plaza Tapatia. This is probably the country's biggest market located in a downtown area and it is certainly among the most interesting. The front part, all under a single, many-domed roof, holds stands selling fruit, vegetables, dry goods, meat, and household items. A wide upper balcony which runs along two sides of the interior is filled with countless small counter-type restaurants where you see the cooking—local variety, as Mexican as they come, delicious and inexpensive. Delicate souls and stomachs take warning: the place is often a madhouse of bustle, definitely not geared for tourists although you are certainly welcome. The place is clean but we can't guarantee that your tummy won't complain afterwards. In the back section of the market, there is a profusion of adjoining stalls in a jumble of goodies, heaps of all kinds of craft items and clothing. You might be nagged by salespersons and bargaining is essential.

The small Plaza de los Mariachis is next to the market, just south and fronting the Cazada Independencia. It is especially active evenings and weekends. You can sit at one of the tables and nurse a beer while listening to the sad or vigorous songs belted out by the resplendent groups. If you are paying, each song is worth about 90¢ but ask the price just to make certain. To the south of the market and behind the Plaza de los Mariachis, there is a *zona de tolerancia,* a euphemism for the red light zone. Usually toned down, things could get tough here, so we advise you to stay out. Anyway, strict morality laws, partially enforced, have taken much of the fun and vitality of what this area used to be.

Continuing our tour of the downtown area, we come upon two gems of colonial churches left off most itineraries. They are located northwest of the cathedral, both on streets named after the respective churches. Santa Monica is five blocks north and two blocks west of the Plaza de los Laureles. A former convent, this richly baroque church has no front, just a long side, replete with carvings, running along Santa Monica Street. Three blocks to the west, San Felipe Neri—which does have a normal facade—is also covered with baroque sculptures with a bonus of gargoyles, all harmoneously blended in colonial style.

Plaza of the Parasols

Directly to the west of the Plaza de los Laureles, we have a pedestrian zone with many stores and shops. The Plaza de las Sombrillas (Parasols), just off Juárez Avenue, fronts a couple of large stores and an outdoor café with parasols (whence the plaza's name), a couple of fountains and the Telegraph Office, a converted colonial building with murals by that arch-atheist, Siqueiros. An underground passage off this plaza and under Juárez Avenue is filled with stalls offering fresh fruit juices, liquados (fruit milkshakes with an egg or two thrown in on request), and watch repairmen. The park of San Francisco is three blocks south of Juárez on the Avenue 16 de Septiembre. The Church of San Francisco has a statue-decorated facade but a plain interior. The nearby chapel of Arazazu is plain on the exterior but the inside shines with resplendent gold leaf, retablos, and architectural decorations.

This about completes the center of Guadalajara, of what can be reached by a reasonably active walker. Heading away from downtown on Avenida Juárez, you go past the ex-convent of El Carmen where expositions and cultural events are held. The federal tourism office is also located here. Crossing the broad Calzada Federalismo, you keep going a few blocks until you see a tall building with many windows on your right. This is the administration building of the University of Guadalajara. Across Vallarta, on your left, there's a white French Renaissance–type mansion, also a part of the university. The auditorium in this building boasts of two powerful Orozco murals, one on the dome and the other one behind the stage. It is usually open to the public unless there is a function going on in the auditorium. The neo-Gothic church of El Expiatorio, still getting finishing touches by master carvers, is located one block in back of the auditorium.

Guadalajara's Own Pink Zone

By continuing west on Vallarta, you will reach a broad avenue with a center walkway filled with trees and fountains: Chapultapec, sometimes called by its old name, Lafayette. The glittering Zona Chapultapec is Guadalajara's answer to Mexico City's Zona Rosa. This is an area surrounding Avenida Chapultapec, an artery running on a north-south axis between the Aurerá superstore and the Niños Heroes monument. Broad and elegant, this is Guadalajara's Champs Élysées but keeping one's sense of proportion. With smart shops, art galleries, international gourmet restaurants, cafés, and excellent bookstores, it represents a fascinating blend of fashion, culture, haute cuisine, and sophisticated leisure. The U.S. consulate is also located in this area. Warning: parking can be tough all around the area.

Guadalajara, a city built on commerce, is maintaining the tradition. There are five huge shopping centers of which Plaza del Sol is the biggest. It is located on Lopez Mateos, south of the Minerva Circle, on the way out of town towards Manzanillo and Morelia (Michoacán). There are over 300 stores here, spread out on some 30 acres in a zone of many hotels and restaurants. Many Tapatíos come here for their purchases. There is usually enough parking space and a wide choice of merchandize at most reasonable prices. You can have bargains on excellent shoes and boots, leatherware, and items you didn't realize you wanted until you saw them.

Guadalajara is also known for its many parks. The two best and most accessible ones should be through rejuvenation by the time you read this. Agua Azul (Blue Water), close to the train station, has lots of tree and garden space, a mini train for kids of all ages, carnivallike rides and Sunday shows in its "Concha Acústica," an open air stage. The Alcalde Park, also spacious, features a good-sized lake where boats are available for rent and huge jets of water break up the scenery. Both of these parks tend to get very crowded on weekends with local families out for picnics and fun. For the biggest park of all and a truly grand spectacle, drive out to the Barrance de los Oblatos, on the road to Zacatecas and Saltillo. About ten miles out of town, you will see a small park, dedicated to Dr. Atl (who was a larger-than-life figure, master of many of Mexico's muralists). From this park you gaze up a couple of huge canyons with a long waterfall the Cols de Caballo (Horse tail) ending up way under your feet before running to the Santiago River which unites with the Rio Verde at the bottom of the barranca.

Tradition of Zapopan

Although with their own separate municipal governments, the suburbs of Zapopan and Tlaquepaque can be considered part of the metropolitan area of Guadalajara.

Zapopan is the center of one of the most colorful and intriguing religious traditions in Mexico. Said tradition centers around the reigning local deity, Our Lady of Zapopan. This Virgin enters Mexican history in 1531, during a battle between the Spaniards and Chimalhuacano Indians. With the issue still in doubt Fray Antonio de Segovia, a Franciscan friar attached to the Spanish forces, climbed a nearby hill and displayed the image of a Virgin. This act so awed the Indians that they surrendered and accepted conversion to Christianity.

An interesting irony: though the Virgin of Zapopan initially appears as a key figure in an Indian defeat at the hands of invading whites, she was to undergo a "conversion" of her own—from Spanish ally to Indian patroness who is deeply reveered by Mexico's Indian population.

Since the Zapopan Virgin is only 10 inches high, she is affectionately known as *la zapopanita* (the little lady of Zapopan.)

The above mentioned tradition is a ceremoniial tour undertaken by the Virgin from June to October of each year. During this period she visits and blesses every section of Guadalajara. This practice began in 1734, when Guadalajara was stricken by a plague. As an extraordinary measure Bishop Gómez de Cervantes authorized visits by *la zapopanita* to all afflicted sections of the city. Since the pestilence ceased wherever the statue appeared, the Virgin was credited with a miracle and declared "patroness against thunders, storms, and epidemics."

The basilica housing the Virgin when she's not "on the road" was dedicated on September 8, 1730. It has a Mudejar tiled dome and an ornate Plateresque facade. The Virgin, clad in a crimson dress and blue mantle, perches over the altar. Her statue has been kept in a silver cup since April 18, 1713, with the original cup replaced by a more artistic one in 1935. The basilica overlooks the main plaza. There is a small Huichol museum and crafts sales room inside the basilica, run by friars who are trying, with mixed success, to convert these Indians in their Sierras.

The whole central area of Zapopan has been completely remodeled and rejuvenated with much junk cleared from the front of the basilica a long ways back, with a huge plaza now giving unimpeded view and access. As part of the reward for its clean-up act, the famous Fiestas de Octubre are now focused on the Benito Juárez auditorium in Zapopan.

Tlaquepaque—A Crafts Center

On the opposite side of Guadalajara from Zapopan, we find the crafts suburb of Tlaquepaque with a population of over 200,000. The heart of Tlaquepaque is a large partially covered square known as the parián. The term comes from Manila's Chinese quarter, of paramount importance to the colonial Mexican trade by the Manila galleon. The numerous restaurants in the parián are over-priced and serve poor quality food. The place is pleasant enough, however, as mariachi bands lean into colorful tunes when there are enough clients, mostly weekends. The musicians' prices have more than kept up with inflation. A single tune costs about $1, while an "hour," usually some eight selections lasting 40 minutes at the most, can vary between $4 and $5.

Tlaquepaque has long been famed as a center for pottery and other native crafts. Good buys can still be found in stoneware, woodcarvings, dresses, handwoven fabrics, leather, and blown glass. And shops there are, in confusing profusion. Over 300 of them at the last count, most catering to tourists. English is spoken in the larger, better-known shops whose prices are consequently higher. As suppliers often deal with several stores, often you will find the same items in different places at varying prices. Shopping around and bargaining could save you many dollars. The nonshipment of purchased items, a problem in the past, has been largely resolved. Although you have to count on several weeks before the goodies get home, they will make it, eventually. Should the items fail to arrive, write to the store as well as the Tlaquepaque Tourism Office (see under *Useful Addresses*) with a photocopy of your receipt. Most stores are open from 10 A.M. to 7 P.M. closed Sunday afternoon. (See under *Shopping* for the names of some of the better shops.)

Tlaquepaque also claims the distinction of being one of Mexico's outstanding centers for witchcraft. And the term isn't meant in the pejorative sense. As in the Land of Oz, there are both good and bad witches. The former, known as *curanderas,* function as combined medical doctors, psychiatrists, and advisers to the lovelorn. Their services are particularly in demand among lovestruck swains and jilted *señoritas.*

Evil witches are known as *brujas* and are authentic purveyors of black magic. You go to a *curandera* if you need help for yourself; to a *bruja* if you want to do in one of your enemies. Though it's easy to sneer, the fact that the institution has endured is in itself a tribute to its efficacy.

A word of warning about the "jewelry" sold under the arcades near the parian: prices change with the speed of lightning and there could be "mistakes" in the exchange rate as well as the purity of the silver. Unless you know your metals and your Spanish is fluent, our advice is to buy jewelry in a reputable shop.

For shopping in Tlaquepaque, the best idea is to wander around on Independencia Street (closed to traffic) and Juarez street, both west of the parian and the plaza. Browse in whatever store strikes your fancy but don't start buying until you have checked out several places. Stroll around the main plaza with its kiosk and San Pedro parish church and visit the Museo Regional de Ceramica (on Independencia Street) where many items are on sale at fixed prices. If you want to combine your shopping expedition with a lively time, plan your trip for a Friday afternoon. That night, there is a Noche Mexicana at the parian with folk dances, singing, fireworks, and, of course, mariachis. Sunday afternoon brings out the natives to the parian with plenty of music, but most of the stores are closed at that time.

The village of Tonalá is just a few minutes' drive east of Tlaquepaque. Many of the ceramics sold in the region are produced here in small factories, each with its own kiln. There are some stores but the place is not geared for tourists in a big way. On Thursday and Sunday mornings, the streets in front of the church are full of ceramics in a bustling crafts market.

PRACTICAL INFORMATION FOR GUADALAJARA

HOW TO GET THERE. There are daily trains from just across the U.S. border at Nogales and Mexicali as well as Mexico City. These trains are equipped with Pullmans and a dining car. It's about $40 for a Pullman from Nogales and $18 for first class passage. Train prices to Mexico City are $15 for a berth and $5 for first class. A daily train goes to Manzanillo in an official time of 8 hours, no Pullman or dining car, for about $1.60.

By Bus. Numerous buses from the U.S. border, Mexico City and just about all major cities in the north and central part of the country. Nogales is some 1,060 miles from Guadalajara and Mexico City 350 miles east. A first class bus to Nogales (much faster if more cramped than the 24-hour-plus train ride) costs around $28 and to Mexico City $10.

By Air. *Mexicana de Aviacion* has direct daily flights to Dallas/Ft. Worth, Los Angeles and San Francisco. *Aeroméxico* flies direct to Houston and New York. *Western* goes daily to Los Angeles. *American* flies daily to Dallas from Monday through Friday. These flights connect to most major U.S. cities and some Canadian ones. *Autotransportes Aeropuerto* runs VW minibuses from the airport to any destination around Guadalajara. One or more passengers going to the same destination pay together. A ride from the airport to downtown costs about $6; to the hotels in the vicinity of the Minerva, some $7.50. If you call them at least 12 hours in advance, they will pick you up to take you back to the airport (tel. 190213 or 190556). Taxis charge about 60% more and you must bargain with them.

EMERGENCY TELEPHONE NUMBERS. U.S. Consulate: 252700; Australian Consulate: 230757; Canadian Consulate: 419319; Mexicano-Americano Hospital: 413141; Santa Maria Chapalita Hospital: 214050; Tourism Office: 145313 or 140156; Police: 06.

HOTELS. In Guadalajara and its metropolitan area hotels classified as *Deluxe* at press time were authorized to charge for a double room, on the average, $60; *First Class,* $32; *Expensive,* $20; *Moderate,* $12; and *Inexpensive* $8.

Deluxe

El Tapatio, off the road to the airport and Chapala, tel. 356050. Scattered 207 units and a host of amenities combine to create a self-contained village. Several bars, gourmet and informal restaurants, disco, ten tennis courts, pool, gym, sauna, jacuzzi, massage, boutiques, travel agency, car rental, baby sitting, 24-hr. medical service, horseback riding, miniature golf. An outstanding Mexican buffet (with strolling mariachis) on Sundays at 1 P.M. A small daily surcharge per room covers all tips (except restaurants).

Guadalajara Sheraton, Niños Heroes and 16 Septiembre, tel. 147272. 222 rooms, all A/C; this is the only Deluxe hotel close to the downtown area; with disco, nightclub, restaurant, bar, pool, most spacious rooms, pleasant lobby, shops in hotel; several car rental agencies within a block; Fiesta Mexicana every night except Tuesday and Sunday.

Camino Real, Vallarta 5005, leading into the Nogales highway, tel. 217217. 224 A/C rooms and bungalows, well spread out, pool, restaurant, nightclub, coffee shop; good for motorists tired and just getting into town from the north.

Fiesta Americana, Minerva Circle, tel. 253434; with 394 units, heated terrace pool, two tennis courts on the 4th floor with lights; Mexican Night on Tuesdays, Italian Night on Fridays, cocktail party for guests on Wednesdays; three restaurants including one with excellent French cuisine, bars, heliport, meeting rooms, commercial center with many shops, very popular lobby bar with live entertainment seven nights a week, nightclub, underground parking, art gallery; striking architecture, inside and out, overlooks the Minerva fountain and statue which are Guadalajara landmarks.

Hyatt Exelaris, Ave. Lopez Mateos in front of the Plaza del Sol shopping center, tel. 227778; with 350 units, heliport, the only ice-skating rink in town; imaginative all-glass exterior, convention centers, marred by empty shop spaces on the street level.

Holiday Inn, Lopez Mateos and Mariano Otero, tel. 315566; tower annex and low building (completely remodeled) totaling 305 units, travel agency, car rental, shops, show-bar, disco, three restaurants—including the rooftop *Jacarandas,* with a spectacular view of the city; Mexican fiesta Sundays.

First Class

Aranzazu, Revolucion and Corona, tel. 133232; across the lovely colonial Aranzazu Church. Two buildings connected by a passage running under Ave. Revolucion; total of 540 units, each building with its pool, parking, bar, restaurant, cafeteria, disco/nightclub for medium-paced action. Some of the rooms have a noise problem, the lobby areas are nothing to brag about and in general, many details could stand improvement. Close to downtown and a bit cheaper than hotels in this category.

Calinda Roma, Juarez #170, tel. 148650; older hotel, partially renovated in a busy downtown area (ask for a room away from the street); 176 rooms, small pool, very pleasant patio upstairs next to the restaurant; polite staff, good location.

De Mendoza, V. Carranza #16, tel. 134646; just off the Degollado Theater; 110 rooms; good view from the upstairs bar onto Plaza Liberacion. Their small pool stays in the shade most of the winter but the area is quiet at night and the downtown location is excellent.

Fenix, Corona 160, tel. 145714; a Best Western affiliate; completely renovated, a favorite of its faithful clientele; tastefully furnished rooms with video and satellite reception, two bars, nightclub, sauna, massage, disco, and several integrated shops; excellent hotel in the downtown area.

Frances, Maestranza 35, tel. 131190; just in back of the Palacio de Gobierno and off the Plaza Libertad, best downtown location; 60 rooms in a building used as far back as 1610 as an inn for traders. Completely restored five years ago; the best lobby in Guadalajara—columns, arches with huge chandelier, fountain, and good piano in lobby bar. Each room or suite is different, ensconced in the contours and shapes of the historic building which has been designated as a national monument; good restaurant, staff with decent command of English.

Lafayette, 2055 La Paz, tel. 301112. In the Zona Rosa (Pink Zone) with 200 units in a 16-story brown stucco building. Two restaurants, nightclub for dancing, bar, pool; TV with satellite reception in all rooms.

Las Pergolas, Morelos 2244, tel. 301727; 200 units, sauna, barbershop, beauty salon, not much of a lobby, restaurant, cafeteria, hourglass pool.

Malibu, Vallarta 3993, tel. 217676. For motorists, near the Camino Real on the way to the Nogales highway. 200 rooms, beauty parlor, local car rental agency, big garden with tables under imposing trees, show-bar, restaurant.

Country Plaza (formerly Jacarandas Colomos), Prolongacion Ave. Americas #1170, tel. 334633. Near the Plaza Patria shopping center; restaurant, bar, pool, boutique.

Castel Plaza del Sol, in the Plaza del Sol shopping center, Lopez Mateos and Mariano Otero, tel. 210515; with 352 A/C rooms, nightclub, jacuzzi, two restaurants, bar, heated pool, solarium, meeting rooms, convention facilities, ample parking.

De Los Reyes, Calzada Independencia Sur 164, just off Lopez Cotilla and very close to the Libertad Market, tel. 130076. New hotel with 171 rooms, noisy on the Independencia side; small pool on the roof, next to one of the two restaurants. Popular with Mexicans, but problems filling the rooms; cheapest hotel in this category.

Diana, Circumvalacion Augustin Yañez 2760, tel. 155510, two blocks from the Minerva Circle; 180 rooms, good Argentine-style restaurant; poor lobby, small pool with no sun in winter; a patio with mariachis under construction.

Plaza Del Angel, Lopez Mateos Sur 2128, tel. 216995; with 179 units all A/C with satellite reception, cafeteria, restaurant featuring international cuisine, nightclub, shops, pool, motor lobby; all new and scheduled for mid-1985 inauguration.

Expensive

Continental, Corona 450, tel. 132030; 127 rooms, close to downtown on a street with heavy traffic; restaurant, ample parking.

Genova, Juarez 123, tel. 137500. 54 rooms in a downtown location; completely renovated but the traffic is still there; restaurant for breakfast only.

Universo, Lopez Cotilla 161, tel. 132815; with 137 rooms and ample parking in the downtown area; geared for the single traveler—rates almost double for two in a room.

Del Bosque, Lopez Mateos 265, tel. 214650; with 43 rooms and 14 apartments, right next to the railway tracks at the Minerva underpass; inexpensive restaurant with Italian and Mexican dishes, pool, parking.

La Estancia Del Sol, Mariano Otero 2407, tel. 316164; with 100 rooms, pool, parking, restaurant/bar, suites in construction for monthly rentals.

Posada Guadalajara, Lopez Mateos Sur 1280, tel. 212022; 68 rooms, some with A/C, pool, restaurant, parking.

Americas, Lopez Mateos Sur 2400, tel. 314415; 102 rooms all A/C with satellite reception, restaurant, cafeteria, meeting room, laundry, parking, bar, two pools, next door to *Tucan* disco.

Internacional, Pedro Moreno 570, tel. 130330; with 102 rooms all A/C, restaurant, bar, car rental, close to downtown.

Posada San Isidro, Ave. Bosques de San Isidro #5, some 10 miles north of town on Highway 54, near a golf course and the Oblatos barranca; 23 units, restaurant, bar, pool, parking.

Moderate

Chapalita, Lopez Mateos 1617, tel. 227710; 93 units units, parking, pool, restaurant, bar.

Colon, Ave. Revolucion #12, tel. 133753; with 78 rooms at a noisy intersection close to downtown; inexpensive restaurant with Mexican dishes and an outstanding model wooden ship in the lobby.

Colonial, Lopez Mateos Sur 2405, tel. 212000; with 24 units, pool.

Canada, Dr. Michel, 218, tel. 192092, just across from the central bus station; 67 rooms with shower or bath, parking.

Del Parque, Juarez 845, tel. 252800; with 77 rooms; designed by the famous architect Luis Barragan, located on a busy street a couple of blocks from the University of Guadalajara. Popular with Houstonians coming down for inexpensive plastic surgery; slowly being renovated.

Guadalajara (motel), Vallarta 3305, tel. 155725; with 68 rooms, most with A/C; pool, restaurant, parking.

Morales, Corona 243, tel. 132969; with 101 rooms, all with shower or bath; close to downtown, a favorite of bullfighters; spacious, pleasant lobby, room phones; no restaurant or bar but plenty close-by.

Nueva Galicia, Ave. Corona 610, tel. 148780; with 91 rooms, all being slowly renovated; restaurant, short walk from downtown, mainly Mexican clientele, parking.

Posada Virreyes, on the highway as you leave town towards Mexico City; tel. 356622; 60 rooms, pool, restaurant.

Rancho Rio Caliente, some 23 kilometers from the Minerva Circle, off the main highway to Tepic and Nogales, past the village of La Primavera; a vegetarian spa with many kinds of cultural programs, lectures in English and a delicious menu. Reservations are essential: Rancho Rio Calente, Apartado Postal 1187, Guadalajara, Jalisco.

SPECIAL EVENTS. Starting in early October and spilling into November, the month-long *Fiestas de Octubre,* a kind of Oktoberfest, enjoys international fame, rivaled in the country only by the Cervantes Festival in Guanajuato. The fiestas are an outgrowth of a religious celebration for the return of the Virgin of Zapopan who is brought back to her home in the basilica of Zapopan on October 12 after a several month long pilgrimage to the city's numerous churches.

The program for the Fiestas de Octubre, which varies from year to year, always has cultural events, expositions, sports, conventions, and other attractions. The best bullfights are put on at this time, national charro championships, a golf tournament, bicycling competition, judo and karate, cross-country motorcycling, a marathon, a tennis championship, squash, boxing, dressage, jumping, an auto rally, expositions of paintings, all kinds of arts and crafts (including sales), a film festival, jazz, all kinds of dancing, a chess tournament, a mariachi festival, industrial and agricultural expositions, a dog show, a magic show, balloons and gliders, Mexican cooking shows, a wine and cheese fair, the voladores (fliers) of Papantla, cockfights . . . there's truly something for everyone.

Many of the events are held in the Benito Juárez Auditorium in Zapopan, others scattered throughout the city and vicinity. Make certain that you reserve your hotel early if you plan on being in Guadalajara during this time. For details and information, contact the Tourist Department or a major hotel.

Tlaquepaque. The *Fiesta de San Pedro* on June 29; activities start around the 14th of the month and last till the 31st. As could be expected, there's an arts and crafts fair with a national ceramics prize, fireworks, cockfights, and table watiers' races.

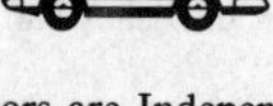

HOW TO GET AROUND. Most of Guadalajara's attractions are downtown, within relatively easy walking distance of one another. To get your general bearings, see map of Guadalajara. The streets dividing the four sectors are Independencia running north-south and Morelos, which becomes

Gigantes going east-west. Street names sometimes change when crossing these axes. For example, Alcalde changes to 16 de Septiembre at Morelos; Unión changes to Américas at Morelos; Munguía changes to Tolsá (officially known as Diaz de Leon) at Morelos. For no fathomable reason, Juárez changes to Vallarta at Munguía.

To reach downtown from the hotels around Lopez Mateos and La Minerva, a taxi should cost you about $3 during the day. (Taxis charge about 25% more at night. It is always essential to agree on the price of the taxi before you get in.) You can also get downtown by bus for 10 or 15 cents U.S. Buses run on Lopez Mateos and down the one-way Hildalgo Street, one of the few major arteries where traffic lights are synchronized. This is the way to drive downtown also, although we suggest leaving your car at the hotel if you are only going to visit the center of Guadalajara. To get back to the Minerva, buses run up the one-way Juárez/Vallarta artery. To reach Tlaquepaque from downtown, taxis charge between $3 and $4. Or catch a bus on Independencia or Revolucion, marked "Tlaquepaque." Zapopan from downtown comes to $4 to $5 by taxi; buses go there from Alcalde—they are marked "Zapopan."

If you want to rest and see downtown in style, hire a *calandria* (horse-drawn carriage) for $5 to $6 an hour. They are located in front of the Regional Museum, the Mercado Libertad and the San Francisco Park, by the church of the same name.

TOURIST INFORMATION SERVICES. All the State of Jalisco Tourism Offices listed here are open from 9 A.M. to 9 P.M. on weekdays, till 1 P.M. Saturday and 3 P.M. on Sunday. There are two offices downtown: one at the ex-convent Del Carmen, Juarez 638 (tel. 140156) and the other at the Plaza Tapatia/Morelos 102 (tel. 145313 and 148686). Their office in Tlaquepaque is at Guillermo Prieto 80 (tel. 351503). In Zapopan, at the Palacio Municipal (20 de Noviembre #103) (tel. 330571). The city government maintains a tourist office in Los Arcos (the arches) just off the Minerva Circle (tel. 163333). The *American Society of Jalisco,* a residents' service club, can help with some information. Their office is at the Holiday Inn and they operate from 9 A.M. to 1 P.M. on weekdays (tel. 314090).

USEFUL ADDRESSES. Consulates: *USA,* Progreso 175, tel. 252700 (they have a long list of English-speaking doctors); *Australia,* Mar Negro 1221, tel. 230757; *Canada,* Colomos 2390, tel. 419319.

Central Post Office and telegraphs, big building on Alcalde and Hospital streets.

Mexicano-Americano Hospital: Colomos 2110, tel. 413141.

Airlines: *Aerocalifornia,* Lopez Cotilla 1423, tel. 261901; *Aeroméxico,* Ave. Corona 196, tel. 145400 and 251010; *Mexicana,* Ave. 16 de Septiembre 495, tel. 132222; *American Airlines,* Avenida Vallarta 1526, tel. 396724; *Western Airlines,* Lopez Cotilla 1701, tel. 303530. These are the companies which fly directly to Guadalajara; many other airlines have offices in town; check the phone directory.

Car Rentals: *Quick,* Niños Heroes 954, tel. 146052; *Avis,* Niños Heroes, 942A, tel. 123451; *Hertz,* Niños Heroes 9, tel. 146162; *Budget,* Niños Heroes 934, tel. 138634; *National,* Niños Heroes 961C, tel. 147175; *Odin,* 16 Septiembre 742, tel. 147120. Most of these agencies are near the Sheraton Hotel. They also have stands at the airport, at the baggage claim area for national flights. Aside from the above, there are several local agencies.

ENGLISH LANGUAGE MEDIA. *The News* from Mexico City is available at major hotels, at Sanborns and some downtown newsstands. *The Colony Reporter* is a paper directed at U.S. residents in this area, with some general articles on Mexico and local events. *The Guadalajara Weekly* is a free paper filled with local happenings. *Welcome* is published by the Autonomous University, national and local focus, tourist oriented.

TOURS. Most travel agencies in town specialize in trips to other areas and airline ticketing. For local sightseeing, try *Panoramex* at Avenida Vallarta 5846, tel. 210637. They have daily tours of the city and Tlaquepaque lasting about 4½ hours, departing at 9:15 A.M. from the San Francisco Park and at 9:30 A.M. from Los Arcos, costing some $5. There are other tours by the same company to Chapala and Tequila.

PARKS. Agua Azul, near the railroad station, off Independencia; lots of trees, carnival-type rides, miniature train, Sunday programs in the open theater. **Alcalde,** on Jesus Garcia, two blocks off Alcalde Street; lake with boats for hire, water jets, lots of space and greenery, picnic grounds, kids' games. **Gonzales Gallo,** off the Calzada Gonzales Gallo, on the way out of town; trees, picnic grounds, kids' games. **Colomos,** out on Pablo Neruda and behind the Unidad Deprtiva Revolucion (sports complex); lots of trees; the Casa de los Colomos has classes in painting, sculpture, dance.

SPORTS. Golf. *San Isidro Golf Club,* off the highway to Zacatecas and Saltillo, km 14.5; 18 holes, tel. 331506. *Club de Golf Santa Anita,* in the village of Santa Anita, a short way out of town on the highway to Colima and Michoacán; 18 holes, tel. (373) 60321. *Club de Golf Atlas,* Chapala Road, km 11, 18 holes, tel. 358298. *Guadalajara Country Club,* Mar Caribe 260, 18 holes, tel. 414045.

Bullfights, at the Plaza Nuevo Progreso, out on Independencia, near the football stadium; corridas at 4 P.M. on Sundays (usually) from October to March. Prices from $1.50 to $20.

Cockfights, daily at 8:30 P.M. at the El Nuevo Palenque Tapatio, on Revolucion 2120, almost in Tlaquepaque. On Friday and Saturday nights, there is often cabaret-type entertainment.

Boxing and wrestling, at the Arena Coliseo, on Medrano near Independencia (2 blocks). The city has produced two world boxing champions, bantamweight Jose Becerra and flyweight Alacran Torres. Friday nights at 9 P.M.; prices, from $1 up.

There are several Lienzos Charros (rodeo rings) in town, the most accessible being the one behind Agua Azul Park. Charro performances *(Charreadas)* are the ancestors of the U.S. rodeos, with the usual starting time Sunday noon. They include such events as *jineteadas* (bullriding), *terna en el ruedo* (two charros lassoing a bull, one by the horns and the other by the legs), and *coleadas.* The latter are equivalent to American "bulldogging" with the difference that a charro brings a bull to earth by the tail rather than by the horns. Most colorful are the costumes of the charros and the *Escaramuza,* the girls' riding team. All is accompanied by mariachi music and a happy atmosphere every Sunday, about noon.

Soccer *(fútbol).* There are two big stadiums in town. One is at the Autonomous University, on Pablo Neruda and Avenida Universidad; the other is the huge, 73,000 enthusiast capacity Estadio Jalisco, on Independencia, near the bullfight ring. From May through July 1986, nine matches of the World Cup Soccer Championship were played in Guadalajara. There are several professional teams in town, playing at the above stadiums. Best season is from late August to May, for the first class division. The favorite local team is Las Chivas. This is the only major league national team which allows no foreign players on its roster.

MUSEUMS AND GALLERIES. **Museo Regional,** next to the Cathedral, pre-colonial ceramics, colonial and Spanish paintings, historical memorabilia, modern crafts, cultural programs. Open from Tuesday to Saturday 10 A.M. to 4 P.M., Sunday till 1 P.M. 10 cents US entrance fee.

Hospicio Cabañas, at the eastern end of the Plaza Tapatía, paintings by Orozco, extensive cultural program, open as above; entrance fee 25 cents U.S. (equivalent).

Auditorium of the University of Guadalajara, on Ave. Juárez, for two Orozco murals, open most of the time when the university is in session; ask the guardian to open up the auditorium and give him a tip as your entrance fee.

Exconvento del Carmen, Juárez 638, temporary art shows of good quality by local artists; open all day and early evening; no entrance fee.

Arte Actual, Justo Sierra 2150C, tel. 152155. The best of the private galleries, selling such well known artists as Tamayo, Cuevas, and Ziniga.

Restaurant/Galeria Piaf, Marseillas 126, tel. 159426; a restaurant with a permanent exposition of modern art, quite exclusive.

La Puerto, Lerdo de Tejada and Union #3183; a new modern art gallery, with special presentations, modern music, rock, jazz.

Acuarelas, Ave. de la Paz 2030, tel. 151520; in the Zona Chapultapec, also a restaurant with live music; only watercolors; open 1:30 P.M. to midnight.

Fiesta Americana Hotel, on the Minerva Circle, tel. 253434; has temporary shows by mostly local artists, changing monthly.

Centro de Arte Moderno, Mariano Otero 375, tel. 163266; the best gallery for shows of a wide variety—paintings, photos, sculptures.

STAGE, MUSIC, DANCE. Sunday band concerts at 6:30 P.M. (practice sessions on Thursdays at the same hour) in the kiosk of the Plaza de Armas, to one side of the Cathedral, by the state band. Sunday 10 A.M. performance by the University of Guadalajara's folk ballet troupe at the Teatro Degollado. Drama and musical programs at the Degollado Theater and the Cabanas Cultural Institute as well as at the various universities; check programs or inquire at the tourism offices.

SHOPPING. For many kinds of "ordinary" purchases, try downtown stores or the sprawling 300 plus stores of the Plaza del Sol Shopping Center, south on Lopez Mateos, across from the Hyatt. Government stores selling crafts at fixed prices are *La Casa de las Artesanias de Jalisco* at the Parque Azul and *El Instituto de la Artesania Jaliscience,* a huge store dealing directly with artisans, at Alcalde 1221. The *Mercado Libertad* has innumerable craft items at variable prices. Just for fun, you could try the weekly Sunday streetside market *El Baratillo* (the little cheap one) on Juan Zavala, east of the Libertad market. Starts early, around 6 AM and lasts till about 2 PM Get there early for possible bargains on items from records to cars.

Guadalajara is knows for its shoe trade which is concentrated on either side of Esteban Alatorre Street, full of stores selling footwear of all qualities and prices. Alatorre Street is located north of the Plaza Tapatía and starts at the

Calzada Independencia. A few especially good stores in town: for antiques, *Antiguedades Cosme* on Hernan Cortes 4137; for fashionable embroidered clothes, *Helen Cerda,* La Villa 2036, in the Chapalita suburb, not too far from the Plaza del Sol; for leather articles and Mexican cowboy clothes (elegant), *El Charro* at Juarez 148 (downtown)—ask to see their selection of boots.

Of course the place to go for crafts is Tlaquepaque. Here's a partial list of the 300-odd stores. Many close between 2 and 4 P.M. and Sunday afternoons. *Sergio Bustamante,* Independencia 238, a beautiful place with original and artistic figures of papier maché as well as bronze and copper, all items in limited editions; his figures sell in places like Macy's and Bloomingdales for much higher prices than here. *Antigua de Mexico,* Independencia 258, with a splendid foyer, lots of metal sculptures, antiques, modern furniture, decorations. *Alfareria La Colonial,* Independencia 225, for a huge selection of lamps of all shapes, sizes and colors as well as ceramics and jewelry. *Rosa de Cristal,* Independencia 232 for all kinds of glassware; in the back of the store, you can watch the hand blown glass fashioned by boys and men who work until around 3 P.M. *Camarasa,* Independencia 163, for the famous hand blown red glassware. *Galeria Mama Carlota,* Independencia 186, for furniture and decorative items, better quality than most other shops. *Maximilian,* Juarez 295, for top quality leather items. *El Tular,* Juárez 417 for wood furniture and *equipales* (leather chairs and tables). *Ceramica Guadalajara,* Juárez 347, for general ceramics and hand-made tiles. *Mia,* Juárez 145–2, for handwoven wool rugs and many other cloth items. *Puente Viejo,* Juárez 159, for ceramics and fanciful tin animals. *Tete,* Juárez 173, one of the most extensive collection of well-made craft items, of the kind that you see in some other stores as well: lamps, hand-blown glass, iron sculptures, ceramics, papier maché figures—the bread-and-butter of Tlaquepaque. *Plateria Tapalpa,* Independencia 208, for fancy jewelry and good leather goods. *Joyería Taxco,* Juárez 134, small, almost boutique-like shop with a good selection of jewelry. *El Aguila Descalza,* Juárez 120, a clothing boutique of expensive but top quality designer clothes, mostly by Josefa. *Hermanos Jimenez,* Juárez 145–1, for a wide selection of all kinds of leather goods, possibility of having tailor-made leather clothes. *Bazaar Hecht,* Independencia 158, clothing, antique (both genuine and copy) furniture, objets d'art all in a tasteful store. *Leo y Hijos,* Independencia 150, specialized leather store which can make leather items on order in a few hours. *Ken Edwards,* Madero 75, the store of the man who introduced stoneware ceramics in this area, brilliant glazes, superb pieces. *Papaya,* Guillermo Prieto in front of the tourism office, for very fashionable clothes, Mexican style, adapted to foreign tastes.

Many of these stores will ship larger items home for you. There a place specializing in getting your goodies home, Pat Murphy's *Ship-World-Wide* at Priscilliano Sanchez 150, tel. 359331.

NIGHTLIFE. Nightclubs. *Gran Salon Astral* of the Hyatt Hotel, Lopez Mateos and Moctezuma, tel. 227778, for the best known Mexican entertainers and occasionally international ones. *Stelaris* of the Fiesta Americana, Minerva Circle at Aurelio Aceves, tel. 253434, high quality entertainment. *El Jaguar* of the Holiday Inn on Lopez Mateos and Mariano Otero, tel. 311727, entertainment Mexican style, geared to both American and Mexican tastes.

Discos. *D'Vinci* of the Holiday Inn. *Disco Osiris,* Lazaro Cardenas 3898, two blocks from the Camino Real, tel. 225067. *The Plantation,* Lopez Mateos Sur 1980, tel. 229992, part of the Restaurant Fritangas. *Pony Express,* part of the

Salon Aztlan, Giralda 100 on Lopez Mateos Sur, also a restaurant in the complex, frequented by younger locals.

Cabarets. These are not really recommended unless you are looking for a bawdy, free-wheeling atmosphere with an occasional fight.

RESTAURANTS. Dining out in Guadalajara is a pleasurable experience, with an abundance of restaurants to suit all palates and pocketbooks. A representative example is listed here. Rather than give price classifications, we state what you might pay, on the average, for a basic meal for one person for food alone; beverages and tip would be extra. Most restaurants accept credit cards. Abbreviations for credit cards are: A, American Express; BC, Bancomer; BM, Banamex; C, Carnet; CB, Carte Blanche; D, Dinners Club; E, Eurocard; I, Inerbank; M, MasterCard; and V, Visa.

Albatros, Ave. de la Paz 1840, tel. 259996; open every day from noon to 7 P.M.; specialties: mixed seafood platter, calamares rellenos (stuffed squid), fresh oysters; all seafood taken from the sea the same day as served; pleasant roofed patio, excellent service, delicious food; basic meal, $10. A, E, M, V.

La Estancia Gaucha, Ave Niños Heroes 2860, tel. 226565; open every day from 1 P.M. till midnight except Sundays when it closes at 6 P.M.; specialties: thick steaks, Argentine style; basic meal, $10. A, BM, C, V.

Tio Juan, Independencia Norte 2248, tel. 384058; specialty: tender kid (goat meat); open daily from 1:30 to 7 P.M.; basic meal, $6; big place; favored by many locals who relish this Jalisco speciality; mariachi or organ music. No credit cards.

Brazz Campestre, Lopez Mateos Sur 6022, tel. 311367; excellent and varied regional cuisine, speciality: filet Brazz, a good sized Hereford cut; basic meal $9. A, BC, BM, D.

Guadalajara Grill, Lopez Mateos Sur 3771, tel. 315622; Mexican and international dishes; open from 1:30 P.M. till midnight every day except Sundays, when closing time is 6 P.M.; mariachis at night; a lively, popular place; basic meal, $8. A, BC, BM, C, V.

Suehiro, Ave. de la Paz 1701, tel. 260094; excellent Japanese restaurant with food prepared at your table; speciality: Teppan yaki (vegetables, house sauces and your choice of seafood, steak, lobster, or shrimp), basic meal $12.50; open every day from 2 till 11:30 P.M.; closed on Sundays. A, BC, BM, CB, E, M, V.

Recco, Libertad 1973 in the zona Chapultapec, tel. 250724; superlative Italian cuisine; specialities: Osso bucco and lasagnas; open every day from 1:30 P.M. till midnight; basic meal, $8. A, D, M, V.

La Vianda, Ave. Chapalita 120, tel. 225926; excellent French cooking, reservations essential; elegant place with piano and violin music; basic meal $12.50; open every day from 1 P.M. till 1 A.M. except Sundays, when the hours are noon till 6 P.M. All major credit cards.

Rio Viejo, Ave. Americas 302, on the corner of Hidalgo, tel. 165321; speciality; chicken a la Rio Viejo; family atmosphere; open from 1:30 P.M., till midnight, closed Sundays; basic meal, $12. A, BC, BM, CB, E, M, V.

Sanborns, Ave. Vallarta 1600, tel. 155899; American and Mexican dishes; open every day from 7:30 A.M. to 1 A.M.; basic meal, $5. No credit cards.

La Mision, Pedro Moreno 1125 (near Tolsa), tel. 261166; speciality; combined meat plate; basic meal $6; open every day from noon to 1 A.M. BM, C, M.

El Tirol, Gomez 25 (near Los Arcos), tel. 152595; speciality: German cooking; basic meal $6; open every day from 11 A.M. till 1 A.M.; no liquor. All major credit cards except A.

El Che, Ave. Hidalgo 1798, tel. 150527; Argentine style steaks with music to match; basic meal $9; open 1 P.M. to 1 A.M. daily except Sundays when closing at 6 P.M. A, BM, C, D, M.

La Copa de Leche, Juarez 414 (downtown), tel. 145347; international cuisine; basic meal $5; trio and piano music; open 8 P.M. to midnight. All major credit cards except D.

La Fuente, Plan de Santos 1899, tel. 247946; international, French, filet mignon, snails Rockefeller; piano and violin music; basic meal $11; open 1:30 P.M. to midnight, closed Sundays. A, BM, C, CB.

Lafayette (off the Camino Real), tel. 217217; speciality: chateaubriand, *cancalaease* (lobster with potatoes and artichokes); quiet live music; basic meal $11; open 1 P.M. to 1 A.M. All major credit cards.

Delfin Sonriente, Niños Heroes 2229, tel. 167441; a seafood retsaurant, family atmosphere; basic meal, $8; open noon to 6 P.M., Sundays till 5 P.M. Credit. M.

Chez Pierre, Niños Heroes 2095, next to the Galeria de Arte Moderno, tel. 156645; French cuisine, prime ribs, Mazatlan shrimp; basic meal $11; open 1 P.M. to 1 A.M., closed Sundays. A, BC, BM, CB, D.

Caporales, Lopez Mateos Sur 5290, tel. 314596; among the best of Mexican cuisine; basic meal, $12; live mariachi music; open weekdays 2 P.M. to 7 P.M., weekends till midnight, all major cards.

El Abañejo Campestre, Juárez 231 (in Tlaquepaque), tel, 359097; Mexican cuisine, especially meats, basic meal $7.50; mariachi and quartet music; open noon to 11 P.M.

El Abañejo, Vallarta 2802, tel. 300307; specializes in meats; marachis; basic meal, $6.50; open 8 A.M. to 11 P.M. A, I, M, V.

Chalet Gourmet, Ave. Americas 925 (corner of Colomos), tel. 169161; speciality: prime ribs, basic meal, $12; open 1 P.M. to midnight every day. All major credit cards.

Restaurant Sin Nombre (without a name), Madero 80; (in Tlaquepaque, tel. 354520 and 359677). No sign whatsoever over the door, only the street number, reservations advised; American run in a renovated colonial mansion, specializes in traditional 19th-century Mexican cooking; there are no menus as the waiters describe the dishes (in English); lots of specialities like chicken casserole and tropical filet (with non-hot chiles); basic meal, $11; outdoor patio dining amid foliage and tropical birds with indoor seating also available; open Monday through Thursday from noon to 10 P.M., Friday and Saturday till midnight, closed Sunday. All major credit cards.

Copenhagen, Lopez Cotilla at the Parque Revolucion, tel. 252803; (another location on Americas and Lopez Mateos); essentially a jazz restaurant with excellent live music, varied international menu; basic meal, $12; open every day from 1 P.M. to 2 A.M. A, C, M, V.

Chalet Suizo, Hidalgo 1983, tel. 157122; specialities; Swiss, international, fondues; basic meal, $8; live music; open 1 P.M. to midnight, Sunday till 10 P.M. All major credit cards except A.

El Meson de Sancho, Marcos Castellanos 114; tel. 252898; Spanish cooking with their special Paella Valenciana; basic meal, $8; open 1 P.M. to midnight; Sunday (when there's a special menu) till 6 P.M. BC, BM, CB, D, E, M, V.

Hacienda de la Flor, Aurelio Ortega 764, Colonia Seattle (in Zapopan, past the Plaza Patria), tel. 333178; a superb place, specializes in the best of Mexican cuisine: lechon ahumado (smoked suckling pig), cordero lechal al horno (baked suckling lamb), chiles en nogada (chiles in walnut-and-spice sauce); basic meal, $11; live music; open 1:30 P.M. to midnight, Sunday till 5 P.M. All major credit cards.

La Zanahoria, Americas 538, tel. 166161; only vegetarian dishes; open 8 A.M. to 10 P.M., Sunday till 5 P.M.; basic meal, $3.50, All major cards except D.

Las Margaritas, Lopez Cotilla and Chapultapec (another location at Dario and Acuna); vegetarian dishes only, open 9 A.M. to 10 P.M.; basic meal, $3.50. No credit cards.

Agora, at the exconvento del Carmen, Juárez 638; international cuisine, basic meal $8; open 8 A.M. to 10 P.M. with a wide variety of entertainment of the Latin American variety around 8 P.M. No credit cards.

Cuates Rosas, Lopez Mateos Sur 646, tel. 213168; specializes in various kinds of meats cooked at your table on small burners; basic meal, $8; open 1 P.M. to 1 A.M. from Monday to Thursday, till 5 A.M. of Friday and Saturday, closed Sunday. Only Mexican credit cards.

EXPLORING THE GUADALAJARA AREA

Many interesting cities and places can easily be reached from Guadalajara by road or air. You can zip by plane to either Puerto Vallarta or Manzanillo in a half hour or to Mazatlán in 45 minutes. The heartland of Mexico is about the same distance from Guadalajara as from Mexico City. (For more information, see *Heartland* chapter.)

The cities to the north and east of Guadalajara have no air links with the capital of Jalisco, so it's either going there by road or flying to Mexico City to make a connection. The thriving cities of Aguascalientes and San Luis Potosí, each with several possible side trips, have good road connections to the heartland cities of Guanajuato and Querétaro as well as to Guadalajara. The old silver city of Zacatecas, relatively close to Aguascalientes and a bit farther from San Luis Potosí, lies about five hours, drive from Guadalajara.

Tequila, the Town and the "Tonic"

A quick half-day trip west will take you to the source of all good or all evil, depending on your inclinations—tequila. There's a town by that name on the main highway to Tepic and Nogales, about an hour's drive from the Minerva Circle in Guadalajara. Some 15 minutes before Tequila, at the village of Amatitan, look for a cemetery on your right—there's a dirt road next to it. By turning off here and following the road a short way, you will come to the old Herradura tequila processing plant. Ask in your best Spanish if you can visit the place—it's a true old-time marvel. Just a bit beyond, there's a new plant which you could also visit. If you have seen these two places while they were processing (there's no firm schedule) you could head back to Guadalajara. Otherwise, keep going on the highway to Tequila. It's a nondescript town. Head straight to the Tequila Sauza plant which is most likely to have a tour going. There are several other large tequila distilleries in town. You could also try the Tequila Cuervo plant. For these tours, best to show up between 10 A.M. and 1 P.M.

You may win some wagers in your local bar if you know exactly what tequila is and how it is made. Tequila is processed from one kind of agave cactus—agave tequilana, the blue magey. There are literally hundreds of species of maguey, some of which produce mezcal. Tequila is a particular kind of mezcal, made *only* from the blue agave which *only* grows in two areas: around the town of Tequila and another place some 40 miles east of Guadalajara. The spikes of the cactus are slashed off at the base, leaving the heart of the plant, called *piña* because of its pineapple-like appearance. (*piña* means pineapple in Spanish) These *piñas,* weighing up to 150 lbs. are chopped up, cooked, shredded, and squeezed dry. Some sugar is added to the resulting juice, fermenting the liquid which is then distilled twice. Now you know what should go into a margarita. Most Mexicans drink their tequila straight with either salt and lime or a sangrita chaser. Before the Spanish, the Indians only had one kind of drink, the fermented pulque, made from another species of cactus. They did not know the process of distillation. In the Aztec culture, only old people could imbibe freely; others were punished by death for getting drunk in any but a very few ceremonial occasions.

Several factors helped to establish the fame of tequila. It was the favorite drink of the miners in the nearby booming silver town of Bolaños in the northern part of Jalisco in the 17th century. About the same time, the thriving port of San Blas demanded tequila to keep crews and passengers happy on the long hauls to California and Alaska. By then, suave palates in Mexico City were also demanding this booze, preferring it over other kinds of mezcal. The government of Guadalajara profited from the fame of tequila—taxes on this liquor paid over half of the cost of the Palacio Federal. Although tequila won some prizes in U.S. competitions in the early part of this century, tequila's fame in America took off with the servicemen on R and R in border towns during World War II.

If you are in the market for opals, keep going another 12 miles beyond Tequila to the town of Magdalena. The main square has several shops selling opals from nearby mines. The Japanese, who think that opals bring good luck, come periodically to look over the crop, so it's unlikely that you will find any bargains. And remember: opals can dehydrate and crack after several months. Bargain and hope for the best.

THE LAKE CHAPALA AREA

The most popular one-day excursion from Guadalajara is a 100-odd-mile round trip which features Lake Chapala with the largest U.S. retirement community in Mexico. On the way back, there are some fine examples of colonial church architecture.

From downtown, take Federalismo towards the south, then Lazaro Cardenas towards the airport. You will have to make a right turn off Lazaro Cardenas as it blends into the highway to Mexico but there are signs. It's about 25 miles to Chapala.

Just before reaching Chapala, you climb a low mountain, part of the cradle of the lake. As you drop down, the panorama unfolds, magnificent on a clear day (but often hazy). The Isla Alacranes (Scorpion Island, but don't worry) peeks just above the surface in front of you while Mexcala Island lies way off to your left. The scene below was the setting for D.H. Lawrence's masterpiece, *The Plumed Serpent* as well as some of his short essays.

Lake Chapala, Mexico's largest lake, currently measures 50 miles east to west and about 20 miles across. The shoreline has dropped several feet since Lawrence's time, leaving much fertile lake bottom exposed for agriculture. The shrinking lake is a result of the ecological disaster of the Lerma River, the only river flowing into Lake Chapala. Due to extensive irrigation upriver, plus Mexico City's unquenchable thirst, the Lerma's input into the lake has become insignificant. Rainfall is now the only refill. Migrating birds still winter around the lake, setting an example for their human counterparts from the freezing north as well as providing exciting binocular-fill to eager birdwatchers.

After passing the turn-off to Ajijic, the highway eases into the town of Chapala (pop. 20,000) and becomes Avenida Madero all the way to the lake and pier. All the commercial life in town lines Avenida Madero, an eager gauntlet for weekend visitors—restaurants, the only downtown hotel, the supermarket, the municipal presidency, the town square with its bandstand in front of the market. All the activity is funneled down to the lakefront. There is a bit of an undistinguished beach with umbrellas to the right backed by a promenade and open-air restaurants. Water lilies and shallow, muddy water discourage all but the most inveterate swimmers.

If you have a choice and want things quiet, come on a weekday; but if the festive bustle of crowds and strolling mariachis attract the soul, make it on a weekend. Most visitors come to Chapala for a relaxing look at the lake, taking perhaps a boat ride from the pier to the nearby Isla Alacranes. The cost is $4 to $7 for the round trip. A meal in a restaurant, mariachi music, a stroll, then it's back home for Guadalajara weekenders.

Tourism began at Chapala at the end of the 19th century when an Englishman built a villa there to take advantage of the thermal waters and scenery. Starting in 1904, the redoutable dictator Porfirio Diaz enjoyed his Easter weeks in Chapala, accompanied by the capital's aristocracy as well as prosperous Tapatios. Chapala was "in" and some of the old-style mansions, now renovated, still grace the waterfront. By 1920 the train tracks reached Chapala but the line functioned for only six years, giving up when a good road finally reached the lake. Train buffs will want to look at the station, still majestic even if inhabited by several families. You will see the station just before the paved road begins on the east side of town running toward San Nicolas.

The Vista del Lago lies just beyond San Nicolas, about 5 miles from Chapala. Upper-crust Tapatios have their weekend homes here, complete with meticulous, spacious lawns and dish antennas for every home. And, of course, a nine-hole golf course, the Country Club de Chapala.

Americans started settling around Chapala after World War II, attracted by the idyllic setting, perfect weather, and cheap prices. The first of the crowd included luminaries such as Tennessee Williams, Robert Penn Warren and ex-king Carol of Rumania.

Haven For Retirees

If you ever consider retiring in Mexico and want to settle in an American colony, the Chapala area is the largest gringo concentration in the country. Chapala, with the close-by villages of Ajijic and Chula Vista (locally referred to as Glendale), can ease the cultural shock: language is not an overwhelming problem and most establishments cater to foreigners. There are three golf courses in the area and the luxury of domestic help is available at very reasonable rates. A very recent book claims that one can live in this area for $250 a month (Thomas McLaughlin: *The Greatest Escape*) but living cost calculations were made in July '82. Current estimates range around $350 to $400 a month in this area for all of one's basic expenses, holding to a moderate lifestyle. But this may very well change by the time you read these lines. Our advice is to contact the Lake Chapala Society as well as the U.S. Consulate in Guadalajara if you are thinking of a long-term stay in the area.

The highway from Chapala to the west starts on Avenida Hidalgo, a block north of the lake, at the town's only traffic light. Heading west a couple of miles brings you to Chula Vista, probably the most completely American settlement in Mexico. Though administratively part of Chapala, Chula Vista is in effect a self-sufficient community with hotel facilities, private housing, a 9-hole golf course, and a non-denominational Protestant church, the Little Chapel by the Lake. While short-term residents will use the hotel (which may have been turned into condos by '87) those planning to settle here have a choice between two types of housing. One area consists of modestly priced bungalows while the other, the so-called "open" housing district, has units ranging from houses only slightly more expensive than the bungalows to lavish estates. The open housing area stretches up the slope of a hill whose summit commands a magnificent view of the lake. Distinguishing between Chapala and Chula Vista, it would be accurate to say that Chapala is a Mexican town with a sizable American colony while Chula Vista is as American as any settlement you'll find in the U.S. sun belt. Yet bordering Chula Vista to the south—and separated from it by the Jocotepec highway—is the completely Mexican village of San Antonio. Though Chula Vista *gringos* and San Antonio Mexicans coexist peacefully, they are culturally light years away.

Ajijic, Artists' Retreat

Three miles west of Chula Vista is Ajijic, the town whose name sounds like a man afflicted with hiccups. Ajijic has traditionally been a writers' and painters' retreat and has also been branded with the hippie label. Where the first image is correct the second is not. There was a hippie influx at one time but it ended abruptly in 1965, which could be correctly described as the Year of the Purge. At the instigation of the Mexican community, resident hippies were unceremoniously escorted to the city limits and subseuqent infiltration has been rigorously discouraged. Those who remained were serious—and successful—

writers and artists, some of them quite prosperous. In the past couple of years there has also been an influx of affluent gays. Ajijic can also be reached via a new cutoff road that begins just before you enter Chapala and exits near Chula Vista.

Along with painting and writing, Ajijic is also a center for native handicrafts. Local shops sell an astonishing variety of goods, including such diverse items as stoneware, woodwork, embroidery, cotton doilies, sport coats, and paintings by talented villagers.

Heading west on the highway out of Ajijic, you soon reach San Juan Cosala, halfway to Jocotepec. There are luxurious homes, the San Juan Racket and Sports Club, and two thermal spas. The Balneario San Juan Cosala was the pioneer—now aging but still worth it for its seven pools of different temperatures ranging from pleasant to unbearable. The more modern Aqua Spa Cosala offers such innovations as jacuzzis in an up-to-date setting.

Jocotepec (pop. 35,000) is the largest town in Lake Chapala's northwest shore but with the smallest number of foreign residents. Devoid of the sports and social facilities offered by the other communities, Jocotepec tends to attract the type of American who came to Mexico to "get away from it all." Apart from its restful atmosphere, Jocotepec's main attractionis is as a center for white serapes. They are on display along a number of streetside shops.

To leave Jocotepec, wind around the plaza following the signs to Guadalajara. Out of town about a mile, you'll see a gas station where you turn right and it's some 35 miles back to Guadalajara, well marked.

About 20 miles before reaching the big town, Santa Cruz de las Flores will pop up on your left. Ask for directions to the church, worth a quick look. But within a block, there is much better. The Capilla del Hospital dates from the 17th century with its splendid baroque facade framing three arched entrances. There is an open-grille gate in front, usually locked as this "chapel" is no longer in use. The town priest will send someone with the key if you want a closer look and enter the capilla.

Santa Anita will be on your right after a few more miles of highway. A road leads straight into town and to the Santa Anita church built of quarried stone in the 18th century. The facade is covered with a profusion of sculptures and three sections of ornate false columns. Good light for photos in the late afternoon.

The highway into Guadalajara turns into Lopez Mateos which you follow past the Plaza del Sol shopping center. Just after you have passed under the railroad tracks, take the exit to the right then around the Minerva to slide into the lateral road which parallels Lopez Mateos. Your first right turn onto Hidalgo shoots you back downtown.

The archaeological site of La Quemada, about 30 km. from Zacatecas, is labeled Chicomoztoc on the road signs. This means "seven caves" in the language of the Aztecs, the last of the Nahuatl-speaking peoples who invaded central Mexico in several waves from the 10th century onwards. All these linguistically related tribes were supposed to issue from seven mythical caves which have nothing to do with La Quemada.

PRACTICAL INFORMATION FOR THE LAKE CHAPALA AREA

Hotels

Ajijic and Chula Vista

Real de Chapala, Paseo del Prado #20; tel. 52519; just off the lake; 85 units, same owners as the Danza del Sol; ample grounds, meticulously kept with trees and flowering shrubs, pool, bars, restaurants, games room, lit tennis courts, horseback riding, nightclub, convention facilities; Saturday barbecues with quartet; Sunday Mexican buffet with mariachis. Except for the last two weeks of December and Easter Week, there are discounts of 30 to 50% on the rooms. *Deluxe.*

Danza del Sol, Zaragoza 165, owned by the Autonomous University of Guadalajara, designed as a convention hotel and only recently open to the public; 45 suites each with one, two, or three bedrooms, tastefully furnished, fireplace. Much larger than the number of suites imply; well landscaped grounds, heated pool, sauna, shops, two lit tennis courts, restaurant with very reasonable prices, including those of drinks; plenty of meeting rooms some of which even include cabins for simultaneous interpretation. *First Class.*

Posada Ajijic, 16 Septiembre #4; 15 units, well managed by Canadians; nonexistent lobby, pool, lush gardens, good restaurant, and bar; plenty of things to including bridge makes this hotel a center of expatriate activities. *Moderate.*

Las Calandrias, motel on the highway, between Aquiles Serdan and Juarez; tel. 52819; 29 spacious apartments with kitchens, parking, pool. *Moderate.*

Las Casitas, motel next door to Las Calendrias, 14 apartments with kitchen, pool, parking, economic monthly rates. *Inexpensive.*

Mariana, a block from the main plaza, 24 rooms and 4 bungalows, Italo Pizza restaurant. *Moderate.*

Motel Villa Formoso, near the Real de Chapala, 22 units all with kitchen, including 10 studio type and 12 with two bedrooms; heated pool, American managed, washing machines, no dogs or children; weekly or monthly rates.

Chapala

Las Brisas de Chapala, just a bit farther from town than the Haciendas on the highway; 41 rooms grouped in two- or three-unit bungalows with a good view of the lake; German owned and favored by foreign tourists; the hotel has its own golf course, ample parking, two pools, restaurant. *Deluxe.*

Chapala Haciendas, about two miles from Chapala on the Guadalajara highway; tel. 52720; 17 rooms, 5 bungalows, all with shower or bath; parking, restaurant, bar, small pool. The restaurant caters to local American residents with Wednesday and Friday night "specials" which includes a good meal and dancing. *Inexpensive.*

Nido, Madero 202, tel: 22116; a half block from the lake on the main street; older hotel with character, large bedrooms, excellent restaurant, pool. *Inexpensive.*

Restaurants

Ajijic. There are many and all cater to American tastes—only the most outstanding and popular are listed. *Posada Ajijic,* right on the lake with a good view of the receding shoreline (now used for parking); lots of aging gringos, jovial atmosphere, food OK but service is slow; large, well-stocked bar with tables next door; a favorite meeting place. *El Meson de Ajijic,* just off the main square; bar/restaurant serving good Mexican food toned down to U.S. tastes;

good atmosphere, live music on Sundays. *El Lugar* (Big Mama's); super bar atmosphere—considered the best by local experts; more than decent food but the kitchen shuts down at 10 P.M. for serious drinking. *Los Naranjitos,* on Hildago; opened in late '85 after losing its lease in Jocotepec; tradition continues with great food, low prices.

Chapala. All the downtown restaurants are within a block or so from the lake and most are geared for weekend visitors from Guadalajara. Meat, fish and seafood everywhere, moderate prices for a resort. *Cazadores,* in a pop-castle mansion on the waterfront has a pleasant atmosphere to go with over-priced meals which are nothing special. The *Beer Garden,* on the "beach," is a huge, somewhat run-down joint with plenty of mariachi ambience on the weekends. The *Hotel Nido* can whip up a delicious soup, catfish (bagre), the local "caviar" (carp roe, called *huevara*) and various lakefish when available, along with other solid meals in one of the cleanest kitchens around. The *Superior* is typically Mexican, favored by locals, an obvious plus. Next door, the *Cafe Paris,* popular with some Americans for breakfast, has an upstairs balcony overlooking the main street; food OK but nothing special. The *La Viuda,* a half block from downtown on the way to Ajijic, has a pleasant garden with tables, varied menu and attracts Americans. For those not too fastidious, cheap, filling Mexican meals are served in a number of mini-restaurants at the market, a couple of blocks from the lake, in back of the bandstand. Best is *Doña Chavela's* at the southwest outer corner of the market. *Acapulquito* is recommended in the string of seafood restaurants next to the yacht club on the lakefront, west of the pier.

Side Trip to Aguascalientes and San Luis Potosí

We head northeast to Aguascalientes and San Luis Potosí for some real exploration of Mexico off the beaten tourist track. Although the roads are good and there are very passable hotels, we may not see another gringo for days.

We exit Guadalajara on Calzada Revolución, which becomes Highway 80 at the city limits. About a mile from town we come to a crossroads with signs reading "Zapotlanejo Libre" and "Zapotlanejo Cuota." Here we take a brief but rewarding side trip to the village of Tonalá, one of Mexico's most outstanding (and overlooked) handicraft centers. Follow the "Zapotlanejo Libre" sign and go left off the main highway about a half-mile later. From this point it's 2½ miles to Tonalá.

Unlike Tlaquepaque, Tonalá's merchandise has not declined in quality. Pottery here is still first-rate and you can get excellent buys in ceramics, papier-mâché, and glass for a fraction of what you'd pay in New York or even Mexico City. Tonalá is also of cultural interest, having been the subject of a 1966 study by University of California anthropologist May N. Díaz.

From Tonalá we retrace our steps to the highway and then go back toward Guadalajara until we reach the "Zapotlanejo Cuota" sign. Turn right here and for the next 26 miles you're on a good toll road that goes as far as Zapotlanejo. Fare 110 pesos.

At Zapotlanejo we rejoin Highway 80. Though this town is undistinguished, the surrounding countryside is glorious, suggesting a combination of the Kerry Mountains and the Blue Ridge.

The hilly region continues for about 15 miles out of Zapotlanejo and then flattens out into a broad plateau. You're now in dairy and farming country that continues for another 35 miles, through the towns of Tepatitlán, Pegueros, Valle de Guadalupe, and Jalostotitlán. The only noteworthy sight along the way is the Panteón de Guadalupe, Jalostotitlán's ornate graveyard.

About 7 miles out of Jalostotitlán the country begins to get hilly again. Set in low, rolling country is our next stop, San Juan de Lagos. San Juan has a celebrated annual fair noted no less for the variety of goods displayed than for its antiquity. Dating back to colonial times, its privileges were confirmed by Charles IV of Spain. In the parish church is an image of the Virgin of San Juan de los Lagos, said to be miraculous. The Virgin is honored in annual *pilgrimages* beginning January 20 and ending February 5. The climactic day is February 2.

A short way past San Juan de los Lagos, there is a turnoff to Aguascalientes, about 70 miles away.

Beyond San Juan de los Lagos there is a dramatic change in terrain as farm country yields to range. In the 29 miles that separate San Juan de los Lagos from Lagos de Moreno, our next stop, it's like making the transition from Midwest to Far West. Sage and mesquite replace cornfields, and in the distance you'll see table-shaped mountains recalling Arizona's mesa country.

Lagos de Moreno was once a well-known stagecoach stop and has retained many colonial characterisitcs. The church is baroque, and a bridge fording the nearby Lagos River was originally built in the 18th century. It's a pleasant sleepy town with a couple of decent hotels. From Lagos de Moreno we can keep going to Ojuelos, then to San Luis Potosí about 95 miles from Lagos de Moreno. There are plenty of steep curves before arriving in San Luis. If we are heading for Aguascalientes, the turn-off is just before reaching Lagos de Moreno on the way up from San Juan de los Lagos.

Here we change course and head north-northwest toward our last stop in the state of Jalisco. This is Encarnación de Díaz, a town with one of the most intriguing parks in Mexico. The plaza is rectangular and surrounded by globular shrubs. These enclose other shrub figures, the latter notable for their ingenious design.

Best time to visit Los Altos is during the months of January and February. This is fiesta time in the area, with no fewer than 8 *alteño* communities sponsoring festivals that last from a week to 12 days.

AGUASCALIENTES

Aguascalientes is a booming business town and the capital of one of the smallest Mexican states having the same name as the city. The state's central location in the country, a dynamic governor and a forward-looking labor leader (no strikes in over 28 years) have succeeded in attracting several international companies: Xerox, General Motors, Texas Instruments, Nissan.

The town was founded in the 16th century to defend the silver convoys from Zacatecas and became a supplier of cattle, leather, and food to the mining community. Legend has it that the state became independent of Zacatecas thanks to a kiss given to the 19th-century dictator Santa Ana by a beautiful lady of Aguascalientes. Be that as it may, Aguascalientes is now economically much more important than Zacatecas. The capital bustles with some 380,000 citizens, twice that of Zacatecas.

And the urban boom is on. The population has more than quadrupled since 1950 and over 60% of the small state's total population lives in the capital. The city is certainly worth a day's visit and nearby one can tour a brandy-making outfit as well as a ranch breeding some of the country's best fighting bulls.

Any visit to Aguascalientes must take in the completely renovated central square. The *cathedral* on one side is an excellent example of 18th-century baroque, its ornate facade playing games with the early morning sun. In the interior, look for the famous painting of the Last Supper by Miguel Cabrera, the most famous of colonial artists, a Zapotec Indian from Oaxaca. For aficionados, there are plenty of other excellent religious paintings from the 17th and 18th centuries.

Next to the cathedral, the *Teatro Morelos* hosted the 1914 gathering of Mexico's revolutionaries in a great convention. After days of high rhetoric but no agreement, Pancho Villa proposed the most macho of solutions to Carranza, his main opponent—that they be both executed, thus permanently resolving their differences. (The offer was ignored by the cautious Carranza who was too afraid even to show up.)

The *Palacio de Gobierno,* the State House, is built of a harmonious combination of red *tezontle* (a porous building stone) and pink *cantera* (a kind of quarried rock). Started in 1665, no one seems to know when it was completed. A sea of interior arcades frame the patio and a massive central staircase. A couple of huge murals, painted by the Chilean artist Oswaldo Barra Cuningham, are so awful that it's almost worth a look—social problems, history, revolutions, idealized solutions all crowd available space and vie for attention.

Four churches are of interest for their architecture and interior. The *Guadalupe,* dedicated to the patron saint of Mexico, is embellished with an ornate baroque facade from colonial times and its second tower is abuilding. The interior is spacious with worshippers almost continuously praying to the most popular of Mexican saints. Both the facade and the interior of the *San Marcos Church* are surprisingly spartan. Ask for entry to the sacristy to view the admirable large canvas of The Adoration of the Kings by José Alzíbar. A beautiful balustrade-enclosed garden in front of the church hosts some of the activities of the yearly San Marcos Fair of national fame.

The Black Christ in the *Temple of El Encino* represents a major attraction for the devout. It is said that the wooden statue's left arm is growing and when it will reach a nearby column, a major disaster will occur. The former cloisters of this church is now a museum dedicated to *José Guadalupe Posada,* Aguascilente's most famous native son. Posada's engravings and etchings reflect the violence of the Diaz dictatorship. His other favorite theme tends to skulls and skeletons, reflecting the Mexican fascination with death. Posada's work influenced the great muralists, Orozco and Rivera. (The museum is open from 10 A.M. to 2 P.M. and 4 to 7:30 P.M. from Tuesday to Saturday.)

A mason and self-taught architect, Refugio Reyes, built several of Aguascalientes' public edifices as well as the eclectic *Church of San Antonio,* his masterpiece. Neoclassic, baroque, byzantine and God knows what other styles were jumbled by Reyes in this church which could almost make Disneyland. The interior is just as complex with paintings and architectural doodads betraying a horror of plain walls.

Railroad buffs will want to visit the nation's biggest train repair shop, a huge complex with thousands of workers doing just about all that is possible to locomotives and rolling stock. A tour can be arranged by the State Tourism Board but for some unfathomable reason, no photography is allowed.

North of town, a few kilometers on the road to Zacatecas, you can visit the *San Marcos winery.* (9 A.M. to 3 P.M. weekdays, till noon on Saturdays; bring someone who speaks Spanish.) Brandy is produced year-round and wine for a month or two, depending on the timing of the grape harvest—usually late August to early October. Beautiful copper distilleries and huge wooden barrels for aging. Buy some brandy at factory prices or for some $3 a bottle of Cham-dor, a surprisingly good Champagne-type wine, not for sale in the U.S. due to labeling problems.

The famous bull breeding ranch, *Hacienda Las Bovedas,* sits a bit farther towards Zacatecas, at the end of a short side road to Valladolid. The matador/owner, Manolo Espinoza Armillita, will show off his beautiful bulls: jet black, potentially as mean as they come, with fighting spirit to spare. Manolo's English is sparse, so you'll need a Spanish speaking guide.

Just beyond the hacienda, the thermal baths at the *Balneario Valladolid* are said to alleviate rheumatism and arthritis. The Olympic pool's water holds at a pleasant 38 degrees centigrade. There are other pools with cooler water, sauna, changing rooms, a snack bar, artificial lakes, and a trailer park.

The *Plaza Vestir,* just south of town, is a unique shopping center for clothes. At the last count, some 120 factories had outlets there, insuring an ample selection at prices cheap even for Mexico. Although the shops in town have fancier items, you can't beat Plaza Vestir for most kinds of clothes, especially wool items, embroideries, crochets, as well as utilitarian goods such as towels and bedsheets of good quality. The complex is located on the highway leading to Guadalajara.

If you are in town on a Sunday, ask at your hotel about a possible *charreada* (very Mexican rodeo) at the old *lienzo charro* near the Parque Centenario. Charreadas are often held on this day—fancy costumes and gentlemen cowboys with skills galore.

A jaunt to the nearby *Sierra Fría* (the Cold Sierra) rewards those blessed with more time, a vehicle and, for longer stays, camping equipment. Lakes aplenty, amid pines and oak, fishing and hunting in tranquil scenery, and spectacular sunsets. Guides are available but there could be a language problem. It is highly recommended that you drop by the *State Tourism Office.* English is spoken there and they can help you with maps and advice as to where to locate a reliable guide, permits to visit the railroad yards and describe the facilities in the Sierra Fría which were being developed at the time of this writing.

PRACTICAL INFORMATION FOR AGUASCALIENTES

HOTELS. In Aguascalientes as well as in San Luis Potosi and Zacatecas, which follow in this chapter, hotels classified as *Deluxe* at press time were authorized to charge, on the average, for a double room, $44; *First Class,* $28; *Expensive,* $17; *Moderate,* $12; and *Inexpensive,* $8.

Hotel Las Trojes, Blvd. Campestre and highway to Zacatecas; tel. 61621; 104 rooms, color TVs with satellite reception in each room, A/C, restaurant, ladies bar, pool, tennis courts, meeting rooms, odds shop, El Cabus disco. A few km. out of town, but the best at the moment; frequented by foreign businessmen. *First Class.*

Hotel Francia, on the main Plaza; tel. 56080; 100 units, A/C, cafeteria, bar, excellent restaurant (serving goodies like smoked trout), meeting rooms. Best central location with great view on to the Plaza. *First Class.*

Hotel Medrano, Blvd. José María Chavez 904; tel. 55500; 49 rooms and 20 bungalows A/C, restaurant, bar, nightclub, pool, cafeteria, nightclub, disco *Zuahiris.* Medium walk from downtown, next to the *Agua's and Charlie's* restaurant of the Carlos Anderson style and flavor. *Moderate.*

Motel La Cascada, Prolongacion Blvd. José María Chavez, next to the Plaza Vestir, tel. 61411; 78 rooms, restaurant, bar, ladies' bar, A/C, plenty of parking, pool. A few km. out of town on the road to the airport and Mexico City. *Moderate.*

Hotel Rio Grande, José María Chavez 101; tel. 61666; restaurant, parking; just off the main plaza; undergoing extensive renovation. *Moderate.*

RESTAURANTS. El Rincon Gaucho, Arturo J. Pani #110 Pte.; tel. 63191; good steaks, music in the afternoons and evenings. **La Vendimia,** Arturo J. Pani #122, tel. 66103; Italian chef, specializes in pastas. **La Tasca,** Arturo J. Pani #126; tel. 57066; small, intimate, good atmosphere in the afternoon, Spanish cuisine. **El Fausto** in the Hotel Frances on the main plaza; tel. 56080; one of the best in town, good cuts of meat and specialities such as smoked trout. **El Caballo Loco,** Venustiano Carranza #306; tel. 57869; bar and steakhouse grill with saloon-type atmosphere near downtown. **Agua's and Charlie's,** the Carlos Anderson fame and quality with friendly service. **Las Buganvilleas,** José María Chavez #101; tel. 51260; in the Hotel Rio Grande, limited but good selection, fine service, reasonably priced. **Los Pirules,** on the corner of Lopez Mateos and Arturo J. Pani; tel. 68934; good for sitting down in the afternoon to slurp up some tequila and trying out typical Mexican snacks. **El Quijote,** on José María Chavez, near the Medrano Hotel; good place, a bit fancy with Spanish and international dishes and some beautifully prepared large fish.

NIGHTLIFE. Safe bets but still jumping are the two discos in the better hotels, the *Cabus* of the Hotel Las Trojes and the *Zuahiris* at the Medrano Hotel. There are plenty of nightclubs but none we really recommend.

FIESTAS AND FAIRS. *Feria de la Uva* (Grape Fair), anytime between August and October; exposition of the state's wine products, processions, parades. *Feria Nacional de San Marcos,* starting either Easter Saturday or the second Saturday of April and running through the first week of May; this is the state's greatest event, very popular—you have to reserve a hotel room several months ahead of time or try the tourism office who will find a private home to put you up. There are cockfights, excellent bullfights, charro rodeos, expositions of local and national products, and gambling galore.

HOW TO GET AROUND. *Aeromexico* has twice daily flights to Mexico City and once daily to Tijuana; flights are planned to Monterrey and Mazatlan. Daily train with Pullman wagons to Mexico City and Ciudad Juarez. Frequent bus connections. About 1½-hour drive to Zacatecas and some 4 hours to Guadalajara.

USEFUL ADDRESSES. *Aeromexico,* Madero 474, tel. 70252. *Avis,* José María Chavez 645, tel. 67934. *Budget,* Lopez Mateos Oriente 413, tel. 64350. *Main bus terminal,* Ave. Circumvalacion Sur and Lopez Velarde. *Travel Agency,* Mexico y el Mundo, Juan de Montoro #203B, tel. 52567. *State Tourism Office,* at the Hotel Francia, in the main square.

SAN LUIS POTOSÍ

San Luis Potosí was founded by Miguel Caldera, one of the first outstanding mestizos of Mexican history. His father was Spanish and his mother a Chichimeca Indian, a generic term which encompasses the hunting-gathering groups of northern Mexico. He achieved fame as a frontiersman during the Chichimeca Wars which threatened to end the incipient Spanish colonization of north-central Mexico, including the rich mines of Zacatecas. Caldera fought when necessary but initiated the policy of "peace by purchase"—giving away food and clothing in order to persuade the wild tribes to settle down. Many years later, the same technique finally ended the Apache depredations.

In 1590 Caldera laid claim to rich silver lodes, thanks to some samples brought to him by friendly Indians. The mountainous area immediately adjacent to the mines was unsuited for a boomtown settlement, so in 1592 San Luis Potosí was founded in the plains. The first part of the city's name comes from the sanctified King of France while *potosí* means great riches in the Quechua language. The Potosí mine of 16th-century Peru (now in Bolivia) was the richest source of silver in the Americas and the founders of its homonym in New Spain were hoping for more of the same. They were to be disappointed, for the mines bonanza lasted but 30 years. However, commerce and ranching were sufficiently advanced by then to insure the permanence of the city and its importance as a regional center.

San Luis Potosí returned to the spotlight at the very beginning of the 1910 Revolution when Francisco Madero was imprisoned in the city. He escaped and from San Antonio, Texas, proclaimed the Plan de San Luis which set the ball rolling against the aging dictator Porfirio Díaz.

Industries Attracted

Today, San Luis (pop. 500,000) is racing to catch the Industrial Age by the coattails. Several large industries have been recently attracted by the city's central location in the Mexican land mass—as well as by tax breaks. An international airport nears completion while the city acquires sophistication. Yet the major attraction remains the colonial atmosphere in the downtown area.

San Luis's colonial churches and civil buildings are concentrated within a few blocks of each other in the downtown area, all easily reached by walking from any central location. The three principal plazas lie on an east-west axis within five blocks of each other while the Jardín (Garden) of San Francisco unfolds but three blocks to the south of the plazas. The Plaza de los Fundadores begins in the east with the Hotel Panorama and its 10th-floor Sky Room with the best overview of the downtown area.

The Plaza de Armas with its bandstand represents the typical colonial source of power and beauty along pre-ordained lines. The cathedral looms on one side, opposite the Palacio de Gobierno (State House). The townhall sticks to one side of the cathedral and the Tourism Office lies caddy-cornered from the State House. The Palacio, from where Juarez ruled Mexico from February to July 1867, holds a room dedicated to the country's most illustrious president. Wax figures dramatically re-create President Juarez beseeched for the life of the defeated Emperor Maximilian. The supplicant, a beautiful lady with the improbable name of Princess Salm Salm, was unable to move the upright Juárez. (Maximilian, the well-meaning but out-of-touch pawn of Napoleon III, was sent to the firing squad.)

The Carmen Church graces a plaza which carried its name. The facade shines as a prime example of the colonial baroque with its sculptures harmoniously disposed if without much breathing room. The Capilla del Rosario (Chapel of the Rosary) opens in golden splendor to your left, a minimarvel on the human scale. The severely classic Teatro de la Paz, designed by the famous architect Tresguerras, stands in reproach to the exuberant Carmen.

The Museo Nacional de Máscaras Regionales (National Museum of Regional Masks), just north of El Carmen, exhibits hundreds of ancient and recent masks from most of Mexico. Open every day except Sunday afternoon and Monday.

The San Francisco Plaza and garden, just south of the main plaza, delights in its fountain and colonial buildings. The church, inside and out, is not to be missed. The Regional Museum, on one side of the square, is worth a quick tour. On the other side, the FONART (government crafts outlet) offers the state's handicraft at most reasonable prices. There is furniture, glassware, ceramics, weavings, wooden toys, and more, all tastefully displayed in a former colonial mansion. This palace, as many churches and civil buildings in San Luis Potosí, is built of a pink to red quarried stone called tezontle. Open during the same hours as the Mask Museum.

If San Luis Potosí's central location is one of the keys in the city's recent industrial awakening, it also creates a problem for tourism. It is a logical stopping place only if you are driving south from the Saltillo-Monterrey area, which few do in this age of jet travel. Zacatecas is the nearest important highlight, 117 miles away, but that city itself is not on any major circuit. Guadalajara lies 220 miles off to the southwest while Mexico City is 263 miles to the southeast, via Querétaro.

Side Trips from San Luis Potosí

There are two possible side trips out of San Luis—one could include diving, archaeology, and bird-watching, while the other leads to a fascinating ghost town reawakening.

Rio Verde (pop. 30,000) lies a bit over 80 miles east of San Luis on Highway 70 to Tampico. Several decent hotels and restaurants are there, should you want to spend the night. A couple of miles before reaching town, there is a sign to Media Luna (Half Moon) to your right. Follow the dirt road next to the irrigation canal to the lake. Called Media Luna for its shape, the lake fills with water from thermal springs which maintain the temperature at a steady year-round 82 degrees F. The waters are crystal clear (except during the rainy season) and reach depths of over 120 feet. You can dive with just a mask or complete scuba gear. Qualified divers can have their tanks filled (and sometimes rent equipment) by contacting Señor Juvencio Martinez at the La Cabaña Restaurant in Rio Verde, tel. 20625, on the right side of the highway just as you reach town.

A few years ago, a mammoth's skull and tusks were wrestled out of the lake. Hundreds of pre-Columbian ceramic pieces have also been picked from the sediment at the lake bottom, a mute testimony to the former ritual importance of this body of water. Just prior to Capt. Caldera's peace efforts, the area was a meeting place of the Chichimec warriors as well as the untamed Huastecs.

Following the main road to Tampico from Rio Verde, you reach Ciudad Valles after 80 miles. The archaeological site of El Tamuín spreads 15 miles beyond. This was the main ceremonial center of the Huastec Indians, a branch of the Mayas, separated from their cousins some 3,500 years ago. South of Ciudad Valles, a little less than 30 miles on Highway 85, take a turnoff to the small town of Quismón. A six-mile dirt road will then lead you to the Sótano de las Golondrinas (Swallows' Cellar), a huge natural hole over 1000 feet deep where thousands of swallows fly in and out at dawn and dusk.

Real de Catorce was one of New Spain's richest mining towns. The bonanza began during the last quarter of the 18th century and continued with ups and downs until the revolution put the mines out of business. The population dropped from a booming 35,000 to a lonely 300 during the early 1910s.

The Ogarrio Tunnel, completed in 1901, is the main entrance to Catorce. It cuts through a hill appropriately named Barriga de Plata (Silver Belly). The 2.2-km.-long tunnel is just wide enough for one car or truck, so a municipal employee phones from one end to his partner at the opposite end to stop traffic when a vehicle enters.

Catorce

You emerge into the sunlight at the head of a peak-enclosed, narrow valley at 9,043 feet. The sides of the hills are denuded of trees—all formerly cut for the mines—and eroded. Catorce clings to the widest available slope, dominated by a huge church and dotted with abandoned roofless houses with carefully fitted stone walls. Tin sheets unfortunately cover homes put back to use when some of the mines recently began small-scale production. The current population is about 800.

The Iglesia de la Parroquia (Parish Church) saved Catorce from complete oblivion. During the 19th century, a cult began there to St. Francis of Assisi. Every year, from September 25 to October 12, thousands of pilgrims trudge or ride to Catorce to thank or supplicate St. Francis for a special favor. Municipal authorities boast that last year some 200,000 pilgrims appeared. This created the usual logistical chaos but all did get to eat and sleep somehow. Affectionately referred to as El Charrito (the little charro or cowboy), the statue of St. Francis represents an ascetic with a brown robe covered with medals and other silver ornaments, each representing a miracle. A large side room in the church is covered with drawings accompanied by a short text explaining some divine intervention of St. Francis in the life of one of the pilgrims.

The Casa de la Moneda (Mint), across the small plaza in front of the church, stamped out silver coins for a few years in mid-19th century. Projects are afoot to turn the building into a cultural center but at the moment, there is only a small museum of photographs in a couple of the rooms on the third floor. Some of the prints show Catorce blanketed by snow which occasionally falls in January.

The Palenque de Gallos (Cockfight Pit) has been recently restored and you need a municipal employee with a key to let you in. Looking like a Roman mini-amphitheater, the palenque is no longer used for cockfights. During the Easter Week of cultural events, plays are presented there.

Wandering along the steep cobblestone streets or the bare hills, you feel the lonely magnetism of the town. A nearby mountain called Wirikuta represents a holy spot for the Huichol Indians where offerings are left to the gods while the hallucinogenic peyote cactus is ritually dug up in the desert below. Some writers and artists are beginning to discover and like Catorce, a tickle which might someday make for a smaller version of Taxco. There is already a modest jewelry production from local silver.

Three versions are current to explain the background of the name Catorce which means the number 14 in Spanish. There were 14 soldiers killed by the Indians in the vicinity during early colonial times; 14 mines were worked during the first bonanza decade; a gang of 14 bandits regularly robbed the silver-laden mule trains leaving the area. Take your pick.

The mines of Catorce were among Mexico's most productive at the beginning of the 19th century, along with those of Guanajuato and Zacatecas. Baron von Humboldt, the German writer-scientist, wrote of Catorce in 1804 when silver production was at its peak and Mexico was in the process of doubling the world's supply. Real de Catorce reached its zenith of glory in 1895 when the dictator Porfirio Diaz came to town for three festival-laden days to inaugurate modern mining machinery.

There are two hotels in town with a total of 15 rooms, often full on weekends and of course during pilgrimage times. The Meson de la Abundancia, with nine rooms and a vital Swedish woman in charge, has plans for renovation and expansion in 1985. The El Real, with six rooms, could fix you up with lodgings even if the hotel is full.

To reach Real de Catorce, drive north on Highway 57, the main road to Saltillo from San Luis Potosí. Just before you reach the town of El Huizache, poor mestizos from the dry desert ranches have set up primitive stands to sell birds and snakes. Hawks are the most popular but you can even purchase a full grown eagle for about $25. Be warned that if you stop, it's the hard-sell method and begging accompanies the sales pitch. Matehuala, 110 miles from San Luis Potosí, has several roadside motels in case Catorce's accommodations are full. Three miles beyond Matehuala, turn left at the sign indicating Cedral and Real de Catorce. Keep going on this paved road through Cedral to the Catorce turn-off, 18 miles from Highway 57. A well-maintained road of fitted stones climbs 15 miles to Catorce, passing the village of La Luz with the operating Santa Ana mine.

PRACTICAL INFORMATION FOR SAN LUIS POTOSÍ

HOTELS. All the motels indicated except for the Posada Potosina are on Highway 57. The hotels are downtown, within walking distance of all the places of interest. **Motel Hostal Del Quijote,** tel. 44444; with 211 units, this is the most plush in town; restaurant, cafeteria, bars, pool, disco. *Deluxe.* **Motel Cactus,** Tel. 21631; 120 rooms with color TV, cafeteria, 24-hr. restaurant, night club. *First Class.* **Hotel Panorama,** V. Carranza #315, tel. 21777, a 10-floor high-rise with 127 rooms, cafeteria, three bars, heated pool, rooftop restaurant. *First Class.* **Motel La Posada,** Highway 70, tel. 44040; 91 rooms, heated pool, restaurant/bar, games for children. *Moderate.* **Motel Real de Minas,** tel. 29311; with 99 units A/C, heated pool, trailer park, restaurant. *Moderate.* **Motel San's,** tel. 27487; with 49 rooms and good restaurant. *Moderate.* **Motel Santa Fe,** tel. 25109; 21 rooms, heated or air cooled, pool, roof garden, restaurant, bar. *Moderate.* **Hotel Concordia,** M. Jose Othon and Morelos, tel. 20666; its 94 rooms are favored by commercial travelers; restaurant/coffee shop. *Moderate.* **Hotel Filher,** Av. Universidad #375, tel. 21562, 48 rooms, cafeteria, bar, restaurant. *Moderate.* **Hotel Napoles,** Juan Sarabia #120, tel. 24819, 84 rooms, restaurant, bar. *Moderate.*

Restaurants: Argentine: *El Fortín de Ciro, La Estancia, El Gaucho.* **Chinese:** *Sam's.* **French:** *La Cachette, Villa Fontana* (also Spanish). **International:** *La Gran Via, P.J. Charlie's, Mona Lisa, Phoenix, Quijote.* **Mexican/International:** *Cantares, Club Britannico, Cherry Grill, La Lonja* (noted for old-fashioned courtesy), *La Virreyna, La Colomba, La Estrella de Dimas, La Mezquita, El Mezquite* (different place). **Mexican/Regional:** *El Campero, Fonda Típica Potosina, El Campanario, El Pastor de San Luis, Cocoyoc, Los Molinos, Los*

Arcos, Los Cazadores Potosinos, Los Jacales. **Seafood:** *Villa Alicia, Mariscos Hector, La Trucha Vagabunda, El Pulpo Manco.* **Coffee Shops:** *Posada Virreyes, Sambos, La Parroquia, Tangamanga.*

USEFUL ADDRESSES. Bus service, main terminal on Diagonal Sur at the Glorieta Juarez. Car rental, *National,* V. Carranza 875A, tel. 25544. *Tourism Office,* Jardin Hidalgo #20 (Main square), tel. 23143 and 42994, open from 9 A.M. to 9 P.M. on weekdays and to 2 P.M. on weekends (open Sundays only in season). U.S. Consular Agency, Carranza 766.

FIESTAS. *National Fair* from August 17 to September 2 to celebrate the city's patron saint; trying to rival Guanajuato's popular series of cultural events as well as to highlight the state's advances in industry, farming and ranching. All of Easter Week, including a *Procession of Silence* on Good Friday, reenacting the Passion of Christ and culminating with the crucifixion. Sept. 26 to Oct. 12, *Festival of St. Francis* (San Francisco) at Real de Catorce. Easter Week at Real de Catorce, with religious and cultural events.

ZACATECAS

Zacatecas lies some 320 km and 5 hours northeast of Guadalajara. You first pass through the Barranca de los Oblatos, crossing the Santiago River. Then, it's hills and valleys until the long, straight dry stretch to Zacatecas.

The capital of the state with the same name, Zacatecas shines as a colonial gem. The streets are paved with flagstones and no modern buildings in the downtown area mar the architectural unity. Most of the town's attractions are easily reached by walking, a good idea since parking can be a problem. A couple of days should be planned to see the town.

The city is dominated by a steep hill called La Bufa, topped by the Church of the Virgin de los Remedios and a pantheon of famous sons. The baroque facade and towers of the cathedral is unique, even in baroque-to-spare Mexico. Two museums are musts, even for museum haters.

As Guanajuato, Zacatecas was built on and by silver. A chunk of silver ore, given to a Spaniards by an unsuspecting Indian, set off the bonanza in the mid-16th century. The town's first decades were difficult as tribes of nomadic Indians preyed on the convoys taking the silver to Mexico City as well as those bringing supplies. But the huge quantities of the precious metal over-rode all problems. Ranching and farming developed in what is now Aguascalientes and Jalisco in order to feed the ever-increasing population of Zacatecas, all busy in bringing the ore out of the mines and refining the silver.

Every available Indian as well as black slaves were pressed into the mines, most to die from overwork and disease at the average age of 35. But wealth was continuously dug from the earth and enough of it stayed in town to build the palaces and churches—monuments to the grandeur of the wealthy, the skills of a few, and the sweat of the countless. Silver production plummeted during the times of political turmoil in the 19th century, rose again under the dictator Porfirio Diaz and was drastically curtailed in the years of the Revolution. Pancho Villa captured Zacatecas in 1914, sealing the fate of the usurper Victoriano Huerta. Villa's victory also sealed his own fate, as in capturing Zacatecas he disregarded the orders of Carranza who was to become the first postrevolutionary president of Mexico.

Zacatecas, at 2,500 meters of altitude, can be cool, so bring adequate clothes. Don't rush around, especially going up stairs or hills—the altitude gets your heart pounding and can lead to a temporary shortness of breath.

The *Cathedral,* in the center of town, is a marvel of baroque sculpture. Its facade and towers are dripping with carving upon carving. Excellent sculptures also decorate the two lateral entrances.

The *old market* is located to one side of the cathedral. Completely renovated and modernized, it is now a fancy shopping center and includes several restaurants. On the upper level, facing Hidalgo Street, there are several glass enclosed shops, an ice cream place, and the Mexicana office. The lower level on Tacuba Street displays souvenir shops—try El Venado for leather goods—and the Cuija restaurant.

On the other side of the cathedral, the *Government Palace* offers a good example of civil colonial architecture. Built in 1727 by Count Santiago de Laguna, the interior stairwell shines with paintings depicting the history of Zacatecas in forceful mural style. The *Santo Domingo Church* and plaza open at the end of a narrow, steep street facing the Cathedral. The church's facade may leave you cold after seeing the cathedral, but take a look at the rich decorations inside, especially the gilded paintings and backdrop of the altar.

The *Pedro Coronel Museum* forms an extension of the Santo Domingo Church, both part of a mid-18th-century Jesuit complex. Provincial museums as a rule are to be skipped except by the most inveterate culture vultures. But this one is an exception. Pedro Coronel is an artist and native son of Zacatecas who has displayed in this museum an incredible collection of art: watercolors by Picasso, Braque, Rouault, Chagall, Léger the best and most complete set of original Goya drawings outside of the Prado, Hogarts, and Daumiers galore . . . excellent Japanese, Chinese, Indian and Tibetan art. Take a good look—it's worth at least a couple of hours. (Open from 10 A.M. to 2 P.M. and 4 to 7 P.M. every day except Thursday.)

Just down Hierro Street from the museum, the massive *Church of San Augustin* has been partially restored. The huge interior space serves well as a lesson in architecture. (Open from 10 A.M. to 2 P.M. and 4 to 5:30 P.M. from Monday to Thursday; Saturdays and Sundays from 10 A.M. to 2 P.M.) From San Augustin you can walk down to Hidalgo Street and back to the Cathedral, passing the ornate 19th-century *Calderon Theater.*

Other points of interest require longer jaunts, a short drive or taxi ride. A well preserved colonial *aqueduct* crosses one of the city's main entrances and ends at the base of an equestrian statue of General Gonzales Ortega, who almost became president of Mexico in the 1860s. A quiet park in back of the statue ends at the former governors' mansion, now the *Francisco Goitea Museum.* A wild painter of a man, Goitea studied in Europe then returned to Mexico to fight alongside

Pancho Villa. His themes are often revolutionary, rendered in typically Mexican style. Some of Goitea's best works as well as those of other artists are on display.

The *El Eden* mine, past the Alameda Park and at the dead end of Dovali Jaime Street, produced unimaginable quantities of gold and silver. Today, a part of the mine has been lit and walkways built for visitors. Tours are held from 1 to 8 P.M., leaving the entrance every half hour or so. Train buffs will love the minilocomotive which takes the passenger wagons into the mine. A cavern deep in the mountain mine jumps to a disco beat from 9 P.M. to 2 A.M., Thursday to Sunday. All kinds of music, not only rock, are played for dancing; there's a decent light show and drinks are inexpensive. The daytime tour of the mine takes about 45 minutes with an English-speaking guide sometimes available. The tour is conducted on the middle of the mine's seven levels—the lower ones are filled with water. After the visit, you can either take the mini-train back to the entrance or an elevator will whisk you to the top level where there is another opening. This top entrance is within 150 meters of the cable car station.

The *cable car* ride over Zacatecas is unique in Mexico. The Swiss system operates from 12:30 to 7:30 P.M. every day except Monday and costs about 75 cents for the round trip. A five-minute ride glides over the city and ends at the peak of *La Bufa* mountain. From there, one takes in the best panoramic view of the city. *Los Remedios Church and Cloisters* are worth a quick look. A paved road,the Paseo Diaz Ordaz, also climbs gently up to the top of La Bufa.

The small town of *Guadalupe* is about 7 kilometers from Zacatecas on the main highway to Mexico City. The Franciscan convent is the town's pride and joy. Founded in the early 18th century, the church and adjacent convent hold one of the best and largest collections of religious paintings from colonial times. An English-speaking guide is often available and he will point out some of the amazing optical tricks in the paintings. The *Chapel of Napoles* shines in a fortune of gold, donated by a lady who owned the El Eden mine. (Open from 10 A.M. to 5 P.M. except Monday and Tuesday.)

PRACTICAL INFORMATION FOR ZACATECAS

HOTELS. Hotel Aristos, Lomas de la Soledad; tel. 21788; 120 rooms, bar, restaurant, sauna, covered pool, banquet and meeting rooms, travel agency, car rental (the only one in town), the Las Burbujas disco, shows in the Bar Intimo. The restaurant serves excellent Mexican and international dishes. Located on the outskirts of town; good view over the city; a favorite with Americans. *First Class.*

Calinda Zacatecas, Blvd. Lopez Mateos and Callejon del Barro; tel. 23311; 133 rooms, bar, restaurant, cafeteria, covered rooftop pool, squash courts, disco, shows (singing). Not too far from downtown. Located on the main highway which cuts through town, roadside rooms can be somewhat noisy. *First Class.*

Zacatecas Courts, Lopez Velarde 602; tel. 20328; 64 rooms, all remodeled, good lobby, restaurant, bar. *Moderate.*

Posada de los Condes, Juarez 18 A, across the street from the State Tourism Office; tel. 21093; 58 rooms, clean, polite service, two adjacent restaurants, and a bar owned by the same family. *Moderate.*

Motel del Bosque, Paseo Diaz Ordaz; tel. 20745; 60 bungalows, restaurant. Located next to the disco El Elefante Blanco and the cable car. *Moderate.*

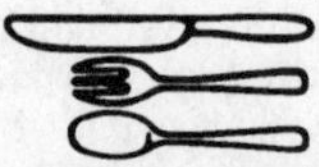

RESTAURANTS. Downtown in the Mercado, **Dom Capone** on Hidalgo Street, specializes in fast-food type pizzas; also in the Mercado but at the lower level, **La Cuija** on Tacuba Street offers Spanish dishes and others in a clean, relaxed atmosphere with quiet live music, excellent service and decent house wine; the only restaurant open in the immediate downtown area at night. There are two **Caballo Loco** restaurants, generally considered the best and most expensive in town, with good cuts of meat and well stocked bars. **El Campanario,** Guerrero 149, lacks atmosphere but specializes in flambé meats and desserts as well as a good paella and marrow soup; under the same management, **La Hacienda del Cobre** on Calzada Lopez Portillo features a trio in a pleasant, outdoor setting. **Las Pampas** on Lopez Mateos and Colegio Militar has good cuts of meat as its name implies and plenty of ambience especially with its nightly trio. For seafood, try **Flipper,** Lopez Mateos 248, or **Villa del Mar,** next to the bus station at Ventura Salazar 340—good service and reasonable prices in a small, popular place. **Hosteria del Conde,** Rayon 101, opposite the tourist office, a steak house with well-stocked bar and excellent coffee. **El Jacalito,** also opposite the tourist office, has an inexpensive, filling daily menu of Mexican dishes of surprising quality, also excellent coffee from an Italian machine, a rare find in town. **Warning:** many of the restaurants close as early as 8 P.M. on weekends; this, however, does not apply to those in the better hotels.

USEFUL ADDRESSES. *Tourism Office,* Juárez 12, first floor, tel. 24170 and 20170, open Monday to Friday from 9 A.M. to 3 P.M. and 5 to 7 P.M. *Travel Agency* (English-speaking guides) Viajes Mazzoco, Hidalgo 307, tel. 22851 and at the Hotel Aristos. *Mexicana,* Ave. Hidalgo 406, tel. 23248. *Central Bus Station,* Ventura Salazar and Lopez Mateos, tel. 21112.

NIGHTLIFE. Both the *Aristos* and the *Calinda* hotels have discos for their guests and outsiders as well as shows. Young people go to the *El Elefante Blanco* disco on Paseo Diaz Ordaz 114, next to the Motel del Bosque and with a great overview of the city. The most unusual disco is the *El Eden,* located inside the mine by the same name at the dead end of Dovali Jaime Street; for different age groups, many kinds of music, inexpensive drinks, a tourist favorite.

FIESTAS AND FAIRS. *Zacatecas Fair,* September 1 to 16, commemorating the founding of the city. Best from September 8. Bullfights, cockfights, charro rodeos, agricultural shows, lots of entertainment. *La Morisma,* on the last Sunday of August. "Native" dances at the top of La Bufa, of the matachine type taught to the Indians by the early missionaries; danced stories of the good guys (the Christians) who win battles over the Muslims (the Moors, whence the name of the festival) be they Turks, Arabs or other bad guys.

HOW TO GET AROUND. There are two daily flights to Mexico City and one to Tijuana everyday on *Mexicana* which also flies daily to Mazatlan except of Saturdays and Sundays. Daily train to Mexico City and Ciudad Juarez with Pullman wagons. Frequent buses to most of the north and center of the country. By road, it's 5½ hours or 320 km to Guadalajara and 1½ hours or 130 km to Aguascalients.

ACAPULCO

Playground Where Fun Reigns

by
SUSAN WAGNER

Susan Wagner is author of Fodor's Fun in Acapulco. *Former travel editor of* Modern Bride *magazine, she has had travel articles published in leading magazines and newspapers throughout the world and has made frequent radio and television appearances on travel programs as an expert on travel to Mexico. She has been studying, visiting, and working in Mexico for many years and claims that she has never had a dull moment during her many visits to Acapulco.*

Acapulco. There's nothing like it in Mexico *or* in the world! Eccentric, mundane, action-packed, tranquil, forthright, beguiling, it's much more than a glittering international playground. It's a multifaceted Mexican city that is among the largest in the country. It's a fun factory that works full shift around the clock around the year. No other resort in the world knows how to manufacture outrageous fun better. Most places that have been blessed with such spectacular scenic beauty and that have added such fabulous facilities for visitors would have stopped right there. But not Acapulco. They take things several steps further and never rest in their efforts to make you have fun every minute of every day of your visit. They make a business of making your vacation unforgettable. That's why Acapulco is so special.

Few places in the world are so permissive. Anything goes, as long as it has nothing to do with breaking the law. This is a place that invites you to let your hair down and kick up your heels, a place where when people say they've danced until dawn, they really mean it! You can stay in your bathing suit past midnight or wear a ball gown to breakfast and no one will bat an eye.

There's so much to see and do that you can plan every day to suit your mood. You can find or make a party from dawn to dusk, or slip away to a secluded spot to revel in unspoiled natural beauty. No matter what you choose, chances are that the temperature will be pleasant and the sun will be shining.

Great weather is Acapulco's ace in the hole. The average year round temperature is 82° F. Generally, the degree of humidity varies more than the temperature throughout the year. Even in the rainy season, August-October, showers are short and most of the rain falls at night. The driest part of the year, December 15 to Easter, is "The Season." Humidity escalates from June to October, but if you don't mind the tropical heat, you can save up to 40% on hotel rates. Generally, everything is open all year round. Christmas and Easter are the most crowded weeks of the year. Book well in advance if you plan to travel during the season.

The weather, the reasonable exchange rates and the amazing attractions are Acapulco's major drawing cards. Of the over one million visitors who arrive annually, many come back every year. Acapulco is not only one of the country's leading resorts for international visitors, it is also the *Numero Uno* destination for Mexican tourists.

Another of Acapulco's greatest assets is that it is thoroughly Mexican. Life goes on as it did centuries ago just off the Costera. The Public Market, Mercado Municipal, is as big as the ones that everyone depends on in other cities, and the downtown area is a bustling tropical port that is also a port of call for cruise ships.

It was the port, not the beaches, that first brought Acapulco world wide attention.

It was popular from the very beginning. The Nahuatl Indians who first lived here called Acapulco "the place where the reeds were destroyed," and indeed it seems that few reeds are left. It was the deep water bay that first brought Acapulco commercial importance. After the Conquest, the Spaniards made it into a leading port for trade with the Orient, and a major take-off point for Spanish colonizers. Hurtado de Mendoza sailed from Acapulco to discover the South Sea Islands and Sebastian Viscaino left from here to discover California. Cortez ordered the settlement of Acapulco in 1531, but it was not until 1799 that Emperor Carlos IV declared it an official city.

A burst of speed in Acapulco's development occurred in the 1950s when an improved highway from Mexico City was completed and the crowds began to arrive. From then on, the tropical snowball has been growing at an amazing speed.

Points of Interest

1) Bull Ring
2) Cici Children's Marine Park
3) La Vista Shopping Mall
4) Convention Center
5) Fort San Diego
6) Market
7) Mexican Naval Base
8) Muelle Pier
9) Old Downtown
10) State of Guerrero Tourist Secretariat
11) Tourist Office

Hotels

12) Acapulco Malibu
13) Copacabana
14) Acapulco Plaza
15) Pierre Marques and Club de Golf
16) Acapulco Princess
17) Casa Blanca
18) Condesa Del Mar
19) Exelaris Hyatt Continental
20) Exelaris Hyatt Regency
21) Calinda
22) La Palapa
23) Las Brisas
24) El Presidente
25) Ritz
26) Villa Vera
27) Acapulco Paraiso

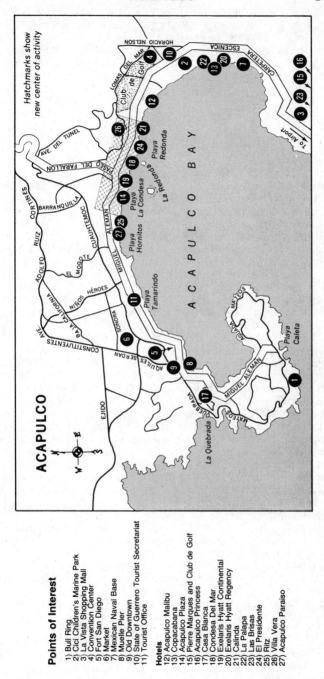

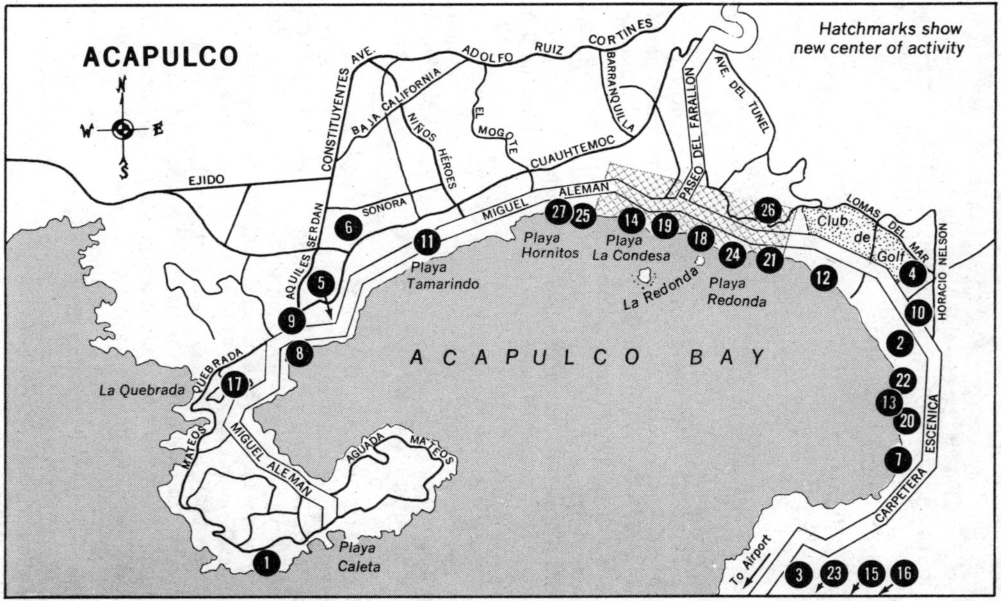

There is so much to see and do that you won't be able to fit it all into one visit. Days are spent in the Great Outdoors. Acapulco nights are legendary. Discos that out-glitter any others in the world stay open until the last guest goes home. Some revellers find that another day has begun before they've climbed into bed! That's one of Acapulco's most delicious qualities. Any night will last as long as you can, and the fun never stops until *you* want it to.

EXPLORING ACAPULCO

Acapulco is one of the world's most beautiful bays. Bordered by the golden Pacific on one side and the towering Sierra Madre mountains on the other, it lies in a breathtaking setting 6 hours drive southwest of Mexico City. Flying time is 45 minutes.

The first view of the bay that you get on the ride from the airport will take your breath away. Every time. The Carretera Escenica (Scenic Highway) is a smooth, flat stretch of highway that passes the Princess and Pierre Marques hotels and begins to climb up the hill. Your first panoramic view will be that of tiny Puerto Marques. The next one, just above Las Brisas Hotel, will be glittering Acapulco Bay in all of its glory. The highway then winds around the hillside, passing the world famous Las Brisas Hotel and residential section and La Vista Shopping Mall.

The wide and wonderful Costera Miguel Aleman, one of the world's most exciting seaside highways, begins at the foot of the hill in front of the Naval Base and winds west around the coast as far as Caleta. Just about everything you may want to see or do is on or just off this amazing highway. The portion between the Hyatt Regency and the Acapulco Paraiso is called "The Strip." It just may be the most fun-packed stretch of highway anywhere in the world.

Beyond it, the road travels through an underpass and winds on past the cruise ship terminal through the downtown area and out to Caleta, the beach that launched the resort of Acapulco into worldwide stardom. Today, this area is called "Traditional Acapulco." It's a perfect place to enjoy a quiet stay away from the crowds.

Past the downtown area, a road winds up to the famous La Quebrada where the daring divers perform and another goes out to Pie de la Cuesta, a primitive beach that is another super scenic 15-minute ride away. Here, you can watch some of the world's most beautiful sunsets. Coyuca Lagoon, a nature preserve where you can swim and ski in fresh water, is across the street.

Turnoffs from the airport road will take you to Barra Vieja, a rustic village with a few seaside restaurants where you can sun and swim. Beto's-Barra Vieja is best. It also has a pool.

Tres Palos, Acapulco's most primitive lagoon and Costa Chica, an area where African descendants live, can be reached from the Highway 200 turn off. Costa Chica is about 150 miles away.

Wherever you go, whatever you do in Acapulco, chances are that you'll get more than your money's worth. The sunshine and beautiful surroundings are free dividends. This is one of the few places in the world where the fun will last as long as you let it.

PRACTICAL INFORMATION FOR ACAPULCO

HOW TO GET THERE. By Air. Major airlines operating from leading U.S. gateways to Acapulco are: *Aeromexico, American, Continental, Mexicana, Western.* Some companies stop in Mexico City for immigration. Two large bags per person are permitted. There are frequent flights from Mexico City every day. Flying time is about 40 minutes.

By Bus. Two bus lines operate frequent schedules from Mexico City. The trip takes about 7½ hours. Some buses are comfortable and air conditioned. *Estrella de Oro:* Deluxe Service. Tel. 5–87–05; at terminal downtown at Cuauhtemoc and Magallanes. *Flecha Roja;* tel. 2–03–51; Terminal at Cuauhtemoc 97.

By Car. An excellent road, Route 95, links Acapulco with Mexico City. Driving time is approximately 5 hours. Tolls total about $3.50. There is a gas station about every hour. Roadside restaurants are not recommended for gringos. There is an Army Inspection Station 60 kms before Acapulco. The highway is patroled by Green Angels who help out with breakdowns. (See *Facts at Your Fingertips.*) The winding old road takes longer but is free. A detour from the new road to the colonial silver city of Taxco takes about 2½ hours.

PHONES AND EMERGENCY NUMBERS. The Area Code for Acapulco is 748. To direct dial from Acapulco (lada), dial 91 + area code (clave) + number for domestic calls; 95 + area code + number for international calls to the U.S. and Canada; 98 + area code to the rest of the world. You'll save considerable money if you call home collect (*a cobrar*). There is a hefty 50%-plus telephone tax in Mexico. Hotels levy a service charge of about 150 pesos for every call. It is cheaper to call at night or on weekends, but there seems to be a skeleton crew of operators then. If you want to get through fast, call during the day, and ask your operator how long it will take to get through. Also ask for time and charges when you finish. Dial 02 for operator-assisted calls within Mexico; 09 for international calls.

Public Phones. Mexico is in the process of changing public phones and raising prices. However, a local call in Acapulco still costs 20 centavos for three minutes.

Emergency Numbers. *Secretaria de Turismo:* Costera Miguel Aleman, No. 54; tel. 4–61–34 or 4–61–36; *U.S. Consular Representative:* Hotel Club del Sol; tel. 5–66–00. If you speak Spanish, *Police:* tel. 2–00–40; *Traffic Police:* tel. 2–50–34; *Red Cross:* tel. 5–09–43; *Fire Department:* tel. 5–00–73; SEME for medical assistance, tel. 4–32–60.

Airlines. *Aeromexico:* Costera Miguel Aleman 286, or on the second floor above VIP's in the Torre de Acapulco; tel. 5–16–25. *American:* Hotel Condesa del Mar; tel. 4–12–44. *Continental:* tel. 4–33–08. *Eastern:* the airport; tel. 4–63–63. *Mexicana de Aviacion,* Hotel Las Hamacas or second floor above VIP's in Torre de Acapulco; tel. 4–68–90. *Western:* the airport; tel. 4–07–16.

HOW TO GET AROUND. Getting around in Acapulco is particularly easy. Most of the leading shops, restaurants, hotels and discos are located along the wide Costera and are easy to find. Those staying on The Strip can walk to most major places along it.

From the Airport. This is just about the only transportation set-up in Acapulco that is complicated, haphazard, and uncomfortable. Private taxis are not permitted to carry passengers from the airport to town, a distance of about 14 miles. As many international flights are scheduled to arrive simultaneously, an already complicated system which is definitely not designed for tourists' comfort, and is certainly stacked against those traveling alone, becomes even more unpleasant.

Here's how the system was designed to run; however, it rarely does. Your porter asks the name of your hotel when you leave customs. He drops your bags at that zone. (Signs indicating which zone your hotel is in are posted overhead.) You then have to leave your bags, buy a ticket on a bus or a combi and come back to board the bus or combi. Tickets are sold at small white booths. As arriving passengers are generally unfamiliar with the system and are confused, booths are crowded and people push, since there is no room to form lines.

Ask which bus or combi will come first and buy that one. The price difference is slight. Bus tickets cost about $1.50 per person one way, $2.83 round trip. Combi tickets cost $2.30 per person one way, $4.25 round trip. Though ticket vendors push buying round-trip transportation, we recommend buying one way only. You call for the return bus pick-up and often have to spend a lot of valuable sun time waiting for the transportation to arrive. Private taxis are permitted to take you from town *to* the airport. The trip costs approximately $8–$10 and you can leave when you wish.

After buying your ticket, go back to your luggage. (Because of the crowds, porters do not wait.) The planeload of arriving passengers has probably made it impossible for the porter to leave your bags near the zone sign. There will probably be a wait for the bus, and you will have to make sure your luggage gets on it. Sometimes private cars appear. They cost approximately $10–$13; $20 for limos, at booth no. 1 outside by the curb.

A direct ride to or from the airport takes 20–25 minutes. However, since buses from the airport make many stops at a variety of hotels, it may take double that amount of time. The good news is that the Scenic Highway affords spectacular views of the bay and if you are staying on The Strip and make different stops, the trip can help in getting you oriented.

So far, no reliable limousine service is available.

Generally, once you get to your hotel the nightmare is over and getting around is easy.

By Taxi. Taxis are plentiful, easy to find, and relatively inexpensive. Most taxis are blue and white sedans or VWs. Their top light is *off* when they're free. It is usually cheaper to flag one down in the street than to get one of the fleet from your hotel, as hotel taxis pay for the right to be part of the hotel fleet and pass the cost along to the customers. However, the difference between a hotel taxi and one from the street is only about $.50 to $1 if you are going anywhere downtown to any point on The Strip. Check the price before you enter. Most hotels have average rates posted at the door. Rates are fixed by zones. The average cost for a ride anywhere along The Strip is about $1.–$1.50. At night, rates are slightly higher. Drivers do not expect tips, though Mexicans often leave small change. They often claim not to have change, so come prepared with a few 100- and 50-peso coins. If you flag a cab down, the price may depend on how much the driver likes your looks, but usually it doesn't exceed what a hotel taxi would charge for the same trip. Often it is half. Some street drivers will ask how much you want to pay. 500 pesos is tops for point-to-point ride between the Ritz and the Exelaris Hyatt Regency. If you want to go shopping and/or sightseeing and have your cab wait, make a deal before you get in. The charge is usually $9–$10 per hour. You also can arrange for a guide for sightseeing. The cost is about $60–$70 per day.

By Bus. Public buses run from the zocalo to Caleta—some go direct; others follow the more scenic "Flamingo" route from the zocalo to La Base, the Naval Base, at the end of The Strip. Some go farther out to Puerto Marques. The cost is about 23 pesos, but the trip may not be the most comfortable one you'll ever take. Other buses operate from the Post Office to Puerto Marques and to Pie de la Cuesta. Sheltered stops dot The Strip. Watch your purse or wallet.

By Car Rental. Average daily price for a small, automatic air conditioned car is $65–$75/day including mileage, depending on the size. Jeeps, often called safaris, are about $40/day.

When making reservations, clearly state that you want air conditioning and automatic drive, and reserve in advance if you are visiting Acapulco in season. Note your confirmation number or ask the company for a written one and have it on hand when you pick up the car. Reservations made in the U.S. have a mysterious way of getting lost.

If you plan to rent a rent a car, pick it up at the airport. In this way, you can avoid the arrival hassle. Almost all companies have space at the airport. Here are their downtown addresses: *Hertz,* Costera Miguel Aleman No. 1945, tel. 5–69–95; *Avis,* Costera Miguel Aleman No. 711, tel. 4–13–42; *Dollar,* Costera Miguel Aleman No. 2148, tel. 4–30–66; *Saad* (jeeps), Costera Miguel Aleman No. 28, tel. 4–34–45; *Sand's,* Costera Miguel Aleman, corner Juan de la Cosa, tel. 4–10–31; *Thrifty,* Fiesta Torguga Hotel, tel. 4–71–17; *Fast* (jeeps), Costera Miguel Aleman, across from Hyatt Continental Hotel, tel. 4–48–44.

TOURIST INFORMATION SERVICES. *Secretaria de Turismo:* Costera Miguel Aleman No. 54, across from CiCi, tel. 4–61–34. It is open from 9 A.M. to 1 P.M. and from 4 P.M. to 7 P.M. They can tell you where to go, what to do and approximately how much it costs. Printed material is almost non existent. There is another city tourist office on the Costera across from Super-Super. They sometimes have maps.

ENGLISH LANGUAGE MEDIA. *The News,* a good English-language newspaper with international news, stock prices, comics, etc., is published in Mexico City daily. It usually hits hotel newsstands and beach vendors around 11 A.M. *Sol de Acapulco,* a local English-language newspaper, comes out weekly. You can find it at hotel newsstands. Major U.S. newspapers are sold at some hotel newsstands such as the Acapulco Plaza, the Hyatt Regency, etc. If you can't find *The News,* go to Sanborn's or Super-Super. Both also have a good collection of American pocket books and magazines.

TV Cable Channel 72 broadcasts news in English at around 9 A.M. and 8 P.M. daily. Watch cable stations for daily schedules. They aren't written anywhere. If the news doesn't come exactly on schedule, leave the set on and hang in there. At least part of it usually shows up. Some cable programs are also in English, but they are mostly old—and we mean *old*—movies. Get used to missing episodes of your favorite soaps.

American and English films with Spanish subtitles are shown around town. A few of the movie houses are *Cine Salon Rojo* on the zocalo; *Variedades* on Calle Hurtado de Mendoza near the Municipal Market; *Cinema Flamboyant,* across from the Acapulco Plaza, and *Cinema Costa Azul* at the corner of Colon and Magallanes. All are air-conditioned and serve snacks. You may have to go in when the film begins, and are not allowed to stay to see it several times as you might back home. Admission is about 700 pesos. There are usually three shows every night from 4 to 10 P.M.

TOURS. A variety of tours can be arranged through travel agencies at most hotels. If you can't find what you want, go to the source: *Turismo Caleta* (the largest travel agency in Acapulco), Andrea Doria No. 2, tel. 4–65–70; *American Express,* Costera Miguel Aleman No. 709A, tel. 4–10–95; *Viajes Acuario,* Costera Miguel Aleman, corner Francisco Pizarro, tel. 5–71–00; *Mexico Travel Advisors,* Costera Miguel Aleman No. 1252, tel. 4–74–00. *Betanzos Tours,* Costera Miguel Aleman No. 98, tel. 4–47–71. Most city tours include main beaches, hotels, residential sections, and shopping areas. Some include the divers at La Quebrada. Arrange through your hotel travel agent. Cost: approximately $15.

Bay Cruises. Several small yachts cruise the bay for a view of the hotel zone and celebrity homes. Cruises leave from downtown docks. The *Hawaiiano* leaves at 11:30 A.M. and returns at 2:30 P.M. There is a stop at a private beach to sun and swim. Restaurant, bar, and cafeteria aboard. Price: about 2,000 pesos. The afternoon sunset cruise leaves at 4:30 P.M. and includes live music and three decks for dancing. Price: 2,000 pesos. The evening cruise leaves at 10:30 P.M. and returns at 2 A.M. It includes dancing to live salsa music, a variety show, and a stop at Palao Restaurant near Roqueta Island for a Hawaiian show. Cost: about 2,000 pesos. Tel. 2–07–85 for reservations.

The *Bonanza* leaves on 2½-hour cruises at 11 A.M. and 4:30 P.M. from its own dock downtown. The morning cruise includes live music and the yacht has a pool on deck. There is a half hour stop for swimming on a private beach. The 4:30 P.M. departure is aboard either the *Bonanza* or the *Fiesta* yacht. It includes live music for dancing. Cost: about 2,400 pesos. The *Fiesta Cabaret* cruise sails away from the same dock at 10:30 every night except Sunday and includes disco music and a Mexican folklore show. Cost: about 3,200 pesos. Tel. 2–20–55, 2–49–47, or 2–62–62. Double-check all times and prices.

The Trimaran *Kontiki* cruises the bay twice a day from the Colonial Restaurant dock downtown below San Diego Fort. Open bar and buffet lunch aboard. Daytime cruises stop at a secluded beach to swim or go shelling. Departs at 10:15 A.M. and returns at 2 P.M. Price: about $19 per person. Sunset cruises leave at 5:30 P.M. and return at 7:30 P.M. Price: approximately $10. Includes two domestic drinks. For reservations telephone 4–65–70 or 4–64–91.

The *Polaris* glass bottom boat cruise will show you colorful tropical fish and the unique underwater statue of the Virgin of Guadalupe. Stop at Roqueta Island for swimming and a buffet lunch. Price: about 2,600 pesos.

Peregrina, a sail boat, cruises the bay twice a day at 10:35 A.M. and 4:30 P.M. Open bar and bilingual guide. Approximately $12; tel. 4–14–93.

Safari Tour of exotic Coyuca Lagoon. The ocean is on one side of the road and a freshwater lagoon, which is a nature preserve, is on the other. A haven for nature lovers. Price: 8,000 pesos; drink and lunch included.

The Divers at La Quebrada. This is a spectacle that you should see at least once. Dives take place both daytime and night. Both are dramatic. Divers plunge 130 feet into 1½-meter-deep waters. The cost to watch outside on the terraced hillside is 50 pesos plus a tip for the divers. Or, you can watch from the nightclub at Miramar Hotel, where the cover charge is 1,500 pesos per person. Check at your hotel desk or at Miramar for show times. Many tours include the divers. It's easier to go on a tour if it's your first time.

PARKS AND GARDENS. Papagayo Park is one of the top municipal parks in the country for location, beauty, and variety. It is part of the renovation of Acapulco program which the state undertook a few years ago. Papagayo (named after the hotel that formerly stood on the grounds) occupies 52 acres of prime real estate along the Costera just after the underpass at the end of The Strip. The park offers much more than beautiful paths and walkways. Though it is primarily directed to children, there is plenty for people of all ages to enjoy. For the kids, there is a life-size replica of a galleon like the ones that sailed into Acapulco when it was Mexico's capital for trade with the Orient. There is a race track with mite-sized Can Am cars; a replica of the space shuttle *Columbia;* bumper boats to ride in the lagoon; and other rides. A cable car will carry you from the park to the beach. The Aviary is the park's most spectacular feature. Hundreds of species of birds can be seen as you walk along shaded pathways. Admission to the park is free. There is a charge of 200–450 pesos for rides, which operate from noon to 8:00 P.M., and 50 pesos to the aviary. Rides are closed on Tuesdays.

The Zocalo. The main square in front of the cathedral is pretty and shaded. Free band concerts take place on Sunday afternoon.

Roqueta Islands. The boardwalk that circles Roqueta does not pass as either a park or a garden, but it is one of the most scenic walks to be taken in Acapulco. The tranquility, the untamed foliage, and the spectacular views give you a Robinson Crusoe feeling.

CiCi (Centro Internacional para Convivencia Infantil) is a water-oriented amusement park for children with daily dolphin and seal shows, a swimming pool with waves, a toboggan ride, and other activities. It is open from 10 A.M. to 6 P.M. every day. Admission is 500 pesos for adults, 300 for children ages 2–10. There is an extra charge of 40 pesos for the toboggan ride.

PARTICIPANT SPORTS. Acapulco is a sportsman's paradise. Name your favorite tropical sport and chances are that you'll find it somewhere in town. Water sports prevail and conditions for them are perfect. Your hotel can arrange almost anything. If it can't, or if you can't find it on the beach, here are a few ideas:

Golf. The Princess and the Pierre Maraues hotels have two spectacular 18-hole championship courses. Greens fees are about $28 for guests and $37 for all others. Price includes cart. Reservations should be made one day in advance. Call 4–31–00 for the Princess; 4–20–00 for Pierre Marques. There is also a public course of nine holes on the north side of The Strip across from the Elcano Hotel. The greens fee is approximately $20. Call 4–07–81 for reservations.

Deep Sea Fishing. Marlin, sailfish, tuna, snapper, yellowtail mackerel, and bonito are prize catches. Boats that accommodate from four to eight people cost about $125–$175 per day. Food and drink are extra. Excursions usually leave about 7:30 A.M. and return about 2 P.M. You can arrange them for yourself by going to *Pesca Deportiva* downtown on the Costera, just down from Sanborn's on the opposite side of the street.

At *Divers de Mexico,* downtown at 100 Costera Miguel Aleman, tel. 2–13–98, you can rent chairs for about $50 or boats from $210–$230. Small boats for freshwater fishing can be rented at *Coyuca Lagoon* across from Pie de la Cuesta, at *Fernando Cadena's, Steve's Hideaway,* or *Tres Marias.* It is better to have your own tackle. Boats cost about $25 per hour.

Parasailing. This fabulous sport began in Acapulco. A boat will pull your parachute high over the Bay for a thrilling view of it all. A seven-minute ride costs about $9 to $10.

Scuba Diving. You can arrange scuba diving excursions at *Divers de Mexico* downtown at 100 Costera Miguel Aleman, tel. 2–13–98, or at *Arnold Brothers* on the Costera in front of San Diego Fort, tel. 2–18–77. At Divers, a four-hour excursion with lessons, equipment and snacks costs approximately $50 per person. If you're already a certified diver, the cost is approximately $40; less if you have your own equipment. Arnold Brothers runs three scuba excursions per day for experts as well as beginners. Two-and-one-half-hour trips cost $45.

Snorkeling. It's best to bring your own snorkeling equipment; however, you may be able to rent some on the beach or at one of the restaurants. *Palao Restaurant* near La Roqueta, *Arnold Brothers* or *Divers de Mexico* have some for rent. The cost is minimal.

Tennis. Most hotels have tennis courts. If yours doesn't, chances are you can play at another hotel. It is generally better to bring your own racquet as most clubs do not have rentals. Court fees range from 500 to 2000 pesos per hour, a bit more for night play. Ball boys get 300 to 500 pesos per hour. Early morning and late afternoon hours are the most comfortable times to play because of the midday heat. Reserve in advance. Here is a brief rundown on a few of the courts: *Acapulco Plaza:* Costera Miguel Aleman across from Flamboyant Shopping Center; five clay courts lit for night play; tel. 5–80–50. *Acapulco Princess:* 9 outdoor, 2 indoor courts lit for night play, tel. 4–31–00. *Club de Tenis Alfredo's:* Avenida del Prado 29; two outdoor lighted flexipave courts; tel. 4–00–04. *Club de Tenis and Golf:* Costera Miguel Aleman, across from Hotel Malibu; four lighted clay courts; tel. 4–07–81. *Exelaris Hyatt Continental:* Costera Miguel Aleman; two lighted indoor courts; tel. 4–09–09. *Exelaris Hyatt Regency:* Costera Miguel Aleman; five outdoor lighted courts; tel. 4–12–25. *Pierre Marques:* five courts; tel. 4–20–00. *Tiffany's Racquet Club:* Avenida Villa Vera 120; five outdoor clay courts; tel. 4–79–49. *Villa Vera:* Lomas del Mar; three outdoor lighted clay courts; tel. 4–03–33.

Water Skiing. Water skiing was invented in Acapulco. Renting a ski boat from the beach costs about $11–$15 per hour. If two people ski simultaneously, it costs the same. You can take lessons at Club Colonial on the Costera across from San Diego Fort; tel. 3–70–77.

Windsurfing. You can rent a windsurfer and take lessons at *Teddy's Beach Club.* Rental cost is approximately $20 per hour. You can rent hobby cats, broncos, jet skis, and even inner tubes along Condesa Beach. Rates range from $10 to $20 per hour. Giant inner tubes go for a few cents. Kayaks and pedal boats can be rented for pennies on Caleta Beach.

SPECTATOR SPORTS. Bullfights take place every Sunday afternoon at 5:30 P.M. at Plaza Caletilla in the old part of town. The best matadors appear in The Season, December to Easter. The best seats are at the railing (*barrera*) in the shade (*sombra*). Top price for a ticket is about $14. Your hotel or a local travel agency can arrange an excursion which includes the ticket and transportation to and from the bullring. You can buy a ticket at Motel Kennedy, tel. 5–85–40. The office is open 10 A.M.–2 P.M. and 4–7 P.M., Wednesdays through Saturdays, and from 10 A.M.–2 P.M. Sundays.

BEACHES. Acapulco has some of the world's most spectacular beaches. Water temperatures are comfortable and just right for bathing all year round. You can find every kind—crowded or secluded, rough or calm, even fresh or salt water. Most of the popular beaches have names, but few tourists are aware of them and you seldom hear anyone using them. Itinerant vendors sell snacks and souvenirs and restaurants serve light meals under palapas everywhere. Generally, you'll be able to find a secluded place to yourself. There's plenty of room to go around. Wear sandals if you plan to walk any distance. The beach is broad and the sand can get hot! Here is a brief rundown from east to west:

Revolcadero Beach extends beyond the Princess and Puerto Marques hotels. It is wide and sprawling. The water is shallow and waves are fairly rough. Serious swimmers will probably want to swim in the pool.

Puerto Marques is a quiet, hidden bay just off the highway. Conditions are ideal for swimming and water sports. Mexican tourists prevail, and Saturdays and Sundays are crowded. The rest of the week is heaven. Rustic restaurants border the beach. You can rent a chair or a hammock and order up a serenade from strolling musicians. Inner tubes, sun fish and water ski boats can be rented.

Icacos Beach stretches from the Naval Base to El Presidente Hotel. It is broad and sloping. Waves are gentle until late afternoon.

Condesa Beach is the most action packed of all. It lies between the Condesa del Mar and the Ritz hotels. Broad and sloping, it is alive with restaurants, vendors, and people every day. Waves are gentle until late afternoon. There is plenty of shade. You can rent everything from an inner tube to a bronco.

Hornos and Hornitos beaches run from the Condesa del Mar to San Diego Fort. Mexican tourists prevail here. They know a good thing when they see one. These beaches are shaded by graceful palms. Swimming conditions are good. Restaurants are within easy walking distance.

Caleta and Caletilla beaches were once the center of Acapulco's action. The sun is strongest in the morning. Conditions are ideal for swimming. These beaches are frequented by Mexican tourists and locals and are least crowded on weekdays. A day in the sun here is fun. You'll get a taste of what Acapulco was like in days gone by. This is a good beach for children. Ferry boats leave for Roqueta Island and Palao Restaurant. Glass-bottom boats will take you to Roqueta.

Roqueta Island. A ferryboat ride costs about $1 and takes about 10 minutes. This is another favorite of Mexican tourists which is a wonderful getaway spot on weekdays. Swimming conditions are excellent. Palao Restaurant, a short walk away is good. They have their own mini beach where you can take a dip between courses and rent snorkel equipment.

Pie De La Cuesta, about 15 minutes out of town where Acapulco's first international airport was located, has remained relatively unpopulated. A few rustic restaurants and hotels border the wide and wonderful beach. Palapas provide shade. You can rent a chair or a hammock and have a meal. Horses can be rented to ride along the beach. Waves are high. Nothing more than a dip at the water's edge is advisable. Ukae Kim Hotel is a little jewel, where non-guests can use the pool area overlooking the beach for 800 pesos a day. Those who want to spend a day swimming or fishing in fresh water or waterskiing on a smooth surface can cross the street to Tres Marias, Steve's Hideaway, or Fernando Cadena's rustic "beach clubs" on La Coyuca Lagoon.

MUSEUMS AND GALLERIES. San Diego Fort has opened as a museum. Pre-Columbian relics found in the area and other historic items relating to the history of the State of Guerrero are on display. Plans include staging folkloric shows twice weekly. An increasing number of galleries are appearing on the scene. Reasonable exchange rates make paintings and sculptures exceptionally good buys. Here are a few of the galleries from east to west.

Intergalerias in the Princess Shopping Mall features works of Sergio Bustamante. Hours are 10 A.M.–1 P.M. and 4–7:00 P.M. except Sundays.

Pal Kepenes, Fabulously original jewelry, sculptures, and other works by this famous and talented local sculptor will soon be displayed for sale in the new shopping center across from Condesa del Mar Hotel. In the meantime, they are on display for sale in his house near Los Rancheros Restaurant on Guitarron No. 140. Call 4–37–38 for a viewing appointment.

Galeria 2010 (Esteban), Costera Miguel Aleman No. 2010, a short walk East of the Malibu Hotel. This is an amazing combination boutique and art gallery. The gallery displays works of contemporary artists in dramatic architectural surrounding. (See *Shopping* section below.)

Sergio Bustamante, Costera Miguel Aleman, across from El Tucan boutique. Two floors of whimsical wood, metal, ceramic, and papier-mâché sculptures by Sergio Bustamante. Hours: 10 A.M.–1 P.M. and 4–7 P.M. except Sundays. Galeria El Dorado, next door, features similar works by an ex-pupil.

Galeria Victor, El Patio Shopping Center, across from the Hyatt Continental, displays sculptures by popular local artist Victor Salmones whose work is world renowned. Hours: 9:30 A.M.–1 P.M. and 4–8 P.M. except Sundays.

Galeria Rudic, across from the Hyatt Continental Hotel on Costera Miguel Aleman. It features works of world renowned Mexican painters and sculptors, such as Zuniga, Leonardo Nierman, Norma Goldberg, and Jose Luis Cuevas for serious collectors. Hours: 10 A.M.–2 P.M. and 5–8 P.M. It is open on Sundays 10 A.M.–2 P.M.

STAGE, MUSIC, AND DANCE. Cultural programs—symphonies, ballets, etc.—are presented in the Acapulco Centro from time to time. Watch for signs announcing special performances.

SHOPPING in Acapulco has almost reached sports status. Many visitors think that Acapulco shopping is sensational. Others think it is not. Dedicated shoppers can find real treasures in Acapulco if they apply a little time and patience. Don't overlook a place that looks old and dusty. That might be the one where you get lucky and find a real treasure or an unusual bargain. Generally, store hours are from 10 A.M. to 1 P.M. and from 4 to 7 or 8 P.M. Many boutiques are closed on Sundays.

Most visitors alternate doses of shopping with doses of sunning. You can shop in typical markets, tiny boutiques, or air-conditioned malls. Many stores have branches scattered throughout town. Most stores are located just a few steps away from the beach, on the Costera or just off it. Open-air souvenir stalls dot sidewalks. Itinerant vendors bring the market to you, but often prices are not lower than the shops. Look for the 9.25 sterling stamp if you're buying silver. Handicrafts and resort wear are present in profusion and are the most popular buys. Leather goods, jewelry, and decorative items for the home run a close second.

Markets give you a chance to engage in the popular sport of bargaining, which is part of the fun. The *Mercado Municipal* is for those who want to take in a lot of local color as they buy. This sprawling market is as typical as any in Mexico and an integral part of Acapulco life. Like any authentic Mexican market, you'll find anything from pets to peanuts and more. The market spreads over several city blocks and, even though it may not appear so, it is arranged in sections. If you are looking for something particular, learn the name of what you want to buy in Spanish and ask people to direct you when you get there. With patience and pointing, chances are you'll find it. If you're just going to browse and/or buy souvenirs, enter through the flower section at the corner of Ruiz Cortines and Hurtado de Mendoza streets. You'll find handicrafts to your right and left, inside and outside. Just before Christmas is a wonderful season to be there. Mexican Christmas ornaments are whimsical, amusing, and cost far less than they do back home.

The *Mercado de Artesanias* downtown offers handicrafts, dresses, serapes, and other typical souvenirs. Although this is strictly for tourists, it has the air of an authentic Mexican market as well. In the ceramics section you can order a lamp base, a plate, or a decorative item and watch a talented artisan paint a design to match your color scheme back home. Don't rely on their packing. It's bad. Small stores called jarcerías on the street at the back of the market on Vasquez de Leon, where locals shop are also fun to browse.

Noa Noa is a smaller handicrafts market on the corner of the Costers and Hurtado de Mendoza, at the turnoff for the Mercado Municipal. It has the same merchandise that you'll find downtown, but less local color.

AFA, Artesanias Finas, is a handicrafts supermarket on the corner of Horacio Nelson and James Cook Avenues. This is an air conditioned place where you can buy souvenirs from throughout the country with credit cards. Though quantity sometimes makes up for quality, and prices are slightly higher than you might find elsewhere, this is probably the easiest place to purchase souvenirs or gifts for the folks back home. Their packing and shipping is about the best.

Resort wear and decorative items are for sale throughout town. The greatest profusion of shops and boutiques lies on both sides along the Costera, between the Malibu and the Condesa del Mar hotels. Most hotels have a few good stores and boutiques. However, if you seek comfort, large fitting rooms and service, you might prefer to shop in one of the malls. If your size is not available, some stores will make up items in a day or two.

Shopping Malls. Mexicans call a shopping mall "*Centro Comercial.*" *There are several good ones for those who like to do all their shopping in one place. Here are a few of the best listed from East to West:*

The Princess. For those who like to shop in controlled environment, air-conditioned places, the Princess has a collection of about 25 shops, which sell everything from souvenirs to jewelry. *Marietta's* and *Pitti Palace* are two of the finest clothing stores. *Emil's* and *Ricardo's* offer good, medium-priced sportswear. *Emi Fors, Ronay,* and *Bulgary* (no relation to the Italian firm) offer good jewelry. *Intergalerias* features the work of Sergio Bustamante, a renowned Mexican artist and sculptor.

La Vista, across from Las Brisas Hotel, is one of the most upscale malls in town. It looks like a Mediterranean village overlooking the Bay. Attractive boutiques and restaurants are linked by paved walkways. This is the most comfortable place to shop in Acapulco. Fitting rooms are more spacious, service is more personal and merchandise is generally of better quality than what you will find along the Costera. *Ore, Marietta, Girasol, Benny's,* and *Antheus* for resort wear; *Oceano Pacifico* for sportswear; *Gucci* and *Aries* for leather goods; and *Tane* for silver are a few of the stores.

The *Centro Acapulco* (the Convention Center) has a handful of stores that are open weekdays from 9 A.M. to 5 P.M.

There are two arcades under *Carlos 'n Charlie's. Sergio's Istar,* one of the top boutiques in town, is at the back of *Fingers Arcade,* the one on the left.

Plaza Condesa is a new shopping mall across from Condesa del Mar Hotel. A show featuring the Flying Indians of Papantla is sometimes there.

El Patio, farther down the Costera, was one of the first shopping malls on the scene and is still one of the best. Chock-a-block with boutiques, galleries, and restaurants, it is cool and comprehensive. *Marietta's* and *Thelma's*—the branches where local ladies have their clothes made—are here along with *Galeria Victor,* one of the prettiest art galleries in town.

El Flamboyant Shopping Center, across from the Acapulco Plaza, has a good collection of upbeat stores and boutiques. *Mar y Mar* offers colorful resort wear. *PQ* carries an upbeat Mexican version of high fashion resort wear.

The *Acapulco Plaza* has a spectacular new steel and glass shopping gallery with over 48 stores and boutiques. *Diva* and *Guess* are particular good. *Pineda de Taxco, Tane,* and other great shops, such as *Scandal* for resort wear and *Emi Fors* for jewelry, are across the entrance way. *Casual Aca, Pitti Palace,* and the hotel sundries shop are also tops.

Most of the most popular separate boutiques lie between the Malibu Hotel and the Diana Traffic Circle. This portion of the Costera is jampacked with them.

Estaban's *Galeria 2010* is a brand new concept. It combines a top boutique with a serious art gallery. Esteban is one of the only Mexican designers exporting to the U.S. He is famous for both resort wear and evening clothes for both sexes. He represents Mexico at the Coty Awards and his fashions show it. His training as an architect also shows in the building, which brings a new dimension to shopping. Husbands can enjoy complimentary drinks, a pool, and a jacuzzi while their wives shop. There is a "Grand Finale" sales room all year round and a knockout collection of original costume jewelry.

Acapulco Joe's across from El Presidente, is king of them all and has gained the coveted status of Numero Uno, the same position that Carlos n' Charlie's holds on the restaurant scene. *Ralph Lauren* (Mexican made), across from Huachinango Charlie's restaurant, runs a close second.

C-83, Marietta's, Emil's, and *Mando's* are a few of the favorites. *Fiorucci* and *Express* have brought a new, trendy look to the scene. *Voban, Favian,* and *Anna's* are three good "high fashion" places. These are just a few. You're sure to discover a personal favorite.

Samy's, downtown on Calle Hildalgo No. 7, is a wonderful hole-in-the-wall where many celebrities shop. Men's and women's resort wear—made to order and off the rack—are offered at reasonable prices. *Benny's,* one of Acapulco's best men's stores, is just down the block.

Don't overlook the bathing suits. Some are terrific and cost far less than they would back home. Mexican tennis clothes are also good and well priced. *Head* and *Fila* franchises are hear.

Here are a few other exceptionally good places:

Leather. *Gucci,* across from El Presidente Hotel, is a Mexican franchise. Some items are undetectable from the genuine ones. *Aries,* beside Eve disco, is also good.

Silver. *Pineda de Taxco, Tane,* and *Emi Fors,* in the Acapulco Plaza, are among the best. *Taxco el Viejo,* in old Acapulco, has a big collection of traditional silver items.

Sundries. Major stores for sundries, cosmetics and toiletries are: *Sanborn's* on The Strip next to Condesa del Mar, *Woolworth's* downtown; the huge brand new *Gigante* and *Super Super,* the big supermarkets just after the Costera underpass. Sanborn's and Super Super are open all day long 8 A.M.–10 P.M. every day, weekends included. Woolworth's is open every day 9:30 A.M.–8:30 P.M. Gigante keeps similar hours.

Farmacias (drugstores) are everywhere, but many are closed on Sundays. If you need an over-the-counter medicine, try *Sanborn's* first.

RESTAURANTS. Acapulco restaurants are legendary. You can dine up on the hill with a view or down by the sea under a thatched roof palapa. You can have fast food or ethnic food, Mexican or American. You can opt for formal (although gentlemen never need ties or jackets), air conditioned gourmet restaurants, or informal open air seaside places where all you need is a bathing suit and a cover up. Choices are endless. All you have to do is select to suit your mood. Fresh seafood and meat head most menus. Mexican specialties like ceviche (marinated fish), enchiladas (rolled baked tortillas with chicken, cheese, or meat inside) or tacos are also popular. Generally, service is good. Acapulco waiters have a special tongue-in-cheek humor and will usually be delighted to join your conversation if you let them.

Average cost for a lunch or dinner in a medium-priced restaurant is $20–$25 with beer or domestic wine. You can still dine in tiny sidewalk places like Pepe's, Las Tablitas and El Rodeo for under $12 for two. Ordering anything imported such as caviar, herring, etc., will push the price way up. Major credit cards, except Diners Club and Carte Blanche are accepted in most places except the very small ones. There is a 15% VAT (Value Added Tax) on food and beverages. Most international visitors lunch by the sea and move across the Costera or up the hill for dinner.

If you want to get double your money's worth and have great people watching along with your meal, switch to Mexican hours. Lunch, generally the main meal of the day, is between 2 and 5 P.M. Dinner is between 9 and 11 P.M. Call ahead for reservations in season between December 15 and Easter.

Leisurely dining in a beautiful sunny setting or with a starry view of the Bay is what Acapulco is all about.

Chinese

Shangri La. Calle Picuda No. 5, just off the Costera. Open 6 P.M. to 1 A.M.; tel. 4–13–00. Cantonese specialties in a shaded, open air garden. Moderate prices.

Japanese

Suntory, Costera Miguel Aleman across from Estacion Acapulco. Open 2 P.M.–1 A.M.; tel. 4–80–88. Authentic Japanese cuisine and garden. Meals are served Benihana style.

German

La Terra za de la Flor, downtown. No nonsense; good, hearty servings of German specialties on a balcony overlooking the zocalo; lunch and dinner.

Italian

Villa Demos. Avenida del Prado No. 6. Open 7 P.M.-midnight; tel. 4–20–40. A tried and true family trattoria that is a favorite with locals and visitors. Dine under the trees in a pretty wooded garden. European atmosphere and good cuisine.

Spaghetti House. El Patio Shopping Center. Open 5 P.M.–1 A.M.; tel. 4–17–88. An informal hideaway; brick oven pizza and other Italian specialties.

Da Raffaello. Avenida Costera Aleman 1221, second floor across from Condesa del Mar. Open 2 P.M.–1 A.M.; tel. 4–01–00. Good Italian specialties overlooking the Costera.

Spanish

El Parador La Vista. Carretera Escenica, La Vista Shopping Center. Open 12:30 P.M.–12:30 A.M.; tel. 4–80–20. Best view of the bay, bar none. The typical appetizers "tapas" are tops.

Sirocco. Costera Miguel Aleman across from Super Super. Open from 1 P.M.–midnight; tel. 2–32–30. Acapulco tradition with authentic Spanish flavor. Paella is the specialty.

Mexican

Los Arcos, Acapulco Plaza Hotel. Air-conditioned. Mexican food with excellent explanations on the menu. Open 6:30 P.M.–12:30 A.M. daily. Live music sometimes. Tel: 5–80–50.

Los Rancheros. Carretera Escenica below Las Brisas Hotel. Open 12:30 P.M.–12:30 A.M.; tel. 4–19–08. A million-dollar view combined with reasonably priced favorite Mexican dishes. Go for the view, not for the food.

La Margarita. Avenida Anahuac No. 110. Brand new; open 6 P.M.–midnight; tel. 4–43–50. The kind of Mexican food that you've come to know and love back home served in a beautiful colonial setting.

Pancho's. Costera Miguel Aleman, near Disco Beach. Open from 1 P.M.–midnight; tel. 4–43–50. The only Mexican restaurant just a few steps from the ocean. You can watch the kitchen prepare your favorite dish.

Gourmet

Note: These are all top dollar restaurants. Meals run about $30–$40 per person, without wine.

Le Gourmet. Princess Hotel. Fine food in plush airconditioned comfort. This is for big spenders who like to dine in refined surroundings. Soft piano music; continental and French dishes à la carte; beautiful presentation. Snails, sea bass, soups, and desserts are superb. Tel. 4–31–00. Be ready to spend $35–$40 or more per person. Open 7 P.M.– midnight daily.

Miramar. A beautiful new open-air restaurant in La Vista, overlooking the bay. Grand proportions and style with the look of a private home. Start with a drink at the bar to appreciate the amazing architecture and the view. A waterfall cascades at one side of the elegant dining room. Continental cuisine prepared by international chefs. Part of Mexico City's prestigious del Lago chain. Open 6:30 P.M.–12:30 A.M.; tel. 4–48–75. Closed Sundays.

Maximillian's in the Acapulco Plaza Hotel is the only air-conditioned gourmet restaurant on the beach. Soft blue decor, comfortable plush banquettes, soft piano music. Continental cuisine presented with European flair à la carte. Mango cheesecake, Crepes Suzette and other delicious desserts. Open 7 P.M.–midnight daily; Tel. 5–80–50.

Normandie. This long-time favorite on the scene is said to be one of the best French restaurants in the country. It has lots of tropical old world charm. Soft blue walls, cream-colored furniture, and classical music are the finishing touches. The menu comprises what is fresh in the market. Open from June–November only, 6 P.M.–midnight. Costera on the corner of Malaespina Street beside Sol de Acapulco. Dinner $15–$20; tel. 5–19–16 or 5–13–35.

Coyuca 22 has a formal feeling although it is open air. It's a quiet world apart on top of a hill in Old Acapulco, with a view of the other side of the bay. You feel as if you are on a private estate. This is not the place to go if you are in a loud party mood. Steak and lobster are the specialties. Open daily from December 1 to April 30, 7:00 P.M.–12:30 A.M.; tel. 2–34–68.

Popular Places

Most of these places have a view of the Costera but that doesn't spoil the fun. They are favorites with locals as well as visitors.

El Campanario. High on the hill overlooking everything. Pretty, giant restaurant with the atmosphere of an elegant Italian villa. Continental cuisine. Mediocre food and slow service, but the views are spectacular. Comfortable bar. Tel. 4–88–30.

El Embarcadero. It looks like a Polynesian jungle, across from Suntory, complete with thick foliage and screaming monkeys. You sit in a shaded open air "Warehouse." The menu is Oriental too. Malaysian shrimp, chicken Rangoon, Bangkok filet tidbits, etc. Open 6 P.M.–midnight; tel. 4–87–87.

D'Joint. Near the cylindrical Calinda Acapulco, this old favorite specializes in roast beef and rib-eye steaks in steakhouse setting upstairs. Downstairs is strictly for hamburgers, sandwiches, and cable TV. Open nightly from 7 P.M. to 1 A.M.; tel. 4–37–09.

Hard Times. Steaks, ribs, and tacos along with lobster and shrimp are served up on the second floor across from the Calinda. You can enjoy them in an air-conditioned dining room or outside under a palm tree that grows through the floor. Open daily 6:30 P.M.–12:30 A.M.; closed Wednesdays; tel. 4–00–64. The sign is hard to find. Look for red neon lights over the narrow street entrance awning.

Chez Guillaume. Just off the Costera across from the Torre de Acapulco at 110 Avenida del Prado. Continental cuisine with French flair under the stars, overlooking the Costera. Air-conditioned bar. If you're dying for caviar, escargots, or a Grand Marniere soufflé, this is the place to find it. Open Mon.–Sat. from 6:30 P.M. to 12:30 A.M.; tel. 4–12–31 or 4–12–32.

Madeiras. Romantic, ultra chic "Town and Country" decor with a breathtaking view near Las Brisas. Reservations are hard to get. Call at least two days in advance in season and be on time! Allow time for a drink at the pretty bar before you go to the table. Tiny croissants and beautiful table settings by famous Taxco silversmiths, Los Castillo. Superb corn fungus crepes, artichokes, and cactus salad. Dinners are prix fixe at $20, without wine. Seatings at 7 and 9 P.M. Tel. 4–43–78 or 4–69–21.

Pepe & Co. Upstairs above the Costera across from the Condesa del Mar. This is one of the town's top favorites. It has the atmosphere of a private club. You can begin and end the evening in the air-conditioned piano bar and dine outside on the balcony in between. Continental cuisine that tastes as good as home cooking. Everybody seems to know everybody. Open for lunch and dinner 1 P.M.–midnight; closed for lunch on Sundays; tel. 4–70–88 or 4–70–89.

Carlos 'N Charlie's. This popular place packs 'em in every day, except Tuesdays. Everyone who comes to Acapulco seems to pass through these portals at least once. It doesn't open until 6:30 P.M. but the line starts to form around 6. A big air-conditioned bar, crazy waiters, and a flip menu make it fun as well as tasty. You're likely to find the waiter at a disco later. No reservations. You have to wait your turn. Tel. 4–12–85.

Seaside Spots

These are some of the most carefree dining places in the world. You need wear nothing more than a bikini with a cover-up. Chances are that you can samba with your shoes off between courses, or life it up as long as you like—even right through the sunset and into the night. Strolling photographers are there to record the mayhem. Most of the most popular seaside places are between the Condesa del Mar and the Hyatt Continental.

Beto's, under a cool palapa, is one of the old time favorites that everybody has loved since the '50s. It has some delicious dishes that other places don't serve, such as quesadillas de cazon (tortillas filled with baby shark meat and fried) and pescado a la Talla (a split snapper barbecued in a delicious sauce). Live music for dancing if the spirit moves you. Occasional live music. Open daily 10 P.M.–midnight; tel. 4–94–73. No *Diners Club* or *Carte Blanche.*

Barbas Negras (Blackbeard's). High up overlooking the ocean, it serves up hearty food that a pirate might like. A big salad bar and he-man-size helpings of lobster thermidor, shrimp, and steaks. Open daily 6:30 P.M.–midnight; tel. 4–25–49.

Mimi's Chili Saloon. When you're dying for a hamburger, onion rings, potato skins, or French fries, this is your place. Two floors of tasty fast food and a crazy happy hour with twofer mango and strawberry margaritas that will knock your block off. Open daily 6 P.M.–midnight.

Paradise. This has to be the craziest place on the Costera. Absolutely anything goes! Pandemonium prevails just off the beach under the sign of the Red Snapper. Live music keeps the party rolling. Waiters go wild when there's a birthday or anniversary to celebrate. A trained chimpanzee will mug for you and the camera. These and other surprises may interrupt your meal but you'll love it! Shrimp and snapper are the most popular dishes. One of these main courses and you won't have to eat for the rest of the day. Open noon–midnight; tel. 4–59–88.

The Crazy Lobster (Langosta Loca) is not crazy at all. It is serious about its food and it's one of the most dignified of the seaside restaurants. Blonde wood furniture and stucco walls give it a sleek look. Sit on the left if you don't want to be bothered by beach vendors. Pretty, pleasant, good value. Open noon–midnight; tel. 4–59–74.

Mahalo, by the beach or Hernan Cortes Street behind the Acapulco Plaza Hotel. New and slightly expensive ($30–$35) but good Oriental specialties are served in a pretty setting to the sound of the waves. Dinner only; opens 6:30 P.M.; tel. 5–20–51.

Huachinango Charlie's. Costera Miguel Aleman, above Eve's disco. Another Carlos 'N Charlie's, this one has a Polynesian flavor and a pretty setting. The view is better than the food. Open for lunch and dinner, 2:15 P.M.–midnight; closed Wednesdays.

Estacion Acapulco. Train buffs can eat things like southern fried pork and ribs or shrimp in cognac sauce. An air-conditioned old dining car. You might have to sit beside strangers, as you would on a real train, as there are no tables for two by the "ride to nowhere" is fun. Across from the Costera from Huachinango Charlie's. Open 12:30 P.M.–1:30 A.M.; tel. 4–32–52. No *Diner's Card.*

Su Casa. It *is* the owner's cozy home. Overlooking the Convention Center and the bay, you get a cosy homey feeling that makes it evident your friendly hosts are present. Simple, easy to order, meat and fish menu. Rose of tomato vinaigrette and conch appetizers are great. Open every night from 6:00 P.M. to midnight; tel. 4–43–50.

Barbarroja (Redbeard). Costera Miguel Aleman across from Fiesta Tortuga. This is really open-end dining under the stars, overlooking the ocean. If pirates had a steakhouse this is what it would look like. Meat, fish, surf and turf plus an air-conditioned piano bar. Open 6:30 P.M.–12:30 A.M. every night. Reserve a table by the sea, the sidewalk is too close for comfort. Tel. 4–59–32.

Sleek and Sexy

Villa Vera Hotel & Racquet Club. A chic restaurant overlooking the Bay, where lunches are lively events and dinners are ultra-romantic. The restaurant has three spectacular views: the bay, the bar and pool area, and the people. Mexican trios at sunset; soft piano music at night. Delicious dishes like pieces of sole with a curry dip and caramel bananas. Open noon–midnight; tel. 4–03–33.

Sunset Beach Club. A pretty swinging place with international flavor overlooking the ocean, next to Eve disco. Head your raft to the edge of the pool and watch the boys or girls go by on the beach below. Swim-up bar, just the right amount of creative chaos. Open noon–6:30 P.M.; tel. 4–00–92 or 4–34–64.

Inexpensive

Pepe's Las Tablitas. On the sidewalk across from Nacional Financiera down from Acapulco Plaza. Specials with chimmichuri and chicken enchiladas with green sauce are tops. Wooden tables, concrete floor; good value served by a Las Brisas graduate; open noon to midnight daily; no reservations.

El Rodeo. A hole-in-the-wall at No. 145 Costera Miguel Aleman, that has a reasonable prix fixe tourist lunch menu that can't be beaten. Prices are low at night, too, and they throw in a free folklore show with cock fights, rope tricks, and dancers. Open noon–midnight.

NIGHTLIFE. Acapulco is the city in Mexico whose night life is world-renowned. Acapulco nights are as star spangled, dazzling and kinetic as they come. If you *really* adjust to Mexican schedules you can have another full day of fun after dark. When the sun goes down, shimmering lights illuminate the bay and Acapulco begins to dazzle like no other city in the world. Discos that outglitter any others stay open until the last guest goes home. Some revelers find that another day has begun before they've climbed into bed! That's one of Acapulco's most delicious qualities. Any night will last as long as you can, and the fun never stops until *you* want it to. Choices of what to do after dinner are endless. Everything from a moonlight cruise around the Bay to a Mexican Fiesta night is available.

Discos

The outrageous discos are what launched Acapulco nights into international fame. They defy any others to outglitter them. Balloons, confetti, video screens and other surprises add to the pandemonium on the dance floor. In season, they're as dark and as crowded as they come, but that only makes everyone more anxious to get in.

Most have door charges of about \$5–\$6 per person, more if there is a special show. Domestic drinks cost approximately \$1.50–\$1.75; imported drinks such as scotch, etc., cost \$3. A bottle of imported champagne costs \$100–\$150.

Getting in may not be easy. Often you have to wait outside in a crowd. The best way to get in on a busy night in season is to look classy, sexy, and dignified. Being past your teens helps. Remember that one of the doorman's jobs is to fill the place with the most attractive people he can find. Go around 11 P.M. on a weekend if you want to get in by midnight. However, if you don't feel like waiting, go to *any* disco. They all offer plenty of pandemonium. All are on the Costera unless stated otherwise. All accept major credit cards except *Diner's* and *Carte Blanche.* And most have boutiques, so you can shop between dances!

The Big Eight are: **Baby O, Bocaccio, Cats, Eve, Fantasy, Jackie O, Magic,** and **Midnight. Fantasy,** beside La Vista Mall in Las Brisas, is crème de la crème and first class all the way. It has floor-to-ceiling picture windows around a dance floor that overlooks the bay and spectacular laser lights. An inside glass elevator takes you to the "sex shop" on the second floor, which sells lingerie. Cover charge is 2,000 pesos plus tax. Tel. 4–67–27.

Baby O, across from the Romano Palace, is king of the discos on or near the Strip. Steep stairs with tiers of tables lead to the dance floor, where disco mania prevails. Video screens add to the fun. The crowd outside may be big, but it's worth waiting if you are determined to dance in one of the hottest places in town.

Bocaccio, five minutes down the Strip, is a superfun, time-tested favorite with Acapulco habitués. The momentum never stops. Party gimmicks, balloons, confetti, ethnic hour, video screens, and electronic boards that can personalize welcomes, birthdays, etc., add to the wonderful pandemonium. Tel. 4–19–00.

Cats, behind Midnight, is a pretty, big, new place that everyone seems to like. Comfortable tables, tiered booths, "trees" with sparkling lights, and videos make it even prettier. Tel. 4–73–35.

Eve, formerly UBQ, is just before the traffic circle. It is the only disco on the ocean. The dance floor may suddenly open so you can dance under the stars. There is a comfortable bar and a few video games.

Jackie O is another old favorite that used to be called Charlie's Chili. Mirrors, leaded glass windows, and plush booths make it look like a private club. There is a bar upstairs. Unaccompanied women are admitted. Tel. 4–08–43.

Midnight, which was Le Jardin, is the most modern-looking of them all. The Villa Vera crowd comes here. More than any other, the people are "the show." Few gimmicks distract from the dance floor. Tel. 4–82–95.

Jackie O, Baby O and Magic have snack bars where you can refuel your engine. Remember, an Acapulco disco rule of thumb is: If you can't get into one, go to another.

Gay Discos

Gay discos are an integral part of Acapulco's nighttime scene. Three of them are just off the Costera across from D'Joint on Avenida de los Deportes. **The Gallery** has an opulent show of female impersonators that is popular with everybody. Shows are at 11:30 P.M. and 1:30 A.M., nightly except Sunday; tel. 4–34–97. **Peacock Alley** probably has the best music in town. The bar and dance floor are under white "palm trees." **Disco 9** is the smallest of the three.

Hotel Discos and Nightclubs

Several hotels have lively disco clubs that also feature shows and big name entertainment. **Cocoloco** and **Tiffany's** in the Princess, tel. 4–31–00; **Club Banneret** in the Calinda, two shows daily except Monday at 11:30 P.M. and 1:30 A.M. Tel. 4–04–10; **Mil Luces** in the Exelaris Hyatt Regency, tel. 4–38–88; two shows nightly at 11:30 P.M. and 1:30 A.M., and **Poseidon Disco Show** in Hotel Torres Gemelas are just a few of them. Check to find out show times.

Rooftop Supper Clubs

Several rooftop supper clubs offer traditional dining and dancing overlooking the bay. The atmosphere is quieter and more romantic. Most feature continental cuisine and live music for touch dancing. Dress codes are slightly more formal (no blue jeans, please), but gentlemen still never need socks, ties, or jackets.

La Joya in the Exelaris Hyatt Continental, tel. 4–09–09; **Numero Uno** in the Exelaris Hyatt Regency, tel. 4–28–88; **Techo Del Mar** in the Condesa del Mar, tel. 4–23–55; and **La Fragata** in the Acapulco Paraiso Hotel are the best. La Joya and Numero Uno sometimes close after the season, so call to check.

Nightclubs

El Fuerte in front of Las Hamacas Hotel has a fabulous flamenco show twice nightly at 11:30 P.M. and 1:30 A.M. every day except Sundays.

Nina's Tropical Disco is for those who like it Latin and lively. This is mostly for Mexicans and anyone who likes the salsa beat. It's open daily from 10 P.M. until 4 A.M. The price is right: 1,500 pesos per person with an open bar of domestic drinks.

Happy Hours

Almost every hotel has a happy hour, especially during the season. Most take place 6–8 P.M. and offer live music for dancing and twofer drinks. The Acapulco Plaza (where you pay by the drink), El Presidente and Condesa del Mar are among the best. This is a time to meet and greet if you're in the mood.

FOR THE KIDS. Big hotels like the Hyatt and the Acapulco Plaza stage special activities for children. Most take place around the pool. Watch for the daily bulletin under your door. **Miniature golf** can be played in front of Super Super at Golfito. There is a **Go Kart** and **roller skating** rink behind Big Boy. It also has electronic games. Downtown, **Chispas** just off the zocalo on Calle Hildalgo also has electronic games. The discos Plus I and Le Dome have Sunday afternoon *tardeadas* for teenagers. The entry fee is 1,000 pesos; only soft drinks are served.

HOTELS. Acapulco's amazing accommodations range from a *De Luxe* category to trailer parks. Almost all of them have more spacious rooms, more beautifully gardened pools, and larger public areas than their counterparts in other parts of the world. And most of them are no more than a few minutes' walk away from a beautiful beach. Almost all have pools, several restaurants, and live music in the bar. Which one you choose and the location play a big part in determining your vacation lifestyle. For those who like to have everything top-of-the-line and on-the-premises, the slightly isolated Princess and Pierre Marques and Las Brisas hotels will fill the bill. Hotels on The Strip from the Exelaris Hyatt Regency to the Acapulco Paraiso are right in the middle of the action. Generally rates go down as you get nearer town. Beyond it is Traditional Acapulco, where some of the hotels that were Acapulco's first drawing cards still stand. These tend to be smaller, quieter, and more relaxing than bigger properties. Most are a short walk from the beach and have small pools. Those that do not have air conditioning have overhead fans.

The season when the weather is best and the rates are highest, is December 15–Easter. If you are planning to go for Christmas, Washington's Birthday, or Easter, book as far ahead as you can to avoid disappointment. Rates go down as much as 40% after that. Especially reasonably priced packages usually become available between July and September. Watch your local newspaper for special offers.

The following is a sample of what is available. Hotels are listed below by the average peak-season rate, in the following categories, based on double occupancy: *Deluxe,* \$150 and up; *First class,* \$100 to \$150; *Expensive,* \$50 to \$100; *Moderate,* \$20 to \$50; *Inexpensive* \$20 and below. Rates quoted are subject to change without notice and are European plan (EP) with no meals, unless otherwise stated.

Deluxe

Acapulco Princess. Playa Revolcadero, Apartado Postal No. 1351. 1031 rooms; tel. 4–31–00. Grand style, self contained, 8 minutes from the airport; ½ hour from The Strip. This is for those who like to have everything, but *everything* on the premises—all 380 acres of it! Tennis, golf, nightclub, disco, restaurants. Spectacular pool area with salt and fresh water pools, beautiful gardens. Golf and tennis.

Pierre Marques. Playa Revolcadero (beside the Princess) Apartado Postal 474; tel. 4–20–00. 340 rooms and duplex villas. Restaurants, golf, tennis, three fresh water pools. All facilities are interchangeable with Acapulco Princess. Shuttle bus between the properties takes 10 minutes. Quieter, sprawling property, beautiful gardens and villas, tranquil setting.

Las Brisas. Box 281, Carretera Escenica 5255; tel. 4–16–50; U.S. reservations (800) 228–3000. 300 Casitas, all with private or shared pool, on the hill overlooking the bay. Pink and white staff-driven jeeps take you from reception to your room and to the beach club below. Tennis courts, restaurants, and health clubs. Elegant and exclusive with the air of a private club. This is the only hotel whose facilities are *not* open to the public. Your neighbor is likely to be a celebrity or an astronaut. No children.

Exelaris Hyatt Regency. Box 565 Costera Miguel Aleman No. 1; tel. 4–28–88. 694 rooms at the foot of the scenic highway at the beginning of The Strip. Tennis courts, restaurants, night clubs. Almost all rooms view the Bay. Elegant atmosphere. A short walk away from "the action."

Villa Vera Hotel & Racquet Club. Box 260 Lomas del Mar No. 35; tel. 4–03–33; U.S. reservations: (800) 421–0767. The prettiest small hotel on the Strip, with 79 photogenic rooms and suites, all different, some with private pools. Cable TV, beautiful gardens, a popular bar, and a pool area with the country's first swim-up bar. One of the town's most popular restaurants overlooks the bay. Tennis courts, plush private-club atmosphere. Facilities are interchangeable with Maralis Hotel on the beach, a 5–7 minute ride away, but guests seldom leave the pool. Management discourages children.

El Presidente. Box 933, Costera Miguel Aleman; tel. 4–17–00; U.S. (800) 228–3278. 422 rooms. Restaurants (the only kosher restaurant in town is open during the season), pools, tennis. The "action packed" part of The Strip begins here.

Condesa Del Mar. Box 933 Costera Miguel Aleman No. 1220; tel. 4–28–81, U.S. (800) 228–3728. Restaurants, pools, tennis, rooftop night club right in the "action" a few steps away from your front door. Never-a-dull-moment atmosphere. Happy Hour pandemonium in the lobby is a sight to see.

Exelaris Hyatt Continental. Box 214, Costera Aleman; tel. 4–09–09, U.S. (800) 228–9000. 435 rooms on eight floors. Restaurants, rooftop night club, pool. Facilities interchangeable with Exelaris Hyatt Regency. Especially beautiful gardens and pool with an island. All rooms have balconies and a view of the ocean.

Acapulco Plaza. Box C-88, Costera Miguel Aleman No. 22; tel. 5–80–50, U.S. (800) 238–8000. 1000 rooms and suites. Full service self-contained resort on The Strip. Tennis, pools, health club, restaurants, cable TV, sparkling, new. Soon-to-be-completed shopping center. Everything you need for fabulous fun in the sun is here. Plenty of action just outside. Five sensational restaurants. Lively happy hour. Oasis Health Club (no children). Five tennis courts.

First Class

Romano's Le Club. Costera Miguel Aleman, corner Tikitiki Street; 300 rooms; tel. 4–77–30. Rococo seaside hotel, lots of groups.

La Palapa. Fragata Yucatan No. 210, tel. 4–53–63, U.S. reservations (602) 957–4200; 400 rooms. All rooms are small suites with ocean view, and kitchenettes. Location on the ocean in a quiet residential section.

Copacabana. Costera Miguel Aleman; U.S. tel. (305) 588–8541. Newest hotel on the beach, ½ block off the Costera. All 420 rooms have ocean view and balconies.

Elcano. Costera Miguel Aleman and Box 430; tel. 4–19–50; 140 rooms with balconies. One of the golden oldies for those in the know. Quiet, well located charm, just off the Costera. One step to the beach.

Malibu. Costera Miguel Aleman No. 20, tel. 4–10–70; 80 rooms with balconies. A good secret to know. The nicest small hotel on the Costera. Time sharing operation. Rents rooms owners are not using; good value.

Calinda/Acapulco. Costera Miguel Aleman No. 1260; tel. 4–04–10; 366 refurbished rooms with balconies. Cylindrical, beach side, newly refurbished.

Fiesta Tortuga. Costera Miguel Aleman; tel. 4–88–89, U.S. (800) 223–2633; 250 rooms. Across the street from the beach in the middle of the action.

Maralisa. Avenida Enrique el Esclavo, Box 721; tel. 4–09–76; 90 rooms on the beach, two small pools. Shuttle buses will take you up the hill. Seaside dining room. Sister hotel to the Villa Vera. A little jewel.

Maris. Costera Miguel Aleman; 84 rooms. Another oldie but goodie.

Ritz. Costera Miguel Aleman just before underpass; tel. 5–73–36; U.S. (800) 458–6888; 278 rooms. Newly remodeled; attractive new seaside dining room. Families like this one.

Sands. Costera Miguel Aleman, corner Juan de la Cosa, 60 rooms; across from Acapulco Plaza and the beach. Small pool. Good value.

Las Hamacas. Costera Miguel Aleman on the curve before town; Box 399; tel. 2–61–66. A pretty, updated old favorite with a small palm-shaded pool. Across the street from the beach.

Caleta. Cerro San Martin, Box 260 R; tel. 2–48–00; 260 rooms. Completely renovated old favorite on Caleta Beach. Sensational view.

Moderate

El Tropicano. Costera Miguel Aleman No. 510 across from Baby O; tel. 4–10–00, U.S. (800) 334–7234. 137 rooms. Pretty little hotel with all amenities. The beach is across the street.

Arbela. Costera Miguel Aleman No. 1270, opposite Golf Club; tel 4–21–64. 50 rooms. Small and well located on the strip.

Auto-Ritz. Avenida Magallanes one half block off the Costera; tel. 5–80–23; U.S. (800) 458–6888; 103 rooms. Good value.

De Gante. Costera Miguel Aleman 265; tel. 5–02–32. 143 rooms. An old favorite across the street from Hornos Beach.

El Mirador. Quebrada No. 74; tel. 2–45–64. 131 rooms. High on the hill; one of the first on the scene. The nightclub, La Perla, has the best view of the world famous divers.

Mozimba. Playa Langosta at the base of the hill to Coyuca 22; tel. 2–15–29. 30 rooms. Newly renovated by U.S. owners.

Casa Blanca. Cerro de la Pinzona; tel. 2–12–12, U.S. (800) 421–0767. 120 rooms. One of the early favorites high on the hill. Quiet and comfortable; spectacular view of the bay; a 5-minute ride to the beach.

Inexpensive

Belmar. Gran Via Tropical, corner Avenida de las Cumbres in Traditional Acapulco; tel. 3–80–98. A short walk down the hill to Caleta Beach. An old favorite with repeat visitors.

Boca Chica. Playa Caletilla; tel. 2–60–14; U.S. (800) 223–5695. 45 rooms. Five-story beautiful location across from Palao Restaurant. Quiet with magnificent view from every balcony. Walk down the hill to the beach or swim from hotel pier.

Vilia. Ave. Roqueta No. 54; tel. 3–33–11. 60 rooms. Chic, well maintained, this was once *the* place to stay. A short walk down the hill to the beach.

Los Flamingos. Avenida Lopez Mateos, Box 70; tel. 2–06–96. 47 rooms. High on a hill in a section that was the ultimate a few years ago. A five-minute ride from downtown and the beaches.

Condos and Villas

There are plenty of spectacular condominiums and villas to rent. Villa rates range from $150 to $600 (and up) per day depending on size, location, and services. One to three couples can share. Three-bedroom condos average $225 per day. *Ron Lavender/Bachur & Associates* can arrange it all. Tel: 5–71–51. You can also call *Sundominiums* (800) 547–6334; *Condoworld* (800) 521–2980; *Creative Leisure* (800) 227–4290 or MaryAnn Rivas, 4–36–60.

Trailer Parks

Playa Suave. Costera Miguel Aleman 739; tel. 5–33–16. Good location; all facilities. Reserve in advance.

Coloso. 5 miles out of town; all facilities.

IXTAPA/ZIHUATANEJO

Ixtapa/Zihuatanejo is a two-town, world class resort that is well on its way to stardom.

If you looked at them on the map a few years ago, you might have said that it would never work. Two sprawling bays at the foot of the Sierra Madre Mountains—Palmar, which is now Ixtapa, and Zihuatanejo, then only a speck of a primitive fishing village, are separated by a jutting rock promontory called Punta Esteban. A dozen years ago, Ixtapa was nothing more than a stretch of palm lined virgin beach and Zihuatanejo was known only by a handful of residents and a few hearty travelers who enjoyed a rustic vacation lifestyle.

However, Fonatur, Mexico's National Trust Fun for Tourism Development, waved its magic wand, building connecting highways and roads, and completing an ultra modern infrastructure. Glittering hotels grew up along Palmar Bay, and international visitors began to discover the spectacular natural beauty that only a handful of hearty travelers had known before. In less than a dozen years, Ixtapa/Zihuatanejo grew into a dazzling duo. This knockout, two-for-the-price-of-one resort is attracting the attention of international travelers. It delights the most sophisticated sun worshippers as well as those who truly like to get away from it all.

Though visitors might still have the feeling of being in a place that is on the threshold of development, all of the comforts and amenities that sophisticated travelers are accustomed to are present. An unspoiled, back to nature ambience prevails.

Even though Zihuatanejo has grown to a population of over 39,000, you have the feeling that it hasn't changed for centuries, and it plays a perfect counterpoint to Ixtapa's modernity. Perhaps nowhere in the world blends the past and the present so harmoniously.

Ixtapa/Zihuatanejo lies 240 km. up the coast from Acapulco. It is an easy 3½-hour drive over a wide highway. Most of the area is sparsely populated and covered with lush tropical foliage. Small towns dot the highway and if you take the time to stop and explore off the main road, you're likely to discover some extaordinarily beautiful beaches. If you were to continue along the coast past Ixtapa, you would leave the state of Guerrero, (which is also home for Acapulco) and be in the state of Michoacán in about two hours.

The area's greatest assets are its natural beauty and the weather. Average year-round temperature is 78°F. It is slightly cooler than Acapulco. Ixtapa/Zihuatanejo is also less humid. June, July, and September are the rainiest months, but showers are usually short and many fall at night.

Dress is also slightly less formal than Acapulco. Men never need socks, ties or jackets. Ladies need a well-put-together look, but the costumes and glitz that one sees in Acapulco is not part of the scene here. Zihuatanejo is still less formal than Ixtapa. There you can get away with jeans or neat shorts and a cover up or tee shirt day and night.

A smooth, broad road links Playa Linda with the Hotel Zone. The Ixtapa Hotel Zone, a row of sparkling hotels, lines Palmar Bay. Paseo de Ixtapa stretches through it past the golf club.

At the end, it turns off to Camino Real Hotel. A smaller road to the left of the entrance to Camino Real leads to a cluster of restaurants, including Villa de la Selva, Kon-Tiki, and the Ibiza disco. The main road continues winding around to Zihuatanejo. Just keep heading for the water. Turn right off the main highway and you'll reach downtown Zihuatanejo. Go straight and you'll reach a small turn off for La Ropa Beach.

Zihuatanejo is four miles (a 6–10-minute ride over a smooth highway) from Ixtapa. The Zihuatanejo International Airport which serves them both is 13 miles from the Hotel Zone.

A smooth, broad road links Playa Linda, the westernmost beach with the Hotel Zone. The Ixtapa Hotel Zone lines Palmar Bay.

Zihuatanejo is a bustling little cobblestone town that is thoroughly Mexican. Residents still consider the Public Market (Mercado Municipal), on Paseo Cocotal, an integral part of their daily lives.

Zihuatanejo means "Place of the Women" in the Nahuatl Indian language. It was once occupied by the Cuitlalteca Indians who had a matriarchal society. In the post-conquest 1500s, it became an important port for Mexico's trade with the Orient. Today, it is a port-of-call for several cruise ships.

Whether you prefer a vacation lifestyle that is old or new, you're sure to enjoy it all.

PRACTICAL INFORMATION FOR IXTAPA/ZIHUATANEJO

TELEPHONES. The area code for Ixtapa/Zihuatanejo is 743. The tax on international calls is over 50%. International long distance calls can be made from the Telephone Office at Ascencio and Galeana, 9 A.M.–2 P.M. and 4–7 P.M. This avoids the surcharge that some hotels charge for placing the call.

HOW TO GET THERE. By Air. *Aeromexico, Mexicana de Aviacion,* and *Western Airlines* operate direct flights from U.S. Gateways to Zihuatanejo International Airport. Aeromexico and Mexicana de Aviacion operate flights from Mexico City. Flying time is approximately 35 minutes.

By Car. There is a new road from Mexico City. Driving time is about 9 hours. Acapulco is 3 ½-hour (237 miles) drive away, over a good road. There are three Government Inspection stops.

By Bus. *Estrella de Oro* and *Flecha Roja* offer frequent departures to Acapulco. The trip takes about 5 hours. They also operate direct service to Mexico City once a day. Estrella de Oro (tel. 4–22–45) departs at 8 P.M.; Flecha Roja (tel. 4–34–33) at 9:30 P.M. Get there ½ hour early. Both terminals are in downtown Zihuatanejo. Estrella de Oro buses are deluxe and air-conditioned.

By Cruise Ship. Zihuatanejo is a port of call for *Princess* and *Royal Viking* lines.

HOW TO GET AROUND. By Car. Rental cars can be found in both Ixtapa and Zihuatenjo. Average daily rate for a medium-size automatic air-conditioned four-door car is \$70–\$80 a day including mileage. Jeeps or Safaris cost about \$50 day. Parking is easy, except for downtown Zihuatanejo. In season, reserve well in advance, specify air-conditioned and automatic, and have your reservation's number ready.

Unless you plan to travel great distances or to visit remote beaches, taxis and buses are far less expensive. A taxi ride from the Hotel Zone to downtown Zihuatanejo costs approximately 700 pesos, to Playa la Ropa, 1,200. "Collective" taxis, which you share with others, (look for the city seal on the side) can be flagged down. The fare to Zihuatanejo from the Hotel Zone is 150 pesos. Taxi fare to the airport is about 2,700 pesos. A Combi costs 850 pesos.

By Bus. Minibuses run between the hotels in the Hotel Zone to Zihuatanejo about every hour. Stops are clearly marked. The fare is about 100 pesos.

Mopeds can be rented for 2,500 pesos an hour in the parking lot in front of the Dorado Pacifico Hotel.

Pedicabs with a fringe on top that accommodate 3 people can be rented for 2,500 pesos an hour in the parking lot in front of Dorado Pacifico Hotel.

SPECIAL EVENTS. *Deep Sea Fishing Tournament:* first week in December; the Semana de Guerrero, a week long series of special events, including a food fair, cock fights, etc., usually takes place in late March or early April.

USEFUL NUMBERS AND ADDRESSES. Airlines. *Aeromexico:* Hotel Krystal, Ixtapa, and Juan Alvarez No. 34, Zihuatanejo, tel. 4–20–18, tel. 4–29–39; *Mexicana de Aviacion;* Vincente Guerrero, corner Nicolas Bravo, Zihuatanejo, tel. 4–22–08; *Western Airlines:* International Airport, Zihuatanejo, tel. 4–33–26; *State Tourism Office:* Avenida del Pescador (Seaside Walk), Zihuatanejo, tel. 4–22–07; *Combi Airport Transportation,* tel. 4–21–70.

Taxi stand: tel. 4–20–80.

Money Exchange: Enturesa Travel Agency, Ixtapa Shopping Center.

Banks. Banking hours are 9 A.M.–1:30 P.M., Monday–Friday. *Bancomer,* La Puerta Shopping Mall, Ixtapa; *Bank of Mexico,* Nicolas Bravo 39A, Zihuatanejo; *Multibanco Comer Mex,* Vincente Guerrero, corner of Ramirez; *Banco Serfin,* Paseo Cocotal 22, Zihuatanejo.

Rent-a-Car offices are at the airport or: *Avis,* Juan Alvarez No. 7, Zihuatanejo, tel. 4–22–75; *Dollar,* Hotel Riviera del Sol, Ixtapa, tel. 4–24–06; *Hertz,* Paseo del Cocotal, Zihuatanejo, tel. 4–30–50 or 4–22–55, and Holiday Inn Hotel, Ixtapa, tel. 4–22–96; *National,* Hotel Krystal, Ixtapa, tel. 4–26–18, ext. 1110.

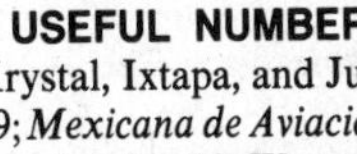

HOTELS. In general, the kind of big, modern hotels that travelers have become accustomed to finding in other Pacific resort areas are located in Ixtapa. Zihuatanejo hotels are smaller and cozier. A few of them meet international standards of sophistication. Unless mentioned otherwise, all hotels are European Plan. Rates are slightly lower in both cities than in Acapulco.

Ixtapa

All hotels mentioned are located on Palmar Bay unless noted.

Deluxe

Camino Real. Playa Hermosa; 450 air-conditioned rooms and suites; 6 suites have private pools. All rooms have an ocean view, a refrigerator-bar. 7 restaurants and bars (La Esfera is tops); four freshwater pools, 4 tennis courts, water sports facilities, and outstanding shopping mall. Elevator to the beach. Creme de la creme. Tel. 4–20–13; U.S. reservations: Westin Hotels (800) 228–3000.

Ixtapa Sheraton. 381 air-conditioned rooms and suites in two towers. All have ocean or mountain view, climate control, FM radio, and refrigerator/bar. Towering atrium lobby with inside glass elevator, 5 bars and restaurants, pool, wading pool for children, water sports. Tel. 4–31–84; U.S. reservations (800) 325–3535. (Closed but scheduled to reopen in February 1986.)

Krystal. 260 rooms and suites, all with individual air-conditioning control, ocean view, private terrace, and color TV. 5 bars and restaurants, pool with a waterfall, tennis courts, racket ball courts, and water sports. Airy lobby, beautiful public areas, tropical decor. Tel. 4–20–13; U.S. reservations (800) 231–9860.

Expensive

Aristos. 250 air-conditioned rooms with balconies; recently completely refurbished and upgraded. Pool, tennis courts, restaurants. Tel: (800) 531–7348.

Dorado Pacifico. 285 air-conditioned rooms, all facing the beach. Pool, children's pool, two tennis courts, 5 bars and restaurants. Shining glass, wood, and stucco decor. Tel. 4–30–60; Telex: 01773655.

Castel Palmar. 110 air-conditioned rooms with individual climate control. Pool, 2 bars, two restaurants, two tennis courts, playground; ideal for families. Tel. 4–23–41; U.S. reservations (800) 854–2026.

Holiday Inn. 238 air-conditioned rooms with ocean view; pool tennis court, water sports, 2 restaurants. Mexican and continental cuisine; disco. Tel. 4–23–96; U.S. reservations (800) 238–8000.

El Presidente. 440 air-conditioned rooms, 2 restaurants, 2 bars, a pool, and tennis courts. Charming Mexican colonial style ambience. Outside glass elevator. Tel. 4–20–13; U.S. reservations (800) 854–2026.

Riviera del Sol. 500 air-conditioned rooms with ocean view; 2 pools, 4 restaurants, 3 bars, a disco; tennis courts and water sports. Tel. 4–24–06; U.S. reservations (800) 223–9868. (Only one of its three towers is operating, but normal operations are expected by the end of 1985.)

Club Mediterranee. Playa Quieta; 375 air-conditioned rooms, all sports facilities, pool, dining room, theater/nightclub. All rooms are part of week-long packages. Tel. 4–20–13; U.S. reservations (800) 528–3100.

Inexpensive

Playa Linda. Playa Quieta. Rock bottom prices. 250 dormitory type rooms that accommodate 1–4 people. Tents can also be rented. There is a fully equipped trailer park with restaurants, bar, sports, and cooking facilities.

Note: Three new hotels were scheduled to open in 1986. **Aquamarina,** a 150-room hotel on the bay, was slated to open in October; **Los Aves,** a 120-room hotel behind Ixpamar Mall, in September; and **Puertas del Mar,** a condo-hotel nearby, in August.

Zihuatanejo

Zihuatanejo has a number of small hotels. Most are small and cozy and have a faithful clientele of repeat visitors, and almost all are within easy walking distance of town and a beach.

Expensive

Fiesta Mexicana, a new hotel on Playa La Ropa, had 32 out of 120 rooms completed and operating at press time.

Villa del Sol. Playa La Ropa. Apartado Postal No. 84, tel. 4–22–39. 17 rooms, most are stylish duplexes with tropical flair. A chic place with a pretty seaside bar/restaurant and the air of an international private club. Water sports and tennis court available. This is a jewel. Some guests reserve a year in advance.

Sotavento. Box 2, tel. 4–20–32. Overlooking Playa La Ropa. 70 rooms high on a hill overlooking the bay. This was one of the area's first and best. Breezy open air lobby and nostalgic style. Big, fan-cooled or air-conditioned rooms, hammocks, two bars, seaside restaurant, room phones.

Posada Caracol. Box 20, tel. 4–20–35. Madera Beach. 60 air-conditioned or fan-cooled rooms, open-air disco. 2 pools, 3 restaurants, Chololo disco, water sports. Colonial decor.

Irma. Box 4, tel. 4–21–05, U.S. (212) 957–7730. Madera Beach. 75 fan-cooled rooms overlooking the bay. 2 pools, beach club restaurant, disco, beautiful terrace. This is an old favorite.

Villas Miramar. Tel. 91–743. Madera Beach. 12 beautiful new suites five minutes from downtown. Colonial style architecture, pool, restaurant. One of the prettiest new places on the scene.

Moderate

Catalina. Box 2, tel. 4–21–37. La Ropa Beach. 30 fan-cooled rooms overlooking the ocean. Elevator from the beach.

Raul 3 Marias. La Noria #4, tel. 4–21–91. 24 fan-cooled units. Small hotel for local businessmen.

Inexpensive

Bungalos Urracas La Ropa Beach. 10 bungalows with kitchens.

Bungalos Allec. Madera Beach. Six fan-cooled bungalows plus a restaurant.

Bungalos Pacificos. Cerro de la Madera. Six small houses with view of the ocean.

Hotel Avila. Juan Alvarez #8. 30 air-conditioned rooms with bath, restaurant.

Hotel Zihuatanejo. Pedro Ascencio 48, tel. 4–26–69. 45 fan-cooled rooms; downtown.

TOURS. Major hotels have travel agencies. If yours does not, try *Turismo Caleta* (tel. 4–24–91) in La Puerta Shopping Mall or *Paseos Ixtapa* in the Sheraton lobby (tel. 4–35–50, ext. 2070). **Horseback riding tours** through the picturesque countryside are conducted from *Rancho La Puerta,* a working ranch, 10 minutes from Ixtapa's hotel zone.

Zihuatanejo City Tour. This includes major points of interest in Zihuatanejo and is a good way to get oriented. It costs about $7 U.S.

Ixtapa Island. A 15-minute boat ride from Playa Quieta or a 45-minute ride from Zihuatanejo. If you go on your own, the fare is 350 pesos round trip from Playa Quieta; 2,500 from Zihuatanejo. An excursion costs approximately $10–$12 U.S.

Tequila Catamaran. You can sail away from La Ropa Beach at 11 A.M. and 3 P.M. for three-hour cruises of the bay with stops for swimming and snorkeling. Tel. 4–25–30.

Playa Las Gatas. A pretty beach, accessible only by water, where you can enjoy swimming, snorkeling, and diving. A few small restaurants offer simple meals. An excursion costs about $10–$12. U.S.

SPORTS. Name your favorite tropical sport and chances are that you can find it.

Parachute rides can be arranged on hotel zone beaches in Ixtapa. A 12-minute ride costs about $10.

Waterskiing, snorkeling, diving, windsurfing, and **sailing** can be arranged on the Ixtapa hotel zone or La Ropa beaches.

Tennis. Most major hotels in Ixtapa have tennis courts. The Palma Real Golf & Tennis Club also has courts lit for night play. Tennis is 950 pesos an hour for day play; 1,150 for night play.

Deep Sea Fishing boats can be rented on the Municipal Beach at Zihuatanejo Pier and at Playa Quieta in Ixtapa. Rates range from $100–$250/day, depending on the size of the boat. Hotel travel agencies can usually arrange excursions, too. Price includes tackle, bait, and a light lunch.

Windsurfing. Windsurfers can be rented on Las Gatas and La Ropa beaches as well as at Las Cuatas Beach Club.

Golf. You can play it at the *Palma Real Golf & Tennis Club* at the end of the Ixtapa hotel zone. There is a par 72, 18-hole championship course, a pool, a restaurant, a snack bar, and a pro shop. Greens fees are 4,800 pesos. Golf carts cost 4200 pesos. Golf and tennis equipment can be bought or rented at the clubhouse. Lessons are available. Tel. 4–22–80.

Scuba Diving. *Carlos* operates day and night diving excursions on Las Gatas Beach. *Oliverio* operates diving excursions on Ixtapa Island. *Casa del Mar* offers 4-hour diving excursions from Zihuatanejo to Barra de Potosi for 15,000 pesos. Price includes lunch and two tanks. Tel: 4–21–19.

Snorkeling. *Salomon Bustos* operates four-hour snorkeling excursions to Playa Manzanillo for 7,000 pesos. The price includes lunch.

BEACHES. The Ixtapa/Zihuatanejo coastline is scalloped and winds around hills and cliffs forming a number of beautiful coves and inlets where conditions are ideal for sunning and swimming. Generally, these beaches are less populated, more unspoiled, longer, and broader than beaches in other leading resorts. Some are more easily reached by car, and some are accessible only by water. You can find a beach to fit your particular preferences, no matter what they are.

Playa Linda. This beach north of Playa Quieta has facilities for campers, mobile homes, and all RVs. Full facilities, bathrooms, rooms and cooking facilities are available. There is a pool and a playground. Horses can be rented.

Playa Quieta is just 10 miles away on the scenic highway. Club Mediterranee is here, but the beach is public. The clear waters and lush vegetation are famous.

Playa Las Cuatas has a moon-shaped "bay" bordered by craggy rocks. Windsurfers, Hobie Cats, jet skis, diving and snorkeling equipment can be rented. There are reasonably priced classes in practically everything. Waterskiing boats are also available. The attractive Beach Club restaurant is open for lunch and dinner.

Palmar, the hotel zone beach, is 2.5 miles of seaside charm. It combines spectacular beauty with all facilities for ultra modern comfort, just a few steps from your door. This is one of the few beaches in the country that you can enjoy at night.

Playa Hermosa at the near end of Playa Palmar is the beautiful beach for the Camino Real Hotel. Towering, picturesque rock formations provide scenic contrast to the curved beach.

Ixtapa Island, a 15–20 minute boat ride from Playa Quieta (where Club Med is), is an unspoiled nature preserve which provides a perfect getaway for scuba divers and those who enjoy uninterrupted sun worshipping in primitive surroundings. When you get off the boat, take the five-minute walk to the other side of the island, which has small restaurants, fine sand, and clear waters.

Zihuatanejo

Municipal Beach. It curves around Zihuatanejo Bay and is a few steps from the downtown shopping and restaurant area. It is lined with cozy hotels and restaurants. Fishing trips and excursions to Ixtapa Island and Las Gatas Beach can be arranged at the pier.

Maderas Beach. Primitive and tiny with gentle waves, it is within easy walking distance of the Municipal Beach. Guests of hotels and bungalows tend to use this one. There are a few restaurants, but you can climb up to hotel dining rooms for lunch.

La Ropa is a bit farther out of town, but the distance is still walkable. Several small hotels line it. Rustic, open-air restaurants frequented by locals and visitors alike dot its edge. Waves are gentle and swimming conditions are ideal. Equipment for water sports can be rented.

Las Gatas. Hearty hikers can walk here from La Ropa Beach in about 20 minutes, but those who want to avoid having to climb sharp rocks take the easy way and come by boat from Playa Quieta or the Municipal Pier. The legend goes that a Tarascan Indian king had a coral reef built so that his daughter could swim safely here. The reef plus warm, crystal clear waters make Las Gatas especially ideal for diving and snorkeling. Instructors are available for both.

SHOPPING

Ixtapa

If you can tear yourself away from the beach, Ixtapa has some great stores and boutiques where you can find plenty of take-home treasures. Handicrafts and resort wear are the most popular items. Store hours are generally open 9 or 10 A.M.–1 or 2 P.M. and 4 or 5 P.M. to 8 or 9 P.M.

Most hotels have a few stores and shops. *Dorado Pacifico* and *Krystal* are particularly good but the small shopping mall in the Camino Real is the most chic of all, hands down. *La Esperanza* has the most carefully chosen selection of fine handicrafts in town. *Vesti Sol* has good belts and accessories. *Tane* has high quality gold and silver jewelry and decorative items.

La Puerta Shopping Mall, across from the El Presidente Hotel, has a collection of good boutiques and is still growing. *Mandarina* and *La Gaviota* have particularly good selections of resort wear and accessories. *Bazaar La Guadalupana* may have more souvenirs per square inch than any shop in the world. *Florence* is a small art and antiques gallery. *Mandiles,* a new shopping mall behind Monmatre Restaurant, is scheduled to open soon. Several exciting new shopping malls and commercial buildings are going up around Plaza Ixtapa behind La Puerta Shopping Mall. When they are completed, there will be over 306 new boutiques. *Calvin Klein, Acapulco Joe, Fiorucci,* and *Roberto's Silver Shop* are just a few. *Off Shore* and *Fernando Huertas,* which feature jewelry and antiques as well as sportswear, in Galeria Ixtapa, and *Soqui,* in Ixpamar Mall, are already open.

Zihuatanejo

Downtown Zihuatanejo is chock-full with inviting shops and boutiques. The best merchandise is often not on display, so it's better to go in and try on. Dedicated shoppers will find their own favorites and plenty of good buys. *La Fuente, La Cucaracha,* and *Cactus* are particularly good. Indians display local crafts in a street market on Juan Alvarez. The State Handicrafts Store, *Casa de Artesanias,* housed in a new glass and chrome building on Paseo Cocotal, has a good selection of crafts.

RESTAURANTS

Ixtapa

Dining out in Ixtapa is pleasant. You can pick a place to suit your mood and probably it will be within easy walking distance. Hotel dining rooms are slightly more formal than other places, but men never need jackets or ties and any well put together look is suitable for ladies. Trying other hotel dining rooms is fun. Some hotels hold special events such as Mexican fiestas or beach barbecues on different nights and generally anyone is invited. An average dinner costs $15–$25. *Diners Club, Carte Blanche,* and *American Express* credit cards are often not accepted.

The La Puerta shopping mall has three restaurants: **Da Baffone.** Air-conditioned and open-air sections. Open for lunch and dinner; Italian specialties; tel. 4–23–15. **Itzel.** Open air, for lunch and dinner. Spareribs, steaks and seafood are the specialties. **La Hacienda.** Air-conditioned and open-air sections. Open for breakfast, lunch, and dinner. Seafood and steaks, plus Mexican dishes; tel. 4–22–11.

Villa Sakura. Next to La Puerta shopping mall. Air-conditioned; authentic Japanese garden and cuisine; dinner only; 6 P.M.–1 A.M.; tel. 4–36–00 or 4–37–06.

Villa de la Selva. Punta Ixtapa, up the hill from entrance to Camino Real Hotel. Picture perfect, knockout decor; stay from sunset through dinner. Seafood and meat specialties; Open 6–midnight; tel. 4–20–96.

Carlos 'N Charlies. Crazy Polynesian setting at the end of the beach beside Castel Palmar Hotel. Serves pork, seafood, and chicken. Open noon to 5 P.M. to midnight, except Tuesdays.

Cuatas Beach Club. A ten-minute drive beyond the hotel zone near Club Med. Attractive place with the air of a private club. Make a day of it. Pretty open air dining by the sea. Seafood specialties and Pescado a la Talla, grilled marinated snapper, a local treat. Open daily 10 A.M.–midnight; tel. 4–27–56.

Several new restaurants will be located in the new shopping malls. **Beto's y Quiques** is already serving steaks and seafood. Paella is their specialty. Open 1 P.M.–midnight.

Los Mandiles serves food with a Mexican flavor in a colonial setting with contemporary touches. Lively live music from Veracruz begins at 8 P.M. Open 4:30–11:30 P.M.

Bogart's, an opulent, ultraromantic Moorish-style restaurant that recalls Casablanca, offers sophisticated dining and continental cuisine. It's a knockout!

Zihuantanejo

Downtown Zihuantanejo is packed with informal, picturesque places to dine. You'll discover them as you stroll. Here are a few of the favorites.

La Mesa del Capitan. Nicolas Bravo No. 18. One of the first. Two floors plus garden dining area; continental cuisine. Tel. 4–20–27.

Puntarenas. Across the bridge on the end of Juan Alvarez Street. Home cooked authentic Mexican food. Pork, chicken, stuffed peppers, hearty plain pipe rack. Lunch only; no reservations; prepare to wait. This is a favorite with locals and visitors in the know. Only open December 15–Easter.

Taboga. Juan Alvarez, corner Cinco de Mayo beside Canaima. Meat and seafood at the main corner; tel. 4–26–37.

Canaima. Paseo del Pescador, Playa Municipal and Cinco de Mayo. Zihua's first, overlooking the town beach and harbor. Rustic, open air dining; hearty food, fresh clams, and lobster specialties. Reserve for dinner; tel. 4–20–03.

Coconuts. Avenida Agustin Ramierez No. 1. Friendly bar and garden restaurant in one of Zihuatanejo's oldest historical buildings. Scrumptious pies and pastries are prepared on the premises. Everybody loves it. Reservations advisable; tel. 4–25–18.

El Castillo. Calle Ejido No. 25. It looks like a corner castle. Friendly bar, international meat and seafood specialties; beautiful table settings; divine desserts. Reserve; tel. 4–34–19.

Garrobos. In the Tres Marias Hotel on Juan Alvarez. Popular place for paella and brochettes. Tel. 4–29–77.

Gitano's. Nicolas Bravo, corner Cinco de Mayo. The seafood comes straight off the fishing boats which tie up at the pier a few yards away. Some meat dishes also available. Tel. 4–23–18.

La Gaviota, on Playa La Ropa, is a mini beach club with a dozen or so tables. Get there early (around 1 P.M.) It's popular with locals and visitors. **El Marlin,** next door, takes the overflow.

A cluster of restaurants have popped up around Ibiza disco, offering dining with a panoramic view of the bay. The **Bay Club** overlooks La Ropa Beach and has a mesquite grill. The setting is pretty. There is live music in the bar below. Open 5 P.M.–11 P.M. Tel: 4–38–44. **Kon Tiki,** next door, also overlooks La Ropa and offers a happy hour 5–8 P.M. for those who like to watch the sunset. Open 1 P.M.–midnight. Tel: 4–24–71.

NIGHTLIFE. Though Ixtapa/Zihuatanejo appears to be a nature oriented early-to-bed destination, you can switch into high gear after dinner and find plenty of action and fun that lasts as long as you let it. Ixtapa hotels often feature shows with big name entertainment. Watch for signs around town.

Discos. Ixtapa's disco scene is booming. Entry fees are approximately $4–$5 per person. Drinks range from about 500 pesos for a coke to 1,200 for imported whiskey and soda. *Christine's,* in front of the Hotel Krystal, is as classy and sassy as they come. Three video screens, smoke, lights, balloons, and other gimmicks make already lively evenings livelier. Open 10:30 P.M.–4 A.M. *Joy,* across the street, is also new and glittering. Comfortable tiers of tables let you watch the action on the dance floor when you're not helping to make it. The fun upstairs includes electronic games and a snack bar. Open 10:30 P.M.– 5 A.M. *La Esfera* in the Camino Real Hotel, is also sleek and lively. Backgammon tables and a comfortable bar are just outside. This is another favorite with locals and visitors. Open 10 P.M.–4 A.M. *Ibiza* is a tiny place with small windows overlooking the ocean on the road to La Ropa. The Zihuatanejo crowd loves it.

PACIFIC RESORTS

Puerto Vallarta, Manzanillo, Mazatlán, and More

by
KAL MULLER

Mexico is bound by three bodies of water of strikingly different character: the Gulf, the Caribbean, and the Pacific. With the exception of Cancun, the most popular coastal resorts are all on the Pacific side, and with good reason. Aside from Cancun's unmatched fine sand, the best beaches are on the west coast, along with weather to match. In this chapter, we look at the three major resorts to the north of Acapulco and we also explore some lesser known (and often cheaper) alternatives along the coast: Melaque/Barra de Navidad, San Blas and Guaymas as well as isolated beaches with little or no infrastructure.

A part of Mexico's 2,000 miles of Pacific littoral, the long stretch of the coast begins at Playa Azul in the state of Michoacán, which lies 230 miles northwest of Acapulco. The coastal highways head northwest from here for over 1,000 miles to Guaymas in the state of Sonora. The main highway either goes through or close to the beaches and resorts along this stretch.

As a rule, there's sunshine everywhere, year-round, and temperatures are kept down by ocean breezes. However, the light, freshening winds can treacherously lead you to believe that you are not being burned to a lobster-red frazzle by the sun's rays, which are a lot more direct than in the northern latitudes. Mazatlán can be 15 degrees cooler than Acapulco—great in the summer, not so good (especially for ocean bathing) in the winter. This coast can at times get muggy humid in the weeks before the onset of the rainy season which starts in June and runs through early October. Rainy season doesn't mean 24 hours of monsoon—it's more like an afternoon shower with plenty of sunshine the rest of the day.

Accessibility is excellent. You can fly to international airports at Mazatlán, Puerto Vallarta, Manzanillo, Hermosillo, or Guadalajara. Hermosillo lies a bit over an hour's drive from Guaymas while it's a half-hour's plane hop from Guadalajara to Puerto Vallarta. There are also air and ferry links, for cars as well as passengers, to Baja California. Lots of buses run between points along the coast. Rental cars are available in the major resorts.

The geography and character of the Pacific resorts show some variety. None can claim Acapulco's sophistication in discos nor the number of luxury hotels. But all three of Acapulco's sisters do have top-rated hotels as well as the best of dining and a variety of entertainment along with the compulsory beaches. Manzanillo's tourist area hugs the shore of two bays, well away from the downtown area, which is a busy port and railhead. The Las Hadas complex is a leader in size, imagination, and luxury, largely responsible for starting off the recent tourism boom in the area. Puerto Vallarta became a jet-set in-spot after the fame it received for the 1964 film *The Night of the Iguana.* Downtown Puerto Vallarta has kept most of its character while channelling tourist development to the immediate north and south along the huge Bahía de Banderas (Bay of Flags). Mazatlán, a longtime favorite of sportfishermen and college students letting off steam, is acquiring sophistication along a lengthy strip backing several beaches to the north of town. At the opposite end of the city, a thriving harbor is the home of Mexico's largest shrimp fishing fleet, modern ferries to La Paz (Baja California) as well as a port of call to several cruise ships.

PUERTO VALLARTA

A Growing Pacific Playground

Puerto Vallarta (pop. 130,000) is fast becoming an international resort as popular as Acapulco or Cancun. Vallarta aims at a sort of compromise between her rivals—less isolated than Cancun, but not blessed with that incredible white-sand Carribean beach; less cosmopolitan, but on a more human scale than big-time Acapulco, whose population is soaring over the million mark. Puerto Vallarta is struggling to maintain a small-town Mexican atmosphere while trying to develop a tourist-oriented flavor.

Contrary to publicity, a charming fishing village is incompatible with an international resort playground. Sleepy fishermen always lose. But Vallarta is still dominated by red-tiled roofs, pastel walls, cobblestone streets and bright bougainvilleas. Hotels and restaurants often go for the traditional high thatch roof even if it has to be redone every two to five years. Fortunately, after one high-rise sneaked into town before anyone realized what was happening, building codes have forbidden nontraditional, modern construction in the city.

Just a couple of years ago, it could be said that Puerto Vallarta was like the Acapulco of the early '60s. But the hustle factor is leaping forward in quantum jumps. However, developers and speculators are hard put to do away with Puerto Vallarta's natural beauty.

Located in the huge curve of the 28-mile Bahia de Banderas (Bay of Flags), the town lies on the same latitude as Hawaii and is blessed with a similar near perfect climate. Parrots squawk for attention amid banana, papaya, and mango trees just outside town. Frigate birds survey the scene from above while pelicans glide for a closer look at the shore.

The climate will always remain a major drawing card, especially during the winter months when birds and humans desperately need to leave the big chill. The vegetation is lush and tropical when let alone. The wide curve of the bay makes for plenty of beaches of varying character.

The town of Puerto Vallarta is located at the edge of the neo-volcanic range which crosses Mexico around the 19th parallel. The western limit of this chain is Cabo Corrientes, the southern tip of the bay. There are plenty of mountains crowding Vallarta. To the south of town, a road has been carved out of the steep mountainside with hotels and condos popping up on any available area. Toward the north and the airport, there is more flat area where the state of Nayarit begins just beyond the airport, across the Ameca River.

A Bit of History

Little is known about the history of Puerto Vallarta. There is an apocryphal account of Francisco Cortés de San Buenaventura, the nephew of the conqueror of the Aztecs, having led the first group of palefaces to this region. We know that the nephew did lead a rugged bunch as far as Tepic but accounts are hazy as to their foray to the coast. One version ascribes the name Bahía de Banderas to the numerous standards or flags borne to battle by the Indians when they confronted the Spaniards here. But no reliable historical text vouches for this.

As the Manila galleons cruised by this coast for 250 years, it is likely that pirates who preyed on the floating treasure house made landings here, trading or fighting with the Indians. No one bothered to record the heroic or dastardly deeds. A definite historical peg surfaces only in 1918 when Puerto de las Peñas (Port of the Boulders) changed its name to Puerto Vallarta to honor a liberal governor of the State of Jalisco. Then back to the sleepy village of fishermen.

"The villages were still predominantly primitive Indian villages and the still-water morning beach of Puerto Barrio and the rain forest above it were among the world's wildest and loveliest populated areas."—*The Night of the Iguana* by Tennessee Williams.

The movie's director John Huston found the spot at a cove called Mismaloya, just south of Puerto Vallarta. Then, when *The Night of the Iguana* was filmed here in 1964, Puerto Vallarta began its road to fame and fortune.

Back in those days, you took a steamboat, a donkey across the mountains, or a DC3 to a weed-infested joke of a landing strip to reach Vallarta. There were about 30,000 natives at the time.

The exotic tropical setting plus the steamy romance of Elizabeth Taylor and Richard Burton were the magnets attracting the first of the beautiful people and later the hoi-polloi. The government built an airport and a paved road link to the main west coast highway. The invading sun and romance-seeking hordes started, especially from the U.S. which still spews out 90% of the town's tourists.

There was a fantastic boom year in 1982 when prices were incredibly low thanks to peso devaluations and inflation had not yet rocketed out of sight. After that, the number of visitors reached the critical mass where more and more would come, no matter what. Unscrupulous businessmen—in hotels and elsewhere—tried hard to kill the goose laying the dollar-covered eggs: overcharges, reservations not honored . . . horror tales abound. The reaction has been muted but the abuses are diminishing, although not yet eliminated. Confirmed reservations through a reputable travel agent are still your best insurance for arriving to a waiting room. If you are willing to take the time, you can probably find your own accommodations in one of the smaller, less expensive hotels.

EXPLORING PUERTO VALLARTA

To help you get your bearings, we will describe Puerto Vallarta and vicinity in three major chunks: the area north of town, the city itself, and the zone to the south. The ocean is always to the west.

The airport, the marina (departure point for all cruises as well as the ferry to Baja) and a strip of hotels make up the northern area. Almost all the 15-odd hotels here are on the beach and constitute self-contained expensive resort units where you can relax, practice water sports, or tan in splendid isolation.

You know when you reached the town itself by the cobblestone-induced rattles which start shaking your vehicle. Vallarta is divided into two distinct and unequal zones by the Cuale River. Most of the population, the commercial district and government offices are to the north of the Cuale. The malecón, a palm-dotted oceanside walk, follows the curve of the bay for about a half mile. It is most popular for late afternoon sunset walks and light or serious drinking in any of a number of watering holes alongside. The only problem is noise as much of the traffic coming to town gets funneled down the one-way street adjacent to the malecón.

Afternoon and evening, the malecón is where the suntanned flower of American youth meet and strike up easy friendships.

Although the locals are pretty well used to the tourists' bizarre outfits, it's still not a very good idea for unaccompanied ladies to display too much flesh—unless native male attention is sought.

The zocalo, the town square with its bandstand, sits back a block from the malecón. The new town hall (with the tourism office) lies to one side of the zocalo. This square is the most popular with the locals when they come out for a stroll at night and husbands are not allowed to ogle the blonde gringas. The Guadalupe Church is another block inland from the zocalo. Top-heavy with an awful concrete crown for the Virgin, this tower is unfortunately the only authentic landmark in town.

Gringo Gulch, formerly the only gilded ghetto, ages well a few blocks uphill from the Guadalupe Church and off the northern bank of the Cuale River. Some rich Americans still maintain homes here but new fashions dictate villas and luxury condominiums on the coastal strip south of town. It is said that Elizabeth Taylor's children sometimes drop in their mother's house, Casa Kimberly, connected by a passageway to Richard Burton's pad across the narrow street. Miss Taylor seldom returns to Vallarta; on her last visit, she stayed at the Camino Real. Of the *Iguana*'s principals, only John Huston has become a full-time resident. Some 1,000 norteamericanos live in Vallarta on a relatively permanent basis, ensconced among the villas of Gringo Gulch or cottages and condos south of town.

On the hillside to the north or in back of Gringo Gulch, where cobblestone streets turn into stairs or dirt paths, the homes of the poorer locals have great views but lack amenities.

Two bridges, each handling one-way traffic, cross the Cuale River, only a stream during the dry season. The town market spreads at the northern end of the upstream bridge. Budget travelers can pick up their fresh fish here, cleaned and fileted at no extra charge. There are also fresh fruit and vegetables at local prices. Many tourist-oriented craft items such as serapes and wool blankets can also be purchased at the market with prices far below the beach hawkers'—half or less.

Cuale Island

Cuale Island, from the upstream bridge to its western tip, is a pleasant walk. The island displays a row of open stalls selling typical tourist items that include stuffed iguanas and armadillos. Resort wear features typically Mexican styles adapted for the mass market. Bargaining is a must. There are several restaurants on the island that cater to visitors. We recommend the Café Franzi, just a few yards west of the downstream bridge. The archeological museum is just beyond—not worth a special trip but do peek in if you're strolling by to see some of the largest obsidian (volcanic glass) pre-Columbian implements we have seen. Open weekdays, 10 A.M. to 5 P.M.

The western tip of Cuale Island almost reaches the sea. Bulldozers were working hard at this writing to give a pleasant perspective to this area. By contrast, the northern part of the island, beyond the upstream bridge, has seen little development. Aside from a restaurant next to the bridge, there is a parched playground with all the swings swiped and a few buildings in disrepair except for a kindergarten. But this piece of real estate is too valuable to leave as is and future development is inevitable. On the river banks off the northern tip of the island, naturally brown-skinned local women pound their wash then spread the clothes to dry in a colorful display.

The economy section of town nestles south of the Cuale, hemmed in by mountains and sea. The short strip which follows the sea is favored by the budget minded: it abounds in small hotels, restaurants, shops and discos. There are a couple of deluxe hotels but most establishments are geared to the less affluent. Pushcarts sell fresh fruit, sugarcane, and seafood; occasionally gargantuan oysters 5 to 6 in. across, to be inhaled in one gulp along with lemon juice and hot sauce.

The beach along here is named alternatively Playa de los Muertos (Beach of the Dead) and Playa del Sol (Beach of the Sun). The morbid name comes from an unsubstantiated battle between pirates and Indians while the saccharine appellation is an effort to put the visitors' minds at rest. Fishermen's wives still roast their husbands' fresh catch, using skewers over coconut husk fires. Pompano, snapper, mackrel, robalo, or bonito can make a wonderful and inexpensive snack as well as a full, healthy meal.

Toward the South

The highway south of town winds its way along the mountains dropping down into the sea. Construction is booming here as any space is enlarged for a luxury condo or high-priced hotel. Some fancy cliff-dwelling villas offer stupendous views at the price of a steep descent to the beach and sea.

A series of huge, vegetation-topped rocks called Los Arcos (The Arches) pop out of the sea about 10 km from town. The name comes from the natural arches in the rocks, passageways big enough to allow a launch through. At Mismaloya, just beyond Los Arcos, you can rent a motorboat to ride around for a few dollars. The sea around the rocks is good for swimming, diving or just enjoying. There is a small village at Mismaloya, a rustic restaurant, and an informal trailer park in spite of a sign forbidding campers. Several crumbling houses on the hill at the end of the bay were the set for *The Night of the Iguana.* But the rustic, exotic atmosphere is long gone. A large, concrete condominium overlooks the other side of the bay and a rusting forest of iron rods graces the flat land at the bottom, another condo—but this one stopped due to a jurisdictional dispute with the local agrarian community. The price of progress.

Public minibuses come out from town as far as Mismaloya every 20 minutes or so. Taxi rates this far are also reasonable. Transportation farther out can be a problem if you don't have your own vehicle, as from here on, taxi fares go up sharply. But the few miles to Boca de Tomatlán are worth the effort and price. Spectacular cascades of tropical vegetation tumble down steep-sided mountains into the sea, only occasionally spoiled by some awful concrete structure. Stop by the Le Kliff restaurant or the Chee Chee for the best views or a meal.

Boca de Tomatlán represents nature's best show in the Vallarta area. A deep, narrow cove pushes inland, its precipitous sides covered with an interlocking tangle of trees and bushes. A river's mouth marks the end of the inlet. The highway cuts inland from here, and there are about 80 miles before you can gaze at the sea again at Chamela.

A number of yachts takes groups daily from the marina in Puerto Vallarta to areas south of the Boca de Tomatlán. Where the light is right, turquoise waters meet the tropical vegetation wall crowding the sea. An occasional white sand beach and minuscule fishing villages break up the shoreline. Local boys who have no use for a tan, throw lines into the sea and almost always come up with a meal. With a forked spear on a rubber sling, they dive for lobsters to sell at restaurants.

Some cruise ships stop at the mini village of Las Animas in a white sand beach cove. Swimming and snorkeling are the preferred activities, along with a short walk to the Quimixto waterfalls. Farther on, at the end of all cruises, Yelapa tries to live up to its South Pacific reputation. There is a small hotel, parasailing, water skiing, and open restaurants on the beach. It is peaceful only when there are no ships anchored.

PRACTICAL INFORMATION FOR PUERTO VALLARTA

WHEN TO GO. High season—the best weather and the expensive prices—are in the winter, from late November through April. During the last two weeks of December and Easter Week, reservations are absolutely essential except for the backpack set or trailer-toters. The other months are not to be scorned. It might get a bit muggy from around mid-May to when the rains start about a month later. The rainy season, which lasts through September, is not unpleasant—usually the weather is clear except for late afternoon showers. Hurricanes almost never reach the area.

HOW TO GET THERE. Most visitors nowadays fly directly to Puerto Vallarta from the U.S., Canada or a Mexican city. There are flights from most large cities in Canada or the U.S., either direct or connecting, on one of several American or Mexican carriers. *Republic Airlines* flies daily from Phoenix and Chicago; *Western* from L.A.; *American* from Dallas/Fort Worth; *Frontier,* six times weekly from Denver, Albuquerque, and thrice from El Paso; *Continental,* three times weekly from Houston. *Mexicana* flies direct, daily, from Chicago, and *Aeromexico* from Dallas, Houston, L.A., San Francisco, and Seattle. Connecting flights are too numerous to list.

Within the country, *Mexicana* and *Aeromexico* offer four daily flights to Guadalajara, six to Mexico City, and at least daily service to Cabo San Lucas, Mazatlan, Monterrey, Nuevo Laredo, and Tijuana. Flights within Mexico are not too expensive even though fares are government regulated with no competition allowed.

Buses are frequent to Tepic, Guadalajara, and Manzanillo with connections to most other major cities. Twice a week there's an overnight ferry to Cabo San Lucas.

Within Puerto Vallarta, there are crowded public minibuses going just about everywhere from the airport to Mismaloya. Very cheap. Taxis were also inexpensive at this writing: from downtown, about $3 to the airport. Popular restaurants, bars, and hotels almost always have taxis at night. Small cars can be rented for $30 to $35 a day, including some insurance plus about 12¢ per km. Car rental agencies require a major credit card and won't do business with under 25-year-olds.

SPORTS. Water sports head the list, as could be expected. Power boats work the beaches where there are concentrations of bored bodies, offering a 5-minute parasail for $15. An exhilarating way to get a birds-eye view of your surroundings. Many of the better hotels will arrange water skiing. The area is not well known for surfing, but if that's a must, contact Gabriel at the *Las Palmas Hotel* for information.

For diving, your best bet is *Chico's Dive Shop,* located on the malecón (tel. 21895)—or contact through a travel agency. A 40 ft. catamaran that holds up to 35 persons takes you to one of two selected dive spots. The set rate is $35 or $45 depending on which tour you take; this includes everything: gear, practice lesson in a hotel pool, guides, the boat, and either a snack or a beach barbecue. The shorter tour is on Monday, Tuesday, Thursday, and Friday to the Los Arcos area, while the longer jaunt on Wednesdays and Saturdays heads farther in the same direction.

Deep-sea fishing is big-time here. There is a tournament at the beginning of the season in early November—contact the Tourism Dept. for exact dates and information (See *Useful Addresses*). There's sailfish and 400 lb. black marlin to troll for. An equipped fishing yacht will cost $200 to $300 for 4 to 8 passengers. Bring your own booze and reserve with anticipation through your hotel.

Land-based activities include tennis in many of the hotels plus the *John Newcombe Tennis Club,* km 2.5 Tepic, the *Los Tules Tennis Club* at the Fiesta Americana and the *Tennis Club Vallarta* near the Posada Vallarta. Horses are available for riding on the beach or for guided jungle trips. Travel agencies can arrange hunting for deer, wild pig, mountain cats, and birds but you should think about this before coming to Mexico (see *Facts at Your Fingertips*).

There was no golf course in Vallarta at the time of this writing although rumor had it that one was to be built near the airport. The *Club de Golf Los Flamingos* is 24 km away, across the state line of Nayarit, just off the highway to Tepic. A superb 18-hole, 72-par course, designed by Percy Clifford; difficult, with plenty of water hazards but four playing levels. There is a practice tee, a pro, a pro shop, lockers, steam baths, caddies or electric carts, equipment rental, a pool, restaurant/bar, and four clay tennis courts. Taxis from Puerto Vallarta charge $10 but the golf course will provide free transportation from the highway at km 1 Tepic, in front of the Sheraton. The greens fee was $15 and due for a raise.

HOTELS. Hotels in Puerto Vallarta are proliferating under a tidal wave of sun-worshipping tourists. But it is just about impossible to luck on a room during the Christmas and Easter holidays. All through the high season—from November to April—we strongly recommend confirmed reservations. Space does not permit listing all the hotels in town. We do include all the better hotels, classified *First Class* or *Deluxe* as well as the special *Gran Turismo* category. Only a reduced selection of lower classified hotels is listed. At press time, hotels in each category were authorized to charge, on the average, the following costs for a double room, plus a federal tax of 15%: *Gran Turismo,* $120; *Deluxe,* $70; *First Class,* $42; *Expensive,* $26; *Moderate,* $18; and *Inexpensive,* $10. However, with the horrendous rate of inflation, prices will doubtlessly increase by the time you read this. If you think that a hotel is overcharging you, or for any other major problem, call the local tourism office from 9 to 9 at 20242 or 20243. Also contact this office, located in the Palacio Municipal (Town Hall) on Juarez Street, to connect with an agency handling villas or condominiums on a weekly or longer basis.

As pointed out earlier in this chapter, the Puerto Vallarta urban area falls into several divisions. We will maintain these divisions when giving the hotel address. Areas north of the cobblestoned city section are labeled in kilometers from downtown Vallarta towards Tepic (i.e., km 2.5 Tepic). To the south, we use the same system (i.e., km 3.5 Mismaloya). For the downtown area, we draw our division at the Cuale River, designating "Cuale North" or "Cuale South" besides the street address.

Gran Turismo

Krystal Posada Vallarta, km 5 Tepic, tel. 21459. 530 units, including suites and villas, this is the biggest hotel in town. But no claustrophobia as it's all spread out among meticulously groomed grounds with balconies and patios galore. You can be passive here and work on a poolside or seaside tan but for the perky, there are endless organized activities: jogging, calisthenics, tennis (three lit courts), horseback riding, fishing, sailing, volleyball, water skiing, and parachute riding. Aside from the usual Fiesta Mexicana ($25) at the hotel's Plaza Mexicana, there's the fiesta Brava ($25), a bloodless bullfight in their own ring complete with brass band, meal and the opportunity to show off your skills with the bull. There are seven restaurants, including the *Japanese Kamakura,* the *Tango* for Argentine steaks accompanied by a trio from the Pampas, and *Los Arcos* for truly gourmet cuisine, often featuring a French, Italian or other gastronomic meals. There is a nightclub, convention center, meeting rooms, travel agency, shops.

Fiesta Americana, km 2.5 Tepic, tel. 22010. With 282 rooms, a large meandering pool, lots of plants and flowers on all the high-rise balconies, 5 tennis courts, a striking lobby covered by a huge peaked and thatched roof, four restaurants, five bars. Good cuisine at the *Morrocco* to the strains of jazz and fresh seafood at the poolside *Oyster Bar* with drinks at the *Bikini Bar* or, for inveterate water freaks, at the *Coco Loco Bar* on an island in the pool. *The Lobby Bar* features live entertainment and nightly dancing. *Los Tules,* next to and managed by this hotel, is a large, private resort club with villas that include all amenities in a 30-acre country club setting and a half mile of beach.

Bougainvilias Sheraton, km 1 Tepic, tel. 23000. Six contiguous 14-story towers bunch together 501 units in Vallarta's biggest building, overwhelming the individualist, loved by the gregarious. Aside from the usual Mexican Night, there is also a weekly Italian Night. There are four restaurants and five bars. At *Las Gaviotas* you can savor a gourmet meal, then saunter over to *El Embarcadero* night club. The usual shops, car rental, travel agency.

Camino Real, km 3.5 Mismaloya, tel. 20002. On the Playa de los Estacas, their fine, secluded beach. A high-rise, 250-unit bundle of luxury, all with a view of the sea. Gourmet dining in the French-style *La Perla* restaurant. Lobby and pool/beach bars; beach parties; weekly Mexican fiestas, and the exotic *La Jungla* disco.

Deluxe

Playa del Oro, km 5.5 Tepic on Avenida las Garzas, next to the marina, tel. 20544. One of the first hotels, now renovated with 392 units, A/C, servi-bars in some rooms and sea views on request and availability basis. Three restaurants, 6 bars, 2 pools, *Quick* car rental, two travel agencies which handle all local tours as well as skin diving. *Kon Tiki* nightclub, Fiesta Mexicana on Saturday nights by the pool. Courteous service, good English at front desk. Excellent value for families or individuals.

Holiday Inn, km 3.5 Tepic, tel. 21700. Main Tower with 230 rooms, 6 suites; Suite Tower with 236 suites, 10 penthouses, all with private terraces overlooking the ocean. There are four restaurants, three bars, *Isadora's* disco, most amenities, and sports.

Plaza las Glorias, km 2.5 Tepic, tel. 22224. 243 standard rooms next to beach, with servi-bars and satellite TV reception. Smallish pool, Fiesta Mexicana on Tuesdays, the *Trattoria* with Italian entertainment and buffet ($21). *Las Pergolas* restaurant for good seafood, lobby bar.

Plaza Vallarta (John Newcombe Tennis Center), km 2.5 Tepic, tel. 24360; with 410 luxury rooms and suites on the beach. The ideal complex for the sports-minded. There are four restaurants, including the excellent French cuisine of *Place Vendome* and the gourmet specialties of *Condesa del Mar;* long list of amenities and activities.

Garza Blanca, km 7.5 Mismaloya, tel. 21023. Features 22 seaside suites, 17 chalets and 34 villas. The cheapest suites were $215 at this writing and the bigger 3-bedroom villas going for $400 a night, so forget about the rating. The hotel is spread out, partially on a steep slope that gives spectacular views on the ocean and mountains. The villas are serviced daily and transportation is provided to the central hotel area. The chalets are split level and, along with the villas, provide private swimming pools. Good restaurant, bar, a couple of shops, a hotel pool and excellent beach.

First Class

Paraiso Perricos, km 5 Tepic, tel. 22325. With 307 rooms, 16 condos, all A/C, 2 restaurants, 2 bars, 2 pools, nightclub, travel agency, car rental. Being on the "wrong" side of the highway (away from the beach), they have to try harder. *Club de Playa* (Beach Club) provides free transportation to the **Holiday Inn's** beach where a sharing arrangement has been worked out. A good price deal if you don't insist on a beachside hotel.

Castel Pelicanos, km 2.5 Tepic, tel. 22107; with 220 almost-on-the-beach units, 2 restaurants, 4 bars, 3 pools, disco. A short walk to beachside pool area, segregated by a wall from pestering vendors.

Las Palmas, km 2.5 Tepic, tel. 20650; with 150 rooms, each with private balcony overlooking the ocean, striking lobby area with multileveled bamboo-railed wooden walkways. Barbeques on Monday and Friday evenings, Mexican fiesta on Wednesdays; pool, 3 bars; an excellent buy for the money.

Buenaventura, Ave. Mexico 1301, Cuale North, on your right just as you reach the cobblestone street ending the highway, tel. 23737. 210 spacious rooms; a five-minute walk to the zocalo. Lobby bar situated under a modern five-story atrium. Large pool, good travel agency; weekly features include a Mexican fiesta, fashion show, and barbecue. Popular *Tucanes Beach Club* offers nightly entertainment.

Conchas Chinas, km 2.5 Mismaloya, tel. 20156; with 32 suites, 8 standard rooms and a penthouse, all with seaview, A/C, kitchenettes with fridge. While most hotels have restaurants as adjuncts, here the situation is reversed. *El Set* (motto: Another lousy sunset in Paradise) is a large, popular restuarant that almost overwhelms the hotel. Conchas has a boutique, pool, and a good beach with rocks in front to break the monotony.

Oro Verde, R. Gomez 111, Cuale South, tel. 21555. Probably the best hotel in this part of town, with 162 units; Swiss-managed, perhaps by the gnomes of Zurich as the lobby has the lowest ceiling we have ever seen; otherwise, quite up to snuff with the compulsory pool, 2 restaurants (*La Barca de Oro* will whip up an "authentic" Swiss fondue), 2 bars; right on the beach, next to the old wave-torn jetty; disco just across the front entrance.

Los Arcos, Olas Altas 380, Cuale South, tel. 21583; a four-story colonial style building with 130 rooms and 9 suites all A/C, with Mexican decor; restaurant, bar, weekly Fiesta Mexicana; the back of the hotel opens onto the beach.

Expensive

Molino de Agua, Vallarta 130, Cuale South, right on the river bank, tel. 21957. Now with 62 units and changing its character, unable to resist the lure of the sea. The original hotel, divided among several units and set in a lush garden, has expanded with the addition of an unimaginative concrete building in which all rooms face the ocean, adjacent to freeform pool. Barbeque on Wednesdays and Saturdays. Restaurant, bar, Jacuzzi.

Posada Rio Cuale, Serdan 242 on the corner of Vallarta, Cuale South, tel. 20450. Lovely small, unpretentious hotel, 24 rooms, clean and well kept; surprisingly good restaurant, bar, and pool.

Tropicana, Amapa 227, Cuale South, tel. 20912. Large hotel for the area, 231 units, half of which look to the sea. This is the last hotel towards the south which is still "in town." Restaurant, bar, travel agency, shops, pool.

Suites Las Garzas, Avenida de las Garzas, km 5 Tepic, between the Posada Vallarta and the Playa del Oro, tel. 21433. Eleven units with kitchenettes, balconies; pool; near the ocean. Good bet for the budget-minded.

Hacienda del Lobo, km 5 Tepic, right on the highway, tel. 29161; 145 rooms, half A/C; restaurant, bar, games room, pool, a lit tennis court.

El Conquistador, km 1.5 Tepic, on the highway, tel. 22088. With 108 rooms, all A/C, satellite reception, bar, pool; frequented by Mexicans as well as Americans; the kids will have fun on the huge slide ending in a pool within the hotel inner patio.

Rosita, Diaz Ordaz 901 (continuation of the Tepic highway into town), Cuale North, tel. 21033. Family hotel with 111 rooms, restaurant, bar, pool. Convenient location just where the malecón starts, although somewhat noisy from the traffic on the streetside rooms.

Cuatro Vientos, Matamoros 520, Cuale North, tel. 20161. A 16-unit hilltop hotel, American owned and managed, superb view. It's a steep climb to reach this hotel in the residential section of town but most visitors who come once return again and again for the excellent service, friendly atmosphere, the view, and the excellent *Chez Helen* restaurant. Prices depend on length of stay. Good exchange rates for your dollars. A best buy if you don't insist on a beachside hotel.

Moderate

Fontana del Mar, Dieguez 171, Cuale South, tel. 20712. In front of and around the corner of its parent hotel, Los Arcos. 41 units, all A/C, pool.

Marsol, Rodriguez 103, Cuale South, tel. 20865. Old hotel with 120 rooms, family style, getting run down; next to the disintegrating pier. Pool, kitchenettes in some rooms; lots of stores and restaurants close by.

Oceano, Galleana 103, Cuale North, tel. 21050, right on the malecón; 52 A/C rooms, restaurant, bar, pool; noisy but right in the middle of the most popular part of town.

Secatur, Hidalgo and Guerrero, Cuale North, tel. 24910. A sort of hotel-school with 14 units, restaurant/bar, near the market.

Encino, Juarez 122, Cuale North on the river bank, tel. 20051. Medium sized hotel popular with budget travelers for its location and price; 75 rooms, four stories with rooftop pool, and restaurant with good view over the river.

Inexpensive

Marlyn, Mexico 1121, Cuale North, tel. 20965. On the street which extends the Tepic highway into town; noisy on the streetside rooms; 37 rooms, some with A/C.

Yazmin, Badillo 168, Caule South, tel. 20087. Good location, fans.

Note: There are several condominiums with apartments for rent along the road south of town, towards Mismaloya. The **Solar Beach Condominiums,** with its own beach, between the Camino Real and the Garza Blanca, tel. 20860, has an average of 15 units for rent, 2-bedroom, 2-bath, individual terraces all looking out to sea, pool, maid service, A/C; expensive. **Quinta María Cortés,** on the Conchas Chinas beach, tel. 21317, has some four apartments for rent, American managed, much appreciated by connoisseurs, exquisite colonial setting. New condos are springing up all the time while older ones often sell all their units.

Your best bet here is to take a drive along the road to Mismaloya and stop to investigate where weekly or daily rates are advertised on roadside signs.

RESTAURANTS. A small list of restaurants compiled by informal survey of local bon vivants is presented here. The emphasis is on atmosphere as well as good food. Hotel restaurants are not included. In view of Puerto Vallarta's culinary explosion (almost as impressive as Mexico's demographic one) a few additional restaurants are listed by category. **Note:** If you feel adventurous in a culinary sense, try local specialties such as turtle soup or *pulpa en su tinta* (octopus in its ink). The local alcoholic beverage is called *raisilla,* which is distilled from a cactus similar to tequila. It has a fine aroma and will curl your eyelids. A *casuela of raisilla* (pot of raisilla) has various tropical fruit floating in it and is sometimes cut with a soft drink. Delicious but be forewarned, it's much stronger than it tastes—it'll sneak up on you without warning.

Mister Pepe's, Badillo 503, Cuale South, tel. 22732; evening reservations are essential. Pepe personally attends to his American clientele who come for the ambience, the food, and the view. An open, rooftop restaurant with a sweeping view over town and ocean, great for sunsets. Piano player sings old favorites. Favorite dishes include giant shrimp, steak with house sauce, and fresh mushrooms, fresh fish filets, coffee and eggnog and nuts. Closed from July to September. Only one seating;—reservations a must.

Kanpai, Carranza 208, Cuale South, tel. 23317. Japanese restaurant also serving Korean and Thai food. Excellent food either inside or in the pretty Japanese courtyard.

Andres, Olas Altas 326, Cuale South, on the beach. New restaurant serving great food on patio overlooking the ocean. Parasails take off right in front of you, and sunsets are spectacular.

Chez Helena, Matamoros 520, Cuale North at the Cuatro Vientos Hotel, tel. 20161. An excellent varied menu in a most pleasant setting with a handsome, talented singer entertaining. Specialties include several interesting Indonesian dishes, lobster and shrimp over spaghetti, fresh fish filet with cheese sauce, beef brochettes with mustard sauce, topped with their flambé café mulatto with ice cream. Accolades from American and European publications, yet, price-wise, this has not gone to their heads.

La Hacienda, Aguacate 274, Cuale South, tel. 20590; good atmosphere, lots of young people, international cuisine, inexpensive.

Las Casuelas, Basilis Vadillo 479, Cuale South, tel. 21658; authentic gourmet cooking, perhaps the best Mexican food in town.

Moby Dick, a half block inland from the start of the malecón, Cuale North. Large restaurant with kitchen in open view, excellent seafood; good selection of white wines, reasonable prices.

Café Franzi, at the lower end of the island in the Cuale; lush vegetation in an outdoor setting, recommended for a relaxing breakfast or lunch.

El Jardín, right at the start of the malecón, in front of the Hotel Rosita. Dishes emphasize good cuts of meat and seafood at reasonable prices; happy hour and tropical music every night.

Carlos O'Brian's, on the malecón; the most popular in town with waiting lines to get in. Why? The food is OK but nothing out of this world. Most customers want the friendly atmosphere which it deserves (but not standing in line for rational beings). It's another of those phenomena where the critical mass has been reached and promotion is the last thing they need.

Las Palomas, on the malecón; slightly raised bar and small restaurant in an open, corner location; popular, lots of life, good for sunsets and very reasonably priced but only one kind of beer served. Good for breakfast and afternoon relaxing and imbibing.

La Cebolla Roja, (The Red Onion), tel. 21087, on the malecón. Food and atmosphere rate with the finest in the city. Not inexpensive, but well worth a visit. Open kitchen, salad bar.

Le Kliff (formerly La Quebrada), 4 km past Mismaloya. A spectacular place on a rocky cliff jutting out into the Pacific with a view to one side onto Los Arcos and Vallarta in the distance. Food is excellent, especially the mixed seafood platter and Mexican specialties; very reasonably priced. Definitely worth the trip from Vallarta.

Chee Chee. near Le Kliff, on a jungle-covered steep slope over the Bay of Tomatlan; tel. 20102. Offers spectacular views, fine seafood, and reasonable prices. Also saltwater pool, sunbathing, shops, and marina. Be aware that all restaurants in this area have steep climbs, which will pose problems for the elderly and the handicapped.

El Eden, located 7 miles up from the Mismaloya Road. Seafood and Mexican specialties served under the second biggest palapa in Puerta Vallarta (the largest is in the Fiesta Americana). This new restaurant is carved out of the jungle along the river. Swimming, diving, sunbathing, and good food make for an exceptional afternoon.

Las Amapas, on the way to Punta Mita, on the right side of the road and set back a little way with no roadside marker. This is by far the hardest restaurant to find, aside from being the farthest from P.V. The specialties of the house are whatever game Don Guillermo has hunted recently—venison, wild pig, armadillo, iguana, mountain cat, badger, rattlesnake—all deliciously prepared. Make sure you ask for the dishes to be prepared *sin chile.* There's beer and the treacherously pleasant *casuela de raisilla* (see above). The dishes are cooked to order, so it might take a while. If Don Guillermo is around and your Spanish up to it, he will tell you how he learned to shoot from his father who picked up the skill by hanging around Pancho Villa—photo for proof as well as the ancient sawed-off .44 magnum revolver. With beers, the unforgettable meal will cost around $5 in this place. Don't look for luxury but it's clean enough.

Other restaurants worth looking into, listed by category include:

Beach restaurants: *El Pirata, El Dorado, La Palapa,* (all on Playa del Sol).

International: North of the Rio Cuale are *Casa Blanca, Sr. Pig* (great prime rib and salads), *Brass* (steaks), *Fuente del Puente* near the bridge. On Isla Cuale in the river is *Franzi's Café* (charming outdoor terrace). South of the river are *Mr. Pepe's* (great view, open only in season, credit cards not accepted), *La Hacienda, La Iguana* (eclectic cuisine), and *Daiquiri Dick's* (beachfront location). South of town in the *Conchas Chinas* sector you'll enjoy *El Set* (spectacular cliffside location, famous for sunsets). Farther south (and well worth the 30-minute drive) is *Chico's Paradise,* with gourmet dining in a wild river valley. Same owner also operates the new *Chico's International.* Also *Le Bistro,* on Rio Cuale Island, and *Chino's Paradise* (not to be confused with Chico's) on Mismaloya Road.

Italian: *Benito's, Pizza Nova, Pietro's* and *Il Mangiare,* both within walking distance of the main plaza.

Mexican: *Las Margaritas* (mariachis), *Patricia,* (both easy on the budget), *Los Molcajetes, El Sarape, Pueblito del Sol* (outdoor patio in colonial setting).

Oriental: *Palacio Oriental* and *Kamakura.*

Seafood: About 20 miles north of town is *Destiladeras,* a delightful beach restaurant. Across from each other on 31 de Octobre, northernmost street of the downtown district, are *Moby Dick* and *Mariscos Mismaloya.* At Mismaloya

Beach itself is *La Gaviota,* featuring fresh catches by local fishermen. A popular south bank entry is *La Langosta,* while *Ostion Féliz,* near the Hotel Rio, is a good north bank selection. A *New Ostion Féliz* has also opened, also on the north bank.

NIGHTLIFE. Top discos are currently *La Onda* (Hotel Pelícanos), *City Dump and Co., Isadora's (Holiday Inn), Capriccio, Sundance, Pompeii,* and *Jungla* at the Camino Real. All major hotels have live music for dancing; among the more popular are *Los Laureles* at the Camino Real, *The Seahorse* at Costa Vida, *The Captain's Table* at Holiday Inn, and *La Estancia* at Posada Vallarta. Also guitar entertainment at *El Nido* sunset bar of *Hotel Cuatro Vientos.*

MUSIC, SHOWS. For the culture oriented, the Camino Real presents a concert program, usually on the first Thursday of the month, but check the date and hour at your hotel. Big-name Mexican entertainers—and occasionally international ones—appear at the plush hotels. There are 3 A/C movie houses downtown, usually showing American films with Spanish subtitles. Many hotels and some restaurants feature Mexican nights with folk dancing, singing, toned-down national dishes and Mexican drinks for an all-inclusive $20 to $30.

CRUISES. Taking a yacht cruise lets you work on the status tan while getting away from the boredom of just roasting on the beach. There are several large yachts and two 60 ft. trimarans piling on the folks at the marina in the mornings for half day or full day cruises. The ships head south, all going past town, Los Arcos, and Mismaloya. Some cruises only go a bit farther, to a cove and beach at Las Animas (near the Quimixto waterfalls), while others continue to Yelapa which is as South Pacific as they come in Mexico. To really enjoy Yelapa, stay in the only hotel's (Lagunita) grass huts after the yacht crowds have sailed off. The boat trips cost between $6 and $17, depending on the length of the excursion and if lunch and/or drinks are included. Make reservations at your hotel travel agency or one downtown.

FIESTAS. May 19 to June 3, celebrating Puerto Vallarta's status as a city; parade with floats marks the beginning, then bullfights, cockfights, charros, dances, big-name Mexican entertainers. **December 12,** the anniversary of the apparition of the Virgin of Guadalupe—that day and for weeks previous, pilgrimages to the church, music in front with local band.

USEFUL ADDRESSES. Federal Tourism Office, Libertad and Morelos; tel. 24243; essentially for complaints. **State Tourism Office,** located downtown on Juarez Street, in an outside corner of the Presidencia Municipal; open from 9 to 9; tel. 20242 and 20243. **Airlines.** Only the first three airlines have offices in town; all have counters at the airport. *Aeroméxico,* Juarez 255; tel. 20031 and 21804. *Mexicana,* Juarez 202; tel. 21707 and 21808. *Republic,* office in Rios Hotel on Morelos and Rodriguez streets; tel. 20267 and 21422. *Continental;* tel. 23095 and 23096. *Western,* tel. 24032. *Frontier;* tel. 23166. *American,* tel. 23787 and 23788.

Car rental. *Hertz,* Paseo Diaz Ordaz 538 at the Hotel Oceano on the malecón and, as all others, at the airport; tel. 20024 and 20056. *Avis,* km 2.5 Tepic; tel. 21412 and 23212. *Budget,* km Tepic; tel. 20556 and 20656. *National,* km 1 Tepic; tel. 21107 and 21226. *Odin,* at the Camino Real; tel. 22825 and 20887. *Rente*

Ford, km 5 Tepic in Automotriz Plaza; tel. 20556 and 20656. *Quick,* km 1.5 Tepic at the Hotel Playa las Glorias and the Playa del Oro; tel. 20006 and 23505. *Travis,* at the airport only; tel. 22324 and 22217.

Post Office, Morelos 444.

U.S. Consulate, Cuauhtlmoc 440; tel. 21143.

Buses. Several bus companies provide frequent service to Tepic, Guadalajara, Manzanillo; all have their respective terminals on or just off Insurgentes Street, Cuale south, in a 3-block area.

THE PUERTO VALLARTA AREA

If you become bored by resort-type activities, had enough sun or are too burned to continue, there are three trips which you could take from Puerto Vallarta. One jaunt takes you north along the coast, the other south following the Pacific and the third goes inland to explore the mountains to the east and south. There are several stopping places along each of the proposed excursions, so you need to go only as far as time, finances, and initiative permit.

To the north of Puerto Vallarta, the highway circles the airport and crosses the Ameca River which marks the limit with the adjacent state of Nayarit. (Puerto Vallarta is in the state of Jalisco whose capital is Guadalajara.) Crossing the state line, there is a time change and you gain an hour when entering the Mountain Standard Time zone. On your left, there are small villages, beaches and restaurants catering to the overflow from Vallarta. A huge new marine complex called Nuevo Vallarta has laid out a system of streets, put up some fancy villas and construction is proceeding on a huge condominium as well as a hotel. The layout of the place takes advantage of the sea arms and lagoons. Could become a chic new resort. A bit farther, you pass Los Flamingos golf course, then the Hotel Playa de Bucerias, probably the best along this stretch. There are excellent white-sand beaches in the vicinity of Bucerias.

Beyond Bucerias, the highway divides. If in a hurry, follow the signs to Tepic; otherwise keep left toward Punta Mita. Lots of curves here as the hills ease down to the sea. About halfway between the turn-off and Punta Mita, be on the lookout for Las Amapas restaurant if you like to eat game. (see *Restaurants*). The road ends at Punta Mita, the northernmost limit of the Bahia de Banderas. There are several open, thatched beachside restaurants here and islands nearby. You can either return to Puerto Vallarta from here, or, about 3 km back from Punta Mita, take an unmarked paved road toward the north. This road, which alternates asphalt surface with short stretches of graded earth, eventually rejoins the main highway to Tepic. Be careful in the dirt stretches during the rainy season.

Just off the highway, there are several villages and the resort town of Rincón de Guayavitos which holds a couple of medium hotels and several inexpensive ones along with restaurants. A very quiet place, hosting mainly Mexican tourists who either can't afford Vallarta or don't like the bustle. Good fishing here. A little farther, at Las Varas, a side road leads to San Blas. We have been told that one can drive through in the dry season with all but the lowest-slung vehicles.

The main highway continues towards Tepic, cutting inland into the hills. At Compostela there is a fork in the road—the left leads to Tepic, about 40 km away; keeping to the right, a toll road points you to the main west coast highway and Guadalajara.

The toll road, some 35 km, costs about $1. Once you are on Highway 15, be prepared for dealing with rushing tractor-trailers. Shortly after sliding into the main highway, you cross a moonscape, the Ceboruco lava field. In 1885 the nearby Mt. Ceboruco erupted, spewing its ravages. The road cuts through a mile of ash boulders with hardly a trace of vegetation. There are places to pull off and climb a bit on the sharp-edged, crumbling rocks. A half-hour farther, at the town of Ixtlan del Rio, inexpensive roadside carts offer seafood along bus stops and heavy traffic.

Just as the highway leaves town, a short track on the left (marked) leads to a set of pre-Columbian ruins. Nothing on the scale of Teotihuacan or the refinement of the Mayas, it's still the best archaeological site of northwest Mexico. The round temple was dedicated to Quetzalcóatl in one of his functions, as Ehécatl, the god of wind. Perhaps this round temple served as a model for the Huichol Indians who still maintain rounded religious structures. The cross-shaped mini-windows are not Christian but probably correspond to the gods of the four cardinal directions.

The worst stretch of highway is coming up—a long, sharp-curved descent, then the same going up several miles. Slow trailers make life miserable and speeds are minimal. Don't take chances if stuck behind a big truck. Sooner or later the road will open up a bit and allow you to pass. Some impatient Mexican drivers pass on blind curves but they also die. Don't follow their example if temptation beckons. The curves and climb end a few miles out of Magdalena, famous for its opals. The mines are nearby and you could end up with a magnificent stone far below stateside cost. But, caveat emptor. Remember that opals can crack once dehydrated. And the Japanese, who have a thing for opals, also come to Magdalena.

Tequila, the town which produces most of the famous brew, comes up about a half hour after Magdalena. The big town is some 35 miles farther, the last stretch speeding over a 6-lane divided highway. Keep going straight and Highway 15 will blend into Avenida Vallarta which takes you to the Minerva Circle. Before getting to the Minerva, there is a railroad overpass—look for the Vallarta signs and turn to follow it.

Cuale Mine

Heading south from Puerto Vallarta, coastal Highway 200 cuts inland at Boca de Tomatlán to get around Cabo Corrientes, the mountainous southern end of Bahia de Banderas. About 40 km out of Vallarta and before reaching the village of El Tuito, you will come to a place called "crucero del Tuito" (crossroads of Tuito). A sign on your left by a dirt road indicates that it's 44 km to the Cuale Mine.

At first, the road winds gently among pines and oak over hills and down valleys. Then after a long climb some 35 km from the paved highway a stupendous view opens from a section of the road carved out of the solid-rock hillside. Called the "relis" (landslide), this stretch was by far the toughest to build. The view, especially in the afternoon, is well worth the effort of coming so far. But watch out for trucks coming from the opposite direction! Although there are places to pull over, at times tricky maneuvering is required, with drops of several hundred feet to one side. Definitely not for faint-hearted drivers.

The large mine, run by the Zimapan Company, consists of a central processing plant which is fed by five huge open pits. In colonial times and again during the Porfiriato, silver and gold were mined in this area. Muleback was the only means to bring in supplies and to take out the precious metals. Nowadays, the ore from the open pits contains some gold and silver but lead, copper, and zinc are of greater commercial value. Heavy trucks shuttle back and forth from the open pits to the processing plant's crusher which handles 50 tons an hour. Chemicals are then applied to concentrate the useful metals which are shipped out for final separation and refining.

If your nerves and vehicle are up to it, you can drive from the mine to a mountain town called Talpa which we will cover on our third trip out of Vallarta. Before you head that way, remember that if it's only 50 km, the road is rough and unmarked. For now, let's go back and continue on Highway 200.

Potent Moonshine

Soon after the turn-off to the mine, the road reaches the village of El Tuito, well known for a moonshine called raisilla. Discreet inquiries could produce a couple bottles of the potent stuff and perhaps even an invitation to visit one of the primitive mini-distilleries, called "tavernas," outside of the village. But this is a man's world where women are not welcome—and absolutely forbidden if menstruating as superstition has it that if a woman having her period gets anywhere near the still, the raisilla will turn sour. Good riders could hire horses here for the exciting journey to Yelapa, several hours away.

Some 30 miles beyond El Tuito there is a turnoff to the left indicating the Cañon de las Peñas, lake and dam. Sixteen kilometers on the dirt road, amidst irrigation ditches, and you arrive at the lake which has been stocked mainly with talapia africana. You can either fish for 'em yourself or settle down in one of the open restaurants for someone else's catch and cold beer.

Back on the highway, you see the sea again at the Bay of Chamela where there are a couple of hotels and family-style restaurants. The bay is frequented mainly by Mexican tourists, so costs are reasonable. Fishermen can be hired with their outboard launches to visit the islands in the bay. One of them is a breeding ground for birds.

Further on, a road on the right indicates the Bay of Tenacatita. There's an excellent hotel there, covered in our trips out of Guadalajara, as is the rest of this coastal area to Manzanillo. Highway 200 sticks close to the coast with spectacular scenery in Michoacán, then on to Ixtapa/Zihuatanejo, Acapulco, and all the way to Guatemala.

Hacienda Jalisco

A visit to the Hacienda Jalisco in the mountains east of Puerto Vallarta offers a fascinating glance at a Mexico unsuspected on the beaches. There is an easy way and a hard way to get there.

The easy way is to fly by small aircraft in 15 minutes from Puerto Vallarta's airport to the Hacienda's strip. There are flights every Monday, Thursday, and Saturday, about $20 one way. (For up-to-date information call Capt. Munguia at tel. 22210.)

The hard way is to drive up, but don't attempt this in the rainy season. From a side road just off the entrance to the airport, it's about 55 km but will take about 5 hours. Best to take someone who knows the way—if not, at least someone who speaks decent Spanish. There are no road signs and hardly any traffic, so ask for directions to San Sebastian from anyone you see. Superb untamed mountain views reward all hassles.

Hacienda Jalisco, at 4,300 ft., is a century-old tastefully renovated former mining headquarters just outside the village of San Sebastian. The interior is all wood, colonial furniture and the rooms have modern baths along with well-stocked fireplaces to take the nip out of the night air. Excellent meals are served in the staid dining area and there is bar service. The most popular activity is exploring the surroundings, by walking or on horseback. The hotel's manager is Bud Accord and he can be contacted at Hacienda Jalisco, San Sebastian del Oeste, Via Mascota, Jalisco (Mexico). No bustle here—phones and electricity are for the distant future. At night, there are flickering gas lights and candles. Reservations in Puerto Vallarta, at the Galeria Uno on Morelos and Corona, tel. 20908. Eight large rooms for rent, with three excellent meals, $75 per couple, $40 single.

The village of San Sebastian is just a couple of miles beyond the hacienda's airstrip. Formerly an important mining town with a population of over 30,000, only some 700 souls still live in this isolated, red tile and adobe village. But rumor whispers that some of the abandoned mines might reopen with modern machinery.

From San Sebastian you can drive (or try to catch a ride) to Mascota, 50 km away on a fair dirt road with pine-filled mountain scenery. Mascota is the largest town in these Sierras, nestled in a fertile, irrigated valley producing guavas, peas, tomatos, peaches, and jalapeño chiles. There are hotels here, restaurants, a charming plaza, and an imposing but unfinished baroque-style church from the 19th century.

Mascota has frequent bus connections to Guadalajara and driving there presents no problems. There are also flights to Puerto Vallarta.

Virgin of Talpa

If you feel like more explorations in the Sierra, head for Talpa, 35 km and an hour away. The miraculous Virgin of Talpa attracts pilgrims year round but there are five major dates when the town's normal population of 6,500 can swell to over 100,000. These dates are Feb. 2, March 19, May 12, Sept. 19, and Oct. 7. Some of the pilgrims walk all the way from Guadalajara. Organized groups march behind their banners proclaiming their origins. Bright and fantastically clad teams perform fanciful dances in front of the church in the Virgin's honor, dances taught by the first missionaries in Mexico, then adapted and elaborated according to whim and imagination.

The statue of the Virgin of Talpa was fashioned from a paste composed of corn stalk and an orchid extract. It was the handiwork of Tarascan Indians who had used this technique before the conquest to make statues of their gods light enough to carry into battle. As her other famous "sisters," the Virgin of Zapopan in Guadalajara and the Virgin of San Juan de los Lagos, Our Lady of Talpa was carried from Michoacán by Franciscan missionaries in the 16th century. She served as a focus of worship for both the Spanish miners in the Sierras as well as the converted Indians. After several decades, when insects and humidity just about finished off the holy image, church authorities ordered Her buried with all due honors.

We are in the year 1644 and it is the duty of a young native girl, María Tenachi, to clean the small church and to respectfully bury the cornstalk statue. Just as she reaches above the altar to take down the Virgin, an intense light emanates from the statue. María falls down unconscious. When her girlfriends rush to her, they see that the insect-riddled statue has been transformed into a solid, resplendent image. Miracle! Once more the Virgin Mary had shown favor to her native American children, just like the Virgin of Guadalupe had done over a century earlier.

Skeptics will say that there are several other colonial statues made of corn-stalk, still well preserved without the role of any supernatural intervention and that the young girl María had an adolescent fit well documented in psychiatry. Be that as it may, a strong cult has grown up around the Virgin del Rosario de Talpa with lasting belief in her miraculous powers to cure, especially in times of fatal epidemics.

Talpa has several hotels and restaurants. A dirt track leading from here drops down to Tomatlán, just off Highway 200, at 120 km and 8 hours away. This is Mexico by the back roads where few Americans venture but where you can see the real rural life of this hospitable country. For those unwilling to brave the rigors and risks of dirt road travel, there are buses from Talpa to Guadalajara.

MANZANILLO

The coastal area of Manzanillo lies more than half-way south along Mexico's long Pacific shore between the U.S. and Guatemala. As points of reference, Guadalajara is 350 kms and 5 hours' drive to the northeast, Puerto Vallarta 280 kms and 4 hours to the northwest and Acapulco 660 kms and about 9 hours to the southeast. The resort section of Manzanillo fringes two wide sand-beach bays immediately north of the city. The Santiago peninsula between these two bays has given birth to spectacular hotels and condos including the you-have-to-see-it-to-believe-it Las Hadas complex, one of the fanciest and architecturally most unusual hotels in the world. But you don't have to spend a fortune to stay in this area—there are dozens of hotels lining the bays with several in each price category.

There is a marked difference between Manzanillo and other coastal resorts in Mexico. The town is quite separate from the tourist places, although there are a few modest hotels in the city itself. The airport, Playa de Oro, is closer to the hotel strips than to Manzanillo proper. The government is spending considerable sums to make Manzanillo the most important Pacific port in Mexico. A superhighway is under construction to Guadalajara but officials are reluctant to come up with a termination date as it all depends on the availability of funds. Several venture an unattributable guess of 1987. In the meanwhile, a new port is being dredged and docks built while in a nearby lagoon a huge thermoelectric plant is already on line.

EXPLORING THE MANZANILLO AREA

Manzanillo (pop. 65,000), is bunched up between steep hills and the sea. Railroad lines crisscross the city to end up at the dock area which is used by both freighters and ships of the Mexican Navy. Next to the docks there is a small harbor with boats for hire (fishing or joyrides) and the departure point for sunset cruises.

Except for a lively *zocalo* (main plaza), the downtown section is lacking in interest. This is a busy port and, unlike Acapulco and Puerto Vallarta, a railhead. Within Manzanillo's city limits commerce definitely takes precedence over tourist-related activity.

Once you're out of town the situation is exactly the reverse. Manzanillo Bay is a treasure house of fine beaches, and tourist accommodations are improving every year. The bay, incidentally, marks a dividing line between black and white sand beaches and readers will be pleased to learn that all beaches beyond the port area are of the latter variety. (Apart from esthetic considerations, black sand is a great heat conductor and mercilessly hard on bare feet.)

The beauty of Manzanillo's beach scene is that you have your choice between millpond tranquillity and moderate surf while the bay protects you from the transgressions of the green wave. Leaving the downtown section you loop around to Playa Azul (not to be confused with the Michoacán beach resort of the same name), the residential area nearest town. At one time a bridge connected the urban area and this section but it was removed when harbor facilities were enlarged. Surf at Playa Azul ranges from minimal to moderate, depending on the season.

Following the westward curve of the bay you come to Santiago peninsula, a promontory that was selected by South American Croesus, Anteñor Patiño, as the perfect site for building his all-white, Mediterranean-style jet-set resort paradise which includes a 200-room hotel, condominium, golf course, and yacht club-cum-marina. Known as *Las Hadas* ("The Fairies"), the multimillion-dollar development was inaugurated in 1974. In late 1983, Las Hadas was brought under the management of the Camino Real Hotels.

Las Hadas, happily, is an ecology-oriented Eden. Housing units are spaced out and surrounded by plants and flowers, and industrial installations are rigidly barred from the area.

Manzanillo long ago outgrew its downtown airport and has gotten a new one nearby. Federal and state governments have invested $7 million on a new layout large enough to receive DC9s, Boeing 727s, or any other type of medium-range jet aircraft. The site is Playa de Oro, about 18 miles north of Manzanillo.

Beyond the peninsula is another bay—Santiago—and two beaches that are usually ideal for mild body surfing. These are Olas Altas (a misnomer meaning "high waves") and Miramar.

Deep-sea fishing is excellent around Manzanillo, the season being from November to May, especially through February. An important yearly fishing tournament takes place in February in what is called the world's sailfish capital. During the daytime, most visitors assiduously work on their tans. In the evening, you can feel the good Mexican atmosphere by walking around the *zocalo* or just sitting around there while the pretty señoritas are on display. The *Bar Social,* an old favorite on the *zocalo,* is great for a cooling beer served with local flavor. A short way from the plaza, *Los Equipales,* Avenida Mexico 275, is a restaurant and bar frequented by both locals and sailors. If you prefer your own kind, stay along the beach strips to sample the restaurants and nightspots.

Short Coastal Trips

With Manzanillo as a base, you can take short trips either up or down the coast to small seaside villages not yet overwhelmed by tidal waves of foreign tourists. Longer trips along the coast bring you to Puerto Vallarta, 280 kms to the northwest, or Playa Azul about the same distance to the southeast by a spectacular ocean-hugging highway. Heading inland, Colima, a small, quiet provincial capital, is worth a visit for a couple of excellent museums as well as spectacular nearby scenery which includes an active volcano along with the sometimes snow-capped Nevado de Colima. From here, it's about 3½ hrs: to Guadalajara.

Heading north on the main highway out of Manzanillo, you pass the airport (5 kms off the road). After the town of Cihuatlán, just inside the borderline of the State of Jalisco, a few minutes bring you to a just-being-discovered resort. Barra de Navidad is a village of about 3,500 that stretches south along a sand bar promontory for about a mile. To the east is a lagoon and to the west Melaque Bay, a body of water harboring a neighboring village named San Patricio. (The complete name of the town is San Patricio Melaque.)

In 1564, an expedition set out from Barra de Navidad under Lopez de Legazpi. After reaching the Philippines, the chief pilot, an Augustinian monk named Andrés de Urdaneta, led a ship in an important first: sailing east across the Pacific. This voyage set the route followed by the Manila Galeon for the next 250 years. Barra de Navidad is also known for its succulent oysters and spicy-hot shrimp "a la diabla" (with butter, garlic and hot sauce).

It is perhaps inevitable that a site so well-favored by nature should have attracted the attention of developers. Presently under way in Barra de Navidad is a project called Pueblo Nuevo. It includes a hotel, two condos, pool, tennis courts, commercial center, yacht club, and canals linking the development area with the ocean.

Dredging was going on in the lagoon in early 1985 as a first step to building a small fishing port. Another marina (besides the Hotel Cabo Blanco's already existing one) was planned inside the lagoon. Neither the Pueblo Nuevo nor the lagoon project has yet affected Barra's easygoing ambience. Laid-back tourists and fishermen mingle easily along the cobblestone streets. There are many outdoor restaurants serving fresh local seafood and modest hotels cater to visitors. A boatmen's cooperative plies its trade with fishing trips, excursions, and running passengers across the lagoon to Colimilla, where there are a couple of good restaurants open during the daytime. From a hill in back of Colimilla you can enjoy a sweeping view of Barra and the narrow channel separating the lagoon from the ocean.

San Patricio Melaque (pop. 5,000) is a bit more of a town, 5 kms from Barra. It is a favorite with Mexican tourists as well as camper-hauling Americans. There are several not-too-fancy hotels and restaurants in this small place which has yet to sell its soul for tourism. From Melaque, you can head for Guadalajara, 298 kms and 4½ hrs. away. On the way, you could stop in the town of Autlán, whose marketplace is famous for tropical fruits and vegetables. Beyond Autlán, you'll cross the Sierras. Some of the vistas are spectacular.

Up the coast towards Puerto Vallarta, there are many good beaches (see *Practical Information*) as well as high-class hotels. This section of the coast ends where the highway cuts inland at the Bay of Chamela. The best yet-to-be-developed attraction here is the Isla Pajarera (Bird Island) where countless seagulls and other birds come to hatch their eggs between mid-March and mid-April. You can hire an outboard fishing boat to go there from Punta Perula, the northern tip of the Bay of Chamela where there are thatched restaurants and a bit of sand beach for swimming.

Pointing south from Manzanillo, the main highway skirts the long lagoon, curving around steep hills. Another good road from town runs past the power station, then between the lagoon and the ocean through coconut plantations and evaporative salt works. Following this road, you reach a small village called Coyutlán which resembles a faintly decaying Jersey beach resort of the '30s. The black sand beach is dotted with several hotels, inexpensive and of moderate classification. Around here and elsewhere along the coast immediately south, the monstrous "green waves" of near tidal proportions batter the coast in the late spring, especially in April and May, before the rainy season calms them down. These breakers are so named because of the mass of marine vegetation they bring up as they pound toward shore. From Cuyutlán you head for the main highway and inland towards the capital of Colima.

A little less than halfway from Manzanillo, there is a junction to Tecoman, at the head of a fertile, tropical valley which grows enough lemons to make Colima the leading producer in the nation as well as giving the state second place in coconuts and bananas. From Tecoman, a 12-km long road leads to the black sand beach resort of Los Pascuales, idyllic except for the yearly green waves. A bit farther down the coast, at Boca de Apiza, the water is a bit rough but the scenery marvellous. There are plenty of thatched restaurants specializing in local seafood. The highway above Boca de Apiza continues into Michoacán.

Spectacular Highway

Because of the rugged mountains of the Sierra Madre, which pushes its steep slopes right into the sea, no attempt had been made for many years at highway construction to the northwest of Playa Azul. Then, thanks to oil-fueled federal budgets during the last few years, there were sufficient funds to combine with engineering skills in order to build and completely pave this portion of the coastal highway. The Sierra's many rivers and creeks represented one of the highway's major obstacles. This was resolved with dozens of long, well-constructed bridges. In spite of the difficulties, this road was so built that you seldom lose sight of the Pacific, breath-taking in its splendor here.

It is recommended that you fill or top off your gas tank before beginning this 140-mile stretch of the coastal highway. If you are coming from the north, there is a Pemex station just inside Michoacán after crossing the Coahuayana River; coming from the south, fill up at Playa Azul. There may be gasoline in one or two small settlements along the way, sold out of large drums, but don't count on it.

For those interested in wildlife, there are many species of birds to be seen and alligators have been reported in the area. At certain times of the year, sea turtles come ashore at night to lay their eggs on the beach. In the past, many of these turtle eggs were gathered and sold, threatening the species with extinction. The situation has been somewhat alleviated, thanks to the Program for the Protection of Marine Turtles. Only a local fishing cooperative has the right to hunt a limited number of turtles. But real progress will be made only when the Mexican public is educated to the fact that, contrary to popular myths, turtle eggs have no aphrodisiac qualities whatever but that they are unusually high in cholesterol.

Although one can drive this 235-km stretch in about four hours, it would be a shame just to zip through. But unless you are planning on sleeping inside your vehicle, be warned that there are only two hotels along the way, both near Playa Azul. Best is the 15-room *Hotel Yuritzi* in Caleta de Campos, 58 km from Playa Azul. Overlooking the bay, all the rooms have a bathroom.

Food is no problem along the way—you only have to bring your own if you plan to camp out on one of the many deserted beaches. There are several settlements along the road with *comedores,* and fish is abundant in many villages.

A word of warning about swimming: There could be dangerous undertows, so it is advisable to seek a sheltered bay or cove unless you want to take your chances in the open Pacific.

The most spectacular stretch of this highway runs between Maruata and Huahua. The road runs at times along cliffs which plunge into the sea, making for spectacular views amidst exuberant tropical vegetation.

The people who live along the coast—fishermen, small-scale farmers with a few head of cattle—are open and friendly. Between the Ostula River and Huahua, the majority are Nahua-speaking Indians, remnants of pre-Columbian migrations or later settlements.

Maruata is perhaps the best place for a leisurely stop. It is located about one-third of the way from the Colima border to Playa Azul. There is a Nahua settlement and several coves with imposing rock formations with seas surging out of caves and between cliffs. A fine sand beach offers protected swimming in calm waters. There are places along the seafront to eat fish and seafood, to have a beer or a soft drink and by asking around you can find some fresh water to wash off after a swim in the sea. Hammocks can sometimes be rented for the night. But in the winter you might need a blanket.

For those with access to an airplane, there is an excellent 1,200-meter by 30-meter paved landing strip right next to town and ending just about at the beach.

Maruata is as close to a tropical paradise as you can find in Mexico, if luxurious but asceptic hotels are not what you need. But who knows for how long Maruata and the coastal stretch of Michoacan will remain "undiscovered," now that it is of easy access by any type of vehicle? For those who want to see an unspoiled and not-yet-commercialized part of Mexico, this new portion of Highway 200 ranks among the most attractive choices.

Playa Azul, a bit of a seedy black sand beach resort, can be reached either via the coastal highway or from Uruapan in Michoacán (see *Heartland* chapter). Heading south from Playa Azul, you pass the smelting and port town of Lazaro Cardenas, a huge industrial creation. It's 122 kms and a bit over two hours to the next resort, Ixtapa/Zihuatanejo. From there, some three hours and 242 kms to Acapulco.

For those not interested in going so far south, let's head back to the junction to Tecoman from Manzanillo. If you keep going straight, you soon climb up to Colima city, capital of the state, population 100,000. On most days as you drive to the city, you'll see the backdrop of a smoking volcano and at times the snow-tipped Nevado de Colima. The capital not only has good hotels and restaurants, but it houses one of the world's most remarkable antique car museums. For this alone (where you can evoke the shade of Scott Fitzgerald among perfectly restored Stutzes and Pierce-Arrows), Colima is worth an overnight stay. Unfortunately, this museum is now closed. But you can see it by making an appointment at the local tourism office (for details, see *Museums* in this section). Should you have a little more time for exploration, you might consider a visit to the nearby town of Comala—famous in the writings of Juan Rulfo and the set for several movies. It is a colonial village, well known for its hand-made furniture and wrought iron. A little farther on the same road, then off another paved road to the right, you will find the attractive Lake Carrizalillo. The local ejido (farmers association) has several clean and inexpensive bungalows there as well as a restaurant which overlooks the lake—with the volcano and often snow-capped Nevado as a spectacular backdrop. Coming back to the juncture of the Comala road, turn right and keep going until you reach the resort of El Jabali, located in the beautiful ex-hacienda of San Antonio. The first 28 rooms (about $80 per person) were completed and in operation in 1985. Eventually, there will be 120 suites and 80 rooms with horseback riding, tennis, pools, restaurants, everything literally "under the volcano." This resort is being built by the Patiño family of Las Hadas fame. A couple of kilometers past the Hacienda of San Antonio, you will find another ejido-run, family-style resort on the Laguna (lake) María with several simple, inexpensive bungalows, a bar, and restaurant. All of this area is in a newly created national park.

PRACTICAL INFORMATION FOR THE MANZANILLO AREA

HOW TO GET THERE. An international airport, **Playa de Oro,** is located 33 kms from Manzanillo and 27 kms from San Patricio Melaque. *Aeroméxico* has daily flights from Mexico City, Guadalajara, Cabo San Lucas, and Los Angeles; three times weekly to Monterrey and Houston. *Mexicana*'s daily flights are to Mexico City and Guadalajara. Road distances and driving times by car on frequent non-stop buses are 350 kms and 5 hours to Guadalajara (via Colima) and 285 kms and some 4½ hrs. to Puerto Vallarta. There are occasional buses going down the coast to Playa Azul in Michoacán.

The VW buses from the airport have little imposed or self-control. Fixed prices are a theory. For what it's worth, the going price per passenger is about $12 to Manzanillo, $9 to Santiago (the hotel zone), $7 to Barra de Navidad/Melaque, $23 to the Club Med at Playa Blanca, and $17 to Tecuan. It's about three miles to the main road from the airport—public buses run along the highway here.

EMERGENCY TELEPHONE NUMBERS. Warning: it is unlikely that at any of the following numbers anyone will speak English, except for the possible exception of the tourism offices. **Barra de Navidad:** 70399 (Presidencia Municipal); **San Patricio Melaque:** 70080 (Presidencia Municipal); tourism: 70100; **Colima:** 21451 (Red Cross); 20227 (hospital); 20293 (police); 24360 and 28360 (tourism). **Manzanillo:** 20096 (Red Cross); 20029 (hospital); 22299 (police); 20181 and 22090 (tourism).

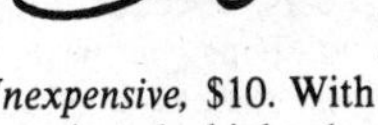

HOTELS. In Manzanillo hotels were authorized, at press time, to charge on the average the following rates for a double room: *Gran Turismo,* $130; *Deluxe,* $75; *First Class,* $42; *Expensive,* $27; *Moderate,* $17; and *Inexpensive,* $10. With the country's rising inflation, however, rates are almost certain to be higher by the time you read this, particularly for accommodations along the ever-growing resort areas. Rates are considerably lower in smaller towns.

Manzanillo

Las Hadas, Apartado Postal 158, tel. 30000; on the Santiago peninsula, owned and managed by the Camino Real chain, Westin affiliated. This fairyland of all-white architecture put Manzanillo on the jet-set map. The hotel has 206 rooms plus 204 more at the adjacent **Puerto Las Hadas.** All the restaurants, bars and services you'll ever need as well as all sports, including golf and tennis. The place has its private marina, in case you decide to cruise down on your yacht with Bo Derek. *Gran Turismo.*

Villas del Palmar, Apartado Postal 646, tel. 30575; on Playa Azul with 186 A/C rooms, pool, water sports, tennis, golf. *Deluxe.*

Condominios Playa Sol, Apartado Postal 414, tel. 30309; on Playa Azul with 120 A/C units, pool, restaurant, parking, disco. *Deluxe.*

Club Maeva, Apartado Postal 442, tel. 30595; on a hillside overlooking Miramar beach, some 10 miles out of town with 514 A/C units, 4 restaurants, disco, large pool, tennis, water sports (including classes), Mexican Night on Saturdays. *Deluxe.*

Club Santiago, Apartado Postal 374, tel. 30413; on the far tip of Miramar beach with 300 units in a complex including villas and condos as well as the Tenisol condo hotel; bar, restaurant, two miles of beach, water sports, tennis, golf, pool. *Deluxe.*

Roca del Mar, next to the Posada on Playa Azul, tel. 20805; just off the entrance to the new harbor, 29 A/C rooms, bungalows on the beach, restaurant, bar, pool, boutique. *First Class.*

Charles y Willie, km 6.5 to Santiago, tel. 22906; opened in early '85 with 40 rooms, all with satellite TV reception, car rental, restaurant, bar, pool. *First Class.*

Villas el Pueblito, Ave. del Tesoro on the Santiago peninsula, tel. 30550; with 52 villas, each 2 or 3 bedrooms, restaurant, bar, car rental, pool, horses. *First Class.*

Colonial, Ave. Mexico 100 (downtown) tel. 21080; with 38 rooms A/C or fans in old-style, pleasant colonial building, restaurant, bar, laundry, parking. *Expensive.*

Las Brisas, Ave. Cardenas on the new port lagoon, tel. 21951; with 66 rooms, some A/C, some fan, some with kitchenettes, pool, parking. *Moderate.*

Motel Star, Ave. Cardenas near Las Brisas, tel. 22400; on the beach with 42 rooms, cafeteria, parking, pool. *Moderate.*

Savoy, Carillo Puerto 60, tel. 20754; with 24 rooms, the best of the economical hotels, on a corner of the main plaza with good views of the port from the top rooms; 24 hr. restaurant. *Moderate.*

La Posada, Apartado Postal 135, tel. 22404; at the entrance to the new harbor with trees and a great tiled patio to the beach; 24 simple rooms, pool; breakfast included. *Moderate.*

Barra De Navidad

Cabo Blanco, Armada and Puerto Navidad, tel. 70182; in the Pueblo Nuevo complex, just before town; 125 A/C units, 3 restaurants, bars, disco, satellite TV, games room, several pools, travel agency, rental of skin diving gear, water skis, fishing boats, medical service, 4 lit tennis courts. By far the best hotel in this area. *First Class.*

Barra de Navidad, Carranza and Legazpi, tel. 70122; with 60 rooms with A/C or fan, restaurant, pool, beach. *Expensive.*

Tropical, Legazpi 150, tel. 70020 with 57 rooms on the beach, some A/C, some fan, bar, restaurant, pool. *Expensive.*

Sands, Morelos 24, tel. 70018; with 44 rooms, all fan cooled; on the lagoon side; restaurant, bar, pool, dock, disco. *Expensive.*

Delfin, Morelos 23, tel. 70068; small with 20 rooms, all with fans; pool, cafeteria. *Moderate.*

Bungalows Karelia, on Legazpi, tel. 70187; on the beach with 10 ample units all with kitchenettes. *Moderate.*

Colima

America, Morelos 162, tel. 20366; newest hotel in town with 80 units, restaurant, two bars, laundry service, steam baths, massage, tobacco shop, pool, beauty salon, soda fountain, parking. *First Class.*

Maria Isabel, Blvd. Camino Real, km 1, tel. 26262; with 88 A/C rooms, bar, two restaurants, pool, parking. *First Class.*

Motel Los Candiles, Blvd. Camino Real, km 1, tel. 22917; with 67 rooms all A/C, restaurant, bar, pool, boutique. *Expensive.*

Costeño, on the exit from town to the Manzanillo highway, tel. 21900; with 64 rooms, some A/C, pool, restaurant, bar, parking. *Expensive.*

Ceballos, Portal Medellin 16 on the main plaza, tel. 21354; 56 rooms. *Moderate.*

Casino, Portal Morelos 11, on the main plaza, tel. 21406; 34 rooms with fans, restaurant, bar. *Moderate.*

Playa Azul (Michoacan)

La Loma (100 rooms, *Expensive*) and **Playa Azul** (56 units, *Expensive*) have fans and A/C. More spartan, but with a good restaurant, is the **Delfin** (*Moderate*) across from the Playa Azul. Families gravitate to the **Bungalows de la Curva** (*Inexpensive*), spacious two-bedroom little huts.

Playa Careyes/Playa Blanca

Club Mediterranée, at Playa Blanca. Weekly packages vary according to the time of the year. One price includes everything except drinks. All kinds of sports and instruction. Reservations through the Club Med offices. *First Class.*

Plaza Careyes, tel. 70010. (Reservations in Mexico City at Amberes 43 in the Zona Rosa, tel. 514–1208.) With 97 units, restaurant with excellent cuisine, bar, pool, disco, horses, all plush and isolated. *First Class.*

San Patricio Melaque

Club Nautico, Madero 1, tel. 70239; with 26 rooms A/C or fan, restaurant, bar, parking; the newest in town. *Expensive.*

Melaque, Paseo de la Primavera, tel. 70001; with 185 fan-cooled rooms, bar, restaurant, pool, billiards; on the beach. *Expensive.*

Posada Pablo de Tarso, Gomez Farias 408, tel. 70117; with 16 bungalows and 11 rooms, some A/C, pool, parking; on the beach. *Moderate.*

Bungalows Azteca, Avante (no number), tel. 70150; with 13 fan-cooled bungalows on the beach, pool, parking. *Moderate.*

Las Brisas, Gomez Farias 102, tel. 70108; with 22 rooms with fans, servibars, parking. *Moderate.*

Vista Hermosa, Gomez Farias 110, tel. 70002; with 47 fan-cooled rooms, pool, parking; on the beach. *Moderate.*

Tecuan

El Tecuan, on the ocean, six miles off the main road north of Melaque, tel. 70132. (For reservations, in Guadalajara tel. 166835.) 40 A/C rooms high on Punta Tecuan, with excellent restaurant (French chef), tennis, pool, two miles of virgin beach, double airstrip for private planes, surf fishing, scuba diving, very secluded. *First Class.*

Tenacatita

Los Angeles Locos de Tenacatita, tel. 70221; about 1½ miles off the main highway; 200 units, all amenities on the quiet bay beach, beautiful view from the terrace of the dining room where international and other cuisine is served. Run by the Fiesta Americana. *First Class.*

SPECIAL EVENTS. Manzanillo: February (pre-Lent)—Carnaval; parade with floats, bullfights, music, dances; February and November—fishing tournaments (see *Sports*); June 1—Navy Day with cannon fire, bands, tours of navy ships.

Barra/Melaque: Mid-January—fishing tournament (see *Sports*); Carnaval, getting bigger and better every year.

Colima: Every Sunday, 6 P.M., band concert at the Plaza Principal; March—fiesta of San Juan with bands, fireworks; late October and early November—state fair with agricultural, cattle, and industrial shows, bullfights, dances, cockfights.

HOW TO GET AROUND. Public buses, very inexpensive, go to most places except for the top hotels. Taxis have no fixed fees—find out at your hotel what your trip should cost and make certain that the driver agrees to the price before you get in.

TOURIST INFORMATION SERVICES. Manzanillo: Ave. Juarez 244, fourth floor, tel. 20181 and 22090; open weekdays 9 A.M. to 3 P.M. and 5 to 8 P.M., Saturdays 10 A.M. to 2 P.M.; closed Sundays.

San Patricio Melaque: Paseo de la Primavera, bungalow 10 of the Hotel Melaque, tel. 70100; open weekdays 9 A.M. to 3 P.M. and 5 to 7 P.M.; Saturdays from 9 A.M. to 1 P.M.; closed Sundays.

Colima: Hidalgo 75, tel. 24360 and 28360; open weekdays from 9 A.M. to 3 P.M. and 5 to 7 P.M., Saturdays 9 A.M. to 2 P.M.; closed Sundays.

USEFUL ADDRESSES. Airlines. In Manzanillo: Aeroméxico, tel. 21267 or 21711; Mexicana, tel. 21970 or 21971; Texas International, 22002 or 22402.

Bus Stations. Manzanillo, at the exit from town towards Colima. In Melaque, G. Farias and V. Carranza. In Colima, Nicolas Bravo and Reforma.

Car Rentals. In Manzanillo all at the airport, plus local offices as follows: *Auto Rentals de Mexico* (Thrifty) at Cruzero de Las Brisas, tel. 21495; *National* at Carratera Santiago km 9.5, tel. 20302; *Avis* at Carratera Santiago km 9, tel. 30194; *Ammsa* at Carratera Santiago km 9, tel. 30418.

TOURS. Manzanillo: *Crucero del Atardecer* (Sunset Cruise) from 5 to 7 P.M. around Manzanillo Bay and Las Hadas, $3 which includes two drinks; departure from the downtown Peralita dock; tel. 22262. The following companies offer tours: *Recorridos Turistocos de Manzanillo* at the lobby of the Playa de Santiago Hotel, tel. 30055. *Bahias Gemelas Tours* at Niños Heroes 652, tel. 21818. Both offer land and sea tours, usually for a 4-party minimum, also 5-hour boat trips with fishing gear for four persons at about $60. Check at your hotel desk for sea tours by *Aquamundo* and *Cooperativa de Prestaciones de Servicios Turisticos*—both also have boat rentals.

Barra de Navidad: The cooperative at the lagoonside wharf will take tours on the lagoon and the nearby bays for about $8 an hour. They also have boats crossing the lagoon to Colimilla, where you can eat, swim, and walk around; round trip, about $5. At the travel agency of the Hotel Cabo Blanco, a "coconut-bullfight" tour can be arranged for $20 per couple. This includes a visit to a working coconut plantation, coco loco drinks, then instructions on how to handle a cape to do your number with (very small) bulls. The same agency arranges sea tours of the coast with fishing for $25 or $30 an hour, depending on the size of the boat.

SPORTS. Manzanillo: Most of the better hotels have tennis courts and there are golf courses next to Las Hadas and the Club Santiago. Ask your hotel to make arrangements. There is a national deep-sea fishing tournament in February and an international one in November. For more information, contact the tourism office or Sr. Adachi at Morelos 118B in Manzanillo, tel. 20073. Good fishing from October through April or May. Fishing boats with basic gear available at about $25 an hour—boats hold 6 to 8 passengers with one or two fishing at one time. For diving equipment rentals as well as boats and instruction, have your hotel contact Aquamundo or Eureka at the Club Santiago.

Barra de Navidad: The Cabo Blanco Hotel has a shop which rents out equipment for water sports. Skin diving equipment with one tank and instructor, flat fee of $15 plus $4 for extra tanks, and $25 an hour for a boat which takes 5 passengers; water skiing, all inclusive, $30 an hour; wind surfing board, $12 an hour; fishing, $25 or $30 per hour, depending on boat size. The same hotel also has the only tennis courts in the area. Annual International Fishing Championship around mid-January. For information, contact the tourism office in San Patricio Melaque, the Hotel Cabo Blanco in Barra or in Guadalajara, call tel. 244043 or 244007. Mainly sailfish, marlin, dorado. Good fishing during the months of October through April. Boats with basic fishing gear can be rented from the boatmen's cooperative at the lagoonside wharf for $8 an hour; you should reserve a half day in advance and the minimum time is three hours; a deposit is required at the time of making the reservation.

BEACHES. Manzanillo: All beaches are located to the east of town where tourism followed. Most of the bay immediately to the east of the new port is called Playa Azul—yellowish sand beach, gentle waves, lots of hotels and restaurants. This beach ends at the Santiago Peninsula where *Las Hadas* is located. On the peninsula, the La Audiencia beach is bordered by vegetation, then urbanized hills; the transparent blue water is quiet and ideal for skin diving and water skiing. The next bay east is reached from the highway by crossing a marine bird refuge. Santiago Beach is quiet, sandy, and with several hotels.

Following the curve of the bay, there is a beach called *olas altas* (meaning highwaves—really moderate most of the time), then Miramar Beach with good sand and moderate waves next to the Club Santiago. South of Manzanillo, there are several black sand beaches: Coyutlán (hotels and restaurants), Boca de Pascuales and Boca de Apiza, both with thatched restaurants serving fresh local seafood. Usually fairly rough seas and undertows around there.

Barra de Navidad/Melaque: The wide Bay of Navidad has but two decent swimming beaches: in front of Melaque and towards the tip of the peninsula which divides the bay from the lagoon. Between these two, there are lots of waves and strong currents, not recommended for swimming but for pleasant walks. Just to the east of Melaque, about 2.5 kms on the dirt road from the main highway, there is a picturesque bay called Cuastecomate with fine white sand beach and several small thatched restaurants for local seafood. La Manzanilla—beach, bay, and small village—is 18 kms from Melaque on the main highway north, then two more kms on a paved side road. A couple of economy hotels and the usual thatched eateries. A few kilometers farther on the main road, another side road leads to the Bay of Tenacatita with fine white sand beach, good fishing, an excellent hotel, a trailer park, and small bayside restaurants. The Bay of Chamela, 72 kms from Melaque, has a couple of modest hotels. The 13-km-wide bay is well known for its large turtles called "*caguamas*" (also a slang term for large bottles of beer). Good fishing here—contact local fishermen for boat rentals. Lots of rocks, islands in the bay all making for rugged scenery but not very good swimming, although there is some sand on the beach at Punta Perula, the northern point and a few other spots scattered around the bay. Just off the highway, there is a great supermarket stocking all you will need for camping. Also a couple of hotels within the bay area.

MUSEUMS. Colima: *Museo de Automoviles Antiguos* (Antique Car Museum), Ave. Revolucion 79. This is a must—350 perfectly restored automobiles, vintage 1884–1950. The museum can only be seen by appointment, easy to arrange. Contact the State Tourism Office at Hidalgo 75, tel. 24360 or 28360. *Museo de la Mascara, Dansa y del Arte Popular* (mask, dance and crafts) on 27 de Septiembre and Manuel Gallardo Zamora; 700 exhibits devoted to the life, dance, art, and music indigenous to peoples of West Central Mexico. Many craft items are for sale at fixed prices. Open from Monday to Saturday 9 A.M. to 2 P.M. and 4 to 8 P.M.; Sundays 9 A.M. to 2 P.M. No entrance fee. *Museo de las Culturas del Occidente* (Museum of Western Cultures) at the Complejo Casa de la Cultura (House of Culture Complex). Excellent pre-Columbian ceramics from Colima, including many of the famous small dogs. Open every day 8:30 A.M. to 7:30 P.M. No entrance fee.

SHOPPING. Manzanillo: Boutiques at the better hotels for chic resort clothing and some craft items; *Boutique Grivel,* Pasaje Oscarana, local 8 and at the Plaza Santiago, Edificio C local 6 for Mexican-style resort wear and some crafts. **Barra de Navidad/Melaque:** *Curiosidades del Mar* on the corner of G. Farias and L. Mateos, Melaque, for all kinds of objects (some quite clever) made from seashells; also *Boutique Ragazzi* for resort wear. In Barra, the shop at the Cabo Blance for resort clothing. **Colima:** craft items at the *Museo de la Mascara* and at *La Codorniz,* Ave. Camino Real 399, tel. 22868. On the main square, in the Portales (archways), the Casa Ceballos Hotel has good copies of pre-Columbian ceramics. At the nearby town of **Comala,** contemporary ceramics and all kinds of crafts at the *Mercado de Artesanias* (Crafts

Market) and at the *Puebla Blanca* (the outlet for the crafts cooperative) just out of town, for hand-made colonial furniture and wrought iron.

RESTAURANTS

Manzanillo

L'Récif, Olas Altas, next to the Vida del Mar hotel, off the Laguna de Miramar, tel. 30624. Basic meal $16; open every day; accepts major credit cards. French-international gourmet cuisine, fresh seafood. The best sea view of any restaurant in the area, superb menu, good choice of wines. Bar open from 11 A.M. to 1 A.M.; lunch from 1 to 5 P.M., dinner 7 to 11:30 P.M.

El Vaquero, Crucero Las Brisas, tel. 22727; specializes in meats, sold by weight for some cuts; basic meal, $10; open from 1 P.M. to 1 A.M. Closed Mondays.

La Chiripada, Colonia Las Brisas, tel. 20722; seafood and meats; basic meal $7; Bacho's bar for live music and dancing.

La Hamburgesa, Davalos 25 (downtown), tel. 21429; hamburgers, naturally at $1 to $2; no credit cards.

Savoy, Puerto and Davalos (downtown), tel. 20754; specializes in Mexican dishes, basic meal $4; no credit cards. Open 24 hrs. a day, every day.

Manolo's, three blocks from the entrance to *Las Hadas,* tel. 30475; international cuisine, salad boat; basic meal $12. Open 6 to 11 P.M every day except Sunday. Garden setting.

Aldea Bruja, km 9 on the Santiago Highway, no telephone. Open every day from 8 A.M. to 8 P.M.; big, thatch covered place, specializing in seafood; basic meal $9; closed Mondays.

Tio Juan, km 7.5 on the Santiago Highway, tel. 30619; meats and seafood; basic meal $8. Open 8 A.M. to 10 P.M.

El Plato, km 10 on the Santiago Highway, no telephone; small thatch roofed; seafood specialities, basic meal $5. Open every day from 10 A.M. to 10 P.M. *Carnet* credit card.

Carlos 'N' Charlie's, km 6.5 on the Santiago Highway; popular new restaurant on the beach; same owners, atmosphere, food as Carlos O'Brien's in Puerta Vallorta.

Ostería Bugatti, km 6 on the highway to Santiago, no telephone; specialities: Italian, oysters, seafood, international cuisine; basic meal $11. Open every day, 1 P.M. to 1 A.M.

Hotel Colonial, Ave. Mexico 100, tel. 21080; specialities: seafood and meats; basic meal $7.

Mexico Lindo, km 2 on the Santiago Highway, no telephone; specialities: quail, meats, grilled fish; basic meal $8. Open 1 P.M. to 1 A.M. with live music (tropical) from 2 to 4 P.M. and 9 P.M. to midnight. *American Express, Visa, Bancomer, Banamex, Carnet.*

Barra De Navidad

La Palapa, at the Cabo Blanco hotel, tel. 70182; good but limited menu of international cuisine, seafood specialities; basic meal, $10 to $15. *American Express, Banamex, Carnet.*

Pancho, Legazpi 53, tel. 70176; on the beach; specialities: camarones a la diabla (shrimp cooked in butter and hot sauce), shrimp in garlic, oysters; basic meal $7; lively atmosphere with the surf as backdrop; no credit cards.

Mozoka, Ave. Veracruz on the lagoon, no telephone; seafood specialities; basic meal $7; no credit cards.

Marisco Natcho, Legazpi 49, no telephone; specialities: seafood and grilled fish; basic meal $7; no credit cards.

El Manglito, Ave. Veracruz no number, no telephone; speciality: oysters from the lagoon; basic meal $7; no credit cards.

Eloy, Morelos 47, tel. 70365; small thatched place jutting over the lagoon, specialities: shrimp and fried fish; try their combination plate for $4; no credit cards.

Bananas Grill, Ave. Veracruz, no number, no telephone; outdoors under thatch, for inexpensive breakfasts, burgers and sandwiches for lunch; very inexpensive, favored by Americans; some of the waiters fluent in English. No credit cards.

Colimilla

Concha, seafood specialities, $8 for the basics.

Hermanos Figueroa, live fish and seafood kept in pens until you order; specialities: crab, turtle soup, shrimp, squid, clams, lobster; basic meal $8.50; no credit cards.

Colima

El Cisne, Constitucion and Zaragoza, downtown, tel. 26088; local and international cuisine, good service; basic meal $9. Open every day, 8 P.M. to midnight; Sunday buffet. *Banamex, Bancomer, Carnet.*

El Tabachin, Del Trabajo and Zaragoza, tel. 21849; elegant place, live music, international and Mexican cuisine; basic meal $9. Open every day except Sunday, 1 P.M. to 1 A.M. All credit cards.

El Tejado, Diaz Miron 584, tel. 23512; with gardens and terraces, specialities: seafood and Mexican dishes; basic meal $9. Open every day, 1 P.M. to midnight. *Banamex, Bancomer, Carnet.*

Los Naranjos, Gabino Berreda 34, tel. 20029; interesting decorations, patio for hot nights; specialities: meats and Mexican dishes; basic meal $6; organ music daily. No credit cards.

San Patricio Melaque

La Tropicana, Punta Melaque, no telephone; big, thatch-covered; speciality: Mexican food; good bar; basic meal $6. Open every day 11 A.M. to 7 P.M. No credit cards.

Kosonoy, Punta Melaque, no telephone; thatch-roofed, Mexican cooking, open evenings, basic meal $6. No credit cards.

La Tesmisa, on the beach, no telephone; Mexican food, open 11 A.M. to 7 P.M.; basic meal $6. No credit cards.

La Piramide, Madero 1, tel. 70239; with bar, Mexican cooking, seafood, basic meal about $4. Open 10 A.M. to 10 P.M. No credit cards.

Aurora, C. Puerto 53, tel. 70075; excellent Mexican cooking but not much seafood; basic meal $4. Open 9 A.M. to 8 P.M. No credit cards.

El Rincon Tropical, L. Mateos 34, tel. 70214; Mexican cooking $4. Open 7 A.M. to 10 P.M. No credit cards.

NIGHTLIFE

Manzanillo

Discos at **Las Hadas** and **Club Maeva,** the fanciest.

Caligula Disco, Carretera Santiago km 15, tel. 30706; open 9 P.M. to 4 A.M., closed Mondays; accepts American Express. Also in the same area, discos **Penthouse** and **Yako's.**

Natcho's Bar, Colonia Las Brisas, tel. 20722; live music, dancing.

Barra De Navidad

La Giff, L. de Legazpi 44, no telephone; open 8:30 P.M. to 2 A.M.; different kinds of music, including disco, romantic, Mexican, tropical; most popular in town but can get a bit bawdy at times.

El Galeon Disco at the Sands Hotel

Mar y Tierra of the Cabo Blanco Hotel but located at the beach, quiet, various kinds of music, live entertainment during the high season.

Colima

Horus Disco, Ave. Rey Coliman 10, tel. 27272; various kinds of music.

La Cabaña, Blvd. Las Palmas 699, tel. 23110; restaurant/bar with live music for dancing, open every day except Monday from 9 P.M. to 3 A.M.

San Patricio Melaque

Albatros on Lopez Mateos 58, tel. 70083, different kinds of music; open 8:30 P.M. to 1 A.M.

Sibonay, on Obregon at the outskirts of town near the highway; a cabaret mainly for local male residents; some shows, lots of drinking; not recommended for single ladies.

MAZATLÁN

The Presidio de Mazatlán was established in 1576 by order of Hernando de Bazán who was the Spanish governor of all of what is now northwest Mexico and the Californias. It was 20 miles southwest of the present Mazatlán, and is now known as Villa Unión. Mazatlán itself was first mentioned as a settlement near the Villa site in 1602, was not incorporated until 1806, and got its first municipal government in 1837. Visitors lose precious little time in tours of plaques marking noted colonial sites.

The port has its history of blockades. The Americans were there in 1847 when the U.S. forces had marched down from the border through northeast Mexico and up from Veracruz to the nation's capital. The liberals blockaded the port when the conservatives were in control in 1859. In 1864 the French bombarded the city, then invaded and remained in control for several years. During the revolution years there was the 1913–14 blockade and the victory of the revolutionary forces in August, 1914.

Following the U.S. Civil War, men from South thought they could infuse Mexico, under the rule of Maximilian, with their patterns of slavery. A colony of rebels who had been led into Mexico by General Joseph O. Shelby went to Mazatlán and Maximilian named a colonizing agent. The Southerners who had hoped for peace were caught between the idealistic crossfire of Juárez and Maximilian and, discouraged, disbanded.

Students of air war will note that the first bombing by a military plane in the Americas happened in Mazatlán, when the city was under siege by the revolutionaries. Icebox Hill (*Cerro de la Neveria*) was the object of the bomb run, but after taking off from the suburban airstrip (now well within the city limits) a sudden lurch caused the hand-held bomb to be released. Survivors will tell you that it landed at Carnaval and Canizales Streets.

Mazatlán, with the finest harbor facilities on Mexico's Pacific coast, has the nation's largest shrimp fleet and the necessary packing plants so that its big haul can be shipped off to its big market, the U.S. It is the port of call for several U.S.-to-Mexico cruise ships and some on round-the-world itineraries. It was popular with sun seekers from the U.S. and Canada long before mid-Mexico discovered its charms. Its tourists knew it when it was a phalanx of new hotels along Olas Altas beach and a clutter of narrow streets lined with homes and commercial houses stretching back from the bay.

Prevented by the harbor estuary from growing southward, it rounded Icebox Hill, where ice was stored for packing the U.S.-bound seafood. Now it is off and away northward.

Tourists arrive by Federal Route 15 running north and south along the Pacific Coast in the northwest or via Federal Route 40, which channels them from Mexico's northeast through Durango. Between

Durango and Mazatlán Route 40 is notably scenic. As 40 is the first lateral highway that motorists from Canada and the U.S. can take to the Pacific shore after entering Mexico, Mazatlán is fortunate. But the highway went there because Mazatlán was there. And from Mazatlán with the increased interest in travel to the Baja Peninsula, the road continues with the use of two ferries to La Paz.

Air service to U.S. and Mexican cities is excellent. There is both taxi and economy bus transportation from the airport to the city. Bus service is especially good from the border to Mazatlán as well as from both Guadalajara and Durango. Trains are being used increasingly.

Mazatlán is one of the few ports from which sailfish or marlin can be caught all year. The port is ranked seventh in the world for its average yearly catch of billfish by sportsmen. Ten thousand sailfish and 5,000 marlin are nothing unusual. A record 973-lb. black marlin was fished out of these waters as well as a 203-lb. sailfish. Anglers in the backwaters south of the city catch rainbow runners, snook, ladyfish, barracuda, and milkfish. A long narrow island separates the Caimanero Lagoon from the sea and provides some of the best wildfowl. Four species of duck as well as quail, dove, and pheasant are found there, and the nearby hills have deer, jaguar, mountain lion, coyote, rabbit, wild boar, and ocelot.

The leading hotels have hunting and fishing tour representatives as well as rental car agencies—Hertz, National, Volkswagen, Aviles, Avis, and Odlin. The city's newest pride is its modern aquarium, a handsome facility displaying more than 250 species of marine life. It's located at Avenida de los Deportes near the malecón.

Natural Harbor

The city of Mazatlán, (pop. 350,000) is built on a wide peninsula with an excellent natural harbor on one side and the open Pacific on the other. Although the hotel zone is quite self-sufficient, those with a bit of interest in Mexico will want to take a trip to the downtown area, which is not tourist-oriented. As Mazatlán is a relatively new town, there is practically none of the wonderful colonial atmosphere found farther south in the country. As elsewhere, the hub of downtown is the central plaza area where you will find town hall (Palacio Municipal) with a tourism office, the Post and Telegraph offices, the central market and, of course, the principal church. Begun in the mid-19th century, the parish church was consecrated in 1937 as a basilica-cathedral. The style is a sort of neogothic with interesting frontal arches and a sumptuous interior. The only other point of interest, the colonial church of San José, is some five blocks from the cathedral following Calle Canizales toward Icebox Hill. This small church, the oldest in town, is on a short street called Calle Campana.

The docks lie to the south of downtown, along Avenida del Puerto. The shrimp boat fleet anchors closest to the mainland. It is from here—near the gas station—that you can catch launches to Isla la Piedra (Stone Island) just across from the harbor. After the shrimp boats, the main dock area berths cruise ships and merchant vessels. The ferries to La Paz utilize the end of the dock area nearest to the ocean.

By following the coast after the wharf, you reach the narrow neck of land where the sports fishing fleet is located. At the very tip of the peninsula, a half hour's climb leads you to El Faro, the lighthouse, 160 meters or 525 ft. above the sea. This is the world's second-highest lighthouse (Gibraltar is first) not so much because of the height of the building as for the elevation above the ocean. Get your breathing back to normal before enjoying the breath-taking views.

Back to sea level, you follow the Pacific, heading generally northwest. Just after leaving the sports fishing docks, the road climbs a hill called Cerro de la Vigía (Lookout Point) with a couple of spots to pull off to enjoy the scenery, especially at sunrise and sunset. A paved road leads to the top of the hill, capped by a meteorological post and another panorama. The coastal drive on the base of the hill begins with the name Paseo Centenario which runs into Paseo Olas Altas (High Waves). This is where the hotels start, along with restaurants, boutiques, and other related activities. Following the coast, Olas Altas becomes Paseo Claussen where the "death divers" take the plunge when there are enough people watching (and tipping). The dive is from a respectable height but don't think that you are in Acapulco's *La Quebrada.* At night, the diving is with torches. A bit farther on the ocean side of the drive, a seedy looking building called Casa Del Marinero gives lodgings to wayward sailors. Around back, you can visit what is called the Spanish Fort with a lonely rusting cannon. Not much of a fort, the place is peaceful; you can sit on the low ramparts and meditate with the rocks and sea.

Rounding a curve, Paseo Claussen becomes Avenida del Mar along the gentle sweep of the bay, backed by hotels and restaurants. Part of the way along, the Fisherman's Monument is no masterpiece but definitely good for a laugh. A naked, net-wielding fisherman peers around a corner where an unclad beauty reclines, holding her left hand as if asking for a donation before the fun can begin. About halfway along the bay, look for the signs to the superb aquarium which sits back a block from the seafront. There is a botanical garden/park and a small zoo right next door. The town's baseball park is close by. The Federal Tourism Office is just beyond the turnoff to the aquarium, on Avenida del Mar which ends at a rock outcrop called Camarón (shrimp) Point. You can't miss it as the rocks support the large, gleaming white Valentino's Disco. In front of Camarón Point, an avenue called Rafael Buelna heads inland, past the Mazatlán Bullring and runs on with a jog to the main highway going towards Culiacán in the north and to the airport and Tepic to the south. Just beyond the road divides with both branches leaving the seafront. The wider part, called Calzada Camarón Sábalo (sabalo is a local species of shad) runs along many shops and the main car rental agencies as well as a plethora of stores before going on along the coast. The smaller road, Loaiza, skirts in back of Los Sábalos Hotel, the Hotel Playa Mazatlán, Las Flores Hotel, and to one side of the Balboa Club before rejoining the Calzada Camarón Sábalo.

Along Loaiza, the municipal tourism office is found across from the Hotel Los Sábalos. Nearby, Sea Shell City calls itself a museum as there are shells from many parts of the world but the place is more a large, two-story store selling all kinds of decorative objects made from shells

—some pure junk, some almost tasteful. Next to Sea Shell City and across from the Hotel Las Flores, the Mazatlán Arts and Crafts Center started out as a place where you could watch craftsmen fashion their specialities but now it's just a complex of shops catering to gringo tastes. The oval-shaped area between Lozaina and Camarón Sábalo is called the Zona Dorada (Golden Zone) for its countless boutiques, restaurants, shops, stores, and offices. This is Mazatlán's greatest concentration of tourist-related activities.

Leaving the hectic Zona Dorada, the Calzada Camarón Sábalo continues past the El Cid Hotel with its golf course, the Holiday Inn, the Oceano Palace Hotel to the spendid Camino Real, the last in the chain of luxury accommodations. One of the town's two bullrings, El Toreo, is just a bit inland from the Holiday Inn. Mazatlán doesn't really need two bullrings but it seems that there are two rival corrida-loving families in fierce competition with one another . . . so much the better for the aficionados. The coastal road continues past the Camino Real over a bridge spanning the mouth of an estuary, then along a beach area beginning to grow condos to end at Cerritos Point. Just before reaching Cerritos, a road to the right joins the main highway heading north to Culiacán and Nogales. At Cerritos Point, the 16-mile seaside boulevard ends with a couple of rustic, thatch-covered restaurants which will undoubtedly metamorphose into chic spots as Mazatlan's tourism follows its manifest destiny to the north along the Pacific.

PRACTICAL INFORMATION FOR MAZATLÁN

HOW TO GET THERE. By Air. *Republic Airlines* has direct daily flights to Phoenix, going on to Chicago; *Western* flies direct to Los Angeles every day except Saturday and Sunday; *Frontier* connects Mazatlán with El Paso, Denver and Albuquerque daily except Monday and Wednesday. *Mexicana* has daily flights to Chicago (via Mexico City), direct daily to Denver, to Kansas City (via Denver), twice daily, direct to Los Angeles, daily to Sacramento (via Los Angeles), twice daily to San Diego (via Tijuana) and daily, direct, to San Francisco as well as every day except Tuesday to Seattle, five weekly flights to Calgary (via Seattle) and to most major Mexican cities, along with *Aeromexico* whose only international flights out of Mazatlán are three times a week to Houston.

By Ferry. Daily, around 5 P.M. to La Paz, with some 17 hours of travel time, passage costing $1.50 to $15 depending on accommodations plus some $25 for an average size car (ferry terminal, tel. 17020).

By Train. Two trains daily from the U.S. border at Nogales and Mexicali as well as from Guadalajara with at least one daily train from each direction equipped with Pullman cars and dining car.

By Bus or Car. There are several daily, first-class buses from major Mexican cities, all quite inexpensive if a bit tiring; the driving distance from Nogales is 1,230 kms, from Guadalajara 525 sometimes mountainous kms and a stunning scenic 295 kms from Durango.

EMERGENCY TELEPHONE NUMBERS. Red Cross: 13690; Police: 13939; Hospital: 14874; Tourism: 14210 and 32545; U.S. Consulate: 12905 and 14488; Canadian Consulate: 37320.

HOTELS. Mazatlán boasts more than 170 hotels in various price ranges. Listed here are the better accommodations, along with a selection of lower cost lodgings. As in Mazanillo, hotels in this area were authorized, at press time, to charge on the average the following rates for a double room: *Deluxe,* $72; *First Class,* $40; *Expensive,* $25; *Moderate,* $16; and *Inexpensive,* $10. Because of rising inflation, however, those rates are most likely to go up during 1987.

Deluxe

Camino Real, Punta del Sábalo, tel. 3111; with 164 A/C units in a stunningly beautiful setting with the best and most courteous service in town; all the amenities you'll ever need including the superb Lafitte restaurant with live music. Small but good beach and a spectacular rocky point with stunning views.

El Cid, Camarón Sábalo, tel. 33333; with 600 spacious A/C rooms plus all the services needed, along with a golf course, a wide beachfront, 11 places to eat, 17 tennis courts, and 5 different-sized pools, elegant new disco.

Los Sábalos, Loaiza 100, tel. 35409; with 185 A/C rooms, also with all possible services in newer hotel with an excellent location on a great beach and at one corner of the Zona Dorada.

Holiday Inn, Ave. Camarón Sábalo 696; tel. 32222; with 200 A/C rooms favored by tour groups and commercial travelers; 3 restaurants, popular lobby bar, disco with live music, most amenities and services.

First Class

Belmar, Olas Altas Sur 166, tel. 14299; with 196 A/C rooms, pool, restaurant, bar; close to the downtown area but also just off a rocky beach which has good seasonal surfing spots.

Costa de Oro, Camarón Sábalo, tel. 35344; with 200 A/C rooms, pool, travel agency, car rental, restaurant, bar; on the best beach in town, close to the Zona Dorada.

De Cima, Ave. del Mar, no number, tel. 14119; with 150 A/C rooms, pool, travel agency, car rental, restaurant, bar, nightclub; decent beach across the coastal drive, a bit of a walk to get anywhere else.

Aqua Marina, Ave. del Mar 110, tel. 17085; with 101 A/C rooms, travel agency, car rental, restaurant, bar; good beach across the road, bit of a walk to the action spots.

Hotel Hacienda, Ave. del Mar and Flamingos, tel. 27000; with 95 A/C rooms, pool, travel agency, car rental, restaurant, bar, disco, nightclub; short walk to a decent beach.

Suites Las Sirenas, Ave. del Mar 1100, tel. 31866; with 72 A/C rooms, pool, tennis, car rental, restaurant, bar; somewhat rocky beach in front.

Playa Mazatlán, Loaiza, 202, tel. 34444; with 425 A/C rooms, pool, restaurant, bar, travel agency, car rental, nightclub, disco; in the Zona Dorada, excellent beach.

Torres Mazatlán, Calzada Sábalo Cerritos, no number, tel. 36330; with 60 A/C rooms stuck out at the very end of the hotel area, too far to walk anywhere; good beach with some strong waves; pool, restaurant, bar.

Aristos Resort, Cameron Sabalo 51, tel. 34611. The Hoteles Aristos chain purchased the Playa Del Rey, Suites Del Rey, and the Tropicana and transformed them into this beautiful complex. The tower rooms, suites, and beach club combine for 393 modern units. Restaurants, bars, pools, nightclub, meeting rooms, long list of amenities. Good beach, short distance from the Zona Dorada.

Yacht Club La Marina, Sábalo Cerritos, no number, tel. 30222; with 103 A/C rooms, pool, tennis, shops, restaurant, bar, travel agency; good beach with waves, far from anywhere except the Torres Mazatlán Hotel.

Club Balboa, Camarón Sábalo, no number, tel. 35633; with 62 A/C rooms, pool, cafeteria, restaurant; good beach, located at one end of the Zona Dorada.

El Pescador, Camarón Sábalo and Atun, tel. 30377; with 125 A/C rooms, pool, travel agency, car rental, restaurant, bar, disco, nightclub; good beach, bit of a walk to the Zona Dorada.

Oceano Palace, Camarón Sábalo, no number, tel. 30666; with 167 A/C rooms, pool, travel agency, restaurant, bar, car rental, cafeteria, disco, car rental, nightclub, good beach, near the Camino Real and a fair ways from the Zona Dorada.

Las Flores, Loaiza, no number, tel. 35033; with 122 A/C rooms, pool, travel agency, car rental, restaurant, bar; good beach; right in the middle of the Zona Dorada.

Expensive

El Dorado, Ave. Del Mar 177, tel. 14718; with 41 A/C rooms, pool, tennis, cafeteria, restaurant, good beach, enough restaurants close by but a good walk to the Zona Dorada or downtown.

Las Arenas, Ave. Del Mar, no number, tel. 20000; with 57 A/C rooms, parking, pool, car rental, restaurant, bar; good beach across the road.

Puesta Del Sol, Camarón Sábalo, no number, tel. 35411; with 72 A/C units, including 22 kitchenettes, parking, pool, travel agency, cafeteria, restaurant, bar; good beach, near the Zona Dorada.

Posada Don Pelayo, Ave. Del Mar 1111, tel. 31888 with 100 rooms, parking, car rental, cafeteria, restaurant, bar, disco, rocky beach in front but a short walk from the Zona Dorada.

Moderate

Arlu, Albatros 2, Colonia Gaviotas, tel. 35212; with 11 A/C rooms, parking, restaurant; no beach very close by.

Marcos Suite, Ave. Del Mar 1234, tel. 35998; with 12 A/C rooms, parking, pool; decent beach a short way although in front it's somewhat rocky; bit of a walk to the Zona Dorada.

Club Playa Mar, Ave. Del Mar 139, tel. 20833; with 61 A/C rooms, pool, parking; good beach across the road.

Suite Caribe Mazatlán, Ave. Del Mar 1020, tel. 31844; with 21 A/C rooms, pool, rocky beach in front but not too far to a better one.

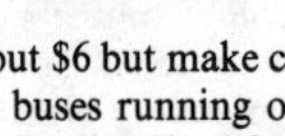

HOW TO GET AROUND. From the airport, which is 23 km or 14 miles to the south of town on Highway 14, there are collective VW buses to any destination in Mazatlán for about $2; taxis to and from the airport cost about $6 but make certain that the price is agreed upon before you get in. There are buses running on the coastal strip all the way from downtown to beyond the Camino Real for some 10 cents U.S. A taxi ride from, say the Camino Real to downtown, or some comparable distance averages about $3. Cheaper by about one-third than taxis, the "pulmonías" are open three- or four-wheel scooter vehicles with a covering on top; bargain for the fare; they can be rented for about $20 an hour.

TOURIST INFORMATION SERVICES. *Federal Tourism Office,* Ave. Del Mar 1000, tel. 14210, open from 8 A.M. to 3 P.M., Monday through Friday, reduced staff on the same days from 5 P.M. to 7 P.M. Good for maps, this is the place to lodge an official complaint. The *Municipal Tourism Office* has two locations, one downtown at the Palacio Municipal on the main square, open 8 A.M. to 3 P.M. on weekdays and in the Centro Commercial Los Sábalos in front of the Hotel Los Sabalos in the Zona Dorada, open the same hours, tel. 32545. There are lots of private tourism information booths in the Zona Dorada, mainly to steer you to various businesses.

USEFUL ADDRESSES. Airlines. *Aeromexico,* Ave. del Mar 117, tel. 13096; *Mexicana,* Paseo Claussen 101B, tel. 27722; *Frontier,* Camarón Sábalo, no number, tel. 34522; *Republic,* Ave. del Mar 80, tel. 16497; *Western,* Camarón Sábalo, no number, tel. 32709. **Car rentals.** All the companies have stands at the airport. *Avis,* Ave. Camarón Sábalo, no number, tel. 36200; *Hertz,* Ave. del Mar 1111 (in the hotel Don Pelayo), tel. 34955; *Budget,* Camarón Sábalo 402, tel. 32000; *National,* Camarón Sábalo (in the Centro Comercial "El Camarón"), tel. 34077. **Consulates.** *United States,* Circunvalacion Poniente 6, tel. 12905 and 14488. *Canadian,* Albatros 705, tel. 37320. **Post Office.** Downtown, on the main square and Juárez.

TOURS. The most popular and inexpensive are the *Fiesta Yacht Cruises,* costing about $3 and motoring around the harbor and bay, with swimming, music, and bilingual guides, lasting some three hours, going by some of the islands offshore with birds and seals (in season). Reservations for these tours can be made in any of the bigger hotels, departures at 10:30 from the dock south of town near the lighthouse, next to the fishermen's docks. There is also a moonlight cruise.

City tours with hotel pickup cost $7. Farther afield, you can take a tour to the old mining town of Copala or "jungle tours" to the swamplands with birdlife in various areas along the coast. To give an example of costs, the company *Autotransportaciones Turísticas* (Calzada Camarón Sábalo, tel. 35301) charges $20 for its tour to Copala with lunch included and $35 for its jungle tour to San Blas' Tovara (see details under *San Blas*) with lunch included.

PARKS, BULLRINGS AND RODEO GROUNDS. *Martiniano Carvajar,* on Ave. del Mar and Miramar for kids and sports; *El Toreo Bullring* by the Holiday Inn; *Monumental Bullring* (also called Mazatlán) on Ave. Rafael Buelna. The bullfight season is from December to Easter. *Lienzo Charro* for Mexican rodeos, at Insurgentes, close to the train station; check for dates at the tourism office.

SPORTS. Golf. At the *El Cid Country Club* on Sábalo Beach Road (18 holes) or at the *Club Campestre de Mazatlán,* south of town on Highway 15 (9 holes). **Hunting.** Lots of game in the hills, migratory birds in season. Contact a qualified guide as, for example, Aviles Brothers, Apartado 221, tel. 13728 or Francisco Meyer. tel. 35936. **Tennis.** If your hotel does not have courts, ask it to make reservations for you at some other hotel or at a public court. Laguna Racket Club (across from Playa Mazatlán Hotel) and the El Cid Racket Club.

Fishing. This is Mazatlán's big sport and one of its main attractions. Use a bit of common sense so that you will not be disappointed with the boat you hire. A decent day charter will cost you around $200; check out the craft before you hire it. There are 11 sport fishing fleets, each having from three to 14 boats. All are docked together near the lighthouse. Boats vary from about 25 to 45 ft. and fishing chairs from two to five. Fishing is good year-round but the weather gets hot around mid-May. Black and blue marlin from May to December; sailfish and dolphin (mahi-mahi) from April to November; striped marlin from November to May. There are many tournaments organized by various U.S. cities. The biggest is put on by the local Chamber of Commerce, in August or September. For more information, write to Miguel Maxemin Coppel, Flota Faro, Apartado Postal 235, Mazatlán. For general information on fishing in Mexico, tournaments, and otherwise, write to Confederacion Maritima Mexicana, Luis Moya 5, Col. Centro, C.P. 06050, Mexico D.F. (tel. 510–1840). Some of Mazatlán's fishing fleets: *Flota Estrella,* tel. 22668 (14 boats), *Flota Faro,* tel. 12824 (8 boats), *Flota Perla,* tel. 17211 (6 boats). **A practical warning:** do not deal with someone who solicits you for a boat charter on the beach or the sidewalks.

The big difference between gamefishing in Mazatlán and the U.S. is that whereas up north you might have thousands of boats out at one time; in Mazatlán the total number is more like 100. And if the fishing is good now, it should be even better if a proposal to ban all commercial fishing in the Sea of Cortez (Gulf of California) should be enacted into law. During the peak season, from mid to end December and around Easter, it is a good idea to reserve your boat through a reputable travel agent.

Water sports. Equipment can be rented from *Club de Buseo* at the Hotel Sábalos, tel. 35333 extension 2172 or *Deportes Aqua Sport* at the Hotel El Cid, tel. 33333 extension 1341.

SPECIAL EVENTS. *Carnaval,* in late February or March, considered by some to be the third best in the world, after Rio and New Orleans (reserve your hotel way in advance). The tradition goes back to 1898 when they used to select a king instead of a queen. Floats, music, fireworks, bullfights, the works. *Mazatlán Fishing Tournament,* in late August or early September.

BEACHES. We start on the port side of the city, go around El Faro, then follow the coast north. **Isla de Piedras.** Accessible by launch from the harbor, departure from near the shrimp packing plants across from the gas station; going across the harbor to a place opposite the cruise ship docks for about 50 cents US; the beach is crowded with locals on weekends and holidays when there's lots of live music and the small thatched restaurants do a booming business in seafood; sand beach, quiet water.

Olas Altas (high waves)—the name applies only a part of the year. This is the first real beach on the long coastal drive, heading generally northwest. Every six months or so, the sand shifts from one part of this beach to another to return later to its original position; good surfing during the summer months; for the non-surfers, a pleasant walk and good sunset watching; plenty of restaurants of various categories on the other side of the coastal drive with various types of cuisine. This beach is within relatively easy walking distance from downtown.

Norte or **Avenida del Mar,** which follows Olas Altas begins at the Fisherman's Monument and ends at Camarón Point. Quiet sand beach makes up the core of the developed seafront drive although there are more hotels and tourist-related activities farther north. Lots of locals and tourists mingling here, mariachis in the busy seasons and a fresh water shower in front of the Hotel Hacienda. Some short stretches with rocks.

Las Gaviotas starts at Camarón Point and the Disco Valentino's; this hotel-backed beach is the closest to the Zona Dorada, the center of tourism in Mazatlán; very good sand beach, sandy, palm-lined, protected from heavy seas by several nearby islands. On this beach you can rent hobie-cats or windsurfing planks, and do parasailing for about $12 for a 5-minute ride. The launch *Super Pato* (Superduck) leaves every two hours from this beach, departing in front of the Hotel Las Flores between 9 A.M. and 5 P.M. to a nearby island where you can swim and return later; cost of round trip, about $2.50.

Sábalo runs to the end of the developed area to Sábalo Point at the Camino Real; with the whitest and widest sand with a trailer park midway next to the Holiday Inn; the beach is backed by a variety of hotels; sometimes decent surf, lots of water sports.

Sábalo Cerritos, the "new" beach zone backed mainly by time-sharing apartments; good white sand beach; the sea can be rough and there are few facilities at the moment.

Escondida (Hidden), good beach, palm trees; out of the crowds, a kind of transition zone with few bathers and no facilities.

Brujos (Witches), good beach, open seas, out in the sticks, quite isolated; on weekends there is some live music and a small thatched restaurant dispenses seafood. The road which runs along the coast from town ends here.

Delfin, reached from the main highway by paved road and so named for a lonely pioneer hotel hoping for the expansion of tourism its way; beyond this, the isolated beaches, only for the adventurous.

MUSEUMS AND GALLERIES. Acuario Mazatlán, Avenida de los Deportes, one block from Avenida del Mar; look for the signs; open Tuesday through Sunday, 10 A.M. to 6 P.M., with 250 species of marine life; admission, $1; botanical garden and small zoo next door.

Sea Shell Museum, on Avenida Loaiza near the Playa Mazatlán Hotel, open 9 to 9 daily; really a store, so there's no admission charge.

Galeria de Arte Moderno, on Camarón Sábalo, for paintings mostly by locals.

SHOPPING. Although there's nothing really unusual for shoppers in Mazatlán, its dozens of shops and boutiques sell a wide variety of beachwear and crafts produced both locally and elsewhere in Mexico. Rather than listing lots of stores, we suggest that if you are in a shopping mood, wander around the Zona Dorada as well as checking out the shops in some of the better hotels. If you are going farther into Mexico, hold off on your crafts purchases and buy only resort clothing. If you are returning home from Mazatlán, by all means stock up on the fanciful and the utilitarian.

RESTAURANTS. The restaurants in the Mazatlán area generally specialize in seafood and steaks. Try the locally brewed Pacifico beer. Most of the restaurants listed here accept major U.S. credit cards. For the cost of a basic seafood meal not including alcoholic beverages (appetizer, entree, dessert), figure $12 to $15, and for non-seafood meals, 25% to 35% less. Unless stated otherwise, these restaurants are open from noon to 11 P.M. but this might vary with the number of clients.

Casa Loma, Ave. Gaviotas 104, tel. 35398; this is a former home with both patio and indoor service; international cuisine and good atmosphere.

El Parador Español, Camarón Sábalo, next to the Hotel El Cid, tel. 30767; Spanish cuisine, such as paella Valenciana.

El Patio, Avenida del Mar 30, tel. 17301; international cuisine, Mexican atmosphere, often with strolling musicians.

El Marinero, Cinco de Mayo 530 just off Paseo Claussen, tel. 17682; seafood and mariachis.

El Camarón, at Punta Camarón, next to Valentino's Disco with another location on Avenida Del Mar, just off the Olas Altas beach; tel. 16626. The interior is decorated with bullfight memorabilia; casual atmosphere and you can wander in just for a drink or the full treatment of their international cuisine, excellent steaks and seafood.

El Bistro at the Mazatlán Arts and Crafts Center in the Zona Dorada, tel. 32031; try their charcoal-grilled steaks and seafood either in their garden or indoors.

Casa de Bruno, Ave. Camarón Sábalo near the Hotel Playa Mazatlán, no phone; some of the dishes are prepared tableside; indoors with colonial decor or on the sidewalk; marimba music at times; friendly staff, barbecued dishes; open till 1 A.M.

El Shrimp Bucket, Olas Altas Sur 11, in the Hotel La Siesta, tel. 16350; one of the Carlos Anderson spots but the crowd is not as young as usual; marimbas, mariachis, dancing; meats, seafood, Mexican cuisine, and very good.

Los Pelicanos, Avenida del Mar 553, tel. 26839; beautiful restaurant on two levels; good food, live music, friendly atmosphere.

Meson del Cobre, Camaron Sabalo, across from the Inn at Mazatlan; open from 7 A.M. till midnight; excellent food in casual atmosphere.

Señor Frog, Avenida del Mar, next to the Sands Hotel, tel. 14367; original decor in what is probably the most fun restaurant in town; meats and seafood; open till midnight.

Doney, on the corner of Mariano Escobedo 610 and Cinco de Mayo, tel. 12651; inexpensive, meats and Mexican specialities, seafood, mariachis often.

Señor Pepper, Camarón Sábalo near the Camino Real for the biggest and best cuts of meat. We usually do not mention hotel restaurants; however we make an exception to recommend the two restaurants at the **Camino Real:** the *Lafitte* for lobsters and prime rib and the *Chiquita Banana* for the freshest and best seafood in town in an open, informal setting right on the beach.

ENTERTAINMENT/NIGHTLIFE. There are bullfights most Sundays from December to May. The high divers perform at *El Mirador* at various times of the day and early night. Mexican Nights with local dishes (toned down for tourists so don't worry about the chilis), national booze, music, and dance are held at the following hotels: *Camino Real, Playa Mazatlán, Los Sabalos, Costa Brava, Paraiso del Mar.* The plushest discos are at the best hotels: the *Camino Real, El Cid* and *Holiday Inn.* These hotels also have top-flight entertainers in their nightclubs. Other good spots include *La Guitarra* at the Hotel Hacienda for shows and live disco music, *Studio A* (also at the Hotel Hacienda) for pure disco, *El Navegante* at the Hotel de Cima for live modern music, *El Carousel* for shows with good Mexican groups; the Restaurant Ney's *Oh Baby* for musical groups, disco music as well as some romantic tunes, *Tony's*

Plaza in the Zona Dorada in front of the Playa Mazatlán Hotel for the piano bar, romantic music, all live and very much alive.

THE MAZATLÁN AREA

As Mazatlán is by far the most important resort city on Mexico's north Pacific shore, we will use it as a base of exploration for other points as far as San Blas, Nayarit to the south and the area of Guaymas, a long ways to the north. We divide the Mazatlán-based trips into three broad zones: the state of Sinaloa including the Los Mochis terminal of the Chihuahua-Pacific Railroad, the San Blas sector of Nayarit and the Guaymas area of Sonora state.

Immediate Vicinity and the State of Sinaloa

Near Mazatlán, there are several small, colonial towns to explore. Heading south on Highway 15, past the airport, take the turnoff toward Durango. Within a few miles, you will come upon the village of Concordia, founded in 1565 and famous for its colonial-baroque San Sebastian Church. Local crafts include pottery, furniture, and leather tanning. Nearby, there are hot water springs at Aguascalientes. Following the road to Durango, the little town of Copala sits in the foothills of the Sierra Madre Occidental. It's colonial and charming with a quiet atmosphere. Take a peek into the church to see the huge retablo (religious painting). By continuing on this highway, you climb into the Sierras; great panoramas, especially from a spot called the *Espinazo del Diablo* (Devil's Spine).

Back to Highway 15, by continuing towards Tepic, you reach El Rosario, uninteresting except for the splendid late-16th-century colonial church dedicated to the Virgen del Rosario (Virgin of the Rosary). The plateresque church was built from silver-mining wealth as Rosario was the main urban center for several dispersed mining camps in the Sierras. A long time ago, the church had to be moved, stone by stone, to a better location. Take a good look at the altar and the 18th-century retablo, claimed to be the best on the Pacific coast. A little farther south, turn to Teacapa, a fishing village with a shrimp-packing plant. This is the departure point for some of the jungle trips featuring birds, wild flowers and tree iguanas in the mangrove swamplands. The beaches at Las Cabras and La Tambora have good sand and are well suited for water sports.

Heading north about 100 km out of Mazatlán on Highway 15, take a paved side road (well marked) to Cosala, some 50 km away. A great little colonial town, still partially living from silver mining though the current economic mainstays are farming and ranching. See the clock at city hall still run by weights hauled up by a rope. If that should fail, there's a sun dial on the old Santa Ursala Church. Stop by the mineralogy museum whose centerpiece is an incongruous mammoth bone.

These are about the only day trips that you can take out of Mazatlán. If you want to explore the state further, be prepared to spend at least one night on the road. Going north on Highway 15, Culiacán, the busy state capital, is 220 km away. There are plenty of hotels of all categories, good hunting nearby for game birds and fishing for largemouth bass at a reservoir. Some 60 km to the west of Culiacán, the beaches of Altata are almost unknown to tourists yet offer hotels, restaurants, and good fishing.

The Adolfo López Mateos reservoir northeast of Culiacán and the Sanalona reservoir east of the city both have bass, catfish, and trout. Ten is the one-man limit per day. Nearby lakes Bataoto, San Lorenzo, Cascabeles, and Mariquita are well stocked and some have snook. Salt-water fishing is best at Altata on the Pacific, 42 miles west of the city. Hunting of Canadian ducks is permitted in October and March in the rice fields near Culiacán.

There are thermal spring resorts at Imala, Macurimi, Carrizalejo, Vigía, and Arenitas.

Going farther north, fishermen after bass will want to take a side road from Guasave to Bacuberito.

LOS MOCHIS AND EL FUERTE

Los Mochis was founded by an American, Benjamin F. Johnston, who built its great sugar refinery, one of the largest in Mexico now, and a home that expert horticulturists can admire. The area is irrigated by waters from the Miguel Hidalgo Dam, which is northward beyond San Blas and El Fuerte. Both are on the Chihuahua Pacific Railroad.

El Fuerte is what Los Mochis isn't. It is a quaint colonial town on the Fuerte River as it comes down through a bountifully rich valley. The El Fuerte valley bolsters the state's pride in having more than 70 percent of its arable land under irrigation. Of this more than 90 percent is mechanized with tractors, seeding machines, combines, and so on. Sinaloa, with only 3 percent of the nation's farm land, accounts for 20 percent of all irrigated land in the republic.

Only 50 miles from Los Mochis, El Fuerte attracts visitors with the Hidalgo Dam catch of catfish, largemouth bass, and carp, the hunting in the surrounding mountains where there are quail, white wing dove, and rabbit all year. White-wing dove season lasts from October through March while for ducks and geese it's November to the end of February.

The town was named for the fort there, but when founded in 1584 by Francisco de Ibarra was known as San Juan de Carápoa.

San Blas, 30 miles from Los Mochis, is the actual rail junction with the Ferrocarril de Pacifico lacing the border with Guadalajara, and the Chihuahua Pacific joining the city of Chihuahua with one of the largest and deepest harbors of the world, Topolobampo.

This San Blas, by the way, is not to be confused with the similarly named San Blas, the tropical seaside town a bit farther south in Nayarit state. While this town devotes itself busily to railroading and agriculture, the other doesn't devote itself to much but languorous living, with a bit of fishing to keep food on the table.

From El Fuerte, San Blas, and the Culiacán fields farther south come tomatoes, rice, chickpeas, cantaloupe, watermelon, sugarcane, wheat, sorghum, chilis, and cucumbers. The crops come in during the winter season and find a wide and receptive market in the U.S. with occasional threats of cutoffs by the big neighbor to the north.

Los Mochis, in addition to its fortunate location surrounded by such agricultural wealth, has fine accommodations to house the *aficionados* of hunting, fishing, and water sports. Fabulous duck, goose, and dove hunting is but 45 minutes from Los Mochis. Gamefish that are highly prized can be caught most of the year with curvina, yellowtail, red snapper, toto, snook, and cabrilla in the catch.

The Botanical Gardens are on the grounds of the home of the city's founder, and there he gathered all varieties of palm, flowers, and shrubs from the world's distant points. It has been officially called Sinaloa Park. The *Country Club* allows hotel guests in the city to use its fine facilities, and tours of the many factories can be arranged for those with a special interest in industry.

It is estimated that 1.6 million game birds migrate to Sinaloa during the U.S. and Canadian winters.

Topolobampo means "tiger water" according to some versions, and in others it is the Indian word for "the lion's watering place." The important thing is that it is only 15 minutes from Los Mochis, on a splendid bay where the porpoise play, and ferries leave for La Paz.

Isla El Farallón in the bay is a refuge for sea lions, which gives some authenticity to the Indian name for their old settlement on the bay. The many other islands are a refuge for a wide variety of water birds. Nearby lagoons, estuaries, and the mouth of the Fuerte River please both visitors and those who pack and ship the shrimp, frogs' legs, butter clams, oysters, scallops, and crab.

The inner bay is fine for water-skiing and along the miles of beaches, shallow to the delight of many, there is profitable shell hunting and beachcombing. Las Animas beach is one of the favorites reached by a 5-minute boat trip from Topolobampo as is Santa María Island.

Guasave is 39 miles from Los Mochis. It was founded in 1595 on a wide fertile plain flanking the Sinaloa River. Special fiestas are held on the first Sunday in October and the last Sunday of November. Boca del Rio and Bocanita beaches are 20 miles from Route 15.

Most visitors arrive in Los Mochis either to get on—or off—the country's most spectacular train ride which crosses the Sierras to Chihuahua. (For a description, see *Chihuahua* chapter.) For those who will spend a night in Los Mochis, here's some practical information.

PRACTICAL INFORMATION FOR LOS MOCHIS AND EL FUERTE

TRAVEL AGENCIES. To arrange tours in the Sierras or along the nearby coast; for the Sierras tours, you get off the train at any one of several stations.

Agencia Flamingos, at the Hotel Santa Anita, Leyva, and Hidalgo; tel. 21613.
Viajes Granados, Leyva 326 bis; tel. 20273.

HOTELS. In the Los Mochis area, hotels were authorized, at press time, to charge, on the average, the following rates for a double room: *First Class,* $28; *Expensive,* $18.50; *Moderate,* $12.50; and *Inexpensive,* $8.

El Dorado Motel, Leyva and Valdez, tel. 51111; with 90 A/C rooms, pool, restaurant, parking. *First Class.*

Santa Anita, Leyva and Hidalgo, tel. 20046; with 130 A/C units, bar, restaurant, parking, travel agency. *First Class.*

Holiday Inn, on Highway 15; with pool and all the basics. *First Class.*

Posada Real, Leyva and Buelna, tel. 22179. *Expensive.*

America, Allende Sur 655, tel. 21355; downtown. *Moderate.*

Beltran, Hidalgo 281 and Zaragoza, tel. 20688; with 42 A/C rooms. *Moderate.*

RESTAURANTS. El Farallon, Obregon and Flores, tel. 21428; nautical decor, murals; seafood. *Moderate.*

Mexico-Español, downtown at Hidalgo Poniente 281, tel. 22983; Spanish cooking; inexpensive.

Madrid, Obregon 414 at Leyva, no phone, Mexican cooking; plain and cheap.

Nayarit

Leaving Mazatlán, follow the signs to Tepic. While still on the flat coastal plain and before reaching Acaponeta, you leave the state of Sinaloa and enter Nayarit.

Nayarit is not really washed by the Sea of Cortés. Its shores face the open Pacific, but the little state gets lumped in with its neighbors to the north anyway. Farther south, really just below the state line, is Puerto Vallarta and the beginning of what the people in Jalisco like to call the Happy Coast.

Together with Sinaloa to the north, Jalisco to the south, and Zacatecas to the east, Nayarit was part of the province of Nueva Galicia for three centuries. Its capital was Compostela, which has since changed its name to Tepic, and the Port of San Blas was the naval center for the missionary/military expeditions which created the bases for the first settlements in Upper California. Then came independence and decline. Nayarit ended up as part of Jalisco and was ruled from Guadalajara.

Back in the days of Benito Juárez, Nayarit was separated and became a federal territory. It became a state of the Mexican Republic in 1917. It is one of Mexico's smallest states.

Nayarit has 180 miles of coastline and is destined to become a big resort area. Highway 15 heads inland south of Mazatlan, then runs parallel to the coast from which it is separated by several miles of swamps. It climbs sharply to Tepic then heads inland to Guadalajara.

Driving in from the north, Acaponeta is the first town in Nayarit. It lies along the Acaponeta River, surrounded by fields in which tobacco, cotton, and sugarcane are grown. The mountains in the background were once rich in silver and gold and no doubt still have some of the metals.

One of the oldest towns in the area, Acaponeta was founded in 1584 by the Franciscans. The town had its troubles, suffering a number of Indian attacks. The mines up in the hills, however, made settlers willing to take their chances with arrows. When the Indians were finally pacified, pirates showed up. In 1688 a band of French buccaneers made off with 20 burro-loads of silver, 40 women, and 2 priests. The priests, it should be noted, were taken to be held for ransom.

About 8 miles west of Acaponeta is Tecuala, a shrimp fishing center over toward the coast. It is a bit swampy in this area, good country for duck hunting. Some 15 miles beyond one arrives at Playa Novilleros, a quiet beach—50 miles long—with excellent seafood.

On beyond Acaponeta, Highway 15 heads almost due south, crossed here and there by little side roads leading to lagoons and bays and fishing villages. The one very much worth visiting is Mexcaltitán, which some archeologists think may be the original home town of the Aztecs. The town is laid out—on a smaller scale—much in the way the Spaniards described the Mexico City of Montezuma.

Mexcaltitán sits like a great lily pad in the lagoon near the mouth of the San Pedro River. The town spreads out to cover its circular island, the streets radiating out like spokes of a wheel. They are only streets in the dry season. With the spring rains they become canals and canoes can be poled up to the central plaza. Those that call this the Venice of Mexico tend toward hyperbole, but the community is unusual. A new 30 km paved road, well marked and 70 km before Tepic, runs to the shore near Mexcaltitán. Frequent launches take you across to the island.

An excellent time to visit Mexcaltitán is on June 29, the Feast of St. Peter and St. Paul. The highlight of the day is a race around the island by a pair of canoes manned by images of St. Peter and St. Paul. The rooting is loudest for St. Peter, for legend has it when he wins the shrimp haul will be good.

On down this way Route 15 leads past Tuxpan and Santiago, two of the biggest towns in the state. This is tobacco country. It is also the land of the Huichol and Cora Indians. Visitors are fascinated by these people, who wander about in their traditional garb and sell attractive handicrafts. These Indians often take seasonal work in the tobacco fields nearby.

Several side roads lead to little shore towns. The most famous of these in San Blas.

THE FAMOUS SAN BLAS AND TEPIC

San Blas might be Bali Hai. It is a little seaside town of swaying palms and thatched huts, of ruined palaces of former days and sleazy *cantinas* where one would expect to find Peter Lorre. It is a haven for those who want to drop out of the world for a while, far better than joining the French Foreign Legion. The curse of the place is gnats. But the bugs are easily discouraged by insect repellent.

San Blas blossomed as a major port during the mid-18th century. It was an important shipbuilding center as well, and here Spain maintained an armada to fight off British and French pirates. Spanish sailors probed the coastline as far north as Alaska. Serra sailed to Loreto in Baja California, then walked to San Diego and farther north, starting the missions in Upper California.

Following Mexico's independence in 1821, San Blas came close to becoming a Mexican Hong Kong. A British importation firm, Barron, Forbes and Co., established itself in the port and managed to run things pretty much as it saw fit. At one time, Barron was the British consul while Forbes held the same post representing the Americans. At times, these two ran afoul of Mexican authorities, with resulting disputes becoming international incidents of sorts. The remote town caught the attention of Henry Wadsworth Longfellow who penned his last poem in its honor:

> But to me, a dreamer of dreams,
> To whom what is and what seems
> Are often one and the same,
> The Bells of San Blas to me
> Have a strange and wild melody
> And are something more than a name.

Just after crossing the bridge over the San Cristobal estuary and before pulling into San Blas proper, there is a knoll on your left. On top, you'll find the ruins of a colonial church and La Contaduria, formerly the most important building, now defended by rusting cannon. A charming place, especially at sunrise and sunset. Good view of San Blas and the sea. (Don't forget insect repellent.) In town and near the estuary, you will find the old Spanish customs house.

From the beach at San Blas on a clear day, three islands can be seen on the horizon. They are the Tres Marías, a penal colony.

Along with the usual shoreside diversions, there is a special treat in the San Blas region. Open motor boats, which can take up to ten adults, leave from the San Cristobal bridge for the two-hour round trip to the clear springs of La Tovara. Launches are available to go up the little rivers through the mangrove jungle, a trip into Tarzan country. The lush vegetation, the birds and beasts seen here are a treat for the eye scarcely matched anywhere this side of Africa.

Tepic

Tepic, the state capital, is a little less than 50 miles from San Blas. It was founded in 1530 by the Spanish conqueror Nuño de Guzmán who named it Villa del Espíritu Santo de la Mayor España. That being a trifle hard to remember, the name was switched to Santiago de Galicia de Compostela. In those early days, the town failed to thrive. When Francisco Vázquez de Coronado was named governor of the area, he moved his capital down the road a piece and took the name with him. What had been Compostela became Tepic, and Tepic eventually became a capital again.

But for a time the capital was moved over to Guadalajara. That annoyed the local folk and for years and years they battled to have their own local government. During the 19th century, Barron and Forbes supported this movement and when Maximilian came over to Mexico to put a crown on his head, he granted autonomy to Nayarit. Benito Juárez, returning to control, allowed things to stand, organizing Nayarit as a federal territory.

All this troubled history is rapidly repeated to the visitor who lingers for anything more than a cup of coffee in Tepic. The most noted site to see in town is the Church of Santa Cruz (Holy Cross), built centuries ago when someone noticed that grass on the site was growing in the form of a cross. The church was built around it and the cross of grass can still be seen. Fray Junípero Serra spent a year at this church and a monument has been built to him here.

Another monument stands in honor of Juan Escutia. He was one of six cadets who wrapped themselves in a Mexican flag and leaped to their deaths from the heights of Chapultepec Castle rather than surrender to victorious American forces during the U.S. invasion nearly a century and a half ago. A school and a market also bear the Escutia name and a plaque marks the house where he was born.

In Juan Escutia Park stands a monument to Amado Nervo, a native son of Tepic who became one of Mexico's most outstanding poets.

Worth a visit is the State Museum, housed in what was once the palace of the Counts of Miravalle and later the headquarters of Barron, Forbes and Co.

It is possible to drive a little way north of Tepic toward Bellavista, on the edge of Indian country. Beyond that, there are few roads. Up in the hills live the Huicholes and the Coras, Indians who live much as their forefathers did. They keep pretty much to themselves but occasionally venture down into Tepic to sell their crafts and to buy batteries for their transistor radios. There are frequent scheduled flights by small plane to the Cora and Huichol Sierra, but there are no facilities of any kind once there. Check at the airport for days and times.

From Tepic, Highway 15 turns inland, running on to Guadalajara.

And at Tepic, a new highway is born. Route 200 goes down the coast to Banderas Bay and Puerto Vallarta. Then it continues on to Acapulco and to the Guatemala border. But this is different geography. It might be said that where Route 200 begins, there ends the shore of the Sea of Cortés.

PRACTICAL INFORMATION FOR SAN BLAS AND TEPIC

HOTELS. In San Blas hotels were authorized, at press time, to charge on the average the following rates for a double room: *First Class,* $37; *Expensive,* $22;

Moderate, $17; and *Inexpensive,* $10. In Tepic rates are a few dollars less for each category.

San Blas

Las Brisas, Cuauhtémoc Sur 160, tel. 50112; with 32 fan-cooled units across from the well known Casa Morales; pool, bar and restaurant working part-time. *First Class.*

Marino Inn. Bataillon (no number), tel. 50340; new hotel with 32 A/C units, parking, pool, restaurant to open sometime in the future. *First Class.*

Casa Morales, Playa Berrego or Apartado Postal 14, tel. 50023; at the marina, one of the two docks from where launches leave to La Tobara (it's longer and a bit more expensive from here); 20 fan cooled rooms in this delightful hotel with parking, pool, garden and restaurant. *Expensive.*

Suites San Blas, Acatima-Fraccionamiento de los Cocos, tel. 50047; with 43 units, parking, pool, games room, disco. *Expensive.*

Motel Posada Del Rey, Calle Campeche 10, tel. 50123; with 12 rooms, fan cooled, pool. *Expensive.*

Bucanero, Juárez Poniente 75, tel. 50110; with 35 rooms in a two-story converted mansion; pool, garden, restaurant, nightclub/disco. *Moderate.*

Los Flamingos, Juárez Poniente 105, no phone; also a trailer park; 20 units, parking, and restaurant. *Moderate.*

Tepic

Fray Junipero Serra, Lerdo Poniente 23, tel. 22525; located on the main square across from cathedral; the best in town, with 97 A/C rooms, restaurant, bar, parking, nightclub, disco. *First Class.*

Motel La Loma, Paseo de la Loma 301, tel. 32222; on the section of the main highway which runs through town; with 34 A/C units, pool, restaurant, cafeteria, bar, parking. *First Class.*

Corita, Insurgentes 310, tel. 20477; with 35 units, restaurant, cafeteria, pool, parking. *Expensive.*

Villa de las Rosas (formerly the *Motel Cora*), Insurgentes 100, tel. 31800; completely renovated 30 rooms, cafeteria, restaurant, parking. *Expensive.*

San Jorge, Lerdo Poniente 124, tel. 21234; with 34 rooms, a half block from the main plaza, restaurant, cafeteria. *Expensive.*

Genova, Zaragoza Norte 51, tel. 21172; with 63 rooms, fan cooled, parking.

Sierra de Alica, Ave. Mexico Norte 180, tel. 26322; 52 fan-cooled rooms a half block from the plaza, bar, nightclub, disco, bar. *Expensive.*

Altamirano, Mina Poniente 15, tel. 37131; 15 fan-cooled rooms just around the corner from the government palace on the main street; clean, good service, cafeteria. *Inexpensive.*

RESTAURANTS

San Blas

Chef Adolfo, Canalizo on the corner with Mercado, no phone; tasty dishes of seafood, meats and Mexican cuisine; open 1 to 8 P.M. No credit cards. Basic meal, $6.50.

El Amparo and **El Pescadito,** both on the main plaza, serve good Mexican cuisine and seafood for about $4 a basic meal; no credit cards.

Tepic

Roberto's, Insurgentes and Colegio Militar, just off the portion of Highway 15 running through town; tel. 32222; excellent international cuisine, open 1 P.M. to 1 A.M., accepts most major credit cards. Basic meal, $9.

Cazadores Nayar, Insurgentes Poniente 276, tel. 30051; specializes in meats; basic meal running about $7.50; open 1 to 10 P.M.; no credit cards.

Chante Clair, Insurgentes and Laureles, tel. 32015; excellent international cuisine, basic meal at $9; open 1 P.M. to midnight; credit cards accepted.

Wendy's Cafeteria, México Norte 178, tel. 26067; simple food at about $2.50; no credit cards.

La Terraza, Highway 15 and Insurgentes Poniente 98, tel. 32180; international cuisine; open 1 P.M. to 11 P.M.; no credit cards.

Mariscos del Farallon, Insurgentes Poniente 276, tel. 31124; the best seafood place in town, average meal running at $7; Open 1 to 9 P.M.; no credit cards.

SPECIAL EVENTS. **San Blas:** May for the fishing tournament; February or March for Carnaval; surfing competition in September. **Mexcaltitán:** June 28 and 29—Fiesta of San Pedro and San Pablo.

BEACHES OF SAN BLAS. Insect repellent is essential in July, August and September. *El Borrego* (the goat), the beach of San Blas; clean, small waves; two estuaries reach to the sea through this area; good sand, hotels, restaurants. *Matenchen,* to the south, on a bay with great view of the mountains, hard, clean sand, gentle slope; small hotels and restaurants. *Los Cocos,* a short distance farther south; lots of palm trees, with a fresh water stream running into the sea; dangerous beach with high waves, sharks, sudden drop-offs; small thatched restaurants operating when there are enough people. *Las Islitas,* about 1½ miles from Matenchen, best for surfing (boards can be rented) especially in September; thatched restaurants.

MUSEUM. *Museo Regional,* Tepic, for excellent pre-Columbian ceramics and contemporary Indian crafts; open Tuesday through Sunday 10 A.M. to 6 P.M.; entrance fee: 50 pesos.

TOURIST INFORMATION. **Tepic,** at the Exconvento de la Cruz, Ave. Mexico, tel. 30724; open weekdays 9 A.M. to 8 P.M. **San Blas,** at the Presidencia Municipal, tel. 50005; open weekdays 9 A.M. to 2 P.M., and 5 to 7 P.M.

GUAYMAS AND SONORA

Sonora is Mexico's second largest, second richest state, a delightful vacationland that has its own band of devoted followers. Yet, for the typical traveler to Mexico, Sonora seems as far away as the moon. This should not be. The place has its own delightful little colonial town that was once a capital, an exciting border crossing, modern cities, great beaches, and excellent fishing. It also has a fascinating history.

Some Sonora History

After both Cabeza de Vaca and Marcos de Niza had a quick look, Francisco Vázquez de Coronado was the first Spaniard to walk on the plains of Sonora. He had been made governor of the provinces to the south, but the natives rid themselves of him by spinning tales of El Dorado and the Seven Cities of Cíbola to the north. In 1540 Coronado set out to find them. He didn't. When he got back home he paid the price for failure and lost his job as governor.

Sonora was discovered, however, and became part of the Province of Nueva Viscaya, which included also Sinaloa, Durango, and Chihuahua. Sonora was largely ignored.

It was more than a century later that Fray Eusébio Francisco Kino led a missionary expedition to Sonora, founding some of the towns in the state. Except for Fray Kino and some miners, no one paid much attention to Sonora for three centuries and more. Indeed, it was the Americans who awakened Mexico's interest in the state. The Americans wanted Sonora for themselves.

Somehow, Sonora was not part of the Mexican territory that ended up under the American flag after the War of 1847. But it was coveted. In the mid-19th century the United States was headed toward civil war. Slavery was the issue. Before secession, the great issue was who would control the Congress in Washington, the free states of the North or the slave states of the South. Each side wanted to bring more territory into the Union. Sonora seemed to be there for the asking.

When the peace treaty of 1853 was drawn up, Mexico included in it a provision under which the United States would move to stop the filibustering, freebooting military attacks into its territory. In Washington, the Senate struck out that clause. Mexico responded by bringing in French colonists to settle along the border and the freebooting went the other way. For a time in the late 1850s the President of the United States tried to get Congress to authorize the establishment of a protectorate over Sonora. But the Americans were facing more serious problems.

Bringing in the French, as it turned out, was not such a good idea for Mexico, either. Within a decade, France was occupying most of Mexico, and Austria's Archduke Maximilian was sitting on a throne in Mexico City playing at being emperor. Even though he was backed by Paris, Max was having trouble with the French, who were demanding exclusive concessions to all the mining rights in Sonora.

The Civil War ended in the United States, and in Mexico the reign of Maximilian came to an end with the emperor facing a firing squad. International squabbles over Sonora faded away only to bloom now and again when the border became a haven for Arizona outlaws. Porfirio Díaz, who dictated in Mexico for 30-odd years, moved to secure the state by settling it. He ran into trouble with the Yaqui Indians who looked on the land as theirs. Don Porfirio rounded up the Yaquis and sent them to Yucatán, about as far away from Sonora as they could be. Surviving Yaquis eventually made their way back. This is an episode most Mexicans overlook when they smugly condemn the way their neighbors to the north treated the American Indians.

For Don Porfirio, developing Sonora was a mistake. From this region came the man who overthrew him. The Mexican Revolution was made by men named Obregón, Calles, de la Huerta, and Rodríguez. Following Díaz's fall, Mexico was ruled for almost a quarter of a century by what historians refer to as the Sonora dynasty.

The revolution brought Sonora prosperity. In much of Mexico, poverty is, in a sense, traditional. The Indian scratching out a living on a corn patch in the central part of the country is living as his ancestors did. He is reluctant to change. But in Sonora, there is little tradition. Most of the inhabitants are new arrivals. They have adopted the most modern farming techniques, irrigated their land, and started feeding the world. After World War II, economists studying Mexico despaired of the country ever being able to feed itself. They particularly deplored the lack of wheat. Today, Sonora grows wheat enough for Mexico and sends a good bit abroad besides.

Highway 2 leads into Sonora from Baja California, crossing the Colorado River and moving from Pacific Time to Mountain Time. The highway hugs the border, and there are a number of crossing points. Interesting is the town of San Luis Colorado, which sprawls along the border fence while on the other side in Arizona there is almost nothing —nothing but a bank and a couple of big supermarkets where the Sonorans used to do their shopping before the peso devaluations.

Nogales, Border Town

The big border town in Sonora is Nogales. Liquor was for a long time the big attraction here. Folks in Phoenix and Tucson would load up the family and head down to the border, Mom, Dad, and the kiddies picking up a gallon each. Now the law has changed. Only a quart per adult can be brought home duty free, and for a time Nogales was suffering a bit. But the border town has rebounded. It still is a fun place to spend a weekend and does a lot of business simply as a port of entry. Winter fruit and vegetables bound for U.S. tables cross the border at Nogales.

Down below Nogales is Magdalena where the grave of Father Kino was recently discovered. He is buried in the San Francisco Church, one of the 110 missions he founded. A million-dollar monument to the memory of this pioneer priest is going up here. From Magdalena a road leads to Cananea, a noted mining center famous (in a Mexican song) for its jail. The 1906 strike by the miners of Cananea was to have a profound effect on the ensuing Revolution. Today, Sonora leads the nation in copper mining, its huge open pits spewing out over half of Mexico's production. Another highway goes off to Puerto Peñasco on the Sea of Cortés where a joint United States-Mexico project is underway to take the salt out of sea water.

Hermosillo (pop. almost ½ million) is the capital of the state, a status it has held on and off since 1831. It is the seat of the state university and benefits from the cultural activities of that institution. The University of Sonora, in turn, has rather strong bonds with the

University of Arizona and Arizona State University, making it anything but parochial in outlook.

The city's name, to those who know a bit of Spanish, sounds as if it means something like "Little Beauty." It doesn't. The name honors José Maria González Hermosillo, one of the leaders in Mexico's War of Independence. Hermosillo was settled in 1742 by Captain Agustín de Vildosola and a contingent of 50 soldiers. They called it Pitic. On the south edge of town, the Plaza of the Three Peoples (*Plaza de los Tres Pueblos*) marks the original settlement.

There is not much left from those bygone days. Hermosillo looks as if it had just been built 20 or 30 years ago. The boulevards are fine, and window shopping is fun. This is a good spot for the horsy set. There is a wide range of leather items for sale, including boots, saddles, and whips.

The local cathedral is attractive only for those who wish to pray. The civic center is spacious and airy, having a variety of architectural styles. Monuments abound to Sonora's famous sons. Among them are Adolfo de la Huerta, who ruled as president in 1920; Alvaro Obregón who followed him; Plutarco Elías Calles, who came next, and finally Abelardo Rodríguez who took over the National Palace four years after Calles left it. "For a while," smile Hermosillo boosters, "we thought our town would be made capital of the republic."

Kino Bay and on South

Some 65 miles west of Hermosillo lies Kino Bay on the shore of the Sea of Cortés. The highway to the coast is excellent and the beaches are magnificent. For many years, Kino Bay was undiscovered except by the RV owners and others who sought the unspoiled and beautiful. A great change has taken place. The area is a convenient distance below Phoenix and Tucson, and a series of fine condominiums have been constructed for the convenience of U.S. owners. As an accompaniment, more and better hotels and motels are going up. Another "last frontier" has disappeared.

An interesting trip from Kino Bay is a run across the narrow channel to Shark Island (Isla Tiburón). This is being developed into one of the finest wildlife and game refuges in North America. Special permits are needed to visit the island, but they are not hard to get. Boatmen usually handle this little chore for their passengers. Only the Seri Indians, for whom Tiburon Island is the traditional turtle fishing grounds, need no special permit.

You might see some of these Indians at Kino Bay selling their fine ironwood carvings of animals. Most of the 750-odd Seris live north of Kino Bay, at Punta Chueca and El Desemboque. Although they have lost much of their traditions, some still hold rituals for a girl's puberty, the capture of a turtle or the finishing of a fine basket. Be warned that Seris ask for money if you take their picture.

Guaymas

Guaymas, (pop. 125,000) a short drive from Hermosillo (and Kino Bay), is a big city, an active port with luxury hotels where visitors come down to get in some serious fishing, spend a wad in a few days, and head home broke but happy.

The port was founded in 1771 and christened San Fernando de Guaymas while a Jesuit mission nearby got the name of San José de Guaymas. This is one of the places where the French had such an impact in the middle of the 19th century. Count Gastón Raousset-Boulbon's adventures in Sonora rival those of William Walker across the gulf in Baja California.

A more recent claim to fame is via the movies. *Catch 22* was filmed here in the Guaymas area. The town also had a role in the early years of the space age. There was a tracking station at nearby Empalme, a town now noted mostly for its stand of cactus.

Guaymas has not one bay, but two: Bacochibampo and San Carlos. San Carlos has the beaches. Bacochibampo is where the boats set out to catch marlin, yellowtail, red snapper, sea bass, and sailfish. In the back country, hunters go after deer, duck, and dove. Higher up in the hills are coyotes and mountain lions. A ferry goes from here to Santa Rosalía in Baja California Sur.

One of the great attractions of Guaymas is simply its beauty. In many of Mexico's ports it can be said the mountains come down to meet the sea, but at Guaymas, the mountains and the desert join with water. The clear air and the rays of sun upon the mountains present panoramas of striking, ever-changing beauty.

Guaymas's sort of off-the-beaten path tranquility will soon come under the heading of "what used to be." Government and private developers have selected this area for intensive tourist development. The beginnings are already under way. Within the next five years quiet Guaymas will attain the status of a major resort. This will include several new, deluxe hotels. Recently completed is a unit of Club Med, its fourth in Mexico (others are at Canucún, Ixtapa, and Playa Careyes, south of Puerto Vallarta), and planned to be the largest.

Already complete is a deluxe clubhouse and an 18-hole golf course. Known as the San Carlos Country Club, the complex has more than a dozen tennis courts with a resident teaching pro, and two swimming pools. The use of a country club and its facilities, as is usual all over Mexico, will be by members only. Hotel guests will be charged admission.

Guaymas Marina, currently the only port in the Sea of Cortés with security dock facilities and electricity, is already engaged in uplifting and expanding its facilities. Fishing boats can be rented for $100–$200 U.S. a day, and smaller outboards for water skiing, fishing, or water-pleasure jaunts.

It is to be hoped that plans for the future will include the provision of some means of adequate public transportation. Guaymas and its beaches are spread out. Up to now the only means of getting around to enjoy all its beauty has been by automobile. The hotels do have car rental agencies. There is an international airport at Guaymas.

South from Guaymas, Highway 15 runs on toward Mazatlán by way of Ciudad Obregón and Navojoa. Obregón is an interesting place that almost might have been lifted out of Kansas and dropped down in Sonora. Ultra-modern with grain elevators, cotton gins, and all other accouterments of the farming industry, Cuidad Obregón even has motels and restaurants that seem to have been imported from the American Midwest.

Alamos is reached by a turnoff from Navojoa. The trip takes less than an hour and is well worth making. Alamos is the most colonial town in Sonora, such a gem of the viceregal era that it has been declared a national monument. A Jesuit mission was founded here in 1630, but the boom started with the discovery of silver in the 1780s. The church dates back to this time, while the mint was built in the 19th century. Take a look at the paintings on the ceiling of the kiosk or bandstand in the plaza in front of the church. At the nearby ghost town of La Aduana, silver ingots were once cast. Alamos's second claim to fame is as the original home of the Mexican jumping bean (caused by a hyperactive larva).

Alamos is reached by a turnoff from Navojoa. The trip takes less than an hour and is well worth making. Alamos is the most colonial town in Sonora, such a gem of the viceregal era that it has been declared a national monument. After World War II, a number of Americans chose Alamos as a place to retire. It is an easy day's drive to the U.S. border, handy to the fishing in Guaymas, and in the midst of some good hunting country. Understandably, the foreign population is growing.

Alamos is a bit like Taxco. While smaller, it is every bit as charming. Silver was found there in the 1680s, but with all the silver in central Mexico, nobody did much about the Sonora mines for nearly a century. Eventually, a town was founded, known officially as El Pueblo Real de la Limpia Concepción de los Alamos. It got its own bishop in 1784, and by 1828 had been declared a full city. For a while it was the capital of the State of the West, as Sonora was once known.

PRACTICAL INFORMATION FOR THE GUAYMAS AREA

HOW TO GET THERE. By Air. The only international flights to Hermosillo and Guaymas are from Tucson, daily. There are direct flights from Guaymas to Guadalajara, La Paz and Tijuana; from Hermosillo to Chihuahua, Ciudad Obregon, Los Mochis, Guadalajara, and Tijuana. Connections to other destinations from these points. All of these flights are either on *Mexicana* or *Aeroméxico. Aerocalifornia* has a direct daily flight from Hermosillo to La Paz. **By Car.** From Tucson, Arizona, via U.S. Highway 19 and Mexico 5; from Tijuana via Mexico 2 through Mexicali and Caborca to Santa Ana, then Highway 15. **By Bus.** Frequent buses from Nogales, Tijuana, and Mexicali. **By Train.** Daily from Nogales and Mexicali.

EMERGENCY TELEPHONE NUMBERS. Hermosillo: police, 40823; Red Cross, 61564; hospital, 21903. **Guaymas:** police, 20030; Red Cross, 20879; hospital, 20122.

HOTELS. In Guaymas and its metropolitan area hotels were authorized, at press time, to charge on the average the following rates for a double room, based on the local economy: *Deluxe,* $56; *First Class,* $37; *Expensive,* $22; *Moderate,* $16; and *Inexpensive,* $9.50. Outside the metropolitan area, rates are a few dollars less in each classification.

Guaymas/San Carlos Bay

First Class

Club Mediterranée at the Playa los Algodones in San Carlos; tel. 60070; with all the facilities and amenities that the Club Med usually implies.

Solimar, San Carlos Country Club, tel. 60231; with 128 A/C units, restaurant, bar, pool, jacuzzi, tennis, golf, sauna, gardens,

Fiesta San Carlos, at San Carlos Bay, tel. 60229; with 33 A/C units, small, very well kept and charming, restaurant, bar, pool, parking.

Nueva Posada San Carlos, at San Carlos Bay, tel. 60015; with 150 A/C units, private beach, restaurant with live mariachi music, bar, terrace bar, pool, parking, gardens, tennis, golf, disco, shops, water sports facilities; located across from the country club with access to its facilities.

Playas de Cortes, two miles off Highway 15 on Bacochibampo Bay, tel. 20121; with 142 A/C units in a well run colonial style building with restaurant, bar, pool, shops, nightclub, parking, car rental, gardens, tennis, water sports facilities.

Motel Armida, on the main highway and Garcia Lopez, just at the entrance to the city, tel. 23050; with 87 A/C rooms, restaurant, bar, pool, disco, jacuzzi, and gardens.

Expensive

Motel Las Playitas, Carretera Varadero Nacional, tel. 22727; with 27 A/C rooms and a trailer park with 120 spaces, pool, beach, boat rental, restaurant, bar, nightclub.

Santa Rita, Calzada García Lopez without number, tel. none, 24 A/C rooms, cafeteria, parking.

Malibu, just out of town on the highway to Hermosillo at km 1983, tel. 22244; with 50 A/C rooms, restaurant, bar, pool, parking.

Alamos

Casa de los Tesoros, Ave. Obregon 10, tel. 80011; with 14 units in a colonial style inn with excellent food and service; small pool, arrangements for horseback riding and hunting, shops, gardens, restaurant, bar, parking; American plan with all meals included; live music daily, Mexican night on Saturdays. *First Class.*

Los Portales, Ave. Juarez 60, on the main plaza, tel. 80111; with 9 rooms; clean, Colonial style. *Moderate.*

Doliza, Madero 72, tel. 80121; with 11 rooms with A/C and 21 trailer spaces, restaurant, bar. *Moderate.*

Motel Somar, Madero 110, tel. 80125; with 7 rooms. *Inexpensive.*

Motel El Viajero, with 10 rooms. *Inexpensive.*

Hermosillo

Holiday Inn, Blvd. Kino, tel. 51112; with 225 A/C units, restaurant, cafeteria, lobby bar, pool, jacuzzi, disco, nightclub, tennis, travel agency, beauty parlor, downtown with its own parking lot. *Deluxe.*

Motel Gandara, Blvd. Kino 1000, tel. 44414; with 116 A/C units, restaurant, bar, pool, gardens, nightclub, travel agency; about two miles north of town. *First Class.*

Valle Grande, Blvd. Kino and Ramon Corral, tel. 44570; with 144 A/C units, restaurant, cafeteria, bar, pool, gardens, travel agency, car rental, beauty parlor, near downtown, parking. *First Class.*

San Alberto, Rosales and Serdan, tel. 21800; with 171 A/C units, restaurant, bar, pool, disco, travel agency, car rental, beauty parlor, gardens. *First Class.*

Motel Autoparador, 2.5 km out of town on the highway to Nogales, no phone; with 29 rooms, restaurant, bar, hydromassage tubs. *First Class.*

Calinda, Rosales and Morelia, tel. 38960; with 111 A/C rooms and restaurant, cafeteria, bar, disco, pool, garden, travel agency. *First Class.*

Bugambilia, Blvd. Kino 712 north of town, tel. 45050; with 109 A/C units, restaurant, pool, garden, car rental. *First Class.*

Motel La Siesta, Blvd. Kino and Carpena, tel. 43989; with 25 A/C rooms, restaurant, bar, parking. *Expensive.*

Motel El Encanto, Blvd. Kino Norte, tel. 44730; with 38 A/C rooms, restaurant, bar, nightclub, pool, gardens, parking. *Expensive.*

Kino, Pino Suarez 151 Sur, tel. 24599; with 114 A/C rooms, restaurant, pool, jacuzzi, steam bath, sauna. *Expensive.*

Niza, Elias Calle 66, downtown, tel. 37196; with 112 A/C rooms, restaurant. *Expensive.*

San Andres, Oaxaca 14, downtown, tel. 20353; with 48 A/C rooms, restaurant. *Expensive.*

America Colonial, on Juárez between Serdan and Chihuahua streets, tel. 22448; with 29 rooms, restaurant, parking. *Moderate.*

Montecarlo, Juárez and Sonora, tel. 20853; with 24 A/C rooms, restaurant, cafeteria, parking. *Moderate.*

Janítzio, Zacatecas #5, tel. 48662; with 40 rooms. *Inexpensive.*

Costa Rica, Blvd. Kino Norte, tel. 46720; with 32 rooms. *Inexpensive.*

Kino Bay

Posada del Mar, Fraccionamiento Bahía de Kino (in Hermosillo, mailing address: P.O. Box 314), tel. 21055 (in Hermosillo, tel. 44193); with 48 A/C units, private beach, restaurant, bar, pool, gardens, parking. *First Class.*

Condominios Mision del Sol, tel. 41180; a condominium owned by Americans and available for rental when the owners are not around; 20 units. *First Class.*

Posada Santa Gema, on the bay, tel. 45576; with 14 A/C bungalows, each with two bedrooms, kitchenettes and overlooking the Sea of Cortes; there is a grocery store on the premises. *First Class.*

Motel Kino Bay, Mar de Cortes and Amelia, tel. 20140; with 24 rooms. *Moderate.*

SPECIAL EVENTS. The following events are without fixed dates: Senorita Sonora beauty contest, Carnaval in Guaymas (floats, dances, cockfights, fireworks). Fiestas de la Vendimia (grapeharvest festival) in June with dances, coronation of the queen, floats. Navy Day on June 1 in Guaymas. In Puerto

Peñasco, sand buggy races in April, October and December, and at the same place, sailboat regattas in March.

HOW TO GET AROUND. By far the easiest way is by automobile, either yours or a rented one; buses are frequent and inexpensive between towns; the train is daily but unreliable and at inconvenient hours. On Tuesdays, Thursdays, and Sundays, there are ferries from Guaymas to Santa Rosalia on the Baja Coast at 10 A.M., taking about 7 hours for the crossing (returning on the same days at 11 P.M.). One way fare for passengers is about $1 for salon class and $2 for tourist class; about $7 for your car.

TOURIST INFORMATION SERVICES. Guaymas: Ave. Serdan between Streets 13 and 14, tel. 21433. **Alamos:** At the Palacio Municipal. **Hermosillo:** Blvd. Kino 1000, tel. 48407 and 47399. All these offices are open 9 A.M. to 2 P.M. and 5 to 7 P.M. daily.

USEFUL ADDRESSES. Airlines. Hermosillo: *Aeroméxico,* Serdan and Rosales (in the Hotel San Alberto) tel. 20928 and 34949; *Mexicana,* Blvd. Abelardo Rodriguez, tel. 43250 and 45350; *Aerocalifornia,* Blvd. Abelardo Rodriguez 24, tel. 26938. Guaymas: Serdan 236, tel. 20123.

Ferry to Santa Rosalia, in Guaymas, tel. 22324 and 23393.

U.S. Consulate. Morelia street in back of the Hotel Calinda, tel. 38925 and 38022, in Hermosillo.

Car rentals. Hermosillo: Autorentas del Pacifico (*Hertz*), Juarez #95, tel. 21830 and 20735; Renta Tur (*Budget*), on the highway to Kino Bay at km 5.5, tel. 43805 and 43033; Rentamovil Internacional (*Avis*), Blvd. Kino and Villareal, tel. 51455. Guaymas: Renta Tur (*Avis*), Calzada Garcia Lopez, tel. 25500; Auto Rental del Pacifico, (*Hertz*), on the main highway at km. 1920, tel. 21000.

ENGLISH LANGUAGE MEDIA. The *Heraldo de San Carlos* and *Sonora Times* are English language newspapers, publishing address: Ramon Corral and Francisco Gonzalez Bocanegra #35 in Hermosillo, tel. 41809 and 44444.

TOURS. There are no local agencies which put together tours within this area. In Guaymas, you can take a yacht tour of the harbor. For more information, contact the tourism office in Guaymas.

SPORTS. Golf: There are three courses in the state of Sonora. San Carlos Country Club at San Carlos Bay, tel. 60231. Club de Golf de Hermosillo at Tamaulipas Final Oriente, tel. 43095. Club de Golf de Ciudad Obregon, just off the main highway at Ciudad Obregon. **Hunting:** Contact Licenciado Javier Artee in Hermosillo at tel. 23239. **Fishing:** For tournaments, contact the tourism office in Guaymas. **Diving:** San Carlos Diving Center, on the main street of San Carlos, mailing address Apartado Postal #655, San Carlos, tel. 60049.

BEACHES. All the main beaches of the state have paved access roads and all the facilities such as hotels and restaurants are at San Carlos and Huatabampito at Guaymas, Puerto Penasco, and Kino Bay. There are miles and miles of secluded beaches all along the Sea of Cortes with difficult access and no facilities.

MUSEUMS. Alamos: *Museo Costumbrista,* open 9 A.M. to 1 P.M. and 3 to 7 P.M.; small entrance fee. **Hermosillo:** *Museo de la Universidad de Sonora,* on Boulevard Luis Encinas and Rosales with pre-Columbian and other exhibits; open Monday-Friday 9 A.M. to 3 P.M.; *Museo Regional,* Dr. Paliza and Comonfort, open Monday-Friday, 9 A.M. to 3 P.M.

SHOPPING. Aside from charro (Mexican cowboy) items in Hermosillo, the best tourist-oriented crafts shops are in San Carlos. *Paul de Mexico,* at the lobby of the Hotel Nueva Posada San Carlos; *Sagitario's Gift Shop,* in front of the entrance to the San Carlos Country Club; *El Pescador Curios Shop* at the Plaza Comercial La Mar; *La Casita* at the Plaza San Carlos; *Bazar* at the Edificio La Marina in San Carlos.

RESTAURANTS. All of the restaurants listed here accept the following credit cards: *American Express, Diners Club, Bancomer, Banamex* and *Carnet.* The cost of a basic meal varies between $15 and $25; alcoholic beverage and tip not included.

HERMOSILLO

Benei of the Holiday Inn on Blvd. Kino Norte, tel. 51112; speciality: prime rib.

Xochimilco, Obregon #5, Villa de Seris, tel. 33484; typical Sonoran dishes.

Jardines Miyako, highway to Kino Bay, km 4.5; excellent Japanese cuisine.

Merendero La Huerto, San Luis Potosi #109, tel. 37887; speciality: seafood.

La Siesta, Blvd. Kino Norte, speciality: fine cuts of beef.

GUAYMAS/SAN CARLOS

Bar L'Club, San Carlos Country Club, San Carlos; international dishes.

El Paradise, Abelardo Rodriguez #20 in Guaymas, tel. 21181; speciality: seafood.

La Roca, restaurant-bar, at San Carlos Bay; seafood.

El Yate, restaurant-bar in San Carlos, tel. 60311; international dishes.

Del Mar, restaurant-bar on Ave. Serdan, no number; international.

NIGHTLIFE. Hermosillo: *Disco Tajji* of the Holiday Inn, open every day from 9 P.M. to 3 A.M. *Bar Ali Baba* at the Plaza Pitic, Blvd. Kino and Roman Yocupicio, open every day 9 to 11 P.M. *Disco Sonovision* of the Hotel San Alberto, open Thursday through Sunday 9 P.M. to 2 A.M. *Bar Cimarron* of the Holiday Inn, open every day. *Bar El Aserradero* of the Hotel Valle Grande. **Guaymas/San Carlos:** *Disco Mar* in the Hotel Nueva Posada San Carlos, open Thursday through Sunday 9 P.M. to 3 A.M. *Bar El Yate,* at the Marina San Carlos, open every night. *Bar Country Club* at the San Carlos Country Club, open every day and night. Bar of the Hotel Playa de Cortes at Bacochibampo Bay, open every night. *Disco Casanova* of the Hotel Armida on Calzada Garcia Lopez, no number, just opened.

BAJA CALIFORNIA

A Peninsula of Paradoxes

by
JIM BUDD

The geography of the place is what boggles the senses. Baja California is longer than the Italian peninsula and nearly as desolate as the moon. It is the richest part of Mexico and the poorest. It is both starkly empty and teeming.

Americans love it. If there are cult movies and cult books, then there must be cult travel destinations. And if there are, Baja California heads the list.

As a playground the rich and famous discovered Baja first. Back in Prohibition days when Hollywood was fresh and new, the movie crowd found what a joy it was to have an international border so close by. Down in Ensenada, Jack Dempsey got involved with a scheme to build a lavish casino, only to see his dreams smashed when the U.S. legalized liquor and Mexico outlawed gambling.

John Steinbeck brought attention to La Paz when he made it the setting for his novel *The Pearl.* Erle Stanley Gardner put aside his typewriter while in Baja to battle the marlin off The Capes back in the 1950s. Dwight Eisenhower became an early fan. Bing Crosby put up some of the money for the first resort hotel in San José del Cabo back when the only way to get there was aboard your own plane.

There are many paradoxes about the American love affair with Baja. During the Mexican War in 1847 the U.S. occupied the peninsula but wanted no part of it once a peace accord was reached. Yet Americans have been lusting after the land ever since. There was a William Walker who invaded La Paz with his private army and decreed himself president of a new republic; the Mexicans saw to it that his administration was brief. In 1910 one Richard Ferris tried something similar, but with Mexico City's approval. He sought to set up a new republic which he would name in honor of Porfirio Diaz, ruler of Mexico for the past 30 years. Revolution brought Diaz down before Ferris got anywhere with his plan.

This gringo fascination with Baja California baffles many Mexicans. A vast and empty peninsula it has, after all, defied mankind for ages.

There are, to be sure, indications of some prehistoric development in these parts. In the rugged mountains that are the backbone of Baja, explorers have come across scores of monumental cave paintings. Hunting scenes many of them are, figures larger than life worked in red, blue, yellow, and black, art of remarkable skill and sensitivity. The paintings are thought to be some 2,000 years old. Who did them no one can say.

Spanish Influence

The first exploring Spaniards arrived to encounter natives remarkable both for their poverty and hostility.

The tale of Spanish penetration into Baja California is a curious one. Within a few years of his conquest of the Aztec Empire, Hernan Cortes dispatched Diego de Becerra to explore what was then believed to be an island west of mainland Mexico. De Becerra ended up being killed by his pilot. Such mutiny might have been a capital offense, but the pilot saw it was quickly forgotten by reporting he had returned from a land where luscious maidens spent their days diving for pearls. Ruling over them, he proclaimed, was a queen of enormous wealth whom he compared to a figure in Spanish fiction of the day, Califia. The legendary Califia gave her name to California.

Cortes was quick to hurry across the sea that now bears his name to learn if the pilot's story was true. Pearls in La Paz he found, but no luscious maidens. Cortes departed the same year he arrived, 1535, leaving behind a settlement at La Paz. Two years later it was abandoned.

The rumors about Califia and her court of beautiful pearl divers, however, lived on. Within the next century and a half any number of Spanish expeditions to Baja were launched. More attempts at settlement were made. All failed.

What the explorers eventually learned is that their island was actually a peninsula about 800 miles long and anywhere from 30 to 150 miles wide. Towering mountains, the tallest being some 10,000 feet high, made it almost impossible to cross. The peninsula was found to possess countless coves and bays, many with excellent harbors. Offshore lay many barren islands, several of them inhabited by colonies of sea lions.

With the exception of its oases, all of Baja California is desert. The Pacific side, especially to the north, is kept cool by ocean breezes and currents, but the land east of the mountains is hellishly hot in the summer. The farther down one goes, the more desert landscape one finds. Joshua trees and barrel cactus dot the countryside. Here grow the ciros which appear to be tree trunks minus branches and leaves. Cardon cactus resembles the saguaro of Arizona. There are vast sandy plains on which Arab horsemen might be at home.

Early Inhabitants

Inhabiting this inhospitable land were sparse tribes calling themselves Kikiwa, Cochimi, Cucapa, and Kumyai, hunters and gatherers —survivors. Many lived in caves. What clothing they wore was made of animal skins.

To save their souls the missionaries came. With great difficulty they established settlements that managed to survive. Padre Eusebio Kino, whose name is revered in Mexico, arrived in 1683, to be followed by Padre Juan Salvatierra who in 1697 built a church that remains in use, the first of the California missions at Loreto. In the decades the followed, 23 missions were established on the peninsula.

Those first missionaries were Jesuits. When the order was expelled from the Spanish Empire in 1768, Franciscans came in to take their place. Junipero Serra was a Franciscan. Landing at Loreto, Serra was unimpressed with what he found. Little more than half the Jesuit missions had proved to be successful. The Indians were anything but pacified. Rather than civilizing them, the Spanish clergy seemed to be killing them with imported European diseases. Serra decided more could be accomplished above the peninsula in the land called Alta (Upper) California.

Independence brought with it a withering of the few missions left in Baja California. They had been an arm of the Spanish church and now all ties with Spain had been severed. Foreign clergymen were deported, mission lands distributed among the few surviving Indians, and the churches converted into parish chapels for which there were no priests. Baja, in effect, became empty again, more empty than when the Spaniards had found it. Little wonder that the U.S. troops who occupied La Paz and Mulege (Loreto had been leveled by a storm and only its church survived) were happy to sail away. Negotiators from Washington could see no point in adding to their conquest this strip which one described as "fit only for cactus and rattlesnakes."

The existence of a new international border was largely ignored for some 20 years. In the 1870s the United States put up a customs station and across the line a few shacks were erected on what, legend has it, was Aunt Jane's Ranch, El Rancho de Tia Juana. The little community was distinguished only by being as far away as anyone in the country could get from Mexico City. It attracted the sort of people who found such distance convenient, as they did in having the American boundary so nearby.

With only some 9,000 people said to be living in the peninsula in the late 19th century, the central government made various efforts to settle Baja California. A group of British pioneers tried near San Quintin and failed. More successful were a group of Russians who arrived in the Guadalupe Valley not far from the border. Mexicali was founded through the efforts of the American-controlled Mexican Land and Colonization Company in 1904. Hordes of Chinese laborers were brought in by the Americans to work on irrigation projects.

Then, in 1910, came the whirlwind of the Mexican Revolution.

The revolution was followed by Prohibition in the U.S. The border area was all but taken over by Americans, Americans who would have fought any attempt at annexation as hard as any Mexican. Repeal was a disaster for the Mexican border towns, but within a decade the U.S. was caught up in World War II. As thousands of recruits swarmed into San Diego, Tijuana blossomed into Sin City, the wickedest town in the Western Hemisphere. In TJ as in the boot camps boys were turned into men.

Of more concern to both Washington and Mexico City was the perceived threat of a Japanese invasion. Worry was that Tokyo might land troops in Baja and head north. Some Americans urged a military occupation. That, of course, never occurred, but Mexico became suddenly convinced of the need to integrate the peninsula with the rest of the country.

The process has been long, slow, and sometimes paradoxical. To make Baja more Mexican it has been allowed in many ways to be less Mexican. The peninsula is a duty free area beyond the pale of Mexican customs (there are some exceptions). This exemption applies all along the border but in Baja it covers two entire states. The federal sales tax is only 6% in Baja; elsewhere (except in border areas) it is 15%. Dollars circulate as freely as pesos in much of the peninsula, although devaluation has had an effect in this respect.

Large federal investments in dams and irrigation systems have made the Mexicali Valley one of the most prosperous farming regions in the country (foreign land holdings have been expropriated). Tender are the grapes grown in the Guadalupe and Califia regions which produce some of Mexico's finest wines. Ensenada has grown into one of Mexico's largest Pacific coast seaports. Tijuana, no longer a sin town, is still heavily dependent on tourism, but it is a growing industrial center as well; here assembly plants turn out quantities of manufactured goods for the American market.

Northern Baja became a state in 1952. The south was to remain a federal territory for 22 more years. During that time seagoing ferries began making regular overnight trips between peninsula ports and the mainland while jets started zipping into La Paz from all over Mexico and the U.S. as well. It was the completion of the 1,061-mile long Transpeninsular Highway, however, that led Southern Baja into statehood.

Tourism is by far Southern Baja's largest industry. There are, to be sure, lush farming areas where the occasional river flows or man has made the desert bloom. Mineral exploitation is beginning to pick up.

Oil and gas fields have been discovered and await development. But tourism is where the action is.

Once tourism meant gamefishing. Off Southern Baja marlin weigh in at half a ton, snook grow nearly as long as a man is tall and a grouper can top 200 pounds. In an average year 40,000 billfish are hooked. Yet these days that is but part of the fun. Hunting is catching on. Duck, goose, and white wing dove winter in Baja. Quail are a favorite target. Then there is tennis and soon there will be golf. Plus all the joys of the seashore.

Fonatur, the Mexican government agency charged with creating new resorts (it gave the world Cancun), is busy putting the finishing touches on projects at Loreto as well as in Cabo San Lucas and San José del Cabo, the two resort towns at the tip of the peninsula coming to be known simply as Los Cabos—the Capes. New hotels have opened and others are being planned as more tennis courts are laid out and land cleared for golf links.

Travelers not pleased with all this progress will find La Paz—another vacation favorite—little changed. La Paz has many fabled seaside resorts. Finally the smaller places, such as Mulege, are much as they were a decade or two ago. They probably will remain that way through the passing of the millennium. Baja remains mostly empty. There may be a highway now, but the off-roaders still come roaring in aboard their four-wheel drives and the annual 1,000-mile race remains a big event. Dune buggy freaks claim there is no better place to test their balloon-tired machines than the miles of empty sand around San Felipe, up where the Sea of Cortes begins. Worrywarts voice concern that tourists will ruin Baja California. Change it no doubt they will, but even that will take some time. For the moment this vast desert peninsula seems able to absorb all who come to visit, and to provide every vacationer with just the right type of holiday.

EXPLORING BAJA CALIFORNIA

One comes first perhaps out of curiosity. Southern Californians grew up near the border and can take it for granted, but for others there is the fascination of seeing another country on the other side. "So Near and Yet So Foreign," read the slogans, which are accurate for once. The Mexican-American frontier is the only place in the world where the First World and the Third World physically meet.

The first trip may be but a glimpse of a few hours; next time there will be a longer stay. There will be an excursion into the interior to see something of "the real Mexico." Then will come a flight to one of Baja California's fabled seaside resorts, then another. Finally there may be the long, sometimes lonely, always fascinating drive down Mexico 1, the Transpeninsular Highway, to its end. That can become an annual pilgrimage. Baja does that to people.

The border towns—Tijuana, Tecate, and Mexicali—are about as different from each other as three cities can be. Crossing formalities are all but nonexistent. Mexican customs normally wave cars through

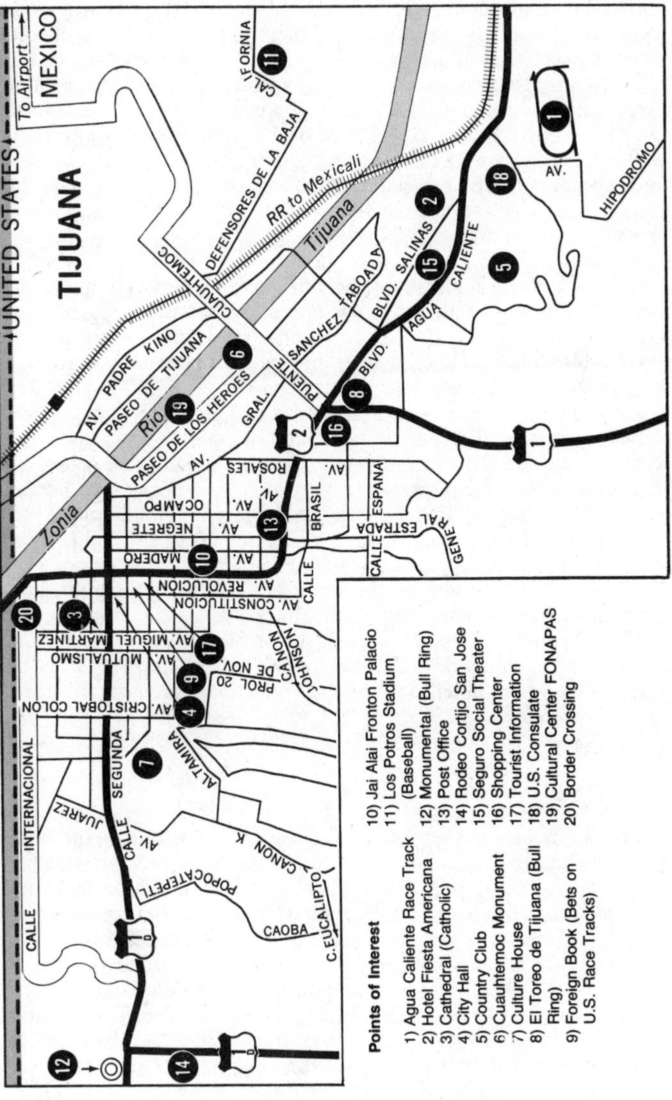

Points of Interest

1) Agua Caliente Race Track
2) Hotel Fiesta Americana
3) Cathedral (Catholic)
4) City Hall
5) Country Club
6) Cuauhtemoc Monument
7) Culture House
8) El Toreo de Tijuana (Bull Ring)
9) Foreign Book (Bets on U.S. Race Tracks)
10) Jai Alai Fronton Palacio
11) Los Potros Stadium (Baseball)
12) Monumental (Bull Ring)
13) Post Office
14) Rodeo Cortijo San Jose
15) Seguro Social Theater
16) Shopping Center
17) Tourist Information
18) U.S. Consulate
19) Cultural Center FONAPAS
20) Border Crossing

without even an inquisitive peer inside. Pedestrians simply stroll through the gate. Going back can be a shade more complicated since U.S. authorities may demand to see some proof of citizenship and may want to know what purchases visitors are bringing home. Mexico's border communities are pretty much open cities. Beyond them—quite a way beyond in the case of Baja—there are secondary checkpoints where inspection is more strict.

Tijuana is visited by more Americans than any other foreign city on earth. Those planning a short stay may prefer to leave their cars in San Diego and hop a bus, or park in one of the many lots on the U.S. side, walk across and grab a taxi; they can get back quicker that way, since autos heading north are often caught in jam-ups at the inspection station (buses get to use a special lane). This is the busiest border crossing in the world.

The heart of Tijuana is about a mile from the border gate. Avenida Revolución is the main street, an attractive if touristy boulevard of shops, restaurants, and bars, some appealing, some not. Carried over from the old days are the three or four strip joints that never close, along with Caesar's Hotel, where, they will tell you, Alex Cardini, an Italian immigrant, concocted the original Caesar salad.

Shopping, not sin, is what brings most people to Tijuana now. Perfumes, cosmetics, designer fashions, and bric-a-brac from the Orient tempt as does an array of wonderful Mexican handicrafts. Along with the shops on Revolución there are more at an American-style shopping mall in the attractive Rio Tijuana development.

In addition to shopping there is marvelous Mexican food to enjoy. Plus the races at the Agua Caliente track and the jai alai games where the betting is wild right on Revolución. There are bullfights almost every Sunday afternoon during the winter.

There is golf and tennis to be played at the Tijuana Country Club and on warm, sunny days the nearby beaches beckon. As far as that goes, all the better hotels have pools. These hotels are not only attractive, but attractively priced.

Teeming Tijuana

The seamy side is there, too, in Tijuana. This is one of the fastest growing cities in Mexico and local authorities have been having a hard time trying to keep up. Much of the place has a honky-tonk look to it with its cheap auto body and car upholstery shops, its curio stands, its crudely painted signs and its slums. Hundreds of Mexicans arrive here from the interior every week, for wage scales are higher along the border than anywhere else in the country and Northern Baja California is Mexico's richest state in terms of personal income. The dream of many of the new arrivals, of course, is to make it across the other side of the border. The boundary fence runs right beside the road to the beach and here and there it is punched through with man-size holes.

Mexico has attempted to stem this illegal traffic by promoting the establishment of assembly plants in its northern cities. Many American manufacturers are taking advantage of lower wage scales in Mexico by carrying out labor intensive operations south of the border. This provides badly needed jobs. Tijuana in particular has benefited from this program and is becoming an industrial city as well as a playground for tourists.

The Rio Tijuana development is the most visible sign of the city's progress. The Tijuana River is one of those streams that flow intermittently. In the bad old days it sometimes would overflow its banks, but most of the time it was a trickle. Squatters were known to settle in the periodically dry bed, with disastrous results when the rains came. Now the river has been given a concrete channel and its banks are landscaped. Handsome public buildings, including the Tijuana Cultural Center, have gone up in the park-like area, along with office complexes and a modern shopping mall.

Tecate, Typical Town

Some 25 miles to the east is Tecate, an entirely different sort of community. Tecate is a typical Mexican small town that just happens to be on the border. Indeed so incidental is the border to local life that the gates are closed from midnight until 7 A.M. Aside from customs and an immigration post, a gas station, and one or two stores, there is nothing on the American side save California 188 which runs to San Diego.

Some 50,000 people live in and around Tecate, yet the town is known throughout Mexico for the beer that bears its name. The brewery is the one big industry. Farming is good around here, especially in the valleys of Guadalupe and Califia which boast some of Mexico's lushest vineyards.

Once this was an area of Russian settlers. They arrived nearly a century ago and had much to do with getting farming started in these parts. As the years passed the immigrants were absorbed and there is little Russian in the neighborhood now.

Tecate's main claim to fame is Rancho La Puerta, a fitness resort catering to well-heeled Americans. The town also attracts residents of San Diego who often drive down for a day to sample the foreign flavor, dine on Mexican fare at one of the many local restaurants, and then poke about the shops.

Mexicali, Northern Capital

Mexicali, 90 miles east of Tecate, is the capital of Northern Baja California and a city almost as large as Tijuana. There the resemblance ends. Little that is honky-tonk is to be found in big, proud Mexicali, market town for what is the Mexican side of the Imperial Valley.

The border cuts right through the heart of Mexicali and neighboring, much smaller Calexico. One can stroll from the commercial center of one city right into the commercial center of its neighbor.

The better hotels, however, are a taxi ride away. Mexicali is growing southward, spreading out. There is now a neighborhood known as Nuevo Mexicali—New Mexicali—centered around the Centro Civico or Civic Center. In some ways this is similar to the Rio Tijuana development. Here are to be found the offices of the state government—

Mexicali is the capital of Northern Baja—as well as an attractive shopping mall.

A surprise to many visitors is the number of Chinese restaurants in Mexicali, and they are quite good. They city actually holds a Chinese food fair every March. All this is the result of private American efforts to develop agriculture in the Mexicali Valley around the turn of the century. The U.S. firm involved brought in hundreds of Chinese laborers to dig the irrigation ditches; many of their descendents now run restaurants, not only in Mexicali but in Tecate and Tijuana as well.

Mexicali is at its best during the winter months for it can get brutally hot during the summer. Winter sees large numbers of snow bunnies—refugees from colder climes who head for Arizona when the temperatures start to fall—coming over for a visit to Mexicali. Many simply stroll along Calle Melgar, browsing in the curio shops and then trying out one of the many Chinese restaurants. Others play a round of golf at the country club and perhaps arrange to stay on over the weekend to take in a Sunday bullfight. Mexicali has some good hotels and their rates are quite reasonable.

The border here also is the point of entry for the boat and trailer set bound for San Felipe 125 miles to the south.

San Felipe, a fishing village of some 5,000 souls, is a favorite playground for Californians, a good many of whom drive down in RVs or come hauling a trailer behind them. Those who prefer hotels will find a couple that are quite good and a few more that are at least clean and comfortable. Reservations are a good idea on weekends and virtually essential over winter holidays. Summer can be blistering.

The little town of sandy streets and humble homes nestles beneath a 1,000 foot high headland that shelters the open bay. The hotels, trailer camps, cafes, bars and curio shops are along the waterfront boulevard, Avenida Mar de Cortes. As is the case with many towns in Baja, the streets all have names but no signs to indicate what they are.

Sportfishing long has been the big appeal here. Seabass and yellowtail are favorite catches, but they are found mostly in the winter and spring. In summer the waters become too warm for many species.

In recent years San Felipe has been attracting the dune buggy and motorcycle set, much to the dismay of old hands who preferred the town when it was not so boisterous. On weekends San Felipe can become pretty wild.

Ensenada, Major Port

Ensenada, across the peninsula on the Pacific side, is only some 60 miles south of Tijuana, reached by a good toll road. It also can be reached from San Felipe via Mexico 5. It attracts a more subdued crowd, although Hussong's, an old fashioned waterfront cantina, gets explosive at times. These days, however, the revelers are likely to be American college kids.

The climate is good throughout the year in Ensenada—better, if anything, in the summer when the sea breezes keep it from getting too hot. This is very much a tourist town and has been since the days of Prohibition when Dempsey and his friends got together to build a

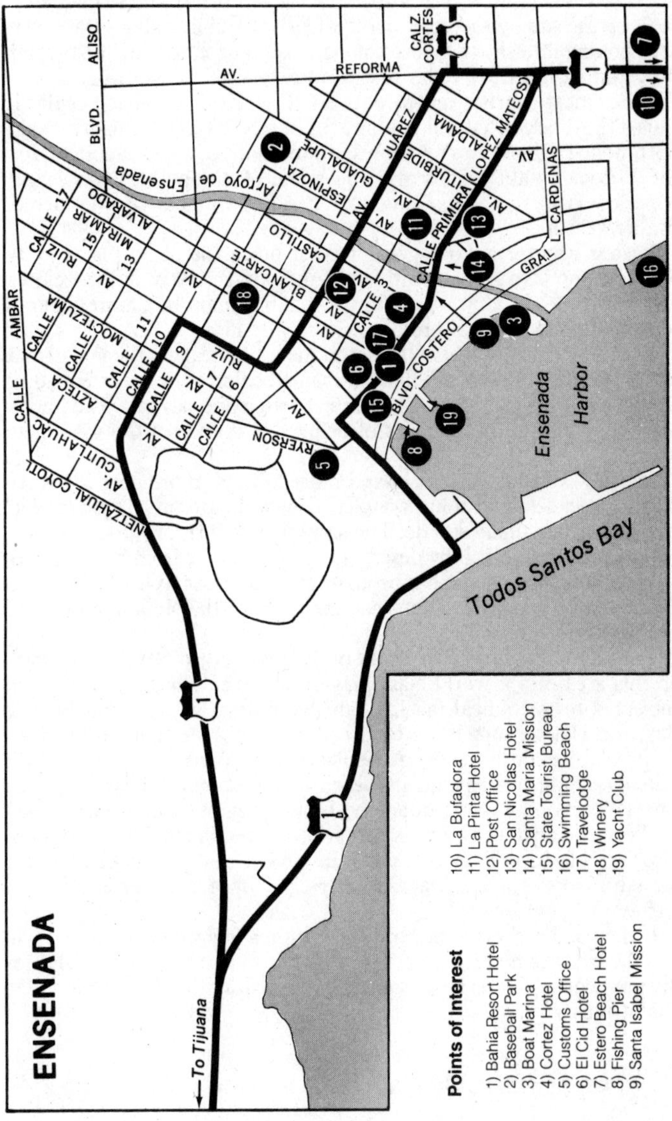
ENSENADA
To Tijuana
Todos Santos Bay
Ensenada Harbor
Arroyo de Ensenada
BLVD. ALISO
AV. REFORMA
CALZ. CORTES
AV. JUAREZ
AV. ESPINOZA
AV. GUADALUPE
AV. ITURBIDE
AV. ALDAMA
CALLE PRIMERA (LOPEZ MATEOS)
GRAL. L. CARDENAS
AV. CASTILLO
AV. BLANCARTE
CALLE 3
AV. RUIZ
AV. ALVARADO
AV. MIRAMAR
CALLE 17
CALLE 15
CALLE 13
CALLE 11
CALLE 10
CALLE 9
CALLE 7
CALLE 6
CALLE AMBAR
CALLE MOCTEZUMA
CALLE AZTECA
AV. CUITLAHUAC
NETZAHUAL COYOTL
AV. RYERSON
BLVD. COSTERO
Points of Interest
1) Bahia Resort Hotel
2) Baseball Park
3) Boat Marina
4) Cortez Hotel
5) Customs Office
6) El Cid Hotel
7) Estero Beach Hotel
8) Fishing Pier
9) Santa Isabel Mission
10) La Bufadora
11) La Pinta Hotel
12) Post Office
13) San Nicolas Hotel
14) Santa Maria Mission
15) State Tourist Bureau
16) Swimming Beach
17) Travelodge
18) Winery
19) Yacht Club

casino by the sea. With gambling no longer legal, the casino has become a convention center of sorts.

The hotels here are located along the waterfront avenue, Lopez Mateos. There is no beach up this way, although there are some nice ones just north and south of town. Most visitors are quite content to soak up the sun by the hotel pools when not ambling about the tourist area poking into shops. Sportsfishing is good here, too, with Ensenada proclaiming itself to be the yellowtail capital of the world.

What most tourists fail to notice is how large Ensenada really is. Baja's third largest city, it is home for nearly 200,000. This is a major port, point of departure for scores of thousands of bales of cotton from the Mexicali Valley. It is also the home of one of Mexico's largest wineries. And, not surprisingly, it has any number of commercial fishing ventures.

Easiest way for anyone going farther down the peninsula is to fly. Shortest hop is to Loreto, still far off in Southern Baja, but the closest jetset resort to the U.S. Resort-in-the-making might be a more accurate term, for much about Loreto is what it promises to be.

This dusty hamlet where the desert meets the sea was the first capital of California, a California that in Spanish colonial times extended up from The Capes all the way to San Francisco and beyond. The imposing parish church here boasts of being the mother of the west coast missions.

Marlin, sailfish, roosterfish, and more have been bringing in sportsmen for decades. The pioneer anglers flew in aboard private planes and, as far as it goes, many still do. The first hotels were more along the lines of fishing camps, plush by desert standards, but far from being luxurious. Although Mexico 1 has brought the motor car to Loreto and this hamlet of 5,000 boasts an international airport, the old hotels are little changed.

The international airport is part of the government program to develop this area into a world class playground. The village itself is to be subjected to no radical facelift, but five miles away, around Nopolo Bay, the 21st century has established a beachhead. Here is the Hotel El Presidente, posh as any Acapulco resort, Windsurfers and Hobie Cats splashing out beyond its beach, bikinied maidens sipping margaritas by its pool. Next door, the Loreto Tennis Center where John McEnroe is the touring pro, is perhaps the finest facility in the country. Not far beyond is Puerto Escondido, now a campers' delight, slated soon to become a leading marina ringed by a Mediterranean-style village.

If the planners' plans materialize, within a few years fine hotels will line the beaches here, interspersed with shops and restaurants. But for the moment Loreto is an escapists' haven, with other hotels more like quaint inns.

La Paz, Southern Capital

La Paz, the capital of Southern Baja, has had an airport for sometime. Hence when the superrich were flying to their hideaway fishing camps aboard private craft, the merely comfortably well off sportsmen

Mexican National Tourist Council

Interior of the cathedral in the capital city reflects the role of religion in daily life.

Mexican National Tourist Council

Both tianguis (native markets) and fishermen are the essence of exotic Mexico.

Mexican National Tourist Council

The allure of Acapulco is evident in this twilight scene of the world-famous resort.

Mexican National Tourist Council

Fiestas and sculptured deities play equal roles in Mexico's cultural heritage.

Mexican National Tourist Council

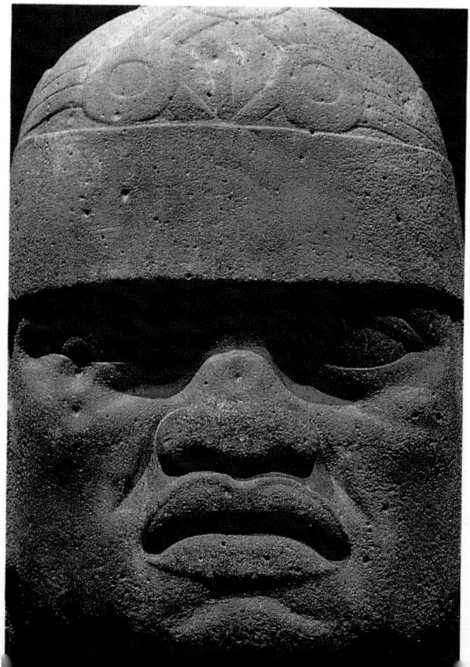

came down aboard commercial craft in order to go out after billfish. As a resort La Paz maintains the flavor of a place that attracts those who holiday on a budget.

But La Paz is not primarily a resort. It is more a political and commercial center, although in no way can it be called bustling. The atmosphere is more that of a colonial city; La Paz seems to be some outpost of empire. There is a sidewalk cafe on its waterfront avenue, and a jumble of shops stocked with duty free merchandise, as if this were a port of call for cruise ships.

Outpost of empire for years is what La Paz was. It is, in many ways, a monument to tenacity. For three centuries, starting with Cortes, the Spaniards made repeated attempts to settle by this lovely bay. They tried and tried again, oyster beds rich in pearls drawing them back after every failure. Only after Mexico declared independence did La Paz become a permanent community. A U.S. occupation force held the port during the Mexican-American War. A few years later William Walker of Tennessee arrived with a private army and declared himself president of a newly decreed republic. His administration was brief, but to hear some folk talk, that was the last exciting thing that happened in La Paz.

The resort hotels of La Paz are out of town a ways on the beach. They are pleasant establishments, all fairly new. Deepsea fishing remains the big attraction.

In Los Cabos, down at the tip of the peninsula, fishing is but one of many ways to have a grand time.

Fishing, to be sure, put the area on most travel maps. Calm seas and sheltered bays make this one of the finest places in the world to go out after the big ones. The mouth of the Sea of Cortes is said to be a natural fish trap swirling with battling monsters of the deep. For those who had the cash, no price was too high to pay for a chance to hook one of these brutes. The finest hotels in the area were built before there was any commercial airport. Guests flew in aboard their own planes. Some sailed down in their yachts.

Baja Capes

But the Baja Capes are beginning to be discovered by others as well. At few places anywhere is the seascape so dramatic as here where craggy rock arches carved by nature mark land's end. There is a special blueness to the water where gulf and ocean meet, and a dry crispness to the air in a world where only cactus grows. A wonderful day can be spent simply sitting on the sands and watching the whales at play.

Cabo San Lucas, Mile One (or, more correctly, Kilometer One) on Mexico 1, is the most exclusive resort area in all of Baja. No longer is it strictly a millionaire's sandbox now that the 727s and DC9s flutter in from everywhere, but there is a feeling of money to the place. Thatched-roof restaurants serve up lobster dinners and romantic trios serenade the hungry. Hotels range from first class to super deluxe so that travelers watching their pesos may need to seek some other town in which to stay. Trailer grounds are parking lots for RVs that qualify as palaces on wheels.

Before the highway and the DC9s, Cabo San Lucas was little more than a pair of dusty streets and a general store. When two cafes opened more or less next to each other, the neighborhood came to be known as restaurant row. None of the hotels has been built within walking distance of another.

Still, what scarcely ranked as a hamlet has grown into a little town. Cruise ships—during the winter several put in each week—have wrought quite a change. Shops, many of them most attractive, have opened up here and there, and visitors now will find quite a good selection of restaurants. Fonatur, the federal agency so busy up in Loreto, has been revamping what it calls the urban infrastructure in San Lucas, and constructing a large yacht marina in the harbor.

Fonatur's big project in these parts, however, is 20 miles away in San José del Cabo. Three hotels already have opened up on the beach at San José, and more are sure to follow. By the time these words see print the first nine holes of the golf course behind the beach should be ready for play and the commercial center fully operational. Already there is a good choice of restaurants in San José and the night life equals that in San Lucas.

The resort development is a few miles outside San José proper. A town of 15,000, this is the only community of any size south of La Paz, rather attractive, although there really is not very much to see. Both the big airlines have ticket offices in San José del Cabo, there are a couple of banks and this is one place to catch a bus bound for Tijuana.

Vacationers who stick to the border country or fly down to any of the big resort areas need not worry about currency or language problems. English is pretty well understood everywhere and dollars accepted as readily as pesos.

For those heading far down the peninsula by road it is another story. Language should be no problem, but it should be kept in mind that not every hash slinger or gas pump jockey will be fluent in English. And dollars will not be welcomed everywhere.

Best idea where money is concerned is to carry a wad of traveler's checks, cashing them in for pesos as the need occurs. Banks offer the best rate, but in a pinch any hotel will change these checks (they make a profit on the transaction). Credit cards will not be accepted everywhere; in the more remote areas there is no way of checking to see if they are valid.

While hundreds of Americans drive the length of Baja every week without incident, wise motorists prepare for the trip as if they were going on safari. (See *Practical Information* section.)

Mexican automobile insurance should be considered obligatory and night driving ruled out (eight out of ten highway accidents in Baja occur after dark). Advance hotel reservations are an excellent idea.

Bus travel is less complicated, but many of the same rules apply. Fares are cheap, about a dollar per hour for the entire 23-hour trip from Tijuana to Los Cabos. The vehicles themselves are not bad although leg room aboard is limited. Frustrating, however, is showing up at the bus station with no certainty any seats will be available. And it may be difficult to locate anyone who speaks English.

First Day's Trip

The first day's trip no doubt will be from Tijuana to San Quintin, a jaunt of about five hours. The toll road from the border to Ensenada, with four lanes, is about on a par with a California freeway. Beyond Ensenada it is two-lane blacktop all the way. Just below Ensenada is the immigration checkpoint where tourist cards must be stamped.

The road here hugs the Pacific side of the peninsula, cutting through the vineyards of Santo Tomás where much of Mexico's finest wine gets its start. Farther on the first stretch of desert begins, cattle country that fades into tomato farms.

San Quintin, with a hotel and three motels, is a beach area well worth at least a couple of nights stay. The bay is lovely and the fishing excellent here. Casting from the shore is popular. During the winter goose hunting is a favorite sport. San Quintin gots its start in the late 1800s when the Mexican government brought a band of British settlers in to colonize the area. Drought undid them and about the only monument to the effort is the lonely English cemetery by the bay.

The trip from San Quintin to Guerrero Negro can take seven hours and an early start is in order. After about 50 miles along the coast the highway turns inland, heading down the desolate center of the peninsula. This is the Baja of the picture books, ciro trees and cardon cactus, dramatic, rugged hills, and vast expanses of blue sky. Santa Ines, about three hours from San Quintin, or Punta Prieta, two hours farther on, are about the only places to stop for a bite to eat.

Guerrero Negro, back on the Pacific, lies just below the 28th parallel, the state line where Northern and Southern Baja meet. Cross the line and switch from Pacific Time to Mountain Time. Marking the spot is a monumental steel eagle, its wings towering 120 feet into the sky. The monument was unveiled to commemorate the completion of the Transpeninsular Highway.

Salt and whales are Guerrero Negro's claim to fame. A company town now controlled by a Japanese-Mexican consortium, Guerrero Negro is the world's largest producer of ocean salt, turning out 20,000 tons a day. Nature does most of the work as the ocean floods into hundreds of evaporating ponds, each one the size of a football field. The seagates are closed and sun and wind do the rest. Left behind is a residue of hard white salt of remarkable purity. Giant shovels scoop the salt into mammoth trucks which dump it into barges. The harbor being shallow here, the barges are hauled out to Cedros Island where their cargo is loaded on freighters for shipment to points around the world.

Where Whales Wallow

Gray Whale National Park is about 20 miles from Guerrero Negro, but since most of the road is unpaved it will take about an hour to get there. From November into March it is well worth the trip, for the park is on the shore of Scammon's Lagoon where the gray whales breed. The animals migrate in each winter from the frigid waters off Alaska, frolic all along Baja's shores down to The Capes, but it is at Scammon's they really get together. This Mexican lagoon is named for an American whaler, a Captain Charles Scammon, who discovered the place in the 19th century and made it his private treasure chest. Eventually his colleagues followed him to the spot and the years of slaughter that followed nearly wiped out the species. Such carnage has now been outlawed and Mexico protects the whales in Scammon's Lagoon to the point where no boats are allowed. The happy creatures, however, can be seen quite well from the shore and a spectacular sight it is.

There is a good hotel and a couple of passable motels in Guerrero Negro as well as several places to eat.

From Guerrero Negro the highway begins a leisurely cut across the peninsula to the shores of the Sea of Cortes. It is about a two-hour drive to San Ignacio, four hours to Santa Rosalia, five hours to Mulege, seven to Loreto. Mulege or Loreto are the best choices as places to spend the night.

San Ignacio, as far as it goes, has a very nice hotel. The community is a true oasis in the desert, surrounded by acres of date trees as oasis towns are supposed to be. Spanish missionaries brought the dates and built the parish church, now two centuries old.

Mexico 1 hits the Sea of Cortes at Santa Rosalia, a century-old French mining town that looks a trifle foreign and out of date. Here is to be found a prefabricated iron church designed by Gustav Eiffel, he who built the famous tower. Like the tower, the church was created for the Paris World's Fair in 1898, the church then being bought by the mining company, crated up and shipped around the Horn. It is one of the world's first prefabricated buildings. While the French departed in the 1950s, they left behind some well-trained cooks. Santa Rosalia is an excellent place to stop for lunch.

Mulege is another oasis community, this one by the sea, the lush green of its vegetation and the blue beyond the shore contrasting sharply with the barren desert hills. One of the spots long favored by fly-in sports fisherman, Mulege has half a dozen small but quite charming inns. It can be a delightful place to linger for a day or two. Big tourist attractions are the Jesuit mission, completed in 1766 and recently restored, and the old territorial prison which still occasionally is used as a jail. For the adventurous, Mulege can be the departure point for expeditions into the hills to see the ancient cave paintings. There are literally hundreds of sites, most of them inaccessible in the extreme, but a few that can be reached by the hearty will to ride a mule. The local hotels can arrange for guides and transportation.

It is a seven-hour drive from Mulege to La Paz. Here once again the highway turns inland to hit Villa Insurgentes and Ciudad Constitución in the midsection of the peninsula. Both are modern farming communities, using well water to irrigate the rich, fertile land of the surrounding Magdalena Valley. The cotton fields in these parts, like the date groves around San Ignacio and Mulege, show how productive Baja's lands could be if only water were more plentiful.

La Paz and Cabo San Lucas, a three-hour drive farther on, are connected to the mainland by ferries, as is Santa Rosalia. That allows for an alternative route when heading back. These seagoing vessels serve a great number of tourists, but they are really in business to carry trucks and commercial cargo. Passenger accommodations are adequate but far from luxurious. It is well to inquire locally about ferry service, make reservations early and be prepared to tip generously to make certain that they are honored.

PRACTICAL INFORMATION FOR BAJA CALIFORNIA

HOW TO GET THERE. Boat and plane, car and train (the latter being the San Diego trolley) all lead into the Baja California peninsula. Best means of transportation depends on how far one wants to go, plus how much time and how much money one has to spend. Overall, Baja is one of the easiest places anywhere in Mexico to visit from the U.S.

By Car. U.S. Interstate 5 hits the border just south of San Diego at Tijuana, becoming Mexico 1, which is the one road that runs the length of the peninsula down to its tip. California 94 crosses at Tecate where Mexico 2 runs west to Tijuana and east to Mexicali. California 111 ends at the border where Calexico becomes Mexicali and Mexico 5 begins, running 125 miles down the east coast of the peninsula to San Felipe; there the pavement ends. About 20 miles above San Felipe is a junction with Mexico 3 which runs northwest up to Ensenada. Visitors in this area will not need tourist cards but motorists should carry Mexican car insurance which may be purchased at border points. Ten miles south of Ensenada is a check point beyond which tourist cards are required.

Baja's highways are quite good by Mexican standards, although, with the exception of the Tijuana-Ensenada Turnpike, American drivers find them narrow and shoulderless. Reassuring is the fact that many trailers and RVs are driven the entire 1,000-mile length of Mexico 1. The highways are patrolled by the Green Angels which provide mechanical assistance if needed. Vehicles should, nevertheless, be in top condition before venturing far into Baja and drivers should carry spare belts, fuses, and hoses. Nighttime travel should be avoided, both because of the danger of cattle on the road and the discomfort of being stranded until dawn should a breakdown occur.

By Train. The *San Diego Trolley* leaves the Santa Fe Depot every 15 minutes during the day (every 30 minutes after 7:30 P.M.) and passes through National City and Chula Vista, stopping directly at the border. On the Mexican side taxis are available for the one-mile trip to downtown Tijuana or to the airport or intercity bus station. The trolley trip takes about an hour.

By Plane. At press time only *Aeromexico* and *Mexicana Airlines* were flying into Baja California airports from U.S. gateways. Often promotional fares are available. At times, depending on the peso dollar parity, considerable savings may be made by flying into the peninsula from Tijuana.

Los Cabos: *Aeromexico* flies in twice a day from Los Angeles, once a day (except Tuesdays) from Tijuana, and three times a week from Houston via Loreto. *Mexicana* has daily flights from San Francisco and Denver. *Aero California,* a regional carrier, operates a daily flight from La Paz.

Loreto: *Aeromexico* flies in daily from Los Angeles and operates three weekly flights from Houston and from Tijuana.

La Paz: *Aeromexico* flies in daily from Los Angeles and Tucson and operates three flights weekly from Houston. *Aeromexico* also has two daily flights from Tijuana, and *Mexicana* has one. *Aero California* has a daily flight from Los Cabos.

Tijuana: *Aeromexico* flies in three times daily from Los Angeles.

By Bus. Greyhound serves Tijuana from Los Angeles and San Diego several times a day. *Mexicoach* (tel. 619/232 5049) has seven departures daily from the San Diego Amtrak depot, stopping both at the Tijuana airport and downtown.

Intercity bus travel in Mexico tends to be confusing for foreigners, but Baja California—where more English is spoken—is an exception. Reserved seats may be purchased the day prior to departure, but only at the bus station. Frequent service is available to all parts of the peninsula reached by highway and fares are quite low. *Autotransportes de Baja California* links Mexicali with San Felipe, Ensenada and Tijuana, while *Tres Estrellas de Oro* serves points along Mexico 1 from Tijuana to Cabo San Lucas.

Tijuana. Central Bus Station, Lazaro Cardenas at Rio Alamar; 86–9515.

Mexicali. Central Bus Station, Centro Civico en Nueva Mexicali, Avenida Independencia; 7–2451.

San Felipe. *Autotransportes de Baja California,* Avenida Mar de Cortes; 7–1039.

Tecate. Avenida Benito Juarez and Calle Abelardo Rodriguez; 4–1221.

Ensenada. Avenida Riveroll between Calles 10 and 11; 8–2322.

La Paz. Gomez Farias at Santos Degollado; 2–5231.

Cabo San Lucas. Zaragoza near Diezyseis de Septiembre; 3–0400.

By Ship. Ensenada is a port of call throughout the year for Western Cruise Lines' *Azure Seas* which sails from Los Angeles twice each week, and for Crown Cruise Line's *Viking Princess* which makes a one day cruise from San Diego several times each week.

Cabo San Lucas is visited once a week throughout the year by Carnival Cruise Lines' *Tropicale* and from November through March by Sitmar Cruises' *Fairsea* and *Fairsky* and January through March by Princess Cruises' vessels. Sundance Cruises' *Stardancer* has weekly sailings during the winter. The *Coromuel,* a ferry, makes overnight sailings between Cabo San Lucas and Puerto Vallarta twice weekly.

La Paz is linked to Mazatlan by ferries making overnight sailings six days a week. Sleeping accommodations are available on the ferries at low fares but there is a little luxury aboard. Tickets must be purchased at the ferry terminal on the day of departure.

EMERGENCY TELEPHONE NUMBERS. To call border cities from the U.S. use these area codes: Tijuana 7066; Mexicali 90376; Tecate 70665; Ensenada 70667. Access number elsewhere is 01152 plus the local area code. Within Mexico long distance access is 91 followed by the area code. Area code for Tijuana is 66, for Mexicali 656, Tecate 665, Ensenada 667, Loreto 683, La Paz 682, Cabo San Lucas and San José del Cabo 684.

U.S. telephones may be reached by dialing 95 and the area code. It is much less expensive, however, to call collect; the English-speaking international operator may be reached by dialing 09; domestic calls may be placed by dialing 91 and the area code or through the long distance operator (who probably speaks no English) at 02. Only local calls may be dialed directly from hotels.

Emergencies are best handled through hotels or local tourist offices where English-speaking assistance is available. The U.S. consulate may be of some help where legal problems arise. While phone numbers for police and hospitals are given here, it should be realized that only Spanish-speaking personnel may be on duty.

Tijuana. Tourist Office: 84–2138; Chamber of Commerce: 88–1088; U.S. Consulate: 86–1001; Police: 85–7090; Hospital: 85–8191.

Mexicali. Tourist Office: 2–4391; Chamber of Commerce: 2–6160; Police 2–4444; Hospital: 5–1666.

San Felipe. Tourist Office: 7–1155; Police: 7–1006; Hospital: 7–1001.

Ensenada. Tourist Office: 4–0142; Chamber of Commerce: 8–2322; Police: 9–1751; Hospital 8–2525

Loreto. Tourist Office: 3–0344; Police 3–0035

La Paz. Tourist Office: 2–1190; Police: 2–0781; Hospital: 2–1111.

Cabo San Lucas. Tourist Office: 3–0494; Police: 3–0057; Hospital: 3–0102.

San José del Cabo. Tourist Office: 2–0233; Police: 2–0361; Hospital: 2–0316.

HOTELS. Good hotels are found the length on the peninsula with truly posh resorts down at the tip. In the border area hotels are cheaper on the Mexican side. Beyond the border, except for La Paz, inexpensive accommodations are scarce. Moderately priced are *La Pinta* hotels along Mexico 1 at Ensenada, San Quintin, Cataviña, Guerrero Negro, San Ignacio, and Loreto and these are about the only places to stay at some points along the highway.

Tijuana

The biggest city on the peninsula offers the widest selection of hotels. Most are south of the downtown area which means a taxi or bus trip for guests without their own cars. Prices begin at $60 for a double at the *Deluxe* hotel; $45 for *First Class;* $30 *Moderate* and $20 *Inexpensive.*

Deluxe

Fiesta Americana. Agua Caliente 4558; 81–7000. New in 1985 with 430 large, comfortable rooms, nightclub, specialty restaurant, coffee shop, health club, tennis, and pool.

First Class

Calinda Quality Inn. Agua Caliente No. 1; 86–5001. Formerly El Presidente, refurbished, with 200 rooms, restaurant, bar, discotheque, and pool.

El Conquistador. Agua Caliente 7000; 86–4801. The 110 rooms are plain, but the restaurant is good, the disco lively, and there is a swim-up bar in the pool.

Lucerna. Paseo de los Heroes; 86–1000. Fairly new, with 170 rooms, specialty restaurant, evening entertainment, and pool.

Palacio Azteca. Deizyseis de Septiembre 213; 86–5401. A 90-room semiresort with specialty restaurant, night club, coffee shop, and large pool.

Rosarito Beach Hotel. Rosarito Beach (about a half-hour drive south of Tijuana); 12–1106. A resort dating back to the Prohibition era, nicely refurbished and classically Mexican. Restaurant, evening entertainment, pool, and tennis.

Moderate

Country Club. Tapachula No. 1; 86–2301. Close to the golf course and race track, with 100 rooms, restaurant, and pool.

La Mesa Inn. Diaz Ordaz and Gardenias; 81–6522. The 95 rooms are plainly furnished, but there is a nice bar, coffee shop and pool.

La Sierra. Diezyseis de Septiembre; 86–1601. A 60-unit motel with restaurant, bar, and pool. Modest but a good value.

La Villa de Zaragoza. Madero 1120; 85–1832. A fairly new motel-like establishment, with a good downtown location by the Jai Alai Palace and just a block from Revolución.

Inexpensive

Caesar. Revolución 827; 86–1616. Downtown and noisy, famed for its long bar and for being the home of the Caesar salad. Somewhat run down.

Leon. Calle Septima and Revolución; 85–6320. A 40-room downtown hotel, little more than a place to sleep.

Mexicali

Although it is quite attractive, few tourists overnight in the capital of Northern Baja California. Those who do find the hotels, while spread out, are somewhat less expensive than in Tijuana.

First Class

Holiday Inn. Boulevard Benito Juarez 2151; 6–3807. A familiar name with some nice Mexican touches. Delightful is the Mexicali Rose steakhouse.

Lucerna. Boulevard Benito Juarez 2151; 4–1000. Large with 200 rooms in the main building or bungalows. Specialty restaurant, coffee shop, piano bar, and mariachi lounge.

Moderate

Calafia. Justo Sierra 1495; 4–0222. One of the newer properties in town with 100 rooms with restaurant, bar, and pool.

La Siesta. Justo Sierra 899; 8–2305. An 84-room motel, with nicely furnished rooms, restaurant, bar, and pool.

Tecate

A border town best known for its beer, Tecate has some lavish resorts as well as more moderate places to stay. Prices are slightly lower than in Tijuana.

Deluxe

Rancho La Puerta. Mexico 2 west of town; 4–1005. A luxury fitness resort where guests usually check in for a week to shed a few pounds and get back into shape. Overnight guests are accepted when space is available.

First Class

Santa Veronica. Mexico 2 east of town; 5–1636. A ranch where fighting bulls are raised, this now also is a resort with a large pool and six tennis courts.

Moderate

El Dorado. Benito Juarez and Esteban Cantu; 4–1101. A pleasant in-town motel with restaurant and pool.

San Felipe

This fishing village on the Sea of Cortes is a favorite with weekending Californians. Prices are slightly lower than in Tijuana. All hotels listed are on the beach.

First Class

Fiesta. 4–0393. Largest property in town with 140 rooms, restaurant, bar, pool and nightly entertainment.

Castel. 2–2822. Fairly new with 120 rooms, restaurant, bar, nightly entertainment, pool and tennis.

Moderate

Villas del Mar. 8–3990. Smaller, with 50 rooms, bar, restaurant, pool and tennis court.

El Cortes. 2–1039. A pleasant enough 65-room motel with a dining room, bar, and horses for rent.

Inexpensive

Riviera. 4–0212. A 20-room hotel that is well managed and charming. Pool, but no restaurant.

Ensenada

This is the favorite holiday town in Northern Baja; hotel prices are about the same as in Tijuana.

First Class

San Nicolas. Lopez Mateos and Guadalupe; 9–1901. An attractive resort with 135 units, restaurant, bar, disco, pool. Deluxe.

El Cid, Lopez Mateos 1000; 8–2404. The decor is Spanish colonial and each of the 50 rooms is different. Restaurant, bar, disco, pool.

Bahia. Lopez Mateos and Riveroll; 8–2101. A long-time favorite with 68 rooms, restaurant, disco-bar, and large pool.

Casa del Sol. Lopez Mateos and Blancarte; 8–1570. A most attractive establishment with 42 units, excellent restaurant, and pool.

Estero Beach, South of Town on Estero Beach; 6–1580. The only complete beach resort in the area, 74 units, restaurant, bar, pool, and tennis.

La Pinta. Floresta and Bucaneros; 6–2601. A 50-unit property with restaurant, piano bar, and pool.

Moderate

TraveLodge. Lopez Mateos at Blancarte; 8–1601. One of the few American affiliated hotels in town with 50 units and a heated pool; the restaurant is across the street.

Dunas. Caracoles 169; 6–3095. Billed as a "hometel," with kitchenette suites actually on the beach.

Quintas Papagayo. Mexico 1 north of town; 8–3675. A bungalow complex, the 30 units equipped with kitchenettes and fireplaces.

Santa Isabel, Lopez Mateos at Castillo; 8–3616. Small, with 31 rooms, restaurant, bar, and pool.

Inexpensive.

Villa Marina. Lopez Mateos and Blancarte; 8–3351. A 60 unit motel with restaurant, pool, and bar.

Flamingo. Lopez Mateos and Rayon; 6–1666. A small, plain hotel handy to everything.

Loreto

The hotels here are far apart and there is little between them. The *Deluxe* establishment charges about $50 for a double room; the other places are *moderate,* charging about $35.

Deluxe

El Presidente. Nopolo Bay; 3–0700. A 250-room resort on the beach and adjoining the Loreto Tennis Center. Fishing and all water sports, tour desk, and shop. Coffee shop, restaurant, entertainment in the lobby bar, discotheque. U.S. programming on room television.

Moderate

La Pinta. 3–0025. A refurbished fishing lodge with 30 charming rooms, nice pool and beachfront location. Two tennis courts, bar and restaurant.

Misión de Loreto. 3–0048. A 52-room inn on the waterfront yet within walking distance of the village. Nice pool, delightful restaurant, and a bar where guests become friends.

Oasis. 3–0211. A 37-room veteran from the days when fishermen flew in aboard their own planes. Cozy, with all services, two tennis courts, game room, and indoor/outdoor dining.

La Paz

Capital of Southern Baja and the state's only city of any size, La Paz has beachfront resort hotels out of town plus a variety of places to stay in the city. The one *Deluxe* hotel charges about $50 for a double; expect to pay $40 in a *First Class* establishment, $30 at a *Moderate* place and under $20 at one that is *Inexpensive.*

Deluxe

Las Arenas, Highway 1, about an hour south of town; no phone (in California call 800–423–4785). Off by itself, all suites, very nice beach, and great fishing.

Gran Baja. Calle Rangel; 2–3900. A concrete high-rise with 256 rooms, restaurant, coffee shop, bars, discotheque, pool, tennis, beachfront, but mediocre management and little charm.

First Class

Palmira. Pichilingue Road; 2–4000, fairly new with 120 rooms, on the beach west of town. Restaurant, bar, discotheque, pool, and tennis courts. Well-run.

Los Arcos. Alvaro Obregon 498; 2–2744. On the waterfront in town with pool but no beach. There are 182 rooms, some in bungalows, U.S. programming on the TV. Coffee shop and restaurant. A favorite with fishermen.

La Perla. Alvaro Obregon 150; 2–0777. Recently refurbished, on the waterfront, with a popular sidewalk cafe and popular night club.

Moderate

La Posada. Reforma and Plaza Sur; 2–4401. A 25-room on on the beach just west of town. Pleasant restaurant and piano bar.

Misiones de La Paz. 6–8220. On an island and reached by boat (no charge). Nice for escapists. Good restaurant, evening entertainment, pool, and beach.

Gardenias. Aquiles Serdan Norte 520; 2–3088. A good enough commercial hotel in town.

Inexpensive

Calafia. Mexico 1, east of town; 2–5811. Restaurant, air conditioned rooms, pool, near the beach.

Lori. Bravo and Madero; 2–1819. Two blocks from the waterfront with clean, air conditioned rooms, restaurant.

Marcasey. Ignacio Ramirez 2016; 2–4484. Small with suites including kitchenettes. Dining room and tour services.

Los Cabos

Cabo San Lucas and San José del Cabo, the capes on the tip on the peninsula, comprise an area with some of the most luxurious resorts in Baja California. Most of the hotels are fairly far apart from each other and some 20 miles separate the two little towns. A double at a *Super Deluxe* resort will cost $120, *Deluxe* $100, *First Class* $60, and there is not anything less expensive in this area. Many hotels are strictly American plan and charge a service fee in lieu of tipping; this will raise the overall rate.

Super Deluxe

Twin Dolphins. Near Cabo San Lucas; (213) 386–3940 (no local phone). Fairly new and quite lavish, all 58 rooms with ocean-view terraces; two tennis courts, 18-hole putting green, own fishing fleet.

Hacienda. Cabo San Lucas; 3–0122. A wide variety of accommodations overlooking what supposedly is the best beach on the capes. Tennis, riding horses, hunting, all water sports, and deep sea fishing.

Cabo San Lucas. Near Cabo San Lucas; (213) 655–7777 (no local phone). Elegant and isolated on 2,500-acre spread with club-like atmosphere. Tennis, putting green, all water sports, hunting, deep sea fishing.

Deluxe

Palmilla. San José del Cabo; (619) 454–0600 (no local phone). Small and elegant, with just 50 rooms, outstanding service, riding horses, tennis, own fishing fleet. No credit cards accepted.

Calinda Cabo Baja. Near Cabo San Lucas; 3–0044. Handsome, with 125 rooms in fairly spread-out units. Getting to the beach requires a hike, but there are three pools and illuminated tennis courts.

El Presidente. San José del Cabo; 2–0038. One of the newest in the area, minibars and U.S. programming on TV in the 250 rooms. Coffee shop, two restaurants, several bars, and a discotheque.

Finisterra. Cabo San Lucas; 3–0000. On the tip of the peninsula, overlooking the Pacific and Sea of Cortes. One of the first hotels in the area, high above the beach, somewhat gloomy.

Solmar. Cabo San Lucas; 3–0023. On the beach at the tip of the peninsula, a charming and friendly hotel with 170 rooms.

First Class.

Castel Cabo. San José del Cabo; 2–0155. New in 1982 with 150 rooms on the beach, all furnished with minibars and television with U.S. programming. Restaurant, bar, and disco.

Calinda Aquamarina. San José del Cabo; 2–0239. On the beach with 100 rooms, lobby bar and restaurant. A Quality Inn and a good value.

Along the Highway

Motorists driving Mexico 1 will encounter motels and hotels every 100 miles or so. Most, however, are small and at times they fill up quickly. Advance reservations and early arrival are advised.

Santa Ines: La Pinta Cataviña Hotel, *First Class.*

San Quintin: La Pinta Hotel, *First Class;* Celito Lindo Motel, *Moderate;* Old Mill Motel and Ernesto's Motel, *Inexpensive.*

Guerrero Negro: La Pinta Paralelo 28 Hotel, *First Class;* Motel Dunas and Motel Baja Sur, *Moderate.*

San Ignacio: La Pinta Hotel, *First Class.* La Posada Motel, *Moderate.*

Santa Rosalia: Hotel El Moro and Hotel Blanco y Negro, *Moderate;* Hotel del Real and Hotel del Centro, *Inexpensive.*

Mulege: Hotel Serenidad, Hotel Mulege, Hotel Terrazas and Old Hacienda, all *Moderate;* Hotel Las Casitas, *Inexpensive.*

Ciudad Constitución: Hotel El Conquistador, Hotel Casino, and Hotel Maribel, all *Inexpensive.*

SPECIAL EVENTS. January and **February** are the best months for whale watching in La Paz, Los Cabos, and Gray Whale National Park at Scammon's Lagoon near Guerrero Negro. The whales can be spotted easily from shore; in La Paz and and Los Cabos boats are available for those who want a closer look. **February** is usually the month for *carnaval,* the pre-Lenten mardi gras celebrated in *Ensenada, San Felipe* and *La Paz.* **March** is the month for the *Mexicali Chinese Food Festival* and other celebrations in that border city. This is also the time for the *Long Beach to Cabo San Lucas Regatta* and the *Tijuana to Ensenada Bike Race.* Dates vary from year to year. The 19th is the date for the *San José del Cabo Fiesta.*

April is the the date for the *Rosarito Spring Fair* in a Tijuana coastal suburb. During the last week of the month the *Newport to Ensenada Regatta* is held. This is the month for the *Transpeninsular Bike Race.* **May** marks the beginning of the sailfish season around Los Cabos. The *La Paz Festival,* marking the foundation of the city, starts May 3. **June** is when the *Los Cabos Marathon Swim* takes place, a nine-hour event in the waters between Cabo San Lucas and San José del Cabo. This is also the month for the *Baja 500* off-road race. During the final week the *Ciudad Constitución Fair* is held.

July is the time for the *Tecate Fair* which takes place the first two weeks of the month. **August** is when the *Tijuana Fair "Baja California on the March"* takes place. **September** is the month Mexico celebrates its independence with fireworks the night of the 15th and parades the 16th in Tijuana, Mexicali, and La Paz. The *Loreto Fiesta* and *Mulege Fiesta* take place the first week of the month, the *Ensenada Festival* during the final week, an event that includes bike races, a sea food fair, and international bartending competition. **October** is the date of the *Tecate Pampolnada* or bull chase, with the animals running through the streets to the ring. **November** sees the running of the *Baja 1000* off-road race. The *Los Cabos Marlin Tournament* attracts top bill fishermen. **December** is when the *Loretto Tennis Festival,* with John McEnroe, takes place.

HOW TO GET AROUND. Airports. VW minibuses operated by concessionaires provide the only transportation from airports. Rates are fixed and quite reasonable. City taxis to the airports are somewhat more expensive, especially in Cabo San Lucas where fares run nearly $25 (it is a long trip) and hotel guests often seek to share a cab.

Rental vehicles. The best way to get around is to have a car of one's own. As an alternative, *Avis, Hertz, Budget* and *National* have offices throughout the peninsula (in Loreto there is only *Budget;* in Ensenada only *Hertz*). Prices tend to be quite high and often only standard shift vehicles are available; in border areas it is much cheaper to rent on the U.S. side (be certain the car has Mexican insurance). Mopeds and scooters may be rented in La Paz and Los Cabos, but it should be remembered they are as risky as they look with no insurance covering victims in an accident.

Taxis are an easy way to get around. Fares are lower than in the U.S., but should be agreed on in advance. Most cabbies in Baja speak some English. Almost all hotels have their own taxi stands.

Buses are a good way to get from Tijuana hotels to downtown and are fairly good in Mexicali, but rattletrap in La Paz. Intercity buses connect all points of Baja California reachable by road and while service is not bad it can be confusing to foreigners. Urban and interurban fares are quite low.

TOURIST INFORMATION. Oddly, more information is available about Baja California north of the border than south of it. Tour operators, car rental firms, and vendors of Mexican automobile insurance all are excellent sources for brochures, leaflets, and maps. Within Mexico hotels usually have considerable literature about the area which is made available only to those who ask for it. Government tourist offices, listed below, normally are open from 10 A.M. until 3 P.M. and 5 until 9 P.M. with no afternoon shift on Sundays.

Tijuana. An information center is operated by the *Chamber of Commerce* at Madero and Calle Primero downtown. The *State Tourist Commission* headquarters are somewhat out of the way in the Rio Tijuana area, but the commission does have booths at the airport, at the border crossing, and on Avenida Revolución.

Mexicali. The Tourist Commission Office is at Calle de Comercio 204 downtown. The Chamber of Commerce has an information booth at Lopez Mateos and Camelias about a mile below the border.

San Felipe. The Tourist Commission is on the waterfront.

Tecate. The State Tourist Commission office is at Callejon Libertad 1305, about five blocks south of the border crossing.

Ensenada. The State Tourist Commission office is on the main street, Lopez Mateos 885, near most hotels.

La Paz. The Tourist Information Office is on the waterfront where Diezyseis de Septiembre meets Alvaro Obregon.

No tourist information offices exist in Los Cabos, Loreto, or other Baja California points.

USEFUL ADDRESSES. Tijuana. *Aeromexico:* Revolución 1236; *Mexicana:* Balarezo 2800; *Aero California:* Plaza Rio Tijuana Mall; *U.S. Consulate:* Tapachula 96; *Police:* Constitución and Calle Octavo; *Hospital:* Avenida Padre Kino, Rio Tijuana development: *Post Office:* Calle Once and Negrete.

Mexicali. *Aeromexico:* Centro Civico, Nuevo Mexicali development; *Mexicana:* Madero 833; *Police:* Centro Civico, Nuevo Mexicali development; *Hospital:* Durango and Salina Cruz; *Post Office:* Madero 491.

San Felipe. As street signs are not posted, it is best to ask directions to locate the police, emergency clinic and post office in this small community.

Tecate. *Police:* Ortiz Rubio and Libertad; *Hospital:* Venustiano Carranza (no number); *Post Office:* Revolución and Cardenas.

Ensenada. *Police:* Ortiz Rubio and Libertad; *Hospital:* Avenida Ruiz and Calle Once; *Post Office:* Juarez 1347.

La Paz. *Aeromexico:* Alvaro Obregon (waterfront) and Hidalgo; *Mexicana:* Alvaro Obregon (waterfront) 340; *Aero California:* Alvaro Obregon (waterfront) 240; *Police:* Constitución and Ignacio Altamirano; *Hospital:* Salvatierra and Bravo; *Post Office:* Constitución and Revolución.

Los Cabos. *Aeromexico* maintains a ticket office only in San José del Cabo; *Mexicana* has offices both in San José and in Cabo San Lucas. *Aero California* has its only office in Cabo San Lucas. While streets in the two towns have names, few of them have signs. The best way to locate police, hospitals, or post offices in either community is to ask.

ENGLISH LANGUAGE MEDIA. Surprisingly, American newspapers and magazines are hard to come by on the Mexican side of the border. In Los Cabos and La Paz they often can be purchased at hotel newsstands as well as at El Presidente in Loreto. *Ensenada News and Views* is published monthly in that city and is a handy guide to what is going on at the moment, as is *The Baja Californian,* issued weekly in La Paz. *About* and *Baja California* are magazines in English of interest primarily for their advertisements.

TOURS. San Diego Mini Tours (619/234–9044) runs morning and afternoon shopping excursions to Tijuana for $17 (with lunch $22) and evening trips that include jai alai games for $18 (with dinner $22.50). *Caliente Tours* (619/260–0060) specializes in trips to the Tijuana track for the dog and horse races, some with meals included; prices vary. *Mexicoach* (619/232–5049) offers a variety of tours including a day in Ensenada for $40. *El Paso Tours* (619/427–8630) has a variety of programs including two days and a night in Ensenada for $81.

Baja Tours (619/357–0200) in Calexico operates trips to San Felipe with sightseeing in Mexicali along the way; prices vary according to accommodations, length of stay, and whether fishing is included.

Ensenada's Santo Tomas Winery takes groups through the premises daily and invites visitors to sample the product, all for free. Call 8–3333 for times.

Loreto's Las Palmas (3–0165) will arrange cruises to see the seals on nearby islands as well as excursions to visit the San Javier Mision up in the mountains.

La Paz: *Viajes Coromuel* (2–8006) features city sightseeing for about $5, half-day outings that include a swim at Pichilingue Beach for $10 and all-day excursions to Los Cabos with lunch for $32. The *Tio Eduardo* leaves the waterfront daily at 8 A.M. for a luncheon cruise to Espiritu Santo Island, returning about 5:30 P.M.; price is about $26. *Viajes Cardon* runs 12-hour whale watching cruises during the season (winter months) for $42 with breakfast and lunch included.

Cabo San Lucas is the departure point for boat trips to *Los Arcos* (The Arches), the rocks at the tip of the peninsula. The trip takes about an hour; hotel tour desks usually charge $10, which includes transportation to the dock as well as the boat ride.

PARKS AND GARDENS. Tijuana: *Rio Tijuana Development,* while not strictly a park, is park-like, an attractive urban renewal along the banks of the often dry Tijuana River. Government buildings, a cultural center and shopping mall are among the structures here. *Guerrero Park,* at Calle 3 and Avenida F is Tijuana's one city park, a couple of blocks of trees and lawn on the fringes of downtown but of no special interest.

Mexicali: *Obregon Park* at Reforma and Irigoyen, and *Constitución Park,* Avenida México and Zuazua, are the only two parks in downtown Mexicali. Both are attractive but of no exceptional interest. *Xochimilco Lagoon,* south of town, is the Mexicali reservoir with picnic and barbecue facilities. *The Mexicali Zoo* is in a park on the south side of the city, at Lazaro Cardenas and Uxmal. *Laguna Salada,* west of town, is a large, attractive lake with boating and picnic facilities, campgrounds, and a drag racing strip.

Tecate: *Hidalgo Park* in the center of town is a typical Mexican village plaza, similar to the *zocalos* found in many towns and cities, but rare in Baja. *Lopez Mateos Park* on Mexico 3 south of town, is where dances and band concerts are held on summer evenings.

Ensenada: *La Bufadora* is a marine blowhole that has become one of Ensenada's top attractions. It is south of town. *El Mirador,* which means "The Lookout" in Chapultepec Hills, is an attractive spot from which to get an overall view of the city and port. *Revolución Park,* Obregon at Calle Septima, is Ensenada's main city park and a popular outing spot for locals, especially on weekends. *Constitución National Park* is a 50-mile drive east of Ensenada, the last half unpaved but passable. Hanson Lagoon is found here and the rugged scenery is spectacular.

Guerrero Negro: *Gray Whale National Park,* midway down the peninsula and just over the Southern Baja California state line, attracts hundreds of motorists from January through March. Here the whales frequently come in quite close to shore. The park is reached by a fairly good but unpaved road.

SPORTS

Tijuana

Bullfights take place every Sunday afternoon at one of Tijuana's two bull rings, the season beginning in May and continuing through mid-September. For ticket information call 84–2126.

Jai Alai games get under way at 8 P.M. every night but Thursday throughout the year. The fronton where the games are played is on the main street, Avenida Revolución. For more information call 82–3636.

Racing takes place at the Caliente track with horses running starting around noon on weekends and the greyhounds nightly starting at 7:30 throughout the year.

Charreadas are Mexican rodeos with amateur cowboy associations competing at one of several rings around town on Sunday mornings. Call 84–2126 for information.

Golf is played at the country club on Agua Caliente Boulevard just south of downtown. Rental clubs, electric and hand carts as well as caddies are available for the 18-hole course open to the public.

Tennis may be played at the country club or at any of several hotels with courts of their own.

Mexicali

Bullfights are held usually twice a month from October through May at the Califia Bullring. For information call 2–9795.

Charreadas, usually are held on Sundays once each month during the winter at one of Mexicali's two rings. Call 8–2330 or 8–2320 for information.

Baseball is played by Mexicali's team in the Triple A Pacific League from mid-October through December. For information call 2–4709.

Golf may be enjoyed at the country club on Mexico 3 south of town. The 18-hole course is open throughout the year. For information call 6–7170.

San Felipe

Fishing is the big sport here with sportsmen going after sea bass, snapper, mackerel, and hundreds of other species. There are half-a-dozen or more places from which to rent small boats. **Baja Tours,** Box 5557, Calexico, CA 92231, tel. (619) 357–0200, runs trips down from the border with two nights in San Felipe. **The Bent Rod** at 715 El Camino Real, Tustin, CA 92680, tel. (714) 838–1420, organizes five days on the Sea of Cortes, departing from San Felipe on Saturday mornings aboard 75-foot boats.

Ensenada

Fishing here is along the Pacific with Ensenada calling itself the "Yellowtail Capital of the World." Best time for angling is April through November, with bottom fishing good in the winter. Charter vessels and party boats are available from several outfitters along Avenida Lopez Mateos, the main street in the tourist zone. The outfitters take care of Mexican fishing licenses.

Hunting for quail, September through December, can be arranged at **Uruapan Lodge,** Gastelum 40 downtown, tel. 8–2190.

Golf may be played at **Bajamar,** an excellent 18-hole course 20 miles north of Ensenada. For information call 8–1844.

Tennis also may be played at **Bajamar** as well as at the **Baja Tennis Club** at San Benito 123 and at hotels that have their own courts.

Charreadas, are regularly scheduled at 3:30 P.M. Saturdays. The ring is at Avenida Alvarado and Calle Dos; call 4–0242 for information.

Loreto

Fishing is what put Loreto on the map as far as many Americans are concerned. Yellowtail, mackerel, and roosterfish are caught during the winter months, marlin, sailfish, and amber jack in the summer, with pompano and snapper biting througnout the year. All hotels can arrange boat charters.

Scuba specialists are **Loreto Divers,** tel. 3–0029. The organization takes clients out to black coral reefs and other exotic spots.

Sailing is best done on Nopolo Bay where Hobie Cats and similar craft may be rented on the beach.

Tennis is at its best in Baja at the **Loreto Tennis Center,** operated by All American Sports and boasting John McEnroe as its touring pro. Located across from the Hotel El Presidente by Nopolo Bay, the center has nine championship courts lit for nighttime play. Expert instruction is available.

La Paz

Fishing, especially for marlin and sail, is best off La Paz from March through September, but is good all year long. Well-equipped deepsea boats, most in the 32-foot catagory, are available for charter. Hotels can make arrangements or sportsmen can contact Jack Valdez at 2–0038 or Hugo Fisher at 2–4011.

Scuba specialists are **Baja Diving Service** at Independencia 107, tel. 2–0719. They run trips to five areas, organize night dives and snorkeling trips also can be set up.

Los Cabos

Fishing is the main reason most visitors head for Cabo San Lucas and San José del Cabo, with local boosters claiming 40,000 marlin are hooked annually in the waters off the capes. Roosterfish, wahoo, tuna, and more also lie in wait throughout the year. All the hotels can arrange for charters and many have their own fleets. There are also independent operators around the Cabo San Lucas waterfront who may or may not charge less (fishing in Los Cabos is never cheap).

Hunting for white wing dove, duck, and quail is catching on in this area, the season being Sept. 15 to Feb. 15. Hotels can make the arrangements for guides and, when necessary, for the rental of guns (importing firearms into Mexico involves considerable red tape).

Scuba trips can be arranged through hotels or at **Enrique's Ultramarine** in Cabo San Lucas. Snorkeling expeditions also can be set up.

Sailing, including windsurfing and paraflying, can be done at most hotels. John Fox, who operates from the beach in front of the Hotel Hacienda, has some of the newest and best equipment.

BEACHES. The seashore everywhere in Mexico is federal property. There are no private beaches and hotels have no authority over their waterfronts. Lifeguards are rarely to be found anywhere; swimmers need to be quite cautious.

Tijuana

The Tijuana Beaches, *Playas de Tijuana,* are just a couple of miles west of the border crossing. Interesting is the marker in the sand and the boundary fence that continues right out into the ocean. *Rosarito,* a waterfront suburb about 15 miles down the coast, generally is considered to have better beaches and a more beach-like atmosphere.

Ensenada

The port city some 65 miles down the coast from Tijuana is on the waterfront, but most of the beaches are south of town while the hotels are in Ensenada itself. *Estero Beach* and the sandy stretch running out a short peninsula to *Punta Banda* and the blowhole at *La Bufadora* are the most popular bathing and sunning spots. Surfers prefer the beaches north of Ensenada, especially those around the village of San Miguel. Summer is the best time for swimming in these parts; the water gets quite cold in winter, even when the air is warm.

San Felipe

Where the Sea of Cortes begins, San Felipe is all beach, its sandy dunes often crowded on weekends with buggies, cycles, and three-wheelers. *Punta Estrella,* 12 miles south of town, and *Las Almejas,* 30 miles to the north, are good spots to go shelling and clamming.

Loreto

The setting is beautiful but the beaches in Loreto are more rocky than sandy. The town itself is on the waterfront as are its three smaller inns. The big Hotel El Presidente is a few miles south on equally rocky *Nopolo Bay. Puerto Escondido,* a favorite with campers, is dramatically beautiful.

La Paz

There are tiny, not very attractive beaches here and there along the waterfront right in town and somewhat nicer sandy stretches in either direction out by the resort hotels. The best beaches, however, are farther out. A favorite is *Pichilingue,* near where the Mazatlan ferry docks. Here there are restaurants, lockers, and camping areas. *Balandra, El Tecolote* and *El Coyote* are more isolated beaches reached by dirt road from Pichlingue. They have no facilities but are popular with campers. *Espiritu Santo,* an island surrounded by beach, is a favorite with day trippers.

Los Cabos

Rafa's Beach, also known as *Playa Medano,* is billed by the Hotel Hacienda, which stands there, as the only safe swimming beach in the area. There are several good places to eat out this way.

Playa de Amor, or Lovers' Beach, no doubt is so named because difficulty in getting there assures some privacy. Although near Cabo San Lucas, it is best reached by one of the small boats called *pangas.* The beach is at the tip of the peninsula, washed by both the Pacific and the Sea of Cortes. The Pacific is dangerous, the Sea of Cortes less so and snorkelers enjoy it.

Cemetery Beach, as odd as its name, is by the graveyard on the outskirts of San Lucas. It is a favorite with campers.

San Cristobal is one of the many lovely Pacific beaches found along nearly impassable Highway 19, which runs from Los Cabos up the west side on the peninsula, looping inward to hit La Paz. Swimming is suicidal at the Pacific beaches, but they make great picnic spots, especially during the whale watching winter months. There are several coves and beaches between Cabo San Lucas and San José del Cabo. *Caleta Linda* is a favorite for snorkeling while *Costa Azul* is rated tops by surfers. The hotels at San José del Cabo are all on a lovely stretch of beach.

CAMP GROUNDS. While there are a number of trailer parks with hookups for recreational vehicles along the length of the Baja California peninsula, there are few organized camp grounds as such. Many campers simply settle in at any likely spot and make themselves at home although using the facilities at trailer camps is recommended. Listed here are parks and informal camping areas found along Mexico 1. Baja's two state tourist commissions have little information of camping facilities; best source of data is the **Automobile**

Club of Southern California, 2601 South Figueroa Street, Los Angeles, CA 90007.

Ensenada area. *California Park,* north of town, tel. 8–2037; *Kings Cornoita,* north of town, tel. 8–1944; *RV Park,* north of town, tel. 8–2302; *Campo Playa,* Lazaro Cardenas and Calle Delante, tel. 8–1818; *Rancho Todos Santos,* south of town, tel. 6–1060.

Santo Tomas. *El Palomar,* north of town.

San Quintin. *Don Diego,* north of town; *Celito Lindo,* south of town.

Cataviña. Hookups are available at the Pemex station.

Guerrero Negro. Hookups are available beside the Hotel La Pinta near the monument marking the state line. Camping is permitted nearby in Gray Whale National Park although no special facilities are provided.

Santa Rosalia. The beaches south of town, around the little village of San Lucas, are popular with campers although no special facilities are available.

Mulege. The *Rio Baja* trailer park is just south of town; *Posada Concepción* is about 15 miles further out, a camping area with facilities on the beach.

Loreto. At Puerto Escondido a few miles south of town is *Tripuí* with space for 70 tents and more than 100 hookups. There is even a swimming pool and tennis court; tel. 3–0362.

Ciudad Constitución. *La Pila,* south of town, has hookups and a swimming pool.

La Paz. *El Cardón* has hookups for 90 vehicles, a pool, and other facilities. On Mexico 1, east of town, tel. 2–0078. There are limited camping facilities on the nearby beaches at *El Mogote, Pichilingue, El Tecolote* and *El Coyote.*

San José del Cabo. Largest and best equipped trailer park in the area is *Brisas del Mar* which is on the beach.

Cabo San Lucas. New trailer park is *Cabo Cielo* (Cape Heaven) on Cemetery Beach. *El Faro Viejo* is about a mile out of town on the road to Todos Santos. Many people simply camp along the many beaches and coves in the area although these lack sanitary and other facilities.

San Felipe. At the top of the Sea of Cortes, has more than a dozen trailer camps with complete hookups, sanitary facilities, showers, swimming pools and tennis courts. Among the best are *El Faro, Sea and Sun, La Jolla, Club de Pesca* and *Ruben's.*

HISTORICAL SITES. Cave paintings dating back no one knows how many centuries before the Spanish conquest, have been discovered in several Baja California caverns. Many of these works compare favorably with those found in Europe. Most of the Baja caves are all but impossible to reach, but dedicated trippers can get to some near Mulege and Loreto. More than 15 of the paintings have been reproduced as murals in public areas at the Twin Dolphin Hotel in Cabo San Lucas.

Missions were built along the length of the peninsula by Spanish friars. Most of them were abandoned in the 19th century but the first, completed in Loreto in 1752, has been in use since it opened. Even more imposing, and also still in use, is the *San Javier Mission,* only 22 miles from Loreto but quite difficult to get to. San Javier, with its elaborate stone work and Moorish design, is considered one of the most striking of the California missions.

The English Cemetery in San Quintin is all that remains of a 19th century British settlement. The Mexican Government at the time supported the project, but the scarcity of water in Baja doomed the pioneers.

The Eiffel Church in Santa Rosalia was designed by the same Gustave Eiffel who built the tower in Paris. It is a prefabricated structure shipped around the Horn back in the days when Santa Rosalia was a French mining town.

Riviera del Pacifico in Ensenada was built as a gambling casino by Jack Dempsey and friends back during the days of U.S. Prohibition. With liquor now legal in the U.S. and blackjack illegal in Mexico, the Riviera is now the local convention center.

MUSEUMS AND GALLERIES. **Tijuana Cultural Center** in the Rio Tijuana development contains a museum of anthropology and history tracing Mexico's past from ancient pre-Hispanic times to the 1910 Revolution and later. It is an excellent introduction to the country.

The State Library in Mexicali at Obregon and Avenida E often doubles as a museum of art with exhibitions of paintings and sculptures.

In Ensenada, Anna's **Galeria de Arte,** on Riveroll 122, and **Artes Bitterlin,** on the corner of Lopez Mateos and Blancarte, have paintings, sculptures, and more for sale.

The La Paz Museum of Anthropology at Cinco de Mayo and Altamirano, has exhibits depicting the peninsula's past, including some reproductions of the cave paintings. Art exhibits sometimes are held here.

STAGE, MUSIC, DANCE, FILM. With the exception of cinemas, which are not plentiful, there is little in this respect. The *Tijuana Cultural Center* contains an auditorium well suited for concerts and theatrical performances, but at this writing it is seldom used. Mexicali and Ensenada each has one good theater where hits from Mexico City occasionally are brought on provincial tours; these, naturally, are in Spanish. Sometimes dance troupes or musical groups, both classical and modern, give performances. Local tourist offices will have information on any such events. La Paz less frequently has such programs; again, the local tourist office is the best source of information. Cinemas in Tijuana, Mexicali, Tecate, Ensenada and La Paz often show fairly recent Hollywood films with the original soundtrack and Spanish subtitles. Price of admission is about 50¢.

SHOPPING. Browsing and buying is a favorite pastime in Baja's bigger tourist areas. Mexican handicrafts are a favorite with most buyers, but Baja is pretty much a duty-free area with imports from around the world. European fashions and cosmetics are among the best buys.

Tijuana's Plaza Rio Mall is an American-style shopping center where the locals buy, *Dorian's* being its largest department store. *Sara* has a branch here although its main store, noted for designer labels, is on the city's main street, Avenida Revolución. Nearby on Revolución is *Le Drug Store,* a shopping complex selling all kinds of handicrafts, souvenirs, T-shirts, and imported cosmetics; it even has a pharmacy. *Tolan* on Revolución is another good place for handicrafts. Better is *Porros* which has decorator quality housewares and ceramics a few blocks from downtown on the corner of Sanchez Taboada and Edmundo O'Gorman. Sport clothes and resort wear can be found on Revolución at *Eduardo's* and *Maya de Mexico* while *Ralph Laren Polo* has a shop nearby on Madero and Calle Septima back of the jai alai palace. A large stock of cowboy boots is to be found at *La Gran Bota* on Revolución.

Ensenada has better quality shopping than Tijuana, with almost all its leading stores along Lopez Mateos, the main boulevard in the tourist area. Outstanding jewelry is to be found at *La Mina de Salomon* (King Solomon's Mine) where an American expatriate fashions the gems. For leatherware, including boots and sandals, look in at *El Escorial* and *Azteca. Fantasias del Mar* is the spot to find seashells that never seem to be lying on the beach. Tops for decorative housewares are *La Cava* (north of town) and *Originales de México.* Best place to start on a hunt for such Mexican crafts as weavings, pottery, wrought iron and wood carvings is *Fonart,* which is operated by a government agency dedicated to preserving handicrafts. Let the search continue at *Casa Colonial, The Barefoot Eagle* and *Monte Carral.* And by all means wander along Blancarte (which runs into Lopez Mateos), stopping in at *El Quetzal* and *El Solecito.* At its western end Lopez Mateos runs into Avenida Ruiz, which is really Ensenada's main drag. Here are to be found some interesting import houses, including *Hong Kong, Regalos Lupita* and *Regalos Avila* (*regalo* means gift).

Mexicali, not being much of a tourist town, is pretty much limited to tawdry curios found just across from the border checkpoint on Avenida Melgar. A nice selection of imported items, ranging from perfumes and cosmetics to porcelain and crystal, is to be seen at *Baldini* on the corner of Comercio and Calle F.

Loreto has two attractive stores, *Kino's* and *La Choya,* almost next door to each other on the waterfront. Both sell fine handicrafts including sweaters serapes, resortwear, ceramics, and the like.

La Paz surprises many first-time visitors, selling as it does so much in the way of imported items. This is because so many Mexicans take the ferry over from the mainland to buy in its duty-free shops what they cannot get at home (travelers heading to the Mexican mainland must pass through customs first). *La Perla,* a big barn of a place at Mutualismo 39, claims to be the largest department store south of Tijuana although *Dorian's* on Diezyseis de Septiembre appears to stock goods of better quality. Nearby, on Callejon Vienteuno de Agosto, the *Plaza Oriental* is a shopping complex peddling treasures not only from Asia, but from Europe and the U.S.A. as well. Men may wish to peek in at *El Trébol* on Independencia 309 and possibly find some bargains. Several stores sell Mexican handicrafts along Alvaro Obregon, the waterfront boulevard, *Delfin* and *La Carreta* being about the best. *The Weaver,* on the main highway between Jalisco and Nayarit, is where Fortunato Silva creates his own fabrics.

Los Cabos, an area almost devoid of shops a few years ago, now has them popping up all over. Quite new is the *Centro Comercial,* an air conditioned mall in San José del Cabo, and the *Tianguis,* a waterfront marketplace in Cabo San Lucas where the merchants cater primarily to cruise ship passengers hunting for souvenirs. Many of the nicest shops are in the hotels; the *Hacienda Mexican Village* in particular is a good place to go looking for gifts, resortwear, and souvenirs. *La Paloma* claims to be the original boutique in Cabo San Lucas and stocks some of the best Mexican handicrafts to be found in these parts. A close rival, however, is *Su Casa* which is next to *Ronnie's T-Shirts.* Since streets bear no names in Cabo San Lucas, addresses are meaningless. Many attractive shops, however, are found more or less in front of the City Hall Plaza. There is a supermarket over this way, too.

RESTAURANTS. Seafood and steak dominate the menus in most Baja restaurants, although Mexicali is regionally famous for its Chinese fare while Tijuana is the best place to sample tacos and enchiladas as they should be prepared. Prices are similar to those north of the border since much of the food is actually brought in from the U.S. Allow $20 for a meal in an *Expensive* place; $15 in a *Moderate* establishment and under $10 in one that is

Inexpensive. Extra will be tips (10 to 15%), and drinks (save by sticking to Mexican liquors; imported booze is heavily taxed even in this duty-free zone). Visa (V) and MasterCard (MC) along with American Express (AE) and Diners Club (D) are generally accepted everywhere along the border but less so further south. A wallet full of traveler's checks will come in handy.

Tijuana

Tia Juana Tilly's, Avenida Revolución at Calle Septima; 85–6024. In the jai alai palace and a good introduction to the Carlos Anderson places found all over Mexico. Others in Tijuana include *Tilly's Fifth Avenue,* also on Revolución, and *Guadalajara Grill* in the Rio Tijuana development. *Moderate to Expensive.* V, MC, AE, D.

Reno, Revolucion at Calle Ocho; 85–9210. Long established and a favorite steak and seafood house for veteran visitors. *Moderate to Expensive.* V, MC, AE, D.

La Langosta Loca, Revolución 914; 85–1313. An attractive seafood house specializing in Pacific lobster and Mexican specialties. *Moderate.* V, MC, AE, D.

Margarita's, Revolución at Calle Tercera; 85–7362. Twelve flavors of margaritas, baked kid and other Mexican dishes served by singing waiters. *Moderate.* V, MC, AE, D.

La Misión, Juarez 82, Rosarito; 2–0202. Half an hour from downtown, on the beach; a favorite, with dinner music, big screen TV in the bar, and an excellent menu. *Moderate.* V, MC, AE, D.

El Abajeño, Agua Caliente 101; 85–6980. A classic Mexican restaurant, tops for carne asada, tamales, and enchiladas. Mariachi music adds to the atmosphere. *Moderate.* V, MC, D.

Puerta del Sol, Sanchez Taboada 9, Rio Tijuana area; 84–2020. An Argentine-style steak house featuring churrasco and baby beef; pleasant surroundings. *Moderate to Expensive.* V, MC, AE, D.

Rodeo, Boulevard Salinas 1647; 86–5640. An American-style steak house made up like the set for a Hollywood movie. A fun place, although the steaks are none too good. *Moderate.* V, MC, AE, D.

Amito's, Brasil and Fresnillo (a block from Agua Caliente); 84–1013. One of several Italian restaurants in town, and possibly the best. *Moderate.* V, MC, AE, D.

Palacio Imperial, Revolución 1233; 85–3560. One of the largest and most attractive of Tijuana's Chinese restaurants. *Moderate;* no credit cards.

Las Macetas, Tijuana Cultural Center; 84–1132. A Mexican restaurant for American tastes, highly recommended for its brunch on Sundays, 10 to 2. *Moderate.* V, MC, AE, D.

El Meson Español, Calle Cuatro 1838; 86–2860. Tijuana's Spanish inn, a good place to order paella and other Iberian dishes. *Moderate.* V, MC.

Chikijai, Revolución and Septima; no phone. A tiny Basque cafe across from the jai alai palace and a gathering place for true *aficionados. Inexpensive.*

Rio Rita, Revolución 744; 81–6181. A curio shop with a bar and Mexican restaurant. Nothing fancy, but not bad. *Inexpensive.*

Yogurt Vision, Calle Segunda 2034; no phone. Healthy snacks, natural shakes, fruit salads, and, of course, yogurt. *Inexpensive.*

Denny's, Revolución 148; 86–3788. A touch of home with burgers and fries on the menu along with tacos and tortillas. *Inexpensive.* V, MC, AE.

Dragon de Oro, Calle Septima 1835; 85–8577. A Chinese place just off Revolución and not half bad. *Inexpensive.*

Mexicali

Casino de Mexicali, Pino Suarez and Calle L; 2–9966. Where the locals go on a big night out. Piano bar and continental menu. *Expensive.* V, MC, AE, D.

La Misión, Lazaro Cardenas 555; 8–7971. Fixed up like an old Spanish mission and serving Spanish, continental, and Mexican dishes. Dancing in the evening. *Expensive.* V, MC, AE, D.

Del Mar, Avenida C and México; 2–8849. An attractive roadhouse specializing in seafood. *Moderate to Expensive.* V, MC.

Chernest, Avenida L No. 1994; 2–6185. An intimate, romantic spot serving international food. *Moderate.* MC, V.

Casa Grande, Aquiles Serdan 1692; 2–4073. Paella and other Spanish dishes are the specialties of the house. *Moderate.* V, MC.

El Dragon, Benito Juarez 1830; 8–1020. This is one of Mexicali's many highly regarded Chinese restaurants. *Moderate.* V, MC, AE, D.

El Nuevo Pekin, Justo Sierra 1101; 8–3730. Another good Chinese restaurant. *Moderate.* V, MC.

Rincon Colonial, corner of Zaragoza and Calle F; 2–1504. Mexican dishes prepared in a gourmet manner. *Moderate.* V, MC.

Casita de Patzcuaro, Lopez Mateos 648. A good place for a light Mexican meal and a favorite with regulars headed for San Felipe. *Inexpensive.*

San Felipe

El Nido, Puerto Padre and **George's,** all along the waterfront, are fine for tacos, steaks, and seafood. **El Pescador,** on a hillside, is a shade more elegant. All are *moderate* and accept V and MC. The **San Felipe Clam Man** on the main street through town is *inexpensive* and always open.

Tecate

El Passetto, Callejon Libertad 200; 4–1361, is probably the top Italian restaurant in all of Baja. The proprietor produces his own wines, which rank with the best. *Moderate.* V, MC.

Pueblo Viego, Hidalgo 140; 4–5310. Highly regarded for its Mexican dishes, especially fare from neighboring Sonora. *Moderate.* V, MC.

El Tucan, Esteban Cantu 1100. An appealing steak house four blocks down from the border. *Moderate.* V, MC.

Restaurant 70, Benito Juarez and Esteban Cantu. This is the best place for Chinese cuisine in Tecate. *Inexpensive.*

Ensenada

El Rey Sol, López Mateos 1000; 8–1733. French cooking in a French-owned restaurant, one of the best of Baja. *Expensive.* V, MC, AE, D.

El Cueva de los Tigres, Playa Hermosa, south of town; no phone. It takes a bit of hunting to find this place and it is well worth the effort. Abalone is the specialty. *Expensive.* V, MC, AE.

Valentino, Costera Boulevard 915; 4–0022. Patio dining, a romantic setting, plus a prize-winning menu. *Expensive.* V, MC, AE, D.

Casamar, Lazaro Cardenas 449; 8–1896, also at Macheros 499; 8–2540. Two long-established seafood houses under the same management. *Moderate.* V, MC.

Del Mar, Lopez Mateos 821; 8–2191. Romantic spot for a candlelit dinner, on the lower level of one of Ensenada's most appealing shops. Seafood is the specialty. *Moderate.* V, MC.

La Gondola, Lopez Mateos 664; 8–3963. A seaside Italian cafe open for breakfast and on until midnight. *Moderate.* V, MC.

Rafael's, Alvarado and Lazaro Cardenas; 8–1195. Margaritas, tamales, tacos, and burritos served in a patio. Good breakfasts in a place that never closes. *Moderate.* V, MC.

El Toro, Lazaro Cardenas 999; 4–0964. Great for steaks and other hearty fare. *Moderate* V, MC.

Cafe Colonial, Segunda 325; 8–3510. A clean if modest place to sample some of the best Mexican cuisine. *Inexpensive.*

Muy Lam, Ruiz 373; 8–1321. Chinese dishes served in the heart of downtown Ensenda. *Inexpensive.* V, MC.

Via Venetto, Lazaro Cardenas 853. Ensenada's best-loved pizza parlor has atmosphere and is *inexpensive.*

La Paz

La Terraza, Alvaro Obregon 1570; 2–0777. A sidewalk cafe that is a local institution. Excellent for breakfast and a late night snack. *Moderate.* V, MC.

La Arboleda, Revolución and Ocampo (no phone). A pleasant and fairly new Mexican restaurant with entertainment in the evening. *Moderate.* V, MC.

La Venta Internacional, Colima and Ramirez; 2–6885. Quite nice, with indoor/outdoor dining, steaks, and seafood. *Moderate to Expensive.* V, MC.

El Molino, Alvaro Obregon and Legaspi; 2–6191. An attractive cafe with a seaside view serving seafood and charcoal broiled steaks. *Moderate to expensive.* V, MC.

Samalu, Rangel between Colima and Jalisco; 2–2481. Mexican dishes and seafood here. A good place for lunch. *Moderate.* V, MC.

La Fabula, Alvaro Obregon between Cinco de Mayo and Independencia. The imaginative local pizza parlor. *Inexpensive.*

Nuevo Pekin, Alvaro Obregon and Victoria; 2–9430. The most attractive of the many Chinese restaurants in La Paz. *Inexpensive.*

San Jose Del Cabo

Damiana, 2–0499. Something of a Mexican hacienda serving haute cuisine a la Mexicana indoors or around the patio. *Expensive.* V, MC.

Playa Palmilla, on the beach a few minute from town. The restaurant has snorkeling and boating equipment, making it popular for lunch. Romantic are the evenings here. *Moderate.*

La Fogata, 2–0480. In town, open for breakfast and on until 10 P.M. Steaks seafood, and Mexican fare dominate the menu. *Moderate.* V, MC.

Bernardo, 2–0197. A Spanish restaurant serving Mexican and international dishes as well. On the beach and open for breakfast. *Moderate.*

Cabo San Lucas

Las Palmas, on Rafa's Beach, is very much an in-spot for lunch and dinner. Lobster, abalone, and other seafood dishes are superb. *Expensive.* V, MC.

Candido's, 3–0666. Open for dinner only with reservations suggested. Something of a country club setting within, refined gathering spot for sportsfishermen and their wives. *Expensive.* V, MC, AE.

Giggling Marlin, 3–1982. Fairly new, lots of fun, where fishermen go when they are feeling ebullient. *Moderate to expensive.* V, MC.

Galeon, 3–0443. An attractive Spanish restaurant across from the marina, open for lunch and dinner, with a somewhat out-of-the-ordinary menu. *Moderate to expensive.* V, MC.

El Delfin. A most luxurious thatched hut beneath which are served large, cooling drinks and well prepared seafood dishes. *Moderate to expensive.* V, MC.

Alfonso's. On Rafa's Beach with a bar fashioned out of the wreck of a sailboat. Steaks here and chicken in addition to the seafood. *Moderate to expensive.* V, MC.

La Balandra, 3–0112. Oldest restaurant in town, this Spanish seafood establishment is on a street known as restaurant row although there are few restaurants here now. *Moderate.* V, MC.

El Rey Sol. Open for breakfast and throughout the day, this is a seafood house, its name notwithstanding. Located across from the marina. *Moderate.*

Patty's. A spot that is geared to American tastes featuring chicken, pork, beef, and shrimp barbecue. *Moderate.*

Cafe Petisa. A favorite spot for a sandwich or pizza. Desserts are a house specialty. *Moderate.*

Taqueria San Lucas. Open for breakfast and lunch only, a favorite hangout of the young at heart. *Inexpensive.*

NIGHTLIFE. Tijuana has toned down its "Sin City" image somewhat. Most visitors spend their evenings, after a good dinner and a tour of the shops, taking in either the races or the jai alai games. And there is entertainment after dark at several hotels, especially the *Calinda* and the new *Fiesta Americana.* There is dancing from 7 P.M. until dawn at the *Regina Disco,* on Avenida Revolución, as well as at the *Aloha,* Revolución 631, and at *Marko,* Balarezo 2000. Nice for dining and dancing are *Los Cristales* at Margarita 6 and *Hot Tip,* on the corner of Salinas and Escuadron Doscientosuno. For those who want the flavor of the old Tijuana, several places along Revolución, among them *Sans Souci, Regio, Bambi* and *Les Girls,* are bars with strip shows around the clock.

Mexicali provides nightly entertainment in the *Lucerna* and *Holiday Inn* hotels as well as at several places along Benito Juarez including the *Cadillac, El Zarape* and *Chic's.* On Juarez also is *La Capilla,* a discotheque with live entertainment, and *El Guaycura* where the recorded sounds are modern. The area known as Nuevo (New) Mexicali has its own *Studio 54 Disco* and a quieter spot called *El Piano Bar.*

San Felipe hotels provide music for dancing (usually recorded) over the weekends while *Cantamar* blasts out weekends with live country music.

Tecate, for all its sleepy, provincial atmosphere, has a disco called *Los Candiles* at Hidalgo 327 and another at *La Hacienda* on Benito Juarez 861. *El Tucan Bar* at Benito Juarez and Esteban Cantu often has live entertainment.

Ensenada is at its best after dark. Tradition demands at least one beer at *Hussong's,* a raunchy landmark cantina. *Bandito's* and *Papa's & Beer,* across the street on Avenida Ruiz, are south-of-the-border fraternity parties. Nice for dining and dancing is *Tortilla Flat,* with a harbor view of the fishing boats coming in. The *Tequila Connection,* at Alvardo 12, and *Chiliki's,* at Lopez Mateos and Balboa, are top discos. Most of the hotels have evening entertainment.

Loreto nightlife is all at the *Hotel El Presidente* on Nopolo Bay where there is live entertainment in the lobby bar and dancing in the disco until the small hours.

La Paz also concentrates its nighttime scene in the hotels. Mariachis play at *La Terraza,* the sidewalk cafe at La Perla, which also has a full-fledged night club, *La Cabaña.* Down the street is the *Okey Maguey* disco. *La Ronda,* at Abasolo and Colima has both live and recorded disco music. There usually is live entertainment at the *Gran Baja* and *Hotel El Presidente.*

Los Cabos is still pretty much an early-to-bed resort area, but that is changing gradually. *Añuiti,* next to the Hotel El Presidente in San José del Cabo, comes close to being a sophisticated supper club with its dine and dance atmosphere. The El Presidente itself boasts the *VideoDisco,* best equipped establishment of its kind on the peninsula. New in Cabo San Lucas is the *Oasis Disco* while *Estella's Bar* plays music guests can talk by as they munch a midnight snack and perhaps play a bit of backgammon.

CHIHUAHUA AND THE COPPER CANYON

Mexico's Wild North

Chihuahua—the city and the state both go by the same name—is located in the north of Mexico, under New Mexico and west Texas. The state of Chihuahua, the largest in the country, is a huge piece of real estate almost the size of Italy. But the land is sparsely populated with only about 3 million inhabitants. This is due to the geography, largely desert or rugged mountains.

The economy is based on cattle ranching, forestry, and mining, especially silver, lead, and zinc. The largest city, Ciudad Juárez, lies across the Rio Grande from El Paso. It thrives on U.S. companies taking advantage of inexpensive labor. The capital, Chihuahua, is expanding rapidly its manufacturing capacity.

Chihuahua was part of Mexico's wild north, the equivalent of the U.S. wild west. Silver was the magnet which drew settlers to this region, starting in the 17th century. Jesuit missionaries in the Sierras and Franciscans in the foothills helped to control the Indians by Christianizing them. There were nevertheless various rebellions which were crushed with bloody effectiveness. The independence movement had no strong echo in Chihuahua but it was here that the fleeing Father

Hidalgo was betrayed, captured, and executed. The state was invaded by American troops during the Mexican War (known here as the War of Intervention) then by the French forces supporting Emperor Maximilian. President Juárez fled north to wait out events in the town which now bears his name. Far worse than these foreign invasions, Apache raids terrorized the state. The rampages went on until the defeat of the last group of Apaches led by Victorio. The winner, the great Indian fighter Colonel Joaquín Terrazas, was every bit as cunning and brave as Americans such as Buffalo Bill, Kit Carson, and Daniel Boone.

During the Porfirio Díaz dictatorship, the rich prospered greatly at the expense of the poor. One man's immense cattle ranch surpassed the size of Belgium, dwarfing even William Randolph Hearst's 875,000-acre Barbicoa Ranch, south of Casas Grandes. With social and economic injustices as a background, the 1910 revolution found plenty of backers in Chihuahua, especially to fill out the ranks of Pancho Villa's army. Opinions of Pancho Villa are still divided in the state; some consider him a hero while for others he was a mere bandit.

The city of Chihuahua is one of the two principal jumping off points for the fantastic train ride across the rugged Sierra Madre mountain range. (The other starting station is at Los Mochis on the Pacific coast.) The city can keep your interest for a day or so and not far away there are spas, Mennonite farmers, pre-Columbian ruins, and cattle ranches —enough to keep any interested visitor busy for several days. And the Sierras can be much more than a one-day train ride. Several good hotels are there which can provide guides and transport—horses or buses—to explore the Tarahumara Indian country as well as the canyons.

Chihuahua is a long ways from Mexico's major cities, over 900 miles from Mexico City, almost 700 miles from Guadalajara, 600 miles from Mazatlán and over 500 miles from Monterrey. The road system is good but long and often boring. But there are direct flights to several major northern cities and connecting flights to the others. Rumors told of an imminent air link with Dallas but this could not be confirmed at press time (late 1986).

EXPLORING CHIHUAHUA AND THE COPPER CANYON

If you enter Mexico at Ciudad Juárez, don't be in a hurry to leave. This is one of Mexico's largest border cities and you'll find a good bit of interest. There are several markets with pottery plus a good variety of other handicrafts and native products. Juárez has two bullrings and bullfights are always a top attraction for tourists. The Mission de Nuestra Señora de Guadalupe (a shrine to Mexico's patron saint) was built more than 300 years ago, with hand-carved beams and 4-foot-thick walls. There is the Museum of Art and History that exhibits the archeology, arts, and crafts of Mexico. San Lorenzo, just east of Juárez, has a festival in honor of Saint Lawrence on August 10. If you can make that, you'll see an unusual ballet with dancers representing Indians and Spaniards.

The border itself is rather fascinating. Until engineers moved in, the Rio Grande had a way of shifting its channel. After a century of trying, Mexico recovered a parcel known as El Chamizal, which for a while had been a part of El Paso. The river had to be rerouted so that it would continue to mark the border.

Highway 45 takes you to Chihuahua City over terrain that looks something like parts of west Texas. At the town of El Sueco, a little more than halfway from Juárez to Chihuahua, you can turn west on Highway 10 and drive 126 miles to Casas Grandes, the ruins of a once great city. Historians and archeologists are still studying this place. There are traces of the Pueblo Indian and Mesoamerican cultures in the 237 acres occupied by the ruins. Recent excavations have uncovered pyramids and the ancient city has a ball court and an irrigation system. About 4 miles away is the town of Nueva Casas Grandes, with gas stations and restaurants.

The city of Chihuahua was founded in 1709, a century before Mexico's War of Independence ended Spanish control. The city has something of a frontier feeling, partly from history and a good bit from its location. A thriving metropolis, it's the center of a vast ranching, timber, and silver-mining district. To the west lie the huge Sierra Madres, a continuation of the Rocky Mountains, and the lands of the Tarahumara Indians. The big cathedral in Chihuahua is an excellent example of colonial architecture. It was begun in 1724, but incessant battles with Indians held up completion until 1826. A colonial aqueduct also dates from the 18th century. Padre Miguel Hidalgo, the priest who launched Mexico's War of Independence from Spain, was captured by Spanish forces, held prisoner in Chihuahua, and executed there in 1811. The building in which he was imprisoned now holds offices of the federal government (Palacio Federal) while the one in which he was executed is the present state capitol (Palacio de Gobierno). The Church of San Francisco was built by Franciscan monks; construction on this baroque edifice began in 1717 and wasn't completed until 1789. Underground passages connect the church and the cathedral.

From Pancho Villa to Mennonites

On the north side of Chihuahua is Quinta Luz, the unusual museum that formerly was the home of revolutionary hero General Francisco Villa—also known as the bandit Pancho Villa. He somehow blended his occupations and made a career of marriage with a variety of ladies, some of whom laid claims to his estate after his assassination in 1923. After considerable study, the Mexican government decided that Luz Corral de Villa was the legitimate widow and she was awarded the home named for her—Quinta Luz. The Quinta is now a museum, filled with Villa's firearms, cartridge belts, and personal effects. On display is the bullet-riddled car Villa was driving when he was ambushed and killed. Many Mexican visitors drive miles out of their way to visit Quinta Luz. The huge mansion was the headquarters for General

Villa's "Golden Ones" during the rough and stirring days of the Mexican Revolution. With the death of Doña Luz in 1981, Quinta Luz was taken over by the government and is now open as the Museum of the Revolution.

For film buffs, there is a mansion copied from Tara in *Gone With the Wind,* located on Calle Cuauhtemoc. As it is a private building, you can only see it from the outside. Don't miss the dramatic monument to Pancho Villa, officially named Monumento a la Division del Norte for Pancho's army. The statue dominates the traffic circle of Avenida Universidad and Avenida Division del Norte. Just outside of town, a swimming and family recreation complex will allow you to let off some energy—but only between March and August, as the weather is too cold during the other months at this Balneario Joaquin Amaro, located in the suburb of Robinson.

Just about an hour's drive west of Chihuahua, the town of Cuauhtémoc serves as a center for the Mennonite farmers living in the countryside. Thousands of Mennonites moved here in the 1920's after living for generations in Germany, Russia, and Canada. Efficient farmers, these German speakers have their own schools and shun all luxuries. They do not speak Spanish, intermarry only among themselves. The families are very large—ten children are nothing unusual—leading to a shortage of farmland. The lack of land here has forced some to move to Belize and Paraguay. Always in distinctive dress, you can't miss these blonde, blue-eyed settlers, riding around in all kinds of horse-drawn contraptions. The Mennonites are famous for excellent cheeses and sausages sold in many area stores, some of which are run by the farmers themselves.

From Chihuahua to Creel through Cuauhtémoc, there is an excellent paved road. Other roads are dirt, and the going may get rough. One of the better roads from Cuauhtémoc leads to the 1000-ft.-high waterfall called Basaseáchic. With a local guide, you can skirt the falls and go down halfway on a path to a vantage point called *la ventana* (the window) for a spectacular view. From the falls, you can continue to the lumber town of Creel, an important station of the cross-Sierras railroad. Creel and its vicinity have several good hotels to be used as bases for further explorations of the Sierras.

Chihuahua-Pacific Railway

This incredible route (it's been called "World's Most Scenic Railroad") grew out of a dream of Albert K. Owen, who visualized more than 100 years ago the rail link from the southwestern United States to the Sea of Cortés port of Topolobampo. It was a means of reducing freight shipping distance overland to the Pacific. Some of the world's top railroad brains and pocketbooks foundered and went under, attempting what they were finally convinced was an impossible job. Mexico bought the foreign rail lines in her territory around 1940 and after 13 years of improving existing roadbeds and studying the problems of the Chihuahua-to-Pacific route, Mexican engineers announced they were ready to start. That was in 1953.

Eight years later, the "impossible" feat had been accomplished and the new line ran across 39 new bridges, through 86 new tunnels, and slithered around countless jagged canyons to reach Los Mochis, 15 miles from the Pacific. The route begins at Chihuahua and runs over more or less standard terrain to the foothills of the high Sierras. Colonel Arthur Stilwell opened that part for his Kansas City, Mexico and Orient Line in the early years of this century. A long stretch from Los Mochis east was completed, also. But the part that turned back the best engineering talent in the United States since the beginning of the dream was the 161-mile gap crossing the wild, high country of the Tarahumara Indians, skirting the deep Copper Canyon, winding around some mountains and going right through a lot of others. In the end, it was the Mexican engineers who were able to conquer their own defiant territory.

Straddling the rail line at an altitude of 7,500 feet is the lumber center of Creel. It once was the end of the line and vast amounts of pine lumber from the region were shipped down to Chihuahua City. You still find lumber camps here and mountains of neatly stacked, rough-sawed boards lie in a flat area just beyond the village, waiting for shipment. If your train stops here long enough, it's well worth a look.

There is a sort of trail that goes to a basin-like valley about half an hour away by truck. Several families of Tarahumara Indians live in caves on the valley floor at the foot of the high cliffs. The area is fresh-washed and green, with everything in startling Technicolor—the sort of place where they would hide rustled cattle in a John Wayne movie. In the winter it's cold, icy cold after the sun sets, and sometimes at nights the little brook crossing the grassy floor of the valley freezes around the edges. Not far from Creel, 30 minutes by truck, is a wonderful little mountain stream that spills along in long, cold stretches before dropping down to a new level. You can get rainbow trout here. Bring your catch to Creel and have a restaurant broil them for you.

Copper Canyon lies over the top, a fairly long run from Creel. The altitude is announced at figures ranging up to nearly 9,000 feet but something like 7,300 is close enough. Trains stop in Divisadero for 10–15 minutes so you can stretch, get out to take photos, and buy Tarahumara crafts from colorfully dressed Indians who sell baskets, weavings, and wood carvings at the station. The canyon is really a vast complex of six huge canyons, so big you can't see it all. But you can line up with an excursion to the bottom almost a mile below, where the quiet Urique River flows through subtropical terrain and you'll be in a different climate from that on top. Pleasant little hotels at the top give you the option of enjoying an overnight in the exhilarating air and continuing your trip on the next day's train.

Winding down toward Los Mochis, you go through the most spectacular part of the trip. You drop down through gorges that seem unreal; the tracks on the other side of the jumbled canyon are where you'll be in a few minutes after rounding the loop turn at the blind end. When crossing the 305-foot-high bridge across the Chinipas River, you almost can't see the narrow bridge looking out of the window and get the spooky feeling of rolling in space high over the big river. They often call it the Chihuahua-Topolobampo train, but Los Mochis is the end of the line. There are five stations to get off the train if you want to spend a while just relaxing or exploring the Sierras: Creel, El Divisadero, Cuiteco, Bahuichivo, and El Fuerte. These places have hotels either close to the station or will send a bus to pick you up. Unless you are willing to risk being stranded without lodgings, it is imperative that you make reservations ahead of time, either from Chihuahua or Los Mochis. (For more information of this train, see the *Practical Information* section.)

Camargo

Ciudad Camargo, 98 miles southeast of Chihuahua City on Highway 45, was originally known as Santa Rosalia. It was founded about 1740. The predominant industry of this region is cattle ranching, but Camargo, with a relatively small population, has meatpacking plants, textile operations, and a flour mill. If you get there on September 4, you can let down your hair for a week-long fiesta in honor of Santa Rosalia, Camargo's patron saint. There are dances, sporting events that include horse races and cockfights, and general merrymaking. There are three mineral springs close to Camargo: Ojo de Jabali, Ojo Salado, and Ojo Caliente. There are facilities (changing rooms, individual pools etc., . . .) only at the Ojo Caliente. Long before the Spaniards came to Mexico, Indians bathed in the medicinal waters said to be effective in clearing up skin and stomach problems. Eighteen paved miles southwest of Camargo is La Boquilla—Boquilla Dam which impounded a big lake on the river that begins as a trickle in the Tarahumara basin near Creel and flows down the slopes of the high Sierras. Interestingly, the official name for this body of water is Lake Toronto. It was so named because the lake was stocked with fish from Toronto, Canada.

Parral

Hidalgo del Parral is an antique mining town on Highway 45, about 190 miles southwest of Chihuahua City and something like 1,000 feet higher. The elevation is close to 5,500 feet. Parral (few people bother with the full name) exploded into world headlines when Pancho Villa was ambushed and assassinated here on July 20, 1923. Nine men waited 103 days for the former revolutionary general to pass the two-room house where they lay in waiting on Calle Gabino Barreda. The all-clear signal was given by a lookout at 8:30 A.M. when Pancho, at the wheel of his 1919 Dodge, and six bodyguards rounded the corner. The killers opened fire with a barrage from rifles and pistols. Villa and four of his bodyguards were killed on the spot. A fifth died a week later. Pancho, with 16 bullets in him, managed to draw one of his pistols in a last gasp move and shoot one of his attackers through the heart. Seven of the remaining eight lit out on horseback and were never bothered. Jesus Salas Barraza stayed behind to announce that he had engineered the assassination "for the good of the country." He was sentenced to 20 years in prison and released a few months later. Old timers in Parral say more than 30,000 attended Pancho Villa's funeral.

This otherwise quiet mountain town came into being when lodes of various ores, principally silver, lead, and copper, were found in the middle of the 16th century. Though the town wasn't officially founded until 1631, some 7,000 men, mainly Indians, were mining the surrounding sierra as early as 1600. In the 19th century, troops of Napoleon III occupied Parral during the brief French intervention. One of the outstanding structures here is a church—la Iglesia de la Virgen del Rayo; Church of the Virgin of the Thunderbolt. A noisy title, but the church is worth visiting. The Church of Our Lady of Fatima was built by the people in appreciation for their successful mining operations. It is made of chunks of ore—a conglomeration of silver, some gold, lead, copper, zinc, with a few other metals from the area. Even the pews of the church are of ore.

Durango

In a sense, Durango is a colonial city gone Hollywood. It was founded in 1563 and apparently named for Durango, Spain. Hollywood discovered it a few years ago and numerous films have been made in the western-type country near the city. John Wayne made several of his westerns here. In the days of the conquest, the Spaniards searched out valuable mineral deposits, rounded up all the Indian "volunteers" who couldn't escape, taught them the rules of Christianity, and put them to work building cities and working the mines. That's why so many of the colonial cities were, and still are, mining centers. Just north of the city is a mountain of iron, one of the largest known deposits in the world. In addition to iron, there are gold and silver deposits that never seem to run out in the ore-rich Sierra Madre Range. Durango has a good climate (6,400 feet altitude) as far as temperature goes but is a little on the arid side with an average annual rainfall of 16 inches. There is enough water, however, to form a stream on which they built the Guadalupe Victoria Dam, creating another good bass lake. The impoundment is a short distance south of the city, by paved road.

A word of warning to summer visitors! The hottest weather has a tendency to bring out the deadly white scorpion, a species found almost exclusively in the Durango area. While other scorpion stings are painful, the venom exuded by this unpleasant customer can be fatal if not treated promptly.

The State of Durango has an ample supply of thermal waters whose therapeutic values were discovered by the Indians before the days of the conquest. In the immediate vicinity of the city of Durango, you have Navacoyán and Valparaiso, whose waters are rich in sulphur, iron, and a number of other minerals reputedly soothing to those suffering from skin ailments, rheumatism, gastroenteritis, neuritis, and some types of anemia. A host of these thermal springs are found in such places as Canatlán, Santiago Papasquiaro, and Tepehuanes, some distance north of Durango along Highway 39, which branches off Highway 45. From the city of Durango, a good and spectacular road drops down to the Pacific resort town of Mazatlán. It is not advisable to drive this road at night.

PRACTICAL INFORMATION FOR CHIHUAHUA AND THE COPPER CANYON

HOW TO GET THERE. Good highways from El Paso, Texas, Monterrey, Durango, and Guadalajara. Passenger train service from Ciudad Juárez and Los Mochis. Direct flights from Ciudad Juárez, Mazatlán, Hermosillo, Mexico City, Monterrey, and Torreon. Flights with one stop from Acapulco, Guadalajara, Ixtapa/Zihuatanejo, Merida, and Tijuana. Possible flights in 1986 to Dallas.

EMERGENCY TELEPHONE NUMBERS. Tourism office—160000; **Police**—129333; **Ambulance**—30509.

HOTELS. Throughout the state of Chihuahua hotels were authorized, at press time, to charge the following average rates for a double room. While classifications may seem low in cost compared with American standards, they are based on the economy of the region. Because of rising inflation and as hotels upgrade their facilities, those listed here are likely to have higher rates by the time you read this. For a *Deluxe* hotel, expect to pay at least $38; *First Class,* $24; *Expensive,* $14.50; *Moderate,* $9.50; and *Inexpensive,* $5.50. All the Sierra hotels have dining rooms with hearty food, and the price of the room often includes all meals.

Chihuahua

Deluxe

Hyatt Exelaris, Niños Heroes and Independencia, downtown; tel. 66000; with 190 rooms, travel agency, car rental, bar, restaurant, disco, cafeteria, nightclub; good atmosphere in the lobby bar.

First Class

Castel Sicomoro, Ortiz Mena 411; tel. 35445; with good central location, 128 rooms, pool, travel agency, two bars, restaurant, cafeteria, satellite TV reception.

San Francisco, downtown at Victoria 504; tel. 67550; with 132 rooms, travel agency, bar, restaurant, cafeteria.

El Presidente, right on the central plaza at Libertad 9; tel. 60606; with 84 rooms, pool, two bars, restaurant, cafeteria, the "Penthouse" disco.

Posada Tierra Blanca, near the downtown area at Camargo and Niños Heroes 100; tel. 50000; with 108 rooms, pool, bar, restaurant, cafeteria, disco.

Mirador, Ave. Universidad 1309; tel. 32205; with 87 rooms near the center of town, pool, travel agency, car rental, bar, restaurant, cafeteria.

Expensive

Apolo, on the corner of Juárez and Carranza; tel. 61101; with 44 rooms, a bar for men only and restaurant open from 2 P.M. to midnight.

Victoria, on the corner of Juárez and Colon; tel. 28893; with 121 rooms, pool, travel agency, car rental, bar, restaurant, cafeteria, disco.

Parador San Migual, on the way into town from the north, on Avenida Tecnologico; tel. 70303; with 45 rooms, travel agency, bar, cafeteria.

Inexpensive

Maria Dolores, near downtown at Niños Heroes 901; tel. 122544; with 25 rooms and restaurant close by.

Roma, Libertad 1015, two blocks from downtown; tel. 127652; with 23 rooms.

San Juan, Victoria 823 near downtown; tel. 128492; with 61 rooms, bar, and restaurant.

Camargo

Los Nogales, Juarez 404; tel. 21247; with 31 rooms. *Expensive.*

Cabañas Santa Rosalia, Juarez and Abasolo; tel. 20214; with 33 rooms. *Inexpensive.*

Victoria, Jimenez and Comonfort; tel. 20791; with 24 rooms. *Inexpensive.*

Near Cuahtémoc

Rancho La Estancia, mainly a hunting lodge/hotel on the outskirts of Cuahtémoc. For reservations write Apdo. Postal 986, Chihuahua, or telephone 122282. *Expensive.*

Tarahumara Inn, Allende and 5th St., Cuahtémoc; tel. 22801; 40 rooms. *Expensive*

Los Mochis

Best Western Hotel Las Colinas, Highway 15 and Blvd. Macario Gaxiola; tel. 20101; 124 rooms, restaurant, cafeteria, bar, disco, pool. *Expensive.*

Hotel Santa Anita, Calle Leyva and Hidalgo; tel. 20046; 130 rooms, restaurant, travel agency, tours. *Expensive.*

Motel Plaza Inn, Calle Leyva; tel. 20075; 40 remodeled rooms; hunting and fishing trips. *Moderate*

In the Sierras, Along the Train Route

Cabañas Divisadero, in El Divisadero; reservations from Chihuahua at Aldama 407, tel. 123362, or through travel agencies. Next to the train station; 35 rooms. *Expensive.*

Misión, in Cerocahui, some 15 miles from the Bahuichivo station. Reservations through travel agencies or at the Hotel Santa Anita in Los Mochis; tel. 20046; 28 rooms, wood burning stoves, rides to the Urique Canyon. *Expensive.*

Parador de la Montaña, in Creel; tel. 160075; for reservations from Chihuahua, tel. 122062, or through travel agency; 36 rooms, central heat. Hotel has a landing strip, bus tours to the Tarahumara, Copper Canyon, Batopilas; good fishing nearby. *Expensive.*

Posada Barrancas, at the next stop after El Divisadero towards Los Mochis. For reservations in Chihuahua, Reforma 1600–2, tel. 165950, or Hotel Santa Anita in Los Mochis, tel. 20046. Has 36 rooms, kerosene stoves, all kinds of tours. *Expensive.*

Posada Hidalgo, Hidalgo 101 in El Fuerte. For reservations in Chihuahua, Reforma 1600–2; in Los Mochis, Santa Anita Hotel. Former hacienda. *Expensive.*

Cabañas Barrancas de Urique, some 25 miles from the train station at Bahuichivo; 21 cabins; bus tours to the canyons and Tarahumaras. Reservations through travel agents or through Apartado Postal 622 in Chihuahua. *Moderate.*

Cabañas del Cobre or **Copper Canyon Lodge,** in Creel; reservations through travel agencies in Chihuahua or through Angelica Lerma, Hotel Victoria, in Chihuahua; tel. 128893. There are 25 lodge-type rooms, fireplaces, games room, tours to a Jesuit mission, Tarahumara Indians, canyons, fishing. *Moderate.*

SPECIAL EVENTS. Feria de Santa Rita (Santa Rita Fair)—second half of May, various expositions by the government showing its advances in the state; cockfights, occasional bullfights, fireworks; at the fairgrounds on Avenida Prolongacion Pacheco. **Expogan**—second half of October; basically a cattle exposition with the *charreria* (Mexican rodeo), cockfights, bullfights, fireworks; a good place to buy all kinds of cowboy clothes and accessories such as saddles. In conjunction with this fair, all the restaurants in town have a *muestra gastronomica* (gastronomic sample) featuring their best dishes at reduced prices; the events take place at the fairgrounds at km 8.5 on the highway to Cuauhtémoc.

HOW TO GET AROUND. Taxis within town are quite inexpensive, $1 to $3 to just about any destination but be certain to agree on the price before you get in; buses are cheap and go to most places within town and to other cities.

By Rail. On the *Chihuahua-Pacific Railroad* (see *Exploring* section), passenger service extends from Chihuahua to Los Mochis in the Mexican state of Sinaloa. The route covers about 410 miles of fascinating country—the rugged homeland of aborigine Indian tribes, including the Tarahumaras.

Two kinds of service link Chihuahua with the Pacific: 1) Autovías or Italian-made *Fiat,* self-propelled diesel electric cars, in tandem, and 2) vísta tren or diesel-powered passenger trains.

The *autovías* leave Chihuahua five times a week but run only as far as Creel. The autovías leave Chihuahua on Monday, Thursday, Friday, Saturday, and Sunday at 8 A.M. arriving at Creel at 2 P.M. These trains return the same days, leaving Creel at 2:30 P.M. and arrive at Chihuahua at 7:35 P.M. (if there are no delays).

Passenger trains leave both the Los Mochis and the Chihuahua terminals every day, making the 400 plus mile run in some 15 hours (if there are no delays). There is a dining car on this train. The regular passenger trains have two classes; numbered reclining seat coach and chair coach *especial numerada* and *primera general*). They leave the Los Mochis and Chihuahua terminals at 7 A.M. and arrive at the opposite end of the line at 8:30 P.M. This means that the last part of each run is at night, especially during the winter. The only way to see it all is to make the trip both ways. If this is impossible, we recommend that you make the trip from Los Mochis to Chihuahua as all of the more spectacular part of the line can be seen in daylight this way. In either direction there is a daytime 10-minute stopover at El Divisadero from where you have the most spectacular view of Copper Canyon, along with Tarahumara Indians who sell their craft to the train passengers.

Small automobiles such as Renaults and Datsuns may be shipped in either direction for about $115. Cars are loaded in boxcars. Count on three days' shipping time. Notice of intent to ship automobile must be given to *Chihuahua-Pacific Railroad Freight Office* at Chihuahua at least 2 days before intended departure date.

No checked baggage is handled on the *autovias* or passenger trains. If desired, automobiles may be parked at the depot parking lot in Chihuahua.

Visitors who wish to go further into Mexico from Los Mochis and rent a car or avail themselves of the excellent *Tres Estrellas de Oro* first class bus service into Mazatlán for a stopover, or on into Guadalajara which has a convenient overnight train connection into Mexico City.

For attractive folders in English on the Copper Canyon trip, schedules, and any late information, write: Emma Rodriguez, General Agent Purchasing Dept., Mexican Government Railways System, 1500 Broadway, Suite 810, New York, NY 10036; tel. 212–382–2262.

If you phone, be prepared to state your needs to an answering machine. If interested, inquire about the occasional rail tours out of the U.S. that incorporate the Copper Canyon trip in their itinerary. Among them are Baja Adventures, Encino Calif.; Sanborn's Tours, Austin, Texas; and Point South R.V. Tours, Northridge, Calif.

Please note that all rates and schedules are subject to change without notice.

TOURIST INFORMATION SERVICES. *City Tourism Office* in Chihuahua Calle Cuauhtémoc 1800, 3rd floor, open 9 A.M.–1 P.M. and 3–7 P.M. Monday through Friday; tel. 16000. *Federal Tourism Office,* Avenida Tecnologico, next to Parador San Miguel, on the highway coming into town from the north; open 8 A.M. to 6 P.M. every day (in theory); no telephone.

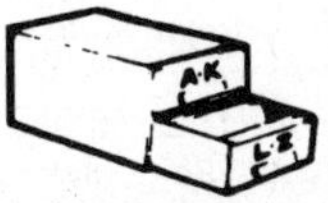

USEFUL ADDRESSES. Airlines. Chihuahua, *Aeroméxico,* Victoria 106, tel. 156306 and at the airport, 122695; *Mexicana,* Edificio Russek, Ave. Juarez 1108/1, tel. 161044 and at the airport, 160551. **Bus station.** Avenida Revolucion and Progreso. **Car rentals.** *Avis,* Ave. Universidad 1703, tel. 141999; *Hertz,* Blvd. Diaz Ordaz 220, tel. 125100; *National,* Central Comercial La Fuente, local 26, tel. 157900, *Thrifty,* Juarez and Colon, tel. 125145. **Hospitals.** *Clinica del Parque,* Calle de la Llave and Calle 12, tel. 122580; *Hospital del Centro,* Ojinaga 816, tel. 160022.

TOURS. The usual tours out of Chihuahua are to the Sierras and these can be arranged by one of the travel agencies listed below. There are also city tours for $6.50 per person, two-person minimum; tour of the cultural places of the city, same price, same conditions; tour of the Mennonite country, $16 per person, four person minimum.

Viajes Cañon del Cobre, at the lobby of the Victoria Hotel on Colon and Juarez, tel. 28893.

Turismo Espectacular de Mexico, V. Carranza 507, tel. 150666.

Viajes Magaña, Calle 15, #103–3, tel. 152912.

Rojo y Casavantes, Bolivar 1000, tel. 154636.

Viajes Dorados, Aldama 316, tel. 162284.

MUSEUMS. *Museo Regional* (Regional Museum) Quinta Gameros, Avenida Bolivar and Calle 3, open from Tuesday to Sunday 9 A.M. to 1 P.M. and 3 to 7 P.M. Small entrance fee. *Museo de la Revolucion* (Pancho Villa Museum), Calle 10 #3017, same hours as above. *Calaboso de Hidalgo* (Hidalgo's Jail) at the Palacio del Federal, open from 9 A.M. to 3 P.M. every day; no admission charge.

SHOPPING. You can get good buys on woven goods such as sweaters and ponchos, silver jewelry, and Tarahumara crafts. *Arte Popular Mexicano,* Aldama 710, tel. 151766; *Artesanias y Gemas Naturales de Mexico,* Calle 10 #3019, tel. 152882, (especially for semi-precious stones); *Mercado de Artesanías Mexicanos,* Victoria 506, tel. 155307; *Artesanias Mexicanas de Jalisco,* Aldama 508, tel. 150716; *Museo de Artes y Industrias Populares,* Reforma 5, closed Mondays.

RESTAURANTS. **La Olla de Chihuahua,** Ave. Juárez 3331, tel. 157894; specializes in meat cuts; basic meal $6; open every day from noon to midnight; accepts credit cards; live music on weekend nights.

La Calesa, Ave. Juárez 3300, tel. 128555; specializes in meat cuts; basic meal $5; open weekdays 1 P.M. to midnight, weekends to 10 P.M. Accepts all major credit cards; live music on weekends.

Los Vitrales, Ave. Juárez 2116, tel. 120915; Cantonese and international dishes, basic meal $6; live music after 9 P.M.; accepts major credit cards except *American Express* and *Diners;* open every day from 1 P.M. to midnight.

Los Parados de Tony Vega, Ave. Juárez 3316, tel. 124141; specializes in meat cuts; live music from 8 to 11 P.M.; basic meal $6; open every day from 1 P.M. to midnight; accepts credit cards.

Robin Hood Pub, Talavera 208, tel. 157283; specializes in meat cuts and incredible sandwiches which can reach three feet in length made from their own bakery, considered the best in the city; also Alaskan King Crab, smoked salmon and rainbow trout; video shows of rock in one side of the restaurant and rock and romantic on the other side; basic meal $7; open 1 P.M. to midnight every day, disco dancing at night; accepts major credit cards.

El Leñador, Tecnologico and Ahuehuete, tel. 136191; meat specialties; basic meal $4; open every day from 1 P.M. to midnight; credit: *Carnet, Banamex, Bancomer.*

El Rey del Taco, Calle 13 and Escorzega, tel. 160940; specializes in tacos; basic meal $3.50; open every day from 1:30 to 11 P.M.; credit: *Bancomer* and *Carnet.*

Quinta Maria Teresa, Independencia 1410, tel. 155953; also an art gallery; specializes in American cuts of meat; basic meal $6.50; open 8 A.M. to midnight; credit: *Bancomer, Banamex, Carnet, Visa.*

Ajos y Cebollas, Colon 207, tel. 163102; also an art gallery; specializes in the authentic cooking of the Sierras and rural Chihuahua, absolutely delicious and most dishes are not too "hot" for American palates; friendly atmosphere; basic meal $3; open from noon to midnight every day except on Monday; no credit cards.

Hosteria 1900, Ave. Independencia 903A, tel. 161990; Mexican crepes; video bar next door; basic meal $4; open daily 1 P.M. to 2 A.M. Major credit cards accepted.

NIGHTLIFE. Discos: *La Mina* in the Hotel Victoria on Ave. Juárez and Colon and the *Robin Hood* at Cuauhtemoc 2207. Cafes with entertainment include *Hobbet,* Ave. Reforma 103, *Gilberto's,* Ave. Division del Norte 2500 and *Ajos y Cebollas,* Colon 207. Hotels: *La Place* piano bar in the Hyatt Hotel Lobby, Independencia 500; and *La Uva* in the Castel Sicomoro Hotel, Ortiz Mina 411, two drinks for one 5–7 P.M.

MONTERREY AREA AND THE GULF COAST TO VERACRUZ AREA

by
JIM BUDD

Broadly speaking, this is the Huasteca country—named for the Huastecs, a tribe whom the Aztecs scorned for their shameful lack of morals. These Indians, who live on in the region, in pre-Hispanic times apparently were more interested in worshipping the goddess of fertility and fleshly pleasures than in building monuments. Their descendants lead more conservative lives.

The Huasteca country includes parts of the states of Tamaulipas, Nuevo Leon, and Veracruz. Best way to see this area is by car. Usually motorists drive down the Gulf Coast Road (Mexico 101 and Mexico 180) to Tampico and Veracruz. Rather than doubling back they will head inland—with a visit to Mexico City if they like—and pick up Mexico 85, the old Pan American Highway which heads for Monterrey and the border.

Some people, however, only get to the border towns, special favorites with "Winter Texans," folks who flee the snows up north to bask in the sun of the Rio Grande Valley. Others opt simply for a few days in Monterrey, Mexico's third-largest city, where the hotels, restaurants, shopping, and nightlife all are terrific. They have a good time, but still they miss a lot of fun.

Fun, really, is what the Huasteca country is all about. It is taking in the races in Laredo, haggling for bargains at the Matamoros market, oléing the matadors in Monterrey, hauling in weighty bass in the lake country northeast of Tampico and lazing in the sun at the Veracruz beaches.

There are sights to see, too. Archaeology is part of a good Mexican holiday and the Huasteca country has it at El Tajin, complete with a spectacular pyramid and stone carvings of human sacrifices. The fortress of San Juan de Ulua in Veracruz might have been a set for one of those old late show pirate movies. Near Monterrey are natural wonders: the Garcia Caves and Horsetail Falls.

EXPLORING THE HUASTECA COUNTRY

The border country is fun, worth spending some time in even for those who are heading farther south. In a way it is all sort of mirror image, stores and shops on the Texas side gaudy with signs in Spanish welcoming Mexican customers and proclaiming a willingness to accept pesos while across the river much of the lettering is in English and discounts are promised for those with dollars to spend.

Nuevo Laredo is Mexico's biggest port of entry on the U.S. border. It can come as something of a shock, zipping down Interstate 35 from San Antonio, crossing the new bridge, leaving the First World, so to speak, and entering the Third. Less of a jolt is driving through downtown Laredo along Convent Avenue, crossing the bridge and ending up on Avenida Guerrero, the main street in Nuevo Laredo. Those who do not want to drive can walk over.

Nuevo Laredo got its start once the Rio Grande became a border river. After Texas broke away from Mexico the Mexicans held the dividing line was farther north, at the Rio Nueces. Caught in no man's land, the settlers wished a plague on both sides and tried to set up an independent republic. Mexican authorities made short work of that. Then, when Texas became a U.S. state, American troops moved below the Nueces, which is what touched off the Mexican War. When it was over the burghers of Laredo who did not wish to be ruled from Austin and Washington founded a new community on the south bank of the Rio Grande (a river the Mexicans call the Rio Bravo).

The railway to the U.S., and then the Pan American Highway, made Nuevo Laredo the big city it is. Liquor laws north of the boundary gave it much of its special flavor. First there was Prohibition, then Texas' own dry statutes drew the thirsty across the bridge. With World War II came regiments of recruits on three-day passes, and they still come pouring in.

The big appeal these days is the racetrack where the ponies run weekend afternoons and the greyhounds four nights a week throughout the year. Then there are the shops, tacky little places, most of them, but a few remarkably posh with handicrafts on sale that are works of art. Nuevo Laredo also is a fine place to get a good meal.

Reynosa, farther to the east, is a crossing point of no great interest. A few miles south of McAllen (the actual Texas border point is a village called Hidalgo), Reynosa is big and industrial, being a major gas processing and oil refining center. There are a couple of hotels and restaurants plus some curio shops around Plaza Hidalgo, but for most tourists Reynosa is simply a town to pass through en route to the fishing camps at the Vicente Guerrero Dam.

Matamoros is much nicer. Across from Brownsville and what is the southernmost part of the continental U.S., Matamoros has an attractive shopping area just beyond the bridge. Downtown, a few blocks away, the city is typically Mexican, belying the old saw about border towns having no personality.

Although roots here go back to Spanish colonial times, this area really began to thrive during the American Civil War. Near Matamoros was the site of Bagdad which, although it was in Mexico, has been described as the biggest port of the Confederacy. From Bagdad Southern cotton went out and arms for Southern armies came in, thus outflanking the Union blockade. Bagdad, you will hear, was a pretty wicked place and it came to a pretty wicked end. A hurricane in 1880 literally wiped Bagdad off the map.

Matamoros itself has little that is historic to see these days. There is the Casa Mata, a small fort that now contains a museum which includes a display of early Huasteca Indian pottery. But perhaps the most impressive feature of this border town is that there seem to be more dental offices than curio shops. With good reason: peso prices are much lower than dollar prices, yet the professionals are on a par with their American counterparts.

Monterrey Spruces Up

Monterrey is that way but even more so. Brewer of beer and forger of steel, Monterrey is the home of nearly three million of the hardest working people in Mexico. It is not an especially tourist-oriented city, but being just a three hour drive from the border—less for those who fly in from Houston or San Antonio—it gets visitors anyway. Few of them go away disappointed.

Urban renewal has made Monterrey, once an ugly place, into quite an attractive city. The 100-acre Grand Plaza extends for several blocks from the classical State House to the ultra-modern City Hall. Dedicated in 1985, the plaza is expected to be an area of intense activity for the next decade as new office buildings and stores open in the area.

The plaza leads into smaller Hidalgo Square and Avenida Morelos, a pedestrian shopping street where automobiles no longer roll. The better stores are along this way, as are many good restaurants, night spots, and many of Monterrey's best hotels. Having the hotels in the

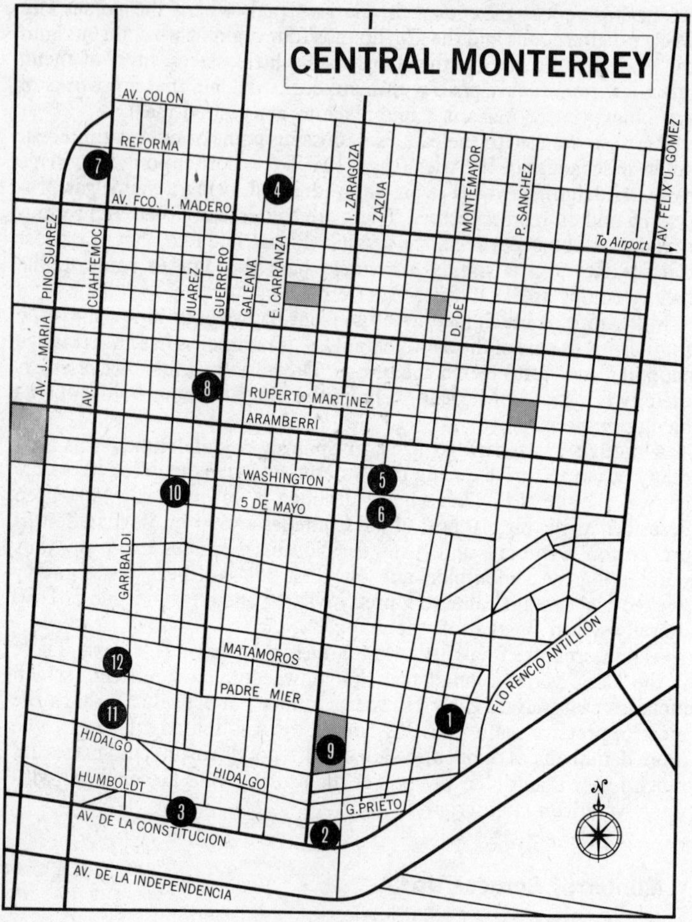

Points of Interest

1) Cathedral
2) City Hall
3) Colon Market
4) Cultural Museum
5) Federal Palace
6) Governor's Palace
7) Independence Arch
8) Juarez Market
9) Plaza Zaragoza
10) Del Roble Church
11) San Luis Gonzaga Church
12) Seguro Hospital

heart of the commercial area is, of course, convenient. Yet for travelers who prefer to be out a ways there are also good places to stay.

Monterrey got its start at the end of the 16th century when the first group of settlers arrived. It struggled merely to survive. Work on the cathedral began in 1635, but it took nearly 200 years to finish the project. The only other ancient structure of note is the Bishops' Palace, erected toward the end of the 18th century as a retirement home for upper strata clergy. Stout and strong, it ended up serving as a fortress; today it is a museum.

Beer is what really made Monterrey. The brewery opened in 1888. Bottles were needed, so a glass factory was built. Cartons were needed in which to ship the bottles, so in went a cardboard plant. Then, to provide caps, a steel mill was opened. Thus industrial might was born.

Gradually culture followed. Monterrey's first museum was its Baseball Hall of Fame. Now there is an art museum as well, along with several galleries. Most spectacular, however, is the Alfa Cultural Center—built by the descendants of those early brewers—where the emphasis is on science and technology.

Monterrey is a place to shop for cowboy boots and lead crystal. It is the place to take in a charro rodeo on a Sunday morning and a bullfight on a Sunday afternoon. It is a city in which to dine well and then stay up late catching a floorshow or stomping at a disco. In that respect Monterrey has no rivals in the Huasteca country.

This, by the way, is where the Huasteca region begins. Huasteca Canyon is just west of the city, high, craggy, dramatic. Out this way, too, are the Garcia Caves, the largest and most majestic in Mexico. The entrance to the caves is reached by cable car and getting there is half the fun. Horsetail Falls, off in another direction, is a lovely spot to go for a picnic or to ride in a pony cart or on a donkey's back.

One heads farther down into the Huasteca country by road. Mexico 85, the old Pan American Highway (first road between Mexico City and the U.S.) runs over to Ciudad Victoria, connecting with Mexico 80 which goes down to the coast. Sportsmen often get no further than the Vicente Guerrero Dam near Ciudad Victoria. The winter months provide top duck and dove hunting along the shores of the man-made lake while the waters teem with bass throughout the year. There are good hunting and fishing camps out this way and they cater mostly to Americans.

The other way to get into the Huasteca Gulf Coast is to head south from Reynosa or Matamoros. Mexico 180 links up with Mexico 80 shortly before that highway enters Tampico. From the border Tampico is about a seven-hour trip; from Monterrey the journey takes a little longer.

Tampico, Tropical Port

To know Tampico is to love it. Raffish, wicked, stately in its fading dignity, Tampico is a set designer's dream of a tropical port. The waterfront around the Plaza Libertad seems to be populated by characters out of central casting all waiting for Graham Greene to put them in a novel. A block or so away is the regal Plaza de Armas guarded by towering palms and a majestic city hall. One gathers that the populations of the two plazas never mix.

With one or two exceptions the better Tampico hotels are away from the Gulf, inland on Avenida Hidalgo as if trying to forget this is a port city. Tampico has a split personality. Originally this was a Huastec settlement; the only museum of note in the area, the one at the Technological Institute, highlights the Huastec culture. The Spaniards came to stay in 1530 when the Franciscans founded a mission. The villages that went up, however, were continually being swept away by hurricanes.

Petroleum made Tampico what it is today. The first oil wells were brought in during 1907 and prosperity of sorts followed. The cathedral on the Plaza de Armas was built with funds donated by Edward L. Doheny, the oil magnate involved in the Teapot Dome scandal of the 1920s. Mexicana Airlines got its start as Latin America's first airline by flying into Tampico from Mexico City back before paved highways had been put in.

Oil did much for Tampico, but in many ways it ruined it for tourism. Time was when Texans would hurry down every chance they got to go after tarpon in the Panuco River. Pollution in the river pretty much ruined that. Once Tampico had an international airport and hotels run by Westin, Howard Johnson, and Holiday Inn. Now the only flights are from Mexico City plus three a week from Monterrey. The former chain hotels are locally managed now.

There still is a bit of game fishing in the Tampico area and the beach at Miramar is nice. Golf can be played at the local country club and visitors are welcome.

Veracruz, an eight-hour drive down the coast, is a bit like Tampico, yet different enough to be worth the trip. Most visitors will want to stop en route and spend a few hours exploring the ruins at El Tajin. This will require an overnight stay either at the Juarez Hotel in Poza Rica or the Tajin Hotel in Papantla.

Papantla is where vanilla comes from. It also is the home of the "Flying Indians" whose pre-Hispanic ritual still is performed every Sunday. The performers, five in all, climb to a tiny platform atop a 100-foot pole. Four of them tie ropes, which have been wound about the pole, to their ankles. Then, while their companion remains on top playing a flute and beating a drum, the four leap into space, gradually whirling toward the ground as the ropes unwind. As might be expected, this is really something to see.

So, too, are the ruins at El Tajin. This is the only archaeological zone of importance in the Huastec country. It is, however, a monument not to the Huastecs but to the Totonacs. It was the Totonacs, then vassels of the Aztecs, who greeted Cortes when he landed at Veracruz.

Historic Veracruz

Although the spot where Cortes first landed is actually some 30 miles up the coast, Veracruz can still claim to be the first European city established on the mainland of the Americas. Throughout most of the colonial era it was the only east coast port of entry into what was then

New Spain and as such was the one gateway to Europe. Seized once by the French, twice by the Americans, looted by pirates and buffeted by storms, Veracruz is rich in history but lacking much that is ancient. The great fort of San Juan de Ulua—built in the time of Charles V to defend the city against buccaneers—is about the only reminder of the turbulent past. In any event, the Jarochos, as the people of Veracruz call themselves, prefer to forget the bad old days. They are too busy having a good time.

This is a city of music, something out of an old Carmen Miranda movie. Veracruz is the home of the bamba, a very special dance, and of trios who play portable harps and tiny guitars. Marimbas throb in the evening outside the sidewalk cafes and even when the mardi gras is not going on (the week before Lent) there is a feeling it is about to start.

Before the air age Veracruz was the first stop on a visit to Mexico. People came by ship and went on to Mexico City by train, often with a wistful look back at the lively port they were leaving. Before Acapulco became such a popular playground, Veracruz was where Mexicans headed when they wanted to spend a few days at the beach. Many still do, for Veracruz is a lot less expensive than the big international resort areas.

The beach at Mocambo a few miles out from the city is delightful. So is Boca del Rio, a fishing village just beyond Mocambo where seafood can be savored at delightful open air restaurants overlooking the river. Many are the good restaurants in Veracruz itself, and there are enough discos and other nightspots to keep revelers happy once darkness falls. Veracruz has its museums, too, plus fishing boats and outings by launch to the beaches at Isla de Sacrificios (Sacrifice Island).

Weather is the one iffy thing in Veracruz. Very iffy. During the winter months what the Jarochos call northers are likely to come whipping in from the Gulf, drenching the city for days. For the philosophical, these storms can be rather delightful, however. Somehow they touch off a certain cheerfulness among the local people, a determination to keep smiling in spite of the clouds. Such attitudes can be catching.

Overall, November through April is the best time to come to the Huasteca country. December and January, to be sure, occasionally are unseasonably cold, but not often. Summers, on the other hand, are almost unfailingly blistering. The border country simmers and Monterrey broils. Tampico and Veracruz usually are blessed by cool breezes, but not always.

PRACTICAL INFORMATION FOR MONTERREY AND THE GULF COAST

HOW TO GET THERE. Most foreign visitors to this area either fly into Monterrey for a long weekend or drive down for an extended stay, taking in as much of the region as their time allows. While all the cities covered here—Monterrey, Tampico, and Veracruz plus the border gateways at Nuevo Laredo, Reynosa, and Matamoros—are served by one of Mexico's two airlines, intraregional service is limited. Only Monterrey is connected by flights from and to the U.S. Rail travel has little to recommend it. Buses, which link all the destinations in the area, will appeal only to the adventurous and the thrifty; language often is the biggest problem since away from the border English is seldom understood.

By Air. Monterrey is connected to Houston by *Continental* and *Aeromexico. Aeromexico* also has daily flights from Los Angeles and San Diego (Tijuana Airport). *Mexicana* flies in daily from Dallas while operating four flights weekly from Chicago and three flights a week from San Antonio.

Nuevo Laredo may be reached via Laredo, Texas, to which *Continental* flies from Houston.

Reynosa is across the Rio Grande from McAllen, Texas, which is served by *Continental* and *Muse* from Houston with *Muse* also flying in from Dallas/Fort Worth.

Matamoros is across from Brownsville, Texas, to which *Muse* flies from Houston and Dallas/Fort Worth and *Ozark* from San Antonio.

By Train. Rail service throughout the area is available, but only the most dedicated train buffs will want to experiment with it. From the border a train leaves Matamoros daily at 6:50 A.M. arriving in Reynosa at 9 A.M. and continuing on to Monterrey, arriving at 2 P.M. From Laredo the *Aztec Eagle* leaves at 7 P.M. and arrives in Monterrey after midnight. A train leaves Monterrey for Tampico daily at 7:40 A.M., arriving at 6 P.M. Veracruz may be reached by train from Monterrey via Mexico City. Fares are cheap, but trains frequently are dirty and often cannot provide seats for all passengers.

By Car. All destinations in this region may be reached comfortably by driving. Highways, with few exceptions, are two lanes and in fairly good condition. Travel after dark should be avoided, however. During daylight hours roads are patrolled by the Green Angels which will provide free mechanical assistance in case of a breakdown.

(For more tips to motorists, see *Facts at Your Fingertips* chapter.)

Rental cars are cheaper in the U.S. but not all agencies will authorize their vehicles being driven across the Rio Grande. Written permission will be required by Mexican authorities if a rental car is to be taken beyond border points.

Nuevo Laredo is across from Laredo, Texas, which is reached by Interstate 35 from San Antonio and U.S. 59 from Houston.

Reynosa, across from McAllen, is reached by U.S. 281 from San Antonio.

Matamoros, across from Brownsville, is reached by U.S. 77 from Corpus Christi.

Monterrey is about a three-hour drive south from Nuevo Laredo via Mexico 85; the city may also be reached from Reynosa via Mexico 40.

Tampico is about an eight-hour drive from Monterrey via Mexico 85 to Ciudad Victoria and Mexico 80 on to the coast. From Matamoros the trip via Mexico 180 takes about seven hours.

Veracruz is an eight-hour drive from Tampico heading down the coast on Mexico 180.

By Bus. The Texas border cities are served by *Greyhound* and *Continental Trailways* with Mexican buses departing from their depots for points south. As mentioned, bus travel in Mexico is cheap (about a dollar for each hour of travel) but confusing. Tickets are for a specific seat on a specific bus; miss the bus, buy a new ticket. Passengers planning intermediate stops before reaching their final destination should buy separate tickets to each point on the journey: Matamoros to Monterrey, for example, and then Monterrey to Tampico. Vehicles, while not up to U.S. standards, are fairly comfortable. Only *First Class* or *Deluxe* (when available) buses should be taken.

Nuevo Laredo. Reynosa and Matamoros all have a central bus station, called *central caminonera,* out on the southern edge these cities. Taxi fares to the station often are higher than the price of the bus ticket itself. This is one reason why it makes sense to board Mexican buses in the Texas terminals which are downtown; also, customs and immigration formalities are handled more expeditiously. When boarding a bus in Mexico, be sure to have tourist cards stamped by immigration at the bridge point of entry. There will be a customs inspection prior to boarding the bus (Mexican border cities are limited duty-free zones) and a secondary check by customs and immigration officials a few miles south of the border cities to see that luggage has been sealed and documents stamped. Usually these procedures are nothing more than a formality, although proof of sufficient funds for travel may be requested. Passengers leaving the U.S. and planning to return should have, naturally, proof of citizenship, or a passport with visa as required by the American authorities.

Travel time by bus is approximately the same as that mentioned above for those driving their own car.

TELEPHONES. *Area codes.* Nuevo Lardeo: 871; Reynosa: 892; Matamoros: 891; Monterrey: 83; Tampico: 121; Veracruz: 29. Only local calls may be dialed from most hotels. In case of extreme emergency help may be summoned by dialing 09 where the international operators speak English.

HOTELS. Good hotels are to be found along both sides of the Rio Grande, although there is a wider selection on the north side of the river. Prices in Mexico tend to be lower, and Mexican inns have the added lure of providing a night abroad. Expect to pay $50 for a double room in the establishment we list as *Deluxe;* $30 at a *First class* hotel; $20 in a *Moderate* place and $15 in one that is *Inexpensive.*

Border Cities

Hacienda, Reforma 5530, Nuevo Laredo; 2–6666. An attractive resort-like motel with ample grounds, pool, bar, restaurant, and 72 rooms. *Deluxe.*

El Presidente, Alvaro Obregon and Amapolas in Matamoros; 3–9440. Colonial; 150 rooms built around a patio and swimming pool. Restaurant, bar, nightly entertainment. *Deluxe.*

Astromundo, Juarez and Guerrero, Reynosa; 2–5625. The name means "Astroworld"; this is a 75-room facility with pool, restaurant and bar. *First Class.*

La Casona, Independencia 513, Matamoros; 6–3740. Central location, pool, restaurant and satellite TV programming. *First Class.*

Fontana, Lauro Villar Highway, Matamoros; 2–4500. A small, pleasant place to stay, on the road to the beach. Restaurant and bar. *Moderate.*

El Rio, Reforma 4404, Nuevo Laredo; 2–3600. Large, with 162 units, this is an American-style motel with pool, children's playground, restaurant, and bar. *First Class.*

Virrey, Hidalgo and Balboa, Reynosa; 3–1050. Centrally located with a good restaurant and appealing bar. *First Class.*

Reforma, Guerrero 822, Nuevo Laredo; 2–3600. Centrally located and a bit noisy with 40 carpeted rooms, all services. *Moderate.*

San Carlos, Hidalgo Oriente 970, Reynosa; 2–1280. An old-fashioned three-story hotel with restaurant, bar, and parking lot. *Moderate.*

Fiesta, Ocampo 559, Nuevo Laredo; 2–4737. One of the best values in town with 35 rooms. *Inexpensive.*

Savoy, Juarez 860, Reynosa; 2–0067. A tiny, nice 22-room inn close to downtown. *Inexpensive.*

Monterrey

The third-largest city in Mexico offers a wide range of accommodations. Most hotels are downtown, close to everything. A double in a *Deluxe* place will cost about $40, *First Class* $35; *Moderate* $25 and *Inexpensive* $18.

Deluxe

Ambassador, Hidalgo and Carranza; 40–9390. Handsome, with 250 rooms, attractive lobby bar, and excellent restaurant. U.S. programming on room TV. Affiliated with Westin.

Gran Hotel Ancira, Hidalgo and Escobedo; 42–4806. Grand dame of Monterrey inns, classically elegant with 300 rooms, two restaurants, bars, evening entertainment in the lobby. U.S. programming on room TV.

Monterrey Plaza Holiday Inn, Constitución 450; 44–6600. The newest in town, 415 rooms, two restaurants, bars, nightly entertainment. U.S. programming on room TV.

Ramada's Hilltop Hacienda, Avenida Alamazan; 76–4481. Something of a resort on the edge of town with pool, tennis, bars, two restaurants and U.S. programming on room TV.

First Class

Chipinque, Galeana Sur 940; 76–1100. An attractive semi-resort up in the hills overlooking the city with 60 units, pool, two tennis courts, appealing restaurant.

Holiday Inn, Universidad 101. 52–2400. Attractive, semi-colonial in design, with 190 units and all services. On the highway coming in from Laredo.

Monterrey, Morelos Oriente 574; 43–5120. An older but recently renovated 200 room Best Western with two restaurants, bars, evening entertainment and U.S. programming on room TV.

Moderate

Jolet, Padre Mier Oriente 201; 40–5500. A 150-room commercial hotel with restaurant and lobby bar, convenient location.

El Paso, Zaragoza Norte 130; 40–0696. An in-the-city motel with restaurant, bar, room television.

Rio, Padre Mier Oriente 194; 44–9040. An old favorite among downtown hotels with 400 rooms, restaurant, bar and extra large pool area.

Royalty, Hidalgo and Carranza; 40–9800. A neighbor of some of the city's finest hotels with 66 rooms, restaurant, bar and pool.

Son-Mar, Universidad 1211; 75–4400. A commercial hotel on the highway coming in from Laredo. Rooms have balconies and television. Restaurant and bar.

Inexpensive

Colonial, Oriente 475; 43–6791. Best in its price range with restaurant, evening entertainment, restaurant, and parking lot.

Quinta Avenida, Madero Oriente 243; 75–6565. Nice enough with 75 air conditioned rooms, restaurant and parking.

Patricia, Madero Oriente 120; 75–0750. Small, with 30 clean rooms.

Tampico

A favorite with weekending Texans, including "winter Texans," the Gulf port of Tampico has a nice selection of hotels. The best places are a taxi ride from downtown. Rate at *Deluxe* properties is about $40 for a double; $30 at a *First Class* hotel; $20 at a *Moderate* establishment and $12 at an *Inexpensive* place.

Deluxe

Camino Real, Avenida Hidalgo 2000; 3–8811. Originally affiliated with Westin, this 100-room hotel boasts fine facilities including pool, bar, restaurant, and nightclub.

Posada de Tampico, Avenida Hidalgo 2200; 3–3050. Originally a Holiday Inn with 130 rooms, large pool, bar, and restaurant. Tennis. A favorite for regional conventions.

First Class

Colonial, Madero Oriente 210; 2–7676. A long time downtown favorite with 150 rooms, restaurant, coffee shop, and bar.

Inglaterra, Diaz Miron Oriente 116; 2–5678. Large (125 rooms) and centrally located, this was once a Howard Johnson's. Restaurant, bar, and nightclub.

Moderate

Impala, Diaz Miron 220; 2–0990. An attractive 80-room hotel with a restaurant.

San Antonio Courts, Hidalgo and Zacatecas; 3–0165. A nice old-fashioned motel with 100 units, restaurant, and pool.

Veracruz

A number of good new hotels have opened up in Mexico's most important port, while older establishments have been refurbished. Rates are similar to those in Tampico.

Deluxe

Torremar, Mocambo Highway 4300; 35–2100. Newest in town, originally a Hyatt, with 185 rooms on the beach, tennis, pool, coffee shop, restaurant, bar, evening entertainment.

First Class

Calinda, Mocambo Highway and Ferrocarrill; 36–0022. A new Quality Inn with 128 rooms plus 26 villas on the beach. Pool, restaurant, bar, and nightly entertainment.

Hostal de Cortes, Boulevard de las Casas and Avila Camacho; 32–0065. Fairly new and close to town with 100 rooms across from the beach. Pool, bar, and restaurant.

Mocambo, Mocambo Beach; 37–1660. A grand old fashioned beach resort, recently refurbished, with indoor and outdoor pool, tennis, restaurant, bar, evening entertainment, and U.S. programming an TV in all 100 rooms.

Puerto Bello, Avila Camacho 1263; 36–1100. Closer to town but across the street from the beach, with pool, coffee shop and delightful piano bar.

Moderate

Colonial, Lerdo 117; 32–0193. On the main square and wonderful for those who do not mind the noise. There are 180 rooms, but suites are so inexpensive as to be worth a fling.

Emporio, Avenida Insurgentes Veracruzanos and Malecon; 35–7520. Overlooking the waterfront but not on a beach; a centrally located old favorite with pool, restaurant, all services.

Inexpensive

Acuario, Valencia and Juan de Dios Peza; 37–4573. An 80-room in town hotel with a pleasant pool, nice restaurant, and bar.

Real del Mar, Avila Camacho 2707; 37–3634. Clean and comfortable with pook, restaurant, all services.

HOW TO GET AROUND. Taxis are the easiest form of transportation within the various cities of this region. Fares are reasonable (although they should be agreed on in advance) and cabs plentiful. Taxis may transport passengers across the border. In Matamoros, vans known as **maxi-taxis** run a fixed route from Mexican customs to the local market. All the cities in this area, including Monterrey, are compact and can best be seen on foot.

Buses are handy and cheap for getting from outlying hotels in Tampico and Veracruz to downtown. Intercity service, primarily because of language problems, is confusing. Those with a grasp of Spanish will still need a sense of adventure and a fair amount of patience. All cities in this region have unified bus terminals (see *Useful Addresses*) from which interurban buses depart. For tips on bus travel, see *How to Get There* at the beginning of this section.

Cars are the best way to tour this region, although within each city often it is better to leave the car at the hotel and take a taxi. Urban traffic in Mexico can be maddening, strange cities confusing, and parking places hard to find. Rental cars are expensive; the most easily available models are subcompacts with standard shift. In border areas it is cheaper to rent on the Texas side, although not all agencies will authorize their vehicles to be taken into Mexico. Any car driven in Mexico should be insured by a Mexican company (insurers have offices at all border points).

Air service within the region is limited to *Mexicana's* three weekly flights between Monterrey and Tampico.

TOURIST INFORMATION SERVICES. Motorists will find vendors of Mexican automobile insurance at the border an excellent source of up-to-date information. A good idea is to get an oil company road map of Mexico in Texas, as maps within Mexico may be hard to find. The State of Tamaulipas maintains tourist information offices on the Mexican side of the bridges in **Nuevo Laredo** (tel. 2–0104), in **Reynosa** (tel. 2–1189) and **Matamoros** (tel. 2–3630. In **Tampico** the office is at Carranza and Olmos Altos (tel. 2–2668). In

Monterrey the Nuevo Leon state tourist office maintains an information booth in the Legislative Palace, at Zaragoza and Matamoros on the Grand Plaza; **Informatur** (tel. 45–0870 or 45–0902 from 9 A.M. to 1 P.M. and 3 to 7 P.M. weekdays, 10 A.M. to 5 P.M. weekends) provides information in Spanish or English. Divertel, 43–5060, for recorded information of what is going on at the moment. The **Veracruz** tourist office is in City Hall on the Plaza de Armas (tel. 32–2151).

USEFUL ADDRESSES. Nuevo Laredo, *Mexicana Airlines:* Heroe de Nacataz 2345, tel. 2–2211; *U.S. Consulate:* Allende 3330, tel. 4–0512; *Police:* Calle Reynosa and Dr. Mier; *Hospital:* Comonfort and Independencia; *Post Office:* Calle Reynosa and Dr. Mier.

Reynosa, *Aeromexico:* Aldama 740, tel. 2–1115; *Police:* Calle Nayarit and Veracruz; *Hospital:* Morelos and Veracruz; *Post Office:* Colon and Porfirio Diáz.

Matamoros. *Aeromexico: Alvaro Obregon 21, tel. 3–0701; U.S. Consulate:* Primera 232, tel. 2–5250; *Police:* Gonzalez and Calle Vienteuno; *Hospital:* Canales and Durango; *Post Office:* Rio Bravo and Calle Once.

Monterrey. *Aeromexico:* Padre Mier 188, tel. 44–7220; *Mexicana,* Hidalgo and Escobedo, tel. 44–1122; *Continental:* Padre Mier 188, tel. 43–7001. *U.S. Consulate:* Constitución Poniente 411, 43–0650; *Hospital:* Universidad and Camelo, tel. 75–1212; *Police:* Gonzalitos and Lincoln, tel. 43–2576.

Tampico. Mexicana Airlines: Diaz Mirón 106, tel. 2–1051; *Police:* Mendez and Sor Juana Ines de la Cruz; *Hospital:* Carranza and Olmos; *Post Office:* Plaza Libertad.

Veracruz. *Mexicana:* Ignacio Allende 1660, tel. 32–2242; *Police:* Zamora 140, tel. 32–2833; *Hospital:* Cordoba and Lafragua, tel. 33–5500; *American Consulate:* Cinco de Mayo 1082, tel. 34–5809.

TOURS. *Good Neighbor Tours* in Laredo (512/724–1000) runs sightseeing, shopping and nightlife outings by bus to Nuevo Laredo and weekly trips to Monterrey. From McAllen, Texas, *Sanborn's,* 2011 South Tenth (512–682–3401), operates frequent motor coach excursions to the border cities, Monterrey, and throughout the Huasteca country. In Monterrey there are free tours of the *Cuauhtemoc Brewery* and *Kristaluxes* crystal factory; check with the tourist office or hotel travel desk for times. Travel desks will also arrange for city sightseeing as well as trips to the Garcia Caves and Horsetail Falls. *Tampico Travel Service* in Tampico and *Viajes Ulua* in Veracruz are the top sightseeing companies in their respective cities.

SPORTS

Nuevo Laredo

Racing at Nuevo Laredo Downs south of town sees horses run Saturday and Sunday afternoons (starting at 2 P.M. Texas time) while the greyhounds go at 8 P.M. (Texas time) Thursdays through Sundays. Programs and announcements are in English and betting is with dollars.

Bullfights are held frequently on Sunday afternoons and often on major Mexican holidays at the Nuevo Laredo Bullring.

Monterrey

Bullfights are held almost every Sunday from November through March at the Plaza Monumental, a covered bullring. Hotel travel desks can arrange for tickets and transport.

Baseball is played April through August by the Monterrey Sultans in the Triple A Mexican League.

Charreadas, Mexican rodeos, are held Sundays starting at noon at the Cryco Lienzo, on Highway 85 south of the city. Admission is about $1. The show is excellent and there is a good Mexican restaurant on the premises.

Golf may be played weekdays at the two courses in the city. The tourist office or hotel travel desks can arrange temporary membership in the local clubs.

Tampico

Fishing for tarpon along the Panuco River once brought hordes of Texans into Tampico; the river, however, has become polluted and most of the tarpon are gone. *Chairel Lagoon,* however, remains a nice spot for anglers with boats and equipment available for rent. The Vicente Guerrero Dam, about a four-hour drive northwest of Tampico, boasts some of the finest bass fishing anywhere.

Hunting for duck and white wing dove is good in this area and excellent around the Guerrero Dam where many camps cater almost exclusively to Americans. The season, depending on species, is roughly October through March. Importing firearms involves considerable red tape (see *Facts at Your Fingertips*)

Golf is good at the local country club. Hotels or the tourist office can arrange for temporary membership.

Baseball is played from April through August by the Tampico team in the Triple A Mexican League.

Veracruz

Fishing is at best fair in this region, but boats are available down by the waterfront or through hotel travel desks. Something different is the riverfishing in Boca del Rio.

Scuba Diving is growing in popularity with *Tridente* one of the outfitters that arranges for boats and trips. The tourist office or hotel travel desks can make arrangements.

BEACHES. Lauro Villar Beach near Matamoros is still referred to by many as Washington Beach, its old name. Usually it is less crowded than the beaches on Padre Island north of the Rio Grande, and it has a reputation for being cleaner. There are many seafood shacks along the sands and the fish is sure to be fresh. **Miramar Beach** is about five miles from downtown Tampico and is a favorite with locals, although it gets few tourists. The sands extend for miles, so it is easy to keep heading north and escape the crowds.

In Veracruz **Mocambo Beach,** about five miles south of town, is by far the best place for a swim in the gulf. The resort hotels are out this way and there is much going on. **Villa del Mar** is in town along Avila Camacho Boulevard and **Costa Verde** is just beyond it. Umbrellas and chairs may be rented for a small fee. Wandering vendors sell *coco locos* (a coconut spiked with gin), beer, and snacks as well as doodads and souvenirs. **Isla de Sacrificios** is an island reached by boat. The beaches are nice and the trip is fun (leave from the

Veracruz waterfront). When the Spaniards arrived the island was used ritually for human sacrifices, hence its name.

HISTORICAL SITES

Matamoros

Casa Mata, Calle Guatemala near Lauro Villar. A thick-walled old fort (the name, roughly translated, means "Killing House") and probably the oldest structure in town. The fort was attacked and taken by Zachary Taylor at the beginning of the Mexican American War. Within are some military displays and Huasteca Indian pottery.

Bagdad, near Matamoros, is the site of a major port through which the Confederates exported cotton and imported arms during the U.S. Civil War. The community was buried beneath the sands by a hurricane in 1880, literally wiped off the map. Treasure hunters enjoy digging among the dunes to see what they can turn up.

Monterrey

Bishops' Palace, Calle Matamoros between Gonzalitos and Carranza, is the city's best known landmark. Built late in the colonial era as a home for retired bishops, the palace was used as a fort during the Mexican American War, the French Intervention of the 1860s, and the Mexican Revolution (Pancho Villa fought there). Today it is a museum.

Cathedral, on the Grand Plaza, on which work was begun in 1635 and completed in 1800, is in part the oldest major building in town. The center facade is noted for its elaborate stone carving. Within are to be found many fine old religious paintings.

State House, or Palacio de Gobierno, is the seat of the Nuevo Leon State Government. Built in 1908, it is where Franklin Roosevelt met Mexican President Manuel Avila Camacho during World War II on the first visit by a U.S. chief executive into Mexico.

Veracruz

San Juan de Ulua, a 16th-century fortress built to defend the port against pirates. This was the final Spanish stronghold in Mexico and not surrendered until 1825. Later it became one of the most notorious prisons in the country. Once an island, the old fortress now can be reached from the waterfront by a causeway.

Santiago Bulwark, Diezyseis de Septiembre and Rayón, is about all that remains of the wall that once protected the city. Within is a small museum.

La Parroquia, the church on the Plaza de Armas in the center of town, was dedicated in 1734. The crystal chandeliers within were ordered by Maximilian for Chapultepec Castle in Mexico City, but arrived in Veracruz after the emperor had been executed.

El Tajin is a good three-hour drive north of Veracruz and very much a worthwhile excursion. The only major archaeological zone in the upper Gulf Coast region, Tajin may have been the most influential center in Mexico a thousand years ago, for this is where cacao beans come from and in pre-Hispanic times cacao beans were money. Also the ball-game, similar to soccer, played throughout Meso-America may have had its origins here. There are several ball courts in the area, carvings on their stones indicating human sacrifice accompanied the contests.

The *Pyramid of the Niches* is the largest structure at El Tajin. Some 60 feet high, it is made up of six tiers into which are carved 365 niches. Some archaeologists believe they originally contained small altars, others speculate they held funeral urns, but no one can say with any certainty.

The two ball courts that have been fairly well restored are full of fascination. Carvings on the panels show players suited up in kneepads and body protectors; they used a hard rubber ball which was not to be touched by the hands. Other panels depict before-and-after scenes of sacrifice.

El Tajin apparently was abandoned around the year 1100, but its builders, the Totonacs, remained a people to be reckoned with for centuries to come. They were the Indians who greeted Hernan Cortes on his arrival.

El Tajin is open daily from 7 A.M. until sunset. There is a small museum at the site. Token admission fee.

MUSEUMS AND GALLERIES. Monterrey: *Bishops' Palace,* Calle Matamoros between Gonzallitos and Carranza, houses the Nuevo Leon Regional Museum with displays relating to the history and culture of the area. Open 10–6 except Mondays; small admission fee. *Monterrey Museum,* Universidad 2202, houses an interesting collection of paintings by Mexican and other artists. Open 10:30–6:30 except Mondays; small admission fee. *Alfa Cultural Center,* Avenida Coatzacoalcos 1000, is in the neighboring suburb of Garza Garcia. Within is a science and industry exhibition and a planetarium. Hours open vary (call 78–0749); admission fee. *Baseball Hall of Fame,* Universidad 2200, at the Cuauhtemoc Brewery, is Monterrey's answer to Cooperstown with photos, bats and uniforms of Mexico's baseball greats. The brewery serves free beer to visitors. Open daily 10–6; free. Monterrey has several art galleries, including *Santa Anita,* Hidalgo Poniente 1113 (44–5021); *Arde,* Padre Mier Poniente 200 (44–8613); *Reto,* Calzada del Valle Oriente 279 (78–4659); and *There Frese,* Paseo de San Angel 326.

Tampico: *Huasteca Museum,* Primero de Mayo near Miramar at the Technological Institute in neighboring Ciudad Madero. The displays highlight the indigenous culture of the Huasteca region in eastern Mexico. Open 10–6 weekdays; free.

Veracruz: *Regional Museum,* Zaragoza 397, houses archaeological displays relating to the area. Featured are some Olmec, Totonac and Huasteca artifacts. Open 10–6 except Mondays. Small admission fee.

National Center of Marine Sciences, Avila Camacho Boulevard, houses an aquarium and other displays related to the sea and oceanography. Open daily; small admission charge. *Carranza Revolutionary Museum/Lighthouse,* on the waterfront at Avila Camacho and Morales, commemorates the establishment of a successful revolutionary government in Veracruz by Venustiano Carranza. Shown are items related to the struggle of the Mexican Revolution. The lighthouse in which the museum is housed no longer functions.

SHOPPING

Nuevo Laredo

The corner of Guerrero (the main street) and Victoria, a few blocks from the bridge, is the best shopping area in town. *Marti's* is truly a class act, with some of the finest handicrafts from all over Mexico—furniture to fabrics to fashions—on display, with a classical harpist tinkling out background music. Somewhat less expensive is *Galva's,* which stocks items in onyx, copper, and brass as well as jewelry. *Deutsch's* specializes in jewelry, much of it made in the store's own workrooms. Farther out, where Guerrero becomes Reforma, is *Rafael de México,* perhaps the largest shop in the city, its showrooms overflowing with dinnerwear and home furnishings. Avenida Guerrero itself is lined with tacky places selling "Mexican curios": paintings on black velvet, plaster matadors, sombreros, and the like. Made-in-Mexico liquor—tequila, rum, vodka and Kahlua—is, of course, a good buy, although Texas charges a small tax when it is brought back across the bridge. Stores in Nuevo Laredo open at 10, the better places closing at 6, but some remaining open until 8.

Matamoros

Calle Obregon, just over the bridge from Brownsville, has some of Matamoros' finest stores. *Barbara* has a bit of the best of everything, ranging from imported perfume and cosmetics to jewelry, hand-embroidered women's wear, carved wood and a vast array of gift items and home furnishings. *Myrta's,* nearby, specializes in textiles and clothing. Other stores sell a wide range of souvenirs and Mexican liquors. *Garcia* and *Arti* have a reputation for being the best. Downtown a large store called *Los Dos Republicas* sells embroidered clothing, tropical shirts for men, Mexican candies, liquor, jewelry, perfume, in short just about everything. It even has a bar on the premises where light snacks are served. The store is on Calle Nueve and Matamoros. A block away is the *Matamoros Market,* fun to wander about and a good place to pick up gifts; haggling is very much in order at the market.

Monterrey

Kristaluxes at José Maria Vigil 400 (take a taxi) is internationally known for its full lead crystal; prices are best at the factory. *Ceramica San Miguel,* Poniente Calle Sur 419 in the suburb of Garza Garcia (again, take a taxi) is a top place to find outstanding ceramics. Cowboy boots and other items of leather are an especially good buy at the many small shops around the Plaza Hidalgo. *Sanborns,* just off the plaza, has an excellent selection of quality handicrafts, including Taxco silver. Calle Morelos, a block from the plaza, has been closed to traffic and now is a pedestrian mall of shops. The *Indian Market* at Bolivar Norte 1150, is a good place to browse and bargain for souvenirs. *Galerias Monterrey,* at Gonzalitos Sur 660, is the city's big American-style shopping center with a large department store and scores of attractive boutiques.

Veracruz

Seashell souvenirs along with dried and varnished frogs, iguanas, and armadillos are sold in great quantities at the many stalls that line the waterfront street known as the Malecon. There is little of redeeming artistic value. Downtown the main shopping street is Independencia, but its stores have little that will interest most foreign visitors.

RESTAURANTS. Travelers with no intention of heading far into Mexico still enjoy crossing the Rio Grande for a good meal. Mexican cuisine is not, by the way, all tacos and enchiladas. Expect to pay around $15 for a meal in a restaurant listed here as *Expensive,* perhaps half that in a *Moderate* place. On the border *Inexpensive* eateries are to be avoided. Remember that drinks and tips wil push up the final tab. Credit cards: Visa (V); MasterCharge (MC); American Express (AE); Diners Club (D). All are open for both lunch and dinner.

Border Cities

Cadillac, Ocampo and Belden in Nuevo Lardeo; 2–9124. A long-time border favorite best known for its bar, but also a place for quail and Caribbean or Pacific lobster. *Expensive.* V, MC, AE, DC.

Drive Inn, Hidalgo and Sexta in Matamoros; 2–0022. In spite of the name this is one of the most plush dining spots on either side of the Rio Grande. Romantic music for dancing, if you will, and hearty Texas fare. *Expensive.* V, MC, AE, DC.

Hacienda, Alvaro Obregon and Amapolas, Matamoros; 3–9440. The elegant spot where the locals go for a power lunch or special night out. *Expensive.* AE, V, MC.

LaFitte's, Calle Matamoros and Victoria in Nuevo Laredo; 2–2208. Sounds French, but this is a seafood house named for the pirate. Shrimp, crawfish, and Caribbean lobster are great. *Expensive.* V, MC, AE, DC.

Winery, Calle Matamoros 308 in Nuevo Laredo; 2–0895. A Mexican version of an English pub and wine bar, clubby in atmosphere, but featuring such south of the border specialties as forged cheese and *tampiqueña* steak. *Expensive.* V, MC, AE, DC.

Louisiana, Bravo 97; 3–5094. The place for frogs' legs, Southern fried chicken, and, sometimes, gumbo. *Moderate.* V, MC.

La Majada, just beyond Mexican customs in Reynosa; 2–0822. The cuisine of northern Mexico, including beef ribs, roast kid, and cold beer, is featured here. *Moderate.* V, MC.

Rio Mar, Guerrero 2403 in Nuevo Laredo; 2–9194. Seafood in all its glory, and plenty of cold Mexican beer. Not very impressive to look at, but Texans who know keep coming back. *Moderate.*

U.S. Bar and Restaurant, Calle Cinco and Gonzalez in downtown Matamoros; 2–1475. One more oddly named eatery, this one being an imitation American steakhouse. Better than the steaks is the seafood. *Moderae.* V, MC, DC.

Monterrey

Time was when the citizens of Monterrey were considered as thrify as Scots, but now expense account dining has arrived. One of the nicest things about the Third City is that it has so many good places to eat. Expect to pay $25 for a meal in an *Expensive* restaurant; $15 in a *Moderate* one and $5 or so in an *Inexpensive* place. Drinks, taxes, and tips, of course, are extra. So is the taxi fare to Colonia del Valle where many of the best restaurants are.

Blue Shell, Gomez Marin 313, Colonia del Valle; 78–5097. Seafood served in elegant and tasteful surroundings. *Expensive.* V, MC, AE.

Cinco Cero, Gomez Morin and Roble, Colonia del Valle 78–6405. Translated, the name means 5–0 and the atmosphere is Hawaiian, the cuisine Polynesian. Very much a local showplace. *Expensive.* V, MC, AE, DC.

Luisiana, Plaza Hidalgo; 43–1561. The original continental restaurant in Monterrey, rich in tradition although not as splashy as some of the newer places. *Expensive.* V, MC, AE, DC.

Residence, Degollado and Matamoros; 42–7230. An elegant townhouse where the movers and shakers of Monterrey gather for lunch. Lovely at dinner. Reservations suggested. *Expensive.* V, MC, AE, DC.

Sahara, Vasconcelos Oriente 124, Colonia del Valle; 78–0828. Arabian dishes and Arabian music served in sheikly style. *Expensive.* V, MC, AE.

Das Bierhaus, Vasconcelos Poniente 455, Colonia del Valle; 78–0870. Teutonic as the Black Forest and nice for a snack or a meal. *Moderate.* V, MC.

Emiliano's, Rio Danubio 355, Colonia del Valle; 78–4618. A newly refurbished spot serving international fare. The bar is a favorite hangout for young executives. *Moderate.* V, MC, DC.

JJ Charlie's, Constituentes Poniente 787; 48–5670. One of the Carlos Anderson group of fashionably informal beaneries, but not one of the best. *Moderate.* V, MC, AE, DC.

Las Pampas, Garza Sada 2401; 58–2127. Argentine steakhouses are the rage all over Mexico. This is one of the really good ones. *Moderate.* V, MC, DC.

Regio, Plaza Hidalgo; 43–6250. More regional cuisine within walking distance of most hotels. A favorite with the locals. *Moderate.* V, MC.

El Tio, Avenida México and Hidalgo; 46–0291. Regional dishes such as broiled kid and beef ribs served in a garden patio. Lovely in the cool of the evening. *Moderate.* V, MC.

El Pastor, Madero Poniente 1067. Unpretentious, specializing in roast kid. *Inexpensive.*

Pico's, Hidalgo 485. Fast food the American way. *Inexpensive.*

Sanborns, just off Plaza Hidalgo, is a Mexico City-based chain of fancy mini-department stores with highly regarded coffee shops. Good for Mexican food or burgers and malts. *Inexpensive.* V, MC, AE.

Tampico

Outside the hotels there are only a few good restaurants in Tampico. A meal at any of them will be in the $15 range with drinks, tips and taxes extra.

Del Mar, Aduana 390 (ground floor); 2–2688. Very much a waterfront cafe, but there are those who visit Tampico simply to dine on stuffed crabs here. V, MC.

Gran Muralla, Hidalgo and Jacaranda; 3–9191. Probably the best of Tampico's many Chinese restaurants. V, MC.

Las Parillas Suizos, Hidalgo and Palmas. Tacos, beer, and similar light fare served in clean, attractive surroundings.

Rincon Gaucho, Hidalgo and Violete; 3–1718. Steaks and chops grilled in the Argentine fashion. V, MC.

Veracruz

Seafood is, of course, what Veracruz is famous for, but there is more to Gulf Coast dining than fish. Prices generally are moderate, about $15 for a meal with drinks, tips and taxes extra.

Las Brisas, in Boca del Rio, a few miles south of downtown, is a joy. Outdoor dining overlooking the Atoyac River. Of course you have to like seafood. V, MC.

Cabaña del Gaucho, Avenida Colona and Alonso de Avila; 33–1259. Steaks served up in the Argentine manner and broiled on a tabletop grill. V, MC, AE, DC.

Los Cedros, Avila Camacho (no number); 33–0804. Lebanese food and international fare in elegant surroundings. A bit expensive. V, MC, AE, DC.

Lorencillo, Avila Camacho near Rayón; 36–1340. The fanciest restaurant in town (with prices to match), international cuisine and a lovely harbor view. V, MC, AE, DC.

La Paella, Zamora 138, is a simple Spanish restaurant, worth trying both for its food and low prices.

La Parroquia, Plaza de Armas. Breakfast on a *bomba* (warmed sweet roll) and coffee with milk served in a glass. Come back for a seafood lunch, then linger over a beer and listen to the mariachis play until the sun goes down.

Prendes, Plaza de Armas; 32–0153. Wags will tell you Cortes dined here. Plain and simple, but the seafood could not be better. Outstanding duck, also. V, MC.

Submarino Amarillo, Avila Camacho at Rayón; 36–1320. The name means "Yellow Submarine" but this is a steakhouse, probably the best one in Veracruz. V, MC, DC.

NIGHTLIFE. Nuevo Laredo's two good restaurants, the *Cadillac* at Ocampo and Beldon, and the *Winery* at Matamoros 308, plus *O'Henry's,* Victoria and Matamoros, get a crowd of late drinkers after the races. Weekends there is entertainment at the hotels *Hacienda* and *El Rio.*

Matamoros provides entertainment at *El Presidente Hotel* just beyond the international bridge. Across the street there is music for dancing at the *Drive Inn.* On Obregon is *Blanca White's,* something of a would-be singles bar. *Mary's* usually has a good show.

Monterrey hotels are where most of the after dark action is. *Scaramouche* in the Monterrey Plaza Holiday Inn is an old fashioned night club, while entertainment at the Plaza's *Mombasa Lobby Bar* is more informal. The *1900 Bar* at the Gran Ancira is a classic Mexican cantina with entertainment, while *Los Vitrales* at the Ambassador next door is more continental. *El Cid* at the Hotel Monterrey has music for dancing, while the *Jaguar* at the Holiday Inn North and the *Chandelier* at Ocampo and Escobedo both feature name entertainment. *La Milpa de Valerio* at Gomez Marin 200 in Colonia del Valle, the *Sapo Cancionero* (singing toad) at Hidalgo Poniente 360, and *El Meson del Gallo,* Padre Mier and Coss, are romantic little places where trios croon. Best discos are *Aja,* Prolongacion Madero Poniente 201; *Sgt. Pepper's,* Rio Orinoco Oriente 105, Colonia del Valle; and *Sharis* in the Ramada Inn.

Tampico nightlife is pretty much limited to what is on at the *Camino Real, Posada de Tampico* and the *Hotel Ingalaterra. Sioux,* at Ejercito and Universidad, is a nice dine-and-dance spot. There are, to be sure, the waterfront dives, but they are just that.

Veracruz' top hotels, the *Mocambo, Calinda* and *Torremar,* all have evening entertainment and the *Hotel Puerto Bello* has a romantic piano bar. *Plaza 44* on the Plaza de Armas is the one good downtown disco, others being the *Perro Salado* and *Capo's* on Avila Camacho Boulevard out toward Costa Verde. Also in Costa Verde is *Hip Pop Potamus* where the girls are really boys.

THE INDIAN SOUTH: OAXACA AND CHIAPAS

Resort Area in the Making

by
KAL MULLER

The two southern states of Mexico, Oaxaca and Chiapas, are most appreciated by those with an interest in archaeology, colonial architecture, rugged mountain scenery, and traditional Indian life. There are also good beaches on the Pacific coast of Oaxaca and a huge new resort development well on its way at Huatulco which may rival Cancun someday. And why not? After all, Cancun some ten years ago was but a fishing village with 117 sleepy souls. Huatulco, 120 km from Puerto Escondido and 145 km from Salina Cruz, ecompasses a 30 km by 7 km piece of real estate with nine bays and 16 km of beaches. In 1987, a Presidente Hotel and a Club Med are scheduled to be in operation, with subsequent sprouting of hotels, services, and an international airport.

The two most interesting towns in this region are Oaxaca, the capital of the state known by the same name, and San Cristobal de las Casas in the cool highlands of Chiapas. Both cities serve as a center for surrounding Indian communities and both are graced with notable examples of colonial architecture. Oaxaca's advantage lies in its closeness to the grand ruins of Monte Alban and Mitla with numerous minor sites nearby. But Chiapas has Palenque, the most luxurious of the accessible ruins, engulfed in rain forest and boasting of some of the best Mayan sculptures on record as well as a stupendous pyramid enclosing a royal tomb.

A two-hour drive from Palenque is Villahermosa, the capital of Tabasco state, which contains an archaeological museum as well as La Venta, an open park displaying huge stone heads and other monoliths of the Olmec culture. (For Practical Information on Villahermosa, see *Yucatan and the Maya Country.*)

The city of Oaxaca is some 300 miles from Mexico City, 250 miles from Veracruz, 415 miles from Acapulco and 840 miles from Merida on top of the Yucatan peninsula. Tuxtla Gutierrez, the capital of Chiapas, is in a low valley 50 miles from San Cristobal de las Casas, 180 miles from Villahermosa, 320 miles from Oaxaca and a bit less than 600 miles from Merida.

EXPLORING SOUTHERN MEXICO

Oaxaca City is a Mexican classic, one of the loveliest of all the country's provincial capitals. For the traveler, the range of attractions is almost unlimited. A joy in itself, Oaxaca is blessed with a marvelous climate, handsome handicrafts, and marvelous monuments to the pre-Hispanic past and the vice-regal era.

The main plaza or zocalo is dominated by a magnificent kiosk where there is live music every night, but Monday. It is shaded by huge, ancient trees and surrounded by sidewalk cafés beneath the arches of colonial-style palaces. The cathedral is to one side, facing its own plaza. The whole area is off limits to vehicles.

A few Americans discovered the place decades ago and never left. There is a sizeable community of foreign scholars of anthropology, archaeology and linguistics. Budget-conscious youth love it, along with the camper-travelers who find they can linger at the tables over a tequila sour for hours. Straight trippers, too, find the lotus-eating life on the plaza spellbinding, trapped by the temptation to do nothing but sit all day and watch the world go by.

On the plaza, the seller comes to the buyer. Peasant men from hillside villages wander past, displaying serapes, colorful blankets that double as beds, coats, rugs, and seat-covers. Their women come along with rebozos, beautifully woven shawls of every description, an entire stock neatly folded and carried on the head. Children, bearing shoeshine kits, lottery tickets, and chewing gum, peddle bits of jewelry made at home with loving care. Yet none of the sellers are pests; a firm no, a wag of the finger, and they go on to some more receptive customer.

The shops on the little side streets offer all these items and more. Machetes are a great favorite—the long knives with legends engraved on the blades: "no drugstore has a cure for bites from this snake." The black pottery from nearby villages is sold today around the world. In Oaxaca it is a bargain. The range of textiles, bolts of cloth, shirts, skirts, and ordinary neckties is unlimited. There are, on the edge of the city, a number of little weavers' workshops and potters' homes, open to the public and fascinating to visit.

Everything is a bargain. In many other places of the Republic, this is no longer so. Silver in Taxco costs the same as it does in Mexico City. Pottery and blown glass from Guadalajara are just as cheap in Ciudad Juárez. But the woolens and cottons of Oaxaca, the silvery-black urns, all cost less in the town where they are made.

Jewelry is a constant favorite. Most of the items are copies of the Mixtec treasures found at Monte Albán. There are gold earrings, pendants, necklaces of Mexican jade and tiny seed pearls. The same items come in gold wash, handsomely worked, yet remarkably cheap.

Churches are the main monuments to the colonial era. The cathedral on the *zocalo* is a rather handsome structure, started in 1553 and completed 200 years later. Squat, due to earthquakes, it is not unattractive. The carved facade is really quite handsome. The clock, installed in the colonial era, is still accurate.

The Church of Santo Domingo is today one of the great art treasures of the Mexican Republic. Outside, the church and the adjoining monastery, built by the Dominicans late in the 16th century, resemble a stark fortress (which it has been on occasion). Within, the church is overpowering. It is a mass of carving covered in gold leaf, a vaulted dome rich in paintings, and 11 different chapels, each seemingly more magnificent than the other. But the best is the Capilla del Rosario, a small gilded church in itself. If the lights are not on when you visit Santo Domingo, one of the keepers might turn them on for you for about $3.

Next to it is a lovely cloistered convent housing the state's Regional Museum, a "must-see" attraction containing most of the priceless gold, crystal and other archaeological treasures discovered in Monte Albán and Mitla. Worth visiting too, by the way, is the smaller Rufino Tamayo Museum on Morelos Avenue. Tamayo, the most famous contemporary Mexican painter, is a native son of Oaxaca. Over several decades, he accumulated pre-Columbian ceramics, the best private collection in the country. Tamayo founded a museum in his home town and gave it most of his pieces which cover the whole range of Indian civilizations prior to the conquest.

Not as splendid as Santo Domingo, the Basilica de la Soledad is dedicated to the Virgin of Solitude, the patron saint of Oaxaca. Located on Independencia and Galeana Streets, the church with its cloisters and park covers a large chunk of real estate. This is one of the most important shrines in southern Mexico, housing the black stone Virgin which is said to have arrived miraculously to this site. The facade of the church is interesting enough, but take in the interior, full of gilt, sculptures and palatable faith. In back of the church, there is a small museum with paintings and countless glass figurines giving thanks for divine help.

The city of Oaxaca was and remains the focus of Indian life, mostly Zapotecs and Mixtecs who live in the valley and nearby mountains. They come to town to buy and sell, especially on Saturdays. While the market is no longer as colorful as in D.H. Lawrence's day (see his *Mornings in Mexico*), it remains an authentic and exotic spectacle. This is the largest Indian market in all Mexico and only Michoacán can rival Oaxaca in the variety and quality of crafts.

There are two markets in town, both open and busy daily but becoming a beehive of activity on Saturday. The *Benito Juárez Market* (two blocks to the southeast of the zócalo) covers a two full-area. You can find some crafts there along with tempting food stalls serving simple meals for natives and budget travelers alike. Two blocks south, there is *Mercado de Artesanías* (Crafts Market) where you can sometimes see Trique Indian women weaving on the backstrap loom. But the authentic action has shifted to the new *Saturday Market* on the southern outskirts of town. It's a short taxi ride or a 15- to 20-minute walk from the zócalo. Late Friday and early Saturday, Indians stream to this place to buy and sell fruit, vegetables, and hundreds of other items. Take a look at the dozens of different kinds of chiles and stacks of tropical fruit. Although mainly a food and household items market (in the most extended sense of the term "household"), you can find crafts here as well. There are striking Indian blouses (called *huipils*) with marked differences according to the village of origin. Best are the delicately brocaded Amuzgo Indian huipils. Many of the woven items are still made with a backstrap loom and pottery is often shaped without a wheel. There are decorative and utilitarian wood carvings, wool rugs with colorful designs, machetes with leather sheaths, clever toys of tin and wood. If you buy clothing, remember that materials may shrink and colors could run. Best to dry clean these items. At the market, bargaining is essential and expected.

It might come as a surprise not to hear much Spanish spoken here. The Zapotec and Mixtec languages have something Oriental about them due to their tonal character where the pitch of the voice changes the meaning of the words.

Monte Albán

As much as its colonial churches and markets, Oaxaca's claim as a major attraction lies in the archaeological site of Monte Albán, located on a hilltop just outside the city. The site was probably chosen for religious purposes as it dominated the fertile land around it. It is doubtful that it was of much use for long-term defense as there is no water available at the top nor evidence of large cisterns. For unknown reasons, the religious complex was abandoned by the Zapotecs to be later used by the Mixtecs who transformed the site into a royal necropolis.

At its height, Monte Albán was the center of a community that ranged over 25 square miles and was home to perhaps 50,000 souls. Today, various ancient buildings line a vast courtyard. These buildings are oriented in the cardinal directions except for what was perhaps an observatory.

Oldest of all is the Temple of the Dancers, erected perhaps some 2,500 years ago. The carvings here of numerous figures on stone slabs were originally thought to represent dancers. In recent years, however, some scholars have come up with the idea that the carvings represent the ill and the deformed, and that the temple was actually a hospital or school of medicine.

Fascinating is the ball court on the southeast end of the courtyard. It resembles many a modern stadium, where a game a bit similar to soccer and basketball combined was played. When it was over, the captain of the losing team might have been sacrificed to insure the favor of the gods.

It is fascinating to speculate about what led to the abandonment of Monte Albán. The period between the years A.D. 650 and 1000 was one of strife and upheavals for all of Mexico's major cultures. Experts agree that one possible cause could have been too many "idle" mouths (priests, aristocracy, artisans) to be fed by too few farmers. There might have been pressures by warlike tribes drifting down into central Mexico from the north. The northernmost of the great Classical centers, Teotihuacán, was abandoned around the year A.D. 650. After about A.D. 900, most of Monte Albán was deserted, serving only for some burials of important nobles and small scale rituals.

Around the 12th century, the Mixtecs, who probably originated in southern Puebla, began to drift into Oaxaca. This was a gradual migration, first in the mountainous regions of the northern part of the state then eventually into the Valley of Oaxaca. As neither the Zapotecs nor the Mixtecs were unified under a single ruler, there were no major battles which sealed the fate of the two groups once and for all. Rather, there were alliances between subgroups, some fighting here and there, along with intermarriages. The Mixtecs converted Monte Albán into a royal necropolis.

Of the 150 tombs uncovered thus far, one, the famed Number Seven, yielded treasure unequaled in the western hemisphere. Discovered 50 years ago, the tomb contained objects of gold, jade, alabaster, pearl, onyx, and rock crystal, now on display in the Oaxaca State Museum.

While the Zapotecs have continuously occupied the Valley of Oaxaca for some 3,000 years, the Mixtecs were late arrivals on the scene. Their workmanship, especially their jewelry, is virtually unrivaled. It might be guessed that they moved in gradually, bringing a fertile source of ideas, culture and craftsmanship which influenced the Zapotecs. Gradually they became more entrenched as Zapotec civilization waned. Eventually, through war and intermarriage, the Mixtec culture became strong in various parts of the Valley of Oaxaca. But the Zapotecs never faded from the scene.

Then came the Aztecs. When Cortés arrived in Mexico, Oaxaca paid some tribute to the Aztecs but was far from being entirely subjugated.

Colonial Oaxaca

The Spaniards never took any great interest in Oaxaca. To be sure, Cortés was so entranced with the place that he established it as his own little fiefdom, taking the title Marquis del Valle de Oaxaca. But the conqueror never did much more than admire the place; he was too restless a man to settle down there. The same is true of his more ambitious lieutenants and their descendants. Although Oaxaca showed up on Aztec tribute lists as a source of gold, after the initial looting of the nobles' treasures, the area never produced the precious metal in large quantities. Nor were any silver mines found to draw the bonanza crowd. It is, even today, one of Mexico's poorest, least developed states.

During the centuries that Mexico was a Spanish colony, Oaxaca developed slowly with the introduction of cattle, other livestock, and wheat along with other grains. Fertile land was expropriated from Indian communities for the benefit of the Spaniards and the Catholic Church. For a few decades, silk was the source of high profits but the trade with China ended this incipient industry. Cochineal proved more durable. This is a red dye made from cactus-dwelling insects, utilized among other things for the famous Red Coats of the British Army. The aniline dyes of the 19th century pushed cochineal production out of the market. But while it lasted, cochineal provided wealth to the eroded mountain lands of northern Oaxaca, a region known as La Mixteca. This wealth, plus Indian labor, is the reason that today you can see huge colonial churches in almost deserted places such as Yanhuitlán, on the main highway from Mexico City to Oaxaca.

Following the departure of the Spanish viceroys, the Catholic Church was the most powerful institution in 19th-century Mexico. Amid squabbling politicians, the Church alone commanded the loyalty and respect of the population. Beyond that, it was a true temporal power. For 300 years and more the wealthy had willed bits of their property to the Church. By 1850, the hierarchy was the greatest landowner in the country as well as the nation's educator and marriage-maker. As an institution it was more than conservative. It was reactionary.

History, or perhaps it might better be said, trouble, largely passed Oaxaca by for three centuries and more. The city languished, vegetating through the colonial era, but involved in the wars of independence and the civil strife in the decades that followed. Then, in a brief moment, Oaxaca gave Mexico a pair of Indian statesmen who were to rule and shape the republic for half a century and more.

Juárez and Díaz, Presidents from Oaxaca

Benito Juárez was one of the world's outstanding men a century ago. He was, to begin with, a Zapotec shepherd boy, born in Guelatao, a town about 40 miles from Oaxaca itself. He might well have lived out his life there except that when he lost a sheep, he ran away to Oaxaca where he met a priest who sponsored his studies for the clergy.

This is one of the little ironies of history, for it was Juárez who all but destroyed the power of the Catholic Church. As a seminary drop-out, he took to law school, became an attorney, a politician, governor of the state, chief justice of the Mexican Supreme Court, and president of the republic. It was quite a ladder to be climbed by a boy who could not speak Spanish, much less read it, until he was 12 years old.

The liberals of the day, Juárez among them, determined that if Mexico was ever to move ahead, the Church must, in effect, render unto Caesar what is Caesar's. It was Juárez who largely was responsible for the Constitution of 1857 and other laws that required the Church to sell its lands; that limited the immunities of the clergy and the authority of the ecclesiastical courts. Priests, nuns, and monks were permitted to renounce their vows; secular education was established.

Pope Pius IX declared the Mexican Constitution null and void.

Backed by their bishops, the conservatives rebelled in what is known as the War of the Reform. The president resigned. Juárez, as chief justice, was called in to take his place. The conservatives were defeated. But they did not give up.

This was when Maximilian was invited to place upon his blond head the Crown of Imperial Mexico. French troops were already in the country, having invaded originally to take over customs collections to pay off back debts. They ended up taking over everything. The United States might have objected, as France was violating the Monroe Doctrine. But the Americans were fighting a civil war of their own at the time.

Juárez ended up huddling on the Rio Grande at the border city that today bears his name. A stubborn, humorless man with an almost religious respect for the law, he refused to submit to a usurper. In the end, he triumphed. The War Between the States ended, and Philip Sheridan was sent with 50,000 troops to the Mexican border. Louis Napoleon of France decided to bring his soldiers home. Maximilian, a noble if tragic figure, ended his days standing before a firing squad in Querétaro. Benito Juárez returned to Chapultepec Castle in Mexico City. The republic was restored.

Juárez's first home in Oaxaca, where he lived as a servant from 1818 to 1828, is a museum today, dedicated to this great Mexican. A large monument and small museum were built to honor Juárez in his home town of Guelatao where there is a peaceful lake. A local legend says that Juárez did not die but vanished into the lake whence he will return someday to lead the Zapotecs.

Conspicuous by their absence are monuments to Oaxaca's other famous son. Only a street and a small bust honors the memory of Porfirio Díaz.

Juárez died in office in 1872. Four years later, Díaz became president. It was a job he held for more than 30 years. He is remembered mostly as a dictator, the target at which the Mexican Revolution was aimed. Today, as old passions fade, the country is beginning to recognize that Díaz, too, made significant contributions to the development of the country. He had, really, only two major failings: he didn't know when to quit and he kept much of the population in misery.

A hero of the Reform War and the battles against the French, Porfirio Díaz never showed the respect for law that was an obsession with Juárez. Failing to be elected, Díaz took the presidency by force and had himself elected. Reelection was prohibited by law. Díaz changed the law.

He was, in his way, a tyrant. He brooked no opposition, and seldom did he have any. He was a great, charming, opulent man, a swarthy mestizo who was loved by the wealthy. To Mexico he brought stability, and with it, progress. Under Díaz the great haciendas flourished, and land that once grew nothing but corn was turned over to sugar, coffee, and bananas for a hungry world.

Foreign businessmen found a warm welcome from Díaz. The British came to build railroads and drill for oil. The French arrived to become merchant princes. Americans ran the country's business, and Mexico began pulling itself up into the family of nations.

But the cost was high. Mexicans were second-class citizens in their own country. The haciendas were manned by peons, Indian serfs who were kept in line by the notorious rural police. In the cities, the foreigner was king. Wealthy Mexicans scorned their own land, spent what time they could abroad, and returned with reluctance to their Hapsburg-like palaces at home. Labor was restive, but Díaz kept a tight lid on the unions.

In 1910, the explosion came. Díaz fled a year later, and revolutionary hero fought revolutionary hero. History today honors them all. Díaz is the only villain. But gradually he is being recognized as the man who gave the country the infrastructure upon which the modern nation is built.

This, then, is Oaxaca, city, valley, state, homeland of the gods, birthplace of statesmen, refuge of intellectuals. To the foreign traveler, perhaps the greatest endorsement comes from the Mexicans themselves. Oaxaca is where they go on holiday. It is a place to relax, unwind, to sit on the plaza or stroll the quiet streets, with at least one visit to the ruins that remind them of a majestic past and the promise of a fruitful future.

The Vicinity of Oaxaca

There are two day trips which can be taken with Oaxaca as a base, in order to see markets, craft villages, colonial churches, and archaeological sites in the Valley of Oaxaca.

Heading south of town on the road to Puerto Angel and Puerto Escondido, you soon (12 km) arrive at the village of Coyotepec, the most famous ceramic center of the state. The speciality here is black pottery with a sensuous glow due to the lead oxide in the clay. Check out the water jugs and whimsical animals in various shapes—there are several outlets around town, often under the sign *alfarería.* About 20 km. farther, the town of Ocotlan is known for its bustling Friday market where bartering is as common as cash purchases. Just at the outskirts of town, matched and plow-trained oxen with yokes are sold in a dusty lot—quite a sight but don't wear your best shoes. Ocotlan is not worth the trip unless you go there on a Friday.

On a different road south of Oaxaca, going at first towards Monte Albán, follow the signs to Cuilapan and Zaachila. At Cuilapan, the Dominicans built a massive monastery and began a church which remains roofless. The epidemics which wiped out the Mixtec Indians left too few hands to support the church. A stone, embedded in a wall, shows Mixtec glyphs and Arabic numerals for the year 1555. In back of the church, a monument commemorates the spot where the Independence hero and president Vicente Guerrero was executed.

A short way past Cuilapan, the small town of Zaachila holds its weekly market on Thursdays. Zaachila was a paramount Zapotec center after Monte Albán had been abandoned. When the Mixtecs moved into the valley around the 14th century, they fused with the Zapotecs but today Zaachila is still bitterly divided between the descendants of the two groups. The church tower has two embedded pre-Columbian Zapotec funerary urns. There are two ancient tombs which were not excavated until 1962; well guarded by townspeople, the grave robbers never sacked them. At first, even archaeologists were physically expulsed and could complete their work only under armed guard. To the locals, the archaeologists became the grave robbers. The treasure trove, almost as valuable as Monte Albán's Tomb 7, included an exceptional polychrome cup with a three-dimensional bird perched on the rim. One of the tombs still has some painted figures but that's all that is left.

The Road to Mitla

To the east of Oaxaca, the short stretch of 40-odd kilometers to Mitla is bordered by many attractions: a weaving center, one of the best colonial churches in the country, a thriving market, and three pre-Columbian sites not including the major ceremonial center at Mitla. As you head out of Oaxaca on the Pan-American Highway to Tehuantepec, you come to two pre-Columbian sites on your right. Dainzu's interest lies in a series of low relief carvings at the base of a platform. Vaguely recalling Monte Albán's *danzantes,* these figures are players of the ancient ball game. Lambityeco, next to the highway, was an important center after the fall of Monte Albán, with residences and tombs of the powerful classes. The site is only partially excavated but worth it for the sculptured stucco figures. Tlacolula, adjacent to the main highway, holds a Sunday market second in importance only to Oaxaca's. If you are in town when a mass is celebrated, look inside the 16th-century church full of gilded decorations and perhaps even a marimba band. Tlacolula is also an important mezcal-producing center, if you want to try some of the potent local brew. Just a bit further on the highway, the site of Yagul lies about a mile on your left. There is a fortress on a hill, a ceremonial center (not spectacular) and lots of tombs. Check out the tombs and the magnificent scenery from the fortress.

Seven kilometers past Yagul, there is a turn-off with one branch of the road going to Mitla. To arrive at the impressive buildings not at all in ruins, you have to pass through town where many woven goods are for sale. At the pseudo-plaza, you will see the Frissell Museum with mostly ceramic pieces, mercifully labeled in English as well as the usual Spanish. The Frissell is housed in a colonial hacienda which also has guest rooms and a restaurant with gringo-style food. The archeological site is about a half kilometer beyond the square, next to a church.

Mitla was started by the Zapotecs, came under strong Mixtec influence, then went back to Zapotec control by the time of the Spanish conquest. The Zapotec language is still spoken in town today. The buildings are noted for their mosaics, diverse panels of geometrical motifs that cover the facades of the various buildings which in turn enclose couryards or patios. These ornaments are unmatched in Mexico. The mosaics are carefully cut and fitted into the walls so that, at first glance, they appear to have been carved out of the wall itself. A group of columns is also unique in Mexico and there are cruciform tombs reached through a sunken patio. An early Spanish chronicle tells of Mitla's thriving at the time of the Spanish conquest, used by both priests and nobles of the Zapotec nation.

Puerto Escondido

A longer trip out of Oaxaca could include sun and sea on the beaches of Puerto Escondido and Puerto Angel. There are two daily DC3-type plane flights to Puerto Escondido and the runway has been extended so that large jets can bring tourists to the development at Huatulco, under construction farther down the coast. If you drive or take a bus, head for Puerto Angel, then to Puerto Escondido as this road is paved while a large chunk of the direct Oaxaca-Puerto Escondido stretch is still a dirt road. Both flight and drive treat you to spectacular mountain scenery.

The fishing village of Puerto Escondido is for relaxing, surfing, or doing a bit of looking around wildlife-filled Manialtepec lagoon and mangrove swamp. It's mostly young people here, staying in inexpensive hotels but there are also better accommodations, not of the luxury class however. At Puerto Angel, the scene is even more laid-back. There is a small naval base here and some coffee is shipped out occasionally. Only one decent hotel—the Angel del Mar, located on a hill overlooking the bay. The sleepy scene may change when the facilities of Huatulco come on-line as this new resort is less than an hour's drive away.

Tehuantepec—Mexico's Narrow Waist

The coastal highway which runs down the Pacific from Acapulco and points northwest to Puerto Angel and Puerto Escondido, follows Oaxaca's littoral to Salina Cruz then cuts a bit inland to Tehuantepec. The Pan-American Highway drops through the mountains to Tehuantepec also.

The Isthmus of Tehuantepec is Mexico's narrow waist where the Gulf of Mexico and the Pacific's lagoons are only 120 miles apart. The southern end is marked by the port of Salina Cruz while the town of Tehuantepec controls the passage to the mountainous interior.

Some 20 years before the arrival of Cortes, the Aztecs had pushed down to this area and onward to the fertile coastal area of Chiapas, where cacao was produced in large quantities. Cacao beans were used in Mexico as money while chocolate was a luxury drink reserved for the Aztec elite. In order to control their trade route, the Aztecs had to establish themselves at the Tehuantepec passage to the highlands. But the Zapotecs had built fortifications close by, near the Tehuantepec River and along the first mountains dominating the inland passage. A strong Aztec army attacked a well-entrenched Zapotec-Mixtec coalition. The defenders used such demoralizing tactics as silent night raids to bring back Aztec bodies for their next day's meal. After a long siege, the Aztecs were defeated or gave up the struggle.

From the time of Cortes, the Isthmus has been envisioned as a potential crossroads of the world, ideal site for a canal linking Atlantic and Pacific. The Isthmus has been coveted ever since. Following the war with the United States in 1847, Mexico was willing enough to yield Texas and California, but when asked to surrender Tehuantepec the Mexicans refused. This was territory they would defend to the last man.

Throughout the 19th century there was talk of building a canal here. Eventually, under Porfirio Díaz, a compromise was reached and a railroad was built. It was opened in 1894 and for nearly 20 years the Isthmus was indeed the crossroads of the world. As many as 60 trains a day ran from Coatzacoalcos on the Gulf to Salina Cruz on the Pacific. At times ships waited for as long as 10 days for dock space in Salina Cruz. The Oaxaca port city became a brawling, bawdy boom town, only to fade and wither with the opening of the Panama Canal in 1915.

Today, Salina Cruz is on its way back up. It is a study in contrasts, tropical and shabby on one side, yet spruced up with modern banks and a couple of handsome stores. Petroleos Mexicanos, the Pemex people, have a pipeline running here from their refinery on the Gulf. Great tankers put into Salina Cruz, plying the coastal routes and keeping the Mexican Pacific coast supplied with gasoline and oil. There is a huge drydock here with the finest installations available between San Diego and Panama City.

Salina Cruz is a free port with a boatyard that turns out fishing vessels used by a dozen countries around the world. Freighters put in here and container installations have been installed; by using the rail facilities, shippers can save 10 days transporting goods from Europe to the Orient.

Yet, except for a look around and perhaps a visit to the beach where the surf is dangerously rough, Salina Cruz has no attraction to the tourist. It is a sailors' town, home of the Mexican hardhat, without a decent hotel or restaurant to its name.

The town of Tehuantepec could be a great disappointment. It is a grubby place, sweltering in the tropical sun. Except for the road running from the highway into the plaza, the streets are paved with dust and populated by pigs, dogs, and naked children.

Song and story tell how Tehuantepec and its neighbor, Juchitán, rival Zapotec towns, are matriarchies runs by Amazons. To be sure, the women do seem to dominate, appearing majestic in their long, flowing skirts and handsomely embroidered jackets. The menfolk, in shabby work clothes, appear tame beside them.

Truth is, men are usually in the fields, for in the tropics there is always something to be planted or harvested. The women are, by and large, tall and handsome. They have a reputation for swapping salty stories and howling at each other in the foulest language. Since their tongue is understood by few outsiders, this would be difficult to verify. What is true is that they dislike to be looked on as curiosities, photographed by blue-eyed strangers. And they let this dislike be known. From this alone comes their fiery reputation, no doubt.

But it's well worth taking a look at their markets where, among other exotica live iguanas are sold for local kitchens. At the Juchitán market, many stalls serve delicious meals where iguana is but one of the specialities. With discretion, patience and a good telephoto lens, it is possible to photograph the ladies at the market without getting mobbed.

For gala occasions, the ladies are decked out in satin and lace, set off by necklaces and earrings of gold coins. As a way to show off their wealth—and a hedge against inflation—the Tehuanas go for buying gold centenarios and other lesser denomination gold coins. Rather then keeping them under the bed, the ladies wear the coins on festive occasions.

The lucky traveler will very likely hit a small fiesta, at least, that brings out the Tehuanas at their best. Along with the big parties, there are the little neighborhood celebrations where a local saint is honored, the Zandunga dance and, instead of playing "Good Night, Ladies," the girls climb up on roofs and hurl fruit at the men down below.

The weddings of the region are something to avoid. Once the mother (not the father) has consented to the union, arrangements are made and the guests brought in to hear both bride and groom make a speech. This inspires others, with brevity considered worse than saying nothing at all.

For an excellent book on this area, see Miguel Covarrubias' *Mexico South, the Isthmus of Tehuantepec.*

If you are driving in this area, be forewarned that the winds, funneled among the Isthmus' mountains, can blow awfully hard. We have seen tractor-trailers blown off the highway.

Tuxtla Gutiérrez

Tuxtla Gutiérrez comes as a pleasant surprise, a delight after a night in Tehuantepec. Some travelers may have skipped the Isthmus and flown here directly. They won't be sorry, either. Tuxtla tends to be underrated by a good many people because it is neither quaint, colorful, nor picturesque. Rather, it is an attractive, modern city, sort of a small Guadalajara with enough bright lights to make an American feel at home. It means a lot, for there are moments when colonial churches, thatched huts, and tiled roofs become oppressive. Tuxtla provides a break. It's a good place to relax, take a swim, and enjoy a movie.

This is the capital of Chiapas, a state whose name Americans might like to recall when Mexicans bring up Texas. Chiapas was, in days of yore, part of Guatemala. That it is a state of the Mexican Republic is due largely to the efforts of Joaquin Miguel Gutiérrez. Hence the city's double name.

Texas, Chiapas, and Guatemala bring to mind a little-known facet of Mexico's history. When New Spain won its freedom from Madrid, its territory included not only what today are large chunks of the United States, but all of Central America as well. The original Mexican Empire of Augustín I took in four of the five republics. Guatemala alone insisted it was an independent entity. There was some squabbling and an army of sorts sent down, but governments in Mexico City were more concerned about holding the National Palace and less worried about the territories below the Suchiate River.

A pleasant hour or so can be spent in Tuxtla's state museum. It is devoted to pre-Hispanic treasures of which the state has many, as well as colonial items.

Not to be missed here is the zoo, the best in Latin America, recently transplanted to roomier quarters on the south side of Tuxtla. On display are animals of the state: monkeys, jaguars, anteaters, ocelots, boars. There is something quite impressive about seeing the creatures here and realizing their cousins may be roaming in the high grass just a few yards from the highway.

Leading north from the state museum on the east side of town is a paved road to El Sumidero, a magnificent canyon carved out by the Grijalva River. This is truly wild country, inhabited mostly by the ghosts of Indians who are said to have leaped out over the walls, falling 1,000 feet or more rather than yield to the Spanish conquerors. Visitors who would like to see what the canyon looks like from below can now take boat tours departing from an *embarcadero* 11 kilometers east of town, near Chiapa de Corzo all the way to a major dam called Chicoasén. You can either hire a boat by yourself or wait until other travelers come along and split the cost.

Chiapa de Corzo

Chiapa de Corzo, a scant 10 miles down the Pan-American Highway from Tuxtla Gutiérrez, boasts some of Chiapas's most accessible yet least visited ruins. This is not really to say that people are perverse. Chiapa de Corzo was one of the earliest Maya settlements and the mounds that have been discovered, while of great interest to scholars, are not particularly impressive to the casual visitor.

Chiapa is the site of one of the oldest of all settlements in Mexico. Apparently it was a city of some kind at least 3,000 years ago, about the time the Olmecs were cutting rock on the Gulf Coast. Over the years it is thought to have become a great trading center, a link between the Mayas to the east and the Zapotecs to the west.

The Church of Jesus Christ of Latter Day Saints (the Mormons) has sponsored considerable study in the Chiapa area. The Mormons believe that the western hemisphere was populated first by the Jaredites, who came to these shores from Mesopotamia, and then by the Lost Tribes of Israel who arrived about 2,500 years ago. The New World Archaeological Foundation has been working about Chiapa to see if any evidence can be uncovered to substantiate a belief that for the moment must be taken on faith. Not one shred of evidence to support their faith has yet been uncovered. And no objects from either China, Africa, or Europe have ever surfaced in a controlled archaeological site. Much less any evidence of influences from outer space.

The little town itself gives no indication of its historic past. It stands by the Grijalva River, a bridge spanning the gorge below offering an impressive view. Most notable landmark is a fountain that was built to resemble the crown of the kings of Spain. There is a small but quite good lacquerware museum to one side of the main plaza where the 16th-century fountain is located. Artisans work in the back and there is a sales room in the museum.

San Cristóbal

San Cristóbal de las Casas is surely the most beloved city in all Chiapas. It ranks with San Miguel de Allende, Taxco, and Alamos as one of those places discovered and promoted by word of mouth largely by foreigners. It is a strange town, brooding, haunting, cold. In Tuxtla, 50-odd miles away, air-conditioning is standard in any decent hotel room. At San Cristóbal, 7,000 feet up in the Chiapas highlands, hotel rooms come with fireplaces, and visitors had better come with sweaters.

San Cristóbal is full of Indians in colorful traditional garb, either selling their crafts, scurrying about their business, or just taking it all in during a day out on the town. Cold as it may get, many of the women and girls walk about barefoot. The town has more than its share of hippies, aging and otherwise. Many Europeans around also, attracted by the traditional cultures, very much alive and prospering nearby. There are enough exotic types around—foreign and native—to make people-watching a major pastime. You might appear as strange to an Indian on his first visit to town as the other way around.

In this Spanish-looking town, Indians stroll the streets much like the Redskins that wander about trading posts in Hollywood Westerns. Here they are Chamulas and Zinacantecos. The latter favor shorts, possibly to show off their muscular legs. The Chamulas go about in trousers that reach the calf. These and the Tenejapans wear woolen tunics as if they were uniforms. All tend to wear flattish straw hats bedecked with ribbons; an expert can tell what group a man comes from by his hat. The ribbons are said to be attractive to the ladies, so much so that, according to non-Indian local wisdom, a married Zinacanteco is supposed to tie up his ribbons while bachelors allow theirs to blow freely in the breeze.

The women have a costume of their own, as well, but it is tame. None of the magnificence of the Tehuanas is to be found there. This is man's country.

All the Indians one sees around town are offshoots of the Mayans, belonging to either the Tzotzil or Tzeltal linguistic groups. The Tzotzils tend to live at higher elevations in the vicinity of San Cristóbal (Chamulas and Zinacantecos among others) while the Tzeltals make their homes on lower slopes.

Every day except Sunday, there is a great deal of activity at the municipal market with many Indians coming to buy and sell. This is the best place for discreet photography as they are often too busy to pay any attention to you. But remember that the Indians either resist photography or will want to be paid. There are two reasons for their resentment to photographers. Some have seen postcards of their fellow tribesmen for sale and they think that you might be taking photos to sell. Trying to tell them different—even in good Spanish which few understand—does no good whatsoever. They want a piece of the action, to get paid on the spot. Another reason for their objections is that many hold to the traditional belief that sickness results from not being "whole," some intangible element missing from their being. Since photography captures something of the person, illness might result.

No problem to photograph the colonial gems around town. The most outstanding example is the Church of Santo Domingo. Built in the mid-16th century, it is one of the finest examples of the baroque in Mexico. The interior is as splendid as the facade. The church was originally erected in 1523 but was demolished and completely rebuilt at the end of the 17th century. The facade makes a poor contrast with Santo Domingo but the interior boasts of an excellent painting by Juan Correa, a baroque pulpit, and many other luxuries. The Church of El Carmen, of simple architectural style, is painted with pastel colors allowed only in Mexico where they fit in very well indeed. A wooden statue in an outside niche has weathered the centuries in remarkably good shape. The Arch or Tower of El Carmen is contiguous with the church. Vehicles and pedestrians used to pass under its gracefully cirved base. Built in 1677, the squat tower shows some Moorish architectural influences.

Follow the street Hermanos Dominguez for two blocks toward the hill where steps lead up to the Church of San Cristóbal, the focal point of the town's yearly fiesta. There is a great view of the city and surrounding countryside.

Many years ago, a Danish archaeologist, Franz Blom, settled in San Cristóbal with his Swiss wife, Gertrude Duby. Working with American universities and foundations, the couple did some excavation work at Muxviquil, a Mayan site on the outskirts of town. They also studied the cultures of the highlands and the jungle Lacandones. After her husband died, Mrs. Blom stayed put and kept working. She is credited by some with keeping the Lacandones alive, a tribe whose numbers were dwindling to less than 200 and appeared doomed to extinction as disease and lumbermen moved in on their territory. Some people criticize Mrs. Blom with holding an overprotective attitude towards the Lacandones, saying that she wishes to keep them isolated from inevitable changes and setting herself up as the only valid expert on the tribe. Be that as it may, she has taken excellent photos of this group. The pictures may be seen at her Na Balom Institute, along with ancient Mayan pieces. This is a museum, guest house, and library where students willing to defer to the old lady are treated warmly. If your interest is superficial, don't bother.

Overlooked at times is the fact that San Cristóbal is the oldest Spanish settlement in Chiapas. It was, in time gone by, known simply as the Royal City and served as capital of the state until 1892 when Tuxtla Gutiérrez took over to punish San Cristóbal for its royalist stance during the War of Independence. The present Municipal Palace (facing the zócalo) functioned as the state capital during the 19th century and remains a fine example of neo-classic architecture. The best example of civil colonial architecture is also off the zócalo. This is the Casa Mazariegos (now the Hotel Santa Clara), the home of the 16th-century conquistador of Chiapas, Diego de Mazariegos. The palace was built in the plateresque style. The long name honors Bartolomé de las Casas, first Bishop of Chiapas and champion of the Indian.

As the conquest of Mexico was consummated, new forms of administration had to be found, new systems devised to run a new empire. Among these was the system of "commending" Indians to various conquerors. The Spaniards were to see that their native charges were well cared for and converted to the Catholic faith that their souls might be saved. In turn, the Indians were to be a labor force that would work the land of the new master.

In effect, the Indians were slaves. And they were treated like slaves. The new masters cared little about saving the souls of their charges and ignored any rights the Indians might have had. Theirs became a system of cruel, crushing exploitation.

De las Casas protested. He spoke out and wrote detailed reports to Madrid about a vile situation, earning himself the hatred of the men who had conquered the land. Spain's enemies in Europe intercepted some of the bishop's writings and circulated them widely, leading to charges that de las Casas was defaming the crown. Nonetheless, to some degree, his efforts met with success. Twenty years after the final defeat of the Aztecs, the King of Spain proclaimed New Ordinances governing the treatment of the Indians in the New World. But to a large extent, the proclamation was ignored.

Nor, it should be noted, can de las Casas be listed as Mexico's first champion of civil rights. To free the Indians from slavery, he suggested Negroes be imported to work the land.

Townspeople are beginning to realize the attraction of the Indians to foreigners but only some 30 odd years ago, the Indians were not even allowed to tread on the sidewalks. The Indians are still very poor but have pride. They may think that you are making fun of them if you dress up in their garb, especially as some male hippies have at times taken to wearing Indian women's blouses.

Palenque

Palenque, site of some of the most notable ruins of the Maya culture, can be reached from Tuxtla Gutiérrez by way of a newly asphalted highway running via Villahermosa. The 250-mile trip takes about 6 to 7 hours, offering vistas of banana, coffee, and cocoa plantations, Tzeltal villages, and orchid jungles. From Tuxtla light airplanes may be chartered to make the trip; they land at an airstrip near the ruins. You can also reach Palenque from the coastal highway which follows the Gulf of Mexico from Veracruz to Villahermosa then shoots up to Merida in the Yucatan Peninsula. From San Cristóbal, a road drops down to Palenque through Ocosingo. At the time of this writing, some 20 km of road has been paved with asphalt, completing the entire length between the two cities. What the road lacks in smooth surface, it more than makes up in scenery—spectacular mountains, valleys, and traditional Indian villages. Figure on 4 to 5 hours for this 110-mile stretch. An hour or so before reaching Palenque, the impressive falls of Agua Azul lie about 4 km on a dirt road to your left (paved at first). Well worth a visit both for the falls and pools of stunning turquoise-blue waters. There is camping and rudimentary facilities.

Palenque was the first major Mayan center to be deserted for reasons still unclear towards the end of the classical period in the 9th century. The Spaniards were in the New World more than 250 years before they stumbled on Palenque. Since then, these ruins have been the goal of many dedicated travelers. Throughout the 19th century explorers hacked their way through jungles, risked malaria and yellow fever to glimpse the fabled lost city.

Some 30 years ago, a rail line was cut through the jungle, running near the ruins. It was not a particularly comfortable ride, the little train chugging along in sweltering heat, and one was never quite certain when the train would be back; seats, nonetheless, were at a premium. Later, light planes began flying to the ruins, as they still do. In those early days passengers could never be quite certain if return reservations would be honored. And the pair of hotels at Palenque were none too appealing. Hammocks were used in place of beds.

Now Palenque is an easy 90-mile trip by bus or car from Villahermosa. Some of the adventure has gone out of visiting the ruins, but creature comforts are considerably improved. Most people get more out of it that way.

First settled about 1,500 years ago, Palenque became the center of a city perhaps 25 miles square. Most of the community would have been rather crude huts long since washed away, but the center is where the ruins of today stand: The Temple of the Cross, the Law Courts, the Palace with its pagoda-like tower, the sunken plaza, and a great pyramid topped by the Temple of Inscriptions. The community flourished for perhaps 500 years, a city-state of the Late Classic period.

In its day, Palenque must have been truly magnificent. The rulers sometimes deferred to the priests who held power through their understanding of astrology and mathematics and decreed when to sow a crop and when to begin a harvest. No doubt they extended this gift of prophecy to other matters as well.

Palenque is considered one of the highest, if not *the* summit, of artistic achievement in Mexico. Other sites may be more massive and imposing but aesthetically Palenque has few rivals. Outstanding are stucco figures of priests or nobles. The bodies were shaped first, then the clothing was added by layers. The drying of the stucco was retarded by the addition of a tree bark to give the artist more time to work on the delicate details.

Aside from working in stucco, the artists of Palenque also carved stone with perfect technique. Among the outstanding examples of this sculpture are the sacred ceiba tree in the Temple of the Foliated Cross, an old priest smoking a pipe (for religious reasons) in the Temple of the Cross as well as the figures of nobles flanking the stairs of the East Court of the Palace and hieroglyphs so intricate that some 19th-century artists gave up when trying to copy them.

Of all buildings in Palenque, the most fascinating is the Temple of the Inscriptions.

The temple stands atop the tallest pyramid in Palenque, which, in itself, is nothing unusual. The pyramids of Mexico, unlike those of Egypt, were built to support temples. But back after World War II, Alberto Ruz Lhuillier, a noted archeologist, began poking around in the temple. The walls, he discovered, continued on down below the floor.

His crew lifted the floor and began digging. Beneath a bit of rubble they uncovered stairwells, filled in with rock and earth 10 centuries before. In all, it took 4 years to go down 72 feet. At that point a thick wall was found. The diggers broke through.

Dr. Ruz later wrote. "Delicate festoons of stalactites hung like the tassels of a curtain, and the stalagmites on the floor looked like the drippings from a great candle. Raised above the floor was an enormous stone slab in perfect condition."

The slab, intricately carved, weighed a good 5 tons. When finally it was lifted it revealed a stone coffin. Within were the remains of what was obviously a great ruler, whose name turned out to be Pacal meaning "shield." His face was covered with a mask of jade mosaic. About the tomb were carvings of the nine lords of the underworld, jewels of jade and pearl, and the bones of half a dozen servants sent to accompany their master on his journey to the world beyond.

Much of this is like nothing ever found in America. No other pyramids are known to have been used as tombs. The figure on top of the slab covering the tomb has been likened to an astronaut at the controls of his spaceship. All of this has led to much foolish speculation about the origins of the Mayan culture. That the Mayans share some cultural traits with other civilizations is possible. But there are far more differences. Why deny the Mayas the evolution and accomplishments of their own culture?

PRACTICAL INFORMATION FOR THE INDIAN SOUTH

HOW TO GET THERE. By Air. The state capitals—Oaxaca (Oaxaca), Tuxtla Gutiérrez (Chiapas) and Villahermosa (Tabasco)—are well connected with each other as well as to Mexico City by air via either *Aeroméxico* or *Mexicana.* Oaxaca has several daily direct flights from Mexico City and daily direct flights from Acapulco, Tapachula (Chiapas), Villahermosa and three direct weekly flights to Tuxtla Gutiérrez. Via connections in Mexico City, there are flights from Chicago, Denver, Philadelphia, Los Angeles. Flights, either connecting or with a stopover, come from Guadalajara, Mazatlán, Mérida, Mexicali, Tijuana, and Toluca. Tuxtla Gutiérrez has direct flights from Mexico City, Oaxaca, Tapachula and Villahermosa; with stopover or connection from Acapulco, Ixtapa/Zihuatanejo and Guadalajara. Villahermosa has direct flights from Cancún, Mérida, Mexico City, Oaxaca, and Tuxtla Gutiérrez; with stopover or connection from Acapulco, Ciudad Juárez, Culiacán, Guadalajara, Ixtapan/Zihuatanejo, Monterrey, Tijuana, Reynosa, San Antonio, and Los Angeles.

Important note: The airport at Tuxtla Gutiérrez is often fogged in and closed to traffic, especially between late November and March. Flights could be delayed several hours or even days.

By Train. There are daily trains from Mexico City to Oaxaca, none too clean, with sleeping cars but no dining car, taking between 13 and 24 hours if there are no major delays. Another rail line runs from Mexico City to Veracruz and on to either Tapachula on the Pacific border with Guatemala or to Mérida in the Yucatan. Estimated times from Mexico City to Palenque run in the 24-hour range and some 13 hours more to Mérida. It is useless to even try to speculate on the time to Tapachula. In this area, rail travel is either for fanatical train buffs or masochists.

By Bus. First class buses are frequent and fast to all major cities from the federal capital and they are inexpensive. Even cheaper are the second class buses both along the major highways and secondary roads.

By Car. Traveling in a private car offers a flexible schedule, the advantage of being able to stop on the spur of the moment or to spend the night. The roads are good if with lots of curves in the mountain areas which means much of Oaxaca and Chiapas. There's not too much traffic but, as always, we strongly discourage night driving. During the months of December to March (and sometimes at other times), the winds around Tehuantepec are strong enough to turn trucks over. Best to sit tight and wait until things settle down a bit or drive very slowly and carefully.

EMERGENCY TELEPHONE NUMBERS. Oaxaca: Federal Tourism Office, 60144 and 60045; State Tourism Office, 63810 and 64828; Hospital (Red Cross), 62056; Police, 62747; U.S. Consulate, 60654.

Tuxtla Gutiérrez: Federal/State Tourism offices, 25509 and 24535; Police, 20530; Red Cross, 20096.

San Cristóbal Las Casas: Tourism Office, 80414; Immigration, 80292; Municipal Police, 80553; Transit Police, 80399.

HOTELS. In the cities of Oaxaca and Puerto Escondido the price range for a double room is, roughly: *Deluxe,* $55; *First Class,* $35; *Expensive,* $23; *Moderate,* $15; *Inexpensive,* $10. You can expect to pay a few dollars less in other sections of the states of Oaxaca and Chiapas. Prices were in effect at time of writing. All are subject to a federal tax of 15%.

Oaxaca

Deluxe

El Presidente, 5 de Mayo #300, tel 60611. The best in town, located in the tastefully renovated 16th-century Convent of Santa Catalina, a few blocks from the zócalo; 91 units, gardens, excellent restaurant and bar, shops, pool, travel agency, car rental, variety shows.

First Class

San Felipe Mision, Jalisco 15, tel. 50100. Located out of town in the suburb of San Felipe; 160 units, all with private terraces; pool with bar, parking, good view of the city, travel agency, shops, live music in the lobby bar, gardens, two good restaurants, popular new disco.

Victoria, on the Pan American Highway km 545 on the Cerro del Fortin, tel. 52633. A bit out of town on a hill with a superb view of the city; 151 units, restaurants, bar, large pool, spacious gardens, tennis, disco.

Mision de los Angeles, Calzada Porfirio Diaz, tel. 51500. A block off the Calzada Niños Heroes; 125 units, large pool with bar, gardens, tennis, games room, restaurant (particularly good for breakfasts), disco/nightclub.

Expensive

Señorial, Portal de Flores, tel. 63933; right on the zócalo, with 136 rooms, restaurant, bar, pool, parking, travel agency and car rental.

Marques del Valle, Portal Clavijero, tel. 63474; on the zócalo, colonial type five-story hotel with 95 rooms, restaurant, bar, and travel agency.

Meson del Angel, Mina 518, tel. 66666, close to downtown with 34 rooms, restaurant, bar, pool, parking; departure point for bus to Monte Albán.

Monte Albán, Alameda de Leon #1, tel. 62777; in front of the cathedral; 34 rooms, pool, restaurant, bar parking.

Moderate

Meson del Rey, Trujano 212, tel. 60033; two blocks from the zócalo; 22 rooms, parking, restaurant.

Plaza, Trujano 112, tel. 62200; a half block from the zócalo; with 19 rooms, restaurant, long distance phone service.

Antequera, Hidalgo 807, tel. 64020; half block from the zócalo; 29 rooms and restaurant.

Isabel, Murguia 104, tel. 64900; four blocks from the zócalo; 64 rooms and restaurant.

Virreyes, Morelos 1001, tel, 65555; four blocks from the zócalo; 31 rooms.

Francia, 20 de Noviembre and Trujano, tel. 64811; half block from the zócalo; 74 regular rooms and 20 more in new annex with A/C, restaurant.

Inexpensive

Principal, 5 de Mayo #208, tel. 62535; five blocks from the zócalo; with 22 rooms.

Puerto Escondido

First Class

Castel Bugambilia, Ave. Juarez #1, tel. 20394; with 100 A/C rooms, restaurant, bar, two pools, beach.

Expensive

Santa Fe, Playa Marinero, tel. 20170; with 24 fan-cooled rooms, crafts shop, boutique, pool, dive shop for equipment rental, restaurant, parking.

Nayar, Ave. Perez Gasca 407, tel. 20113; a short uphill walk from the beach area; 24 fan cooled units, restaurant, gardens, parking.

Paraiso Escondido, Union #1, tel. 20444; with 20 A/C rooms, restaurant, bar, pool, parking, garden, crafts shop, travel agency, car rental, boutique, tobacco shop.

Rincon del Pacifico, Perez Gasca 900, tel. 20056; with 26 fan cooled rooms, restaurant, garden.

Inexpensive

Las Palmas, Perez Gasca no number, tel. 20230; on the beach with 40 fan-cooled rooms, cafeteria, restaurant, bar.

Posada del Puerto, Ave. Hidalgo 104, tel. 20264; with 16 rooms, fan cooled and with bath, parking.

Tuxtla Gutiérrez

First Class

Castel Flamboyant, Blvd. Dominguez km 1081, tel. 29311, a bit out of town on the way to the airport, 119 A/C units in some questionable pop architecture but with lots of amenities: restaurant, bar, pool, tennis, lots of live music, movies on closed circuit TV, cafeteria, parking, and disco/nightclub.

Expensive

Bonampak Tuxtla, Blvd. Dominguez 180, tel. 32050; at the edge of the downtown area and near the Madero Park; 112 units including some bungalows, some rooms A/C, pool, bars, restaurant, beauty and barber shop, cafeteria, gardens, steam bath, tennis, parking, travel agency, crafts shop, films on closed circuit TV.

Gran Hotel Humberto, Avenida Central Poniente #180, tel. 22080; near the central plaza; 119 A/C rooms, restaurant, cabaret/nightclub, bar, small parking lot in the tallest building in town.

Posada del Rey, Primera Oriente Norte #310, tel. 22911; just off the northeast corner of the main plaza; 48 rooms, some A/C, some fans, rooftop bar and restaurant, travel agency, car rental.

San Cristóbal De Las Casas

Expensive

Posada Diego de Mazariegos, Adelina Flores #2, tel. 81825; a block from the central plaza; 53 units spread among two colonial buildings, the most prestigious hotel in town; excellent service, large rooms in the older area, courtyards, some rooms with fireplaces, restaurant, popular bar and coffee shop/cafeteria.

Santa Clara, on the zócalo in the former home of Diego de Mazariegos (the conquistador of Chiapas and the founder of San Cristobal) tel. 81140; some very large rooms, patio with fountain, restaurant, bar, cafeteria, crafts shop.

Parador Ciudad Real, Diagonal Centenario 32, tel. 81886; at the entrance to town from Tuxtla Gutierrez; 48 rooms in elegant or junky decor, according to your tastes, good service, restaurant, bar, parking.

Bonampak, Calzada Mexico #5, tel. 81621; at the entrance to town near the Parador Ciudad Real, 34 rooms, restaurant, bar, parking.

Moderate

Posada del Cid, Carretera Internacional km 1171, tel. 81181 at the entrance to town with 48 rooms, restaurant/bar, parking, disco.

El Molino de la Alborada, Apartado Postal 50, tel. 80935; about 1½ miles from downtown; 11 cottages all with fireplaces, view of town; horses for rent, hotel bus to town several times a day, restaurant, all under American management.

Palacio de Moctezuma, Leon and Juárez #16, tel. 80352; with 23 rooms (some are quite small), courtyard with flowers and flowers, four blocks from the main plaza, parking, restaurant, bar.

Español, Uno de Marzo #15, tel. 80045; two blocks from the main square; 36 rooms in a colonial setting with patio/garden, some rooms with fireplaces (charge for the wood), restaurant, bar, parking.

Rincon de los Arcos, Ejercito Nacional #66, tel. 81313; with 18 rooms, disco, restaurant/bar, parking.

Parador Mexicanos, Cinco de Mayo 38, tel. 81515; with 25 rooms, restaurant, bar, parking, tennis (only place in town), beautifully colonial.

Palenque

Expensive

Casa de Pacal, Juarez 10; no telephone, on the main street; 16 small A/C rooms, clean, restaurant, bar.

Chan Kah, at km 6 from town towards the ruins; no telephone; 14 fan cooled bungalows in a great tropical setting, multi-leveled pool fed by stream water, restaurant, bar, parking.

Moderate

Nututun Viva, Carratera Ocosingo km 3, tel. 50100; with 60 nice A/C rooms, parking, restaurant, bar, crafts shop, trailer park, natural pool from curve in the river.

Tulija, at the entrance to town, tel. 50104; with 84 rooms either A/C or fan cooled, pool, restaurant, bar, parking.

Inexpensive

Misol Ha, Juarez 14, tel. 50092, in town next to the Pakal with 28 small rooms, some A/C, some fan cooled.

Vaca Vieja, on the corner of Cinco de Mayo and Chiapas towards the outskirts of town, tel. 50388; with 18 clean rooms, fan cooled or A/C.

SPECIAL EVENTS

Oaxaca

Guelaguetza, in the city of Oaxaca during the last two Mondays of July, a big bash, now geared mostly far tourists but worthwhile to see all the states' traditional costumes and dances; essential to reserve tickets for the dances and hotel space well in advance.

Vigen de la Soledad, Dec. 16 to 18, fiesta to honor the city's patron saint with processions, floats, dances, bands, fireworks.

Christmas festivities in the city include the *Noche de los Rabanos* (Radishes' night) on December 23 with expositions of sculptured radishes in the zócalo; these sculptures include Nativity scenes; on Christmas Eve, *posadas* or representations of Joseph and Mary's wanderings to seek lodgings before the birth of Jesus. The fiestas end with a grand finale around the zócalo with floats, giant puppets, music, and fireworks lasting until midnight mass.

Spring Festival from March 21 for a couple of weeks with the Symphony Orchestra of Mexico City playing in town and neighboring villages famous for their colonial churches or in archaeological sites.

29 April in San Pedro Comitancilla, traditional fiesta including the famous Zandunga dance.

The following fiestas in the isthmus of Tehuantepec are called *velas,* literally meaning "candles" from the old habit of making candles for religious celebrations. They all include the famous Tehuana ladies in their resplendent costumes and solid gold jewelry as well as dances typical to the region! **Juchitán**—17–31 May, 13–16 August and 3–6 September; **Tehuantepec**—22–25 June, 2–5 and 13–17 August; September 29.

Chiapas

15 to 23 January, *Fiesta de San Sebastian* in Chiapa de Corzo with many processions, colorful and carrying the saint, dances with masks particular to this

fiesta and representing Spaniards, and a mock naval battle in the Grijalva River on the 21st.

Beginning after Easter Week in San Cristobal de las Casas, *Feria de la Primavera y de la Paz* (Spring and Peace Fair) with cockfights, bullfights, fireworks, and interesting cultural events.

24–25 July fiesta of the patron saint of San Cristobal at the church on the hill dominating the city; pilgrimages to the church by all taxi drivers as the saint is also their patron; early morning pilgrimages for each of the eight days preceding the fiesta from the various neighborhoods of the city; lots of music and fireworks.

The following fiestas in the two Indian communities located nearest to San Cristobal are most colorful but it is strongly advised that you do not try to photograph; all the rituals involve praying in churches, fireworks, lots of eating and drinking: 20–22 January, fiesta of San Sebastian in **Zinacantan;** 22–24 June, fiesta of San Juan in **San Juan Chamula;** 9–10 August, fiesta of San Lorenzo in **Zinacantan.** 30 December–1 January, changing of civil authorities in the Indian communities

Carnaval and Holy Week, moveable dates in both Indian communities with lots of color and action, horse races, running across fire as a purification rite, traditional music.

In the town of Palenque, the annual fiesta of Santo Domingo from August 1 to 5 with a country fair, cockfights, fireworks, charreadas (Mexican rodeo), bullfights, lots of music, and a crafts show.

HOW TO GET AROUND. Air connections between the state capitals are frequent and there are scheduled flights from Tuxtla Gutiérrez to Palenque. Small plane chartered flights (four passengers, $80 to $100 per person, 4 person minimum) are available from Palenque, from San Cristobal and Tuxtla Gutiérrez to the jungle ruins of Bonampak and Yaxchilan, at times stopping at a Lacandon Indian village, weather conditions permitting. There are two daily flights from Oaxaca to Puerto Escondido. *Mexicana* now flies direct to Puerto Escondido from Mexico City. Buses are frequent and inexpensive between all places mentioned in this chapter, except for Bonampak and Yaxchilan. Within cities, taxis are available, not very expensive but be certain that the price is agreed upon before getting in the vehicle.

By Bus. Daily service from Oaxaca to Puerto Escondido and Puerto Angel is available. Be sure to take the line using the Miahuatlán-Pochutla-Puerto Angel route. Complete paving of this formerly very rough highway was finished in 1982. It can now be navigated safely by the ordinary motorist.

By Car. At least a week should be allowed for a trip from Mexico City to San Cristóbal de las Casas and back; this includes a day's sightseeing in Oaxaca each way and a day in San Cristóbal.

The main highways of the area are excellent, lightly traveled two-lane roads. Gasoline stations, however, are far apart and on occasions the gas stations run out of gas. It is well to keep the automobile well-fueled at all times. There is a paucity of restaurants along the highways. The drive from Mexico City to Oaxaca takes about 8 hours.

From Oaxaca to San Cristóbal de las Casas is a tiring 12-hour drive. Preferably, it can be broken up with stops in Tehuantepec and Tuxtla Gutiérrez. Driving at night is dangerous in Mexico. Cattle at times wander the highways, unlighted vehicles lumber along, potholes are unseen, and detours may be missed.

Oaxaca can be reached from Tapachula in about 12 hours.

Puerto Escondido and Puerto Angel are both seaside towns that can be reached by car from Oaxaca City via Miahuatlán and Pochutla, or by taking Hwy. 200 from Acapulco. A direct road links Oaxaca City with Puerto Escondido, but is not recommended. It is only partially paved and exceedingly rough over the unpaved portions. The direct Oaxaca City-Miahuatlán-Pochutla-Puerto Angel road is now completely paved and offers spectacular scenery. The new highway below Puerto Angel has been opened so now you can drive on to the Tehuantepec peninsula and on to Tapachula on the Pacific, the border with Guatemala.

BEACHES. Oaxaca, Puerto Escondido, and immediate vicinity offer several beaches with a medium range of hotels and facilities nearby. The nearby beach of Zicatela has good surfing, especially from June through September. Diving equipment can be rented at the Hotel Santa Fe. Near Puerto Angel, there are some decent if somewhat isolated beaches. Farther down the coast, the Huatulco beaches are excellent with facilities in the works for '86 but check before going. At Salina Cruz, the seas are rough and bathing not very recommended. Most af the beaches of Chiapas are black sand with minimal facilities, not yet developed for tourism.

INFORMATION. Oaxaca. The state government maintains three modules of information in the capital, the city of Oaxaca: at the *Palacio Municipal* (Independencia and Vigil, tel. 63810), at their central office (Cinco de Mayo and Morelos, tel. 64828) and at the airport, (tel. 68101 and 62337). The hours are Monday–Friday 9 A.M. to 3 P.M. and 6 to 8 P.M.; Saturday, 10 A.M. to 1 P.M. During holidays and fiesta times, these modules and several temporary ones are open from 9 A.M. to 8 P.M.

Puerto Escondido. Tourism Office on Ave. Perez Gasca, tel. 20175, open Monday–Friday 8 A.M. to 1 P.M. and 5 to 8 P.M. Saturday, 8 to 11 A.M.

Tuxtla Gutiérrez. *Delegacion Federal de Turismo,* Avenida Central Poniente #1498, tel. 24535; open 9 A.M. to 3 P.M. On the main highway coming to town from the west, the state tourism authorities maintain an information module (Carretera Federal Highway #190) at Blvd. Belisario Dominguez #950, tel. 20732 and 27773; open every day from 8 to 8 every day. There is also an information booth at the airport.

San Cristóbal de las Casas. At the Palacio Municipal on the main square, tel. 80414; open 8 to 8 every day except Sunday when they close at 3 P.M.

Palenque. At the Palacio Municipal and at Catazaja (where the main highway forks with a branch to Palenque) both open from 8 A.M. to 2 P.M., and in the afternoon at Catazaja from 3 to 6 and at the Palacio Municipal from 5 to 8.

USEFUL ADDRESSES. Oaxaca. U.S. Consulate. Crespo 213, tel. 60654. Airlines. *Aeroméxico,* Hidalgo 513; tel. 63765 and 63229; *Mexicana,* Fiallo and Independencia; tel. 68414 and 65796; *Aerovias Oaxaquenas,* Armenta and Lopez #209; tel. 63824 and 63833. VW Combis to the airport, tel. 67878 and 60363. Buses to Monte Albán, from the Hotel Meson del Angel, Mina 518 at Diaz Ordaz, tel. 65327 (about $1 round trip). Post Office, facing the Cathedral square on Independencia. Railroad station, Calzada Madero, tel. 62676.

Chiapas. Airlines, *Aeroméxico,* Segunda Oriente Sur #130, tel. 22155 and 31000; *Mexicana,* Avenida Central Poniente #206, tel. 20020 and 25402. Airport Llano de San Juan, tel. 20601. *Federal Airport,* tel. 20076 and 26667. *Aviacion de Chiapas,* Cuarta Calle Poniente and Primera Avenida Norte, tel. 25529 and 21379. Bus Stations. First Class, Segunda Norte and Segunda Poniente; Second Class, Segunda Sur and Septima Oriente. Car rentals. *Gabriel Rent-a-Car,* Boulevard Belisario Dominguez #780, tel. 20757; *Autos Badia,* Segunda Sur Poniente #1472, tel. 20956; *Tuchtlan Turistico,* Boulevard Belisario Dominguez km 1777, tel. 27828; *Tuxtla Rent-a-Car* (Budget), Cuarta Oriente Norte #201A, tel. 25506.

San Cristobal de las Casas. *Aero Chiapas,* at the airport, tel. 81192. First class bus terminal, at Insurgentes and the Pan-American Highway. Post Office at Crescencio Rosas and Cuauhtemoc. In **Palenque** for air charter to Bonampak and Yaxchilan (about $300 for one to four passengers) at *Aviacion Chiapas,* Ave. Juarez 163, tel. 50210.

TOURS. Oaxaca. There are tours available for the city, to the archaeological sites, nearby towns, market, specialized crafts, or colonial churches. Tours are also taken to Puerto Escondido. Some agencies: *El Convento* at the Presidente Hotel, tel. 60611; *Viajes Chimali,* Alcala 201, tel. 66869; *Camacho Tours,* Diaz 311 local A, tel. 69246. There is usually a stipulation of two persons minimum. Typical costs per person for the city tour $6.50, Monte Albán $7.50, Mitla $7.50. At Puerto Escondido, there are boat tours lasting all day, jungle cruises to the lush Manialtepec Lagoon, leaving in the morning from in front of La Posada Restaurant.

Chiapas. Several travel agencies in Tuxtla Gutiérrez run city tours, to the Sumidero Canyon, to Chiapa de Corso, and to San Cristóbal. On your own you can go down to the dock on the river in Chiapa de Corso for a fantastic boat ride at the bottom of the canyon to the Chicoasen Dam, a ride lasting some three hours and costing $3 per person. Boats usually leave when there are enough passengers; between six and nine is a usual load. City and environs tours cost about $12 per person, six person minimum, with lunch often included. The tour to San Cristobal, lasting 10 to 12 hours costs about $15 without lunch. Some agencies: *Tuchtlan* at the Hotel Tuchtlan, Segunda Sur Oriente #422, tel. 29772; *Marabasco,* Boulevard Belisario Dominguez on the corner with Plaza Bonampak, tel. 27815; *Santa Ana Tours,* 16 Septiembre #6, tel 80298; *Wagon Lits,* Hotel Flamboyan, tel. 29311.

San Cristóbal de las Casas has no travel agency as such, but if you want a guide who speaks the Indian languages and knows the area like the palm of his hand, have your hotel contact Sergio Castro. He lives at 16 Septiembre #32 without a phone but with the best collection of regional costumes and other Indian items, plus he speaks good English.

Palenque has guides who sometimes put together VW bus tours to Bonampak; two days, sleep in hammocks and barely adequate food unless you pay extra. Costs about $250 total for 6 to 8 persons. Same type of tour to Yaxchilan, including a two-hour trip up the Usumacinta River, total cost about $350. Check at the Hotel La Cañada or at the Municipal Tourism Office.

MUSEUMS. Oaxaca. *Museo Regional,* next to the Santo Domingo Church with the unsurpassed pre-Columbian collection from Monte Albán plus plenty of other things, all in the ex-convent. Open Tuesday to Sunday, 10 to 6; small admission charge. *Tamayo Museum,* Morelos and Palacios, far-ranging collection of pre-Columbian ceramics from many cultures. Open Wednesday through Monday; small admission charge. *House of Benito Juárez,* Carranza and Diaz, open from Tuesday through Sunday 9 to 2 and 4 to 6; small admission charge. *Aripo,* the State Handicraft Center, Garcia Vigil 809; run by the state government for the sale of crafts and the exhibition of weaving on wooden looms. Open Monday through Saturday 9 to 1 and 4 to 7, Sunday 9 to 1. *INAH,* Pino Suarez 715, frequent expositions of diverse types of art; open Monday–Friday 8 to 3. *Alianza Francesa,* Morelos 1308, expositions of paintings; call tel. 63934 to check hours. *Cafe Sol y Luna,* Murguia #105, a restaurant with student atmosphere, slow service, art shows and live music. *Casa de la Cultura,* Gonzales Ortega 403, all types of courses and expositions, check their program but everything is in Spanish. *Frissell Museum* at Mitla, small, affiliated with the University of the Americas with—for once—the pieces also labeled in English; decent pre-Columbian stuff but nothing outstanding; crafts shop featuring amber items and other local crafts; open from 9 to 6 every day.

Chiapas. In Tuxtla Gutiérrez, the *Regional Museum* for Mayan and colonial art, located in the Parque Madero; open 9 to 7 Tuesday through Sunday (the park also has a nature house and a botanical garden). An excellent zoo, perhaps the best in Latin America, is located just out of town, off the highway to San Cristóbal; very few cages, most animals in liberty in spacious places which resemble their habitat; open 8:30 to 5 Tuesday through Sunday. In Chiapa de Corzo, the *Lacquer Museum* is to one side of the main square, open Tuesday through Sunday, 9 to 2 and 5 to 7.

Palenque. the museum at the archeological site is open from 10 to 4, definitely worth a visit. In **San Cristóbal de las Casas,** the *Na Balom,* on Calle Vicente Guerrero, has some pre-Columbian pieces, contemporary Indian items, and a good library dealing with the region; open Tuesday through Sunday, 4 to 5:30; donations expected. *Museo de Trajes,* 16 Septiembre #32, a private collection of the best of the local Indian costumes and other items; open 6 to 7 every day; free entrance; owner speaks English.

SHOPPING. Oaxaca. The state and the city are best known for weavings and ceramics; there is also some jewelry, copies of the items found in Tomb 7 at Monte Albán. Stores and markets abound with bargaining the accepted norm. In the capital, the *Saturday Market,* located on the outskirts of town near the second class bus station, is open every day and busy in the mornings, but, as the name implies, busiest on Saturdays. The *Mercado Benito Juárez,* the old market, is still busy selling food and crafts as well as household items; it is located a couple of blocks from the main square. The *Mercado de Artesanias* (Crafts Market) is found two blocks south of the Juárez Market, on the corner of Garcia and Zaragoza. Some good stores for shopping in town: *Yalalag* on M. Acala #104; *Victor's* at P. Diaz #111; *Fonart* (government store) at Garcia Vigil and M. Bravo #116; *Casa Brena* at Pino Suarez #700; *El Petate* on Alcala near Santo Domingo. For excitement and bustle, try one of the weekly town markets in the vicinity. The best known and most frequented by tourists is at Tlacolula on Sunday; some others: Tuesday at Ejutla and Atzompa; Wednesday at Etla and Zimatlan; Thursday at Zaachila; Friday at Ocotlan.

Chiapas. Tuxtla Gutiérrez. *Bazaar Ishcanal,* Plaza de las Instituciones, a government run fixed price store of all types of crafts, open from 9 to 2 and 4 to 8 Monday through Saturday, Sunday from 9 to 2. San Cristóbal de las Casas is known above all for its fine weavings of different patterns according to the Indian group. Best to buy directly from the Indians or do some comparison shopping among the many stores along Calle Real de Guadalupe where there are also many Guatemalan items and crude but strong leather goods. The store called *San Jolobil* is a pseudo-Indian cooperative with stores both at the Santo Domingo church and downtown. In Palenque, there are some Lacandon arrows (cheapest at the ruins) and reproductions of the Palenque sculptures at the shop *Arte Maya* at the Hotel La Cañada.

RESTAURANTS. Restaurants usually serve both regional cooking (can be good but seldom superlative) and international cuisine (not often a gastronomic high). The open-air cafes around the plaza are more for a drink, snacks, people watching, and looking over strolling vendors' wares than for serious eating. Meals are certainly available but tend to be somewhat overpriced due to location. If you want to join the crowds and eat there anyway, the *comida corrida* (set meal menu offered at mid-day, sometimes with a limited choice) is most economical. The best of the local dishes include the multi-spiced local *mole oaxaqueña* served on pork or fowl and tamales, steamed corn dough filled with various goodies. The home produced rot-gut is mezcal, undistinguished in flavor but cheap and sold in colorful places, sometimes in exotic ceramic containers. Most locals drink beer, mineral water or soft drinks with their meals. Unless specified, credit cards are not accepted at the following restaurants. Abbreviations: AE, American Express; D, Diners Club; BC, Bancomer; BM, Banamex; C, Carnet; V, Visa.

Oaxaca

El Refectorio of the Hotel Presidente, at 5 de Mayo #300, tel. 60611; the most authentic high class colonial setting with a basic meal coming in at around $15; accepts most major credit cards.

Hotel Mision de los Angeles' restaurant has a nice view, excellent breakfast, and very good international dishes; highly recommended; good service.

El Jardín, Portal de Flores, tel. 62090; on the zócalo; the most popular outdoor café for both tourists and locals, serving regional and international dishes, good service but make sure that you sit outside—the interior is uninspired not to say depressing; basic meal $6.50, open 9 A.M. to midnight; AE, BC, BM, C.

Guelatao, Portal Benito Juárez 102; tel. 62311; on the east side of the zócalo; favored by the young and at times hippy set due to the inexpensive set meals and slow service, local and international cooking, basic meal $6, open 8 A.M. to 11 P.M. every day.

El Asador Vasco, Portal de Flores #11, tel. 69719; on the zócalo; a decent grill—try their mole or shrimp with garlic; as you are paying for the view overlooking the square, try for a balcony table; basic meal $7, open 1 to 11 P.M.; all major credit cards.

Del Portal, Portal Benito Juárez 112; tel. 62092; with regional and international dishes; basic meal $6; open 12:30 to 11 P.M. AE, BC, BM, C.

Mi Casita, Hidalgo 616, tel. 69256; on the second floor, overlooking the zócalo, specializes in regional dishes and filling snacks, good atmosphere, popular with locals; basic meal $6; open 1 to 8 P.M.

Meson del Taco, Hidalgo 805, tel. 62729; specializes in tacos, naturally; basic meal $4.50; open 6:30 to 11 P.M.

El Regio de Oaxaca, Emiliano Carranza and Palmeras, tel. 51996, in the Colonia Reforma, specialized in good northern cuts of meat; basic meal $7.

Doña Elpidia, Miguel Cabrera 413, tel. 64292; three blocks from the zócalo (there's no sign over the door, so ask); good regional home cooking in a family atmosphere in a most pleasant patio with attentive service but no English; basic meal $5; open every day from 8 to 10:30 A.M. and 1:30 to 4:30 P.M.

Cafe el Sol y la Luna, Murguia 105; no phone; student atmosphere, good live music some nights, specializes in over-rated Italian dishes and salads, mediocre food and slow service, basic meal $5; come for the atmosphere and a drink, not a meal.

Cafe Tavos, on Alcala, a half a block south from Santo Domingo, no phone; small place specializing in honest Mexican cuisine; basic meal $5; open 8 A.M. to 9 P.M. every day except Sunday when they close at 5 P.M.

Catedral, Garcia Vigil at Morelos; tel. 63285; specializes in good cuts of meat, inexpensive set menu, nice ambience; basic meal $8; open 8 A.M. to 11:30 P.M.

La Morsa, Porfirio Díaz 240; tel. 52213; specializes in seafood; basic meal $12; open Monday through Saturday 1:30 to 5 P.M. and 7:30 to 11 P.M.; BC, BM, C.

Ajos y Cebollas, Ave. Juárez 605, tel. 63793; good atmosphere, specializes in cheese and wine, expensive basic meal at $15; open noon to midnight; BC, BM, C.

Estancia Guaucha, Alcala 303, tel. 65038; specializes in Argentine style meats; basic meal $8; open 1 to 11 P.M. every day. BC, BM, C.

Tuxtla Gutiérrez

Café Avenida, Avenida Central 226 and Primera Poniente; the best place for locally grown, freshly roasted coffee but little else, open 7 A.M. to midnight.

Flamingos Cafeteria, Primera Poniente Sur #168, tel. 20922; international, try their paella; inexpensive basic meal at $3.

London, Primera Norte and Cuarta Poniente, tel. 31979; excellent meats and seafood; open 1:30 P.M. to 1 A.M.; live music; basic meal $17; BC, BM, C, V.

Las Pichanchas, Ave. Central Oriente #837, tel. 25351; outstanding variety of regional dishes; live marimba music, regional dances Thursday nights; open 2 to 5 P.M. and 8 P.M. to midnight; BC, BM, V.

San Cristóbal de Las Casas

Posada Diego de Mazariegos, at the hotel by the same name, tel. 81621; specializes in filet cuts and meat brochettes; basic meal $7; open for breakfast, lunch, and supper 7 to 11 P.M.; AE, D, V.

Toluc, Madero #9 just off the zócalo, tel. 82090; specializes in red snapper, meats, and chicken; extremely popular restaurant and owner.

Plaza, Hidalgo #1, tel. 80887; with a view of the plaza and pleasant ambience; national and international cooking; open 9 A.M. to 11 P.M. daily; basic meal $5.50. BC, BM, C, V.

La Galeria, Hidalgo #3, tel. 81547; a half block from the zócalo; a coffee house serving light food including hamburgers; has art exhibits and a shop with crafts; open 9 to 9; friendly service; inexpensive.

El Paredon D'Scorpio, Alvaro Obregon #5, tel. 82222; specializes in Mexican dishes and meats; basic meal $3.50; open 8 A.M. to midnight; organ music and at times a live marimba; BC, BM, C.

El Puente Blanco, Centenario (no number), tel. 81874; specializes in meat dishes and Mexican food; basic meal $3.50; open 8 A.M. to midnight; BC, BM, C, V.

Palenque

El Paraiso, km 2 to the ruins, no phone; large, open-aired, and thatch-covered; crafts shop; seafood and regional dishes; basic meal $7.50.

La Selva, on a dirt road just at the entrance to town and a part of the Hotel La Canada; tel. 50363; seafood, good fresh water fish, and meats; basic meal $8; singing or marimba music Thursday through Sunday.

Chan Kah, on the way to the ruins from town, no phone, specializes in beef and fish; basic meal $12.

Nututun, on the highway to Ocosingo past the turnoff to the ruins, tel. 50100; specializes in fresh water fish, seafood and meats; basic meal $12.

El Mayab, on the outskirts of town; tel. 50140; meats and fish; basic meal $6; open 8 A.M. through dinner.

Restaurant Maya, facing the zócalo in the center of town; tel. 50042; the usual meat and river fish; basic meal $6.50.

NIGHTLIFE/ENTERTAINMENT. Oaxaca. Every evening at the bandstand in the zócalo, you have a free concert from about 7 to 8:15; on Tuesday, Thursday, and Sunday (when there's also a noon performance), it's the State Band playing semi-classic music with lots of marches; on Wednesday, Friday, and Saturday, it's the *State Marimba Band* doing tropical music; not to be missed. The *El Presidente Hotel* has Friday and Saturday buffets with regional dances, starting about 7 for some $8.00. The *Cafe El Sol y la Luna* has live Latin American music several nights a week. The *Monte Albán Hotel* puts on regional folk dance shows every evening at 8:30, costing $1.50 without the meal. The *Macedonia de Acala* has many concerts throughout the year. Discos: *Kaftan's* at the Hotel Mision de los Angeles with shows from Thursday through Saturday; *Victoria,* at the Hotel Victoria; *Yonque Video Disco* at Jalisco # 15 and the *Pasha* located three blocks from the Mision de los Angeles Hotel, on the corner with Belizario Dominguez. In Puerto Escondido, try the disco *Picapiedra.*

YUCATAN AND THE MAYA COUNTRY

Elegance Amongst the Ruins

by
JIM BUDD

The development of Cancun as a world class playground has changed things around considerably on the Yucatan peninsula. Not so long ago Mérida was the hub through which travelers passed en route to the Maya ruins; the peninsula's Caribbean coast was nearly as remote as Vanuatu. Now the pristine coral beaches along the Mexican Caribbean are what lure vacationers in; Maya ruins are but one of the attractions to be found near Cancun.

Yet it is the ruins that are remembered. They fascinate, these monuments to a vanished civilization built by the forefathers of the unconquered people who live on in Yucatan, in Quintana Roo, in Campeche, and beyond. For the Mayas really never were beaten. Some of their lands were occupied, to be sure, here and there by Spanish conquistadores; the Caribbean coast for centuries was dotted with pirates' dens, ruled by buccaneers who swore allegiance to no flag but the Jolly Roger.

This is truly another Mexico, "our sister republic," as mainlanders sometimes call the peninsula in grudging admiration. Turmoil and rebellion (in the 1800s Yucatan wanted to follow the Texas example by breaking away and joining the U.S.A.) explain why the peninsula is three states where it had been one. That divide-and-rule policy of the federal government was only moderately successful. For most of its history the Yucatan area simply was ignored, allowed to develop along its own lines as best it could. Airplanes connected the peninsula with the rest of the country before highways ever did. So remote was Caribbean Quintana Roo that it became a state only in 1974 (before that it had been a federal territory).

Cancun is in Quintana Roo, as are Mexico's two Caribbean island resorts, Cozumel and Isla Mujeres. They are near the northeast tip of the peninsula. To the south is Chetumal, capital of the state; just across the border is Belize, which before it became independent was British Honduras.

Westward to the Gulf of Mexico stretches the peninsula, a flat, riverless cap of limestone sticking out like a thumb from the mainland. Mérida, with some half-million inhabitants, is the only big town in the area. The Mayas, during their great classic period 1,500 years ago, were far more ambitious builders. The peninsula is speckled with the remains of their splendid ceremonial centers: Tulum, near Cancun, Chichen Itza, and Uxmal outside of Mérida, along with lesser known spots such as Edzna in Campeche and on to justifiably famed Palenque in the jungles of Chiapas.

Palenque and booming Villahermosa are not, strictly speaking, part of the Yucatan peninsula. They are, however, part of the Maya country; anyone visiting this area probably will want to take them in. Bus tours and air tours of the region frequently begin in Villahermosa, continue on to Mérida and wind up in Cancun. Motorists driving down from the U.S. learn when they reach Villahermosa that they are entering Maya lands. It is, of course, far easier to fly into Cancun, rent a car and set out to circle the peninsula. Roads are good and distances short. Chetumal is only a four- or five-hour drive from Cancun, and Campeche five or six hours from Chetumal. It takes but three hours to reach Mérida from Campeche, and from Mérida Cancun is only four or five hours away. With all there is to see along the route, of course, a full day with an early start should be allowed for each segment of this circle trip.

EXPLORING THE MEXICAN CARIBBEAN

The story still is told of how a computer discovered Cancun: Back in the 1960s, with the birth of the jet age, tourism began booming in Mexico. Until that time it had almost been ignored by the country's officialdom. Then, rather suddenly, the gnomes who gather statistics at the Banco de Mexico, the central bank, noticed that tourism was

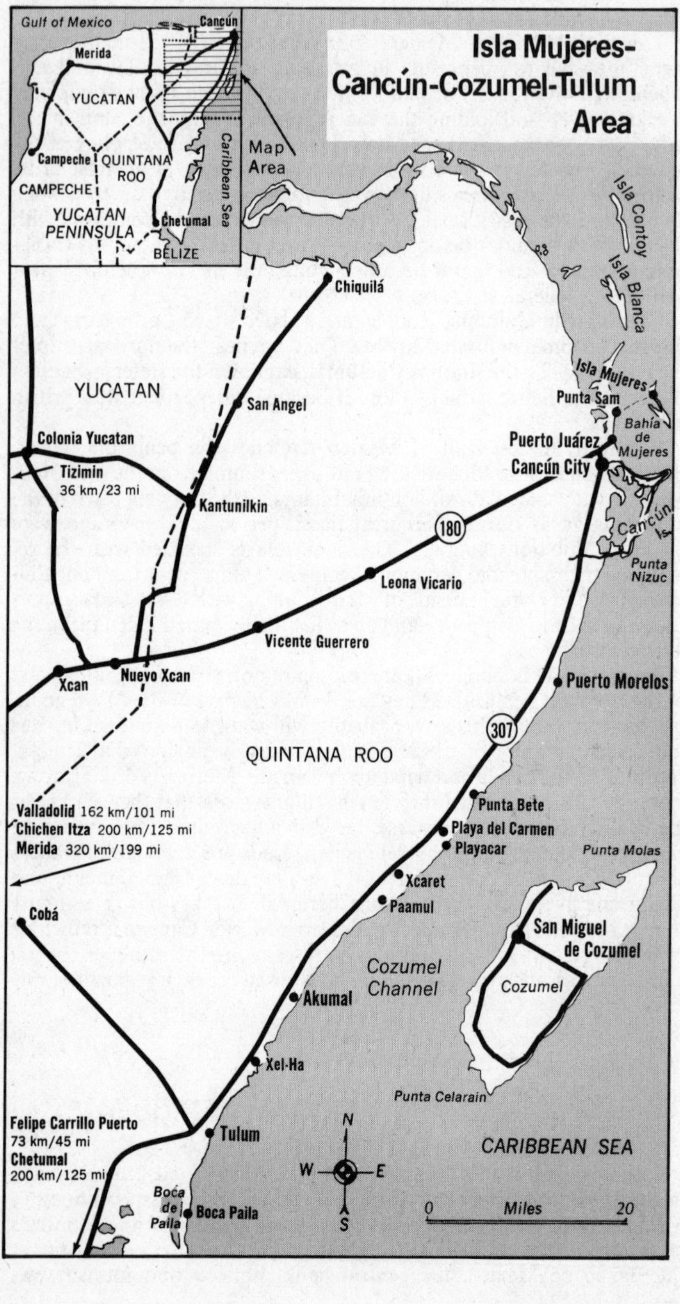
Isla Mujeres-Cancún-Cozumel-Tulum Area
Gulf of Mexico
Cancún
Merida
YUCATAN
Campeche
QUINTANA ROO
CAMPECHE
YUCATAN PENINSULA
Chetumal
BELIZE
Caribbean Sea
Map Area
Isla Contoy
Isla Blanca
Chiquilá
Isla Mujeres
Punta Sam
Bahía de Mujeres
Puerto Juárez
Cancún City
Cancún Is.
Punta Nizuc
YUCATAN
San Angel
Colonia Yucatan
Tizimin
36 km/23 mi
Kantunilkin
180
Leona Vicario
Vicente Guerrero
Xcan
Nuevo Xcan
Puerto Morelos
307
QUINTANA ROO
Punta Bete
Playa del Carmen
Playacar
Punta Molas
Valladolid 162 km/101 mi
Chichen Itza 200 km/125 mi
Merida 320 km/199 mi
Xcaret
Paamul
Cobá
San Miguel de Cozumel
Cozumel Channel
Cozumel
Akumal
Xel-Ha
Punta Celarain
Felipe Carrillo Puerto
73 km/45 mi
Chetumal
200 km/125 mi
Tulum
CARIBBEAN SEA
N
W
E
S
Boca de Paila
Boca Paila
0 Miles 20

starting to bring in as many dollars as some of the leading exports. It also was creating jobs faster than any other industry, for with every new hotel that went up there was a need not only for banquet managers and room clerks but for maids and bellboys, bartenders, airport porters, guides, and taxi drivers. Puerto Vallarta, an isolated, unknown fishing village, had become world famous. Many people still remembered when Acapulco was nothing but a steamy tropical port. Lately there were times when no vacant hotel rooms could be found there at any price.

What Mexico needed, the bankers came to realize, was more Acapulcos and more Puerto Vallartas.

Setting out to create them was another matter. Resort areas as a rule just happen. Hollywood really discovered first Acapulco and then Puerto Vallarta. Vacation crowds flocked where the stars had gone. Governments cannot simply decree that a place will become an international playground. Yet the Mexican Government decided to do just that.

Cancun, An Ideal Holiday Spot

Where? That was the question. To find the answer teams of experts scoured the republic for likely locations, punched their findings into a computer and awaited the answer.

Anyone who has been to Cancun may ask what all the fuss was about. Simply seeing Cancun one might wonder why it was not discovered eons ago. A 12-mile-long elbow-shaped sandbar backed by a jungle lagoon, its perfection is evident to anyone who sees it. Here the tranquil, turquoise Caribbean laps beautiful beaches of cool, talcum-white coral sand. This, legend had it, was the Eden of Maya kings, as nearly ideal for a seaside holiday as any spot on earth could be.

The computer had even more arguments in favor of Cancun. It is closer to most U.S. cities than many Caribbean islands and that could mean the opening of new markets for Mexico. The region was remote, isolated and empty, crying for development. Yet not only was it beautiful, but blessed by wonderful weather. In Cancun, statistics showed, hurricanes hardly happen.

The task of converting this potential paradise into a resort, however, was enormous. In the matter of what technicians call infrastructure, Cancun had nothing. No roads, no airport, no telephones, no electric power, no water lines, nothing. This was a land of coconut plantations and chicle forests, the only settlement being a collection of huts, shacks, and a customs house at Puerto Juarez.

Old Cancun hands never tire of telling what things were like when the first hotels opened in 1974. Every item had to be trucked in or flown in, and there were times when such necessities as beer didn't arrive. Installing the telephone system and getting Telexes to work took longer than expected, so that reservations were being booked by radio. Biggest problem was service. The friendly, cheerful Maya villagers recruited to make beds and wait on tables often never had seen sheets or tablecloths before (the Mayas sleep in hammocks). More experienced hands brought in from other parts of Mexico tended not to stay too long.

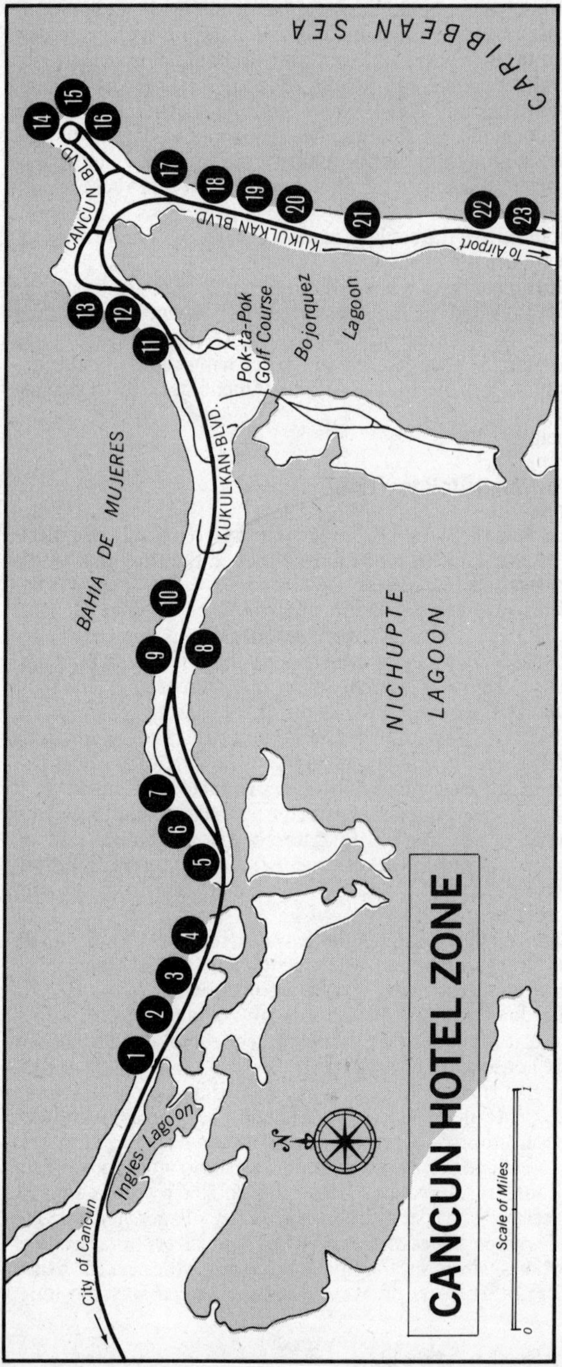

Cancun Hotels
Aristos 18
Calinda 5
Camino Real 14
Caribe Mar 3
Carrousel 4
Casa Maya 7
Club Lagoon 8
Club Mediterranee 23
Club Verano Beat 1
Cristal 16
Fiesta Americana 13
Hyatt Cancun 20
Hyatt Regency 15
Maya Caribe 10
Miramar Mision 19
Playa Blanca 2
Playa Sol 17
El Presidente 11
Vacations Clubs 6
Villas El Presidente 21
Villas Tacul 9
Viva 12
Sheraton 22

Living costs were high and such benefits of civilization as radio, not to mention television, were still unknown in Cancun.

Memories of those days are fading fast. Vacationers get some of the feeling of how things were when they arrived. Ultra-modern as the international airport is, it lies in what appears to be the middle of nowhere surrounded by scrub. Board a van for the 15-mile trip to your hotel and you zip along a good two-lane blacktop cutting through the wilderness. Then, just when you least expect it, comes the first glimpse of the sea, turquoise, jade, aquamarine, powdery blue, changing shade with every ripple. In the distance looms the skyline like a mirage.

The planners who laid out Cancun decided from the outset to go for luxury and elegance. No neon signs here; signs, in fact, are so discreet it can be difficult to identify the hotels. The rule against highrises, to be sure, has been relaxed; guests, it was found, prefer to take elevators than to hike over a few acres to their rooms. Regulations regarding space, on the other hand, remain very much in effect. No crowding in Cancun. In many cases quite a little stroll is required to get from one hotel to its neighbor next door.

Hotel Zone

This is the hotel zone, or the island, as some people call it. Technically the hotel zone is on an island, a 12-mile-long strip of beach connected at either end to the mainland by bridges so short most people never notice them. There are some 20 hotels out this way plus more than a fair sprinkling of condo units, about 4,500 rooms in all. More constantly are being built. It will be a long time before construction cranes disappear from the Cancun skyline.

With the sea on one side and a lagoon on the other, just about every hotel room in this area looks out on the water. The zone has room for only one long street, Kukulkan Boulevard, which extends the length of the island. Here and there along this avenue on the lagoon side are a few restaurants, shops, and various marinas. The lagoon, peaceful, calm and clear, seems made for waterskiing, jet skiing or learning how to windsurf. Scuba boats, fishing boats and tour boats put out from these parts.

Dominating the skyline is the microwave tower (Cancun these days has instant communication with the rest of the world) soaring over the Convention Center. With a capacity for 1,200 people, the center is in reality an inflated building, a great white dome that resembles half a balloon, which, in a manner of speaking, it is. The center provided Cancun with its first shopping mall. Now there are several, all of them full of stores and restaurants.

There is golf, too, at the Pok-a-Tok Club, its 18-hole course designed by Robert Trent Jones and open to the public.

The hotel zone, then, is a carefully planned strip of hotels—but not wall-to-wall hotels by any means—rising along one of the most beautiful stretches of beach in the world. Beyond the Sheraton everything still is pretty much jungle (plus ruins of a small Maya ceremonial center) but it will not be that way forever. Fonatur, the agency that developed Cancun, has plans to keep on developing. If all goes according to program, by the end of the century there will be hotels along the entire stretch of the island.

Luxury hotels they will be. All is luxury in the hotel zone. Only First Class, Deluxe and Super Deluxe establishments are allowed. Cancun was designed to earn dollars for Mexico, and earn many of them as fast as it can. In that respect it has been an enormous success. Occupancy levels are higher here than at any other resort area in the country.

Activity Abounds

A big reason for this is that there is so much to do in Cancun. The golf course is the only one along Mexico's Caribbean shores. Almost every hotel in the hotel zone has a tennis court or two, often several, usually equipped with floodlights for after-dark play.

Every conceivable type of water sport is available in Cancun, from sailing and waterskiing to scuba diving and paraflying. Here one can charter a boat for a day of gamefishing (marlin and sail during the spring months) or try learning how to master a windsurfer or a jetski.

More passive folk may simply opt for a picnic cruise over to nearby Isla Mujeres, by day or night, or sign on for a ride in a houseboat through the lagoon up in the wilderness where all is still jungle. Of the bus tours to the Maya ruins, the jaunt to Tulum is best. Tulum is spectacularly beautiful and right on the beach. The ride there takes only about two hours and includes a pleasant lunch stop. The ruins at Chichen Itza are more impressive, to be sure, but for many people the trip is so long as to be exhausting while the time at the site itself is too brief.

Nightlife in Cancun finally has come into its own. For a time it appeared there was so much to do during the day that vacationers were too weary to stay up very late. As it is, evenings begin a bit earlier here than in the rest of Mexico, with the restaurants filling up around 7 P.M., something unheard of in Acapulco. After dinner there is a nice choice of discos and piano bars.

Cheap spots are rare. Cancun was designed to be pricey.

Budget travelers, however, need not feel barred. If rates in the hotel zone are too high, there are always less costly places downtown, over on the mainland, in what is called Cancun City. The beaches in the hotel zone are public, after all, and only a short bus ride away.

Cancun City is home for some 100,000 souls, from hotel general managers to busboys. It simply did not exist back a few years ago, proving all that was predicted about resort promotion leading to regional development. The city was as carefully laid out as the hotel zone, each neighborhood carefully planned as a residential unit centered around parks and plazas. Avenida Tulum is the main drag although many of the hotels and restaurants are along Avenida Yaxchilan. And for all its planning, Cancun City is not an especially pretty place. It looks like what it is, a boom town with many of its buildings all but put up overnight.

It is only fair to say that for many travelers Cancun is something of a disappointment. To these people the hotel zone is simply too carefully planned. In the eyes of some it is sterile and lacking in charm and grace.

As for Cancun City, to many visitors it comes off simply as junky. Happily for these folk, Cancun alone is not the Mexican Caribbean. The great joy of the region is its ability to provide about any kind of surroundings that a body might want. There are, to begin with, the real islands, Isla Mujeres and Cozumel. And there are any number of delightful spots just off the highway to Tulum.

Cozumel Started it All

Cozumel is Mexico's original Caribbean playground. In a manner of speaking it has been attracting visitors since 1518 when the first Spanish explorers landed there. A year later Cortes had his fleet from Cuba meet there and form up to sail on to Veracruz to begin the conquest of Mexico.

World War II brought about what might be called the second discovery of Cozumel. The U.S. built an airstrip there from which planes could hunt U-boats. The Americans spent their off hours snorkeling and diving in the exceptionally clear waters about the reefs and went home lavishly praising the island from which they could visit another world. Eventually Jacques Cousteau, the undersea guru, came to find out what all the excitement was about and pronounced Cozumel one of the finest diving areas in the world. With that a minor rush began.

Scuba diving is still very much what Cozumel is all about. The island has something of a tropical ski town ambience to it. Young men congregate at the many open sided cafes to nurse beers and talk about their adventures off Palancar Reef, to exchange night dive experiences and worry over regulators that are acting up. Where there are young men such as these one also always finds young women.

Over the years a number of rather luxurious hotels opened on the island, although it was only recently that the first international chain, Sheraton, put in an appearance. Now Cozumel is a favorite stop for cruise ships and this has given rise to great numbers of shops. Basically, however, the island is little changed.

Just over the horizon from the mainland. Cozumel is 30 miles long and about 12 miles wide. Most of it is empty. Back when the Spanish first visited the place they estimated it had a population of 40,000 and there are, to be sure, many Maya relics scattered about the bush. Yet following the Conquest the Spaniards paid little attention to the island, allowing it to languish.

The one town (most folk simply call it *El Pueblo,* the village) is a fishing community grown big. Duty-free shops line the waterfront avenue, although actual bargains are rare; still, they do quite a business with cruise ship passengers who put in for a day.

Most of the resort hotels are north of town. The luxury establishments south of it, being closer to Palancar Reef, cater more to divers. Many of the young diving addicts, however, stay at the less expensive lodgings in town. Dive shops, and there are many, arrange to get them out to the boats.

While taxis are plentiful on Cozumel, getting around comfortably means renting wheels. When it comes to wheels, almost everyone opts for a motorbike. These can be dangerous—the more so since insurance is not available—but they are cheap and too much fun to resist. Rental cars also are available.

Young at heart is Cozumel. It's all jeans and T shirts with none of the cultivated elegance of Cancun. Vacationers not out on the dive boats seem to spend their days polishing their windsurfing techniques. The well-heeled go out deepsea fishing, with islanders insisting they cater to serious sportsmen while the Cancun boats handle first-timers. Billfish usually bite only during the spring. Tuna and barracuda are the gamefish the rest of the year.

Almost everyone sets aside a day for what are called Robinson Crusoe cruises. These are picnic excursions up the island coast to some stretch of isolated beach. As the area is now a sealife sanctuary, the crew no longer dives for fresh conch and lobster en route. What they bring along, however, they grill to perfection.

Enjoyable, too, is taking the ferry and heading over to the mainland to wander about the Maya ruins at Tulum. The ruins on the island itself are far less impressive and more difficult to get to.

Sightseeing on Cozumel itself is pretty limited. A single road loops around the center of the island, running over to the windward side where there is one small inn with a pleasant enough restaurant. The beaches here are beautiful and largely deserted; swimming on this side is almost suicidal.

Evenings start early on Cozumel and often end early as well. The sporting types like to be up at the crack of dawn. Those who want more in the way of after dark fun, however, need not turn in early. Some of the larger hotels have entertainment after dark and there are a few discos in town plus a country music lounge and a lively backgammon bar.

Isla Mujeres (Isle of Women)

Isla Mujeres is even more laid back. This smallest corner of Mexico's Caribbean triangle is best known in Cancun as the place where the day cruise yachts head for, but it has a handful of hotels of its own, most of them in the budget category. Five miles long and just a half-mile wide, Isla coddles vacationers who want to linger long and stretch their pesos far.

One Francisco Hernandez de Cordoba became the first Spaniard to set foot on what is now Mexican territory when he arrived on the island in 1517. It was he who named the place, dubbing it the Isle of Women because of the hundreds of feminine figurines—fertility symbols—he found there. Traces of Isla Mujeres' Maya past are still to be seen here and there on the island, including the remains of what may have been a lighthouse. To anyone but an archaeologist, however, they are nothing but so many stones.

More interesting are the ruins of the mansion built by Fermin Mundaca, one of the last of the pirates of the Caribbean. The tale is told of how Mundaca, smitten by a local señorita, promised to give up his wicked ways and went so far as to build a magnificent hacienda to prove he meant what he said. The girl was unimpressed and Mundaca lived out his final years there alone. Yet even death dealt Mundaca a low blow. He died suddenly while visiting Mérida and is buried there, while the grave he left for himself on Isla Mujeres remains empty.

While air taxi service to Isla Mujeres can be arranged, most people get there aboard the ferries that connect the island to Puerto Juarez and Punta Sam, both a short bus ride from downtown Cancun.

The hotels are clustered around the village at the north end of the island. Only two have beaches suitable for swimming. Most folk rent motorbikes for getting around. The alternatives are taxis, rental bicycles, or bringing over a car from Cancun since none are rented on Isla Mujeres itself.

Avenida Rueda Medina on the waterfront is the main drag, extending for five or six blocks. Inland the village runs only three or four blocks before hitting the other shore. Playa los Cocos, the beach on the north shore, is about a half-mile from the center of what there is to town.

Best beach is El Garrafon, some five miles distant on the southern end of Isla Mujeres. This is the national park where the tour boats from Cancun put in. Snorkeling among the tropical fish that feed on the reefs just off shore (equipment may be rented at the park) is a memorable experience that lures many people into finding out more about scuba diving, which just about equals the best Cozumel has to offer.

Divers, whether beginners or experts, find all kind of facilities on Isla Mujeres. For the courageous there is the Cave of the Sleeping Sharks, which is just that. The beasts, man-eaters if given a chance, slip into the cave and tune out the world. Divers can join them and caress them if they wish; suvivors will have quite a story to tell when they get home.

Less mind boggling is playing among the turtles and perhaps trying to ride them at the turtle pen by Playa Lancheros. Turtles are one of Isla Mujeres' principal products. From the pens the animals go to those who turn them into steaks, soup, wallets, and combs. Deepsea fishing can be arranged on Isla Mujeres; the catch is likely to be tuna, grouper, and barracuda, with billfish biting during the spring.

Nightlife on Isla Mujeres has been described as sitting on the beach and watching the sun go down. Actually, it is a trifle more exciting than that. People often eat late—there are some nice little restaurants in town—linger over dinner, and perhaps then head out to one of the island's three discotheques. For variety there is a movie theater that occasionally shows a Hollywood film.

To some escapists even this sounds like too much civilization. For those people there lies the almost untouched mainland coast beyond Cancun.

Puerto Juarez, Punta Sam

Puerto Juarez and Punta Sam, where the Isla Mujeres ferries put in, are so close to downtown Cancun that they are served by the municipal bus system. Yet in atmosphere they are a million miles away. Juarez is budget hotels and budget restaurants; Sam, five miles north, is thatched huts with hammocks instead of beds. Sam is the end of the road and looks it. Beyond the peninsula stretches northward to its end and all is vast and empty.

South of Cancun Highway 307 beckons toward adventure. The road hugs the coast for nearly 100 miles to the Maya ruins at Tulum, swings inward to a settlement sacred more to contemporary Mayas—Chan Santa Cruz is now called Felipe Carrillo Puerto—and on to Chetumal on the Belize border.

A car of some sort is pretty much necessary to explore this route although the backpacking set do it by bus. First stop would be Puerto Morelos, only 20 miles from Cancun. Cruise ships put in here and from Puerto Morelos the car ferry sails to Cozumel every morning. The beach is lovely and the waters ideal for snorkeling and scuba diving. The two small hotels here both specialize in catering to divers. They have all the necessary equipment plus boats and guides going out to the reefs. But that is all there is.

Punta Bete offers about the same, but its three little hotels usually host fairly well-heeled beachcombers; the only way to get to Punta Bete is by car. The diving is good here, all facilities are available and the crowd is congenial.

Playa del Carmen, like Puerto Morelos, is served by intercity buses and is a busy little community. From here passenger ferries depart for Cozumel and there are several little restaurants around doing a thriving business with folk waiting for the boat. There is a nice little hotel here, too, and a pleasant beach.

Akumal is nothing less than luxurious. The hotel here does well hosting guests who want to be off somewhere isolated while making no sacrifices to comfort. Originally, in the pre-Cancun era, this was a camp for wealthy underwater explorers who flew in aboard small planes and set out to hunt for wrecks buried beneath the waves. Rather fascinating is the underwater museum here which any snorkeler can visit. On display are ancient cannon and other artifacts shown more or less in the same condition as the underwater explorers found them. Akumal now is where tour groups come for lunch after exploring the ruins at Tulum.

Maya Ruins of Tulum

Tulum is one of the most beautiful and fascinating of the many ancient Maya sites found on the Yucatan peninsula. It is truly unique. This was the only Maya city built right on the coast, the only one protected by a wall, and the only one known to have been inhabited when the Conquistadores arrived.

Although archaeologists have found indications Tulum was settled 1,500 years ago, most of the present buildings are no more than 800 years old. They belong to the late postclassic period when the Maya civilization was in its decline. Certain artistic refinements found elsewhere are missing here, but the excellent state of preservation more than makes up for that. And the castle, *El Castillo,* that dominates the area, is impressive. The castle has now been identified as a temple to Kukulkan, the feathered snake diety introduced by the Toltecs, the Indian horde that swept in from central Mexico, conquered the Mayas only to be absorbed by them. The Toltecs have vanished; the Mayas live on.

Believers in unidentified flying objects and others convinced that the earth once was visited by tiny aliens from some other planet have made Tulum a shrine of their own. They hold in greatest reverence the Temple of the Descending God. Over the doorway is a carved figure that does indeed appear to be tumbling from the heavens. More prosaic scholars claim this represents either the setting sun or a bee (the Mayas were and are great producers of honey).

Still it is a fact that Maya myth maintains Tulum was first built by prodigious dwarfs. Many of the lesser temples are indeed tiny. Entranceways do seem designed to accommodate little people. Archaeologists, however, insist low doorways were so designed that those who entered would be forced to bow if not crawl, this being only proper when approaching a god.

Tulum in its final days is believed to have been a seaside trading center. It may have been a haven for the Chontal, a Maya group from the Campeche side of the peninsula who operated a merchant fleet of canoes that made regular trips to Central America. Or Tulum may have been a satellite of Coba, once a city of 50,000 about 25 miles inland.

Side Trip to Coba

A detour to Coba, with the possibility of spending the night there, has much to recommend it. The towering pyramids, soaring above the rain forest, are the most majestic in Mexico. The setting of what was a great city on the shores of five lakes is ghostly in its beauty.

Coba was inhabited more than 2,000 years ago, but it seems to have got its start as a true city about 600 A.D. The remains of 30 wide roads—they must have been more impressive than today's highways, although they were used only by human bearers since the Mayas had no beasts of burden—indicate this was a great center of commerce. There was considerable trade, apparently, with the Mayas of Tikal in what is now Guatemala.

Tallest pyramid at Coba towers up 125 feet and contains at its top a temple honoring that mysterious figure found at Tulum, the Descending God. There is another pyramid nearby, this one with a now empty tomb. All about are remnants of temples and stelae. These stelae are carved slabs which archaeologists believe tell the history of Coba. They depict some rather tyrannical rulers, lords—and, in one case, a lady—standing imperiously on the backs of either captives, subjects, or slaves.

Coba is quite extensive. Two or three miles separate one group of ruins from the next. Not too much in the way of excavation has been done. Those that have been carried out show that this was one of the greatest Mayan city-states.

Back near Tulum there are a couple of final opportunities to frolic in the Caribbean. Xel-Ha, a park, is a natural aquarium and a wonderful place to snorkel. Equipment is available for rent along with locker rooms and showers. The restaurant here is pleasant enough and there are a number of souvenir shops.

X-Caret, nearby, in many ways is equally beautiful but far more primitive. Campers sometimes make a temporary home here.

Beyond Tulum the highway turns inward. After a rather monotonous hour of driving, one comes into the town of Felipe Carrillo Puerto, formerly Chan Santa Cruz. It does not look like much, but in reality this was the last Maya ceremonial center. During the height of the 19th century Maya rebellion—the War of the Castes—this was the chief command center; only priests and top leaders were permitted to live here. Once the rebellion was put down the name of the place was changed; Felipe Carrillo Puerto was a Yucatan governor during the turbulent days of the Mexican Revolution and he ended up before a firing squad.

Chetumal, An Isolated Capital

It is about a two-hour drive from Felipe Carrillo Puerto to Chetumal, the road passing through little Maya villages and skirting Bacalar Lagoon. It is quite a pretty drive. Of course one can fly into Chetumal from Mérida or take a bus from Cancun, but ideally it is best to have a vehicle of one's own. None can be rented in Chetumal and there is a good bit to see.

Founded in 1898, Chetumal has changed little from the days when it was a territorial capital so isolated it could be reached only by ship, plane or buses bouncing over unspeakable dirt tracks. Smuggling then was the main industry and to some extent it still is. In its territorial days Quintana Roo was placed beyond the pale of Mexican customs, there being no practical way to ship domestic goods in. The exemptions have been whittled back a good bit (one must, however, stop for a customs check when crossing out of Quintana Roo), but the streets still are lined with shops selling imports either heavily taxed or simply unavailable in the rest of Mexico. It is pleasant finding that there are a couple of first class hotels as well as several budget inns in Chetumal.

Bacalar Lagoon is the prettiest place to visit. It extends for some 50 miles, fresh water mingling with the sea to make this "The Lake of Seven Colors," shades shifting from pale turquoise to cobalt blue. There is an old Spanish fort out this way. Built in 1733 to ward off pirates, it later became a Maya stronghold during the Caste Wars.

Fun, and something of an adventure, is driving ten miles or so for lunch in Corozal across the border in Belize. Although now independent, what was once British Honduras still has a colonial flavor to it, something you notice right at the border. The crossing formalities are fairly strict and you will need your tourist card and proper identification. It is best to leave all luggage back in your Chetumal hotel so as not to have to bother much with customs. Corozal is little more than a few wooden houses built on stilts. Tony's Motel is the best place to eat. While Orange Walk, considerably larger, is just 30 miles further in, the road is so bad getting there could take two hours.

Highway 307 ends in Chetumal and Highway 186 begins. Running due west, 186 runs on through Campeche state into Tabasco and its capital, Villahermosa, where, it might be said, the Maya country begins.

EXPLORING THE MAYA COUNTRY

Cancun's modern sun worshipers bump into the Maya past of the Yucatan peninsula almost everywhere they turn. A couple of hotels actually have the remains of ancient temples on their premises and the nondescript ruins at El Rey lie on the lagoon just a few miles down the road from the Sheraton. Almost everyone signs up for an excursion to Tulum and many are tempted by tours going off in the other direction to Chichen Itza, a much more extensive site.

Mérida, capital of Yucatan state—a five-hour drive from Cancun—generally is regarded as the best place to get a hold on what is known of Maya history. But for those who really want to delve into the long ago, Villahermosa is the place to start.

Villahermosa is a former hellhole, a onetime steamy river port that Graham Greene made the setting for *The Power and the Glory.* Greene would never recognize the place today. This is a boomtown made rich by oil. Pedestrian malls, luxury hotels and an elegant shopping center are part of the scene. The only reminder of the religious persecution Greene wrote about is the singular lack of churches. That, too, is changing. Dominating the skyline is the soaring belltower of what one day will be the Cathedral of Our Lord of Tabasco. (Villahermosa is capital of Tabasco, although the sauce named for the state is made in Louisiana.) The church, being built along colonial lines, is far from completion. One can recapture the feeling of the old days by taking a luncheon cruise aboard the *Capitan Beulo;* this converted river boat chugs along the Grijalva into the jungle that surrounds the city, and when it does Greene's description of the countryside comes very much alive.

Travelers head for Villahermosa to view the monolithic sculptures created by the Olmecs and then go on to see the imposing Maya ruins at Palenque.

Some 3,000 years ago the Olmecs created the first advanced civilization in the Americas. They even developed a form of writing which, sadly, no one today is able to read. As a result no one knows much about the Olmecs. All that can be said is that they developed a culture that thrived in humid, inhospitable lands, and then, quite suddenly, they vanished.

They left their sculptures behind. There are huge basalt heads, nine feet high and weighing 60 tons, the features negroid (was there some connection with Africa?) that look for all the world like football players in old-fashioned leather helmets.

These carvings and others were found half-buried in mangrove swamps where there is no stone. They must have been hauled from quarries at least 60 miles away. How that was done remains a mystery. In 1957 the Olmec works with great difficulty were brought to Villahermosa and set up in a park named La Venta in tribute to the Gulf Coast site where they originally were found.

The park is an outdoor museum. The massive stone heads and other carvings are on display in a setting much like the one in which they originally were found. There are jaguars and individuals half human and half beast. Supposedly the Olmecs believed themselves to be descended from a jaguar god. There is a great altar before which sits a glaring Buddha-like figure. Any Olmec communication with Asia would be unlikely, but no one can say for certain.

A light and sound show in the evening is a good reason for visiting La Venta a second time (bring insect repellent for both day and nighttime visits). Artificial light reveals subtleties in the sculptures all but invisible during the day. The spoken commentary is in Spanish only and too banal to be worth translating.

If the Olmecs themselves were not racially the forefathers of the Mayas, culturally their influence was great. The Mayas picked up their numerical symbols from the Olmecs, played a similar ritualized ball game, worshipped the same rain god and, like the Olmecs, showed their piety by gashing themselves and letting their blood flow.

Maya Origin Obscure

The origin of the Mayas is as great an enigma as that of the Olmecs. Generally it is assumed that the Indians of the Americas crossed into Alaska during the Ice Age and gradually made their way south. Yet the Mayas, short of stature and large of head, are so distinct from their neighbors as to seem like an entirely different race. Speculation runs wild. Are they a lost tribe of Israel? Children of Atlantis? Simply another tribe? No one really can say.

What can be said is that the Mayas were the creators of one of the greatest of the ancient civilizations. Their grasp of mathematics still astounds. They came up with the concept of zero and a sophisticated numerical system long before the Europeans. They understood the mysteries of the planets and the stars to an incredible degree. The ruins of their cities still inspire awe. One finds not only temples adorned with murals and sumptuous tombs for the princely dead, but what were once grand highways and well engineered drainage canals. The Mayas were the Greeks of the New World, inhabitants of city-states sometimes allied but often at war with each other. Then around 900 A.D. it all came to an end. Here again, no one really knows why.

Corn—or maize, if you will—was first domesticated about 10,000 years ago. As millennia passed, tribes of hunters and gatherers settled down to become villages of farmers. Basic to the success of agriculture is knowing when to plant, knowing when the rains will come. The secrets were learned from the stars, but learned by very few. Those who could divine the coming of the seasons were men of magic, magicians who became priests. Priests who ruled, for no man is more powerful than he who holds the secret to his people's survival.

Only he who controlled arms might challenge a priest. Once a village had a bulging granary it was a tempting target for raiders. Defenders needed to be recruited and trained. Defensive troops can easily become an offensive army. A village may survive on what it grows, but it becomes rich by looting from others. Warrior chiefs who led the looting became kings.

The great Maya cities now in ruins, archaeologists say, were not so much inhabited places as ceremonial centers. One can guess that they grew in splendor as princes and priests sought to outdo each other. Temples arose atop pyramids. Great palaces were built. The peons who huddled in huts much like those still seen in Maya villages did the work. Did they ever rebel? Were the periodic decline and fall of Maya cities the result of peasant uprisings? Or did proud kings slaughter arrogant priests only to find that with them they had killed the secrets of when to sow? The stories may be told in the glyphs carved on walls and on the stelae at many sites. Of late some progress has been made in deciphering them.

The calendar was the first code to be cracked, and with the calendar the numerical system gave way. The Mayas did their sums with a series of dots and dashes. A shell stood for zero and they calculated in units of twenty rather than ten. As civilization flowered it became the custom of city–states to erect a stela every twenty years. Recorded on these stone monuments is a notation of important happenings during the previous two decades. Rulers are recognized easily; in magnificent dress they often stand upon the backs of more unfortunate souls. Glyphs representing these rulers can be picked out, and after careful study patient archaeologists get some idea of their accomplishments.

The Mayas showed their first signs of greatness around 300 B.C. which was about when the Olmecs went into their final decline. Yet since centuries were to pass before the Mayas were to enter into what is now regarded as their classic period. And the first of their great centers went up in the cool highlands of Central America far from the sultry swamps so favored by the Olmecs.

Palenque, about 90 miles southeast of Villahermosa, is such a place. Its great flowering came about midway in the classic era, starting around A.D. 600. (See *The Indian South.*)

Most visitors to Palenque head out from Villahermosa early in the day and return about dusk. For those who want to see more-Palenque, surrounded by jungle hills, is most impressive early in the day—there is a choice of several small, modest hotels.

Bonampak, one of the most famous Maya sites and also one of the most inaccessible, can be reached by air taxi from Palenque. A small site surrounded by jungle, Bonampak is noted for murals that really bring the Maya past to life. However, it must be added that Bonampak is not worth the trip. One should know about Bonampak, but the fact is that reproductions of the murals—the best are in Mexico City's Museum of Anthropology—are better than the real thing. Bonampak was discovered in 1946 and since then efforts to enhance the murals have only faded them. The site itself is small and unimpressive.

Very much worth while, on the other hand, is pushing on from Palenque into the Chiapas highlands. It will take the better part of a day to get to San Cristóbal de las Casas—the trip is spectacularly beautiful—and a couple more days will be needed just to wander around before backtracking to Villahermosa. This is the home of the

Highland Maya, people who even more than their cousins in Yucatan maintain their customs, traditions and ancient way of life.

Yucatan is different culturally as well as geographically. The Maya city-states went into decline around A.D. 900. Toward the end of that century the Toltecs swept into Yucatan, conquered the Mayas there and, in the end, were absorbed by them. The Mayas in Chiapas were largely left alone. (See *Pre-Columbian Heritage* chapter.)

Arrival of Spaniards

When the Spaniards arrived, their earliest expeditions were driven from the shores by fierce native warriors. Then in 1527, nearly a decade after Cortes had conquered the Aztecs, Francisco de Montejo won royal permission to subdue Yucatan. He met with no quick success. Routed from what is now the coast of Quintana Roo, Montejo decided he was too old for the conquest business and turned it over to his son. Montejo junior opted to attack the peninsula's other shore. It was he who settled Campeche and from there moved south. Some 20 years were required for the Montejos to establish Spanish rule on the Yucatan peninsula. Victory was won not so much by arms as disease. Smallpox and measles decimated the Mayas.

Many of those who survived retreated inland. Only the eastern coast of the region really came under Spanish domination. The great battles were still to come as missionaries waged what has come to be called the spiritual conquest and here the casualties in some respects were the highest of all. Every Mayan book that could be found was destroyed. The zeal of the church in destroying what it considered works of the devil is completely understandable considering attitudes at that time, but the loss to humanity was enormous.

The religion of the Mayas never was entirely stamped out. Often it blended with Christianity, the gods of the ancients taking on the names of the saints. Mass became another ritual. The Maya civilization had been in decline for 500 years before the Europeans came. It continued to decline in bush villages, but never did it disappear.

On the coast Spain ruled for 300 years. Pirates were the worst worry, especially in Campeche, but they never threatened the system. What brought that down was Mexican independence. Yucatan was then a separate jurisdiction, ruled directly by the Spanish crown. But when the Viceroy of New Spain yielded to the mainland freedom fighters, the governor of Yucatan resigned as well. After some debate, and in return for considerable autonomy, Yucatan chose to throw in its lot with Mexico and with some reservations joined the new federation.

It was an attempt to impose a strong central government in Mexico that led Texas to break away from Mexico in 1836. Four years later Yucatan followed its example. Like Texas, Yucatan sought to join the U.S. Washington declined the offer, but Yucatan refused to make its peace with Mexico City. In an effort to defend independence the rulers of the peninsula—great landholders descended from Spanish conquerors—chose to arm the Mayas.

War of the Castes

That, from the landholders point of view, turned out to be a dreadful mistake. It touched off a civil struggle that lasted for generations. This was the War of the Castes.

Under Spanish rule the people of the colonies were classified according to birth. At the top were the Peninsulars, the natives of Spain, who ruled. Then there were the Creoles, offspring of Peninsulars born in the colony. Beneath them were the Indians and those of mixed blood; every combination had a name. These were the *castas,* the castes. In the 1840s the Indians, the castes, were given arms to defend the Creoles. Instead, they rose up against them.

What began as a rebellion grew into a movement to re-establish a kingdom of the Mayas. Yucatan's Creoles quickly terminated their own secessionist movement, rejoining the Mexican federation with Campeche as a separate state. Troops came in from the mainland, but the Mayas, while they retreated, never surrendered.

Chan Santa Cruz (Little Holy Cross in Maya Spanish) in what is now Quintana Roo became the Maya capital. Here a small wooden cross is said to have spoken to the Maya rebels, urging them to fight on. Fight they did for more than half a century. The Mexican Revolution, the great social upheaval that broke out in 1910, finally brought an end to the fighting. Federal troops being occupied elsewhere, simply withdrew. The Mayas were left running their own affairs.

The more enlightened rulers brought in by the revolution reached something of an informal compromise. The lands ruled by the Mayas were broken off from the state of Yucatan and made a federal territory, Quintana Roo (named, somewhat ironically, for Andres Quintana Roo, a 19th-century figure who had been instrumental in convincing Yucatan to join the Mexican Union). Chan Santa Cruz became Felipe Carrillo Puerto in honor of a Revolutionary governor of Yucatan who was deposed and shot by his enemies. After that the Mayas were pretty much left to their own devices. As the decades passed, younger Mayas began pressing not to be left so much alone. The benefits of development were wanted and jobs needed. Thus Cancun was built and in 1974 Quintana Roo became a state. But in much of Quintana Roo the Maya people live as their ancestors did.

Campeche, A Photographer's Delight

Campeche, which is about a six-hour drive from Villahermosa, is where the Spanish conquest of the Yucatan peninsula began. It also is where the 19th-century secessionist movement, that inadvertently gave rise to the War of Castes, was often strongest. Travelers starting out on a circle tour of the peninsula will make Campeche their first overnight stop after leaving Chetumal. The same is true of travelers coming by road from Villahermosa. Air tours skip it, which is something of a shame. Campeche is the most photogenic city in Mexico.

Ramparts and walls are the reason for this. Pirates were the reason for the walls. In colonial times Campeche was the richest, most thriving port on the peninsula. As such it was a tempting target for buccaneers. Rather quickly it became a fortified city. Not too many years ago, in a misguided effort to modernize, many of the walls were pulled down. The Seagate and Landgate still stand, however, as do parapets and drawbridges.

Campeche is mostly a town for strolling about. The local tourist office and two museums are located within some of the old fortifications. The museums themselves, one of archaeology and the other of history, offer rather mediocre exhibits and the tourist office has little in the way of information, but exploring their interiors can be interesting.

Rather curious in this setting are the would-be space-age-designed state government buildings. They, too, are a result of the effort to modernize Campeche and as such are monuments to failure. The salt air and tropics have been less kind to these structures than to the Spanish walls.

There are a couple of first class hotels in Campeche and some rather charming inns in the moderate category. Missing is any beach. Present are some passable restaurants. Campeche is a fishing center famous throughout Mexico especially for its shrimp.

The ruins of the Maya center at Edzna are about an hour's drive from Campeche. Of late Edzna has been attracting attention as possibly the place were the Maya calendar—actually more accurate than the one the world uses today—may have been devised. The fact that the sun reaches its zenith over Edzna on what would be Maya New Year's Day has led to this theory. In other respects the ruins, largely undisturbed since they were discovered, will impress only archaeology buffs.

Oft-Built Uxmal

Uxmal, on the other hand, must not be missed. One of the greatest of all Maya sites, it is perhaps 90 minutes from Campeche on the way to Mérida (which is only an hour beyond). While it would be easy enough to stop, view Uxmal and continue on to Mérida, far more rewarding is spending the night at one of the pleasant hotels here, seeing all at leisure and returning in the evening for the light and sound show.

Uxmal, tour guides will tell you, means "Thrice Built." They will then add Uxmal was rebuilt at least five times. The center first flourished sometime in the 7th century, about the era when Palenque was getting started. It was abandoned, reoccupied and left on a couple of occasions. No one can say with any certainty why. The invading Toltecs in the 10th century seized what may well have been little more than a ghost town, held on there for awhile and evacuated. Finally Uxmal became a rather pure Maya ceremonial center of the postclassic era. It was deserted for the last time some 90 years before the Spanish conquest began.

The architecture is what sets Uxmal apart. Lines are clean and uncluttered and the buildings themselves in excellent repair. It would seem that the successive waves of groups that made Uxmal theirs chose to honor the designs. In some cases efforts were made to improve upon them, but seldom were they radically changed.

Worshipped here with great fervor was Chac, the elephant-snouted rain god whose face appears throughout Yucatan. The people of Uxmal had good reason to be reverent toward him, for water in these parts is scarce. There are no cenotes or sink holes. The Mayas dug cisterns for collecting rainwater when it came. Drought may be the reason Uxmal was abandoned so often. The theme of the light and sound show centers upon the dependence of the people on rain.

Really the best thing about this spectacle is the way the artificial light brings out details of carvings and mosaics so easy to miss when the sun is shining. There are, for example, replicas of Maya huts reproduced in stone on one facade in the quadrangle. They resemble almost identically the huts still to be seen in many Maya villages today. And by moonglow the unique rounded Pyramid of the Magician, said to have been built overnight by a magical dwarf, takes on added beauty.

Staying at an Uxmal hotel allows one ample time to visit other Maya ruins in the area. Kabah can be taken in while driving over from Campeche. It is rather fascinating because of its Temple of the Masks with an entire facade covered by big-nosed images of Chac. The Arch of Kabah is notable as well. This is one of the finest of the Maya arches. Technically the Mayas never mastered the true keystone arch, but with their engineering skills they came quite close.

Allow some time to wander about the contemporary Maya towns such as Mani and Ticul. Many homes in these parts are the same sort of thatch oval huts the Mayas have been living in for literally thousands of years. Men and women favor the traditional garb that, while not pre-Hispanic, has been worn for centuries. For the male this is simply white shirts and slacks cut in the traditional manner. The female outfit, with embroidered blouse and rebozo shawl, is more distinctive and certainly more attractive than the store-bought stuff the younger generations frequently prefer. The Maya tongue, far from being a dead language, is heard more frequently in the streets of these towns than is Spanish.

Mani is infamous as the place where the Spanish Bishop Diego de Landa lashed religious backsliders and burned the Maya books. It is also the venue of a well where the wicked mother of the magical dwarf who built the Uxmal pyramid is said to live. Wicked because she sometimes made the well run dry and demanded babies be tossed in as sacrifice to get the water flowing again. Ticul is an excellent place to stop for lunch. Its main restaurant, *Los Almendros* has a reputation for serving the best Yucatan regional cuisine to be found anywhere.

Mérida—Contemporary Maya Capital

Mérida, one of Mexico's most delightful cities, too often gets short shrift from visitors. It is made the base from which the nearby ruins are toured, the buses leaving right after breakfast and returning at dusk. Much better it is to overnight at the ruins—there are good hotels at both Uxmal and Chichen Itza—and see Mérida for what it is.

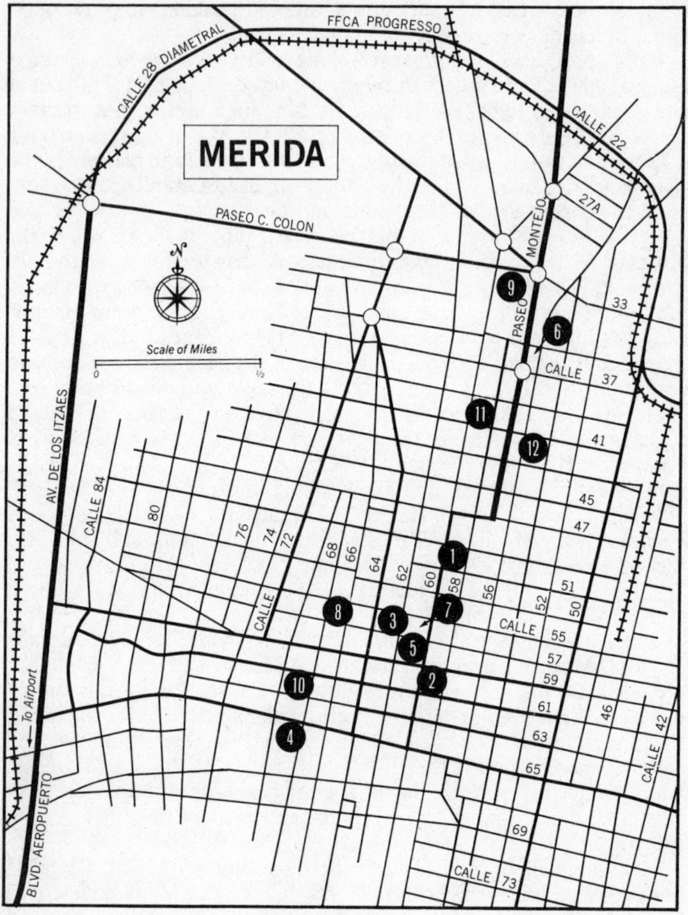

Hotels

1) Los Aluxes
2) Caribe
3) El Castellano
4) Cayre
5) Colonial
6) Conquistador
7) Gobernador
8) Hacienda Inn
9) Holiday Inn
10) Maria del Carmen
11) Montejo Palace
12) Paseo de Montejo

The sobriquets of the past apply no more (one wonders if they ever did). Mérida no longer can be described truthfully as "The White City" or "The City of Windmills" (the windmills, the kind seen on Kansas farms rather than those of Holland, have pretty much been replaced by electric pumps). Nor is it fair to call this the "Paris of the Americas" as some guides have been known to do.

Mérida instead is the sometimes bustling, sometimes somnambulant capital of contemporary Maya Yucatan. Mostly it is an old-fashioned kind of place and, compared to Cancun, is blessed by old-fashioned prices.

Mérida was once Tiho and was the last of the Maya strongholds to fall to the Spanish. Following victory the Montejo family settled here. They renamed the Maya center, then in ruins, for a town in Spain. Still standing is the Montejo home, a monument to the conquest. Built in 1550, the facade is dominated by huge bas-reliefs showing Spanish knights planted upon the heads of vanquished Mayas; it reminds one of the carvings at some of the ruins depicting Maya princes strutting on the backs of what were either captives, slaves or hapless subjects.

The Montejo home, now a bank and an interesting place to change money, is on the main plaza. The plaza itself is quite charming, a park of manicured laurel trees and S-shaped benches designed for confidential chats. Towering over the scene is the cathedral. Stark, bare and unadorned outside, with gunnery slits instead of windows, the building looks more like a castle than a church. When it was started in 1561 the cathedral was indeed built for defense. Within, the decor is stark as well, the sacred interior having last been sacked during the raucous days of the Mexican Revolution.

City Hall (Palacio Municipal), also on the plaza, dates from the Montejo era. The State House (Palacio de Gobierno) is of much more recent construction and is noted for its interesting murals over the staircase. Completed in 1978 by Fernando Castro Pacheco, the paintings trace some of the history of Yucatan.

A block or so north of the plaza, on Calles 57 and 60 is the Peon Contreras Theater, which has been recently restored. Apart from the frequent programs presented there, the theater is notable as a tribute Mérida's once fabled wealth. In colonial times Yucatan was a source of dyewood much prized in Europe; Mérida merchants thrived. Then, starting in the 19th century, henequin or sisal made Yucatan landowners rich. Montejo Boulevard uptown is lined with the baronial town houses of the sisal lords. These mansions were built along French lines, which is why Mérida sometimes has been compared to Paris.

Sisal, a natural hard fiber used in manufacturing rope, largely has been replaced by synthetics. Yucatan has suffered considerably as a result of falling prices for its principal export. Montejo Boulevard is a trifle shabby now.

More grand than ever, nonetheless, is the Mérida Museum of Anthropology which inhabits one of the mansions on Montejo Boulevard. The mansion itself—at one time it was used as the governor's residence—is the most splendid on the avenue. The exhibits within are well done and an excellent introduction to the Mayas. Of special interest are artifacts recovered from the sacrificial cenote at Chichen Itza, and displays showing how the pre–Hispanic Mayas deformed the skulls and crossed the eyes of their infants to produce what they considered more beautiful adults.

One of the nicest ways of seeing Mérida is to take a tour in a horse-drawn carriage. They are easily found around the main plaza and for about $10 (the fee at press time) take passengers for a ride through the downtown streets out to Montejo Boulevard and back again. The drivers generally speak enough English to be able to point out the principal sights.

Shoppers will find themselves tempted at every turn in Mérida. Guayaberras, attractive tailored shirts that are almost the uniform of males in Yucatan, are an especially good buy. They are available for women, too, and are comfortable attire in these warm climes. Items of straw, sandals, pottery, and rubbings from the temples make attractive souvenirs.

Dining out is another special pleasure in Mérida. The cuisine of Yucatan is quite distinctive from that found in the rest of Mexico. There are local beers highly prized (although rarely available) in the rest of the country, and one can even go native at breakfast. (See *Restaurants Section.*)

Chichen Itza

Chichen Itza is about a 90-minute drive east of Mérida on the highway that leads to the Caribbean resorts. A one- or two-night stop at the site is highly recommended. The hotels at Chichen are delightful and the Maya ruins the most extensively restored and, in some respects, the most extraordinary of the pre–Hispanic centers.

While the earliest buildings here date back to the classic era having been erected some 1,500 years ago, Chichen Itza is most of all a Maya-Toltec center. The Toltec invaders from the mainland made this their religious capital and it is a monument both to their warlike ways and to the genius of the Mayas. Nowhere is this better seen than at the pyramid called El Castillo (The Castle) that dominates the site.

El Castillo is topped by a temple to Kukulkan (known as Quetzacoatl in mainland Mexico), the diety represented by a feathered snake that led the Toltecs on their migration to Yucatan. By the base of one balustrade is carved a great serpent head. At the spring and fall equinox, March 21 and September 21, light and shadow strike the balustrade in such a way to form a shadow picture representing Kukulkan undulating out of his temple and wriggling down the pyramid to bless the fertile earth. The engineering skill that went into this amazing project boggles the mind.

Nearby is a ballcourt, similar to those found at other ancient centers in Mexico, but bigger. The game played was something like soccer (no hands were to be used) and it fascinated the Europeans; indeed it might be said that one of Mexico's gifts to the Old World was team sports and rubber balls. To the Mayas and their neighbors ballgames apparently had religious significance. A carving at the court shows what appears to be a player being sacrificed by decapitation, blood spurting from his severed neck to fertilize the earth.

More sacrifices took place at the Sacred Well, a cenote about a half mile from the main ceremonial area. Once it was believed that virgins were hurled into these waters to appease the rain gods, but diving archaeologists have since discovered skeletons belonging to individuals of all ages. Also found were artifacts of gold and jade, items highly precious to the Mayas. The cenote undoubtedly holds more treasures. Trees and shrubs have been washed into the well over the centuries and their remains have prevented divers from getting to the bottom. Since the pool is fed by a network of underground rivers, it cannot be drained.

With its Caracol (Snail) observatory, its Court of Columns and seemingly numberless temples, Chichen Itza has much to see and explore. The light and sound show in the evening is not as well done as the one at Uxmal, but it provides a form of after-dark entertainment.

Just a couple of miles from Chichen Itza is the Cave of Balancanche, a Maya shrine discovered in 1959. It was virtually undisturbed since the time of the conquest. Within is to be seen the largest collection of artifacts yet found in Yucatan, mostly vases and jars once filled with offerings. An image of the rain god rises about a small underground lake in which blind fish swim. Guided tours, which depart on the hour (noon and 1 P.M. are skipped; the last tour leaves at 4 P.M.) are mandatory for visitors to the cave. Even then one must be in fairly good physical shape, for considerable crawling is required. Claustrophobics should avoid Balancanche.

Izamal, with its huge Franciscan monastery built atop a truncated pyramid, requires some doubling back to see. It is north of the highway to Mérida, and really of interest only to tourists who wish to leave no sight unseen. The dogged Bishop de Landa had the monastery built to supplant the heathen temple which once stood there. It is one of the largest religious structures in Mexico. The road continues north to Yucatan's spooky Gulf Coast and the village of Dzidzantún where many of the fair, blue–eyed inhabitants claim to be descendants of pirates. The cemetery contains a gravestone inscribed "Jean Lafitte 1780–1827."

From Chichen Itza east toward the Caribbean the highway winds through Valladolid. Second-largest city in the state of Yucatan, Valladolid is picturesque, pleasant and provincial. It has a couple of inexpensive hotels and passable places to eat. A turnoff here leads north to Rio Lagartos (Alligator River). Flamingos in grand flocks make this neighborhood home. Seeing these long-necked pink birds soaring above the water and watching them settle in great red clouds makes the detour worthwhile. Rio Lagartos, with its palmy beaches, supposedly one day will be developed into a seaside resort. Yucatan authorities have been talking about that for years. More likely it will be promoted among sportsmen. Tarpon fishing and hunting for deer and boar are excellent here.

From Rio Lagartos motorists can either take a shortcut back to Mérida or return to Valladolid and head east into Quintana Roo. Cancun and the Mexican Caribbean are no more than two hours away.

PRACTICAL INFORMATION FOR THE YUCATAN

HOW TO GET THERE. Most international travelers fly into Yucatan directly from the U.S. Mérida is about a 90-minute flight from Mexico City while Cancun is two hours distant. By road it takes some 25 hours to reach Mérida, with another four or five hours to get to Cancun. Coach tours offer a chance to see and visit much that is fascinating along the route. Regular buses and trains, however, will appeal only to the adventurous or the penniless. The peninsula's Caribbean coast is touched by numerous cruise ships. Ferries connect Isla Mujeres and Cozumel with the mainland and a local commuter airline serves Cozumel.

By Air. Domestic air fares in Mexico generally are lower than international tariffs. Much depends on the peso-dollar parity at the time. Once or twice a year domestic fares are raised, often without advance notice, to compensate for inflation. Within Mexico no discounts are offered on round trip flights but excursion fares are in effect on some routes. Best bargains are the VTI, VTP and VHI packages sold by *Mexicana Airlines* and *Aeromexico.* Available only at ticket offices within Mexico, these include some ground arrangements and provide discounts of up to 40%. On international routes all airlines usually charge the same, but there frequently are special promotional and seasonal tariffs as well as excursion rates and discounts included in packages. A good travel agent will have the latest information on the lowest fares.

Cancun

American Airlines from Dallas/Fort Worth; *Eastern* from Atlanta; *United* from Chicago; *Continental* from Houston; *Aeromexico* from Houston, New York, Mexico City, Merida, Monterrey and Villahermosa; *Mexicana* from Miami, Philadelphia, Dallas/Fort Worth and Mexico City.

Cozumel

American Airlines from Dallas/Fort Worth; *Eastern* from Atlanta; *Continental* from Houston; *United* from Chicago; *Aeromexico* from Houston, Mérida and Mexico City; *Mexicana* from Miami, Mérida and Mexico City; *Aerocozumel* from Cancun.

Mérida

Aeromexico from Houston, Miami, Cancun, Chetumal and Villahermosa; *Mexicana* from Cozumel and Mexico City.

Campeche

Mexicana from Mexico City except Tuesdays and Thursdays.

Chetumal

Aeromexico from Mexico City and Mérida.

Villahermosa

Aeromexico from Cancun, Merida and Mexico City; *Mexicana* from Mexico City.

By Bus. The entire Yucatan peninsula is served by ADO *(Autobuses de Oriente)* as well as local lines. Buses stop at ferry terminals. Fares are quite low. Confusion is the major hazard in bus travel, especially for passengers who do not speak Spanish. Patience is a necessity; at some points there is no way of knowing whether seats will be available until the bus actually arrives. The vehicles themselves, while not luxurious, are scarcely more uncomfortable than airplanes; the difference is that the ride is longer. Tickets must be purchased at the station.

Cancun. Plaza Caribe (between Uxmal and Tulum, downtown), tel. 4–3927; *Mérida.* Calle 69 between Calles 68 and 70, tel. 1–0888; *Campeche.* Avenida Gobernadors at Chile, tel. 6–3344; *Chetumal.* Heroes 162, tel. 2–0369; *Villahermosa.* Francisco Javier Mina No. 297, tel. 2–1446.

By Train. Mérida and Campeche are the only points in this area served directly by rail. The trip from Mexico City to Mérida takes at least 37 hours and often a good bit longer. Equipment is ancient and none too clean; toilets, in particular, often are a mess. There is no dining car service. Tickets must be purchased on the day of departure; no advance bookings are accepted. Individual berths and roomettes are available and fares quite low, but train travel to Yucatan has little to recommend it.

By Car. Motoring is an excellent way to see and enjoy the Yucatan peninsula. Those driving in from the U.S. probably will follow the Gulf Coast highway to Villahermosa, Campeche, and Mérida, going on to the Caribbean coast. There are a number of opportunities for side trips. Roads are two-lane blacktops in reasonable condition and are patrolled by the Green Angels which provide emergency mechanical assistance if it is needed. Because of the chance of being stranded in case of a breakdown, plus other hazards, driving after dark should be avoided. Rental cars are available from *Avis, Budget, Hertz, National* and others at all commercial airports as well as from downtown locations. Local outfits, as opposed to franchisers of internationally known names, frequently offer lower prices but are often lax about keeping vehicles in good condition. Easy to obtain are subcompact VW beetles and similar vehicles. Large, automatic, air conditioned cars, which are very expensive, should be reserved in advance. When all extra charges are added in, car rental costs are higher in Mexico than in the U.S. Promotional tariffs and weekend rates are almost non-existent. Insurance should be considered mandatory; uninsured drivers involved in accidents may be detained until they come up with the cash to cover damages they have caused.

By Ship. Cozumel boasts that a different cruise ship ties up at the local pier almost every day of the year. Among those making regularly scheduled visits from Miami are Norwegian Caribbean Lines' *Skyward* and *Starward,* and Royal Caribbean Cruise Lines' *Song of Norway;* from St. Petersburg Commodore Cruise Lines' *Boheme* and from Tampa, October through May, Bahama Cruise Lines' *Veracruz.* Bahama Cruise Lines' *Bermuda Star* departs every Saturday from New Orleans, November through April. Many of these vessels also put in at Puerto Morelos, a peninsular port about 40 miles north of Cancun.

EMERGENCY TELEPHONE NUMBERS. Area code for Cancun is 988; for Cozumel, 987; for Chetumal, 983; for Mérida, 992; for Campeche, 981, and for Villahermosa, 931. Within Mexico dial 91 for access to long distance lines. To call Mexico from abroad first dial 01152. Public telephones, where they are available, cost one peso, making them an exceptional bargain. From public telephones long distance calls must be placed collect. Dial 09 to reach an international operator (they speak English); 02 for domestic service (operators speak only Spanish). Directory assistance is 04; only Spanish is spoken. Only local calls may be dialed from most hotels. Where possible international calls should be made collect as this avoids hefty Mexican taxes and all but a minimum hotel service charge.

English-speaking personnel is available at tourist offices. In Cancun at 4–3340; Cozumel 2–0357; Isla Mujeres 2–0188; Mérida 4–9290; Chetumal 2–1581; Campeche 6–3847, and in Villahermosa 3–8000. The U.S. consulate in Cancun is at 4–1638; in Mérida at 5–5011. Other consulates in Mérida include the British at 1–6799, Canadian 7–0460, Swiss 7–2095, and Netherlands 3–2410.

For police (who speak only Spanish) in Cancun call 4–1913; in Cozumel 2–0480; on Isla Mujeres 2–0082; in Campeche 6–4025; in Chetumal 2–1984; in Mérida 3–4019, and in Villahermosa 3–2125. The police will assist when an ambulance is needed. In an absolute emergency help can be summoned by calling the English-speaking international operators, dialing 09.

HOTELS AND ACCOMMODATIONS. Good to excellent places to stay are to be found throughout this area, although only Cancun is overflowing with hostelries in the **Super Deluxe** class. Happily for those on a budget, even Cancun has inexpensive inns. Categories are established by the Tourism Ministry and prices set accordingly. Rates listed here are for the high season, Dec. 15 through April; off season rates usually drop by one–third.

Cancun

All hotels here are new, few of them more than ten years old. The finest properties are in what is called the hotel zone, a strip of beach backed by a lagoon. Budget inns are downtown. At press time *Super Deluxe* rates were $120, *Deluxe* $100, *First Class* $65, *Moderate* $40, and *Inexpensive* $25.

Super Deluxe

Camino Real, Kukulkan Boulevard, hotel zone; 3–0100. Westin Hotels' low-rise pyramid faces out on two beaches and its own minilagoon. Spread out, it requires much walking. TV with U.S. programming, room bars and room safes. Instruction in Windsurfing, scuba and tennis (four lighted courts). Three restaurants, disco and music nightly in the lobby bar. Across from the convention center and near shopping malls.

Krystal, Kukulkan Boulevard, hotel zone; 3–1133. Handsome, with American TV and bars in the 360 rooms, nice beach, huge pool, tennis. Facilities include a supper club and an outstanding disco. Handy to convention center and shopping malls.

Sheraton, Kukulkan Boulevard, hotel zone; 3–1988. Farthest out of the big hotels, this is a two-building complex with 340 rooms and 140 condo suites. U.S. TV and mini-bars in the rooms, indoor and outdoor pools and six lighted tennis courts. Strong activities program with no extra charge for most events. Two restaurants, lobby bar and disco.

Hyatt Regency, Kukulkan Boulevard, hotel zone; 3–0966. A 14-story high-rise with mini-bars and U.S. programing on room television. The Regency Club offers premium accommodations at premium rates. Three restaurants, three bars, evening entertainment. Tennis. Near convention center and shopping malls.

Fiesta Americana, Cancun Boulevard, hotel zone; 3–1400. A striking horseshoe encircling the pool, this hotel is built to resemble a picturesque Mediterranean village. TV with U.S. programing and minibars in all 280 rooms. Several restaurants and lounges, tennis, but a small beach. Near shopping malls and the convention center.

Miramar Misión, Kukulkan Boulevard, hotel zone; 3–1280. Pleasant with minibars in the 225 rooms, two restaurants, night club, piano bar, tennis, and miniature golf. Somewhat far out but normally less expensive than other Super Deluxe Hotels.

Deluxe

Hyatt Caribe, Kukulkan Boulevard, hotel zone; 3–0044. One of Cancun's first hotels and still a favorite with 203 rooms and 63 beachside villas. A cozy, friendly place with evening entertainment.

Calinda Quality Inn, Kukulkan Boulevard, hotel zone; 3–1600. Somewhat bare bones are the 280 rooms, but the stretch of beach here is exceptionally nice and the water sports program outstanding. Entertainment nightly. Tennis courts.

El Presidente, Cancun Boulevard, hotel zone; 3–0200. Nice is the location adjoining the golf course. In all, there are 380 rooms in the hotel and next door condo complex. Two pools; tennis courts.

Viva, Kukulkan Boulevard, hotel zone; 3–0800. A 250–room condo-hotel which resembles an apartment house but which does feature nice accommodations. Piano bar; tennis courts.

Casa Maya, Kukulkan Boulevard, hotel zone; 3–1248. An even larger condo –hotel with 100 rooms and 200 suites that are reasonably priced. Three pools, tennis courts and evening entertainment.

Villas Tacul, Kukulkan Boulevard, hotel zone; 3–0000. A small complex of two-, three- and four-bedroom villas, the largest of which are on the beach. Tennis courts. Very exclusive.

Club Lagoon, Kukulkan Boulevard, hotel zone; 3–0811. This is a village-like complex with 90 rooms and 20 suites, strong on charm and big with watersports, but rather spotty management.

Club Mediterranée, Punta Nizuc (south of hotel zone); 4–2900. One of a worldwide chain of French–managed vacation villages where the basic rate covers meals and activities as well as a bed; most guests check in for at least a week and walk–ins are not encouraged.

First Class

Aristos, Kukulkan Boulevard, hotel zone; 3–0011. In many ways this 260-room establishment is *Deluxe* but charges only *First Class* prices. While maintenance is lax there are two restaurants, nightly entertainment, tennis courts, and a pleasant bit of beach.

Playa Blanca, Kukulkan Boulevard, hotel zone; 3–0344. One of the first hotels in the area, this 72-room Best Western is close to downtown Cancun. There is an indoor-outdoor restaurant-bar, tennis court, and an excellent water sports marina.

Maya Caribe, Kukulkan Boulevard, hotel zone; 3–0602. With 120 rooms this is a small, rather charming hotel surrounded on three sides by tropical gardens.

Decor is Spanish colonial; most units have balconies. Nightly entertainment. Tennis.

Castel Flamingo, Kukulkan Boulevard, hotel zone; 3–1544. New in 1985, 90 units overlook a nice stretch of beach. Coffee shop, specialty restaurant, and several bars. U.S. TV in the rooms. Isolation gives an exclusive feeling.

Carrousel, Kukulkan Boulevard, hotel zone; 3–0388. A condo-hotel with kitchenettes in most of the 110 rooms. There is a restaurant, cocktail lounge and snack bar. The hotel is a favorite with families.

Club Verano Beat, Kukulkan Boulevard, hotel zone; 3–0722. An all suite condo-hotel with 90 units, tennis and squash courts, and one of Cancun's best discos.

Dos Playas, Kukulkan Boulevard, hotel zone; 3–0500. A smaller condo-hotel with 58 units, restaurant, tennis courts.

America, Avenida Tulum, corner of Brisa, downtown; 4–1500. The only first class hotel downtown; free shuttle service to the beaches; large pool.

Moderate

Plaza Caribe, Avenida Tulum, corner of Uxmal, downtown; 4–1377. Somewhat garish, but the 112 rooms are air conditioned and carpeted. Coffee shop, restaurant, lobby bar, and pool.

Maria de Lourdes, Yaxchilan 1357, downtown; 4–1242. A small (50 rooms) inviting inn, air conditioned, and well cared for. Restaurant, nightly entertainment, pool, and steam baths.

Batab, Avenida Chichen Itza 52, downtown; 4–3822. The 68 rooms are air conditioned and there is a restaurant on the premises, but this is really a commercial hotel for business travelers.

Komvaser, Avenida Yaxchilan No. 15, downtown; 3–0849. Nice, with hot plates in all 55 rooms. Indoor–outdoor restaurant and a pool.

Inexpensive

Soberanis, Avenida Coba at Tulum, downtown; 3–0782. The 65 rooms are large and there is much tile, insuring that this place is clean but making it look like a bathhouse.

Antillano, Avenida Tulum and Claveles, downtown; 4–1132. With 48 air conditioned rooms, a pool, restaurant, and two bars, this is one of the most attractive of the inexpensive hotels.

Atlantis, Avenida Coba and Bonampak; 4–1622. There are 26 suites, the largest of which have fully-equipped kitchens. Pool and delicatessen.

Cotty, Avenida Uxmal 44, downtown; 3–0550. A nice, neat little place, air conditioned, providing a bed to sleep in but little more.

Crea, Kukulkan Boulevard, hotel zone. Guests have to be under 30 to stay at this beachfront government-run hostel. There are 700 beds and rates include meals. Management is somewhat bluenosed.

Beyond Cancun

Back before Cancun was a gleam in some planner's eye, the first resort hotels opened on the Caribbean coastline of the Yucatan Peninsula. Others have come in more recently. They appeal to guests who prefer to stay away from the crowds. There are few better places in the world for scuba diving or simply snorkeling. The beaches are super, the nights long and quiet.

Deluxe

Akumal, just off Highway 307, 60 miles south of Cancun; 4–3522. Originally a club for underwater explorers, now a 50-room resort with diving, sailing, and fishing featured. This is a lunch stop on most tours to the Tulum ruins.

Pez Maya, on Boca de Paila, which is about five miles east of Highway 307 via dirt road, the turnoff being some 30 miles beyond Tulum (many guests arrive by air taxi), tel. Cozumel 2–0411. A posh fishing camp catering to light tackle anglers seeking to hook permit and bonefish.

First Class

La Ceiba, in Puerto Morelos, just 12 miles from the Cancun airport; 2–0379. A delightful grouping of a dozen duplex cabins with an excellent restaurant. Scuba and snorkeling are big here. Riding horses available.

Molcas, at Playa del Carmen, 40 miles south of Cancun; 1–9222. Fairly new, built along Mexican colonial lines with 40 rooms, large pool, nice gardens and a good restaurant. Playa del Carmen is where the Cozumel ferries put in.

Boca de Paila, off Highway 307 about ten miles south of Tulum; 2–3030. A pleasant eight-unit fishing camp where sportsmen stay on the American plan.

Villa Arqueologica, in Coba, 25 miles inland from Tulum; 3–0800. A 40-room establishment hard by a group of Maya ruins and a lake, this is one of several hotels run in Mexico by Club Med for archeology buffs. Pool, tennis, and a good restaurant.

Moderate

Ojo de Agua, at Puerto Morelos, a dozen miles south of Cancun (no phone). There are 20 bungalows cooled by ceiling fans, pool, restaurant/bar, and equipment for snorkeling and scuba diving.

Jean Lafitte Cabins, off Highway 307 about 25 miles south of Cancun; tel. Mérida 3–0845. A wonderful place to play Robinson Crusoe in style. There are 25 fan-cooled cabins with all amenities, a restaurant/bar, large pool plus snorkeling and scuba gear available.

Inexpensive

Marlin Azul, about five miles from the Lafitte Cabins and under the same management. This complex is only about one-third as big, has a bar and restaurant but no pool.

Crucero Ruinas, at the Tulum ruins off Highway 307. A plain but comfortable place from which to explore the Maya ruins at leisure. With no pool, there is not much else to do. The restaurant is quite good.

Isabel, Puerto Juarez, five miles north of downtown Cancun. Some of the 40 rooms have air conditioning and there is a bar and restaurant. Cancun and its beaches are only a bus ride away.

Isla Mujeres

The Isle of Women—for so it is called in Spanish—is said to get its name from sculptures of females the early Spanish explorers found there. It became a laid-back Caribbean resort long before anyone ever heard of Cancun and remains a favorite with budget vacationers. Reached by ferry from Puerto Juarez, Isla Mujeres is about five miles long and half-a-mile wide. The hotels, such as they are, lie scattered about the one little village on streets with no names. Prices, according to category, are about the same as in Cancun.

First Class

El Presidente Caribe, 2–0122. The only hotel on the island with any pretensions of being luxurious, this five-story landmark is located on its own little islet and reached by a causeway. Rooms are air conditioned; there is entertainment nightly, a pool, windsurfing, sailing, and good scuba diving.

Moderate

Posada del Mar, 2–0198. Across from the beach, this is a well-maintained older establishment with 46 air conditioned rooms and bungalows. There is a bar and restaurant on the premises.

Rocamar, 2–0101. Across the island from the ferry terminal on a beach which is not good for swimming. Still, it is quite nice and the air conditioned rooms have balconies with a seaview. Restaurant and bar.

Inexpensive

Berny, 2–0025. A block or so up from the ferry terminal and not on the beach. Most of the 35 rooms in the three-story building are air conditioned and pleasant. Bar and restaurant.

Rocas del Caribe, 2–0011. On the west side of the island where the beach is not good for swimming. Many of the 34 rooms are air conditioned and have balconies with a sea view. Restaurant.

Poc-Na, an extremely attractive privately run hostel with dorms for men and women. One can choose either a hammock or bunk (sheets cost extra). The restaurant is open for breakfast and dinner.

Cozumel

Some 12 miles out, Cozumel is a limestone slab that is Mexico's only true Caribbean island resort. A scarcity of fresh water has hampered development, which adds to its charm. Most of the island, which is 30 miles long, 10 miles wide, is empty. There is one settlement with the better hotels a few miles north or south of it. The less expensive places to stay are in the village. Scuba diving is the big attraction, along with other water sports including game fishing. A room in a first class hotel will cost about $75; in a moderate establishment $50, in a modest one $35, and under $25 in an inexpensive hotel.

First Class

El Presidente, about six miles south of town; 2–0322. Managed by the country's largest chain, this 200-room resort is one of the best on the island. Excellent snorkeling from the beach. The restaurant is outstanding. Tennis.

Sol Caribe, four miles south of town; 2–1711. A 220-room resort managed by the Fiesta Americana group, noted for excellent diving facilities, lighted tennis courts, but also for catering more to cruise ship passengers than to guests.

La Ceiba, four miles south of town; 2–0379. The 120 rooms have television that receives U.S. programming; there is a tennis court, restaurant, cocktail lounge, and some of the best snorkeling and diving facilities on the island.

Mayan Plaza, northernmost hotel on Cozumel; 2–0627. Fairly new with balconies overlooking the sea on all 94 rooms. Swim-up bar in the pool, a restaurant on the ocean, and a nice beach.

Cabañas del Caribe, north of town; 2–0072. Bungalows by the sea, 56 of them in a beachfront coconut grove. A good place to learn windsurfing.

El Cozumeleño, north of town; 2–0149. A rather plain, somewhat gloomy 80-room resort on the beach catering primarily to groups. Restaurant, bar and tennis courts.

Moderate

La Perla, south of town; 2–0188. With just 24 rooms, this is a cozy inn by the sea that attracts a young crowd and is a good place to meet new friends.

Canatrel, north of town; 2–0144. With 100 rooms, this is one of the island's oldest hotels. The years have not been kind to the property.

Cozumel Caribe, north of town; 2–0288. Much larger, with 180 suites and 65 room. Tennis courts and an attractive stretch of beach.

Playa Azul, north of town; 2–0033. The hotel has seen better days, but the 40 rooms and 20 bungalows have a certain charm.

Mara, just north of town; 2–0300. One of the best in its price range. All 50 rooms have large balconies with a seaview. Dive shop and scooter rentals on the premises.

Colonial, Quinta Avenida Sur; 2–0506. An attractive in-town hotel with rooms and suites that include fully equipped kitchenettes.

Villablanca, south of town; 2–0730. Just 20 rooms here but there are tennis courts on the premises. A favorite with divers on a budget.

Inexpensive

Paraiso Caribe, Avenida Quinta Norte 599; 2–0740. Some of the 37 rooms are air conditioned, the others have fans. Pool, garden, coffee shop, and bar.

Mesón San Miguel, on the main square in town; 2–0333. A recently refurbished 97-room hotel, air conditioned, with swimming pool.

Galapago Inn, south of town; 2–0627. With 20 rooms, this small hotel caters almost exclusively to divers. A nicely run place with many pleasant touches, but no air conditioning.

Vista del Mar, Avenida Melgar 45; 2–3333. Two stories with balconies and a sea view for all 40 rooms. No air conditioning but a nice coffee shop.

Maya Cozumel, Calle Cinco Sur 4; 2–0011. Although the 30-room hotel has a pool, it lacks air conditioning and has no restaurant.

Baracuda, south of town; 2–0002. A 34-room divers' hangout with balconies overlooking the water and refrigerators in the rooms. The coffee shop serves breakfast only.

Chetumal

Capital of Quintana Roo (the state in which all Mexican Caribbean resorts are located) and 230 miles south of Cancun, Chetumal gets visited mostly out of curiosity. It looks as remote as it is, but the nearby Bacalar Lagoon is lovely and it can be fun driving over the border for lunch in Belize (which formerly was British Honduras). Year–round rates at press time were *First Class* $35, *Moderate* $20, *Inexpensive* $12.

First Class

El Presidente, Avenida de los Heroes at Aguilar; 2–0542. The only chain property in town, this hotel seems to be managed by corporate exiles. However, it is air conditioned and usually has entertainment nightly.

Continental Caribe, Avenida de los Heroes 171; 2–1100. While old, this property has been refurbished and kept up to date. It also is air conditioned and has nightly entertainment.

Moderate

Real Azteca, Belice 136; 2–0720. All rooms are carpeted and air conditioned in this pleasant little inn. The restaurant serves Arabic as well as continental dishes and there is nightly entertainment in the piano bar.

El Dorado, Avenida Cinco de Mayo 22; 2–0318. The rooms are spartan but most of them are air conditioned. There is a piano bar but no restaurant.

Inexpensive

Posada Veracruz, Paseo Veracruz 362; 2–3152. Small, with clean, fan-cooled rooms, this inn appeals primarily to backpacking travelers in from Belize and Guatemala.

Crea, Avenidas Alvaro Obregon and General Anaya. A youth hostel run by the government for vacationers under 30. This is a dormitory setup with rather strict rules.

Mérida

Capital of Yucatan state and the big city on the peninsula, Mérida frequently serves as a base for exploring the Maya ruins that are no more than an hour or two away by road. A better idea for those who have the time is to arrange to stay right at Chichen Itza and Uxmal. Still, Mérida itself is not to be missed. Two nights there will not be regretted. Most hotels are located downtown or out on or near elegant Montejo Boulevard. Downtown is better for visitors who enjoy strolling about on their own, poking into the shops and trying out little restaurants. Rates at press time were *Deluxe,* $55; *First Class,* $35; *Moderate,* $20, and *Inexpensive,* $12.

Deluxe

Holiday Inn. Colon at Montejo; 5–6877. New in 1980, with U.S. television programing and minibars in the 210 rooms. Pool, tennis, excellent restaurant, shopping arcade, and evening entertainment.

First Class

Casa del Balam, Calle 57 No. 455, downtown; 1–9474. An old but well-maintained property, neo-colonial in design with 54 attractive rooms, restaurant, bar, and pool.

El Castellano, Calle 57 No. 513, downtown; 3–0100. A 170-room hotel, more attractive inside than outside. Room music, restaurant, bar and pool.

Montejo Palace, Montejo Boulevard 483; 1–1641. A highrise with balconies for most of its 90 rooms. A fun place with rooftop night club and sidewalk cafe.

Misión Mérida, Calle 60 No. 491, downtown; 6–9667. Long a landmark in Mérida and recently refurbished, the Misión has plain, simple rooms on 12 floors, a small pool, two restaurants, bar, and nightly entertainment.

Autel, Calle 59 No. 546, downtown; 1–9175. A new urban motel short on charm but long on comfort. Room music, television and mini–bars. Restaurant, cocktail lounge, and pool.

Maria del Carmen, Calle 63 No. 550, downtown; 3–9133. Fairly new and modern with 70 rooms looking out on the pool. Restaurant, bar, and shops.

Pan Americana, Calle 59 No. 455; 3–9111. A recently reopened Merida landmark, quiet but close to downtown, with 110 rooms, large pool, restaurant, and nightly entertainment.

Moderate

Paseo de Montejo, Montejo Boulevard 482; 3–9033. Under the same management as the Montejo Palace but more of a bargain. The 92 rooms have television and mini–bars. Steak house, coffee shop, and sidewalk cafe.

Colon, Calle 62 No. 483, downtown; 3–4355. A wonderful old inn with 54 rooms, restaurant, bar, and pool all just a block from the main plaza.

Bojorquez, Calle 58 No. 483, downtown; 1–1616. Owned by a tour operator of the same name, this was once the Maya-Excelsior, in its day one of Mérida's best hotels. Now it caters primarily to bus tours. Pool, bar, and discotheque.

Cayré, Calle 70 No. 543, downtown; 1–1652. Quite charming this, with 100 rooms, pool in a garden, restaurant, bar, and shops.

Del Gobernador, Calle 59 No. 535, downtown; 1–3514. One of Mérida's newest; the 59 rooms have balconies looking out on a small pool. Nice coffee shop but motel-like atmosphere.

Colonial, Calle 62 No. 476, downtown; 3–6444. Old but well maintained with music in the 52 rooms. Pool, a delightful restaurant, and bar.

Alfonso Garcia, Calle 86-B No. 587, near airport; 1–6496. Once the villa of a Mexican movie star, this is a most unusual hotel, home to a flock of flamingos and peacocks. There are 80 rooms, restaurant, and bar.

Aluxes, Calle 60 No. 444, uptown; 4–2199. A fairly new 109-unit commercial hotel with pool, specialty restaurant, coffee shop, and most other services.

Caribe, Calle 59 No. 500, on Parque Hidalgo downtown; 1–9232. One of Mérida's real delights, old fashioned but with television and music in the 60 rooms, small pool, lovely restaurant/bar, all in an ideal location.

Inexpensive

Gran, Calle 60 No. 496, on Parque Hidalgo downtown; 1–7620. A relic from a gracious bygone age with 36 rooms. The setting is ideal with the main plaza, shops and many restaurants nearby, but the hotel can be noisy.

Del Parque, Calle 60 No. 495, downtown; 1–7840. Just 21 rooms but a friendly convivial sort of place.

Dolores Alba, Calle 63 No. 464, downtown; 1–3745. Only eight rooms and one of Mérida's tiniest inns. Nice restaurant.

San Luis, Calle 61 No. 534, near downtown; 1–7580. With 40 rooms, a pool, and fair restaurant and bar.

Mucuy, Calle 57 No. 481, downtown; 1–1037. Ten rooms with three beds in each. Pleasant garden but no air conditioning.

Centenario, Calle 84 No. 498; 3–2532. A 33-room inn in a residential area, nice for visitors who like to get away from the tourists.

Peninsular, Calle 58 No. 519, near downtown; 3–6902. New, with pool and restaurant, a trifle more pricey than others in this category.

Nacional, Calle 61 No. 474, downtown; 1–9275. Only some of the 80 rooms are air conditioned. Restaurant and pool.

Sevilla, Calle 62 No. 511, downtown; 1–5258. The 45 rooms surround a garden patio. Charming colonial atmosphere.

Posada Toledo, Calle 58 No. 487; 3–1690. Best of several pensión type inns in Mérida. Just 12 fan-cooled rooms. Very friendly.

Chichen Itza

Best way to really see these magnificent Maya ruins is to stay at one of the nearby hotels and wander about the area at leisure. Many of the hotels are exceptionally nice. All are located on the main highway within hiking distance of the ruins (taxis are available). Rates, by category, are the same as in Mérida.

First Class

Villa Arqueologica, one of the several Club Med-managed inns at the archeological sites in Mexico. New, with pool, tennis and good food. Rooms are nice but quite compact.

Mayaland, a long-time favorite with 66 spacious rooms and the flavor of old Mexico throughout the premises. Restaurant, cocktail lounge, shops, and pool.

Misión, an attractive, renovated colonial inn with 50 large rooms, a nice pool, and good restaurant.

Moderate

Dolores Alba, nearly two miles from the ruins, this small inn has some air conditioned rooms, pool and indoor/outdoor dining. Excellent for budget travelers.

Uxmal

Although the ruins here are only some 50 miles south of Mérida, the evening light-and-sound program makes an overnight stay a good idea. Indeed, with the ruins at Kabah, Sayil and other sites nearby, a two-night stay might be in order. All hotels are *First Class;* rates at press time were about $35.

Villa Arqueologica, rather new, one of several archaeological site hotels managed by Club Med, with pool, tennis court, and a French restaurant. Rooms are compact but comfortable.

Hacienda Uxmal, large, with 85 rooms in a colonial style setting. The pool, restaurant, and bar are in the midst of lush tropical gardens.

Misión, an attractive, recently renovated 50-unit hotel with large rooms, restaurant, bar, and a nice pool. Popular with tour groups.

Campeche

No more than a three-hour drive from Mérida, or 90 minutes south of Uxmal, Campeche, with its massive gates and crumbling walls, is a monument to the days when pirates roamed the Spanish Main. Hotels are centrally located. Rates: *Moderate,* $24; *Inexpensive,* $10.

Moderate

El Presidente, Ruiz Cortines No. 100; 6–2233. Although this chain hotel is fairly new, it is somewhat rundown. There are 120 rooms and suites plus a pool, restaurant, bar, and entertainment most evenings.

Baluartes, Ruiz Cortines No 80; 6–3911. A striking 100-unit seaside hotel overlooking the gulf, with fair accommodations, restaurant, coffee shop, lobby bar and occasional nighttime entertainment.

López, Calle 12 No. 189; 6–3344. Half of the 40 rooms are air conditioned. The restaurant/bar is nice enough and the management eager to please.

Colonial, Calle 14 No. 122; 6–2222. The owners claim this 30–room hotel was the home of Campeche's colonial governors. A few rooms have been air conditioned since then, but not all. Bar and restaurant.

Cuauhtemoc, Calle 57 No. 2; 6–5182. The Empress Carlotta slept here during the final days of Maximilian's reign. Renovated since then, there are 24 fan-cooled rooms.

Inexpensive

America, Calle 14 No. 122; 6–4588. Here are 30 fan-cooled clean rooms, little more.

Villahermosa

Oil has turned this tropical riverport into one of Mexico's most modern, fastest-growing provincial capitals. Most of the older hotels are downtown, near the river while the newer places are uptown by the parks. Rates at press time: *Deluxe,* $45; *First Class,* $30; *Moderate,* $18; *Inexpensive,* $10.

Deluxe

Holiday Inn, Paseo Tabasco 1407, Tabasco 2000 complex; 3–4400. Part of the uptown civic center/shopping mall development, with 276 rooms receiving U.S. television, coffee shop, specialty restaurant, bars, and nightly entertainment.

Hyatt, Juarez 106, uptown; 2–8808. Quite new with U.S television and mini–bars in all 210 rooms. Pool, coffee shop, restaurant, night club and discotheque.

First Class

Viva, Paseo Tabasco 1201, uptown; 2–5555. Attractive and well-run with television in its 260 rooms, pool, coffee shop, restaurant, lobby bar, piano bar, and disco.

Choco's, Constitución and Lino Moreno, downtown; 2–9444. Pleasant, with television in the 80 rooms. Restaurant, bar, and some evening entertainment.

Cencalli, Paseo Juarez at Calle Tabasco, uptown; 2–6000. Potentially quite nice, in a park setting with 116 large, comfortable air conditioned rooms. Pool, restaurant, bar, and disco.

Maya Tabasco, Avenida Grijalva, uptown; 2–1111. The 100 rooms could stand redecorating, but the pool is large and there is outdoor/indoor dining.

Moderate

Miraflores, Reforma 304, downtown; 8–6000. Smallish and unpretentious, with music in the 70 air conditioned rooms; restaurant and piano bar.

Manzur, Madero 422, downtown; 2–2499. A longtime favorite, primarily a commercial hotel, with 115 rooms, restaurant, and bar.

Plaza Independencia, Independencia 123, downtown; 2–1299. Plain on the outside but quite nice within. Television and piped music in the 62 rooms; restaurant, coffee shop, and entertainment most evenings.

Maria Dolores, Reforma at Aldama, downtown; 2–2211. An older commercial hotel with no frills but a nice restaurant.

SPECIAL EVENTS. February is the month for *carnaval,* the pre-Lenten mardi gras celebrated with special fervor in Mérida, Cozumel, Campeche, and Chetumal. **March 21,** *The Equinox,* is the day when light blends with shadow to make it appear Kukulkan, the feathered serpent, is crawling out of his temple and down his pyramid to fertilize the earth. This amazing spectacle also takes place in September, but often is rained out. **April** is when regattas sail from Florida to Texas to Isla Mujeres, followed by several days of racing around the island. Actual dates vary from year to year. **May 3,** the *Day of the Holy Cross,* is celebrated with fiestas in Felipe Carrillo Puerto (midway between Cancun and Chetumal) and in Celestún, Maxcanú and Xoccel (all near Mérida: there are fireworks, parades and a blending of Maya and Christian tradition. The final ten days of May are the date of the *Becal Fiesta* in Becal near Mérida. **May** and **June** are when billfish tournaments are held in Cancun and Cozumel, attracting sportsmen from all over the continent.

June is the month the *National Windsurfing Championships* are held in Cancun. **July 31** is the first day of the week-long *St. Ignatius Fiesta* in Chetumal. Day after day there are processions, parades, cockfights, fireworks and dances. **November 2** is the *Day of the Dead (All Souls Day),* blending Maya and Christian beliefs as candles and special foods are placed on home altars and all night vigils held at many cemeteries to welcome spirits returning for a brief visit from the Great Beyond. **November's** first week is the date of the *Cancun Fair* which includes carnival rides, cockfights and various exhibits. While it appeals mostly to local residents, it provides an interesting change of pace for visitors as well. **December 14** is when the *Christmas Fair* begins in Campeche. It continues through New Year's Day. **December 26** is when the circus traditionally arrives in Cancun. Held in a tent, it is an old-fashioned kind of show that can be great fun.

HOW TO GET AROUND. Good two-lane highways connect major points in the Yucatan area and a circle tour by road has much to recommend it. Rental cars are available but must be returned to where they were rented from to avoid substantial drop-off charges. Driving is easy. Buses are cheap, but they will appeal only to the adventurous. There are organized tours to almost everywhere as well as individual driver guides who may be hired. Air service within the region is fairly good.

At the major airports minibus and taxi service is provided to hotels at fixed rates, about $5 for a cab, $3 for a seat in a minibus. The airports are small and ground transportation clearly marked. Airports also have tourism information offices which may be able to help find hotel rooms. Dollars may be exchanged for pesos at favorable bank rates in the airports at Cancun, Cozumel, and Mérida.

Cancun

By Bus. Easiest way to get from one hotel to another or to the shopping malls or the convention center as well as downtown is by bus. These vehicles run between the Sheraton and downtown, passing by every five minutes or so and charging about 25 U.S. cents (of course you pay in pesos).

By Taxi. Cabs are found outside all the larger hotels as well as cruising; fares are fixed by zones. Expect to pay about $1.50 within the hotel area, $4 from the hotel zone to downtown. Tipping is not customary.

By Rental Vehicles. Most internationally known firms as well as many local ones have booths at the airport and outlets in the hotels. Jeeps and compact, standard shift cars are the most easily obtained; advance reservations are a good idea when a specific type of auto is required. The local firms sometimes offer lower rates, but their cars tend to be of the rent-a-wreck variety.

Special are the MGs that may be rented for about $65 a day at Plaza Quetzel in the hotel zone (tel. 3–1650) and the horseless carriages available for $15 per hour at Plaza Caracol, also in the hotel zone.

Mopeds and scooters may be rented at the Hotel Krystal and at several other locations (for cash only), but they are not recommended for Cancun. There have been many accidents and no insurance is available.

Limousines as such cannot be found in Cancun since they are not manufactured in Mexico. Large, late-model air conditioned cars with English-speaking drivers may be hired from *Best Day* by calling 4–3713.

Isla Mujeres

By Ferry. Boats leave both Puerto Juarez (just north of downtown Cancun) and the Isla Mujeres dock hourly on the half hour from 6:30 A.M. to 6:30 P.M. Better not wait for the last boat; there may be no room. Fare for the 45-minute ride is less than a dollar.

From Punta Sam, about five miles north of Puerto Juarez, car ferries leave at 7 and 10 A.M., 12:30, 6, 8:30, and 11 P.M. Return trips from the island depart at 6, 8:30, and 11:30 A.M. and 5, 7:30 and 10 P.M. Fare is about 50 U.S. cents.

By Taxi. Since the maximum distance is five miles, fares are low, seldom more than $3.

By Moped. Scooters rent for about $5 for two hours, $20 per day; credit cards are accepted for deposits but payment must be made in cash. The scooters are great fun, but risky, with no insurance available to cover medical bills.

Cozumel

By Air. Aerocozumel flies between Cancun and Cozumel (and vice versa) every two hours, more or less.

By Ferry. Departing Playa del Carmen, 40 miles south of Cancun, at noon and 4:30 P.M. and leaving Cozumel for Playa del Carmen at 9 A.M. and 4:30 P.M. The trip takes 75 minutes and the fare is less than a dollar. There is a car ferry leaving Puerto Morelos (about 12 miles south of Cancun) at 6 A.M. and returning from Cozumel at 1 P.M. Fare for the three-hour trip is about a dollar; there is no service on Mondays.

By Taxi. Cabs are plentiful on Cozumel. They charge about $2.50 for trips between the resort hotels and town.

By Rental Vehicles. Standard shift subcompacts and jeeps are available at the airport and in town from a variety of firms including several with international reputations. Mopeds and scooters, however, are the favorite with most visitors. These can be obtained at almost any hotel for about $20 per day.

Chetumal

By Taxi. Cabs are plentiful and fares within the city seldom exceed $2.50. **Rental Cars** are not available.

Mérida

By Bus. Within the city buses are confusing, crowded and uncomfortable; several days are needed to master the route system. Intercity buses stopping at the ruins of Chichen Itza and Uxmal are acceptable. There are frequent departures from the *Central Bus Terminal* at Calle 69 between Calles 68 and 70 (tel. 1–9150).

By Taxi. Available on the main plaza, by Hidalgo Park, outside the Montejo Palace Hotel on Montejo Boulevard, cabs also may be called from shops and restaurants. Minimum fare is about $1.50.

By Carriage. Known as *calesas,* these horse–drawn vehicles are found primarily around the main plaza. Drivers, who usually speak some English, charge about $10 for 90 minutes of sightseeing.

By Rental Car. Most internationally known firms as well as several local ones have booths at the airport and offices downtown. Automatic, air-conditioned vehicles should be reserved in advance. A car is of little use in Mérida itself—the city is compact and parking spaces scarce—but driving is one of the best ways to get to the ruins and see the countryside.

Campeche

By Taxi. Most of what there is to see in Campeche is within walking distance of the hotels, which is just as well; cabs are sometimes hard to find.

By Rental Car. Hertz has an office in the Belmar Building on Calle 59, tel. 6–4855.

Villahermosa

By Bus. The Paseo Tabasco line runs between the riverfront downtown to the parks uptown. Fare is about 25 U.S. cents but the vehicles are often ramshackle and crowded.

By Taxi. The best way to get around, although cabs cost a bit more in this oil town, anywhere from $2.50 to $5.

By Rental Car. Most of the well-known firms along with some local outfits have offices at the airport and in the various hotels. An auto is of little use in the city, where the streets are confusing and parking spaces few. A car is handy, however, for driving to the Palenque ruins and seeing the surrounding countryside.

TOURIST INFORMATION SERVICES

Cancun

The State Tourist Department has a stand at the airport and another by the convention center in the hotel zone; the latter is open from 9 A.M. to 1 P.M. and 5 to 9 P.M. daily. The main office is located downtown at the corner of Avenidas Tulum and Chichen (tel. 4–0650). *Cancun Tips,* a useful local giveaway, has its own information office at El Parian Mall in the hotel zone and downtown on Avenida Tulum next to the Ki-Huic Market; these offices are open 10 A.M. to 2 P.M. and 4 to 8 P.M. except Sundays.

Isla Mujeres

The government tourist office booth is on the village plaza about two blocks from the ferry terminal. It is open 10 A.M. to 2 P.M. and 5 to 8 P.M.

Cozumel

The government tourist office, open from 10 A.M. to 2 P.M. and 5 to 8 P.M., is on Rafael Melgar, the waterfront avenue, in the clearly marked Fideicomiso building. Two publications, the *Blue Guide* and *Cozumel: What to Do, Where to Go,* are distributed free in most hotels and full of handy information.

Chetumal

The government tourist office, open from 10 A.M. to 2 P.M. and 5 to 8 P.M., is at Obregon 457, tel. 2–1581.

Mérida

Main office of the state tourism authority is at Avenida Itzaes 490 (tel. 4–6596), which is fairly far from downtown. There are information stands at the airport, in the State House *(Palacio de Gobierno)* on the main plaza, in the Peón Contreras Theater at the corner of Calles 57 and 60 downtown, and on Montejo Boulevard at the corner of Calle 43, the latter three open from 8 A.M. until 6 P.M.

Campeche

The government tourist office, open 9 A.M. to 2 P.M. and 5 to 8 P.M., is at Plaza Moch Couoh (tel. 6–3847) on Avenida Ruiz Cortines near Hotel Baluartes.

Villahermosa

Information is available on the waterfront at Madrazo and Zaragoza. The main office of the Tourism Commission is at Retorno Via 5 No. 104 in the Tabasco 2000 complex; tel. 2–3171.

USEFUL ADDRESSES

Cancun

Aeromexico: El Parian Mall in the hotel zone and Avenida Tulum 3, downtown; tel. 4–1231. *Mexicana,* Avenida Coba 13, downtown, tel. 4–1265. *Aerocozumel,* tel. 4–2562; *American,* tel. 4–2947; *Eastern,* tel. 4–2870; *Continental,* tel. 4–2540, and *United,* tel. 4–2858, all have offices only at the airport.

U.S. Consular Service, Edificio Venus, downtown, tel. 4–1638. *Police,* City Hall *(Palacio Municipal),* Avenida Tulum, downtown, tel. 4–1913. *Central Hospital,* Avenida Tulum, downtown. There is a bank at the Parian Mall in the hotel zone and several others on Avenida Tulum downtown.

Isla Mujeres

Police, on the plaza about two blocks from the ferry terminal, tel. 2–0082. *Emergency Health Center,* three blocks up from the ferry terminal, tel. 2–0117. *Post Office,* about two blocks up from the Hotel Posada del Mar. The island's two banks are about a block up from the ferry terminal.

Cozumel

Aeromexico, Rafael Melgar 13, tel. 2–0422. *Mexicana,* Rafael Melgar Sur 17, tel. 2–0263. *Eastern,* tel. 2–0646; *Aerocozumel,* tel. 2–0928; *Continental,* tel. 2–0646, and *United,* tel. 2–0468, have offices only at the airport.

Police, Rafael Melgar south of town, tel. 2–0480. *Central Hospital,* Avenida Circunvalación, tel. 2–0525. *Post Office,* Rafael Melgar. Banks are located on Rafael Melgar and just off it on Primera Avenida and Quinta Avenida.

Chetumal

Aeromexico, Carmen Ochoa de Merino 6, tel. 2–1922. *Police,* Insurgentes at Belice, tel. 2–1984. *General Hospital,* Avenida Quintana Roo at J.J. Siordia, tel. 2–1977. *Post Office,* Elias Calles 2. There are banks at Obregon 479, Blanco 184, Heroes 6 and Heroes 34 as well as along Avenida Juarez.

Mérida

Aeromexico, Montejo Boulevard 460, tel. 7–9000. *Mexicana,* Calle 58 at 61, tel. 1–4959.

U.S. Consulate, Montejo Boulevard 460, tel. 5–5409. *British Consular Service,* Calle 58 No. 450, tel. 1–6799. *Canadian Consul,* Fraccionamiento Campestre, Calle 1–F–249, tel. 7–0460. *Police,* City Hall *(Palacio Municipal)* on the main plaza, tel. 1–3782. *Post Office,* Calle 65 at 56. *Emergency Hospital,* Calle 65 No.

546, tel. 1–6638. Banks are located along Montejo Boulevard and on Calle 63 just off the main plaza.

Campeche

Mexicana, Calle 10 No. 365, tel. 6–1894. *Police,* Avenida Diezyseis de Septiembre at Calle 61, tel. 6–2234. *Emergency Hospital,* Avenida López Mateos at Calle 55, tel. 6–4342. *Post Office,* Calle 59 at Calle 12. Several banks are located along Avenida Diezyseis de Septiembre.

Villahermosa

Aeromexico, Carlos Pillicer 511, tel. 2–6991. *Mexicana,* Avenida Madero 109, tel. 2–1169. *Police,* Diezyseis de Septiembre at Periferico, tel. 3–9142. *Emergency Hospital,* Paseo Usumacinta at Ayuntamiento, tel. 3–3593. *Post Office,* Lerdo at Saenz. Banks are to be found on Paseo Madrazo and at the Tabasco 2000 complex.

ENGLISH LANGUAGE MEDIA. *Cancun Tips,* distributed free at the airport and at most hotels, has 200 pages of ads and information on the resort. The *Blue Guide* and *Cozumel: What to Do, Where to Go* are both useful for visitors to the island and free. Free also, but more limited in scope, is *Maya Fiesta,* distributed in Mérida.

The News, published daily in Mexico City, is available at the better hotels and at some newsstands in Cancun, Cozumel, and Mérida. Some U.S. newspapers are available in Cancun. Magazines and paperback books may be found in some shops and newsstands in Cancun, Cozumel, and Mérida. Some hotels receive U.S. television programing via satellite; these are noted in the hotel listings.

TOURS. Sightseeing excursions to at least one of the archaeological zones in the area should not be missed. Popular, too, are cruises, most of which go over to Isla Mujeres; seasick pills are a good idea on these.

Cancun

Don Diego, a trimaran, and the catamaran *Cancun 5–0* sail daily at 11 A.M. from the marina at the Playa Blanca Hotel. The five-hour trip costs $25 and includes snorkeling at Isla Mujeres' Garrafón Beach, drinks, lunch and—for those who volunteer—swinging on the spinnaker. Tel. 3–0606. *Aqua-quin,* also a trimaran, makes a similar voyage for a similar price from the marina at the Camino Real. Tel. 3–0100. *El Corsario,* a 50-foot motor sloop, heads for Isla Mujeres from the marina at the Hotel El Presidente. Price again is $25 and while there is no spinnaker to swing from, the vessel is more steady. Tel. 3–0200. "*Booze Cruise*" aboard the *Don Alejandro* leaves the Mauna Loa marina at 6 P.M. for a ride up the lagoon and partying on a secluded beach. Dance music is played on board and, as the name indicates, the $25 includes drinks for an open bar. Tel. 3–0072. *Tropical,* a motor yacht, leaves at an early 9 A.M. for Isla Mujeres, stopping both at the village and at Garrafón Beach. Passengers get a bit more tour for their $25, including drinks, lunch and free use of snorkeling equipment. Tel. 3–1488. *Fiesta Maya,* a motor yacht, departs at 10 A.M. from its own pier, taking a route through the lagoon and on to Isla Mujeres. The boat's glass bottom allows non-snorkelers to view marine life. There is dance music played on board, but the $25 fare does not include drinks or lunch.

To Tulum. A two-hour bus trip offered by several operators, all charging about $20. Tulum was the only Maya city to have been built right on the beach.

There is ample time to explore the site. Most tours include a lunch stop at the Akumal Hotel, plus time for snorkeling at Xel-Ha, a lagoon that is virtually a natural aquarium filled with tropical fish.

To Chichen Itza. One of the largest and most spectacular of the Maya ruins, more than a few hours are needed to appreciate it. The bus tours, costing $40, arrive at midday when the sun is hottest. Sightseers are given an hour or so to wander around, then taken to a nearby hotel for lunch and a swim. Air tours also are available, but the best bet is overnighting at the site.

To Cozumel. Flying over and back in a day costs $40, but after an hour or so of poking around the shops on the island, there really is not much to do on a brief visit.

Cozumel

Robinson Crusoe Cruises, of which there are several, depart each morning from the main pier in town, sailing along the coast of the island for a seafood picnic on a remote stretch of beach. Tickets, available at most hotels, cost $25.

Tulum. Sightseers are put aboard the 9 A.M. ferry and met in Playa del Carmen for a short bus ride to the ruins. Tulum was the only Maya center built right on the beach. The small site can be seen in a short time. Lunch at the Akumal hotel and snorkeling at the Xel-Ha lagoon is included, with passengers returning aboard the 4:30 P.M. ferry, all for $40.

Chichen Itza. Less than an hour away by small aircraft, Chichen Itza is one of the largest and most impressive of Yucatan's ancient Maya sites. At $80 the trip is expensive, worth the price only to those who are seriously interested. Visitors do get to see more than those who come in by bus from Cancun.

Seeing the Island. At $12.50, sightseeing on Cozumel Island is cheap enough, although there isn't much most people will not have seen on their own. Included is a stop at the San Gervacio Maya ruins, interesting only to those not planning to see the ruins at Tulum or Chichen Itza.

Chetumal

While there are no organized sightseeing operators in Chetumal, and English-speaking guides may be difficult to find, hotels can arrange for taxis to take visitors around at a flat rate, about $25 per day, $15 per half day. Worth seeing is Bacalar Lagoon, one of the most beautiful jungle lakes in Mexico. The Maya ruins in the area, little restored, give visitors the feeling of being discoverers. The Belize border is just south of Chetumal and it can be fun to drive over to the little town of Corozal for lunch (remember to bring all travel documents).

Mérida

Although every other store front in Mérida seems to be a travel agency with sightseeing services, those in the hotels are generally the most reliable and furnish the best guides. These hotel operations may be more expensive, but since a tour really depends on the quality of the guide, the extra money is well spent.

Carriages. A buggy ride is a wonderful way to catch the flavor of the Yucatan capital. Passengers usually are taken from the main plaza out along stately Montejo Boulevard and back. The drivers provide a bit of commentary in broken English but it can be great fun. The 90-minute ride costs about $10 (per buggy).

City tour. This will cover some of the same territory seen from the buggies as well as a stop at the excellent Museum of Anthropology and a mandatory bit of shopping. Cost is about $10 per person.

Plaza walks. A two-hour guided stroll in the area of the main plaza. Included is the Montejo House (built by the conquerors of Yucatan), the fortress-like cathedral and the state house. La Ceiba Tours at the Holiday Inn, tel. 4–0075, charges $5 per person for these walks.

To Chichen Itza. Since it is only a 90-minute drive from Mérida, this large ancient Maya center can easily be visited in a day. Overnight stays, however, are recommended. The ruins are best appreciated in the early morning and late afternoon. Two-day tours often include stops at Valladolid, Yucatan's somnolent second city, and Izamal with its huge colonial monastery built over the remains of a Maya pyramid.

Uxmal. Only an hour from Mérida, this site also easily can be visited on a one-day tour for $25, lunch included. Here again, however, a one- or two-night stay should be considered. The evening light-and-sound show is quite good and Uxmal can be a base from which to visit the nearby Maya ruins at Kabah, Sayil and Labna.

Progreso and the Coast. A $25 excursion to the nearby port and beach at Progreso and then up to Rio Lagartos where flocks of flamingos are to be seen. The flamingos make it all worthwhile.

Villahermosa

La Venta. Guided tours through the park museum to view the colossal sculptures done by the Olmecs some 3,000 years ago cost about $5 with transportation and admission fees included. Sightseers also take in Tabasco 2000 (Villahermosa is the capital of Tabasco), impressive urban development on the edge of the jungle.

Jungle Cruise. The yacht *Capitan Buelo,* once a working river boat, now takes passengers on luncheon voyages up the Grijalva twice each afternoon except Mondays. While the food is ordinary at best, the cruise is, one imagines, something like going up the Congo or the Amazon. Lunch runs about $7 and the boat trip itself is included.

Palenque. A Maya center hidden in the Chiapas jungle, Palenque is one of the most spectacular archaeological zones in Mexico. It costs about $30 for the all-day sightseeing tours that depart Villahermosa early (the ruins are 90 miles away) and return in the evening. Lunch is included on these excursions. Hotel travel desks will arrange for tours.

PARKS AND GARDENS

Cancun

Cancun itself has no areas that can properly be called parks, although the residential areas near downtown are dotted with attractive public gardens.

Xel-Ha. Pronounced "shell-hah," this national park is 75 miles south of Cancun. Xel-Ha is a great natural aquarium. The gin-clear lagoon here is home for many species of brightly colored tropical fish. Snorkeling equipment is available for rental. Sightseeing tours to Tulum usually put in for a while at Xel-Ha for rest and relaxation.

Contoy Island. A national park and bird sanctuary reached from Cancun by charter boat (there are no regularly scheduled trips), Contoy is a heavenly place for a picnic. Numerous species of pelicans, frigate birds, terns, and egrets are among the fowl that make Contoy home.

Isla Mujeres

El Garrafón. On the southern tip of the island, El Garrafón is a national park where most tour boats from Cancun put it. It is about four miles from the village and a wonderful place to snorkel. Reef fish are abundant. Snorkeling equipment may be rented here. Services include lockers, changing rooms and showers. There are a number of seafood restaurants in the park.

Cozumel

Chankanaab. A new national park midway along the island's lee shore, Chankanaab includes a protected marine reef, a clear fresh water lagoon and a botanical garden. Scuba and snorkeling equipment may be rented and there are changing rooms with showers. The restaurant on the grounds is quite good.

Mérida

The Plaza. Following Spanish custom, the heart of Mérida is the town square. In this case it is a delightful garden where ancient laurels are clipped into geometrical patterns. Benches are molded concrete affairs, two seaters designed for face-to-face chats.

El Centenario, out on the western end of Calle 61, is Mérida's principal park, complete with a small zoo, miniature train ride, boating on an artificial lake, and tables for picnics.

Las Americas, out a few blocks from Montejo Boulevard, features trees from every country in the hemisphere.

Hidalgo and Santa Lucia are two of the loveliest of Merida's many charming little plazas. Both face on Calle 60 and are marvelous places to lounge, loaf, read a newspaper or get a shoeshine.

Villahermosa

La Venta, quite remarkable, is a park museum displaying monolithic sculptures by the Olmecs, the mysterious people who thrived along the Gulf Coast 3,000 years ago. The works on display were brought from nearby swamplands to Villahermosa so that more people could see them. The evening light and sound show is worth seeing even if you do not understand the Spanish commentary, for the statues take on new forms under artificial light (be sure to bring insect repellent).

Garido Park, adjoining La Venta, is a pleasant spot by the Lagoon of Illusions. It contains the state fairgrounds and an open air theater. Oddly, it is named to honor Tomas Garrido, a dictatorial governor of the early 1930s who is best recalled for his fierce persecution of organized religion.

Children's Park, on the other side of La Venta, is open to adults as well. It is a wonderful place for youngsters to frolic on the shores of the lagoon.

La Choca, on the shores of the Carrizal River, is Villahermosa's newest park, part of a petroleum-financed development called Tabasco 2000. It has its own miniature railway, picnic grounds and an outdoor theater.

SPORTS

Cancun

Resorts in the hotel zone offer all the water sports plus, in almost all cases, tennis. As these are concessions, outside clients are welcome. Some of the best facilities are found at the **Playa Blanca Marina** (phone 3–0344), **Club Lagoon Marina** (3–1111), **El Presidente Marina** (3–0200), **Viva Marina** (3–0019) and the **Aquaquin Marina** at the Camino Real (3–0100). The **Mauna Loa Marina** (3–0072), on the lagoon, is the only marina with jet skis. **Scuba Cancun** (3–0315), as the name implies, specializes in diving. **Aventurismo** (3–0315) and **Pez Vela** (3–0992) operate Cancun's largest fleets of game fishing boats.

Prices vary from place to place and haggling may produce results. At press time fishing charters cost $350 per day. A two-tank scuba dive trip cost $50; a resort course in diving was $55. Snorkeling gear rented for $12 for a day; $6 for two hours. Windsurfers were available at $12 per hour and a three-hour windsurfing lesson cost $42. Hobie Cats rented at $35 per hour, or $45 with an instructor. Waterskiing cost $20 for 30 minutes while parasailing fees were $20 for ten minutes.

Golf is at Pok-Ta-Pok, an 18-hole course designed by Robert Trent Jones. Cost, including green fees and cart rental, is about $25. Private lessons and clinics are available.

Bullfights are held at a small bullring on Wednesday afternoons during the winter months. Tickets run about $15 and may be purchased at hotel travel desks.

Isla Mujeres

Mexico Divers, near the main dock in the village, has a full line of scuba diving equipment, provides lessons and operates both day and night tours to the reefs. **El Canon** and **Aquamundo** also have rental equipment available. On the other end of the island at El Garrafón National Park, **El Garrafón Dive Shop** rents both scuba and snorkeling equipment. There are a number of excellent places to dive around Isla Mujeres. Prices are lower than in Cancun.

Cozumel

The hotels south of the village, especially *La Ceiba, El Sol Caribe, El Presidente* and the *Galapago Inn,* make a specialty of catering to **scuba divers** and maintain well-equipped dive shops on their premises. In town *Dive Paradise,* Calle Dos Sur and *Discover Cozumel,* on the waterfront, are among the best scuba outfitters. There are good dive shops at Chankanaab National Park for those who want to explore the reef there. Dive shops also rent snorkeling equipment.

Windsurfers and jetskis may be rented on the beach in front of the *Hotel Mayan Plaza* north of town. *El Sol Caribe* and *El Presidente* also have windsurfers. The *Club Nautico* north of town (tel. 2–1113) has **sports fishing** boats available for charter. Price depends on the size of the boat.

Bicycles as well as motor scooters may be rented on Cozumel. *Rentadora Cozumel,* (tel. 2–1120) will deliver bikes to customers' hotels.

Miniature golf may be played at *Playa Festival* on the waterfront next to the Barracuda Hotel.

Mérida

Scuba diving in the cenotes or sink holes that open into Yucatan's underground river system is the specialty of *Dive Mayab,* Calle 53 No. 469, tel. 3–7142. Cenote waters are very clear. Divers, who must be certified, will find these cenote adventures unforgettable. Prices, which include ground transportation and equipment rental, begin at $50.

Hunting for duck, deer and boar is excellent along the north coast of Yucatan just a few miles from Mérida. Arrangements, especially regarding the importation of firearms, are complicated. *Garcia López* at Calle 11 No. 201 (phone 5–1225) or *La Ceiba* at Montejo Boulevard 481 (4–0075) are experts at cutting through red tape and setting up expeditions.

Golf is played at *La Ceiba Country Club* about ten miles north of Mérida on the Progreso Highway.

Bullfights are not regularly scheduled events in Mérida, but when they take place they do attract some of Mexico's top matadors. Hotels and travel agencies sell tickets.

Baseball is played from mid-March through mid-August at the stadium adjoining the *Carta Clara* brewery at Calle 14 No. 70. Mérida boasts one of the best teams in the Mexican League.

BEACHES. First, a reminder that beaches in Mexico are federal property, open to the enjoyment of all who wish to use them. Hotels have no authority over the seashore on which they front. Swimming is at one's own risk, for lifeguards are all but non-existent.

Cancun

Strictly speaking, the hotel zone is all beach, and some of the most beautiful beach in the world at that. The Caribbean is somewhat more gentle on the stretch from the Playa Blanca Hotel (near the mainland) to the Convention Center. Beyond the Sheraton Hotel the beach, backed by jungle, is virtually deserted and not especially attractive.

Just a short bus ride north of town on the mainland is Punta Sam, a pleasant bit of shoreline backed by some inexpensive seafood shacks and a favorite with budget vacationers staying in the downtown hotels.

South of town Highway 307 hugs the shore for 80 miles until it reaches Tulum. Puerto Morelos, where the cruise ships dock, and Playa del Carmen, from which the Cozumel ferry departs, have excellent facilities including hotels. Beyond Playa del Carmen is Paamul, wonderfully isolated. Acumal, with all facilities, is an ideal beach for snorkeling, as is nearby X-Caret where a lagoon joins the sea. The Maya ruins at Tulum overlook one of the most beautiful little coves on the Mexican Caribbean.

Isla Mujeres

Los Cocos on the northern end of the island is a nice swimming beach just beyond the village and is where most vacationers staying on the island congregate.

El Garrafón, near the southern tip of the island, is where most of the tour boats from Cancun put in. The water teems with tropical fish and the snorkeling here is excellent.

Playa Lancheros, midway along the island, is noted for its turtle pens where those who wish may try riding a turtle. Up a winding path are the remains of the Mundaca estate, built by one of the area's more successful pirates.

Cozumel

The best swimming and sunning beach stretches along the lee shore of the island north of Cozumel's one in town and it is in this area that most of the larger resort hotels are found. South of town the sea is more appealing to snorkelers and scuba divers. Just off from the Hotel La Ceiba, for instance, is the sunken hulk of an airplane, not an actual wreck but the remnant of a set from an underwater adventure film. Last stop is **San Francisco Beach,** one of the prettiest stretches of sand on the island and the place where the tour boats put in for their picnics.

The island's one road swings across to the east and skirts the shore of the open Caribbean. There are many delightful little coves over here—El Mirador, Punta Chiquero and Chen Rio among them—and few people, but the sea is rough here and dangerous for swimming.

Chetumal

Although the city is on a bay, the best beach is at **Calderitas** about five miles north of town. Even better swimming is to be found at the **Cenote Azul,** a sinkhole of blue transparent water some 25 miles inland.

Mérida

Progreso, the port 20 miles north of Mérida, is where the locals go for a dip when temperatures soar. This is the Gulf of Mexico and its beaches suffer by comparison to the Caribbean.

Campeche

While Campeche is on the Gulf it has no beaches worthy of the name. There are a few sandy strips that can be found driving south along Highway 180, but they are not worth looking for.

HISTORICAL SITES. Token admission fees, never as much as a dollar, are charged at many areas. Guides normally are available only at Chichen Itza, Uxmal and Palenque.

Cancun

El Rey is a minor archaeological site about five miles south of the hotel zone and on the lagoon. It appeals to tourists who want to say they have seen a Maya ruin and then get back on the beach. Apparently this was a small grouping of temples built around 800 years ago. To be seen are the remains of several small pyramids and a few other buildings.

Tulum, about 80 miles from Cancun, is one of the most majestic of the ancient Maya centers. Most of the structures were erected around 1200 A.D. and the city was still inhabited when the Spaniards arrived. It is the only major Maya settlement on the shoreline. Dominating the site is the Temple of Kukulkan, the feathered snake diety known to the Toltecs and Aztecs as Quetzalcoatl. The Spanish called the temple *El Castillo,* The Castle, and indeed it does look like a fortress. Nearby is the small Temple of the Descending God. Above the doorway is a carved figure plummeting headfirst toward earth; guides are fond of speculating that this may have been a visitor from outer space.

Coba, 30 miles inland from Tulum, is a bit more than four hours from Cancun. Founded about the time Tulum was, it grew to be a far more important city with perhaps 50,000 inhabitants. Today many of the ruins remain enveloped by the jungle, but the great pyramid towers over the bush and the setting by five lakes make this one of the most beautiful of the ancient Maya monuments.

Isla Mujeres

Mayan Temple on the southern tip of the island is the only remnant left from pre-Hispanic times. Apparently this was one of many island temples dedicated to the fertility goddess. Sculptures in female form found by the Conquistadores inspired the name Isla Mujeres—Isle of Women.

Mundaca Home, or what's left of it, was built by Fermin Mundaca, one of the last pirates of the Caribbean. Enamored by an Isla Mujeres señorita, Mundaca constructed an elegant hacienda both to impress his lady love and prove he was going straight. The girl, or so the story goes, would have nothing to do with retired buccaneer, leaving Mundaca to grow old on his estate alone. The remains of the estate are just inland from Playa Lancheros.

Cozumel

There are several Maya ruins on the island, but they are not especially impressive. Usually they are visited by vacationers who simply want to say they have seen a ruin and get back to playing.

Mérida

Cathedral, also on the plaza, was completed in 1598. From without, the building looks more like a fortress than a church and within it is stark, something of a reminder of Yucatan's past troubles.

Montejo Home, built in 1549 by the Montejo family that led the conquest of Yucatan, this is now a bank office, but has been splendidly restored. The facade is carved with the arms of the Montejo family as well as those of Spain and has two Spanish knights depicted in stone as standing on the heads of the conquered Mayas. On the south side of the main plaza.

San Barnardo Hacienda, which dates back to the 19th century, is a restored henequin plantation where visitors get an idea of how things used to be in these parts.

Chichen Itza

One of the largest and best restored of Yucatan's pre-Hispanic centers, Chichen Itza was a Maya city conquered by the Toltecs from central Mexico. As such it blends two of the early cultures of Mexico.

El Castillo, the Pyramid of Kukulkan, dominates the site, rising up 75 feet with a temple on the top. It is from this temple that Kukulkan, the feathered serpent, appears to crawl down the pyramid in a play of light and shadow during the equinox twice each year. El Castillo, is of Toltec influence.

Ball Court, this one larger than those found at other pre-Hispanic centers, is where ritual games were played that at least occasionally ended in human sacrifice. Wall carvings depict a beheaded player fertilizing the ground with blood spurting from his neck.

Sacred Well is not really a well at all but a cenote, or sinkhole, opening onto an underground river. Here humans were thrown into the waters as a sacrifice to the rain god. Where once it was believed the victims were lovely virgins, bones recovered in recent explorations reveal that people of all ages, including children, were hurled to their deaths here.

El Caracol, or The Snail, is now generally regarded as a Maya observatory. This is one of the older structures at the site, although it was later modified by the Toltecs.

Uxmal

While not as extensive as Chichen Itza, Uxmal generally is considered architecturally more attractive. It is also more purely Mayan, having been abandoned prior to the Toltec conquest.

Pyramid of the Magician, which dominates the site, is oval rather than square and the front is much steeper than the back. Legend has it the pyramid was built by a dwarf magician who completed the job in a single night. Archeologists, not surprisingly, dispute this tale, maintaining that there are several pyramids here, one having been built over the other.

Governor's Palace is the name given by the Spaniards to Uxmal's most splendid structure. It may very well have been just that, or the residence of a prince or high priest. Almost 320 feet long and decorated in carved stone mosaic, the palace is regarded by many experts as the finest of all Maya buildings.

Nunnery, while named by the conquerors, could have been just that, or at least quarters for the priesthood. There are four buildings here, laid out in a rectangle, and while the style of each is different, they rather complement each other. This is where the light-and-sound show takes place each evening.

Kabah, Sayil and Labna are other ancient Maya sites fairly close to Uxmal. Uxmal itself has more than half-a-dozen buildings worth exploring. Travelers really fascinated by the mystery of the Mayas will want to take in the other centers. Kabah is famed for its superb Temple of the Masks honoring the rain god. Sayil, only partially cleared from the jungle, boasts a palace that some say might have been inspired by the Greeks. Labna is noted for an impressive ceremonial arch which is almost Roman in concept.

Campeche

Ramparts, including walls, portals, and forts erected in the 17th century as a defense against raiding pirates, today make Campeche one of the most photogenic cities in Mexico. Especially noted are the Sea Gate on Calle 59 and Diezyseis de Septiembre, near the water front, and Land Gate, five blocks inland. Fort Soledad, on the northeast corner of the old wall, is now a regional museum.

Well of the Conquerors, about two miles northeast of the walled city, on Avenida Obregon, supposedly is where a Spanish expedition put in for water in 1517. The nearby Church of San Francisco is said to mark the spot where the first Catholic mass was said on the mainland of the Americas.

Edzna, about 40 miles west of Campeche, is a Maya center that has been attracting great interest of late. There are indications that the Maya calendar—one of the most accurate ever devised—was invented at Edzna. Being somewhat out of the way and with its ruins generally unrestored, Edzna is little visited. Those who do get there find the five-tiered pyramid known as the Acropolis most impressive.

Villahermosa

Palenque is nearly 100 miles from Villahermosa, but is is very much considered one of Villahermosa's attractions if not the major reason tourists visit Villahermosa. A Maya ceremonial center surrounded by dense jungle, Palenque is quite distinct from the ruins found on the Yucatan peninsula. Many experts consider that artistically the Mayas reached their zenith at Palenque. Architecturally they came up with many innovations as well, changing traditional designs to permit larger doors and bigger rooms. Here also is the only Maya pyramid yet found in Mexico to have been used as a tomb. (For details on this and other sites in Palenque, see chapter on *The Indian South.*)

La Venta Park Museum on Boulevard Grijalva near Paseo Tabaco—a fine display of monolithic Olmec sculptures in a well-designed park setting; open every day 9–4:30; small admission fee. Sound and light shows were slated to begin in 1985; tel. 21879.

Olmec/Maya Museum or **CICOM,** between the Periferico Carlos Pellicer and the Grijalva River. Excellent art selection from Olmec, Mayan and other pre-Columbian cultures; open daily except holidays, 9 to 8; free.

As for Villahermosa itself, while it has been around since 1596, it was, until recently, little more than a grubby river port in the tropics. Today it is a boom town and its historical sites are just now being built.

MUSEUMS AND GALLERIES. Admission fees, where they are charged, are less than a dollar.

Cancun

Anthropology Museum, in the Convention Center, although small, is a good introduction to the area's Mayan past. Displayed are artifacts including pottery, jewelry and stucco masks. While the labeling is in Spanish, bilingual personnel on the staff will be happy to answer any questions. Open 10 A.M. to 2 P.M. and 5 P.M. to 8 P.M. except Mondays.

Cedam Museum, Kukulkan Boulevard downtown in the Bahia condo complex. On display are treasures plucked from the deep by underwater explorers, everything from canons to pieces of eight. Open daily from 11 to 8.

Orbe Galerias, Plaza Caracol Mall, hotel zone. On display and for sale are works by leading Mexican artists. Open 10 to 2 and 5 to 9, tel. 3–1571.

Mérida

Regional Museum on Montejo Boulevard at Calle 43 is the most splendid mansion on a street of splendid mansions. On display within is quite an extensive collection of Mayan artifacts including items recovered from the Sacred Well at Chichen Itza. Since all the labeling is in Spanish, taking a guide along is a good idea (the museum is included in most city sightseeing tours). Open daily except Mondays 8 A.M. to 8 P.M., Sundays 8 A.M. to 2 P.M.

Crafts Museum, on the corner of Calles 50 and 61, contains a collection of Yucatan handicrafts ranging from pottery to basketry, as well as traditional costumes. Many items are on sale. Open 10 A.M. to 2 P.M. and 4 to 8 P.M. (mornings only on Saturdays) except Sundays.

Campeche

History Museum is in Forte Soledad on the eastern end of Calle 8. The fort was once part of the city ramparts and within are many reminders of Campeche's pirate-plagued past. These include cutlasses, sextants and models of ships. Open daily except Mondays 9 A.M. to 2 P.M. and 4 to 8 P.M. (mornings only on Sundays).

Archaeology Museum is in Fort San Miguel a couple of miles west of downtown on the Villahermosa Highway. The fort, complete with drawbridge, is really more interesting than the contents of the museum itself. Exhibited are pieces of pottery from all over Mexico and a display showing how the Mayans deformed the skulls of their infants. Open the same hours as the History Museum.

Villahermosa

Art Center, in the same general complex as the museum, includes the José Gorostiza Gallery and the Miguel Angel Gomez Sculpture Garden, both reflecting Villahermosa's petroleum prosperity. Open 10 A.M. to 8 P.M. daily except Sundays (mornings only on Saturdays).

Cicom Archaeological Museum, part of the Center for Investigation of the Olmec and Maya Cultures, is on the Malecon by the Grijalva River. New and well laid out, the museum displays a large collection of Olmec and Maya artifacts as well as pieces from other pre-Hispanic cultures throughout Mexico. Open daily except Wednesdays 9 A.M. to 7 P.M.

Museum of Folkways *(Museo de Cultura Popular),* Zaragoza 810, contains displays showing how people live in Tabasco river settlements. It is small but fascinating, and includes a replica of a Chontal hut complete with sound effects. Open same hours as Art Center.

STAGE, MUSIC, AND DANCE

Cancun

Ballet Folklorico, a dinner theater arrangement beginning with a buffet of regional specialties at 7 P.M. followed by the show at 8:30. The ballet comprises two hours of folk dances from all over Mexico and is eminently enjoyable. At the Convention Center nightly except Sundays. Tickets are about $22.

Mérida

Peon Contreras Theater, on Calles 57 and 60, just a block or so from the main plaza, is a turn-of-the-century Italian-designed opera house at which there are presentations almost every night of the week. These include symphonies, jazz concerts, piano recitals, modern dance, ballet, and theatrical works.

Regional Dances are presented each Monday evening at 9 P.M. in the Jardin de los Compositores just behind the Municipal Palace (City Hall) which is on the main plaza. Free

Tributes to the Big Bands are staged Tuesday evenings at 9 at Santiago Park, Calles 59 and 72. Played are popular dance tunes from the Big Band era. Free.

Concerts for Strings take place 9 P.M. Wednesdays in the Santa Ana Park, Calles 47 and 60, and feature music from Mexican and Spanish operettas as well as works by Yucatan composers.

Yucatan Serenades on Thursday evenings at 9 P.M. at Santa Lucia Park, Calles 55 and 60, presents some of the best entertainers appearing at the moment in Mérida, along with soloists, trios and the state orchestra. Free.

Villahermosa

Esperanza Iris State Theater, a new facility by the banks of the Rio Grijalva, often has something going on every night. Usually there are plays (in Spanish, of course), but occasionally concerts or performances by dance groups, folk singers or opera.

The outdoor theater in *La Choca Park* and the *Convention Center* in the Tabasco 2000 development also now and then are venues for entertainment.

SHOPPING. The State of Quintana Roo—in which Cancun, Isla Mujeres, Cozumel, and Chetumal are located—is something of a duty-free area (tobacco and alcohol are not tax exempt). This is a holdover from the not-so-long-ago era when the region truly was remote and merited special concessions. Even today when flying or driving into the rest of Mexico one may be subjected to customs inspection. Actually there are few bargains that will appeal to foreign tourists; most of the imported items that are on sale consist of Danish cookies, Dutch cheese and American canned peanuts. Some of the better shops stock European perfumes and fashions, which simply are not available in the rest of the country (except in Baja California and along the U.S. border). The siesta is an honored tradition in Quintana Roo and the rest of the peninsula. Shopping hours generally are from 10 A.M. to 1 P.M. and 5 to 8 P.M.

Cancun

The major hotels all have shops on the premises which are handy but sometimes a trifle pricy. Then there are various malls in the hotel zone. The *Plaza Caracol* is the most elegant and is fully air conditioned. *El Parian,* by the Convention Center, is more downscale with many stalls where bargaining is quite in order. Other malls include the *Mauna Loa* complex, *Quetzal* and the *Costa Blanca.* Downtown, Avenida Tulum is the major shopping artery. *Pama* at Tulum and Lluvia, *Cactus* at Tulum 13, *La Casita* at Tulum 37, and *Charlie* at Tulum No. 1 all stock a wide variety of goods ranging from handicrafts and jewelry to resort wear for men and women. *Geraldine* at Tulum 29 and *Nicte-Ha* at Tulum 53 specialize in jewelry. *Aca Joe* at Tulum 15 is Mexico's leading resort wear designer while *Valentino's* at Tulum 7 carries internationally known designer labels. *Plaza Mexico* on Avenida Tulum is a downtown mall where various shops each feature handicrafts from individual Mexican states. *Don Quijote* at Tulum 27 is an excellent place to find books, magazines, records, cassettes, postcards, and even stamps. The *Farmacia Turistica* in the Caracol mall is a drug store along the lines of those in the U.S.

Isla Mujeres

This tiny island offers limited shopping, but there are a few places of special note in the village. Since the streets are unblemished by names, addresses are meaningless. *The Drug Store,* near the plaza, has everything from film and sun tan lotion to pills and ointments. *Super Betino,* also near the plaza, carries food and drink for those who would dine in their rooms, plus sports wear, cosmetics, and a line of pharmaceuticals. *Casa del Arte* is a good place to pick up rubbings from Maya temples along with jewelry and handicrafts. *La Playita,* on the waterfront, has a fair line of resort wear.

Cozumel

Cruise ships putting in just about every day have made Cozumel's one village a community of shopkeepers. Many of the boutiques are identical to their neighbors, but a few are somewhat special. *Cinco Soles,* on the waterfront toward the north end of town, features an outstanding collection of fashions, handicrafts and jewelry; no siesta break here, either. The *Handicraft Market,* half a block up from the market, is a good place to find souvenirs while *La Concha,* Cinco Avenida Sur just off the plaza, specializes in quality work by top artisans. Nearby on the same street, *Roberto's* is noted for prized black coral while *Van Cleef* sells fine gold jewelry. *Aca Joe* on the waterfront is a good bet for resort wear. *Emma,* a boutique on Juarez near the plaza, goes in for high fashion. *El Sombrero,* on the waterfront, is a fine spot to find boots, belts, bags and other leather items.

Chetumal

The capital of Quintana Roo is dotted with little shops featuring imported goods, but offering little that would be of interest to foreign tourists. *El Parador,* at Avenida Heroes 129, for instance, is perhaps the largest shop in town with a stock of car stereos, tennis rackets, toasters, and typewriters, imports that appeal to Mexican shoppers.

Mérida

Without a doubt this is the best place to browse and buy items made of straw—handbags, hammocks, baskets, mats and Panama hats—in the entire region. Tailored shirts called guayaberras and leather huarache sandals are also to be found at attractive prices. Calles 58, 60 and 62 running off the main plaza, are the best shopping streets. Guayaberras are everywhere. *La Poblana,* Calle 65 No. 492 is perhaps the best place in town to find hammocks, while *Becal* at Calle 56 No. 522 has an excellent assortment of Panama hats, many of them quite inexpensive. *Las Mariposas,* Calle 55 No. 499, is local headquarters for frocks by Georgia, who also has a nice collection of folk art. Worth seeking out also is *Originales Patric,* now at Calle 16 No. 104 (take a taxi), with the finest in rubbings from the Maya temples; these make ideal gifts. Finally, the public market on the corner of Calles 56 and 67, has a bit of everything plus plenty of local color.

Campeche

The state-run *Artesans House* in Fort San Carlos where Calle 8 begins along the waterfront is a good place to find regional crafts including Panama hats, embroidered blouses and basketry. Especially attractive are items of tortoise-shell, but these are not allowed in the U.S. since tortoises are considered an endangered species. The public market is on Avenida Lopez Mateos, about seven blocks from the waterfront along Calle 63.

Villahermosa

Many downtown streets in the neighborhood called Zona Luz have been turned into pedestrian malls, interesting for window shoppers. *Mis Recuerdos* on Juarez, *Artesanias Tabasco* on Aldama and *Villa Arte* on Gil y Sanchez, all of them between Reforma and Lerdo de Tejada, are the best souvenir shops in the Zona Luz. More in the way of handicrafts can be found at the Cicom Museum complex. *El Puerto de Liverpool,* a branch of the big Mexico City department store chain, is on Paseo Tabasco in the Tabasco 2000 complex.

RESTAURANTS. Distinctive gastronomy, no doubt a reflection of its Mayan heritage, is a feature of the Yuctatan peninsula. The coastal areas, to be sure, place a strong emphasis on seafood, but even Cancun and Cozumel have restaurants specializing in *huevos motuleños* and *cochinita pibil,* the former being fried eggs and refried beans on a toasted tortilla, the latter pork baked in banana leaves. Generally, the cuisine of the Yucatan area is less piquant than that of the mainland.

The basic price for a meal will run about $25 in a *Deluxe* establishment, $20 in an *Expensive* place, $10 in a *Moderate* restaurant and $6 at an *Inexpensive* cafe. Drinks (remember that anything imported is extremely costly), and tips (15% at *Deluxe* and *Expensive* spots, 10% elsewhere) can easily double the bill. Neither jackets nor neckties are required anywhere, but overly casual attire (shorts, skimpies), while tolerated in many places, is appreciated nowhere. *Visa* (V) and *MasterCard* (MC) all almost universally accepted, *American Express* (AE) and *Diners Club* (DC) less so. Just as you would not attempt to pay for a meal with pesos in the U.S., don't expect to use dollars in Mexican restaurants; traveler's checks are best cashed at banks or hotels (banks give a much better rate).

Cancun

Unless noted otherwise, the restaurants listed here are open for luncheon as well as dinner. Generally, however, vacationers snack poolside at lunchtime and go out somewhere for dinner. Since it gets dark earlier in Cancun and Americans usually outnumber Mexicans, anytime after 7 P.M. is an acceptable time to dine. While most of the better hotels have a number of dining rooms and accept outsiders, we are listing only independent restaurants here. The majority of these are downtown.

Deluxe

Maxime, Pez Volador No. 8, hotel zone, 3–0438. Dinner only; reservations required. French country-style dining by the Mexican Caribbean. Decor is antique and elegant, the cuisine continental. The piano bar is charming. AE, DC, MC, V.

Mauna Loa, Kukulkan Boulevard, hotel zone. Dinner only; reservations required. A Polynesian spectacular that includes a hula floor show, a night at the Mauna Loa is a Cancun tradition. AE, DC, MC, V.

Bogart's, across from the Convention Center, hotel zone, 3–1133. Dinner only; reservations suggested. This is Cancun's answer to *Rick's Cafe Americain* of *Casablanca* fame. The menu is outstanding. AE, MC, V.

Expensive

Pancho's, Kukulkan Boulevard, hotel zone, 3–1010. Tropical and Mexican, lots of fun for lunch, better still at night for dining and dancing under the stars. MC, V.

Compass Rose, Kukulkan Boulevard, hotel zone, 3–0963. The decor is nautical as is the food, along with Oriental specialties from a Mongolian oven. AE, DC, MC, V.

Carlos 'n Charlie's, Kukulkan Boulevard, hotel zone, 3–1304. A link in Mexico's largest chain of wild and rather wacky dining spots, especially nice at night with dancing from 10 P.M. on. AE, DC, MC, V.

Cancun 1900, at the Convention Center; 3–0038. The decor is old-fashioned-saloon, the atmosphere casual and fun, the food quite good. MC, V, AE.

Torremolinos, Tulum at Xcaret downtown, 4–3639. Spanish fare here, with brunch served starting at 10 A.M. MC, V.

La Habichuela, Margaritas 27, downtown, 4–3129. Dinner only; reservations suggested. A garden restaurant serving steaks and seafood, this is a favorite with folk who live in Cancun. MC, V.

Angus, Kukulkan and Nader downtown, 4–2251. Dinner only. The setting is nothing special, but the steaks may well be the best in town. AE, MC, V.

Moderate

Augustus Caesar, Claveles 13, downtown, 4–1261. Italian food of all kinds is served here in classic, air conditioned surroundings. AE, MC, V.

Chocko's and **Terre** with two locations, one at the Convention Center in the hotel zone, the other at Claveles 7 downtown, 4–1394, specializes in lobster and seafood. MC, V.

Brujo's, Claveles 9, downtown, 4–1591. Dinner only. Mexican cuisine prepared in the Texas manner. Live music nightly adds to the fun. AE, MC, V.

Patagonia, Coba 18, downtown, 4-1860. Argentine Churrasco and Caribbean lobster are among the specialties. AE, MC, V.

Don Juan, Coba 11, downtown, 3–1966. Something like a Monterrey steakhouse laid out like a Mexican hacienda. The happy hour is from 6 to 8 P.M.

Karl's Keller, Plaza Caracol, hotel zone, 3–1104. Sausage and strudel with a Teutonic flare. MC, V.

Mandarin, Sun Yax Chen 53 (no phone). Traditional Cantonese cuisine in a pleasant setting. MC, V.

Inexpensive

Dan's, Tulum 83, downtown, 4–1885. Cancun's home of the great American hamburger, french fries, hot dogs, and steak sandwiches. Open for breakfast.

Almendros, Tulum at Sayil, downtown 4–0807. A branch of Mérida's highly regarded Yucatan-style restaurant, an excellent place to sample regional cuisine. MC, V.

La Posta, Crisantemas 10 near Coba downtown, 4–2105. A bit of the Old West serving both Mexican and American specialties. Open for breakfast.

Papagayo, Claveles 31, downtown, modest yet cheerful, open for breakfast as well as lunch and dinner.

Rolandi, Coba 12, downtown. Easily the best place in town for a good pizza, plus excellent pasta in a pleasant garden setting. MC, V.

Isla Mujeres

Dining out is one of the principal activities of the island, which is fine as long as you enjoy seafood. The restaurants are located at both ends of the island, either in the village or out by Garrafón beach.

Expensive

Maria's Kankin, at Garrafón Beach, is a bit of Gaul by the sea owned by a French lady named Maria. Her peppered turtle steaks and lobster parisienne long have been considered reason enough to cross over to the island. Luncheon only. MC, V.

Gomar, two blocks from the waterfront, is a lovely place for dinner if you are staying on the island. The setting is romantic and the cook excels at his job. Dinner only. AE, MC, V.

Moderate

El Garrafón, at Garrafón Beach, serves fish, lobster, and shrimp in a casual open air setting overlooking the sea. Lunch only. MC,V.

Buho's, on the beach just north of the village offers steaks as well as seafood and provides dance music in the evening. AE, MC, V.

Ciro's, is a lobster house just up the street from the docks. Steaks are on the menu here, too. MC, V.

Villa del Mar, across from the dock, is another popular Isla Mujeres seafood house.

Inexpensive

La Peña, across from the plaza, features pizzas, sodas, and Mexican specialties.

Cozumel

Most of the restaurants are in the island's one town. As is the case in Cancun, on Cozumel most vacationers take a light lunch and show up for dinner as early as 7 P.M. The rest of Mexico dines much later.

Deluxe

Morgan's, on the plaza, is open for both lunch and dinner, with music in the evening (tel. 2–0584 for reservations). The place to go for a big night out. AE, V, MC, D, CB.

Expensive

Grips, on the waterfront at the north end of town, is a delightful establishment serving dinner only, on the terrace and indoors. As the hour grows late it becomes a disco. V, MC, AE, CB.

Carlos 'n Charlie's (and Jimmy Kitchen) has an odd name, but being one of Anderson's places that is expected. One flight up on the waterfront with a nice view of sea and stars. V, MC, D, AE, CB.

Sports Page, corner of Quinta Avenida and Calle Dos, brags it is very American, serving fried chicken, steaks, and seafood. Open for breakfast as well as lunch and dinner. V, MC, AE.

Moderate

La Laguna, Chankanaab National Park, is open for lunch from 10 to 4. Seafood is the specialty at this thatched-roof, open-air restaurant on the beach. V, MC.

B.B.Q.s, on the waterfront between Calles Cuatro and Seis, is an American-style place featuring ribs, steak, and chicken. Open for lunch and dinner with country music at night. V, MC, AE, D.

El Portal, on the waterfront by the ferry dock, opens starting at breakfast. A casual, open-sided cafe, this is a good spot to try Yucatan specialties. V, MC.

Pepe's, a block from the waterfront and just off the main plaza, is a big, busy open-sided restaurant, nice for both lunch and dinner. MC, V.

Rolandi, on the waterfront, north end of town, serves the best pasta on the island in a delightful garden (don't be discouraged by the seedy entrance). V, MC, AE, D, CB.

Inexpensive

Las Palmeras, on the waterfront near the ferry dock and open all day, this is a favorite for snacks as well as meals.

Such is Life, Adolfo Rosado Salas, three blocks from the plaza, serves Italian sandwiches and Mexican specialties; this is a favorite with scuba divers on a budget.

Las Tortugas, Avenida Diez Norte 82, a short walk from the plaza, is tops for tortas and tacos. This is another divers' den.

Chetumal

While the capital of Quintana Roo is no gourmet rendezvous, there is a handful of surprisingly pleasant places to eat in the city. The traditional late dining hours of Mexico are observed more closely in Chetumal, but so is the custom of eating whenever one is hungry.

Moderate

Mufa, Heroes at Obregon. Shish kebab and other Middle Eastern dishes are on the menu with a choice of dining within or at the sidewalk cafe. MC, V.

Los Milagros, Zaragoza 271, also a sidewalk cafe, this one open for breakfast. Many Yucatan specialties are on the menu. MC, V.

Fogata, Juarez 49, a traditional Mexican restaurant open only in the evening. MC, V.

Inexpensive

Sergio's, Obregon 182, is Chetumal's pizza and spaghetti parlor; one of the most popular spots in town.

El Caribe, near Heroes down by the beach, is a pleasant place for a lunchtime snack.

Mérida

Although the locals sup lightly in Mérida, a good evening meal for visitors is often a wonderful way to end a busy day of sightseeing. A siesta and a late meal (9 P.M.) are much in order.

Expensive

Le Gourmet, Ponce Perez 109; 7–1970. The name says it all. This is one of Mérida's classic mansions converted into a fine place to dine. Nice piano bar, too. Evenings only. AE, DC, MC, V.

Chateau Valentin, Calle 58 No. 499-D; 5–6367. Here again, a mansion has been converted into a French restaurant. This one, too, has a piano bar. Reservations recommended; dinner only. AE, MC, V.

De Fernando, Calle 60, corner of 35; 1–5859. This restored townhouse specializes in regional dishes prepared to international standards; luncheon and dinner. AE, MC, V.

Moderate

Almendros, Calle 59 No. 434; this is something of a shrine to Yucatan gastronomy. A noisy dining hall at midday, it tends to be more sedate in the evening. MC, V.

Las Palomas, Calle 56 between 55 and 53; 3–1545. Another of the wonderful old converted mansions; lunch and dinner. MC, V.

Siqueff, Calle 59 No. 553, 1–5859. Middle Eastern fare as well as international specialties are served here in intimate surroundings; lunch and dinner. MC, V.

Patio Español, Parque Hidalgo just off Calle 60; 1–9232. Indoor-outdoor dining with both Spanish and regional food served at its best; lunch and dinner. MC, V.

La Casona, Calle 60 No. 435; 4–8348. Italian cuisine made with homemade pastry is served here. Nicest at night. AE, MC, V.

Kon-Tiki, Colon at Calle 14; 5–4409. Chow mein and other Cantonese specialties are to be found here at Mérida's only Chinese restaurant. MC, V.

Pancho Villa's, Calle 59 No. 509; 3–0942. This is a relaxed theme restaurant with evening entertainment; dinner only. AE, MC, V.

Inexpensive

La Prosperidad, corner of Calles 53 and 56. Bamboo wall and thatched roof are for real, not to create atmosphere. This is a cantina that has hit the big time.

Mexican and regional specialties are on the menu and there is a free lunch at the bar. Best at night. MC, V.

Cafe Express, Parque Hidalgo off Calle 60. Tops for snacks and sandwiches, this seems to be everyone's favorite gathering place.

Soberanis, on the main plaza and also at Calle 56 No. 617. The place does not look like much from the outside, but seafood lovers say there is no better place for fish and shrimp. MC, V.

Los Arrecifes, Montejo Boulevard near Calle 43, is a modest sidewalk cafe, serving Mexican specialties and grilled meats. MC, V.

Pop, Calle 57 No. 501. A pleasant place for a budget breakfast, lunch, or dinner.

Campeche

Seafood is the specialty here, Campeche being famed throughout Mexico for its shrimp. *Congrejo moro* or stone crab is another local prize. The restaurants themselves don't look like much. Local folk put greater store in good food than atmosphere.

Moderate

El Refugio de Lorencillo, Las Palmas 49, is a cab ride from any hotel but well worth the price. The setting is memorable and they have steaks as well as seafood on the menu. MC, V.

Miramar, corner of Calle 59 and Deizyseis de Septiembre, on the waterfront, while not impressive, brings the customers back day after day.

Kalua, Calle 12 No. 150, is a relative newcomer, small but noted for its good cooking.

Villahermosa

Petroleum has brought some major changes to the dining scene in Villahermosa. The selection, to be sure, remains limited, but time was not so long ago when there was no selection at all. Dinnertime is anytime between 7 and 10 P.M.; lunch never before 1 P.M.

Expensive

Los Guayacanes, by the Cicom Museum on the waterfront; 2–1530. A nice international menu here in a restaurant worthy of Mexico City. AE, DC, MC, V.

Grijalva Grill, Grijala Boulevard; 3–2214. Another of the Carlos Anderson chain of theme restaurants, this one a favorite of visiting oilmen from Texas. AE, DC, MC, V.

El Mesón de Castilla, José Pages Lergo No. 125; 2–5621. Spanish and international cuisine served in an attractive Iberian setting. AE, MC, V.

Country Steak House, Cedro No. 209; 2–7979. Steaks, as the name implies. AE, MC, V.

Moderate

Capitan Beulo, the riverboat that departs on luncheon cruises up the Grijalva daily at 1:30 and 3 P.M. The food is not so great, but the trip is not to be missed.

Chon Chupon, Parque La Choca; 3–3593. A seafood house in the city's newest park. MC, V.

Old Canyon, Tabasco 2000 complex; 2–7744. Made up to look like a saloon out of the Old West, with good steaks, hamburgers, and beer. MC, V.

Mesón del Duende, Diezyseis de Septiembre No. 303; 2–0724. The name means "Inn of the Dwarf" and this is a rather charming place with a good international menu. MC, V.

Inexpensive

Parilla Holandesa, Fidencia No. 713. In this case the name means "Dutch Grill" yet the menu is mostly Mexican. Grilled cheese is a specialty, and the Dutch are famous for their cheese, get it? MC, V.

Los Pepes, Madero 610, opens for breakfast and closes pretty late at night.

NIGHTLIFE

Cancun

An evening in Cancun usually begins with cocktails in any hotel lobby bar (happy hour normally ends at 7 P.M. as this is when the fashionable drinkers arrive), followed by a long and leisurely dinner and then on to the discos, which get jumping about 11 P.M. One can wind up the night touch-dancing or holding hands in a cozy piano bar. All the places listed here are in the hotel zone; downtown Cancun rolls up the sidewalks before midnight.

For a change of pace there is a Mexican fiesta every night of the week at one of the big hotels and a "pirate cruise" at sundown over to Isla Mujeres. See your hotel travel desk for details.

Live Music

Friday Lopez, Hotel Fiesta Americana, is the American singles bar scene on the Mexican Caribbean. Two bands take turns here starting about 7 P.M. and going on and on. There is a dance floor plus good burgers and barbecue.

Reflejos, Hyatt Regency, has romantic dance music from 7 P.M. until late at night. Sophisticated and elegant, the appeal is to a more mature crowd.

Lone Star, Avenida Yaxchilan downtown, is country music for dancing and fun. Stays open until everyone leaves. Opens at 8 P.M. (but the crowds come later).

La Terraza, Hotel Viva, features nostalgic music from the age before amplifiers were invented. It opens at 7 P.M.

Casa Salsa, Plaza Caracol Mall, is a restaurant that turns into a late night haven for lovers of Jamaican and Afro-Cuban music. Best to show up here after 11 P.M.

Discotheques

Aquarius, next to the Hotel Camino Real, opens at 10:30 P.M. and likes to think of itself as Cancun's most elegant disco. Phone 3–0100 for reservations.

Cocay, Hyatt Regency, opens at 10 P.M. and is one of the area's newest discos where nondancers can sit, talk, and hear each other. Phone 3–0044 for reservations.

El Caberet, Hotel Fiesta Americana, may just be the loudest and wildest disco in Cancun. Phone 3–1400 for reservations. Opens at 10 P.M.

Christine, Hotel Krystal, is the newest disco in Cancun and probably the most spectacular in all of Mexico. Call 3-1133 for reservations.

Tabano's, Hotel Sheraton, opens at 10 P.M. and tries to be quite chic. Call 3–1988 for reservations.

Mine Company, Hotel Viva, is Cancun's first disco and is something of an institution. A favorite with locals. No reservations accepted here.

Isla Mujeres

Discotheques account for all the nightlife there is on the island. They open early, some at 7 P.M. The choices are *Calipso* on Ruez Medina, *Buho's* at Carlos Laza No. 1, and *Tequila Disco* at the corner of Hidalgo and Matamoros.

Cozumel

Just as dinner starts earlier in these parts than in other areas of Mexico, so does the nighttime action. Even then it is limited, as the sporting types either sign up for night scuba dives or want to get an early start in the morning.

Neptuno, on the waterfront at the corner of Once Sur, is the newest disco in town and the best equipped. The crowds start lining up about 10 P.M.

Scaramouche, also on the waterfront, has been a popular favorite with the disco crowd for several years. It, too, gets going around 10 P.M.

Grips, on the waterfront, and **Morgan's,** on the plaza, both are restaurants that turn into discos, starting about 11 P.M. Each appeals to dancers with money to spend.

La Fragata, on the waterfront next to Pepe's, is a romantic bar with live music played from 6 to midnight.

Chetumal

The discos at the **Continental Caribe** and **El Presidente** hotels are the best in town, but they tend to be rather dismal save on weekends. **Los Globos,** west of town, is a popular roadhouse.

Mérida

The nightlife scene here is more varied than even in swinging Cancun. It should be remembered, of course, that Mérida is no resort town. Things tend to be more conservative here and places often close up a bit earlier. Standard evening entertainment is taking in performances of regional dances; these are presented both at a downtown hotel and at a rather touristy nightclub. Making a second night in Mérida worthwhile is the chance to enjoy one of the free shows which are presented at 9 P.M. weekday nights at one of the parks in the city. All in Spanish, of course, these range from quite professional entertainers to something close to an amateur hour; always they are charming, fun, and give one the feeling of really experiencing the Mérida lifestyle.

Tulipanes, Calle 42 No. 462; 7–2009. Every group tourist who passes through Yucatan, it seems, is bused here for a mediocre dinner and a folkloric floor show. And everyone appears to have a fine time.

Mision Mérida, the hotel at Calle 60 No. 491, presents regional dances with dinner every night. The Mision also has a disco. Call 9–9500 for reservations.

Club Romanticos, Reforma at Colon, is as romantic as the name implies. It opens at 9 P.M. and features crooning trios and dance music.

Trovador Bohemio, Calle 55 No. 504 by Santa Lucia Park, (3–0385) is another delightful little bar where romantic trios sing soft and gentle tunes.

Aloha, Hotel Montejo Palace, Montejo Boulevard 483; (1–1641) is the biggest and brassiest nightclub in town. Opens at 10 P.M.

La Conquista, Hotel Paseo de Montejo, Montejo Boulevard No. 482 gets started at 9 P.M. with dance music and a floor show at 11.

Dracmas, Calle 60 No. 319; 5–5478, and **Barba Azul** on Montejo Boulevard, phone 1–0677, are Mérida's top two discos.

Campeche

The choice here is the piano bar at the *Hotel Baluartes* or the disco at the Hotel *El Presidente.*

Villahermosa

Between them, the hotels offer a good variety of nightlife. There are piano bars at the *Miraflores, Viva* and *Plaza Independencia;* discotheques at the *Viva, Hyatt,* and *Maya Tabasco;* and nightclubs at the *Hyatt Holiday Inn,* and *Plaza Independencia.* Other nightspots outside the hotels can get a bit rough in this oiltown.

USEFUL PHRASES AND VOCABULARY

Spanish is a relatively easy language to learn. Here are a few basic rules on pronunciation.

		as in:	example:
1) **Vowels** are pronounced precisely, with exceptions noted below:			
a		father	mas
exception:	ai/ay	life	aire, hay
	au	out	autobós
e		then	necesito
exception:	ei	weigh	seis
	eu—no equivalent word in English, but sounds like:	eh-oo	neumático
i		police	repita
exception:	before a, e, o, u	yes	viaje, bien, edificio, ciudad
o		none	noche
exception:	oi	boy	oigo
u		good	mucho
exception:	before a, e, i, o	was	cuarto, puedo, cuidado, acuoso
	(silent when used with: qui, que, gul, gue)		aquí, queso, guía, embrague
2) **Consonants** are pronounced similarly to English, except:			
c before a, o, u		kick	casa, poco, película
before e, i		see	dice, décimo
g before a, o, u		go	gazpacho, langosta, gusto
before e, i		house	gerente, ginebra
gu		before a	guava agua
h (silent)		Esther	hablo
j		hill	mejor

ll	young	llame
ñ	onion	señor
q (always followed by silent "u")	pi**qu**e	mante**qu**illa
rr rolled	th**r-r**-ee	a**rr**oz
x as in English, except in a few proper names when between vowels or beginning a proper name	**h**ut	México, Oaxaca,
	zest	Xochimilco Xochicalco
y before vowels	yet	ayer
when meaning "and"	me	y
z	lose	azul

3) **Accent marks** are used to indicate which syllable is stressed, or to distinguish between two words, i.e., el (the) or él (he).

General

Good morning/good day.	Buenos días.
Good afternoon.	Buenas tardes
Good evening/good night.	Buenas noches.
I am glad to see you.	Mucho gusto en verle.
I don't speak Spanish.	No hablo español.
Do you speak English?	Habla usted inglés?
A little bit.	Un poquito.
How do you say in Spanish?	Cómo se dice en español?
Do you understand me?	Me entiende usted?
I understand.	Entiendo.
I don't understand.	No entiendo.
What did you say?	Cómo dice?
More slowly, please.	Más despacio, por favor.
Repeat, please.	Repita, por favor.
Write it down, please.	Escriba, por favor.
I don't feel well. I am sick.	No me siento bien. Estoy enfermo.
I need a doctor.	Necesito un médico.
How are you?	Cómo está usted?
Fine. And you?	Perfectamente. Y usted?
Very good.	Muy bien.
I have the pleasure of introducing Mr. . . .	Tengo el gusto de presentarle al señor . . .
Pleased to meet you.	Mucho gusto en conocerle.
The pleasure is mine.	El gusto es mío.
Pardon me. Excuse me.	Perdóneme. Con permiso.
Do you have a match?	Tiene usted un fósforo?
Can I take your photo?	Puedo tomar su fotografía?

Where is the . . . ?	Dónde está . . . ?
I don't know.	No sé.
Where can I change my money?	Dónde puedo cambiar mi dinero?
Where do you come from?	De dónde es usted?
Can you tell me?	Puede usted decirme?
What do you wish?	Que desea usted?
What is the matter?	Que pasa?
Sit down, please.	Siéntese, por favor.
You are very kind.	Usted es muy amable.
It doesn't matter.	No importa.
Call me/phone me.	Llámeme por teléfono.
Is Mr. . . . in?	Está el Señor . . . ?
What is your name?	Cómo se llama usted?
Let's go.	Vámonos.
Good-bye.	Adiós.
Till we meet again.	Hasta la vista.
Until later/so long.	Hasta luego.
Many thanks.	Muchas gracias.
Don't mention it/You're welcome.	De nada

address	dirección
American	americano
aspirin	aspirina
better	mejor
boat/ship	barco
book	libro
bookstore	librería
boy	niño, muchacho
building	edificio
bullfight	corrida de toros
bullfighter	torero
business	negocio
chair	silla
church	iglesia
cigarette	cigarro
clean	limpio
cleaning	limpieza
come here	venga acá
come in	entre
depart	salir, partir
do	hacer
dry	seco
dry-clean	lavado en seco
expensive	caro
eye	ojo
eyeglasses	lentes, anteojos
few	pocos
film	rollo, película
find	encontrar
forbidden	se prohibe
from	de
garden	jardín
gentleman	caballero, el señor

girl	niña
go	ir
good	bueno
guide	guía
handbag	bolsa de mano
hard	duro
heavy	pesado
high	alto
hospital	hospital
house	casa
husband	esposo
know	saber
lady	la señora, dama
look	mire, vea
look out	cuidado
lost	perdido
man	hombre
more	más
me	mi
my	mio, mia
name	nombre
new	nuevo
no more	nada más
no/non-	no
of	de
office	oficina
old	viejo
painting	pintura
please	por favor
policeman	policía
pretty	linda, bonita
quick	rápido, pronto
rain	lluvia
school	escuela
see	ver
single	solo, sencillo
smokers	fumadores
smoking	fumar
suitcase	maleta
sweet	dulce
there is, are	hay, son
thick	grueso
thin	delgado
time	tiempo
too	también
trip	viaje
United States	Estados Unidos
up	arriba
very	muy, mucho
wallet	cartera
watch	reloj
water	agua
weather	clima
welcome	bienvenido

wet	mojado
wife	esposa
with	con
with me	conmigo
without	sin
woman	mujer
yes	sí
young lady	la señorita
your	su

Calendar

Months (meses):	
January	enero
February	febrero
March	marzo
April	abril
May	mayo
June	junio
July	julio
August	agosto
September	septiembre
October	octubre
November	noviembre
December	diciembre
Days (días):	
Monday	Lunes
Tuesday	Martes
Wednesday	Miércoles
Thursday	Jueves
Friday	Viernes
Saturday	Sábado
Sunday	Domingo
Year (año)	
next year	el año que viene (or: el año próximo)
last year	el año pasado
Seasons	
winter	el invierno
spring	la primavera
summer	el verano
fall	el otoño

Time (tiempo)

At what time?	A qué hora?
What time is it?	Qué horas son?
It's 10 A.M.	Son las diez de la mañana.
It's noon.	Son las doce.
It's 1 o'clock	Es la una.
It's 3:15.	Son las tres y cuarto.

It's 4:30.	Son las cuatro y media.
It's 5:45.	Son las seis menos cuarto.
It's 6:50.	Faltan diez para las siete.
At 8 o'clock sharp.	A las ocho en punto.
About 9 o'clock.	Cerca de las neuve.
At 10 P.M.	A las diez de la noche.
It is midnight.	Es la medianoche.
I will be a little late.	Llegaré un poco tarde.
Whenever you please	Cuando guste.
In a little while.	Dentro de poco.
minute	minuto
hour	hora
ago	hace
2 days ago	hace dos días
today	hoy
tomorrow	mañana
day after tomorrow	pasado mañana
yesterday	ayer
day before yesterday	antier
morning	mañana
afternoon	tarde
night	noche
for tonight	para esta noche
last night	anoche
week	semana
next week	semana próxima
next week	semana pasada
when?	cuándo?
now	ahora
late	tarde
early	temprano
next time	la próxima vez
how long	cuánto tiempo?
always	siempre
in a minute	al momento

Hotel (hotel)

Where is the hotel?	Dónde está el hotel?
Where is a first-class hotel?	Dónde está un hotel de primera clase?
Where is a motel?	Dónde está un motel?
Where is the inn?	Dónde está la posada?
I would like a single room	Quiero un cuarto sencillo.
I would like a double room.	Quiero un cuarto para dos.
I would like a room with twin beds.	Quiero un cuarto con camas gemelas.
I would like a room with double bed.	Quiero un cuarto con cama matrimonial.
I would like a room with bath.	Quiero un cuarto con baño.
I would like a room with shower.	Quiero un cuarto con regadera.
I would like a room with a bathtub.	Quiero un cuarto con tina.
I would like a room with a view.	Quiero un cuarto con vista.

I would like a room with air conditioning.	Quiero un cuarto con air acondicionado.
I would like a quiet room.	Quiero un cuarto tranquilo.
What is the price?	Cuál es el precio?
Is there a garage?	Hay garage?
Is there a laundry of dry-cleaning service?	Hay servicio de lavandería o tintorería?
Is there a pressing service?	Hay servicio de planchar?
Is there a drugstore?	Hay una farmacia?
Is there a beauty shop?	Hay un salón de belleza?
Is there a barbershop?	Hay una peluquería?
I would like a haircut.	Quiero un corte de pelo.
I would like a shampoo and set	Quiero un champú y peinado.
May I use your telephone?	Me permite usar el teléfono?
Where is the phone?	Dónde está el teléfono?
Where is the ladies' room?	Dónde está el baño de damas?
Where is the men's room?	Dónde está el baño de caballeros?
Open the door.	Abra la puerta.
Will you please send the baggage up?	Favor de hacer subir el equipaje.
Will you please send the baggage down?	Favor de hacer bajar el equipaje.
Put it here.	Póngalo aquí.
This isn't working.	Esto no funciona.
Close the window.	Cierre la ventana.
Keep the change.	Quédese con el cambio.
My bill, please.	Mi cuenta, por favor.
key	llave

Restaurant (restaurante)

Where is a good restaurant?	Dónde hay un buen restaurante?
I reserved a table for two.	Reservé una mesa para dos.
A menu, please	El menú, por favor.
I am hungry.	Tengo hambre.
I am thirsty.	Tengo sed.
What do you wish?	Qué desea usted?
Bring me . . .	Tráigame . . .
I like my meat . . .	Quiero la carne . . .
medium rare	media cocida
rare	tierna, cruda
well done	bien cocida
I would like a little more of that.	Un poco más, por favor.
The check, please.	La cuenta, por favor.

Breakfast (desayuno)

Juices (jugos)	
Tomato	de tomate
Orange	de naranja
Grapefruit	de toronja
Pineapple	de piña

Eggs (huevos)	
Mexican style	a la mexicana
Mexican ranch style	huevos rancheros
soft-boiled	tibios
poached	pochados
scrambled	revueltos
with sausage	con chorizo
hard-boiled	cocidos
fried	fritos
omelet	omelet
with bacon	con tocino
with ham	con jamón

Bread (pan)	
rolls	bolillo
sweet rolls	pan dulce
toasted	tostado
butter	mantequilla
syrup	jarabe, miel
corn griddle cakes	tortillas
crackers, cookies	galletas
French toast	a la francesa
marmalade	mermelada
honey	miel de abejas

Beverages (bebidas)	
coffee	café
black	negro
with cream	con crema
without milk	sin leche
Sanka	Sanka
Expresso	café express
tea	té
iced tea	té helado
chocolate	chocolate
milk	leche
bottle of pure water	botella de agua pura
mineral water	agua mineral
mineral water, uncarbonated	agua mineral, sin gas

Lunch (comida) **and Dinner** (cena)

Appetizers (entremeses)	
marinated fish	ceviche
refried beans with melted Cheese topping	frijoles refritos con queso
smoked salmon	salmón ahumado
fruit cocktail	coctel de frutas
baby cactus	nopalitos
avocado dip	guacamole
herring	arenques
shrimp cocktail	coctel de camarones
olives	aceitunas

Soups (sopas)

bean (spicy)	frijoles, picante
chick pea	de garbanzos
lentil	lentejas
cold veg.	verduras
consomme	caldo
pea	chìcharo
garlic	ajo

Fish & Shellfish (pescados y mariscos)

salmon	salmon
trout	trucha
tuna	atún
crayfish	langostino
clam	almeja
oysters	ostiones
eels	angulas
red snapper	huachinango
bonito	bonito
lobster	langosta
crab	cangrejo, jaiba
shrimp	camaron
snails	caracoles
halibut	lenguado
smoked codfish	bacalao

Meat & Poultry (carne y aves) Mexican Specialties:

tamales with beef	tamales con carne
tacos, Enchiladas, and Tostadas with chicken or beef	con pollo; con carne
chopped meat, creole style, fried green bananas and rice	picadillo a la criolla
meatballs	albóndigas
stuffed peppers	chiles rellenos
tortillas with meat, cheese and sauce	enchiladas
chicken and rice	arroz con pollo
chicken or turkey in Mexican chocolate sauce	mole poblano or mole de pavo (or: de guajalote)

Vegetables (legumbres)

potatoes	papas
fried	fritas
with cheese	con queso
spinach	espinaca
beans	frijoles
string beans	ejotes
peas	chícharos
asparagus	espárragos
mushrooms	champiñónes, hongos
carrots	zanahorias
lettuce	lechuga

radish	rábano
celery	apio
garlic	ajo
corn	elote
sweet potatoes	camotes
tomato	jitomate
rice	arroz
squash	calabaza
beets	betabeles
cabbage	col
onion	cebolla
eggplant	berenjena
cauliflower	coliflor
sauer kraut	choucrut
artichokes	alcachofas
avocado	aguacate

Desserts (postres)

cheese	queso
Spanish cream	natillas
custard	flan
ice cream	helado
sherbet	nieve
cake	pastel
fruit salad	ensalada de frutas
stewed fruit	compota
fruit tart	pastel de frutas
candy	dulces
pudding	pudín

Fruit (frutas)

apple	manzana
banana	plátano
strawberries	fresas
raspberries	frambuesas
pineapple	piña
coconut	coco
lime	lima
lemon	limón
papaya	papaya
melon	melón
mango	mango
guava	guayaba
grapes	uvas
watermelon	sandía
fruit cocktail	coctel de frutas
plums, prunes	ciruelas

Beverages (bebidas)

cactus plant drinks:	Tequila, Mezcal, Pulque, Margarita, Tequila cocktail
beer	cerveza
Bohemia	(light, native)
Carta Blanca	(light, native)

Dos Equis XX	(dark, native)
brandy	coñac
champagne	champaña
cider	sidra
gin	ginebra
wine	vino
white	vino blanco
red	vino tinto
Spanish wine punch	Sangría
rum	ron
soda	soda, Tehuacán
sherry	jerez
liquor	licor
soft drinks	refrescos
ice	hielo

Miscellaneous

sugar	azúcar
salt	sal
pepper	pimienta
mustard	mostaza
oil	aceite
vinegar	vinagre
butter	mantequilla
knife	cuchillo
fork	tenedor
spoon	cuchara
teaspoon	cucharita
sauce/gravy	salsa
tip	la propina
waiter	el mesero
waitress	la mesera; señorita
sour	agrio
spicy	picante

Mail (correo)

post office	oficina de correos
stamps	timbres, estampillas
airmail stamp	timbres, estampillas de correo aéreo
register	registrado
letter	carta
postcard	tarjeta postal

Getting Around

By car (por carro)

How do you get to . . . ?	Cómo se va a . . . ?
Where are you going?	A dónde va usted?
How far is it to . . . ?	Qué distancia hay a . . . ?
It is near/very near.	Está cerca/Está muy cerca.
It is far/very far.	Está lejos/Está muy lejos.
Which way?	Por dónde?

This way/that way.	Por aquí/Por allí, Por allá.
Go straight ahead.	Vaya usted derecho.
Turn right/left.	Doble usted a la derecha/a la izquierda.
Keep to the right.	Tome su derecha.
When are you returning?	Cuándo volverá usted?
Is the road paved?	Está pavimentado el camino?
No parking.	Se prohibe estacionarse.
Maximum speed.	Velocidad máxima.
Go ahead.	Siga
Stop	Pare, alto

By Air (por avión)

We want a reservation.	Queremos una reservación.
One way.	Viaje sencillo.
Round trip.	Viaje redondo
When does the plane leave?	A qué hors sale el avión?
When does the plane arrive?	A qué hors llega el avión?
Is the plane on time?	Llega el avíon a tiempo?
Is the plane late?	Llega tarde el avión?
No smoking.	Se prohibe fumar.
Check my luggage, please.	Revise mi equipaje, por favor.
airline	línea aérea
airport	aeropuerto
flight	vuelo

By train (por tren)

Where is the railway station?	Dónde está la estación de ferrocarriles?
train	tren
timetable	itinerario
conductor	conductor
What is the fare?	Cuá es la tarifa, por favor?

INDEX

General Information

Airport departure taxes, 33
Air travel
  to Mexico, 9–10
    from Britain, 10
    from Canada, 10
    from U.S.A., 9–10
Archaeological sites, 6
Archaeology. *See* Pre-Columbian Heritage
Arts, 71–82
  literature, 77–80
  music, 80–82
  painters & paintings, 71–77
    Orozco, 73–74, 75
    Rivera, 72–73, 75–76
    Siqueiros, 74, 76
Auto travel to Mexico, 11–15, 20
  aid to motorists, 13
  fly & drive, 15
  general information, 11
  insurance, 13
  missing license plates, 14
  parking meters, 14
  police, 14–15
  practical tips, 11–13
  precautions, 20
  repairs, 14
  service stations & restrooms, 13–14
  witnessing an accident, 14
British visitors' information, 17–18
Bullfighting, 108–118
Bus travel to Mexico, 10
Climate, 1–2
Clothing, 18–20
Colonial cities, 5–6
Costs, 20–21
Credit cards, 8, 18
Currency & exchange, 7–8, 18
Customs procedures, 33–34
Electricity, 29
English language media, 33
Folklore, 83–100
  arts & crafts, 96–98
  fiestas & ferias, 85–88
  folk costumes, 93–96
  folk music & dance, 89–93
  pottery, textiles & straw, 98–100
Food & drink, 101–107
  central & coastal Mexico, 106
  northern Mexico, 105–106
  southern Mexico, 107
Geography, 1
Getaway resorts, 4–5
Handicapped travelers, 31
Health precautions, 32–33
History of Mexico, 37–46
Holidays, 24–25
Hotels, 25
Hours of business, 24
Independent travel, 6–7
Information sources, 17
Insurance, 8–9, 13
Jai Alai, 118
Language, 2, 52–53. *See also* tourist vocabulary
Laundry & dry cleaning, 30
Legal system & Mexican law, 53–54
Mail & postage, 33
Major cities & resort areas, 3
Map of Mexican states, 518–519
Map of Mexico, 516–517
Meeting the Mexicans, 17
Mexico City area, 4
Package tours, 6–7, 16–17
Packing, 18–20
Passports, 15
People & customs, 46–55
Pets, 25
Population, 2
Pre-Columbian Heritage, 56–70
  Aztecs, 68–70, 121
  Mayas (Mayans), 63–68
  Mixtecs, 59–60
  Olmecs, 57–59
  Toltecs, 62–63, 66
  Zapotecs, 59
Religion, 51
Restaurants, 26
Seaside playgrounds, 4
Seasonal events, 21–24
Senior citizens' information, 30–31
Ship travel to Mexico, 10
Shopping, 27–29
Soccer, 118–119
Sports, 108–119. *See also* alphabetical listings
Students information, 30–31
Telephones, 30
Time zones, 29
Tipping, 26–27
Tourist vocabulary & useful phrases, 493–504
Tour operators, 16–17
Train travel to Mexico, 10–11
Travel agents, 15–16
Traveler's checks, 7–8, 18
Trip planning, 6–7

Geographical & Practical Information

(The letter H indicates hotels & other accommodations. The letter R indicates restaurants.)

Acaponeta, 319–320
Acapulco, 239–262
  background & history, 239–242
  beaches, 249
  children's activities, 259
  dance & ballet, 250
  emergency telephone numbers, 243
  English language media, 245–246
  exploring, 242–243
  hotels & other accommodations, 259–262

Acapulco *(continued)*
condos & villas, 262
deluxe, 260
first class, 260–261
inexpensive, 261–262
moderate, 261
information sources, 245
map, 241
museums & art galleries, 250
music, 250
nightlife, 257–259
parks & gardens, 247
restaurants, 253–257
ethnic, 253–254
gourmet, 254–255
inexpensive, 257
popular places, 255
seaside spots, 256–257
shopping, 250–253
sports (participant), 247–248
sports (spectator), 248
telephones, 243
theatre, 250
tours, 246
transportation in, 243–245
airport, 244
auto rentals, 245
buses, 245
taxis, 244–245
transportation to, 243
Agua Azul, 418
Aguascalientes, 226–230
fiestas & fairs, 230
HR229
information sources, 230
nightlife, 229
Ajijic, 222–223, H224, R224–225
Akumal, 442, H461
Alamos, 329, H330
museums, 333
Altata, 317
Angahuán, 195
Autlán, 294

Bacalar Lagoon, 444
Background & history
Acapulco, 239–242
Baja California, 334–348
Bajio (The) & West Central Mexico, 166–168
Chihuahua & The Copper Canyon, 371–372
Guadalajara, 200–201
Mexico City, 120–121, 124
Monterrey area & The Gulf Coast, 383–384
Oaxaca & Chiapas: The Indian South, 403–404
Yucatan & The Maya Country, 455
Bacochibampo Bay, 328
Baja California, 334–370
background & history, 334–338
beaches, 361–362
camping, 362–363
emergency telephone numbers, 350–351
English language media, 358
exploring, 339
historical sites, 363–364
hotels, 351–356
information sources, 357–358
maps, 340, 343
museums & galleries, 364
nightlife, 369–370
parks & gardens, 359
restaurants, 365–369
shopping, 364–365
special events, 356
sports, 359–361
tours, 358–359
transportation in, 357
transportation to, 349–350
Baja Capes, 345–349
Bajio (The) & West Central Mexico, 166–199. *See* alphabetical listings for H, R & other information
Balancanche, 455
Barra de Navidad, 293–294
beaches, 302
emergency telephone numbers, 297
hotels, 298–299
nightlife, 305
restaurants, 303–304
shopping, 302
special events, 302
sports, 301
tours, 301
Barra Vieja, 242
Basaseáchic (waterfalls), 374
Bay of Chamela, 289
Bay of Tenacatita, 289
Boca de Apiza, 295
Boca del Rio, 389
Boca de Paila, H461
Boca de Tomatlán, 277–278
Bonampak, 447
Bucerias, 287

Cabo San Lucas, 345–346
camping, 363
emergency telephone numbers, 351
restaurants, 368–369
special events, 356
tours, 358–359
Caleta de Campos, 195, H295
Camargo, H379
Campeche, 449–450
beaches, 478
emergency telephone numbers, 458
historic sites, 480
hotels, 466
information sources, 471, 472
museums & galleries, 481–482
nightlife, 492
restaurants, 489
shopping, 484
special events, 467–468
transportation in, 469–470
transportation to, 456–457
Cananea, 326
Cancún, 433, 435–439
ballet, 482
beaches, 477
emergency telephone numbers, 458
English language media, 472
historic sites, 478
hotels, 458–460
information sources, 470, 471
map, 436
museums & galleries, 481

nightlife, 490
parks & gardens, 474
restaurants, 485–486
shopping, 483
special events, 467–468
sports, 475–476
tours, 472–473
transportation in, 468
transportation to, 456–457
Cañon de las Peñas (lake & dam), 289
Casas Grandes, 373
Ceboruco (mt. & lava field), 288
Chamela, 289
Chapala (town), 221, H224, R225
Chetumal, 444
beaches, 478
emergency telephone numbers, 458
hotels, 463–464
information sources, 470, 471
nightlife, 491
restaurants, 487–488
shopping, 484
special events, 467
tours, 473
transportation in, 469
transportation to, 456–457
Chiapa de Corzo, 415
information sources, 427
special events, 424–425
tours, 427
Chichen Itza, 63, 66–67, 454–455
historic sites, 479
hotels, 465–466
Chihuahua (city), 373–374
emergency telephone numbers, 378
hotels, 378–379
information sources, 380–381
museums, 381
nightlife, 382
restaurants, 381–382
shopping, 381
special events, 379
tours, 381
transportation in, 380
transportation to, 378
Chihuahua-Pacific Railway 374–376, H379
Chihuahua (state/city & The Copper Canyon, 371–382
background & history, 371–372
emergency telephone numbers, 378
exploring, 372–377
hotels, 378–379
information sources, 381
museums & galleries, 381
nightlife, 382
restaurants, 382
shopping, 381
special events, 379
tours, 381
transportation in, 380–381
transportation to, 378
Cholula, 127, 147
Chula Vista, 222, H224
Ciudad Camargo, 376
Ciudad Constitucíon, 348
camping, 363
hotels, 356
special events, 356
Ciudad Juaréz, 372
Ciudad Obregón, 329
sports, 332
Ciudad Victoria, 387
Coba, 443, 478, H461
Colima, 293, 296
hotels, 299
information sources, 300
museums, 302
nightlife, 305
restaurants, 304
shopping, 302
special events, 300
Colimilla, 294, R304
Comala, 296
shopping, 302–303
Concordia, 316
Copala, 316
Copper Canyon, 375
Cosala, 316
Coyotepec, 410
Coyutlán, 294
Cozumel, 439–440
beaches, 477–478
emergency telephone numbers, 458
English language media, 472
historic sites, 479
hotels, 462–463
information sources, 470, 471
map, 434
nightlife, 497
parks & gardens, 475
restaurants, 487
shopping, 483–484
special events, 467
sports, 476
tours, 473
transportation in, 469
transportation to, 456
Creel, 374, 375, H379–380
Crefal, 192
Cuale Mine, 288–289
Cuauhtemóc, 374, H379
Cuernavaca, 127
art galleries, 151
historic sites, 146
hotels, 133–134
museums, 149–150
nightlife, 164
parks & gardens, 141
restaurants, 161
shopping, 155
Cuilapan, 410
Culiacán, 317

Dainzu, 411
Dance & ballet
Acapulco, 250
Guadalajara, 215
Mexico City, 152
Dolores Hidalgo, 174
Durango, 377
Dzidzantun, 454

El Cubilets, 173
El Desemboque, 327
El Divisadero, H379
El Fuerte, 317
El Garrafon (beach & nat'l park), 441, 475
El Jabali, 297

El Rey, 478
El Rosario, 316
El Sumidero (canyon), 415
El Tajin, 63, 388, 397–398
El Tamuín, 232
El Tuito, 289
Emergency telephone numbers
  Acapulco, 243
  Baja California, 350–351
  Chihuahua & The Copper Canyon, 378
  Guadalajara, 209
  Mexico City, 129
  Monterrey area & Gulf Coast, 391
  Oaxaca & Chiapas: The Indian South, 421
  Yucatan & The Maya Country, 458
Encarnacíon de Díaz, 226
Ensenada, 342–344
  beaches, 361
  camping, 363
  emergency telephone numbers, 351
  English language media, 358
  historic sites, 364
  hotels, 353–354
  information sources, 357
  map, 343
  museums & galleries, 364
  nightlife, 369
  parks & gardens, 359
  restaurants, 367–368
  shopping, 364–365
  special events, 356
  sports, 360
  tours, 358
  transportation in, 357

Felipe Carrillo Puerto, 444
  special events, 467

Garcia Caves, 387
Gray Whale Nat'l Park, 347–348, 359
  special events, 356
Grutas of San Cristóbal, 431
Guadalajara, 200–219
  background & history, 200–201
  emergency telephone numbers, 209
  English language media, 214
  hotels, 209–212
  information sources, 213
  map, 202–203
  museums & galleries, 215
  nightlife, 216–217
  parks, 214
  restaurants, 217–219
  shopping, 215–216
  sightseeing, 201–206
  special events, 212
  sports, 214–215
  stage, music & dance, 215
  tours, 214
  transportation in, 212–213
  transportation to, 209
Guadalupe, 237
Guanajuato, 168–173
  cemetery, 171
  festivals, 171
  hotels, 172–173
  museums, 170
  restaurants, 173
  shopping, 170
  tours & sightseeing, 171
Guasave, 318
Guaymas, 328–333
  emergency telephone numbers, 330
  hotels, 330
  information sources, 332
  nightlife, 333
  restaurants, 333
  special events, 331
  sports, 332
  tours, 332
Guelatao, 409
Guerrero Negro, 347
  camping, 363
  hotels, 355
  parks & gardens, 359

Hacienda Jalisco, 290
Hermosillo, 326–327
  emergency telephone numbers, 330
  English language media, 332
  hotels, 331
  information sources, 332
  museums, 333
  nightlife, 333
  restaurants, 333
  shopping, 333
  sports, 333
Hidalgo Dam, 317
Hidalgo del Parral, 376–377
Historic sites
  Baja California, 363–364
  Mexico City, 143–145
  Mexico City environs, 145–147
  Monterrey area & The Gulf Coast, 397–398
  Yucatan & The Maya Country, 478–481
Horsetail Falls, 386
Hotels
  Acapaulco, 259–262
  Baja California, 351–356
  Chihuahua & The Copper Canyon, 378–379
  Guadalajara, 209–212
  Mexico City, 129–133
  Mexico City environs, 133–136
  Monterrey area & The Gulf Coast, 391–394
  Oaxaca & Chiapas: The Indian South, 421–424
  Yucatan & The Maya Country, 458–467
Huasteca Caves, 386

Ignacio Allende Dam, 177–178
Information sources
  Acapulco, 245
  Baja California, 357–358
  Bajio (The) & West Central Mexico, 199
  Chihuahua & The Copper Canyon, 381
  Guadalajara, 213
  Mexico City, 139
  Monterrey area & The Gulf Coast, 394–395
  Oaxaca & Chiapas: The Indian South, 426–427

Yucatan & The Maya Country, 470–472
Isla El Farallón, 318
Isla Mujeres, 440–441
beaches, 478
emergency telephone numbers, 458
historic sites, 479
hotels, 461–462
information sources, 470, 471
map, 434
nightlife, 491
parks & gardens, 475
restaurants, 486–487
shopping, 483
special events, 467
sports, 476
transportation in, 468–469
transportation to, 456
Isla Pajararera, 294
Isla Tiburón, 327
Ixtapa, 263–271
beaches, 268–269
English language media, 267
hotels, 265–266
information sources, 265
nightlife, 271
restaurants, 270
shopping, 269
special events, 265
sports, 268
telephones, 264
tours, 267–268
transportation in, 265
transportation to, 264–265
Ixtlan del Rio, 288
Izamel, 455
Izapa, 432

Jalostotitlán, 226
Janitzio, 191–192
Jocotepec, 223
Juchitán, 413–414
special events, 424

Kino Bay, 327, H331

La Aduana, 329
Lagos de Moreno, 226
Lake Carrizalilo, 297
Lake Chapala & area, 220–225
La Paz, 344–345
beaches, 362
camping, 363
emergency telephone numbers, 351
English language media, 358
hotels, 354
information sources, 357
museums & galleries, 364
nightlife, 370
restaurants, 368
shopping, 365
special events, 356
sports, 361
tours, 358
transportation in, 357
transportation to, 349
La Quemada, 223
Las Animas, 278
Las Cabras, 316
Las Hadas, 292, 293
La Tambora, 316
La Venta, 57–58, 445–446, 481
Leon, 173, H173–174, R174
Libraries
Mexico City, 147–148
Mexico City environs, 148
Loreto, 344
beaches, 362
camping, 363
emergency telephone numbers, 351
English language media, 358
historic sites, 363
hotels, 354
nightlife, 370
shopping, 365
special events, 356
sports, 360
tours, 358
transportation in, 357
transportation to, 350
Los Altos, 226–227
Los Arcos, 277
Los Cabos, 345
beaches, 362
English language media, 358
hotels, 355
information sources, 357–358
nightlife, 370
shopping, 365
special events, 356
sports, 361
tours, 358
transportation in, 357
transportation to, 350
Los Mochis, 317–318, HR319
Los Pascuales, 295

Magdalena (Jalisco), 220, 288
Magdalena (Sonora), 326
Mani, 451
Manzanillo, 291–293
beaches, 301–302
emergency telephone numbers, 297
hotels, 298
information sources, 300
nightlife, 304–305
restaurants, 303
shopping, 302
special events, 300
sports, 301
tours, 301
transportation to, 297
Manzanillo & area, 291–305
beaches, 301–302
emergency telephone numbers, 297
hotels, 297–300
information sources, 300
museums, 302
nightlife, 304–305
restaurants, 303–304
shopping, 302–303
special events, 300
sports, 301
tours, 301
transportation in, 300
transportation to, 297
Maps
Acapulco, 241
Baja California, 340, 343
Guadalajara, 202–203

Maps *(continued)*
  Mexico City, 122–123
  metro map, 125
  Monterrey, 386
  Yucatan & The Maya Country, 434, 436, 452
Maruata, 296
Mascota, 290
Matamoros, 385
  beaches, 396
  historic sites, 397
  hotels, 391–392
  information sources, 394–395
  nightlife, 402
  restaurants, 400
  shopping, 399
  transportation in, 394
  transportation to, 390–391
Mazatlán, 306–316
  background & history, 306
  beaches, 313–314
  emergency telephone numbers, 310
  entertainment/nightlife, 315–316
  exploring, 307–309
  hotels, 310–311
  information sources, 312
  museums & galleries, 314
  parks, bullrings & rodeo grounds, 312
  restaurants, 314–315
  shopping, 314
  special events, 313
  sports, 312–313
  tours, 316
  transportation in, 311–312
  transportation to, 309
Media Luna (lake), 232
Mérida, 451–454
  emergency telephone numbers, 458
  English language media, 472
  historic sites, 479
  hotels, 464–465
  information sources, 470, 471–472
  map, 452
  museums & galleries, 481
  nightlife, 491
  parks & gardens, 475
  restaurants, 488–489
  shopping, 484
  special events, 467
  sports, 476–477
  theatre & music, 482
  tours, 473–474
  transportation in, 469
  transportation to, 456–457
Mexcaltitán, 320
  special events, 324
Mexicali, 341–342
  emergency telephone numbers, 351
  hotels, 352
  information sources, 357
  museums & galleries, 364
  nightlife, 369
  parks & gardens, 359
  restaurants, 367
  shopping, 365
  special events, 356
  sports, 359–360
  tours, 358
  transportation in, 357
Mexico City, 120–165
  art galleries, 151
  background & history, 120–121, 124
  dance & ballet, 152
  emergency telephone numbers, 129
  English language media, 139
  exploring, 126
  historic sites, 143–145
  hotels, 129–132
  information sources, 138–139
  libraries, 147–148
  map, 122–123
  metro map, 125
  museums, 148–149
  music, 152
  nightlife, 162–164
  parks & gardens, 140–141
  restaurants, 155–161
    Argentine, 158
    American, 160–161
    British, 158–159
    European, 160
    French, 159
    Italian, 159–160
    Mexican, 156–157
    Oriental, 161
    Spanish, 157–158
  shopping, 152–155
  special events, 136–137
  sports, 142–143
  theatre, 151–152
  tours, 139–140
  transportation in, 137–138
    airport, 137
    automobiles, 138
    buses, 137–138
    peseros, 138
    subways, 137
    taxis, 137
  transportation to, 128–129
  zoo, 141
Michoacán, 290
Mismaloya, 277
Mitla, 411–412
  museums, 428
Mocambo, 389
Monte Albán, 58–60, 406–407
Montebello Nat'l Park, 431
Monterrey, 385–387
  historic sites, 397
  hotels, 392–393
  information sources, 394–395
  map, 386
  museums & galleries, 398
  nightlife, 402
  restaurants, 400–401
  shopping, 399
  sports, 396
  tours, 395
  transportation in, 394
  transportation to, 390–391
Monterrey area & The Gulf Coast, 383–402
  background & history, 383–384
  beaches, 396–397
  emergency telephone numbers, 391
  exploring, 384–388
  historic sites, 397–398
  hotels, 391–394
  information sources, 394–395
  museums & galleries, 398

nightlife, 402
restaurants, 399–402
shopping, 398–399
sports, 395–396
tours, 395
transportation in, 394
transportation to, 390–391
Morelia, 185–189
hotels, 195–196
information sources, 199
museums, 198
parks, 188
restaurants, 197
shopping, 188, 189
sightseeing & churches, 186–188
Mulege, 348
camping, 363
historic sites, 363
hotels, 356
special events, 356
Museums & galleries
Acapulco, 250
Baja California, 364
Bajia (The) & West Central Mexico, 198
Chihuahua & The Copper Canyon, 381
Mexico City, 148–149, 151
Mexico City environs, 149–151
Monterrey area & The Gulf Coast, 398
Yucatan & The Maya Country, 481–482
Music
Acapulco, 250
Guadalajara, 215
Mexico City, 152
Yucatan & The Maya Country, 482

Nayarit (state), 319–324
Nightlife
Acapulco, 257–259
Baja California, 369–370
Chihuahua, 382
Guadalajara, 216–217
Mexico City, 162–164
Mexico City environs, 164–165
Monterrey area & The Gulf Coast, 402
Oaxaca & Chiapas: The Indian South, 431
Yucatan & The Maya Country, 490–492
Nogales, 326
Nopolo Bay, 344
Nueva Casas Grandes, 373
Nuevo Laredo, 384–385
hotels, 391–392
information sources, 394–395
nightlife, 402
restaurants, 400
shopping, 398–399
sports, 395
tours, 395
transportation in, 394
transportation to, 390–391
Nuevo Vallarta, 287

Oaxaca & Chiapas: The Indian South
background & history, 403–404, 406–410
beaches, 426
emergency telephone numbers, 421
exploring, 404–420
hotels, 421–424
information sources, 426–427
museums & galleries, 427–428
nightlife, 431
restaurants, 429–431
seasonal & special events, 424–425
shopping, 428–429
tours, 427
transportation in, 425–426
transportation to, 420–421
Oaxaca (city), 404–410
beaches, 426
emergency telephone numbers, 421
hotels, 421–422
information sources, 426
museums, 427–428
nightlife, 431
restaurants, 429–430
shopping, 428
special events, 424
tours, 427
transportation in, 425–426
transportation to, 420–421
Ocampo, 189
Ocotlan, 410
shopping, 428
Ocumicho, 195

Pachuca, 127
historical sites, 146
hotels, 134–135
museums, 151
Pacific Resorts, 272–333. *See* alphabetical listings for H, R & other information
Palenque, 65–66, 418–420, 480–481
hotels, 424
information sources, 426–427
museums, 428
restaurants, 431
shopping, 429
tours, 427
Papantla, 388
Paracho, 194
Paricutín (volcano), 193–194
Parks & gardens
Acapulco, 247
Baja California, 359
Mexico City, 140–141
Mexico City environs, 141
Yucatan & The Maya Country, 474–475
Parral. *See* Hidalgo del Parral
Pátzcuaro (town & lake), 166, 189–193
hotels, 196–197
information sources, 191, 199
museums, 198
restaurants, 198
shopping, 191, 193
sightseeing, 191–193
Pie de la Cuesta, 249
Playa Azul (Manzanillo), 292, 295, 296
Playa Azul (Michoacán), 195, H299
Playa Blanca, H299
Playa Careyes, H299
Playa del Carmen, 442, H461
Playa Novilleros, 320

Puebla, 127
art galleries, 151
historic sites, 147
hotels, 135
libraries, 148
museums, 150
nightlife, 165
restaurants, 162
shopping, 155
zoo, 141–142
Puerto Angel, 412
Puerto Escondido, 344, 412
beaches, 426
hotels, 422
information sources, 426
transportation in, 425–426
Puerto Juarez, 441, H461
Puerto Morelos, 442, H461
Puerto Peñasco, 326
special events, 332
Puerto Vallarta, 273–287
background & history, 273–275
climate, 279
cruises, 286
entertainment, 286
exploring, 275–277
fiestas, 286
hotels, 280–284
deluxe, 281–282
expensive, 282–283
first class, 282
gran turismo, 281
inexpensive, 283–284
moderate, 283
information sources, 286–287
music, 286
nightlife, 286
restaurants, 284–286
sports, 279–280
transportation in, 279
transportation to, 279
Punta Bete, 442
Punta Chueca, 327
Punta Mita, 287
Punta Perula, 294
Punta Sam, 441

Queretaro, 179–182
auto rentals, 182
hotels, 181–182
information sources, 181
museums, 181
nightlife, 182
Palacio Federal, 181
restaurants, 182
shopping, 181

Real de Catorce, 232–234, H234
Restaurants
Acapulco, 253–257
Baja California, 365–369
Chihuahua & The Copper Canyon, 382
Guadalajara, 217–219
Mexico City, 155–161
Mexico City environs, 161–162
Monterrey area & The Gulf Coast, 399–402
Oaxaca & Chiapas: The Indian South, 429–431
Yucatan & The Maya Country, 484–490
Reynosa, 385
hotels, 391–392
information sources, 394–395
nightlife, 401
restaurant, 400
transportation in, 394
transportation to, 390–391
Rincón de Guayavitos, 287
Rio Lagartos, 455
Rio Verde, 232
Roqueta Islands, 247, 249
Ruiz Nat'l Park, 194

Salina Cruz, 413
San Blas (Sinaloa), 317, 320–321
beaches, 324
HR323
information sources, 324
special events, 324
San Carlos Bay, 328
hotels, 330
nightlife, 333
restaurants, 333
shopping, 333
sports, 332
San Cristóbal de las Casas, 416–418, 447–448
emergency telephone numbers, 421
hotels, 423
information sources, 426–427
museums, 428
restaurants, 430
tours, 427
transportation in, 425
San Felipe, 342
beaches, 362
camping, 363
emergency telephone numbers, 351
hotels, 353
information sources, 357
nightlife, 369
restaurants, 367
special events, 356
sports, 360
tours, 358
San Ignacio, 348, H355
San Javier Mission, 363
San José del Cabo, 346
camping, 363
emergency telephone numbers, 351
restaurants, 368
special events, 356
San José Purua, 189
San Juan Chamula
special events, 425
San Juan Cosala, 223
San Juan de los Lagos, 226
San Juan del Rio, 183
HR184
shopping, 183
San Juan Parangaricutiro, 195
San Lorenzo, 372–373
San Luis Potosí, 230–232
fiestas, 235
hotels, 234
information sources, 235
restaurants, 234–235
San Miguel Allende, 174–179

churches, 175–176
cultural center, 175
hotels, 178–179
restaurants, 179
shopping, 177
sports, 177–178
tours & sightseeing, 176
San Patricio Melaque, 294
emergency telephone numbers, 297
hotels, 299–300
information sources, 300
nightlife, 305
restaurants, 304
shopping, 302
transportation to, 297
San Quintin, 347
camping, 363
historic sites, 363
hotels, 355
San Sebastian, 290
Santa Clara del Cobre, 193
Santa Cruz de las Flores, 223
Santa Ines, H355
Santa Rosalia, 348
camping, 363
historic sites, 364
hotels, 356
Santiago, 320
Santiago Peninsula, 291–293
Santo Tomás, 347
camping, 363
Scammon's Lagoon, 347–348
special events, 356
Shark Island. *See* Isla Tiburón
Shopping
Acapulco, 250–253
Baja California, 364–365
Chihuahua & The Copper Canyon, 381
Guadaljara, 215–216
Mexico City, 152–155
Mexico City environs, 155
Monterrey area & The Gulf Coast, 398–399
Oaxaca & Chiapas: The Indian South, 428–429
Yucatan & The Maya Country, 483–484
Sierra de Patamban, 195
Sierra Fría, 228
Sierras (The)
tours, 318–319
Sonora (state), 324–333
background & history, 325–326
beaches, 332
emergency telephone numbers, 330
English language media, 332
hotels, 330–331
information sources, 332
museums, 333
nightlife, 333
restaurants, 333
shopping, 333
special events, 331–332
sports, 332
tours, 332
transportation to, 329
Special & seasonal events
Baja California, 356
Bajio (The) & West Central Mexico, 199
Chihuahua & The Copper Canyon, 379
Guadalajara, 212
Mexico City, 136–137
Mexico City environs, 136–137
Oaxaca & Chiapas: The Indian South, 424–425
Yucatan & The Maya Country, 467–468
Sports
Acapulco, 247–248
Baja California, 359–362
Guadalajara, 214–215
Mexico City, 142–143
Monterrey area & The Gulf Coast, 395–396
Yucatan & The Maya Country, 475–477

Talpa, 289, 290–291
Tampico, 387–388
beaches, 396
hotels, 393
information sources, 394–395
museums & galleries, 398
nightlife, 402
restaurants, 401
sports, 396
tours, 395
transportation in, 394
transportation to, 390–391
Tapachula, 431–432
Taxco, 127
art galleries, 151
historic sites, 147
hotels, 134
museums, 150
nightlife, 165
restaurants, 162
shopping, 155
Tecate, 341
hotels, 352
information sources, 357
parks & gardens, 359
restaurants, 367
special events, 356
Tecoman, 295
Tecuala, 320
Tecuan, H300
Tehuacan, 127, H135–136
Tehuantepec (town), 413
special events, 424
Tenacatita, H300
Tenochitlan, 69–70
Teotihuacan, 60–62, 121, 126
historic sites, 145
Tepic, 321–322
hotels, 323
information sources, 324
museums, 324
restaurants, 324
Tepotzotlan
museums, 151
Tequila, 219–220, 288
Tequisquiapan, 183
HR184
shopping, 183
Theatre (stage)
Acapulco, 250
Guadalajara, 215

Theatre (stage) *(continued)*
Mexico City, 151–152
Yucatan & The Maya Country, 482
Ticul, 451
Tijuana, 338–341
beaches, 361
emergency telephone numbers, 351
exploring, 339–341
hotels, 351–352
information sources, 357
map, 340
music, film & theatre, 364
nightlife, 369
parks & gardens, 358
restaurants, 366
special events, 356
sports, 359
tours, 358
transportation in, 357
Tingambato, 199
Tlacolula, 411
shopping, 428
Tlaquepacque, 207–208
shopping, 208
special events, 212
Tonalá, 208, 225
Topolobampo, 317, 318
Tours
Acapulco, 246
Baja California, 358–359
Chihuahua & The Copper Canyon, 381
Guadalajara, 214
Mexico City, 140
Monterrey area & The Gulf Coast, 395
Oaxaca & Chiapas: The Indian South, 427
Yucatan & The Maya Country, 472–474
Transportation in
Acapulco, 243–245
Baja California, 357
Chihuahua, 380
Guadalajara, 212–213
Mexico City, 137–139
Monterrey area & The Gulf Coast, 394
Oaxaca & Chiapas: The Indian South, 425–426
Yucatan & The Maya Country, 468–470
Transportation to
Acapulco, 243
Baja California, 349–350
Chichuahua, 378
Gaudalajara, 209
Mexico City, 128–129
Monterrey area & The Gulf Coast, 390–391
Oaxaca & Chiapas: The Indian South, 420–421
Yucatan & The Maya Country, 456–457
Tula, 62–63, 127
historic sites, 146
Tulum, 442–443, 478, H461
Tuxpan, 320
Tuxtla Gutiérrez, 414–415
emergency telephone numbers, 421
hotels, 422–423
information sources, 426
museums, 428
restaurants, 430
shopping, 428–429
transportation to, 420–421
Tzaráracua Falls, 194
Tzintzuntzán, 190, 199

Uruapan, 193–194
hotels, 197
information sources, 199
museums, 198
restaurants, 198
Uxmal, 67–68, 450–451
historic sites, 480
hotels, 466

Valencia Silver Mine, 170–171
Valladoid, 455
Veracruz, 388–389
beaches, 396–397
historic sites, 397
hotels, 393–394
information sources, 395
museums & galleries, 398
nightlife, 402
restaurants, 401–402
shopping, 399
sports, 396
transportation in, 394
transportation to, 390–391
Villahermosa, 445–446
emergency telephone numbers, 458
historic sites, 480–481
hotels, 466–467
information sources, 471, 472
museums & galleries, 482
nightlife, 492
parks & gardens, 475
restaurants, 489–490
shopping, 484
theatre & music, 482
tours, 474
transportation in, 470
transportation to, 457
Villa Insurgentes, 348

X-Caret, 443
Xel-Ha, 443, 474
Xochicalco, 63, 146

Yagul, 411
Yanhuitlán, 408
Yelapa, 278
Yucatan & The Maya Country, 433–492
background & history, 455
beaches, 477–478
emergency telephone numbers, 458
English language media, 472
exploring
Maya Country, 445–454
Mexican Caribbean, 434–444
historic sites, 478–481
hotels, 458–467
information sources, 470–472
maps, 434, 436, 452
museums & galleries, 481–482
nightlife, 490–492

parks & gardens, 474–475
restaurants, 484–490
seasonal & special events, 467–468
shopping, 483–484
sports, 475–477
stage, music & dance, 482
tours, 472–474
transportation in, 468–470
transportation to, 456–457

Zaachila, 410–411
Zacatecas, 235–238
fiestas & fairs, 238
hotels, 237–238
information sources, 238
nightlife, 238
restaurants, 238
transportation, 238
Zapopan, 206–207
Zapotlanejo, 225
Zihuatanejo, 263–271
beaches, 268–269
English language media, 267
hotels, 266–267
information sources, 265
nightlife, 271
restaurants, 270–271
shopping, 270
special events, 265
sports, 268
telephones, 264
tours, 267–268
transportation in, 265
transportation to, 264–265
Zinacantan
special events, 425
Zitacuaro, 189

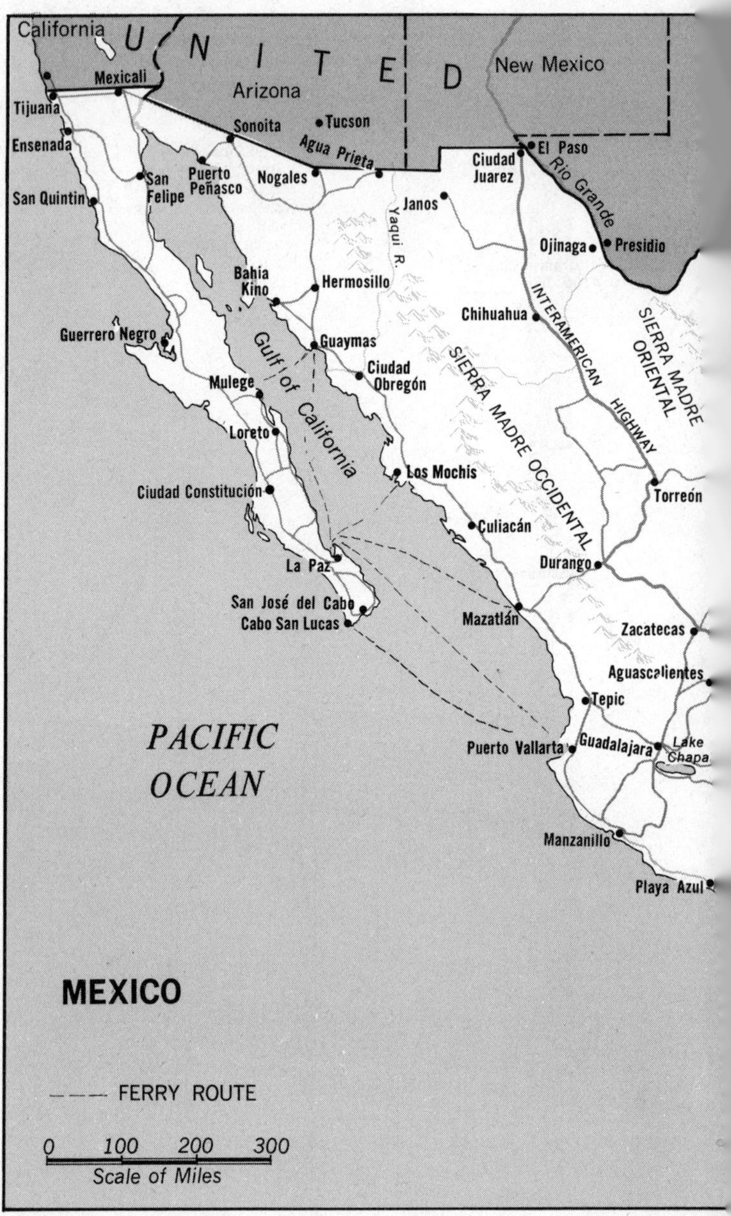

California
U N I T E D
Arizona
New Mexico
Mexicali
Tijuana
Ensenada
Sonoita
Tucson
Agua Prieta
Nogales
San Felipe
Puerto Peñasco
San Quintin
Ciudad Juarez
El Paso
Rio Grande
Janos
Yaqui R.
Ojinaga
Presidio
Bahia Kino
Hermosillo
Guerrero Negro
Guaymas
Chihuahua
Gulf of California
Ciudad Obregón
SIERRA MADRE OCCIDENTAL
INTERAMERICAN HIGHWAY
SIERRA MADRE ORIENTAL
Mulege
Loreto
Los Mochis
Torreón
Ciudad Constitución
Culiacán
Durango
La Paz
San José del Cabo
Cabo San Lucas
Mazatlán
Zacatecas
Aguascalientes
Tepic
PACIFIC OCEAN
Puerto Vallarta
Guadalajara
Lake Chapa
Manzanillo
Playa Azul
MEXICO
FERRY ROUTE
0 100 200 300
Scale of Miles

TATES
Texas
Louisiana
Miss.
Mississippi R.
New Orleans
Houston
San Antonio
illa Acuña
Piedras Negras
Nuevo Laredo
Laredo
nclova
Mier
Reynosa
Brownsville
Matamoros
Monterrey
Saltillo
Gulf of Mexico
Ciudad Victoria
Soto La Marina
Mante
zache
Tampico
Valles
San Luis Potosi
Tuxpan
Salamanca
Queretaro
Pachuca
Morelia
MEXICO
Veracruz
Puebla
Toluca
Orizaba
Iguala
Taxco
Coatzacoalcos
Villahermosa
Altamirano
Zihuatanejo
Huajuapan de León
Oaxaca
Tuxtla Gutierrez
Usumacinta
Acapulco
SIERRA MADRE DEL SUR
Tehuantepec
San Cristóbal de las Casas
Pinotepa Nal.
Puerto Escondido
Puerto Angel
Gulf of Tehuantepec
Ciudad Cuauhtémoc
Tapachula
GUATEMALA
Guatemala
HONDURAS
San Salvador
EL SALVADOR
BELIZE
Belize
Francisco Escárcega
Chetumal
Campeche
Yucatan Peninsula
Mérida
Felipe Carillo Puerto
Cozumel
Cancun
Puerto Juarez
Isla Mujeres

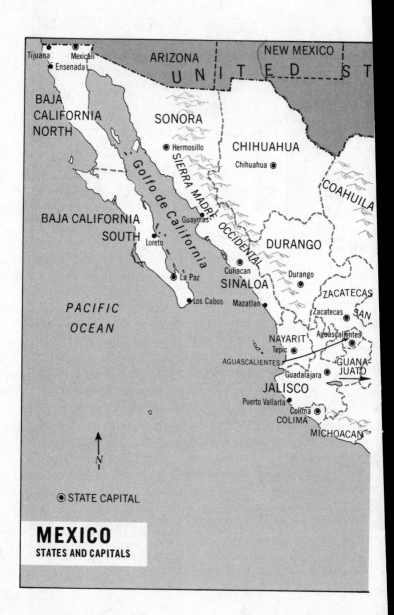

MEXICO
STATES AND CAPITALS